THE AVIATION FACTFILE

MODERN MILITARY AIRCRAFT

THE AVIATION FACTFILE

MODERN MILITARY AIRCRAFT

GENERAL EDITOR: JIM WINCHESTER

THUNDER BAY
P·R·E·S·S

San Diego, California

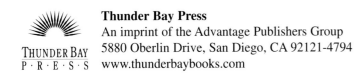

Thunder Bay Press
An imprint of the Advantage Publishers Group
5880 Oberlin Drive, San Diego, CA 92121-4794
www.thunderbaybooks.com

All notations of errors or omissions should be addressed to Thunder Bay Press, Editorial Department, at the above address. All other
correspondence (author inquiries, permissions) concerning the content of this book should be addressed to Amber Books Ltd., Bradley's Close,
74–77 White Lion Street, London N1 9PF, England, www.amberbooks.co.uk.

ISBN-13: 978-1-59223-225-3
ISBN-10: 1-59223-225-6

Library of Congress Cataloging-in-Publication Data.

Modern military aircraft/general editor, Jim Winchester.
     p. cm -- (The aviation factfile)
  Includes index.
  ISBN 1-59223-225-6
  1. Airplanes, Military. I. Winchester, Jim. II Series..

UG1240.M64 2004
623.74'6'03--dc22

2004062125

Printed in Singapore

3 4 5 08 07 06

Contents

INTRODUCTION

Fighters

Today's few remaining combat aircraft manufacturers identify five generations of modern fighter aircraft, although there is disagreement on the details. The first generation fighters were the early jets such as the F-86 Sabre, Hunter and the MiG-15 and -17. The second generation was usually supersonic and featured integrated electronics and guided missiles – examples include the F-4 Phantom, MiG-21 and Mirage III. Third generation fighters such as the F-16, Mirage 2000 and MiG-29 introduced digital electronics and integrated systems. Many had 'fly-by-wire' control systems. The fourth generation encompasses the new fighters such as

Above: The Eurofighter Typhoon features canard foreplanes to enhance manoevrability.

the Gripen, F/A-22 and Typhoon. These are characterised by some degree of stealth and totally integrated weapons, controls, displays and sensors. Russian manufacturers in particular claim that their latest prototypes represent a fifth generation. Despite these technological breakthroughs, the world's air forces still field large numbers of second-generation and quite a few first-generation fighters.

Bombers

The definition of 'bomber' has blurred over time to encompass light attack

aircraft such as the Embraer AMX and the A-4 Skyhawk, and those equipped largely with air-to-ground missiles rather than just bombs. The medium bomber category is now occupied by fast, manoeuvrable aircraft such as the Tornado IDS, Su-34 and the F-15E. The Boeing B-52 has outlived all its contemporaries, and will continue to do so if plans to re-engine the surviving H models come to fruition. The Tupolev 'Bear' series beat the B-52 for production longevity, rolling out of Russian plants at a slow rate from the 1960s to the 1990s. The large supersonic bombers, the US B-1B and the Russian Tu-160 may look similar, but the latter is much larger and more powerful, if much rarer. At over $2 billion apiece,

Top left: The Sukhoi Su-27IB is just one of a formidable family of strike aircraft.

Top right: The Lockheed F-117 Nighthawk first saw major action during Operation Desert Storm in 1991.

Above: The giant An-124 Ruslan 'Condor', the largest production aircraft in the world, provides an important strategic airlift capacity.

only the world's sole remaining superpower could afford something as 'out of this world' as the B-2A Spirit. New generation guided weapons have allowed such Cold War leftovers to take on roles such as close air support that were previously the domain of tactical bombers and attack aircraft.

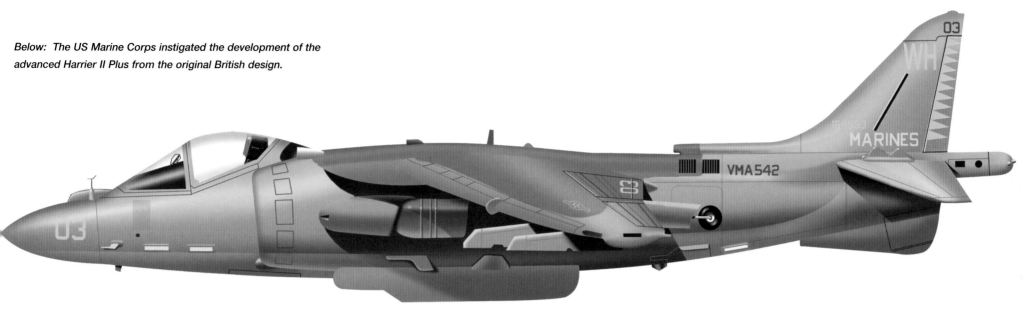

Below: The US Marine Corps instigated the development of the advanced Harrier II Plus from the original British design.

Transports and tankers

No air force or army fights without logistic support, today largely provided by strategic and tactical airlift. Most heavy military freighters follow the high-wing four-jet layout established by the Lockheed C-141. The tactical equivalent is the C-130, found in almost all western air forces, and used from the Sahara to the Antarctic. There is no direct Eastern Bloc counterpart to the C-130, but Antonov's An-24/26 and An-12 are almost as ubiquitous in the former Eastern Bloc and the Third World. In-flight refuelling revolutionised military aviation. To refuel the once-great bomber fleets, the USA built specialised tankers and most other nations converted airliners or bombers

themselves. The invention of the 'buddy pod' in the 1950s allowed even the small air forces to have a tactical air refuelling capability.

Naval aircraft

Developments in aircraft-carrier design and operation revitalised naval aviation from the 1950s onwards. The angled landing deck and the mirror landing system improved safety, while nuclear propulsion and nuclear weapons made the US 'super carriers' the most powerful and versatile military vehicles ever created. The near to medium future will see the creation of more 'large deck' carriers as several navies put the fourth (or fifth) generation of fighters to sea.

Below: Lockheed C-130s overflying burning oil wells during the 1991 Gulf War. This versatile aircraft has seen more than 40 years of service in many roles.

AERMACCHI

MB.339

● Advanced trainer ● Light strike ● Frecce Tricolori aerobatic aircraft

A beautiful aircraft and a delight to fly, the Aermacchi MB.339 is the standard Italian air force trainer which has also been developed into a potent light-attack warplane. It is familiar on the air show circuit thanks to its appearances with the Italian national aerobatic team Frecce Tricolori, whose dramatic flight manoeuvres have entertained crowds in 32 countries.

▲ The MB.339 has followed in the footsteps of the older MB.326 as a well-harmonised jet trainer. It is not as advanced as the BAe Hawk series, but is a better performer than the MB.326.

AERMACCHI MB.339

Tip tanks ▶
Like the MB.326, the MB.339 has wingtip fuel tanks. The attack-dedicated MB.339C has larger tip tanks.

▼ Prototype 'K'
The MB.339K only exists as a prototype. This was a single-seat dedicated light-attack variant with a limited air-to-air capability.

▲ Neat cockpit
The MB.339 has a neat cockpit of conventional layout. Unusually, the ejection seat has two handles on either side for firing.

▼ Straight wing
Unlike the higher performance Hawk and Alpha Jet, the MB.339 has a straight wing with a swept leading edge. This gives more stable handling.

▲ Italian air force
The largest user of the MB.339 is the Italian air force. Pilots complete 180 hours on the MB.339 after flying the SF.260 light trainer. They then convert to fast jets.

FACTS AND FIGURES

➤ The MB.339 introduced a 33-cm (13-in.) stepped SICAMB/Martin-Baker Mk 10 'zero-zero' ejection seat.

➤ Lockheed sought to sell licence-built MB.339s to the US as the 'T-bird II'.

➤ Just one of many export customers, Eritrea bought six MB.339Cs in March 1996.

➤ Six Argentine MB.339A fighter trainers were used as warplanes against the British in the 1982 Falklands War.

➤ The MB.339K is a single-seat version designed exclusively for light attack.

➤ Operators of the MB.339 include Dubai, Ghana, Malaysia, Nigeria and Peru.

PROFILE

Aermacchi's fast trainer

Based upon Aermacchi's earlier MB.326 used by 12 nations, the MB.339 looks 'hot' but has very docile handling qualities. This makes it ideal for flight instruction yet highly adaptable for combat duties. The MB.326 is first and foremost a trainer which has taught thousands of fast-jet students how to fly. In service with seven air forces, it was an unsuccessful competitor in the Pentagon's JPATS competition for a new primary trainer for the US Air Force and Navy.

But the MB.339 has considerable military potential, and a single-seat attack version has been evaluated. The two-seat 'lead-in fighter trainer' variant is designed to carry a wide variety of weapons to teach future fighter pilots how to fire them, and can be used as an effective light-attack and anti-shipping strike aircraft. The MB.339C has been ordered by the Royal New Zealand Air Force, which purchased 18 in May 1990 to replace the successful but ageing British Strikemaster. The single-seat MB.339K is unlikely to see operational service.

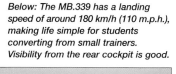

Above: The Italian air force aerobatic team, the Frecce Tricolori, show just how impressive the performance of the MB.339 can be in the hands of expertly trained pilots.

Below: The MB.339 has a landing speed of around 180 km/h (110 m.p.h.), making life simple for students converting from small trainers. Visibility from the rear cockpit is good.

MB.339A

Type: tandem two-seat trainer and close-support aircraft

Powerplant: one 17.78-kN (3,990-lb.-thrust) Piaggio-built Rolls-Royce Viper 632043 turbojet

Maximum speed: 898 km/h (552 m.p.h.)

Range: 1760 km (1,091 mi.)

Service ceiling: 14,630 m (48,000 ft.)

Weights: empty 3215 kg (7,073 lb.); loaded 5895 kg (13,970 lb.)

Armament: provision for two 30-mm or multi-barrel 7.62-mm (.30 cal.) guns, AS.11/AS.12 or Magic missiles, or up to 1935 kg of bombs (including two 340-kg (750-lb.) bombs on inboard pylons) or fuel tanks

Dimensions:
span 10.86 m (36 ft.)
length 10.97 m (36 ft.)
height 3.99 m (13 ft.)
wing area 19.30 m² (208 sq. ft.)

MB.339PAN

The Gruppo Pattuglia Aerobatica Nazionale, better known as the Frecce Tricolori, have used the MB.339PAN since 1982. This is a special version for the team, with the tip tanks removed for agility.

Compared to the MB.326, forward vision for the instructor in the rear seat is greatly improved. Both cockpits have full pressurisation and dual controls. A gunsight can also be fitted to the rear cockpit to allow an instructor to monitor his student's shooting during weapon training.

This flamboyant colour scheme is reserved for the team. The normal paintwork for the air force's MB.339s is a light grey with high-visibility 'dayglo' panels.

Systems fitted to the MB.339C version include laser rangefinder, Kaiser head-up display and weapon aiming computer.

The main undercarriage retracts into the wing. It has an anti-skid braking system and is capable of operation from semi-prepared surfaces.

Twin ventral strakes are fitted to the rear fuselage to enhance stability at high angles of attack.

Despite its age and lack of power, Aermacchi opted for the Rolls-Royce Viper turbojet.

ACTION DATA

MAXIMUM SPEED

Advanced trainers convert pilots from flying basic trainers, which typically have a maximum speed of around 500 km/h (300 m.p.h.), to jet fighters, which usually have a maximum speed at sea level of over 1000 km/h (600 m.p.h.). These speeds allow them to perform light-attack missions with a reasonable amount of success.

MB.339A	898 km/h (557 m.p.h.)
L-39 ALBATROS	850 km/h (527 m.p.h.)
ALPHA JET	916 km/h (568 m.p.h.)

WEAPONS

Secondary light-attack capability is vital to many small air forces, and all the main designs have some ability to drop light bombs or missiles, either for weapon training or operational use. The MB.339 can fire anti-ship missiles or rocket pods.

MB.339A	ALPHA JET	L-39 ALBATROS
1935 kg (4,257 lb.)	2500 kg (5,500 lb.)	1000 kg (2,200 lb.)

MAXIMUM TAKE-OFF WEIGHT

The MB.339 is less capable than the best advanced trainers, such as the Alpha Jet and the Hawk, but more capable than the cheapest, and its maximum take-off weight reflects this. The Alpha Jet has twin engines and a high standard of equipment, giving it a high take-off weight.

MB.339A 6350 kg (13,970 lb.)

L-39 ALBATROS 4700 kg (10,340 lb.)

ALPHA JET 8000 kg (17,600 lb.)

Aermacchi light civil and training aircraft

■ **MB.308:** This light two-seat sport aircraft was developed in the early 1950s. It was powered by a Continental C90 four-cylinder air-cooled engine and had a wooden fuselage.

■ **MB.320:** The MB.320 was a six-seat twin-engined touring machine with a wooden wing. Most of the fuselage behind the nose was also of wooden construction to reduce costs.

■ **MB.323:** Powered by a Pratt & Whitney radial air-cooled piston engine, the MB.323 was a basic trainer seating two in tandem. Although it was a fine design, it never entered service.

■ **MB.326:** The MB.326 was a very popular design which achieved wide export success as well as being licence-built in Australia and Brazil. It also used the Rolls-Royce Viper turbojet engine.

AERO

L-39/L-59 ALBATROS

● Czech-built trainer ● More than 2800 built ● Ground-attack variants

The L-39 Albatros, successor to Aero's earlier L-29, continues to be Russia's standard trainer. More than 2000 L-39s were delivered to the former Soviet Union between 1973 and 1989. The type has also sold well outside the former Eastern Bloc. Serving with the air forces of at least 16 other countries, the Albatros has been progressively modernised, and resulted in the more capable L-59 and a number of proposals for other variants.

▲ Aero built
3,600 L-29 Delfins to fill the training requirements of the Warsaw Pact countries. The company was eager to produce a successor, and flew a prototype L-39 in 1968.

PHOTO FILE

AERO L-39/L-59 ALBATROS

Trainer with teeth ▶
An L-39ZA of the Slovak air force. This ground-attack version has a secondary reconnaissance role and can carry a centreline camera pod. L-39ZA/ARTs with Elbit avionics were produced for Thailand.

▼ Greater capability
The improved L-39MS has a stronger fuselage, a new engine, upgraded avionics, powered controls and larger tip-tanks.

▲ More than 20 years' service
The L-39 first took to the air in 1968 and entered service in 1974. The Soviets alone ordered 2,094.

▼ L-39MS demonstrator
The first L-59s were designated L-39MS. Five were delivered to the Czech air force.

Export success ▶
Most customers for the Albatros came from Soviet allies, although since the end of the Cold War other countries, like Tunisia, have purchased the type.

FACTS AND FIGURES

➤ By removing the rear seat and fitting target-towing equipment, Aero created the L-39V for use with a KT-04 target.

➤ Czechoslovak L-39s were divided between the Czech and Slovak air forces in 1992.

➤ The second biggest customer, after the Soviets, was Libya with 181 machines.

➤ The L-39ZO replaced Warsaw Pact MiG-17s, MiG-21s and Su-7s in the weapons training role.

➤ A two-seat trainer variant of the L-159, the L-159T, is planned by Aero.

➤ The Czech air force has ordered 72 L-159s.

PROFILE

Trainer for WarPac and the world

By adding an undernose GSh-23 23-mm gun pod to the L-39ZO trainer, Aero created the L-39ZA ground-attack and reconnaissance platform. Wing pylons have a capacity of 1500 kg (3,300 lb.).

Many versions of the L–39 have been produced since the original L-39C entered service with the Czechoslovak air force in 1974. The L-39ZO has a built-in cannon and four wing hardpoints, plus a stronger undercarriage. The -39V is a target tug and the ZA is a ground-attack version. They are all powered by the 16.9-kN (4,400-lb.-thrust) AI-25 turbofan. Aero built a version of the ZA with Israeli avionics, including a head-up display, and

navigation/attack system, for Thailand. Another derivative, the L-139 with a Garrett TFE731 engine and other new systems and equipment, was developed to meet the American JPATS trainer specification.

By 1990 Aero had developed a new model powered by a DV-2 engine. The increased thrust gives the L-59 (known initially as L-39MS) greatly improved performance. The aircraft has a more sophisticated cockpit for advanced training, including weapons

delivery techniques. It was also designed to be easier to maintain. Egypt was the first export customer, ordering 48, and Tunisia has bought 12. For the Czech air force, Aero is producing the L-159, a single-seat attack version with a 28-kN (6,300-lb.-thrust) Garrett F124 engine.

L-39C ALBATROS

This L-39C basic and advanced trainer appeared at the 1990 Battle of Britain Salute at Boscombe Down. A factory demonstrator, it gave a spirited display in this colourful paint scheme.

The L-39's Ivchenko turbofan is fed by two high-set air intakes behind the cockpit. Their position was chosen to minimise the FOD (foreign object damage) ingestion.

The L-39C's optional underwing stations are for external fuel tanks. On the L-39ZO, ZA, MS and L-59, four are fitted and are intended for air-to-ground ordnance or camera equipment.

Flown in 1968 and placed in production in 1972, the L-39 is a generation behind types like the BAe Hawk. It is probably more comparable with the Aermacchi MB.326.

The L-39C is the basic training variant of the Albatros. The pilot and instructor sit in tandem in separate cockpits. Each has a Czech-designed ejection seat.

The L-39's undercarriage is robust enough for use on semi-prepared strips.

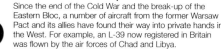

A major change in the L-59, apart from a new engine, was a multi-mode pulse-Doppler radar installed in the nose. This greatly increased the aircraft's capability.

Since the end of the Cold War and the break-up of the Eastern Bloc, a number of aircraft from the former Warsaw Pact and its allies have found their way into private hands in the West. For example, an L-39 now registered in Britain was flown by the air forces of Chad and Libya.

Most L-39 variants are powered by a single Ivchenko AI-25TL turbofan. This produces 16.87 kN (4,400 lb. of thrust). The L-39MS/L-59 introduced a Lotarev DV-2 engine of 21.57 kN (4,850 lb.-thrust).

A feature of the L-39, except for the L-39MS/L-59, is an electrically-operated variable-incidence tailplane. Elevators are also fitted, although these are manually actuated with a small trim tab.

Ex-military trainers in private hands

■ **DE HAVILLAND VAMPIRE T.Mk 55:** This ex-Swiss air force aircraft wears the colours of a Sea Vampire T.Mk 22. Private owners often repaint their aircraft in unauthentic markings.

■ **HAWKER HUNTER T.Mk 68:** Some ex-military jets are used as executive aircraft. This British-registered Hunter is used by its owner to fly to his holiday home in Majorca.

■ **HUNTING JET PROVOST T.Mk 5P:** This ex-RAF Jet Provost carries advertising for an accessory retailer. Flying ex-military jets is expensive and sponsorship helps to cover costs.

■ **LOCKHEED T-33A SHOOTING STAR:** Based at Duxford in Cambridgeshire, this ex-USAF trainer carries the US registration N33VC to avoid having to be certificated in the UK.

L-59E Albatros

Type: advanced trainer and light attack aircraft

Powerplant: one 21.57-kN (4,850-lb.-thrust) Povazski Strojarne/ZMK DV-2 turbofan

Maximum speed: 875 km/h (543 m.p.h.) at 5000 m (16,500 ft.)

Climb rate: 1500 m/min (4,920 f.p.m.) at sea level

Range: 1210 km (750 mi.) at 5000 m (16,500 ft.)

Service ceiling: 11,730 m (38,470 ft.)

Weights: empty 4030 kg (8,866 lb.); maximum take-off 7000 kg (15,400 lb.)

Armament: one GSh-23 23-mm cannon, plus up to 1500 kg (3,300 lb.) of rockets, bombs and air-to-air missiles

Dimensions:
span	9.54 m	(31 ft. 4 in.)
length	12.20 m	(40 ft.)
height	4.77 m	(15 ft. 8 in.)
wing area	18.80 m²	(202 sq. ft.)

COMBAT DATA

THRUST

With considerably more thrust than the other machines, the L-59E has enough power to be a very useful attack aircraft, as well as one of the world's best jet trainers.

L-59E ALBATROS — 21.57 kN (4,850 lb. thrust)

G-4 SUPER GALEB — 17.79 kN (4,000 lb. thrust)

IA-63 PAMPA — 15.57 kN (3,500 lb. thrust)

ORDNANCE

In the weapons training and light attack roles the L-59E is again the most capable aircraft. It can carry a considerably larger weapon load than its competitors.

L-59E ALBATROS 1500 kg (3,300 lb.)

G-4 SUPER GALEB 1280 kg (2,820 lb.)

IA-63 PAMPA 1160 kg (2,550 lb.)

CLIMB RATE

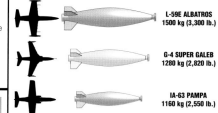

Argentina's FAMF/FMA IA-63 Pampa is able to climb as quickly as the L-59E, but is struggling to find export sales. The L-59E has stunned air show crowds with its performance.

L-59E ALBATROS 1560 m/min (4,920 f.p.m.)

IA-63 PAMPA 1560 m/min (5,117 f.p.m.)

G-4 SUPER GALEB 1860 m/min (6,100 f.p.m.)

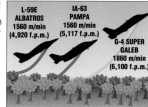

AÉROSPATIALE (SOCATA)

TB 30B EPSILON

● Piston-engined trainer ● Armée de l'Air service ● Turbine version

▲ *Though
the Epsilon sold in large
numbers to the Armée de l'Air, exports have
been limited. A turbine-engined variant, the
Oméga, followed but has failed to find a buyer
in the highly competitive trainer market in a
period of shrinking defence budgets.*

Derived from the TB 10 Tobago, the TB 30 Epsilon was proposed in both TB 30A and TB 30B versions with 194-kW (260-hp.) and 224-kW (300-hp.) engines. France's Armée de l'Air selected the 30B as its new basic trainer in June 1979; the first prototype flew the following December. Fully aerobatic, the Epsilon is designed to prepare students for more advanced training in the Alpha Jet.

AÉROSPATIALE (SOCATA) TB 30B EPSILON

▼ **Epsilon prototype**
After the first TB 30 prototype had flown in 1979, the design was fitted with a new tail and modified wings. VO are the last two letters of the aircraft's civil registration F-WZVO.

▲ **Turbine-powered TB 30C**
SOCATA's Epsilon prototype was fitted with a Turboméca TP319 turboprop as the TB 30C. Further modified, this became the Oméga.

TB 31 Oméga ▶
SOCATA developed the Oméga as a private venture, the first example flying in 1989.

◀ **Retractable gear**
A retractable undercarriage was a feature of the TB 20 Trinidad that was carried over to the TB 30.

African exports ▶
Former French colony Togo was one of two Epsilon export customers. Three aircraft were delivered in 1986, followed by an attrition replacement in 1987.

FACTS AND FIGURES

➤ SOCATA's TB 31 Oméga prototype first flew on 30 April 1989 and was a rebuild of the original Epsilon prototype.

➤ The Oméga features Martin-Baker ejection seats and g limits of +7/-3.5.

➤ Togo's four Epsilons are the only TB 30Bs to feature underwing hardpoints.

➤ Portuguese Epsilons feature a cathode ray tube (CRT) display for radio and navigation data.

➤ Between the Epsilon and Oméga there is 60 per cent component commonality.

➤ Total Epsilon sales totalled 172, including two demonstrators.

PROFILE

France's basic trainers

In addition to the 150 TB 30Bs bought by the French air force, Aérospatiale's SOCATA subsidiary produced one for Portugal, where OGMA assembled a further 17. They are used for the first 120 hours of pilot training.

The French aircraft are operated by the Armée de l'Air's basic flying training school at Cognac, where trainees spend 66.5 hours flying the Epsilon as part of their 23-week course. *G* limits of +6.7/-3.35 allow aerobatic manoeuvres to be carried out.

An export version of the Epsilon can carry a wide range of armament on its four underwing hardpoints, including machine-gun pods, rocket or grenade launchers or two 125-kg bombs. Togo is the only operator, with four delivered, the last in 1987.

The original TB 30B prototype was flown in 1985 with a Turboméca TP319 turboprop, before being modified and fitted with a 364-kW (488-hp.) TP319-1A2 Arrius as the TB 31 Oméga. With its new canopy and space for

Above: Colourful tenth anniversary markings are worn by this Armée de l'Air Epsilon seen in 1994.

ejection seats, the Oméga offered higher performance than the Epsilon, including a top speed of 519 km/h (322 m.p.h.). However, the French air force selected the Tucano to replace its Magister trainers and SOCATA has so far failed to find a launch customer.

Below: Portugal's air force ordered 18 Epsilons in 1987. The first was delivered in January 1989, and the rest were assembled in Portugal by OGMA.

TB 30B Epsilon

Type: two-seat basic primary/basic trainer

Powerplant: one 224-kW (300-hp.) Lycoming AEIO-540-L1B5D flat-six piston engine

Maximum speed: 380 km/h (236 m.p.h.)

Endurance: 3 hours 45 min

Climb rate: 564 m/min (1,850 f.p.m.)

Service ceiling: 7010 m (23,000 ft.)

Weights: empty equipped 932 kg (2,050 lb.); maximum take-off and landing 1250 kg (2,750 lb.)

Armament: (export) up to 300 kg (660 lb.) of bombs, machine-gun pods or grenade launchers

Dimensions:
span	7.92 m	(26 ft.)
length	7.59 m	(24 ft. 10 in.)
height	2.66 m	(8 ft. 9 in.)
wing area	9.00 m²	(97 sq. ft.)

TB 30B EPSILON

Groupement Ecole 315 at Cognac/Châteaubernard took delivery of its first Epsilons in 1984. Employing the type as an *ab initio* pilot trainer, the unit had 150 of the aircraft by late 1989.

Unlike the high-performance Oméga, the Epsilon is not fitted with ejection seats and has a framed canopy. The cockpit is arranged to prepare student pilots for conversion to the Alpha Jet advanced trainer.

That the Epsilon is a derivative of the TB 10 Tobago four/five-seat light plane is most evident in the tailfin design. Changes introduced on the second prototype included increased wing span and rounded wingtips. Development of the TB 30 began in 1977 to an Armée de l'Air requirement.

The Epsilon's fuselage is a light alloy semi-monocoque structure. Fixed surfaces are metal skinned, while the elevators and rudder are covered with polyester fabric.

One of Lycoming's (later AlliedSignal's) large and successful family of air-cooled flat-configuration piston engines powers the Epsilon.

Epsilons built for export can carry a variety of stores on four underwing pylons; up to 80 kg (176 lb.) each on outer hardpoints and 160 kg (352 lb.) each on inner pylons.

The rear instructor's seat in this dual-control aircraft is raised 70 mm (3 in.) to improve visibility. The two-part canopy slides to the rear. Aft of the cabin is a small baggage compartment.

COMBAT DATA

POWER

Chile's ENAER Pillán shares the Epsilon's AlliedSignal (Lycoming) air-cooled, flat-six engine of 224 kW (300 hp.). SIAI-Marchetti's SF.260, derived from a civil light aircraft, has a smaller engine.

TB 30B EPSILON	SF.260W WARRIOR	T-35A PILLÁN
224 kW (300 hp.)	194 kW (260 hp.)	224 kW (300 hp.)

MAXIMUM CLIMB RATE

Climb rate is an area in which the Epsilon outperforms the other types, thanks to its good power-to-weight ratio. This also gives the type superior manoeuvrability.

SF.260W WARRIOR 381 m/min (1,250 f.p.m.)

T-35A PILLÁN 465 m/min (1,525 f.p.m.)

TB 30B EPSILON 564 m/min (1,850 f.p.m.)

MAXIMUM ORDNANCE

The Pillán has strengthened wings able to carry almost 500 kg (1,102 lb.) of stores. Both the Epsilon and Warrior are restricted to 300 kg (661 lb.), though the Epsilon has four hardpoints stressed to hold 480 kg (1,058 lb.).

TB 30B EPSILON	SF.260W WARRIOR	T-35A PILLÁN
300 kg (660 lb.)	300 kg (660 lb.)	499 kg (1,100 lb.)

Turbine-powered trainers today

■ **EMBRAER TUCANO:** Brazil's turbine-powered EMB-312 has sold well in export markets and served as the basis for the Shorts-built, Garrett-engined Tucano sold to the RAF, Kenya and Kuwait.

■ **ENAER T-35DT AUCÁN:** Like the Oméga, the Aucán was a derivative of a piston-engined trainer, the Pillán. Chilean company ENAER developed the Pillán from the Piper PA-28 Dakota.

■ **PILATUS PC-9:** One of the Tucano's main competitors has been the Swiss PC-9. In 1997 the type was chosen by the USAF and US Navy to fill the need for a trainer to replace the T-34C and T-37B.

AGUSTA (SIAI-MARCHETTI)

S.211

● Advanced jet trainer ● Light attack aircraft ● Low cost

Developed originally by SIAI-Marchetti, the S.211 joined a new stable of military trainers in January 1997 when ownership of the company was transferred from Agusta to Aermacchi. First flying in April 1981, by 1988 it had been sold to four countries. An upgraded version, known as the S.211A, lost out to Beechcraft's modified Pilatus PC-9 in the JPATS competition to supply a new primary trainer for both the US Air Force and Navy.

▲ *Besides its principal role as a trainer, the S.211 is also fully combat-capable, a feature that has contributed to its adoption by a number of air forces looking for a versatile dual-role aircraft.*

AGUSTA (SIAI-MARCHETTI) S.211

◄ **JPATS**
An uprated S.211A was unsuccessfully shortlisted for the US Joint Primary Aircraft Training System (JPATS).

▼ **Lightweight performer**
Although a jet, the S.211 weighs little more than turboprop trainers, yet can out-perform them in most respects.

◄ **Service in the Far East**
S.211s were acquired by three Far Eastern nations – Brunei, the Philippines and Singapore – which operate them as trainers.

▼ **For export only**
Despite being of Italian origin, the S.211 has not been adopted by the country's own air force.

▲ **First flight**
Work began on the project in June 1977, with the first prototype, registered I-SITF, taking to the air on 10 April 1981.

FACTS AND FIGURES

➤ The Republic of Haiti, in the Caribbean, acquired a small number of S.211s in 1985. They were sold five years later.

➤ The S.211 was developed as a private venture by SIAI-Marchetti.

➤ JPATS S.211As were required to have a 14,400-hour fatigue life.

➤ Pratt & Whitney's JT15D turbojet engine also powers the USAF's Beech T-1A Jayhawk trainer.

➤ JPATS S.211A construction would have been split 50-50, with assembly in the US.

➤ Agusta proposed an S.211 variant with an improved navigation/attack system.

Lightweight, low-cost trainer

Economical operating costs and jet performance were the goal of the S.211. Weight is kept low by the extensive use of composite materials in its construction, and its reasonably high performance is accompanied by safe stalling and spinning characteristics, which are essential in a trainer.

In its alternative attack role, the S.211 can carry a useful ordnance load, including a wide range of rockets and gun pods, on four wing stations. Sales have proved disappointing, with only

the Philippines, Singapore and Haiti having bought a total of 52 aircraft by 1988. Since then, Brunei has been the only other customer. Most of Singapore's 30 S.211s were assembled locally, and the Philippine Aerospace Development Corporation was responsible for assembling 14 of the 18 aircraft delivered to the Philippine air force. The improved variant, the S.211A, was developed in partnership with Grumman and put forward unsuccessfully for the US JPATS competition. It featured a

Left: One of the three SIAI-Marchetti company demonstrators, wearing this distinctive desert camouflage, is seen poised for touch-down.

Below: Serialled I-SIJF, the second prototype flew three months after the first machine. Both aircraft wore this distinctive SIAI-Marchetti company livery.

14.2-kN (3,195-lb.-thrust) JT15D-5C engine for a higher top speed of 766 km/h (475 m.p.h.). Climb rate, range, service ceiling and *g* loadings were all improved, and weapon load was increased to 1090 kg (2,400 lb.).

S.211

Type: basic trainer and light strike aircraft

Powerplant: one 11.12-kN (2,500-lb.-thrust) Pratt & Whitney Canada JT15D-4C turbofan

Maximum speed: 667 km/h (414 m.p.h.) at 7620 m (25,000 ft.)

Initial climb rate: 1280 m/min (4,200 f.p.m.)

Range: 1168 km (724 mi.) on internal fuel

Service ceiling: 12,200 m (40,000 ft.)

Weights: empty 1850 kg (4,070 lb.), maximum take-off 3150 kg (6,930 lb.)

Armament: two 20-mm or four 12.7-mm (.50 in.) or 7.62-mm (.30 in.) gun pods, four rocket launchers, or up to 600 kg (1,320 lb.) of bombs

Dimensions:
span	8.43 m	(27 ft. 8 in.)
length	9.31 m	(30 ft. 6 in.)
height	3.80 m	(12 ft. 6 in.)
wing area	12.60 m²	(136 sq. ft.)

S.211

The Philippines acquired 18 S.211s, of which four were built in Italy, the remainder being assembled locally. All were assigned to the 100th Training Wing at Fernando, Luzon.

Following in the footsteps of other modern jet trainers, the S.211 features a high-mounted tandem cockpit that, in addition to offering excellent visibility, provides space for full navigation and communication equipment. Both pilot and instructor sit on Martin-Baker ejection seats, which are designed to punch through the canopy.

A mid-mounted supercritical wing gives the S.211 exceptional performance and manoeuvrability at high load. The ailerons feature a blunt trailing edge to enhance their effectiveness and control response.

Philippine aircraft are operated by one squadron. Half of them were delivered in natural metal and wear orange bands on the nose, rear fuselage and wings.

The main flight controls are mechanical, being operated by push rods. Secondary systems, such as the undercarriage and wheel brakes, are actuated hydraulically.

Fuel is carried internally in the wings and fuselage, with a total capacity of 802 litres (212 gal.). The aircraft can also be equipped with twin wing tanks containing 132 litres (35 gal.) each, which are normally used for ferry flights.

Powering the S.211 is a single Pratt & Whitney JT15D-4C twin spool turbofan, previously used only on business jet aircraft. Of advanced design, this engine has a good bypass ratio and gives excellent fuel consumption.

ACTION DATA

CLIMB RATE

Current jet trainers possess excellent performance and manoeuvrability. The S.211, although capable in its own right, is not quite in the same league of performance as the C.101 Aviojet or MB-339, both of which are used by their respective countries' national air display teams.

AERMACCHI MB-339A 2010 m/min (6,620 f.p.m.)

CASA C.101CC AVIOJET 1494 m/min (4,900 f.p.m.)

AGUSTA (SIAI-MARCHETTI) S.211 1280 m/min (4,200 f.p.m.)

THRUST

Not quite as powerful as rivals such as the CASA Aviojet or MB-339, the S.211 nevertheless has an exceptional power-to-weight ratio, being one of the lightest operational jet trainers around. All three aircraft were designed as low-cost machines.

AGUSTA (SIAI-MARCHETTI) S.211 11.12 kN (2,500 lb. thrust)

CASA C.101CC AVIOJET 19.13 kN (4,300 lb. thrust)

AERMACCHI MB-339A 17.79 kN (4,000 lb. thrust)

G LIMIT

Today, the vast majority of combat trainers in service have been designed to withstand high *g* loadings, thereby providing performance as close as possible to that of front-line aircraft. The S.211 is capable of pulling more than 6 *g*.

AERMACCHI MB-339A +8 *g*

CASA C.101CC AVIOJET +7.5 *g*

AGUSTA (SIAI-MARCHETTI) S.211 +6 *g*

European training/light attack aircraft

■ AERO L-39 ALBATROSS: Originating from former Czechoslovakia, the L-39 has proved a highly successful light attack/training aircraft.

■ BAe HAWK T.Mk 1: RAF Hawks serve with training and weapons conversions units, and some are configured for the air defence role.

■ CASA C.101CC AVIOJET: This dedicated attack version of the C.101 trainer first flew in November 1983.

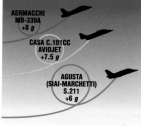

■ DASSAULT/DORNIER ALPHA JET: Jointly developed by France and Germany, the Alpha Jet remains in service with both countries' air forces.

AIDC

AT-3 Tsu Chiang

● Basic trainer ● First jet developed in Taiwan ● Display mount

▲ *Considerable*
pride in the development of the
AT-3 is reflected in the formation of a display
team equipped with the type. The team is based
at the Air Force Academy at Kangshan.

After building a version of the Pazmany PL-1 trainer, the Aero Industry Development Center (AIDC) produced its own turboprop basic trainer, the T-CH-1 Chung Tsing. In the early 1970s the AIDC started building more than 200 F-5 fighters for the Taiwan air force, and in 1975 it started work on its own jet aircraft design. Flown for the first time in September 1980, the AT-3 is the Taiwanese air force's standard basic trainer.

AIDC AT-3 Tsu Chiang

Learning curve ▶
The Tsu Chiang is proving to be an excellent training tool for introducing potential front-line pilots to advanced fast jet aircraft.

▲ **Clear view**
Visibility for the pupil and instructor, vital in training aircraft, is achieved with a large canopy.

Dedicated attack ▶
The single-seat version (above) developed for the close support role is known as the AT-3B.

▼ **Basic design**
Though offering little in the way of advanced design features, the AT-3 was a major step forward for the Taiwanese aviation industry.

▲ **Air-to-air**
Though a basic trainer, when required the AT-3 can be fitted with wingtip launch rails for Sidewinder air-to-air missiles and pylons for the delivery of a wide range of bombs and rockets.

FACTS AND FIGURES

➤ The first flight of the AT-3 took place on 16 September 1980 at the AIDC test facility in Taiwan.

➤ A contract was placed for 60 aircraft by the ROCAF who are the prime operators.

➤ For attack duties a single-seat close air-support version was developed.

➤ Seven external stores pylons are available to carry a wide range of bombs and missiles.

➤ Fewer than four hours of maintenance is needed on the AT-3 after a one-hour flight.

➤ An attack version designated A-3 Lui Meng was developed but then halted.

PROFILE

Taiwanese jet trainer

Although a fairly conventional aircraft, the AT-3 represented an ambitious step on the part of the AIDC. It also helped pave the way for the company to develop its own supersonic fighter design in the shape of the Ching-Kuo, when the US government prohibited the export of advanced fighters to the country.

Of the 60 AT-3s delivered between 1984 and 1990, 20 have been modified as AT-3B attack aircraft. Equipped with a version of the F-16's APG-66 radar and fire-control system, they have a weapons bay under the rear cockpit which can carry machine-gun packs.

Other stores can be carried on a fuselage centreline pylon and four wing pylons, and there are wingtip rails for air-to-air missiles. Another attack variant, the single-seat A-3 Lui Meng, was built in prototype form only. The appearance of the AT-3B led to the original model being redesignated the AT-3A. It serves with the Taiwan air force

Above: Taiwanese air force student pilots receive 120 hours' instruction on the AT-3 before advancing to a front-line squadron.

(ROCAF) academy, and pilot cadets fly it for the first part of their jet training. The attack version equips the air force's No. 71 Squadron at Tainan.

Above: The bright colours of this AT-3 signify its allocation to the Taiwanese display team based at Kangshan.

AT-3B Tsu Chiang

Type: two-seat basic trainer

Powerplant: two 15.57-kN (3,500-lb.-thrust) Garrett TF3 731-2-2L turbofan engines

Maximum speed: 904 km/h (561 m.p.h.) at 11,000 m (36,000 ft.)

Initial climb rate: 3078 m/min (10,100 f.p.m.)

Range: 2279 km (1,413 mi.)

Service ceiling: 14,625 m (48,000 ft.)

Weights: empty 3856 kg (8,483 lb.); take-off 7938 kg (17,464 lb.)

Armament: two wingtip AAMs; 2721 kg (5,986 lb.) of bombs can be fitted

Dimensions:
span	10.46 m	(34 ft. 4 in.)
length	12.90 m	(42 ft. 4 in.)
height	4.36 m	(14 ft. 4 in.)
wing area	21.93 m² (235 sq. ft.)	

AT-3 Tsu Chiang

The first military jet developed in Taiwan, the AT-3 is proving to be highly suitable as a fast jet trainer. A single-seat attack version has also been developed and is in limited service with the ROCAF.

The pilots are seated on zero-zero ejection seats which allow the crew to escape from the aircraft at ground level if necessary.

The two turbofan engines are easy to maintain, helping the AT-3 to be operated in the bustling environment of a flight training academy.

Of conventional construction, the AT-3 consists of a light-alloy structure with heavy-plate machine skinning over the semi-monocoque fuselage.

Visibility from the cockpit is exceptional. The large canopy and the raised position of the ejection seats allow excellent crew co-ordination.

Although the AT-3 is only a trainer, a state-of-the-art radar is installed which is compatible with later aircraft on to which the student progresses.

A well-equipped cockpit instrument panel is fitted for each pilot featuring multi-functional displays, and for attack duties a sophisticated head-up display.

In a more offensive role, the AT-3 can be fitted with wingtip missiles for air combat. Pylons can also be attached to the wings to allow bombs to be carried.

The high visibility day-glo patches on this AT-3 signify that this AT-3 serves in the flight training role, preparing cadets for fast-jet operations.

ACTION DATA

RANGE

The long range of the AT-3B is a reflection of the aircraft's dual role as a battlefield attack type. Restricted to purely training duties, the Spanish Aviojet offers a more modest range and consequently has no secondary attack role in Spanish service. Although the largest of the three the T-4's range is only fair.

AT-3B 2279 km (1,413 mi.)
C.101CC AVIOJET 519 km (322 mi.)
T-4 1297 km (804 mi.)

MAXIMUM SPEED

The twin-engine layout of the AT-3 allows a high performance to be achieved, which undoubtedly eases conversion to front-line jets for the Taiwanese pilots. Although Japan's T-4 is the best performer, this is reflected in the high cost of the aircraft which has reduced its export potential.

AT-3B	904 km/h (561 m.p.h.)
C.101CC	834 km/h (517 m.p.h.)
T-4	1038 km/h (644 m.p.h.)

SERVICE CEILING

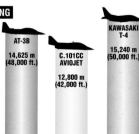

With the normal limited thrust of typical training types, a surprisingly good performance is achieved by the AT-3B. By operating at a high altitude a saving in fuel is possible, while increasing the safety margin for the pilot.

AT-3B 14,625 m (48,000 ft.)
C.101CC AVIOJET 12,800 m (42,000 ft.)
KAWASAKI T-4 15,240 m (50,000 ft.)

Defending the Republic

T-CH-1 CHUNG TSING: The first military aircraft of indigenous Taiwanese design, the T-CH-1 was heavily influenced by the T-28 Trojan. A reconnaissance variant is still in service.

F-104G STARFIGHTER: Purchased from surplus European stocks, the F-104 has been progressively updated. The aircraft will remain in front-line service for the foreseeable future.

F-5E TIGER II: First delivered in 1973, the F-5E at present is the most potent aircraft in the Taiwanese inventory, the twin-seat F-5F is also in service in a dual trainer-attack role.

AIRTECH
CN.235

● Twin turboprop tactical transport ● Excellent STOL performance

I t looks like a mini-Hercules, and performs like one. Designed and built in Spain and Indonesia, the Airtech CN.235 is a highly capable, very successful short-range tactical transport. Intended to operate from short, semi-prepared fields, this twin-turboprop machine has proven itself a highly effective and economical aircraft, suitable for a variety of uses from cargo-hauling through casualty evacuation and VIP transport to armed maritime patrol.

▲ Airborne troops drop from doors fitted to both sides of the fuselage of a CN.235M military transport. The aircraft can carry and deliver up to 46 fully equipped paratroopers.

AIRTECH CN.235

Airborne assault ▶
The CN.235's high swept tail and large rear loading ramp were designed to allow the delivery of cargo by parachute.

▼ Armée de l'Air
The French air force operates eight CN.235s alongside larger Transall C-160s and Hercules.

▲ Saudi CN.235
Saudi Arabia is one of the smaller operators of Airtech's CN.235, with just two transport and two luxury-interior VIP versions.

▼ U.S. powerplants
Like all CN.235s, this United Arab Emirates aircraft is powered by two General Electric CT7-9C four-blade turboprop engines.

Coastal persuasion ▶
The CN.235MPA Persuader is a maritime patroller that has search radar, FLIR surveillance sensors, and six wing pylons for armament.

FACTS AND FIGURES

➤ The first CN.235s to be delivered began coming off the Indonesian production lines in December 1986.

➤ Military CN.235s can land on airstrips less than 500 m (1,650 ft.) in length.

➤ As a commuter airliner, the CN.235 can carry up to 44 passengers.

➤ The coastal patrol CN.235MPA can carry up to 3500 kg (7,700 lb.) of torpedoes or anti-ship missiles on six underwing pylons.

➤ In the medevac role the CN.235 can carry 24 stretchers and four attendants.

➤ The cargo bay is 9.65 m (31.8 ft.) long and has a deck area of 22.82 m² (246 sq. ft.).

PROFILE

Multi-role Spanish-Indonesian airlifter

Spain's Construcciones Aeronauticas SA, or CASA, is one of the oldest aircraft manufacturing companies in the world. Founded in 1923, it seems an unlikely complement to Indonesia, one of the world's newer aviation nations. But in partnership with Industri Pesawat Terbang Nusantara, or IPTN, it has set up the joint company known as Airtech, specifically to develop and produce the twin turboprop CN.235 light/medium short-haul transport, and a successful partnership it has become.

Development work began in 1980. First flown on 11 November 1983 in Spain and on December 30 of that year in

Indonesia, the CN.235 follows the standard layout of a modern military transport, with circular-section pressurized fuselage, high wing and tail, and rear loading ramp.

The CN-235's excellent rough-field STOL performance has seen it achieve considerable success on the export market. By the mid 1990s, more than 200 had been sold to at least 17 military customers and another 30 or more to civil operators.

The majority of CN.235s sold have been tactical transports, but a number have been fitted out as VIP transports, and the CN.235MPA Persuader is a specialized maritime patrol variant.

Above: South Korea has taken delivery of 12 CN.235s, and is one of more than 17 countries that operate the aircraft.

Right: The Moroccan air force operates six CN.235s in the general transport role, plus one example for VIP duties.

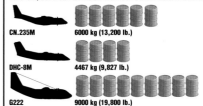

CN.235M Series 100

Type: short-range military transport

Powerplant: two 1394.5-kW (1,870-hp.) General Electric CT7-9C turboprops

Maximum cruise speed: 460 km/h (285 m.p.h.) at 4500 m (14,750 ft.)

Maximum climb rate: 579 m/min (1,900 f.p.m.)

Range: 1500 km (930 mi.) with max payload; 4355 km (2,700 mi.) with 3550-kg (7,810-lb.) payload

Service ceiling: 8110 m (26,600 ft.)

Maximum takeoff weight: 16,500 kg (54,120 lb.)

Payload: 48 troops or 46 paratroops or 24 stretchers or 6000 kg (13,200 lb.) of cargo

Dimensions:
span	25.81 m	(84 ft. 7 in.)
length	21.35 m	(70 ft.)
height	8.18 m	(26 ft. 10 in.)
wing area	59.10 m²	(636 sq. ft.)

CN.235M

Standard military version of the CN.235, seen here in Spanish colors. The Spanish air force operates 26 of these aircraft.

The CN.235 has a conventional cockpit, and is usually flown by a two-person flight crew of pilot and copilot.

From the 31st production aircraft the CN.235 has been fitted with a more powerful variant of the General Electric CT7 turboprop.

The high-lift wing is of conventional alloy, but the leading- and trailing-edge flaps are made from advanced composite materials.

The landing gear is carried on sponsons on the fuselage sides, and does not intrude into the cargo compartment. It is suitable for operation from semi-prepared surfaces.

The fuselage is of conventional semi-monocoque construction, and is largely built from aluminum alloys.

The upswept tail and tall fin was incorporated into the design to allow the large rear cargo door.

The lower part of the divided rear door swings down to serve as a cargo ramp for loading larger cargoes, such as NATO standard containers. The ramp can be opened in flight to allow parachute delivery of equipment.

721 19

ACTION DATA

PAYLOAD

The CN.235 has several rivals in the short-range tactical transport field. It has a larger payload than the similar-sized Canadian DHC-8M, but it cannot match the much bulkier Italian Alenia G222.

CN.235M	6000 kg (13,200 lb.)
DHC-8M	4467 kg (9,827 lb.)
G222	9000 kg (19,800 lb.)

TAKEOFF DISTANCE

While the CN.235 is a good short-field performer it needs more runway than the DHC-8M, which sacrifices cargo load for performance. The far more powerful G222 performs even better.

G222 662 m (2,170 ft.)
DHC-8M 960 m (3,149 ft.)
CN.235M 1060 m (3,510 ft.)

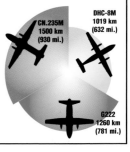

RANGE

The CN.235 has a longer range with maximum load than its rivals when carrying a full load, although the G222's capacious fuselage can lift around three tons more than the Spanish/Indonesian transport. The Canadian DHC-8 was designed as a passenger carrier, and so does not perform as well when carrying heavy freight loads.

DHC-8M 1019 km (632 mi.)
CN.235M 1500 km (930 mi.)
G222 1260 km (781 mi.)

Roles of the CN.235

VERSATILITY: The CN.235's roller-equipped cargo bay can carry a variety of fittings depending on the aircraft's mission.

MEDEVAC: The CN.235's circular section pressure fuselage with rear loading ramp is easy to convert to a 24-stretcher ambulance configuration.

MARITIME PATROL: The CN.235MPA has added radar, night vision and electronic sensors, and can carry weapons.

TRANSPORT: The CN.235 can carry troops or cargo in standard LD3 containers, or a mix of both.

ALENIA (AERITALIA)

G222

● Italian twin-engined tactical transport ● Operators worldwide

PHOTO FILE

ALENIA (AERITALIA) G222

▲ Cargo capacity
The G222 can lift a maximum payload of nine tons. It can air-drop palletised cargo or up to 32 fully-equipped paratroops.

▲ Export success
Ten customers have bought the G222 and use the transport aircraft in a variety of roles.

C-27 Spartan ▶
The USAF operates the C-27 Spartan in Central America.

◀ Calibration craft
Surprisingly agile for an aircraft of its size, the G222 is a popular Italian air show performer. This example is a G222RM instrument calibration aircraft and is one of four built for the Italian air force.

Short take-off ▶
The G222 excels at flying into and out of short, rough airstrips. It can take off in less than 1000 m (3,200 ft.).

Originally designed by Fiat in the 1960s and flown for the first time in July 1970, the G222 had to fulfil the Italian air force's requirement for an aircraft that was able to cope with short, semi-prepared airstrips, mountainous terrain and extreme weather. The Aeronautica Militare Italiana (AMI) remains the type's biggest user, but the G222's ruggedness and adaptability have also won orders from other military operators and development continues.

▲ An Italian M151
jeep is driven onto a G222 transport. Although only 100 examples of Italy's standard tactical lifter have been built, around half have been exported to seven other air arms.

FACTS AND FIGURES

➤ After operational evaluation by the Italian air force, a production G222 was flown in late 1975 and 46 machines were ordered.

➤ A NATO competition in the mid-1960s resulted in the G222.

➤ Two prototypes (MM582 and 583) were flown on 18 July 1970 and 22 July 1971.

➤ A collaborative manufacturing effort between Italian aerospace firms produced components for the G222.

➤ Four versions are in service with the Aeronautica Militare Italiana.

➤ Libyan Rolls-Royce Tyne-powered G222s use engines from ex-RAF Belfasts.

PROFILE

Italian tactical airlifter

Many G222s were delivered in special configurations for the Italian air force. Four were completed as flight inspection aircraft, with equipment to analyse the accuracy of radio navigation aids. A further eight were built as aerial firefighters and two as electronic warfare machines. One has been modified as a maritime patrol aircraft for the Italian customs service. The standard military transport can also be adapted to other roles. Quick-change kits turn it into an aeromedical

aircraft, and in this form it has been used to support Red Cross operations as far afield as Kampuchea and Peru. Export customers include Argentina, Dubai, Nigeria, Somalia and Venezuela, and 20 were completed with Rolls-Royce Tyne engines for Libya. In 1990 the USAF selected the G222 to support US forces in Latin America. These aircraft were assembled by Alenia and sent to Chrysler Aerospace for installation of mission equipment.

In 1996 Alenia and Lockheed agreed to develop a modernised

version as the C-27J, with upgraded systems similar to those installed in the latest four-engined, high-technology C-130J Hercules.

Below: Alongside the regular transport, the Italian air force operates three specialised versions. This is the G222VS (Versione Speciale), which is equipped with various antennas for the electronic warfare role.

Above: Italy operates the G222SAA (Sistema Aeronautico Antincendio) firefighting version. The G222RM (Radio Misure) calibrates airfield radios and radars.

G222TCM

Type: light/medium tactical transport

Powerplant: two 2535-kW (3,400-hp.) Fiat-built General Electric T64-GE-P4D turboprops

Maximum speed: 540 km/h (335 m.p.h.)

Initial climb rate: 520 m/min (1,700 f.p.m.)

Take-off run: 662 m (2,170 ft.) at maximum take-off weight

Range: 1371 km (850 mi.) with maximum payload

Service ceiling: 7620 m (25,000 ft.)

Weights: empty 15,400 kg (33,880 lb.); maximum take-off 28,000 kg (61,600 lb.)

Payload: maximum 9000 kg (19,800 lb.)

Dimensions:
span	28.70 m	(94 ft. 2 in.)
length	22.70 m	(74 ft. 5 in.)
height	9.80 m	(32 ft. 2 in.)
wing area	82.00 m²	(882 sq. ft.)

G222TCM

The AMI bought 46 aircraft and operates the largest number of G222s. This is a standard transport, wearing the markings of 46ª Aerobrigata Trasporti Medi (Medium Air Transport Wing), based at Pisa-San Giusto.

The G222 normally carries a crew of three – a pilot, co-pilot and a flight engineer/radio operator. A loadmaster can also be carried in the cargo hold.

Under licence from General Electric, Fiat produced the T64-GE-P4D engine for the G222. Libyan aircraft are powered by Rolls-Royce Tyne engines.

The cargo hold can carry a maximum of 44 troops or 32 paratroops or 9000 kg (19,800 lb.) of freight. Both the flightdeck and hold are partially pressurised (and air-conditioned) to give an environment which is equivalent to that at 1200 m (4,000 ft.) when flying at 6000 m (19,700 ft.).

De-icing strips line the leading edges of all wing and tail surfaces. The leading edges of the propeller blades and the spinners are de-iced electrically. A mixture of hot air and electrical heating keeps the engine intakes clear of ice.

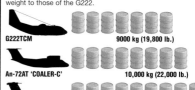

Paratroops are usually deployed via two doors, one on either side of the rear fuselage, but can use the rear doors if necessary.

As on most modern tactical airlifters, the upswept rear fuselage of the G222 contains rear loading doors which can be opened in flight for air-dropping cargo.

46 82

ACTION DATA

MAXIMUM PAYLOAD

In service use performance considerations are likely to restrict the Antonov An-72 and Kawasaki C-1 to loads of a similar weight to those of the G222.

G222TCM	9000 kg (19,800 lb.)
An-72AT 'COALER-C'	10,000 kg (22,000 lb.)
C-1	11,900 kg (26,200 lb.)

TAKE-OFF RUN

Outstanding short take-off performance is a feature of the C-1, but it is not as rugged as the G222 or An-72 and is therefore restricted to better prepared airstrips. In addition, the jets are again weight restricted, while the G222 performs as shown with a full payload.

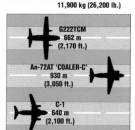

G222TCM	662 m (2,170 ft.)
An-72AT 'COALER-C'	930 m (3,050 ft.)
C-1	640 m (2,100 ft.)

RANGE

With maximum payload and maximum fuel, the efficient turboprop engines of the G222 allow it to outperform its jet rivals in range. With full payload, the jet transports – especially the 'Coaler-C' – offer only limited range, which is fine in a tactical scenario but restricts their overall versatility. The jets have the advantage of flying faster sectors, however.

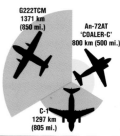

G222TCM	1371 km (850 mi.)
An-72AT 'COALER-C'	800 km (500 mi.)
C-1	1297 km (805 mi.)

International G222 operators

ARGENTINA: Comando de Aviacion del Ejercito (Argentine Army Aviation Command) took delivery of three G222s in 1977. They played no part in the Falklands War.

DUBAI: Part of the United Arab Emirates, Dubai was the first export customer for the G222. Only one aircraft was delivered, in November 1976, and this remains in service.

LIBYA: Libya's 20 G222s were fitted with Rolls-Royce Tyne turboprops to overcome the American embargo on supplying T64 engines. They were used during the intervention in Chad.

SOMALIA: Somalia originally ordered six G222s, but only two were delivered, in 1980. They suffered from shortages of spares and were both destroyed during the 1993 civil war.

AMX INTERNATIONAL

AMX

● Tactical striker ● Light-attack aircraft ● Reconnaissance

▲ Showing that it can help make light fighters, as well as trainers and executive aircraft, has been an important factor for EMBRAER. It makes the air intakes, pylons, wings and reconnaissance pallet.

Deemed good enough to replace two able old warriors, the Fiat G.91 and Lockheed F-104 in Italian air force service, the Aeritalia/Aermacchi AMX was originally conceived as a small multi-role light-attack aircraft in 1976. EMBRAER of Brazil joined the Italian concern and this collaboration eventually proved fruitful. The aircraft entered service with Italy's 51 Stormo in October 1989 and Brazil's 1 Esquadrao in October 1989.

AMX INTERNATIONAL AMX

▲ Light fighter
For nations such as Italy, the AMX is a good compromise between light-strike advanced trainers like the MB.339 and heavy-strike aircraft like the Tornado.

▲ Night mission
Provision for forward-looking infrared or passive night goggles gives the AMX night strike capability, which would be much further enhanced by a TIALD pod.

▲ Maximum load
Optimized for tactical strike, the AMX usually carries cluster bombs, rocket pods or Skyshark dispenser weapons.

◄ Two-seater
The AMX-T two-seat conversion trainer is fully combat capable, though it has shorter range than the single-seater.

Modern design ▶
Despite its plain appearance, the AMX is a modern design, with low maintenance requirements and good reliability. The aircraft can stand at 15 minutes readiness for 30 days with limited servicing.

FACTS AND FIGURES

➤ Series production of the AMX began in July 1986, and the first aircraft rolled out on 29 March 1988.

➤ Brazilian AMXs have two 30-mm cannon, and Italian ones have one 20-mm Vulcan.

➤ An engine problem resulted in the crash of the prototype AMX on 1 June 1984.

➤ The AMX can carry weapons on seven hardpoints and boost this figure to 12 by using multiple stores carriers.

➤ Brazilian AMXs carry the MAA-1 Piranha missile for self defense.

➤ A proposed electronic warfare AMX with HARM missiles has not been developed.

PROFILE

AMX Latin light striker

Designed from the outset to undertake the strike role, the AMX International is the result of European and South American collaboration to build a wholly new airplane for the Italian air force, and has proven remarkably successful. The Italian requirement was made known in 1977 and, rather than buy 'off-the-shelf' or opt for a refurbished older type, the decision was taken to design a new aircraft.

Both the larger Italian

aerospace manufacturers pooled resources in April 1978 and Brazil joined in July 1981, with the object of securing the Italian design as a follow-up to the MB.326.

The AMX began flight testing in May 1984. Trials set out to establish that the planned low-level delivery of a variety of ordnance (up to 2722 kg (5,988 lb.)) over a 370-km (230-mi.) range was a viable alternative to big and expensive hardware. This was indeed proven but the AMX lacks radar and has no all-

Another highly successful collaborative program for Italy and Brazil, the AMX has yet to win export orders in the face of severe competition from the Hawk 200.

weather capability. But with the AMX/A-1 in service in Italy and Brazil, and a trainer version, the AMX-T, undergoing flight-tests, the development program promises some interesting new models, with an anti-shipping or electronic warfare variant still possible.

Brazil's AMXs are the most modern strike aircraft in Latin America, and the type may well be ordered by other nations in the region. It offers a performance capability between Brazil's F-5s and Mirage IIIs.

AMX

Type: close support fighter-bomber.

Powerplant: one 49.10-kN (11,000-lb.-thrust) Rolls-Royce Spey Mk 107 turbofan.

Max speed: 914 km/h (567 m.p.h.)

Service ceiling: 13,000 m (42,640 ft.)

Range: 890 km (552 mi.)

Weights: empty 6700 kg (14,740 lb.); loaded 12,500 kg (27,500 lb.)

Weapons: one M61-A1 20-mm cannon or two DEFA 554 30-mm cannon; and up to a 2722-kg (5,988-lb.) bomb load.

Dimensions:
span	8.87 m	(29 ft.)
length	13.23 m	(43 ft.)
height	4.55 m	(15 ft.)
wing area	21 m²	(226 sq. ft.)

AMX

The Fuerza Aera Braziliana designated the AMX as the A-1. The first Brazilian unit was 1 Esquadrao of 16 Grupo de Aviaco de Caca at Santa Cruz.

The wing has spoilers in front of the ailerons, which augment the ailerons as well as act as lift-dumpers and airbrakes. The wing has leading-edge flaps and trailing-edge Fowler flaps to give short-field takeoff capability.

The wingtip store station is for defensive air-to-air missiles, such as the Sidewinder.

An OMI/Selenia head-up display and Alenia multi-function display help ease pilot workload. The cockpit has HOTAS (Hands on throttle and stick) controls.

Italian AMXs have a small FIAR Pointer radar based on the ELTA EL/M, and any future advanced variants will probably have a FIAR Grifo multi-mode system. Brazilian aircraft will probably receive the SCP-01 radar soon.

The canopy is a one-piece sideways hinging unit, which allows excellent all-round vision. The pilot sits on a Martin-Baker ejection seat.

AMX is powered by a single Rolls-Royce Spey 168 turbofan built under license in Italy. This reliable engine is similar to the model which was used in the Buccaneer.

Low-intensity strip lights are fitted to the rear fuselage to aid formation flying at night.

ACTION DATA

AIM-9L SIDEWINDER
Used by several NATO countries, the AIM-9L is one of the most advanced Sidewinder models, able to attack targets from the front if they are flying fast enough. The AMX carries a pair of Sidewinders on wingtip pylons. Sidewinder has an 11-kg (24-lb.) blast fragmentation warhead triggered by a laser proximity fuse.

GBU-12
Paveway II GBU-12 is a laser-guided 500-lb. (227 kg.) bomb, which is extremely accurate. It homes in on reflected laser energy from a designator. Although the AMX has no laser designator, it is earmarked to receive a podded system such as the GEC TIALD or Thomson-CSF ATLIS to allow the pilot to mark targets.

MK-83
A conventional unguided 'dumb' bomb, the Mk 83 is a steel-cased 447-kg (1,000-lb.) weapon filled with 202 kg (450 lb.) of H-6 explosive. Used in conventional mode, the bomb is fitted with M904 nose fuses and M905 tail fuses. It can be fitted with a Ballute type tail section for delivery as a retarded bomb and is normally carried underwing.

Brazil's fighter-bombers

■ **EMBRAER XAVANTE:** The Xavante, a license-built Aermacchi MB.326, is an advanced trainer with light-strike capability and armed with machine guns, cluster bombs and rocket pods. About 100 remain in service. The Xavante can also be equipped with a Vinten camera pod for performing reconnaissance missions.

■ **NORTHROP F-5E:** Used in the light-attack role, Brazil is planning to upgrade its F-5s with the same SCP-01 radar and OMI/Alenia HUD as used in the AMX. They have already been supplied with air-to-air refueling probes. Brazil's 36 F-5Es are based at Santa Cruz and Canoas.

■ **MIRAGE IIIDBR:** The nation's primary interceptor, the Mirage III has also been upgraded with canards and new avionics. They are armed with Matra R530 missiles and DEFA 30-mm cannon. With the introduction of AMX, it is unlikely that the Mirage will be used in air-to-ground roles despite its capability.

ANTONOV
AN-12 'CUB'

● Tactical airlifter ● Flying command post ● Electronic warfare

Antonov's An-12 'Cub' is a big, tough, practical transport often called the 'Soviet C-130' because it closely resembles the West's Lockheed Hercules. The Ukrainian-designed An-12 is a high-wing, four-engined, rear-loading freighter that won wide acceptance in the Soviet military, served the airlines and was copied in China. This versatile machine also operated in Afghanistan and worked as an electronic warfare jammer and testbed.

▲ Like the C-130, the An-12 was the first transport properly designed for the forces that used it, featuring a high wing, turboprops, rough-field capability, large rear loading doors and a wide fuselage. The utility of such machines has ensured that the An-12 is still in service today.

ANTONOV AN-12 'CUB'

▲ **Driver's seat**
The An-12 cockpit is a spartan place to work, but it is well laid out and offers the pilot a good view for landing.

▲ **Soft landing**
With its long flaps and low-pressure tyres, the An-12 can easily touch down safely on rough strips at high weights.

Himalaya flyer ▶
India's An-12s operate in the Himalayan range, but the lack of pressurisation in the hold often limits their operations there.

▲ **Still going strong**
The An-12 still remained in service in the mid-1990s: this Aeroflot machine is flying from Zhukovskii.

Aeroflot visitor ▶
Intercepted by an A-7 from the carrier USS Midway, this An-12 was on a reconnaissance mission.

FACTS AND FIGURES

➤ Many An-12s have been converted for duty as test and research platforms, including engine testbed work.

➤ When production ended in 1973, about 900 An-12s had been built in the USSR.

➤ The prototype Antonov An-12 made its maiden flight in 1958.

➤ China produces the An-12, known as the Y-8, in Xian and has exported the type to Sri Lanka and Sudan.

➤ Afghan rebels succeeded in downing an An-12 with Stinger missiles.

➤ Four tonnes of electronic warfare gear is carried by the 'Cub-C' jammer.

PROFILE

Supreme Soviet tactical airlifter

Antonov's An-12 'Cub' is the hard-working transport which pilots say cannot be replaced. Although this burly, turboprop heavyweight has been out of production for a quarter of a century (its American equivalent, the C-130, is still being built), pilots agree that plans to replace the 'Cub' with jet transports were premature.

The 'Cub' is an enduring presence in the former Soviet Union and is still relied upon to transport military supplies, while also being used for secondary missions. In addition, Aeroflot continues to operate a small number of An-12 civil freighters.

The An-12 is not fully pressurised like the C-130 and uses a different method of rear loading, which sometimes requires additional ground equipment. The An-12 cannot land on a rough, unpaved surface near the battlefield in the short distance of 1500 m (4,920 ft.) that is required by the C-130. But when support equipment is available and airfields are used, the An-12 is a champion freight-hauler for a plane of its class.

Aeroflot found the An-12 essential, as a large area of the USSR was totally inaccessible to more conventional aircraft.

The Czech Republic and Slovakia both retained an An-12 each after the division of Czechoslovakia. Although the Slovak An-12 ('2209') is used, the Czechs have retired their aircraft despite having no replacement.

Y-8

The Shaanxi Y-8 is a Chinese-built version of the An-12. Amazingly, this aircraft is still in production and the latest version, the Y-8C, was first flown in 1990 and is widely used by Chinese operators.

Like most modern tactical transports, the An-12 was powered by four turboprops, namely the Ivchenko AI-20. Hot air from the engines was used to de-ice the wing and tail.

The wing design for the An-12 was derived from that of the An-10, but held more fuel in its 26 tanks. A high wing design was chosen to allow vehicles to drive around the aircraft easily and for the pilot to see the ground. It also kept the propellers clear of debris on rough airstrips.

A crew of five were accommodated in the front of the An-12 in a pressurised cockpit. The crew consisted of two pilots, a navigator, flight engineer and radio operator.

Some aircraft had an additional pressurised 12-man compartment fitted behind the flight deck to accommodate cargo handlers and vehicle crews.

The fuselage can accommodate vehicles such as the ZSU-23-4 tracked anti-aircraft gun or PT-76 light tank.

The tail turret is based on that of the Tu-16 'Badger' medium bomber and contains two 23-mm cannon. It has a tail warning radar, but not a gun-laying radar. The turret is pressurised for the gunner. Remaining aircraft often have the guns deleted.

Most An-12s had clamshell-style doors, but a few had a C-130-style rear loading ramp door.

An-12 'Cub'

Type: passenger/cargo transport

Powerplant: four 2983-kW (3,940-hp.) Ivchenko AI-20K turboprop engines

Maximum speed: 670 km/h (416 m.p.h.)

Cruising speed: 550 km/h 342 m.p.h.) at 7620 m (25,000 ft.)

Range: 5700 km (3,542 mi.)

Service ceiling: 10,200 m (33,500 ft.)

Weights: normal take-off 54,000 kg (119,050 lb.); maximum take-off 61,000 kg (134,482 lb.)

Armament: (on some military An-12s) two 'NR-23' 23-mm cannons in a rear turret

Dimensions:
span	38.00 m	(124 ft. 8 in.)
length	33.10 m	(108 ft. 7 in.)
height	10.53 m	(34 ft. 7 in.)
wing area	121.70 m² (1,310 sq. ft.)	

COMBAT DATA

MAXIMUM CRUISING SPEED

With turboprop engines and a bulky fuselage, tactical transports are not designed for speed. The more streamlined fuselage of the An-12 gives it a slightly higher speed than the C-130, but in practice most transports rarely reach their maximum speed.

An-12 'CUB' 670 km/h (416 m.p.h.)

C-130 HERCULES 595 km/h (370 m.p.h.)

C.160 513 km/h (319 m.p.h.)

LOAD

The Antonov has impressive load-carrying capability, and can haul more than a C-130. Perhaps the only weakness of the An-12 is that loading the aircraft is slower than a C-130 or a Transall C.160 due to the absence of a rear loading ramp. The Transall is only a twin-engined design but still manages to carry a fair payload.

An-12 'CUB'	C-130 HERCULES	C.160
20,000 kg (44,092 lb.)	16,194 kg (35,702 lb.)	16,000 kg (35,274 lb.)

RANGE

The An-12 has less range than a C-130, but it still has an adequate radius of action for a tactical transport, especially considering that operations in Europe do not require long stretches without refuelling. Jamming An-12s could stay on station for long stretches at a time.

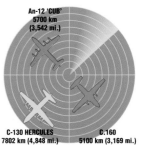

An-12 'CUB' 5700 km (3,542 mi.)

C-130 HERCULES 7802 km (4,848 mi.)

C.160 5100 km (3,169 mi.)

An-12 missions

TARGET TANK: The object of the An-12 mission was to attack Pakistani troops and armour during the 1971 conflict.

BOMBING RAID: India converted several of its An-12BPs to serve as makeshift bombers; 16 tons of palletised bombs were pushed out of the rear doors.

EJECTION TEST: The An-12 has also been fitted with a special tail cone used for firing ejection seats to test their effectiveness.

ELECTRONIC JAMMER: An electronic warfare variant known to NATO as 'Cub-C' has active jamming gear for blocking communications and radar, and can also dispense 'chaff' barriers to give false returns on radar.

ANTONOV

AN-24 'COKE'/AN-26 'CURL'

● Twin-turboprops ● Personnel transport ● Tactical airlifters

Designed to satisfy an Aeroflot requirement for a turboprop transport, the An-24 'Coke' also sold in some numbers to military operators as both a passenger and freight carrier. It led directly to development of the An-26 'Curl', a dedicated military tactical transport, which has proven itself to be a rugged and capable performer. In China, unlicensed production of both aircraft has been carried out under the designation Xian Y-7.

▲ *Antonov's*
twins serve in some numbers
with both military and paramilitary operators.
The majority of An-24s are passenger
transports without rear loading ramp doors.

Czech 'Curl' ▶
This aircraft demonstrates the distinctive
bubble observation window of the type.

▼ Paradropping
With its large rear door and
blister observation window,
the An-26 is optimised for
the parachute deployment
of troops.

▲ Jet APU
The jet exhaust of the APU is clearly seen within the polished
section of the starboard engine nacelle of this Czech An-26.

Abraded underside ▼
During rough-field operations debris is thrown up at the
underside of the fuselage, as shown by this weathered aircraft.

▼ African 'Coke'
At least five An-24s were
supplied to Sudan, but all
seem to have been
withdrawn from use.

FACTS AND FIGURES

➤ Very few operators use the An-24 in a freight role; most use the aircraft as a 50-seat passenger transport.

➤ Under the designation An-24P, one 'Coke' was modified for fire-bombing.

➤ Antonov claims a corrosion life of 30,000 hours for the An-24 fuselage.

➤ The An-26 was the first Soviet-designed transport aircraft to have a fully pressurised hold.

➤ During 1996, Russia had 20 Elint-dedicated An-26s on strength.

➤ Angola's and Mozambique's air forces have used An-26s as attack aircraft.

PROFILE

Antonov's lightweight airlifters

Having first flown on 20 December 1959, the An-24 'Coke' was a direct competitor to the F27 Friendship. Both aircraft were fundamentally airliners, but both sought military customers, in which quest the 'Coke' came off best. Antonov designed the An-24 with the emphasis on strength and reliability, rather than on lightweight and economical operations.

Early aircraft featured a gas turbine auxiliary power unit (APU) in the rear of the starboard engine nacelle, but this was replaced in the An-24RV by a small turbojet which improved take-off performance. This installation was also a feature of the An-24RT dedicated freighter.

Designed as a tactical airlifter, the An-26 has enjoyed far greater success. It has greater power, an upswept rear fuselage which incorporates a large cargo door, and is fully equipped for the rapid loading and off-loading of freight, light vehicles or paratroops.

Unusually, the An-26 has a second skin of titanium beneath the fuselage, to protect it during rough field operations. The aircraft has also been developed into a number of special versions, especially for the electronic intelligence, signals intelligence and electronic warfare (Elint, Sigint and EW) roles. All machines in this category are given the NATO designation 'Curl-B'.

Left: Early in 1996, the Libyan Arab Republic Air Force had eight An-26s on strength as transports.

Above: Hungary flies the An-24V in the conventional passenger role, alongside An-26 tactical airlifters, as illustrated.

A flight crew of three is required to operate the An-24. The aircraft represents a departure from previous Soviet design philosophy by having a radar nose instead of the extensively glazed navigator's position normally associated with Soviet transports.

Mounted high on the wing, the powerful turboprops and their propellers are kept away from flying debris. An-24RT and RV machines have an auxiliary turbojet replacing the APU in the starboard nacelle. This provides all electrical power on take-off, allowing the main engines to deliver more thrust to the propellers, as well as providing residual thrust.

In addition to its five An-24RVs, in March 1996 the Czech air force also had in service four An-26s and a single, Elint-dedicated An-26Z-1M 'Curl-B'.

AN-24RV 'COKE'

When it was formed in 1992, the Czech air force received a number of An-24s from the former Czechoslovak air force. The aircraft are generally used as staff transports.

2904

In cross-section, the fuselage of both the An-24 and An-26 takes the form of a rounded triangle. This allows maximum floor width, while retaining a nearly circular cross-section which is structurally desirable for a pressurised cabin.

Most military An-24s are flown as pure passenger transports and are designated An-24V, or RV with turbojet APU. A cargo variant was produced as the An-24T (An-24RT) with rear loading and twin ventral fins, but it found few customers.

As a passenger transport, the An-24 was supplied with a small entry door in the port rear fuselage. The ventral fins fitted to An-24Ts were sometimes applied to An-24Vs, as on this example.

'Curl' colours

AFGHANISTAN: In 1978 the first of about 20 An-26s and a number of An-24s was delivered to the Afghan air force. Some were destroyed by rocket fire, but the survivors remain airworthy.

MALI: An-26s were first received in 1983 and continue to fly alongside a number of An-24s. 'Cokes' and 'Curls' have proved popular among African nations.

YUGOSLAVIA: After the divisions within Yugoslavia, the An-26 fleet now flies with Serbian forces. Having stood at 15 in the mid-1980s, numbers totalled 25 by 1996.

ANTONOV

AN-30 'CLANK'/AN-32 'CLINE'

● Twin turboprop ● Aerial survey and transport ● 'Open Skies' flights

▲ *A versatile family of medium-range aircraft has been built up around the An-32. Meanwhile, modifications to the An-30 have taken it beyond the simple photographic survey mission capability.*

No organisation has been responsible for a wider range of transport aircraft than the Ukraine's Antonov design bureau. Developed from the An-24RT, the An-30 is a specialised aerial survey aircraft used in small numbers by Russia and a handful of the former Soviet allies. The An-32, on the other hand, is a widely operated tactical transport. With its powerful engines it is particularly useful in hot, mountainous countries.

ANTONOV AN-30 'CLANK'/AN-32 'CLINE'

▼ **Fire-killer**
Firefighting An-32Ps have a total water capacity of 8000 kg, which is carried in removable tanks. They can also carry rain-making equipment.

▲ **Nose job**
A weather radar is contained within the solid nose of the An-32; this replaces the glazed nose of the An-30. The high-mounted engines are also unique to the An-32.

▲ **'Open Skies'**
The Czech Republic uses this An-30 for 'Open Skies' overflights of other nations.

▼ **Indian air force**
India was the first customer to take delivery of the An-32 and received its first aircraft in 1984.

▲ **Glass nose**
Nose glazing has been a feature of many former Soviet designs. This is usually to aid navigation over the vast, featureless tracts of the former USSR and also, on the An-30, for photography.

FACTS AND FIGURES

➤ A computer aboard the An-30 is programmed with the route and controls the aircraft during surveys.

➤ In basic fit the An-30 cabin has four camera apertures and a light-meter.

➤ An-30s are also used for mineral prospecting and environmental studies.

➤ Western experts first received details about the An-32 in May 1977 and it appeared at the Paris Air Show that year.

➤ 'Cline' is the NATO reporting name of the An-32; 'Clank' is that of the An-30.

➤ An air ambulance version of the An-32 is equipped with an operating theatre.

PROFILE

Exceptional Antonovs

Externally, the most obvious difference between the An-30 and An-24RT, from which it was developed, is the glazed nose and raised cockpit canopy of the 'Clank'. Internally, though, the later model carries survey cameras along with a darkroom and map-making equipment, or other geographical survey equipment. An even more specialised version is the An-30M Sky Cleaner. This has fuselage-mounted pods which dispense granular carbon dioxide into clouds in order to produce rain over drought-stricken regions or forest fires.

The An-32 was developed specifically for operations in hot-and-high conditions. In addition to much more powerful engines than the An-30's 2103-kW (2,820-hp.) AI-24VTs, it has a new wing with triple-slot curved flaps and automatic leading-edge slats.

The type's ability to operate from airfields as high as 4500 m (14,750 ft.) above sea level, plus rough-field landing gear and a self-contained mechanised loading system, makes it an ideal tactical transport, fire-fighting, ambulance and agricultural aircraft. As a result of its outstanding performance and the difficult conditions in the country, the An-32 is the standard tactical transport of the Indian air force, which has named it the Sutlej.

Right: An-30 pilots have a far better field of view than their An-24 colleagues. The raised cockpit was primarily installed to provide more space for the navigator and survey equipment

Right: Bulgaria flies the An-30 in its basic survey role. Antonov designed the aircraft specifically for survey work in relation to map production.

AN-32 'CLINE'

India was a natural customer for the 'Cline', with its mountainous terrain and high temperatures. The Indian contract was fulfilled by Antonov from its GAZ 473 factory at Kiev before any other deliveries began.

Without lower glazing through which to view navigational landmarks on the ground, accurate navigation becomes difficult. The An-32 and some An-24 and -26 aircraft have a large observation window.

By mounting the powerful AI-20 engines above the wing, the propellers inlets remained clear of runway debris. An-32s are expected to operate from rough airfields and foreign object damage could be disastrous under marginal take-off conditions.

Very deep nacelles characterise the An-32. These house the retracted main undercarriage and the high-set engines. The right-hand nacelle also contains a small auxiliary turbojet.

A 3000-kg capacity hoist is fixed in the cabin to aid freight handling, together with a removable roller conveyor. The cabin can accommodate 12 pallets, 50 passengers or 42 parachutists.

An-32s may be called upon to operate in icy, mountainous conditions. As indicated by the substantial de-icing boots on all leading edges, this was one area of improvement over the An-26.

A crew of three, consisting of pilot, co-pilot and navigator, fly the aircraft from a pressurised and air-conditioned cabin. A flight engineer may also be carried.

Two huge ventral fins are carried beneath the tail. These aid directional stability and provide some protection from the slipstream for paratroops.

'Clanks' and 'Clines' in service

■ **An-30 'CLANK':** This is a camouflaged aircraft in Romanian air force service. Several eastern European air forces fly An-30s and some may serve in Vietnam.

■ **An-30 'CLANK':** Many aircraft flying in Aeroflot colours are used on military operations and aircraft such as this one are probably committed to the military in times of crisis.

■ **An-32 'CLINE':** Solid nose, high-set engines, forward bubble observation window and enlarged ventral fins distinguish the An-32 from the earlier An-30, -26 and -24.

ACTION DATA

PAYLOAD

Although the An-32 can carry less than the G222 and C.160, when taking off at high altitude with a full payload it retains its take-off performance. Both of its competitors must carry less fuel or cargo in order to operate from similar altitudes.

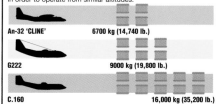

An-32 'CLINE'	6700 kg (14,740 lb.)
G222	9000 kg (19,800 lb.)
C.160	16,000 kg (35,200 lb.)

RANGE

With maximum fuel the An-32 exhibits good range. A full fuel load is likely to be at the expense of some payload, however. Despite this, range remains a creditable 1200 km (745 mi.) with a full payload.

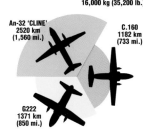

An-32 'CLINE' 2520 km (1,560 mi.)

C.160 1182 km (733 mi.)

G222 1371 km (850 mi.)

TAKE-OFF DISTANCE

At sea level the take-off performance of the An-32 is not particularly spectacular, since it does not have the STOL features of the other aircraft. Under hot-and-high conditions, however, its lift-off performance is excellent.

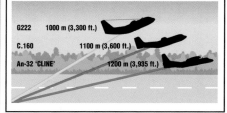

G222	1000 m (3,300 ft.)
C.160	1100 m (3,600 ft.)
An-32 'CLINE'	1200 m (3,935 ft.)

ANTONOV

AN-124 RUSLAN 'CONDOR'

● Giant airlifter ● Fly-by-wire controls ● Humanitarian missions

A true giant of the air, the Antonov An-124 Ruslan, known as the 'Condor' in the West, is the largest production aircraft in the world, dwarfing even the Lockheed C-5 Galaxy. In fact, this aircraft is so large that the cockpit is almost 9 m (30 ft.) high when the aircraft is on the ground. The An-124 is a successful military airlifter of great strategic importance because of its ability to carry tanks, missiles and heavy equipment over long ranges.

▲ *Ruslan continues to draw a crowd wherever it goes. Here it is seen on approach to Farnborough for its first appearance at the international airshow. The aircraft has proven to be of immense value to Russian forces.*

ANTONOV AN-124 RUSLAN 'CONDOR'

◀ Nose loader
Although the An-124's nose takes a full seven minutes to open, it enables loading of the aircraft from either end. A ramp allows easy and rapid loading of vehicles. Both front and rear ramps are stressed for a 70,000-kg (154,000-lb.) main battle tank (MBT).

▲ Lotarev turbofans
The Lotarev bureau developed the D-18T engines. These were the first large Soviet turbofans.

Aeroflot airlifter ▶
Like the An-22 'Cock', which the AN-124 was designed to replace, many examples of the Ruslan fly in civilian Aeroflot markings. It seems that the majority are assigned military tasks, however.

▼ Multi-wheel landing
Seen on approach, the multi-wheel main landing gear and twin nosewheel units of the An-124 are apparent.

▲ Civil charter
Several 'Condors' are available for charter throughout the world. A huge crane is required to maneuver and load this payload.

FACTS AND FIGURES

➤ In 1990, a Ruslan carried 451 passengers when hauling Bangledeshi refugees from Amman to Dhaka.

➤ The prototype An-124 Ruslan made its maiden flight on 26 December 1982.

➤ About 40 An-124s have been manufactured for civil and military use.

➤ Four years of argument ensued before Aeroflot and the Russian air force could agree on the An-124's fuselage section.

➤ An An-124 carried 171,219 kg (376,682 lb.) of cargo to 10,750 m (35,250 ft.).

➤ The An-124 inspired the world's only larger transport, the six-engine An-225.

PROFILE

High-capacity Ukrainian airlifter

Named Ruslan after Pushkin's famous giant and known to NATO as 'Condor', the Antonov An-124 is one of the most impressive aircraft ever built. Developed to meet a joint airline and military need for a heavy lifter, this behemoth transport has a number of features to ease the loading of its cavernous hold.

These features include a rear loading ramp and an upward-hinging visor-type nose, which allows loading from both ends simultaneously. The interior of this transport is so voluminous that 3000-kg (6,600-lb.) capacity winches and 10,000-kg (22,000-lb.) capacity travelling cranes are part of its regular on-board equipment. The aircraft can be made to kneel, giving its hold a floor slope of up to 3.5 degrees to assist in loading and unloading. The flight deck and an upper cabin, which accommodates 88 passengers, is fully pressurized, while the cargo hold is only lightly pressurized. A relatively high-tech airplane of exceptionally clean and efficient design, the An-124 has a fly-by-wire control system and uses composite materials in its structure, bringing about a significant weight saving. Despite its enormous size, the Ruslan is designed to operate from semi-prepared strips, including hard-packed snow or even ice-covered lakes.

Below: Admiring onlookers lend scale to the huge Ruslan. The aircraft flies regularly to airfields around the world.

Above: Production of the An-124 continues at a rate of two to three per year. No other military customers have come forward, and cargo airlines seem content to charter aircraft as required.

An-124 Ruslan 'Condor'

Type: four-engine strategic transport

Powerplant: four 229.47-kN (51,622-lb.-thrust) ZMDB Progress D-18T turbofan engines

Maximum speed: 865 km/h (536 m.p.h.)

Cruising speed: 800 km/h (496 m.p.h.) to 850 km/h (527 m.p.h.)

Range: 16,500 km (10,230 mi.) with max. fuel

Service ceiling: approx. 11,000 m (36,080 ft.)

Weights: empty 175,000 kg (385,000 lb.); maximum take-off 405,000 kg (891,000 lb.)

Accommodation: 6 crew; 88 passengers and up to 150,000 kg (330,000 lb.) of freight

Dimensions: span 73.30 m (240 ft. 5 in.)
length 69.10 m (226 ft. 7 in.)
height 20.78 m (68 ft. 2 in.)
wing area 628 m² (6,757 sq. ft.)

AN-124 RUSLAN 'CONDOR'

Most An-124s wear a color scheme similar to this, whether they are nominally in military or civilian service. This aircraft carries Aeroflot markings.

Hinging at this point, the entire nose section of the aircraft swings upward and over the cockpit. The nose loading ramp is triple hinged.

Antonov produced a wing of exceptional design for the An-124. It features full-span leading-edge slats, huge three-section flaps, four airbrakes inboard and eight spoilers outboard, as well as two-piece ailerons.

Ten fuel tanks are contained within the sealed wing box. Between them they hold 229,999 kg (505,998 lb.) of fuel. In 1987, a 'Condor' set a 20,151-km (124,934-mi.) closed-circuit distance record in 25 hours and 30 minutes.

Using an unusual pear-shaped fuselage cross-section, Antonov was able to produce a cargo hold that is 4.40 m (14 ft. 5 in.) high, 6.40 m (21 ft.) wide and has a usable length of 36 m (118 ft.). This latter figure does not include the rear loading ramp, which is also stressed for load carrying.

At the rear of the aircraft, a pair of clamshell doors open hydraulically, allowing the deployment of a rear loading ramp. This may be fixed at an intermediate position for loading from truck-bed height.

Aviation giants

■ **ANTONOV AN-225 MRIYA 'COSSACK':** Although it has recently been used as a spares source for An-124s, the An-225 was the heaviest and largest (apart from wingspan) aircraft ever produced. It was designed to carry the Buran spacecraft.

■ **HUGHES H-4 HERCULES:** Howard Hughes' 'Spruce Goose' is still able to boast the largest wingspan of any aircraft. It flew only once, for a distance of about one mile, and represented the ultimate large passenger flying boat airliner.

■ **LOCKHEED C-5 GALAXY:** Before the An-124, the C-5 was the largest aircraft, with the exception of wingspan. The An-124 is now the world's largest production aircraft and has carried a 53 per cent greater payload than the C-5B to 2000 m (6,550 ft.).

ACTION DATA

PAYLOAD

Antonov's An-124 has the largest payload of any military airlifter. It carries considerably more than the Lockheed C-5B Galaxy, which is its closest rival. The An-225 is a considerably larger aircraft than the Ruslan, but the single example built now lies derelict.

An-124 RUSLAN 'CONDOR' 150,000 kg (330,000 lb.)
C-5B GALAXY 118,387 kg (260,451 lb.)
An-225 MRIYA 'COSSACK' 250,000 kg (550,000 lb.)

31

ATLAS

CHEETAH

● Mirage III upgrade ● South Africa's indigenous fighter

Familiar on the outside, the high-tech Atlas Cheetah fighter is new on the inside. Developed from the Mirage III at a time when South Africa had little choice but to improve its existing aircraft, the Cheetah retains the exterior of the famous French fighter. But, within, it is modernized for combat against any opposition. With this aircraft, the South African Air Force (SAAF) remains a first-class fighting arm today.

▲ Based on the Mirage III fighter-bomber, the Cheetah introduces modern weapon systems, avionics and aerodynamics into a proven airframe to produce a highly capable combat aircraft.

ATLAS CHEETAH

◀ **To the Moon, Atlas**
The first Cheetahs to be delivered were two-seat Cheetah Ds converted from Mirage IIIDZs and D2Zs. In total, 16 Cheetah Ds were produced, some of them from Mirages and Kfirs supplied secretly by Israel. The Cheetah closely resembles the Kfir C7.

▼ **Operational role**
The Cheetah Ds have full weapons capability. One of their wartime roles would be laser designation for Cheetah Cs.

▲ **Operational conversion**
Initially, the two-seat version was used mainly to convert new pilots to the Cheetah. They were first used by No. 89 Combat Flying School.

◀ **African attacker**
The Cheetah D is the most potent attack aircraft in the southern part of Africa and carries many locally made weapons.

▲ **Hot landings**
Like the Mirage, the Cheetah has a high landing speed; a braking chute reduces the landing run.

FACTS AND FIGURES

➤ The Cheetah was revealed to the public on 16 July 1986.

➤ The Atlas Cheetah became operational in 1987, while South Africa was still under an international arms embargo.

➤ The Israelis supplied much expertise and help in the development of the Cheetah.

➤ The Cheetah's cruciform braking parachute is easier to manufacture and pack than round chutes.

➤ Improved instruments, weapons and navigation systems are incorporated.

➤ The Cheetah was modified from the highly successful French Mirage III.

Modern day African warrior

In July 1968 the South African manufacturer Atlas unveiled a much-modified Dassault Mirage III, renamed Cheetah. Developed with Israel's help, the Cheetah resembles that country's Kfir fighter. South Africa has now converted about 38 single- and two-seat Mirage IIIs into Cheetahs, and is using them as the front-line cutting edge of its air combat force.

In addition, to the two cannon found on single-seat versions, the Cheetah carries a remarkable variety of smart air-to-air and air-to-ground weapons guided by an indigenous designator pod.

This pouring of a new wine into a familiar bottle has produced a first-rate warplane with superb performance. The pilot of the Cheetah sits at the controls of a formidable craft, capable of holding its own in any battle. The Cheetah is also a delight to fly, and pilots revel in being turned loose to fling this powerful ship around the sky.

Recognized by its new wing with its dogtoothed leading edge and by its canard foreplanes, the Cheetah is expected to be in service for years to come.

Aerodynamic modifications include Kfir-style small nose side-strakes and canards mounted behind the engine intakes. These give the aircraft excellent agility.

The most obvious distinguishing feature of the Cheetah is the longer nose, giving the Cheetah C an overall length of 15.62 m (51 ft. 3 in.) compared to 15.03 m (49 ft. 3 in.) for the Mirage III.

The two-tone gray color scheme with a diamond on the upper side was first introduced on the Cheetah C, although it is worn by at least one Cheetah D. The first Cheetahs were Cheetah Ds, followed by the single-seat Cheetah E, which was withdrawn from service in 1992. One Cheetah R reconnaissance version was also built. The Cheetah C is the most sophisticated of the Cheetah variants and was only unveiled in the early 1990s. A dedicated air defense variant, the C also retains significant ground-attack capability.

The canard foreplanes enhance maneuverability and low-speed handling, which improves safety on the landing approach.

CHEETAH C

Most of South Africa's Cheetahs are flown by No. 2 Squadron, The Flying Cheetah, based at AFB Louis Trichardt in the northeastern part of the country.

The longer nose of the Cheetah C probably houses an Israeli-designed EL/M-2032 radar. This can pick up an air-to-air target at 20 miles and can track targets while scanning for others.

Improvements introduced on the Cheetah include a fixed refueling probe for refueling from Boeing 707 tankers, and a one-piece windscreen for greater visibility. The ejection seat is the same Martin-Baker Mk 6 fitted to the Mirage III.

The Cheetah's air-to-air armament consists of short-range Kentron V3C Darter AAMs, which can be aimed using the pilot's helmet-mounted sight. Medium-range AAMs are now being developed.

Today the Cheetah C is powered by the Atar 9k-50 engine, but these may be replaced by MiG-29 or Mirage F-1 powerplants.

Cheetah EZ

Type: single- or two-seat fighter

Powerplant: one SNECMA Atar 9C turbojet engine rated at 41.97 kN (9,440 lb. thrust) dry and 60.80 kN (13,675 lb. thrust) with afterburner

Maximum speed: 2338 km/h (1,450 m.p.h.) at 12,000 m (39,400 ft.)

Cruising speed: 956 km/h (593 m.p.h.) at 11,000 m (34,000 ft.)

Range: 1200 km (745 mi.)

Service ceiling: 17,000 m (55,750 ft.)

Weapons: two DEFA 30-mm (1.18-in.) cannons (single-seat aircraft only); plus up to 4000 kg (8,800 lb.) of other weapons

Weights: empty approx. 7400 kg (16,280 lb.); maximum take-off approx. 16,500 kg (36,300 lb.)

Dimensions:
span	8.22 m (27 ft.)
length	15.65 m (51 ft. 3 in.)
height	4.55 m (14 ft. 11 in.)
wing area	34.80 m² (374 sq. ft)

ACTION DATA

SPEED

The basic Mirage airframe of the Cheetah is very clean, giving the aircraft Mach 2 performance for short periods and making it noticeably faster than the F-16. There have been studies into replacing the old Atar 9 engine with the RD-33 of the MiG-29.

CHEETAH E	2338 km/h (1,450 m.p.h.)
MiG-29 'FULCRUM A'	2445 km/h (1,516 m.p.h.)
F-16C	2124 km/h (1,317 m.p.h.)

WEAPONS

The Cheetah, Fulcrum and Fighting Falcon were all designed to be good air-to-air fighters but each has a significant ground-attack capability. The Cheetah typically carries eight 227-kg (500-lb.) bombs, but can also be equipped with LGBs, ASMs, cluster bombs and rockets. The two-seaters do not have the internal cannon.

CHEETAH E	MiG-29 'FULCRUM A'	F-16C FIGHTING FALCON
2 x 30-mm (1.18-in.) cannon, 4000 kg (8,800 lb.) of bombs	1 x 30-mm (1.18-in.) cannon, 3000 kg (6,600 lb.) of ordnance	1 x 20-mm (0.78-in.) cannon, 6894 kg (15,070 lb.) of bombs

CEILING

The origins of the Cheetah in the Mirage III are reflected in the high altitude performance of the Cheetah. The more modern twin-engine MiG-29 has the same maximum altitude as the Cheetah, while the F-16, with one engine and the smallest wing area of the three aircraft, has the lowest ceiling.

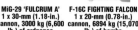

CHEETAH E	MiG-29 'FULCRUM A'	F-16C FIGHTING FALCON
17,000 m (55,750 ft.)	17,000 m (55,750 ft.)	15,240 m (50,000 ft.)

World-class Atlas aircraft

■ **IMPALA:** The first jet combat aircraft built in South Africa was the Atlas Impala Mk 1, a license-built version of the Aermacchi MB.326. The Impala Mk 2 was the single-seat attack version.

■ **AM-3C BOSBOK:** The Bosbok (Bushbuck) was originally a Lockheed design, but the license was passed to Aermacchi and then to Atlas. They were used as spotters for the army.

■ **XH-1 ALPHA:** The Alpha was a prototype aircraft designed to test the systems for the Rooivalk. It was basically an Alouette III with a new fuselage and cockpit and a 20-mm cannon.

■ **CHS-2 ROOIVALK:** The Rooivalk (Red Kestrel) is a dedicated attack helicopter with a secondary air-to-air (anti-helicopter) role. It has not yet been ordered by the SAAF.

ATLAS

IMPALA

● Licence-built MB.326 ● Two variants ● Active service in Africa

▲ Of the top-selling MB.326 family, South Africa's Impalas have perhaps seen the most action, having been used extensively in the skies over Angola and Namibia.

Atlas Aircraft of South Africa was formed in 1965 specifically to build the Aermacchi MB.326M trainer. The first kit-set example flew in 1966, and Atlas soon started manufacturing the aircraft as the Impala, completing a total of 151. In 1970, Aermacchi flew the first MB.326KC single-seat attack version. Atlas started building it in 1974 as the Impala Mk 2 for the South African Air Force, at the time embroiled in counter-insurgency campaigns.

ATLAS IMPALA

▼ **Prototype Mk 2**
In all, 100 Mk 2s were built, including the first seven by Aermacchi, plus a further 15 kits of components. This aircraft, serialled 1000, was the first, entering service in 1974.

▲ **Versatile design**
The MB.326 design has proved highly versatile and has been widely exported and licence built in several countries.

▼ **Maximum local content**
This, the 28th Impala Mk 2, was the sixth produced without Italian parts. Underwing rocket pods are carried.

▼ **Over south-west Africa**
Impalas saw extensive service in South Africa's bush wars in Angola and Namibia.

▲ **Kit-set beginnings**
In the 1960s, Aermacchi supplied Atlas with 16 kits for a version of the MB.326GB suitable for training and the COIN role. This was known to the Italian company as the MB.326M and to Atlas as the Impala Mk 1. A further 135 aircraft followed.

FACTS AND FIGURES

➤ In March 1996, Impalas were in service with No. 8 Squadron and a No. 85 Combat Flying training unit.

➤ Impala production totalled 251, of which 151 were two-seat Mk 1s.

➤ Angolan missions included night intruder raids on supply convoys.

➤ An Impala returned from a raid on Angola with an unexploded SA-9 surface-to-air missile lodged in its jetpipe.

➤ In early 1996, 20 Mk 1 and 40 Mk 2 aircraft remained in SAAF service.

➤ SAAF Cheetah pilots must complete 700 hours on the Impala before selection.

PROFILE

Impalas in Angolan skies

Replacing the de Havilland Vampire in the South African Air Force, the Impala Mk 1 entered service from 1966. It was used mainly as a trainer for fighter pilots who had completed their initial training on North American Harvards (now being replaced by PC-7s). From 1968, it also equipped the South African Air Force's 'Silver Falcons' display team. Like the Mk 1s, the first Impala 2s were built from kits, but again Atlas steadily increased the proportion of local content in the aircraft. The 100 aircraft delivered differed from the original MB.326K, which was powered by a 19.57-kN (4,400-lb.-thrust) Viper 680, in using the same engine as the Mk 1. The Mk 2 was used extensively for ground-attack and close-support missions in Namibia and Angola. In addition to the two built-in guns, it carried 120-kg (260-lb.) and 250-kg (550-lb.) bombs, rocket launchers and tactical reconnaissance pods, often with auxiliary fuel tanks. Probably the most enduring contribution made by the Impala programme to South Africa's fortunes was its role in establishing the local aircraft industry when many states refused to sell arms to the country.

Above: A tactical camouflage scheme adorns the Mk 2s in recognition of their counter-insurgency (COIN) role.

Below: Two-seat Impala Mk 1s were generally finished in this all-over silver scheme. Aircraft 499 was among the second batch of 40 aircraft built using Italian components.

Impala Mk 2

Type: advanced training, COIN and armed reconnaissance aircraft

Powerplant: one 15.17-kN (3,400-lb.-thrust) Rolls-Royce Viper 20 Mk 540 turbojet

Maximum speed: 890 km/h (552 m.p.h.) at 1525 m (5,000 ft.)

Climb rate: 1981 m/min (6,500 f.p.m.)

Range: 130–1040 km (80–650 mi.), depending on weapons load and mission profile

Service ceiling: 14,325 m (47,000 ft.)

Weights: empty 2964 kg (6,520 lb.); maximum take-off 5897 kg (12,973 lb.)

Armament: two 30-mm cannon plus up to 1814 kg (4,000 lb.) of stores

Dimensions:
span	10.15 m	(33 ft. 4 in.)
length	10.67 m	(35 ft.)
height	3.72 m	(12 ft. 3 in.)
wing area	19.35 m²	(208 sq. ft.)

IMPALA MK 2

This licence-built MB.326KC served with the SAAF's No. 4 Squadron, a unit of the Active Citizen Force, based at Lanseria/Durban. Around 40 were still in SAAF service in March 1996.

The Impala Mk 2's pilot was strapped into a Martin-Baker zero-zero rocket ejection seat. Impala losses over Namibia and Angola were comparatively light.

To create a single-seat version of the MB.326 trainer, Aermacchi made minimal changes to the airframe, simply fitting a smaller cockpit canopy and fairing over the rear seat. An extra fuel tank filled part of the redundant space.

In the COIN role, the Impala Mk 1 often carried two 12.7-mm (.50 cal.) machine-gun pods and two 80-mm rocket pods. Mk 2s were used for armed reconnaissance, with an underwing camera pod and drop-tank.

From the outset, the MB.326 was powered by Rolls-Royce's highly successful Bristol Siddeley-designed Viper turbojet, which was fitted to several Western trainer/light-attack types. Whereas Aermacchi fitted a more powerful version of this engine to the single-seat MB.326K, Atlas retained the variant used in the trainer.

Although the SAAF adopted their current national marking, incorporating the springbok, after World War II they retained the red, white and blue fin flash, a legacy of the RAF, for some years.

Two 30-mm DEFA cannon added a ground-strafing capability to the COIN abilities of the single-seat Impala Mk 2. SAAF aircraft have also carried machine-gun pods under the wings.

Drop-tanks of up to 227 litres (60 gal.) capacity can be fitted on the underwing pylons to increase combat radius in the COIN role. The ordnance load limit is 1814 kg (4,000 lb.) on four pylons.

COMBAT DATA

MAXIMUM SPEED

The Impala, the design of which dates back to the MB.326 of the 1950s, is showing its age in terms of performance. Its maximum speed is less than that of both the MB.339, a development of the MB.326, and the Hawk Mk 200.

IMPALA Mk 2	890 km/h (552 m.p.h.)
MB.339K	900 km/h (558 m.p.h.)
HAWK Mk 208	1017 km/h (630 m.p.h.)

ORDNANCE LOAD

The Impala's ordnance load is a little less than that of the later MB.339, but considerably less than the Hawk 200's. The Hawk, in its single-seat guise, has developed into a considerably more capable aircraft than the original two-seat trainer variant. Not only can it carry a heavier load, but also a wider array of weapons.

IMPALA Mk 2	MB.339K	HAWK Mk 208
1814 kg (4,000 lb.)	1935 kg (4,250 lb.)	3175 kg (7,000 lb.)

COMBAT RADIUS

While the Hawk 200 has a limited combat radius in a low-level mission with a 'typically' moderate ordnance load, it would be able to fly further than both the Impala and MB.339 with comparable loads. The MB.339 has twice the combat radius, but with half the weapons load on its wing pylons.

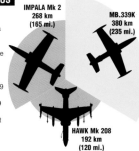

IMPALA Mk 2
268 km (165 mi.)

MB.339K
380 km (235 mi.)

HAWK Mk 208
192 km (120 mi.)

South African Air Force aircraft

■ **AÉROSPATIALE ALOUETTE III:** First delivered to the South African Air Force in 1967, this widely-exported Alouette remains in use in the communications and training roles.

■ **ATLAS CHEETAH:** A home-grown development of the Mirage III, the Cheetah uses Israeli avionics and radar as well as South African-designed equipment. Around 60 are in service.

■ **DASSAULT MIRAGE F.1:** Fewer than 30 F.1s remain in service with the SAAF, in the air defence and ground-attack roles. First delivered in 1975, they soon scored kills over Angolan MiGs.

BEECH

C-12

- Multi-role turboprop light transport ● Derived from civil design

Initially supplied to the US Army and USAF in 1975 as a light transport, the Beech C-12 is today in service with all three US services and 18 other air arms (in some cases in its civil guise) in a wide variety of roles. The Beech B200 Super King Air, from which the C-12 is derived, was developed from the commercial Model 100 in the early 1970s. The new type featured a T-tail, longer wings and many internal refinements. Later versions have further improvements.

▲ *Beechcraft's C-12F replaced the CT-39 Sabreliner as an operational support aircraft and featured more powerful engines, a cargo door and improved passenger facilities.*

BEECH C-12

▼ **Special duties**
Not all C-12s supplied to air arms are used as transports. Some are camouflaged and used for aerial surveillance and other tasks.

▲ **Navy transports**
A total of 78 Beech A200Cs was purchased by the US Navy and Marine Corps as UC-12Bs. They first entered service in 1980 as personnel and utility transports.

▼ **Mission support**
Designated UC-12J, this bigger and more powerful Beech 1900C is one of six used by the US Air National Guard for mission support from 1987.

▲ **Army Hurons**
The US Army employs its C-12A/C/D Hurons in the utility role, supporting Army units and US embassies around the world.

Upgraded aircraft ►
When the US Army took delivery of the more powerful C-12C/Ds with PT6A-41 turboprops it upgraded its large fleet of C-12As to the same standard. This C-12D features increased-span wings and cargo doors.

FACTS AND FIGURES

- ➤ It took Beechcraft four years to develop the Model 200 Super King Air/C-12 with its large T-tail, from the Model 100.

- ➤ The first C-12 entered service with the US Army at Fort Monroe in July 1975.

- ➤ Two USAF C-12s are operated by US Customs for anti-smuggling surveillance.

- ➤ Extensive aerial arrays identify the RC-12 variants used by the US Army for electronics special missions.

- ➤ The Beech B200C/C-12F can fly faster, higher and further than the A200 model.

- ➤ Cargo doors and provision of wingtip fuel tanks are features of the C-12D.

PROFILE

Military utility 'off the shelf'

Beech developed its Super King Air 200 over a four-year period from 1969, using the successful King Air 100 executive turboprop transport as a basis. It had more powerful engines, a T-tail and increased wingspan as well as equipment changes. It was bigger, faster and more capable than the King Airs already in service with the US Army as the U-21. A contract was placed for 34 of the new aircraft as C-12s, for the US Army and USAF. In most respects these were

standard Super King Airs from the production line, but with modified avionics and equipment to meet military requirements as staff transports.

In 1978 the US Navy bought the first of 78 C-12s for use as personnel and utility transports. In order to accommodate freight items these UC-12Bs had a large cargo door (1.32 m/4-ft. 4-in. by 1.32 m/4-ft. 4-in.) on the port side. They also had 634-kW (850-hp.) Pratt & Whitney PT6A-41 engines and a taller undercarriage assembly.

Below: This UC-12B was operated by the US Marine Corps headquarters and based at the Naval Air Facility at Washington, DC.

Above: A number of South American air arms, including that of Argentina, have purchased Super King Airs as affordable surveillance and maritime patrol platforms.

The US Army converted a number of its new C-12Ds for special electronic missions and battlefield surveillance as RC-12s. These have a large array of aerials and pods.

C-12F

Type: utility transport

Powerplant: two 634-kW (850-hp.) Pratt & Whitney Canada PT6A-42 turboprops

Maximum speed: 545 km/h (338 m.p.h.) at 7620 m (25,000 ft.)

Initial climb rate: 747 m/min (2,450 f.p.m.)

Range: 3641 km (2,260 mi.) with maximum fuel at 10,670 m (35,000 ft.)

Service ceiling: more than 10,670 m (35,000 ft.)

Weights: operating empty 3656 kg (8,043 lb.); maximum take-off 5670 kg (12,464 lb.)

Accommodation: two pilots, plus eight passengers or 1201 kg (2,642 lb.) of cargo

Dimensions:
span	16.61 m (54 ft. 6 in.)
length	13.36 m (43 ft. 10 in.)
height	4.52 m (14 ft. 10 in.)
wing area	28.15 m² (303 sq. ft.)

SUPER KING AIR B200

Ireland's Air Corps is one of 18 air arms apart from the US services that has operated Beech C-12/Super King Airs. Three B200s were used for maritime patrol missions and as transports and multi-engine trainers.

The semi-monocoque fuselage structure of the Super King Air 200 is of light alloy. The cabin is air-conditioned and fully pressurised. Large windows along the fuselage and on the flight deck give good visibility.

Accommodation is provided for two pilots and up to 10 passengers in the standard transport layout. When mission equipment is carried for maritime patrol, accommodation is reduced to a maximum of six, depending upon the duration of the flight.

The B200 has a cantilever T-tail structure of light alloy, with swept vertical and horizontal surfaces. The fixed incidence tailplane has de-icing 'boots' on the leading edges. Each elevator has a trim tab.

IRISH AIR CORPS — AER CHÓR na h-ÉIREANN   240

Two Pratt & Whitney Canada PT6A turboprops each drive a three-bladed, metal, constant-speed fully-feathering and reversible propeller.

The tricycle undercarriage has twin main wheels on each leg that retract forwards into the engine nacelle. The nose leg has a single, steerable wheel that retracts rearwards into the nose section.

This standard Super King Air 200 has a passenger entry door at the rear of the cabin on the port side. It has integral steps built into the back of the door that lower to the ground. Some USAF, US Navy and US Army C-12s have large (1.32-m/4-ft. 4-in. high and 1.32-m/4-ft. 4-in. wide) cargo access doors.

ACTION DATA

PASSENGERS

The usefulness of the C-12F as a liaison transport is limited by its size. This role is largely the preserve of larger, 19-seat machines like the C-12J (derived from the Beech 1900) and C-26A Metro, both civil designs that have been adapted for military roles.

C-12F 8 passengers

C-12J 19 passengers

C-26A METRO 19 passengers

MAXIMUM CRUISING SPEED

Though the C-12J is a larger aircraft it lacks the high cruising speed of the smaller C-12F. The Fairchild C-26A has a similar speed performance to the Beechcraft C-12F.

C-12F	536 km/h (338 m.p.h.)
C-12J	471 km/h (292 m.p.h.)
C-26A METRO	515 km/h (319 m.p.h.)

TAKE-OFF RUN TO 15 M (50 FT.)

Both the 19-seaters here require almost 1000 m (3,300 ft.) in which to get airborne and attain a height of 15 m (50 ft.). The smaller C-12F uses just under 800 m (2,600 ft.) of runway to do the same, making it more useful from smaller airports. Take-off performance varies according to the load being carried. Heavier loads need longer runways.

C-12F	786 m (2,580 ft.)
C-12J	991 m (3,250 ft.)
C-26A METRO	991 m (3,250 ft.)

USAF/ANG light transports

■ **BRITISH AEROSPACE C-29A:** BAe's well-known 125 Series 800A executive jet was adopted by the USAF in the late 1980s for the Combat Flight Inspection and Navigation (C-FIN) role.

■ **FAIRCHILD C-26A:** When the US Air National Guard (ANG) needed a new operational support transport aircraft, the Metro 3, a 19-seater regional airliner was chosen in 1988.

■ **GATES LEARJET C-21A:** In the early 1980s the then Military Airlift Command operated the CT-39 Sabreliner for high-priority, time-sensitive cargos. The Learjet replaced these from 1984.

■ **SHORTS C-23:** For the distribution of spare parts around Europe, USAFE bought 18 Shorts 330 Sherpas (C-23As). Ten were later bought for the ANG, while the Army bought ex-civil C-23Bs.

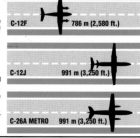

BEECH

T-1A JAYHAWK

● Civil design ● Tanker-trainer ● Military 'biz-jet'

BEECH T-1A JAYHAWK

▲ Classic lines
The Jayhawk displays the low-set wings and the rear-mounted engines that have become the hallmarks of current 'biz-jets.'

▲ Bright future
Having been in service for only a relatively short period of time, the Beech Jayhawk is expected to have a long military career with the USAF.

Japanese use ▶
By early 1994 Japan's Air Self-Defence Force had also purchased the improved American Jayhawk to use as a light utility transport aircraft.

▼ Improved design
One of the military modifications specified involved the wings of the Jayhawk being strengthened in order to withstand the damaging effects of a heavy birdstrike. The pilot's cockpit glazing was also improved as a precaution.

▲ Training for all
The type having passed its trials with 'flying-colours' the USAF quickly ordered 148 Jayhawks. A final total of 180 examples is anticipated.

Cutting an unusual shape in the sky with its all white colour scheme and swept-back wings, the T-1 Jayhawk is fast becoming the standard training tool for the United States Air Force. The shortage of T-38 Talon trainers coupled with a shrinking defence budget saw the United States Air Force undertake the unusual step of purchasing a civilian business jet for its training purposes. The aircraft required only minor modification.

▲ Despite its civilian origins the Beech T-1 Jayhawk has proved suitable for the rigours of military training. Crews have found the aircraft a forgiving teaching tool.

FACTS AND FIGURES

➤ The T-1A Jayhawk provides the USAF with an advanced trainer for instructing future tanker/transport pilots.

➤ A shortage of T-38 Talons saw the adoption of the Jayhawk in US service.

➤ Increased fuel capacity is one of the major changes to military Jayhawks.

➤ During training flights a senior instructor pilot is accompanied by at least four students to reduce operating costs.

➤ Jayhawks are the first aircraft delivered under the new pilot training programme.

➤ The Jayhawk is based on the civilian Beech Jet 400.

PROFILE

America's pilot provider

The Beech T-1 Jayhawk is now entering service in increasing numbers and providing the USAF with a unique training tool. In line with the current trend of using civilian aircraft for military applications, future USAF tanker and transport pilots now receive training at Reese AFB at a much reduced cost to the American taxpayer. One source of economies is that several trainees can be taken on each sortie under the guidance of one senior instructor pilot.

Alterations to the aircraft were required before it entered military service. These saw an increase in the strength of the wing leading edges and a revised cockpit windscreen. To reduce maintenance demands a single refuelling point was also installed on the aircraft. USAF examples are limited to the training role and therefore feature six fewer windows in the cabin area because of their reduced seating capacity.

In a somewhat ironic move given the original Mitsubishi design of the Jayhawk, the Japanese Air Self-Defence

Above: America's training fleet has worn a host of colour schemes, but the overall white is now used.

Force (JASDF) followed the American example and bought the aircraft for the training role. Beginning in early 1994, the JASDF took delivery of three Beech 400Ts (equivalent to the T-1A) to use for pilot training. These aircraft are equipped with extra fuel tanks and thrust reversers to simulate the handling of large transport aircraft for their pupil pilots.

Above: Having completed another sortie, a student enters the landing circuit at Reese AFB, where the first aircraft was delivered in 1992.

T-1A Jayhawk

Type: advanced jet trainer/utility jet

Powerplant: two 12.9-kN (2,900-lb.-thrust) Pratt & Whitney Canada JT15D-5B turbojets

Maximum speed: 854 km/h (529 m.p.h.) at 8840 m (29,000 ft.); cruising speed 828 km/h (513 m.p.h.) at 11,890 m (39,000 ft.)

Range: 3575 km (2,340 mi.) with four passengers and maximum internal fuel load

Service ceiling: 12,495 m (41,000 ft.)

Weights: empty 4588 kg (10,094 lb.); maximum take-off 7157 kg (15,745 lb.)

Accommodation: one instructor pilot; four students

Dimensions:
span	13.25 m	(43 ft. 5 in.)
length	14.75 m	(48 ft. 4 in.)
height	4.19 m	(13 ft. 9 in.)
wing area	22.43 m²	(241 sq. ft.)

T-1A JAYHAWK

This T-1A Jayhawk is based at Reese AFB in Texas, operating under the TTTS (Tanker/Transport Trainer System). The aircraft is proving to be an extremely practical training tool. Future orders for additional aircraft are currently being considered by the USAF.

Pilots destined for the vast transport and tanker fleet of the United States Air Force are instructed on the Jayhawk in an effort to develop the necessary skills required for handling large aircraft. This has resulted in a huge saving in training costs.

A high-set tail allows the Jayhawk excellent handling qualities at high altitudes where most operational training takes place. Very few modifications were made to the flight control systems of the aircraft.

10078

Avionics equipment in the nose of the aircraft was relocated to the cockpit, also added was a turbulence-detection radar.

To improve the safety record of the aircraft the wings of USAF Jayhawks were strengthened, along with the pilot's windscreen.

A distinguishing feature of the aircraft is its small undercarriage. This was seen as a weight-saving measure but also allows the aircraft to be maintained without requiring gantries.

Positioned high on the rear fuselage are the Pratt & Whitney Canada JT15D turbofan engines. These received little modification prior to the entry of the Jayhawk into military service. Maintenance personnel have found the aircraft to be extremely reliable.

ACTION DATA

MAXIMUM SPEED

Matched against other military trainers the T-1 Jayhawk offers a maximum speed that is far in excess of its propeller-powered equivalents. Despite this performance, high speed is seldom used on training flights.

T-1A JAYHAWK	854 km/h (529 m.p.h.)
C-12F	545 km/h (338 m.p.h.)
KING AIR C90A	457 km/h (283 m.p.h.)

RANGE

Additional fuel tanks were a requirement before the USAF would accept the Jayhawk into service. Despite the addition of wing tip tanks to the Beech C-12 variants the huge range of the Jayhawk cannot be equalled by its contemporaries.

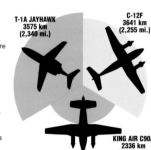

T-1A JAYHAWK 3575 km (2,340 mi.)

C-12F 3641 km (2,255 mi.)

KING AIR C90A 2336 km (1,450 mi.)

MAXIMUM TAKE OFF WEIGHT

In its role as a training aircraft the Jayhawk requires a large take-off weight. Despite its relatively small size the Jayhawk matches this need surprisingly well. Compared to the King Air, which is also used in the utility role, the Jayhawk compares very favourably.

T-1A JAYHAWK 7157 kg (15,745 lb.)

C-12F 3641 kg (8,010 lb.)

KING AIR C90A 2336 kg (5,139 lb.)

Serving their country

■ **CESSNA CITATION:** Operational with the Spanish Navy, the Citation is used as a navigation trainer and light transport aircraft. One model is used for reconnaissance duties.

■ **GRUMMAN GULFSTREAM:** The large dimensions of the Gulfstream III have made it an ideal platform for liaison and VIP duties. This example serves with the Danish air force.

■ **NORTH AMERICAN SABRELINER:** Currently reaching the end of its service with the United States armed forces, the T-39 Sabreliner continues to serve with South American air arms.

BELL/BOEING

V-22 OSPREY

● Assault transport ● Vertical take-off ● Multiple roles

Us Marines have a phrase for it: they call it 'Vertical Envelopment'. The idea is to bypass a defended coast by flying troops over the top, fast, landing them in the enemy rear before the foe can react. And nothing can move Marines as fast as the revolutionary V-22 Osprey, which flies like an aeroplane but takes off and lands like a helicopter.

▲ *The prototype V-22 Osprey is seen transitioning to horizontal flight. It is this unique ability which will revolutionise the speed of US Marine Corps amphibious assaults.*

PHOTO FILE

BELL/BOEING V-22 OSPREY

Sea ▶ trials
The Osprey has shown that it can operate from any deck large enough to give sideways clearance to the twin rotors.

▲ Osprey's forerunner
The Bell XV-15 was the culmination of a long line of experimental convertiplanes, and was the direct ancestor of the V-22.

Global reach ▶
The V-22 can be refuelled in flight. It can be deployed over intercontinental distances in less than a day – which is something that no helicopter can do.

▲ High-tech
The Osprey comes equipped with a modern 'glass' cockpit, dominated by multi-function controls and computerised video displays.

Marine ◀ assault
The most enthusiastic supporters of the V-22 are the US Marines, who see the aircraft as adding greatly to the ability with which they can carry out amphibious assaults.

▲ Folding wings
The Osprey takes up a lot of space, which is at a premium aboard even the largest carrier. To make more room, the rotors fold and the wing swivels in line with the fuselage.

FACTS AND FIGURES

➤ The V-22 first flew on 19 March 1989, taking off vertically from Bell's research facility at Arlington, Texas.

➤ First transition from vertical to horizontal flight took place on 14 September 1989.

➤ The V-22 has twice the speed and twice the range of a comparable helicopter.

➤ V-22s can be deployed anywhere in the world within 36 hours.

➤ A typical helicopter needs three times as much maintenance as the V-22.

➤ Ospreys can carry a seven-ton load slung beneath the fuselage at speeds of up to 375 km/h (235 m.p.h.).

High-speed assault

A Marine commander assaulting a defended shoreline needs to get his troops and equipment ashore fast. But landing craft are slow and make easy targets, and helicopters are horribly vulnerable to enemy fire. Until now, the only way to minimise the time the helicopters are at risk has been to launch them from as close to shore as possible, but that exposes the irreplaceable assault ships to danger from the enemy's long-range artillery and missiles.

The Osprey has changed all that. With its rotors pointing upwards, it can take off and land vertically on ship or ashore. But tilting the rotors forwards converts them into propellers, allowing the Osprey to fly twice as fast as the fastest helicopter.

Operating in conjunction with speedy air-cushion landing craft, the V-22 can deliver troops or weapons over much greater distances than a helicopter. An amphibious task force commander can now launch his attack from over the horizon, and still have his troops ashore in a shorter time than would have been possible with helicopters and landing craft.

The tremendous width of the Osprey's rotor blades is clear in this photo of a landing on a 'Wasp'-class assault ship.

The V-22's prop-rotors are 11.58 m (38 ft.) in diameter. Immensely strong to resist combat damage, one provides enough lift to keep the aircraft in the air alone if necessary.

The wing is fitted on a pivot. Swung fore and aft and with the rotors folded, an Osprey takes up no more room than a large helicopter.

MV-22A Osprey

Type: two-crew multi-role convertiplane transport

Powerplant: two 4593-kW (6,150-hp.) Allison T406-AD-400 turboprops

Maximum speed: 556 km/h (345 mi.) at sea level

Combat radius: 1880 km (1,168 mi.) search and rescue; 1000 km (620 mi.) amphibious assault

Rate of climb: 332 m/min (1,100 f.p.m.) vertically

Service ceiling: 8000 m (26,250 ft.)

Weights: empty 14,433 kg (31,820 lb.); loaded 24,948 kg (55,000 lb.)

Payload: up to 25 fully equipped troops or 4500 kg (9,920 lb.) cargo internally, or 6800 kg (15,000 lb.) external load

Dimensions:
span (inc rotors) 25.76 m (84 ft. 6 in.)
length 17.32 m (56 ft. 10 in.)
height 6.63 m (21 ft. 9 in.)
rotor area 210 m² (2,260 sq. ft.)

XV-22 OSPREY

Although facing Congressional opposition, the V-22 has been described by senior Marine officers as 'our number one aviation priority'.

Test aircraft are often fitted with sensitive flight testing instruments to measure the aircraft's performance in all areas of the flight regime.

The Osprey is manned by a pilot and co-pilot. They control the aircraft by means of an electronic fly-by-wire system.

The Osprey's engines are immensely powerful, in order to lift the aircraft free of the ground without any aerodynamic assistance.

The huge paddle-bladed prop-rotors are a compromise between long helicopter-type rotors and much smaller aircraft-type propellers.

Osprey's twin tail is set high on a boom, in order to leave room for the rear door and loading ramp.

The extensive use of composite material means that the V-22 is about 25 per cent lighter than a metal aircraft of comparable size and lifting power.

ACTION DATA

TAKE-OFF PROCEDURE

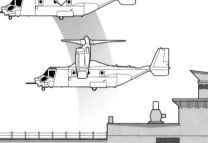

Osprey can take off vertically or with a short take-off run. Transition from vertical flight to horizontal is automatic. As the aircraft's forward speed increases, control is switched from the aircraft's rotors (as in a helicopter) to the conventional flaps and ailerons (as in an aircraft).

PAYLOAD EFFICIENCY

A CH-53 helicopter can carry up to 55 troops in the assault role.

Although its capacity is only 25, the V-22 can make three trips to a helicopter's one, landing 75 troops in the same time that the CH-53 lands 55.

Landing comparison

MARINE ASSAULT: An amphibious assault using Ospreys and air-cushion landing craft can stand offshore a safe distance from enemy defences, and still land troops more quickly than helicopters and landing craft.

ENEMY THREAT: Most modern artillery pieces have a range of between 17 and 30 km 10 and 20 mi.), putting at risk any vessel coming within that range.

CLOSE RANGE: Conventional assaults are limited by the slow speed of conventional landing craft. To get troops ashore in under an hour, the assault fleet has to be within a few thousand metres of the coast, well within artillery range.

V-22 OSPREY

CH-53

OBJECTIVE: THE BEACH

LARGE ASSAULT SHIP

AIR-CUSHION LANDING CRAFT

ASSAULT SHIP 5 KM OFFSHORE

LANDING CRAFT

BOEING

B-52G/H STRATOFORTRESS

● Strategic bomber ● Nuclear/conventional weapons ● Global reach

onceived as the giant silver sword of the United States Air Force Strategic Air Command the B-52 Stratofortress was the biggest purely jet-powered bomber of its time, and has been flying for almost 50 years. Flown for decades on atomic alert, its only combat use has been the massive conventional bombing campaigns in Southeast Asia and the Persian Gulf.

▲ Displaying its enormous wingspan a B-52 gets airborne trailing a thick plume of smoke as its eight turbojet engines strain at full power to lift its 229,000 kg (504,860 lb.) into the air.

BOEING B-52G/H STRATOFORTRESS

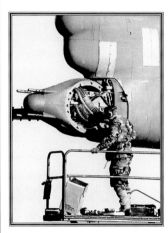

◄ Sting in the tail
Most versions of the B-52 had a fearsome rear defence of four '50-calibre' guns. These were aimed using the radar mounted above.

◄ Extending the range
By using inflight refuelling, the B-52 can cover any part of the globe from just a few bases. This veteran is seen on its way to Vietnam in 1972.

Modern day warrior ▶
Two fully-laden B-52Gs launch from Riyadh in Saudi Arabia for another mission against massed Iraqi armoured divisions during the Gulf War of 1991.

◄ Nuclear deterrence
The B-52 has an important role as a launch platform for nuclear missiles. Here a SRAM is launched from the massive weapons bay.

A fistful of throttles ▶
The B-52's cockpit is dominated by the central engine control panel. Every dial and lever is multiplied eight-fold.

FACTS AND FIGURES

➤ The B-52 has a crew of five, including two pilots, navigator, electronic warfare officer and bombardier.

➤ Boeing manufactured 744 'Buffs' and finished the last aircraft in October 1962.

➤ A B-52 can reach any target in the world within 18 hours.

➤ During Operation Desert Storm, B-52s flew 1624 missions, and dropped 5,829,000 kg (12,850,740 lb.) of bombs.

➤ Each B-52 contains 90 km (56 mi.) of electrical wiring.

➤ In 1959, three B-52Bs flew non-stop around the world in under 50 hours.

PROFILE

America's 'Big Stick'

The longest-serving front-line warplane in history, the B-52 Stratofortress was the right aircraft at the right time. It first flew on 15 April 1952 and became the backbone of the West's nuclear preparedness; had the need arisen, hundreds of B-52s would have headed for Russia to drop hydrogen bombs on key strategic targets.

The special 'Big Belly B-52D' could also carry 108 conventional bombs, and during the Vietnam War 129 B-52s, of several models, carried out the December 1972 'Christmas bombing', designed to force North Vietnam to the conference table. Since then, the B-52 has been extensively modified. New engines and

electronics have extended the life of the 'Buff' (Big Ugly Fat Fella) into the 1990s. B-52Gs flew the longest combat missions in history during Operation Desert Storm, from Louisiana to the Middle East. Today, B-52Hs have both nuclear and conventional roles.

The 'Buff' is one of the best-loved of all aircraft and can operate at high level or at very low level on terrain-avoidance under-the-radar missions.

During the first Gulf War B-52s pounded Iraqi targets from as far afield as England and Diego Garcia in the Indian Ocean.

B-52H STRATOFORTRESS

Known in the USAF as the 'Cadillac', the B-52H is significantly upgraded compared to the early Stratofortresses. With more modern turbofan engines it outperforms its predecessors in both range and payload. Built to carry nuclear-tipped ballistic missiles, it is still a vital weapon in the USAF arsenal.

'Buffs' can mount up to 24 340-kg (750-lb.) or 454-kg (1,000-lb.) high-explosive or cluster bombs on wing pylons.

The radar-directed rear guns are controlled remotely by a gunner who aims via a screen in the forward cockpit.

The immensely strong wings of the B-52 not only support the eight engines but are also filled with fuel, giving the 'Buff' enormous range.

The B-52's wings can flex several metres up and down. Outriggers under the wingtips stop them from hitting the runway when carrying a full load of fuel and weaponry.

The flight deck of the B-52 has two levels. The upper deck houses the two pilots. Behind them sit the electronic warfare officer, who handles all the countermeasures equipment, and the tail gunner, who fires by remote control.

On the lower level, facing forwards, are two navigators. One handles the route navigation, while the other operates the upgraded radar and weapon control systems.

The enormous bomb-bays of the B-52 can accommodate clips of a wide range of armament, ranging from 227-kg (500-lb.) bombs to giant nuclear weapons.

The B-52 has a bicycle-type main undercarriage. This caters for crosswind landings and take-offs by crabbing, so that the aircraft's fuselage slews down the runway.

B-52H Stratofortress

Type: five-seat long-range strategic bomber

Powerplant: eight 75.62-kN (17,014-lb. thrust) Pratt & Whitney TF33-P-3 turbofans

Maximum speed: 958 km/h (595 m.p.h.) at 3096 m (10,160 ft.)

Range: 16,000 km (9942 mi.)

Service ceiling: 16,765 m (55,000 ft.)

Weights: empty 138,799 kg (306,000 lb.); loaded 229,000 kg (504,860 lb.)

Armament: one 20-mm M61A1 tail cannon; 81 454-kg (1,000-lb.) bombs, or 20 AGM-86 or AGM-129 cruise missiles, or four to six nuclear bombs

Dimensions:
span	56.39 m (185 ft.)
length	49.05 m (160 ft. 11 in.)
height	12.40 m (40 ft. 8 in.)
wing area	272.3 m² (2,932 sq. ft.)

COMBAT DATA

BOMBLOAD

The B-52H can carry a vast array of weaponry. Its load can include up to 20 nuclear cruise missiles or 81 free-fall bombs as well as anti-ship missiles or conventional cruise missiles. Designed during the Cold War, the B-52 carries its bombload over a great range and would have penetrated into the heart of the Soviet Union if necessary.

VICTOR 16,000 kg (35,275 lb.)

B-52H STRATOFORTRESS 38,250 kg (84,330 lb.)

Tu-95 'BEAR' 20,000 kg (44,100 lb.)

Barksdale AFB is a major Strategic Air Command facility, and is the location of the USAF 8th Air Force headquarters.

BARKSDALE AFB

The B-52s were refuelled by tankers flying from Lajes in the Azores.

Launching from northern Saudi airspace, the B-52s attacked key military targets in northern Iraq, around the oil centres of Kirkuk and Mosul.

The longest raid in history

On the first night of the first Gulf War, B-52Gs took off from Barksdale AFB in Louisiana, flew to northern Saudi Arabia and launched cruise missiles against Iraqi targets. They then flew all the way back to their base, having flown non-stop for more than 35 hours.

The Mediterranean flight path was chosen to avoid overflying other countries as much as possible.

BOEING

E-3 AWACS SENTRY

● Flying radar station ● Commands and controls the air battle

Boeing's E-3 Sentry is a flying radar station. This aerial headquarters patrols the skies and scans the military situation below, monitoring friendly and hostile aircraft. Inside the metal cocoon of the E-3's fuselage, technical experts work magic with radar and electronics to detect enemy warplanes, plot their course, and guide friendly fighters to shoot them down.

▲ A number of E-3 AWACS are assigned to NATO. Radar operators, communications technicians and battle analysts from each member state serve aboard each Sentry aircraft.

BOEING E-3 AWACS SENTRY

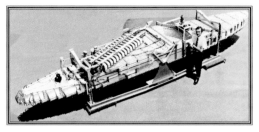

▲ **Giant radar**
This is the huge antenna for the APY-2 radar. On one side is the radar itself; on the other is the IFF equipment for detecting whether aircraft are friendly or hostile.

▲ **Flight deck**
E-3 pilots may expect to spend a good deal of time at their stations: AWACS missions often last 10 hours or more, flying basically a racetrack orbit.

▼ **Operator station**
The cabin of the E-3 is packed with consoles. From here, operators monitor air traffic on large screens which display output from the long-range radar.

▲ **Long endurance**
Inflight refuelling allows the E-3 to stay aloft for a day or more. On very long missions extra flight crew are carried to avoid over-exhaustion.

◄ **NATO's air force**
In addition to American, British and French E-3s, NATO also has its own AWACS squadron, crewed by airmen from the member nations.

FACTS AND FIGURES

➤ The Boeing E-3 Sentry took to the air for the first time on 5 February 1972.

➤ Originally, the Sentry was expected to be an eight-engined aircraft.

➤ The AWACS radar can see over the horizon, detecting enemy aircraft hundreds of kilometres away.

➤ In all, 68 AWACS were built for the US, NATO, Saudi Arabia, Britain and France.

➤ The disc-shaped radar dome atop the AWACS is larger than many aircraft.

➤ The Sentry was the last version of the Boeing 707, which went out of production in 1991 after 37 years.

Eye in the sky

Getting the edge over the enemy by using a large aircraft for surveillance was a hot idea in 1955 when the Lockheed Super Constellation became the first Airborne Warning and Control System (AWACS). Today's E-3 is a modern AWACS aircraft which flies at jet speeds carrying up to 17 technicians who use the latest hi-tech wizardry. To the pilots up front, the E-3 is an upscale version of the Boeing 707, the great and beautiful

aircraft which revolutionised air travel. But to the technicians who sit out back, the E-3 AWACS is the eyes and ears of the battlefield commander, watching, analysing and directing. During Operation Desert Storm, 30 air-to-air victories were scored by Allied

fighters who were guided into action by AWACS crews. With its long range and endurance, the E-3 Sentry can spy on an entire battlefield or, if necessary, an entire nation as they did keeping tabs on the conflict in Bosnia.

Versions of the Sentry built for the UK, France and Saudi Arabia have much fatter and far more fuel-efficient engines than their USAF cousins.

British and French aircraft have a refuelling probe above the flight deck. The standard American boom receptacle is also retained.

Royal Air Force Sentries are equipped with wingtip ESM pods which house a Loral passive radar detection system.

The APY radar operates in various modes, including over-the-horizon, pulse-Doppler, passive and maritime.

E-3A AWACS SENTRY

Introduced into USAF service in 1977, the Sentry was selected to equip a multinational NATO unit based in Germany under Luxembourg registration. The first of 18 aircraft was delivered to the NATO Airborne Early Warning Force in 1981.

Key to the E-3's capability is the Westinghouse AN/APY-1 or -2 radar. Its huge antenna, mounted above the fuselage, rotates six times per minute.

E-3s generally carry a mission crew of 16, under the overall mission commander. These include radar operators, communications specialists and weapons controllers.

AWACS has a flight deck crew of four, comprising pilot/aircraft commander, co-pilot, navigator and flight engineer.

USAF and NATO Sentries are powered by four Pratt & Whitney TF-33 turbofans. British, French and Saudi E-3s are powered by larger and more fuel-efficient CFM-56 engines.

In order to control the air battle, AWACS is fitted with 13 HF, VHF and UHF communications links controlled by the computerised and digitised J-TIDS (Joint Tactical Information Distribution System).

NATO ⊕ OTAN

LX-N 90444

E-3A AWACS Sentry

Type: airborne warning and control system

Powerplant: (USAF and NATO aircraft) four 93.36-kN (21,000-lb.-thrust) Pratt & Whitney TF-33-P-100/100A turbofans

Maximum speed: 853 km/h (550 m.p.h.) at 6096 m (25,000 ft.)

Normal operating speed: 563 km/h (350 m.p.h.) at 12,192 m (40,000 ft.)

Endurance: six hours, flying at 12,192 m (40,000 ft.), 1609 km (1,000 mi.) from base

Service ceiling: 8850 m (29,000 ft.)

Weights: empty 77,966 kg (172,000 lb.); loaded 147,420 kg (325,000 lb.)

Dimensions:
span	44.42 m (145 ft. 9 in.)
length	46.61 m (152 ft. 11 in.)
span	12.73 m (42 ft. 5 in.)
wing area	283.3 m³ (3,050 sq. ft.)

COMBAT DATA

ENDURANCE

The E-3 Sentry's exceptional endurance means that it is capable of flying unrefuelled surveillance missions lasting six hours at distances in excess of 1600 km (1,000 mi.) from its home base.

E-2 HAWKEYE	E-3 AWACS SENTRY	A-50 'MAINSTAY'
6.25 hours	More than 11 hours	8 hours

OPERATING ALTITUDE

The Sentry has a surprisingly modest service ceiling, being bettered by the smaller propeller-driven Hawkeye. Even so, at its working operating heights above 8000 m (25,000 ft.) the E-3 can 'see' for several hundred kilometres.

E-2 HAWKEYE	E-3 AWACS SENTRY	A-50 'MAINSTAY'
90,000 m (30,800 ft.)	85,000 m (29,000 ft.)	10,000 m (31,000 ft.)

RADAR RANGE

The Sentry's most important attribute is its amazing radar. Capable of detecting several thousand targets at extremely long range, it can also simultaneously direct and control 100 or more allied aircraft making intercepts.

E-3 AWACS SENTRY	650 km (400 mi.)
E-2 HAWKEYE	550 km (340 mi.)
A-50 'MAINSTAY'	350–400 km (220–250 mi.) (estimated)

Multi-mode radar control

PDNS: Pulse-Doppler Non-elevation Scan is the basic radar mode, used to measure the distance of airborne targets several hundred miles away.

MARITIME: Advanced signal processing systems allows AWACS to pick-out ship-sized targets amid the chaotic clutter of radar returns from the surface of the sea.

INTERLEAVED: AWACS can switch between modes several times per second. This allows the big aircraft to scan for aircraft and surface targets simultaneously.

BOEING
E-6 MERCURY

● Global mission ● Submarine communications ● Last of the 707s

BOEING E-6 MERCURY

▲ Mercury roll-out
An admiring crowd gives scale to the first production E-6, showing the huge size of this special communications aircraft.

▲ On the flightdeck
Cockpit systems are similar to those of the standard 707, except for the F108-CF-100 engine controls and the highly accurate navigation equipment. Air-refuelled missions may last up to 72 hours, and a relief aircrew is carried for these extended flights.

▲ Communicating from Mercury
Relief systems operators may also be accommodated, since the E-6 has eight bunks. An area is also set aside for the in-flight repair of faulty systems.

▲ Winging through the clouds
Missions are carried out at high altitude and over long ranges. The CFM engines are more powerful than the similar units fitted to the E-3 Sentry.

Wingtip sensor array ▶
High-frequency communication probes are fixed under the wing, and the wingtips are fitted with pods containing ultra-high frequency satellite receivers.

Maintaining communication links with American missile submarines at sea is the unique job of the Boeing E-6 Mercury. The E-6, formerly known as Hermes, was the final version of the Boeing 707 off the production line in Renton, Washington. The 707 airframe, which was originally designed in the 1950s, encloses the hi-tech communications system known by the nickname TACAMO (Take Charge and Move Out).

▲ Equipped with the latest communications systems, the E-6 Mercury will remain a vital component in the US chain of command well into the next century. A crew of 18 operators is required to control the systems.

FACTS AND FIGURES

➤ The maiden flight of the series prototype aircraft took place on 19 February 1987; the aircraft have seen combat.

➤ On 2 August 1989 the first operational E-6 Mercury entered service.

➤ Two squadrons, each with eight E-6s, are operated by the US Navy.

➤ The E-6 carries extra bunks for relief crewmembers because of its long endurance flights of up to 72 hours.

➤ Boeing manufactured 18 E-6s for service with the US Navy.

➤ Training for Mercury pilots is carried out in Waco, Texas, by civilian contractors.

PROFILE

Co-ordinating the submarine fleet

For several years the US Navy used the EC-130Q Hercules in the TACAMO role, which maintains low-frequency communications between American commanders and their nuclear submarines. However, a more modern aircraft, especially one that could provide extra space and improved crew comfort, was required as a replacement for the ageing Hercules. Navy experts decided that the Boeing 707-320 airliner offered the most suitable basis for the new aircraft, and issued a contract in 1983.

The 707 airframe, from which the E-6 was developed, provided maximum commonality with the E-3 Sentry AWACS

(Airborne Warning and Communications System) aircraft, for ease of servicing. The huge CFM56 engines, chosen because of their outstanding fuel efficiency, resulted in ultra-long endurance while on patrol. In fact, since it can be refuelled aloft, the endurance of the Mercury is limited only by its engine oil capacity. To communicate with submarines, the Mercury uses two trailing wire antennas which are hardened against the effects of nuclear blast and are deployed from its tailcone (1220 m (4,000 ft.) long) and underfuselage (7925 m (26,000 ft.) long). When the aircraft flies a tight orbit these antennas hang vertically down and

allow communications to be transmitted to submarines towing their own aerial array. After defence cuts in the 1990s, and as the threat of nuclear war becomes increasingly unlikely, the Navy has more E-6s than it needs and may assign some of them to secondary duties such as training or transport.

Above: Departing Renton for the short flight to Boeing Field in Seattle, the US Navy's first Mercury flew in 1987. The first two operational aircraft flew into NAS Barbers Point, Hawaii in August 1989 to serve with VQ-3 squadron in the Pacific theatre.

Above: Just visible at the extreme rear of this E-6's fuselage is the orange tip of the VLF trailing wire antennas. A tight orbit is flown to keep the wires vertical during use.

E-6A Mercury

Type: strategic communications aircraft

Powerplant: four 106.76-kN (24,000-lb.-thrust) CFM International F108-CF-100 (CFM56-2A-2) turbofan engines

Maximum speed: 981 km/h (608 m.p.h.)

Maximum cruising speed: 842 km/h (522 m.p.h.)

Range: 11,760 km (7,291 mi.)

Service ceiling: 12,800 m (42,000 ft.)

Weights: empty 78,378 kg (172,431 lb.); maximum take-off 155,128 kg (341,281 lb.)

Dimensions: span 45.16 m (148 ft. 2 in.)
length 46.61 m (152 ft. 11 in.)
height 12.93 m (42 ft. 5 in.)
wing area 283.35 m² (3,049 sq. ft.)

E-6A MERCURY

Some US Navy E-6s have been seen in this grey and white colour scheme, but most operational aircraft are painted an overall white. All Mercurys carry minimum markings.

Five communications stations are situated in the fuselage above the wing. A vast array of radio equipment is carried, including secure voice communications, which even allow secure communication between crew members via the intercom.

A flight crew of four is standard, and they are the only crewmembers who have an outside view. The fuselage has no windows, apart from tiny portholes in the emergency escape doors.

The crew rest areas, with bunks, galley and a toilet, are housed in the forward section of the fuselage. Such amenities are vital if the crew is to remain efficient on missions of up to three days.

Efficiency and reliability were the main factors behind the choice of CFM International engines. Internal fuel capacity is an enormous 70,308 kg (154,678 lb.) enough for a 10½-hour mission at 1850 km (1,150 mi.) from base.

In addition to the satellite communications downlink equipment, the wingtip pods also contain electronic support measures systems.

62782

Very low-frequency (VLF) trailing wire aerials are stowed in the rear fuselage. One retracts into the tailcone while the other is stored within the rear fuselage.

NAVY

COMBAT DATA

RANGE

Aircraft of this type are often required to fly long distances on detachment to various parts of the world. Once there, they use air-to-air refuelling to stay airborne for long periods.

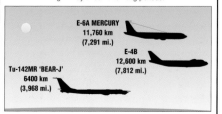

E-6A MERCURY
11,760 km
(7,291 mi.)

E-4B
12,600 km
(7,812 mi.)

Tu-142MR 'BEAR-J'
6400 km
(3,968 mi.)

Airborne relay station

TALKING TO SUBS: The E-6 is primarily tasked with providing communication links with the US Navy's ballistic missile-firing submarine fleet in a post-nuclear strike environment.

SECONDARY ROLE: As well as the wartime submarine communications role, the E-6 fleet has a secondary task of providing back-up VLF communications in parts of the world out of the range of ground-based transmitters.

RELAYING MESSAGES: Supported by the USAF's KC-135 tanker fleet, the Mercury can relay communications between ground stations, satellites, an E-4 command post aircraft and the submerged submarine fleet.

BOEING

E-4

● Airborne command post ● Four built ● Based on the 747 airliner

K nown as the AABNCPs (Advanced Airborne National Command Posts), or National Emergency Airborne Command Posts (NEACPs or 'Kneecaps'), the E-4 'Doomsday Planes' were always associated with the prospect of nuclear attack during the Cold War. The four USAF E-4Bs continue to provide an aerial command centre for US leaders in the event of not only nuclear war, but any major conflict or crisis.

▲ Boeing
received its first E-4 contract in 1973, and delivered the first aircraft the following year after an internal refit by E-Systems. The first upgraded E-4B was redelivered in 1980.

BOEING E-4

▼ Continuing role
Despite the end of the Cold War, the E-4 has a continuing role during national emergencies.

▲ Communications gear
In terms of its communications systems, the E-4B is the world's best-equipped aircraft. Thirteen external communications systems, covering seven wavebands, use power from a 1200-kVa electrical system powered by an engine-driven generator.

▼ 'Air Force One'
The most recent 747s delivered to the USAF were two VC-25A Presidential transports based on Boeing's 747-200B airliner. The callsign 'Air Force One' is used when the President is aboard.

▲ Advanced technology
The E-4B's highly advanced range of communications systems are optimised for maximum reliability.

▲ Maximum endurance by IFR
The E-4s have in-flight refuelling capability via a receptacle above the nose of the aircraft.

FACTS AND FIGURES

➤ Four E-4Bs belong to the 1st Air Command and Control Squadron of the 55th Wing at Offutt AFB, Nebraska.

➤ E-4s are limited to 72 hours' endurance by their engines' lubricating oil capacity.

➤ The E-4 made its first flight without mission equipment on 13 June 1973.

➤ Including the VC-25s, the USAF operates six 747s; plans to buy ex-airline 747s for the National Guard were cancelled.

➤ Originally, the airborne command post requirement called for six E-4s.

➤ The E-4's systems are held in 1613 'black boxes' – three times the number in an E-3.

Presidential 'Doomsday Plane'

Right: Three of the four E-4Bs were delivered as E-4As, without the dorsal antenna.

U ntil recently an E-4 was kept on alert at Andrews Air Force Base, Maryland – a short helicopter journey from the White House. In the event of an attack on the United States, the President and his staff would have boarded the E-4 to direct American forces from the comparative safety of the air.

The E-4 uses the familiar Boeing 747 airliner's fuselage to accommodate the President (in his role as Commander-in-Chief of US forces) and key members of his battle staff. They reside in the flying equivalent of the White House's Situation Room.

This 'war readiness aircraft' is equipped with nuclear thermal shielding, protection against EMP (electromagnetic pulse) and a large variety of communications systems, covering seven wavebands from super-high to very-low frequency. If necessary, the aircraft can broadcast to the US population over the national radio network or link up to commercial telephone networks to send emergency messages.

Initially, the E-4As of the mid-1970s used equipment from EC-135J Project 'Looking Glass' command post aircraft. But when the current E-4B entered service in 1980 it had considerably more equipment, including SHF (super-high frequency) satellite communications gear in a distinctive dorsal blister. The result was a command post and flying 'situation room' aircraft.

Although the Cold War has ended, the E-4 remains available for deployment worldwide in times of crisis.

Above: Whenever the US President travels abroad, an aircraft from the E-4 fleet accompanies 'Air Force One' at a discreet distance in case an emergency situation arises.

E-4B

Type: national emergency airborne command post (NEACP)

Powerplant: four 233.53-kN (52,500-lb.-thrust) General Electric F103-PW-100 (CF6-50-E2) turbofans

Cruising speed: (typical) 933 km/h (578 m.p.h.) at 6096 m (20,000 ft.)

Endurance: 12 hours (without in-flight refuelling); 72 hours (with in-flight refuelling)

Ferry range: 12,600 km (7,812 mi.)

Cruise ceiling: 13,715 m (45,000 ft.)

Weights: max. take-off 362,874 kg (799,992 lb.)

Accommodation: two flight crews, each of four plus; total accommodation for 94 crewmembers, including a battle staff of 30

Dimensions: span 59.64 m (195 ft. 7 in.); length 70.51 m (231 ft. 4 in.); height 19.33 m (63 ft. 5 in.); wing area 510.95 m² (5,498 sq. ft.)

E-4B

73-1676 was one of three E-4As delivered in the mid-1970s and was upgraded shortly after delivery to E-4B standard. All equip the 1st Air Command and Control Squadron, based at Offutt Air Force Base, Nebraska.

The E-4B carries two flight crews on potentially long missions, each consisting of an aircraft commander (pilot), co-pilot, navigator and flight engineer. A special navigation station and crew rest area are provided on the upper deck, behind the cockpit.

The most obvious external identification feature of the E-4B is the dorsal fairing on top of the forward fuselage. This contains the satellite/super-high frequency (SHF) antenna. The aircraft has nuclear thermal shielding and protection against EMP weapons.

The main deck is divided between a flight crew section and four operating compartments for the President and his battle staff. These are the NCA (National Command Authority) area (similar in role to the White House Situation Room), conference room, battle staff area and C³I (command, control, communications and intelligence) area.

When the Boeing 747 was selected to fill the SS-481B Support System requirement in 1973, it was chosen because of its size and the fact that it was an 'off-the-shelf' design. Airframe costs were therefore kept to a minimum. The E-4s are painted in this all-over anti-flash white finish.

UNITED STATES OF AMERICA

31676

One of the 46 external antennas is an 8-km (5-mi.) long, retractable very-low frequency (VLF) aerial trailing behind the aircraft. VLF is used to communicate with submerged submarines.

E-4Bs are powered by four General Electric CF6 turbofans (military designation F103). The first two aircraft were delivered with Pratt & Whitney JT9Ds (F105s).

In times of crisis

THE PRESIDENT AND THE NCA: If the US was attacked, some leaders would be taken to the underground command centre in Virginia, while others, including the President, would board an E-4B in order to direct American forces. A National Command Authority (NCA) would co-ordinate the army, navy and air force.

72 HOURS' ENDURANCE: The E-4 can remain airborne for three days and nights, refuelled by USAF tankers. The key to its capability is the extensive array of communications systems fitted, covering seven wavelengths.

EMP AND NUCLEAR SHIELDING: In order to perform its role as a communications centre, the E-4 is protected against nuclear thermal damage and electromagnetic pulse weapons.

EARLY COMMAND POSTS

BOEING EC-135C/J: E-4s replaced various versions of the EC-135 (itself based on the KC-135B tanker), which had performed the Project 'Looking Glass' task since 1961. 'Looking Glass' was the Strategic Air Command's (SAC) commitment to have a command post in the air at all times to direct SAC's manned and ballistic missile assets in time of war.

BOEING
EC/RC-135

● Strategic reconnaissance ● Intelligence gatherer ● Command post

For decades the Boeing RC-135, the aerial espionage cousin of the KC-135 tanker, has been vanguard of the secret world of reconnaissance, giving its crews hours of boring routine interrupted by seconds of sheer terror. During tensions with the Soviet Union, the 'spy in the sky' RC-135 often flew within a kilometre of Moscow's territory. The EC-135 is similar, but is packed with radios to act as a flying command post during a nuclear war.

▲ The EC-135 is based on the same aircraft as the RC-135, but contains different equipment. Most of this is for communications with other US military forces. There is usually a General on board who can control the war from the air.

BOEING EC/RC-135

◄ High-tech telephonist
The job of most of the crew on the EC-135 is to make communication connections with ground stations or other aircraft.

▼ Command post
The airframe of the EC-135 is festooned with antennas for the many radios.

▼ Missile watchers
The two RC-135S Cobra Ball aircraft specialise in tracking and photographing missiles. A unique feature is the black painted wing, which reduces glare for photography of re-entry vehicles. Aerials are used to gather data from missile launchers.

▼ Inflight refuelling
Tanking is vital to the RC-135's ability to stay on station for many hours at a time.

▼ The 'Hoover'
This RC-135U is known as the 'Hoover' because of its ability to 'suck up' every electronic signal. Only two remain in service, flying from Offut AFB, Nevada.

FACTS AND FIGURES

➤ The systems operators in the RC-135 are known as Ravens.

➤ The first RC-135 reconnaissance craft became operational in August 1966.

➤ Strategic Air Command RC-135s flew more than 6200 intelligence-gathering sorties during the Vietnam War.

➤ EC-135s have a trailing antenna which can be reeled out to a length of 10 km for communication with submarines.

➤ Several EC-135s carried a special nose radome to track the Apollo spacecraft.

➤ The RC-135S can hunt for enemy mobile missile launchers in wartime.

PROFILE

America's super snooper

The Boeing RC-135 strategic reconnaissance aircraft is the offspring of the Boeing KC-135 Stratotanker and is closely related to the spectacularly successful Boeing 707 airliner. Designed as an electronic eavesdropper, the RC-135 collects SIGINT (signals intelligence), including an enemy's radar emissions, radio communications or missile telemetry.

The closely related EC-135 was an airborne command post for Strategic Air Command, and

the E-6 Mercury still provides the same service for the US Navy's missile submarines. RC-135s of the US Air Force's 55th Wing deploy worldwide to snoop on potential adversaries in global trouble spots. During the Cold War, they flew closer to the USSR more often than any other Western aircraft. During Operation Desert Storm, the RC-135 gathered vital intelligence on Saddam Hussein's forces. Using radios, radar and electronic equipment to spy

Below: The nose of the RC-135 is covered with bulges containing intelligence-gathering equipment.

Above: Despite the end of the Cold War, the RC-135 fleet is as important as ever to the United States. During the wars in Vietnam and the Gulf it proved it was just as good at collecting intelligence in a tactical war, as it was in the type of superpower stand-off for which it had been designed.

on potential opponents, the RC-135 continues to be vital to the overseas interests of the United States.

RC-135V

Type: multi-engine long-range reconnaissance aircraft

Powerplant: four 80.07-kN (17,960-lb.-thrust) Pratt & Whitney TF-33-P-9 (JT3D-3B) turbojets

Maximum speed: 990 km/h (614 m.p.h.) at 10,000 m (33,000 ft.)

Operational radius: 4300 km (2,666 mi.)

Service ceiling: 12,375 m (40,600 ft.)

Weights: empty 47,650 kg (104,830 lb.); loaded 144,000 kg (316,880 lb.)

Accommodation: reconnaissance versions of the Stratotanker carry electronic sensors and monitoring crews of up to 35

Dimensions:
span	39.88 m (131 ft.)
length	41.53 m (136 ft.)
height	12.70 m (42 ft.)
wing area	226 m² (2,432 sq. ft.)

RC-135V

Known collectively by the codename Rivet Joint, the US Air Force has a fleet of 14 RC-135Vs and RC-135Ws for gathering electronic intelligence. Together they keep watch on potentially hostile nations on a global basis from bases around the world.

Large cheek fairings on either side of the fuselage contain flat antennas. These 'listen out' across a wide range of frequencies for signals which are analysed by the onboard crew.

The crew of the RC-135 is large: there are two pilots and two navigators on the flight deck, with about 17 systems operators in the cabin.

As well as 'listening' with extraordinary sensitivity, the RC-135 can also 'talk' thanks to satellite communications aerials fitted on the spine.

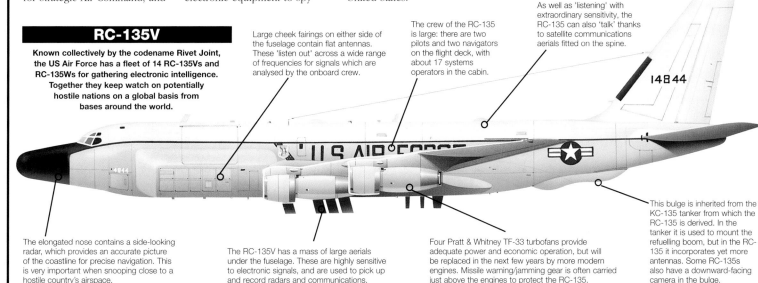

The elongated nose contains a side-looking radar, which provides an accurate picture of the coastline for precise navigation. This is very important when snooping close to a hostile country's airspace.

The RC-135V has a mass of large aerials under the fuselage. These are highly sensitive to electronic signals, and are used to pick up and record radars and communications.

Four Pratt & Whitney TF-33 turbofans provide adequate power and economic operation, but will be replaced in the next few years by more modern engines. Missile warning/jamming gear is often carried just above the engines to protect the RC-135.

This bulge is inherited from the KC-135 tanker from which the RC-135 is derived. In the tanker it is used to mount the refuelling boom, but in the RC-135 it incorporates yet more antennas. Some RC-135s also have a downward-facing camera in the bulge.

RC-135 missions

COMINT: Communications intelligence is the interception and recording of military communications. RC-135s may carry foreign language specialists to help in this work.

ELINT: Electronic intelligence gathering is the detection, location and classification of radars. The information may be passed to attack aircraft which can steer around potentially dangerous radars.

TELINT: The Cobra Ball aircraft gather telemetry intelligence. This entails recording signals from foreign missile tests and photographing the re-entry vehicles.

COMBAT DATA

MAXIMUM SPEED

Compared to the main British and Russian intelligence gatherers, the RC-135 is faster. Although in the deadly game of strategic reconnaissance, endurance and equipment capability are the telling factors.

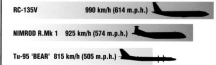

RC-135V **990 km/h (614 m.p.h.)**
NIMROD R.Mk 1 **925 km/h (574 m.p.h.)**
Tu-95 'BEAR' **815 km/h (505 m.p.h.)**

SERVICE CEILING

The three aircraft have similar ceilings. Operations are normally undertaken at around 10,000 m (33,000 ft.), at which height they are high enough to 'peer' a long way into the target territory.

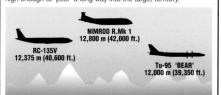

NIMROD R.Mk 1 **12,800 m (42,000 ft.)**
RC-135V **12,375 m (40,600 ft.)**
Tu-95 'BEAR' **12,000 m (39,350 ft.)**

RANGE

Designed as a long-range bomber, the Tu-95 'Bear' has exceptional endurance. For longer missions RC-135s are supported by aerial tankers providing inflight refuelling to prolong the sorties.

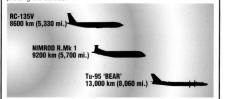

RC-135V **8600 km (5,330 mi.)**
NIMROD R.Mk 1 **9200 km (5,700 mi.)**
Tu-95 'BEAR' **13,000 km (8,060 mi.)**

BOEING

KC-135 STRATOTANKER

● USAF tanker ● Passenger and cargo capability ● Long serving

Taking a huge risk, Boeing proposed, built and funded a military jet tanker/transport prototype in 1954. The aircraft was ordered into production as the KC-135, and one of the greatest success stories in military aviation had begun. Stratotankers have since served around the world, supporting all types of USAF missions, and have been involved in combat operations over Vietnam and in the Gulf War.

▲ Flying the KC-135 requires great skill and courage. The crew must either rendezvous with receivers at long range and at high altitude, or maintain an accurate course so that the receiver aircraft can fly to them.

BOEING KC-135 STRATOTANKER

◀ **Producing Stratotankers**
KC-135 production was a priority as the USAF was equipped with increasing numbers of fast, jet-powered bombers which were supported by propeller-driven tankers that could not keep up with them.

▲ **New developments**
A KC-135A in its original natural metal colour is refuelled by the KC-135R development aircraft. New engines gave the 'R' improved performance.

▼ **A-7D top-up**
Tactical jets are able to fly much longer attack missions with pre- and post-strike refuellings.

▲ **French tanker**
French C-135Fs were adapted to the probe-and-drogue system of refuelling.

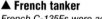

◀ **Flying 'gas station'**
A pristine KC-135A, with its large cargo door visible on the forward fuselage, is seen early in its life.

FACTS AND FIGURES

➤ When the 93rd Air Refuelling Squadron of the 93rd Bomb Wing received the KC-135 in 1957, each tanker cost $3,670,000.

➤ KC-135s powered by the old J57 turbojet are nicknamed 'stovepipe' aircraft.

➤ A 54,000-piece kit is required to convert a KC-135A to KC-135R standard.

➤ On 19 November 1988, 'Cherokee Rose', a KC-135R, established 16 time-to-height records in four weight classes.

➤ New refuelling pods allow KC-135s to support probe-equipped receivers.

➤ The US Air National Guard received its first jet tankers, KC-135As, in 1975.

Boeing's immortal jet tanker

Boeing and the USAF confidently expect that the KC-135 will be refuelling bombers, fighters, reconnaissance aircraft and transports beyond the year 2025.

The aircraft, which began as the private-venture Boeing Model 367-80 (or 'Dash-Eighty'), has been constantly updated, keeping pace with modern technology and remaining as safe and efficient now as it was on 15 July 1954 when the 'Dash-Eighty' first flew.

The addition of a Boeing-developed refuelling boom and a slightly wider fuselage produced the Model 717, known to the USAF as the Boeing KC-135 Stratotanker. Few modifications, the most important being a taller fin, were needed during the production of 732 aircraft. All of the surviving airframes have undergone a continuous evolution.

A host of special variants was produced, including the KC-135Q, a specialised supporter of the SR-71A; the KC-135E, a KC-135A re-engined with TF33 engines from old 707 airliners; and the KC-135R, which was powered by F108 engines and had a 150 per cent increase in

fuel available for transfer at a radius of 4630 km (2,870 mi.).

France was the only export customer for the Stratotanker and bought 12, designated the C-135F, to support its Mirage IV fleet. In USAF service the KC-135 will fly for many more years performing its unglamorous but vital role.

Above: These Early Strategic Air Command KC-135As maintain operational readiness. They have the original short fin.

Below: The amount of time spent on station for a vital asset such as the E-3 Sentry may be increased from hours to a few days with regular KC-135 refuellings.

KC-135R STRATOTANKER

Strategic Air Command began to receive the KC-135R in July 1984 and it represented a big leap in performance over earlier variants. The grey colour of this early delivery aircraft has largely been replaced by a dark-green over grey or overall mid-grey scheme.

A large door on the left forward fuselage hinges upwards to allow cargo or passengers to be loaded. Up to 37,650 kg (82,000 lb.) of palletised freight may be accommodated.

CFM International F108-CF-100 turbofans, each of 97.86-kN (22,015-lb.-thrust), power the KC-135R. This extra thrust provides an all-round performance improvement, including an impressive take-off, with the KC-135R becoming airborne 61 m (200 ft.) before the KC-135A has left the runway.

All of the Stratotanker's refuelling systems are mounted below floor level, which gives the aircraft great flexibility by allowing the carriage of cargo or up to 80 passengers, or any combination of the two.

In order to keep the KC-135 in service for as long as possible, a programme was initiated in 1975 to re-skin the lower wings. The airframe fatigue life was increased by 27,000 hours.

Upgraded aircraft, beginning with the KC-135E programme, have increased-span tailplanes which were taken from 707 airliners.

Using a small control column the boom operator 'flies' the boom towards the receiver aircraft. The 'boomer' lies on his or her stomach on a couch.

Boeing's air-refuelling boom has control surfaces similar to those of an aircraft. It is also telescopic, so that a safe distance may be maintained between the tanker and the receiver.

10310

U.S. AIR FORCE

Tanking tactics

TWO RACE TRACKS: Flights of fighters set up a race-track at 90 degrees to the track of the tankers. Each flight waiting its turn to refuel.

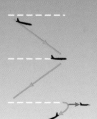

ACTIVE LEVEL: A series of tankers stack at 325 metre intervals above an active refuelling level. When the active tanker can give no more fuel it leaves the pattern and the remaining tankers all move down by one level.

LAST TANKER, LAST FLIGHT: If all goes according to plan, the last tanker in the stack should refuel the last flight of fighters and still have enough fuel remaining for the return to base.

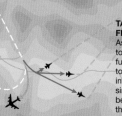

TANKERS RETURN, FIGHTERS FLY ON: As the tankers return to base, the fully fueled fighters are free to penetrate deeply into enemy territory. A similar operation may be mounted to get them home.

BOEING/GRUMMAN

E-8 J-STARS

● Stand-off surveillance ● Battlefield intelligence ● Gulf War veteran

▲ *Seventeen*
mission crew-members operate consoles displaying colour-coded images of enemy terrain and vehicles. A mission crew commander is usually a lieutenant colonel or colonel.

Grumman's E-8 is a command post in the sky, able to detect, locate, track and classify enemy ground formations at long range. Flying for 12 hours at a time near the battlefield, this modified Boeing 707 uses Joint STARS (Surveillance Target Attack Radar System) to watch events unfold and to gather data. Rushed into service in the first Gulf War, the contribution made by the E-8 was enormous.

BOEING/GRUMMAN E-8 J-STARS

◀ **Tested in action**
The two E-8A prototypes were hastily deployed and saw active service in the first Gulf War despite still being part-way through their test programme. Production E-8Cs have improved avionics.

▲ **Production deliveries**
Production E-8C serial number 90-0175 is one of a fleet of E-8s ordered by the USAF/US Army.

▼ **Ground Station**
The US Army truck-mounted Ground Station Module relays data from J-STARS to tactical operations centres on the ground for use by Army commanders.

▲ **Gulf War operations**
In the Gulf the two E-8A prototypes were flown by the 4411th Joint STARS Squadron and were useful in locating 'Scud' missile sites.

◀ **Fighter escorts**
With no weapons or defensive systems, E-8 J-STARS are usually escorted by F-15 Eagles on HVACAP (high-value asset combat air patrol) during a mission.

FACTS AND FIGURES

➤ USAF plans call for Joint STARS aircraft to be assigned to the 93rd Airborne Surveillance Control Wing at Robins AFB.

➤ The first production E-8 (the third ship, an E-8C) appeared on 22 March 1996.

➤ An eight-hour sortie can cover an area of one million sq. km (400,000 sq. mi.).

➤ The first two E-8s were not modified to receive air-to-air refuelling, though later aircraft will be equipped for this.

➤ The two Desert Storm E-8s flew 54 missions and logged 535 flight hours.

➤ One E-8B airframe was delivered before the cheaper E-8C version was chosen.

PROFILE

Army eyes over the battlefield

Although still being developed, two E-8 Joint STARS aircraft were rushed to Riyadh, Saudi Arabia, in 1990. Their job was to provide Operation Desert Storm commanders with a 'real-time' method of tracking the enemy's armour and other military vehicles.

The sophisticated SLAR (side-looking airborne radar) aboard this converted Boeing 707 airliner is able to distinguish even stationary objects on the ground over a distance of 250 km (155 mi.), giving military

an unprecedented ability to follow the enemy's every move on the battlefield.

E-8 development began in the late-1980s when advances in radar technology made it possible to design this 'air-to-ground' equivalent of the already proven E-3 AWACS (Airborne Warning and Command System) 'air-to-air' command centre. Operated jointly by the USAF and US Army, improved versions of this Grumman-modified airframe have also been on duty over the Balkans on behalf of United

Nations forces. Cruising at 800 km/h (496 m.p.h.), the E-8 Joint STARS aircraft maintain continuous C³I (command, control, communications and intelligence) operations monitoring hundreds of ground targets at a time.

The USAF and US Army have a requirement for 20 E-8Cs. Whether all these aircraft will be funded remains to be seen. One factor in the progress of the conversion programme has been the availability of suitable secondhand 707 airframes.

E-8A J-STARS

Type: multi-crew battlefield command and control aircraft

Powerplant: four 84.53-kN (18,960-lb.-thrust) Pratt & Whitney JT3D-7 turbofan engines

Maximum cruising speed: 973 km/h (603 m.p.h.) at 7620 m (25,000 ft.)

Endurance: 11 hours, or 20 hours with one inflight refuelling

Range: 9266 km (5,745 mi.)

Service ceiling: 12,800 m (39,000 ft.)

Weights: maximum take-off 151,315 kg (332,893 lb.)

Accommodation: pilot, co-pilot, flight engineer, navigator, plus 10 mission crewmembers

Dimensions:
span	44.42 m (145 ft. 8 in.)
length	46.61 m (152 ft. 10 in.)
height	12.93 m (42 ft. 5 in.)
wing area	283.35 m² (3,046 sq. ft.)

E-8A J-STARS

N8411 was the second E-8A airframe and was allocated the military serial number 86-0417. Production machines are designated E-8C and are converted from Boeing 707 ex-airliners.

The plan to use newly constructed Boeing 707-320C airframes for the production E-8B was changed on cost grounds; converted airliners are being used instead, the result being the E-8C.

E-8Bs were to be powered by new GE/SNECMA F108 turbofan engines, as fitted to re-engined KC-135R tanker aircraft. However, efforts to cut costs have resulted in the E-8C with rebuilt TF33 engines.

E-8As carried a flight crew of four: a pilot, co-pilot, flight engineer and navigator/self-defence suite operator.

The 7.93-m (26-ft.) 'canoe' fairing below the fuselage contains the Norden synthetic aperture radar that forms the heart of the J-STARS system.

E-8As carried ten operator consoles. E-8Cs have 17 consoles and one dedicated to defensive electronics. The standard mission crew is 21, but this can be increased to 34 for longer missions.

The teardrop fairing known as the 'fiddle' was only fitted to E-8As. It contained the Flight Test Data Link used over long distances during Desert Storm to convey information to central command in Riyadh.

US AIR FORCE-US ARMY
Joint STARS

N8411

The E-8 airframe is that of the Boeing 707-320C, the final version of the famous airliner. These lack the ventral fin of earlier models.

J-STARS surveillance

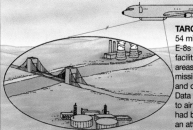

QUICK DEPLOYMENT: Based in Riyadh, the E-8's deployment proved invaluable during Desert Storm. The Norden radar set is able to cover an area of 50,000 km² (19,000 sq. mi.).

TARGETS: Flying 54 missions, the two E-8s targeted oil facilities, assembly areas, 'Scud' missile sites, tanks and other vehicles. Data was passed on to air forces which had been assigned an attack role.

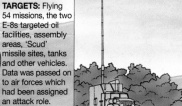

GROUND STATION MODULE: The US Army's GSM receives relayed information from the J-STARS about the enemy's movements and passes this on to ground forces.

COMBAT DATA

MISSION ENDURANCE

The E-8 can stay aloft for 11 hours before needing to refuel using the standard USAF air-to-air refuelling system. Flights of up to 72 hours' duration are possible, onboard supplies and crew fatigue being the governing factors. All three types are also capable of air-to-air refuelling.

E-4
12 hours

E-6 MERCURY
10½ hours

E-8 J-STARS
11 hours

BRITISH AEROSPACE

SEA HARRIER FRS.MK 1

● V/STOL fighter ● Anti-shipping strike ● Carrier air defence

F irst ordered by the Royal Navy as a multi-role, carrier-borne fighter in 1975, the Sea Harrier went on to prove itself in various missions in the Falklands conflict. It was not taken seriously at first, but the Sea Harrier has proved capable of undertaking reconnaissance, anti-ship missile attacks and air defence missions with efficiency. It has been exported to India, and recently upgraded by Britain with more advanced radar and missiles.

▲ India has so far been the only export customer for the Sea Harrier, and operates these capable aircraft from its aircraft-carriers Viraat and Vikrant. Royal Navy Sea Harriers currently serve aboard the carriers Invincible, Illustrious and Ark Royal, sharing the ship's flight deck with Sea King helicopters.

BRITISH AEROSPACE SEA HARRIER FRS.MK 1

▼ Sidewinder armament
On Royal Navy combat air patrol missions the Sea Harrier's principal air-to-air weapon is the AIM-9L Sidewinder infra-red homing missile.

▲ Royal Navy's defender
The key to the success of the Sea Harrier is the excellent integrated avionics and head-up display system. Pilots claim it is still one of the best in service in a fighter aircraft.

▼ Long-range patrol
These five Sea Harriers carry a typical long-range air combat training load of Sidewinder acquisition rounds and underwing drop-tanks.

▲ Fleet training
Prospective Sea Harrier pilots were trained on two-seat Sea Harrier T.Mk 4s for flight technique and Blue Fox radar-equipped Hunter T.Mk 8Ns for advanced intercept training.

Thrust-vectoring manoeuvrability ▶
The key to the Sea Harrier's success lies in its unmatched ability to alter the direction of its engine nozzles in flight and outmanoeuvre faster aircraft.

FACTS AND FIGURES

➤ In Royal Navy service the Sea Harrier filled the gap left when the McDonnell Douglas Phantom FGR.Mk 2 was retired.

➤ The Sea Harrier can carry the Sea Eagle anti-ship missile or a nuclear bomb.

➤ India operates 26 Sea Harrier Mk 51s armed with MATRA 550 missiles.

➤ The first operational Sea Harrier Squadron was No. 800 aboard HMS Invincible in 1980.

➤ Six Sea Harriers were lost in the Falklands, but none during air combat.

➤ Royal Navy FRS.Mk 1s have been upgraded to F/A.Mk 2 standard.

PROFILE

Vertical take-off superfighter

A first-class naval strike fighter in its own right, the Sea Harrier was originally developed from the RAF's own Harrier GR.Mk 3. Rather than being a land-based aircraft, the Sea Harrier was designed from the outset to serve aboard the Royal Navy's 20000-tonne ASW carriers.

Soon after its 1980 service entry with the fleet, the Sea Harrier became involved in the 1982 Falklands War, performing faultlessly in air defence, strike

and reconnaissance duties. Embarking for the South Atlantic first aboard HMS *Hermes* and later aboard HMS *Invincible*, the two squadrons of Sea Harriers equipped with the Blue Fox radar and Sidewinder missile returned after their successful 'Operation Corporate' with 22 aerial victories and no aerial combat losses. Sea Harriers continue to be the Royal Navy's sole fixed-wing combat asset, but now also serve in numbers

aboard the aircraft-carriers of the Indian navy as FRS.Mk 51s. The Indian navy may adopt an Israeli radar and advanced active radar missile for its Sea Harriers to acquire long-range air-to-air engagement capability.

For pilot training the Sea Harrier utilises a specially built land-based replica of the Royal Navy's carrier deck 'ski-jumps', used during short take-offs with increased payloads.

Sea Harrier FRS.Mk 1

Type: carrier-based V/STOL fleet defence fighter and strike aircraft

Powerplant: one 9752-kN (21,950-lb.-thrust) Rolls-Royce Pegasus Mk 104

Maximum speed: 1328 km/h (735 m.p.h.)

Combat radius: 750 km (465 mi.) with four AIM-9L Sidewinder AAMs

Service ceiling: 15,545 m (51,000 ft.)

Weights: maximum take-off weight 11,884 kg (26,145 lb.)

Armament: underfuselage mounts for two 30-mm ADEN cannon; maximum ordnance of 3629 kg (7,984 lb.) on underwing pylons

Dimensions:
span	7.70 m	(25 ft. 3 in.)
length	14.50 m	(47 ft. 7 in.)
height	3.71 m	(12 ft. 2 in.)
wing area	18.68 m²	(201 sq. ft.)

SEA HARRIER FRS.Mk 1

This Sea Harrier is in the colours of No. 801 Squadron, based at RNAS Yeovilton, known to the Royal Navy as HMS *Heron*. The code '000' shows that it is the aircraft assigned to the squadron commander.

For naval operations the Sea Harrier has all its easily corroded magnesium components replaced.

The Sea Harrier's cockpit is raised to provide room for extra marine avionics. The FRS.Mk 1 also features weather-proof protective coatings on important components.

The distinctive tail houses a Marconi radar warning receiver in the leading edge of the vertical surface, as well as various receiver aerials in the tailcone.

Two ADEN 30-mm cannon pods are carried under the fuselage. Under the wings each outer pylon mounts twin AIM-9L Sidewinder heat-seeking air-to-air dogfight missiles.

The naval Harrier carries an advanced Blue Fox all-weather radar in the nose. This can detect fighters up to 40 km (25 mi.) and ships up to 150 km (90 mi.) distant, but cannot 'look down' to search for aircraft flying low over water.

A single Rolls-Royce Pegasus Mk 104 turbofan with two swivelling exhausts either side of the fuselage creates 9752 kN (21,950 lb. thrust).

The unusual bicycle undercarriage with wing-mounted outriggers provides the plane with stable vertical landings on aircraft-carrier decks in all weathers.

COMBAT DATA

MAXIMUM SPEED

The Sea Harrier and the Matador are from the same family of aircraft and therefore have a similar top speed. The 'Forger' is slower despite having one engine dedicated to forward speed.

SEA HARRIER FRS.Mk 1	1328 km/h (735 m.p.h.)
AV-8S MATADOR	1176 km/h (729 m.p.h.)
YAK-38 'FORGER'	1009 km/h (626 m.p.h.)

CLIMB RATE

At sea level the Sea Harrier has a blistering climb rate, ideal for a quick launch from a carrier to intercept incoming aircraft. The Yak-38 takes much longer to reach operating altitude.

SEA HARRIER FRS.Mk 1
14,540 m/min
(47,700 f.p.m.)

AV-8S MATADOR
8840 m/min
(29,00 f.p.m.)

YAK-38 'FORGER'
4500 m/min
(14,760 f.p.m.)

BOMBLOAD

Although it is powered by three engines the Yak-38 can only manage to carry a relatively light warload. The Sea Harrier can be equipped with a wide variety and a fair weight of weapons.

SEA HARRIER FRS.Mk 1
3629 kg (7,984 lb.)

AV-8S MATADOR
2404 kg (5,289 lb.)

YAK-38 'FORGER'
2000 kg (4,400 lb.)

In the Falklands

AIRFIELD DESTRUCTION: Avoiding Argentinian fighters and 35-mm anti-aircraft guns, Sea Harriers flew low over Goose Green, hitting a stationary FMA Pucará with cluster bombs.

SIDEWINDER STRIKE: The Israeli-built Dagger was faster than the Sea Harrier, but a combination of pilot skill and the deadly Sidewinder missile accounted for 11 Dagger kills.

SURPRISE ATTACK: Sea Harriers ambushed Argentinian Agusta 109 and Puma helicopters over Mount Kent, strafing them.

BRITISH AEROSPACE

HAWK

● Advanced jet trainer ● Light multi-mission fighter

▲ Steam rises from the catapult as a T-45 Goshawk is prepared for launch. The US Navy's carrier-capable version of the Hawk brings to 15 the number of countries using this best-selling trainer.

The Hawk is one of the most successful advanced trainers in the world. Used by the Royal Air Force and 14 other air arms worldwide, this lithe and exciting jet is also a carrier-capable advanced trainer for the US Navy and is being developed into a versatile family of lightweight fighters. But the Hawk is also a high-flying ambassador of goodwill: the all-red Hawks of the RAF's Red Arrows have entertained more than 50 million spectators in the past 18 years.

BRITISH AEROSPACE HAWK

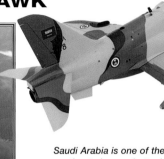

Desert warrior ▲
Saudi Arabia is one of the largest Hawk users operating trainer and attack versions. Its Hawks wear a disruptive brown/sand coloured camouflage scheme, enabling them to blend into the desert.

▲ Red Arrows
The famous Red Arrows aerobatic display team perform a formation loop at an air display.

◄ Aerobat
The RAF use the Hawk as an advanced trainer with a secondary role as a light fighter armed with heat-seeking missiles, and an externally fitted 30-mm gunpod.

▲ Pilot's classroom
The comfortable Hawk cockpit combines the simplicity of the aircraft that students would be familiar with from basic training with features of advanced combat jets that they all aspire to fly.

▼ Gulf warrior
During the Gulf War, Kuwaiti Hawks took part in light strike sorties against Iraqi positions inside Kuwait. This trainer Hawk is in service with the neighbouring state of Abu Dhabi.

▲ Alpine trainer
The Swiss air force selected the Hawk to replace ageing de Havilland Vampire trainers. The Hawk will take pilots from flying the turboprop PC-7 to the mighty F/A-18 Hornet.

FACTS AND FIGURES

➤ The Hawk made its maiden flight on 21 August 1971.

➤ Eighty-eight Hawks were modified to carry the Sidewinder missile and were designated Hawk T.Mk 1A.

➤ The Red Arrows display team has operated the Hawk since 1979.

➤ RAF No. 100 Squadrons uses the Hawk for target-towing duties. The towing equipment is attached under the fuselage.

➤ The Hawk trainer has been exported to the Middle East, Africa, Europe and the Far East.

➤ Finland purchased over 50 Hawk Mk 51s which were assembled by Valmet.

PROFILE

The world's favourite trainer

B ritish Aerospace (originally Hawker Siddeley) developed the beautiful, capable Hawk to replace the RAF's standard trainer, the Gnat. As a trainer the Hawk is simple and practical, yet offers the high performance associated with military jets. Several air forces now use the Hawk to train pilots, and after a protracted period of development the US Navy is employing the McDonnell-built T-45 Goshawk trainer version.

Pilots found that flying this sleek jet was almost like flying

the hottest, fastest fighter. Inevitably, fighter versions followed. Now the Hawk can be used as a trainer or fighter by a small air force unable to afford more expensive jets.

Although hardly in the category of a MiG-25 or an F-15, the Hawk is potent as a lightweight fighter and would give a good account of itself in battle. The Hawk 100 two-seater

Blasting a target with SNEB rockets is part of the tactical weapons course for RAF pilots. The Hawk can carry four rocket pods.

is a trainer with full military capabilities. Half-a-dozen nations are using versions of the Hawk 200, a single-seater which is a pure combat version fitted with the APG-66H multi-mode radar.

This aircraft is seen in the grey-green colours of the early 1980s. Current weapons trainers are painted all-over grey.

The leading edge of the Hawk's wing is swept back at 26°.

Hawk T.Mk 1A

Type: two-seat trainer/light fighter

Powerplant: one 23.34-kN (5,200-lb.-thrust) Rolls-Royce/Turboméca Adour Mk 151-01 turbofan

Maximum speed: 1040 km/h (645 m.p.h.) at sea level

Range: 2500 km (1,800 mi.) with two drop-tanks; combat radius 1038 km (620 mi.) with a 1361-kg (3,000-lb.) warload

Service ceiling: 14,000 m (46,000 ft.)

Weights: empty 3990 kg (8,800 lb.); maximum 7755 kg (16,200 lb.)

Armament: two AIM-9L Sidewinder air-to-air missiles plus up to 500 kg (1,100 lb.) ordnance; maximum load 3000 kg (6,600 lb.)

Dimensions:
span	9.39 m	(30 ft. 9 in.)
length	11.17 m	(35 ft. 4 in.)
height	3.99 m	(13 ft.)
wing area	16.69 m²	(180 sq. ft.)

HAWK T.MK 1

The first customer for the Hawk was the RAF, which uses the type for advanced jet and tactical weapons training. RAF Hawks now use a new gloss-black colour scheme to make them more visible.

A Micro-Detonating Cord (MDC) runs through the top of the canopy. This shatters a fraction before the ejection seat is fired.

The Hawk is powered by a non-afterburning Rolls-Royce Adour turbofan engine, which has proved reliable and economical in service.

The airframe of the Hawk is immensely strong. It is stressed to 9g, the same as an F-16 or a MiG-29 fighter.

The Hawk cockpit has two Martin Baker ejection seats. The raised rear seat gives an instructor a good view of his student in action.

Hawks are clear-weather aircraft; basic versions lack radar.

The Hawk can carry a variety of external stores, from the tanks and rocket pods seen here to cannon packs and air-to-air missiles.

The airbrake fairs neatly into the Hawk's belly. It is of great value in training prospective fighter pilots the techniques of combat manoeuvring.

COMBAT DATA

MAXIMUM SPEED

Current advanced trainers are usually capable of high subsonic speeds. Their light weight and good power-to-weight ratios generally mean that they are very quick to accelerate, and give them the ability to perform as well as faster and more powerful machines.

HAWK T.Mk 1	1040 km/h (645 m.p.h.)
ALPHA JET E	1000 km/h (620 m.p.h.)
MB.339C	817 km/h (510 m.p.h.)

COMBAT RADIUS

Although the small size of trainers prevents them from carrying a great deal of fuel, their small, efficient engines mean that even when carrying a useful warload (typically, two 454-kg bombs and two air-to-air missiles) aircraft like the Hawk can strike at targets at considerable range. This extra capability allows the Hawk to turn from trainer to attack duties.

HAWK T.Mk 1 1038 km (745 mi.)

MB.339 500 km (310 mi.)

ALPHA JET E 1000 km (620 mi.)

ARMAMENT

HAWK T.Mk 1 3000 kg (6,600 lb.)

ALPHA JET E 2500 kg (5,500 lb.)

MB.339 2000 kg (4,400 lb.)

They cannot match the latest front-line jets for sheer armament-lifting ability, but advanced combat trainers usually have a fairly respectable weapons load, and form an effective reserve force to more powerful combat jets.

A family of Hawks

■ **HAWK T.Mk 1** is the basic two-seat trainer version, capable of fast-jet training missions as well as weapons training. This version can carry a wide variety of weapons, but has no sensors and only basic avionics.

■ **HAWK 100** is a more advanced two-seat trainer and light-strike aircraft, with optional forward-looking infra-red systems. The cockpit is more advanced than the standard version, and the wing has extra pylons.

■ **HAWK 200** is the most advanced and deadly of the family. Although no bigger than other Hawks, it can be equipped with a full array of sensors, including radar and a laser rangefinder, and can deliver a wide range of weaponry.

■ **T-45 GOSHAWK** has been selected by the US Navy as its combat trainer for the 21st century. Based on the Hawk, it has upgraded systems, an arrester hook and tougher landing gear to withstand carrier launches and landings.

CASA

C.101 AVIOJET

● Spanish twin-jet trainer ● German/US design help ● Exports

▲ An impressive array of weapons including a cannon, bombs, rockets and napalm are displayed before the C.101 prototype. A secondary strike role has impressed export customers.

Designed as a trainer and light strike aircraft to replace the Hispano HA200 and HA220 Saeta, the C.101 flew for the first time in June 1977. Since then it has been sold to Chile, Honduras and Jordan and, naturally, to the Spanish air force as its primary trainer. While its main role is to take trainee pilots all the way from primary training to the operational conversion stage, a built-in provision for armament makes it a useful strike aircraft.

CASA C.101 AVIOJET

◄ **Royal Jordanian C.101**
Jordan was the last C.101 customer, in 1987, taking delivery of 16 C.101CC-04s at a cost of US$90 million, including spares and training. Used for training, they have an attack capability.

▼ **Chilean A-36 Halcón**
CASA granted ENAER a licence to build the C.101CC-02 as the Halcón (Hawk) attack aircraft, armed with BAe Sea Eagle anti-ship missiles.

▲ **On the attack**
The first attack C.101 variant was the dual-role C.101BB attack/trainer, which features six wing hardpoints and an optional DEFA 30-mm cannon.

▼ **Exports to South America**
Chile took delivery of four CASA-built and eight ENAER-built C.101BBs, designating them T-36. Ranging radar was fitted in the aircraft's nose.

▲ **Colourful prototype**
Bearing a civil registration EC-ZZZ, carried from 1982, the C.101 pylon-equipped prototype displays a colourful demonstration scheme. Ventral fins are a feature of exported aircraft.

FACTS AND FIGURES

➤ CASA unsuccessfully proposed a C.101 variant for the US Joint Primary Aircraft Training System (JPATS) requirement.

➤ Total C.101 production comprised 149 aircraft, including prototypes.

➤ Once Chile's A-36s were delivered, the T-36s were relegated to pilot training.

➤ In a reciprocal deal, Chile licence-built the C.101 while CASA assembled 41 Pillán trainers for the Spanish air force.

➤ The AGM-65 Maverick air-to-surface missile is compatible with the C.101DD.

➤ Germany's MBB designed the Aviojet's rear fuselage and tail section.

PROFILE

Blackbird: the Iberian instructor

In its initial C.101EB form for the Spanish air force, the Aviojet was an unarmed trainer designated E.25 Mirlo (Blackbird). The 88 delivered equip the central flying school and training and trials units, as well as the 'Team Aguila' aerobatic display team.

To improve performance at high altitudes, the C.101BB attack/trainer has a more powerful engine. It also carries a ranging radar, has up to six weapons pylons and can have a 30-mm cannon or two 12.7-mm

(.50 cal.) machine-guns in a fuselage bay below the rear cockpit. In addition, this bay can be used for reconnaissance or electronic warfare equipment.

Both Chile and Honduras opted for the C.101BB. ENAER built eight of the Chilean air force's 12 T-36s, and has gone on to produce all but one of its 23 C.101CCs, a dedicated attack version which is designated A-36 Halcón (Hawk) in Chilean service. Honduras purchased four C.101CCs and the Royal Jordanian Air Force bought 16.

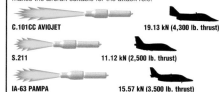

Above: Spain took delivery of 88 C.101EB-01s from 1980. After initial training on the E.25, pilots receive weapons tuition on the SF-5Bs.

A developed version, the C.101DD, was flown in May 1985 with an uprated engine and more sophisticated navigation/attack systems, like a head-up display (HUD) and hands-on-throttle-and-stick (HOTAS) controls. So far, it has failed to find a customer.

Above: In 1985, CASA flew the C.101DD advanced trainer with uprated engines and new avionics and cockpit systems. By 1996, a launch customer had yet to be found.

C.101CC Aviojet

Type: advanced trainer and light attack aircraft

Powerplant: one 19.13-kN (4,300-lb.-thrust) Garrett TFE731-5-1J turbofan

Maximum speed: 834 km/h (517 m.p.h.) at 4575 m (15,000 ft.)

Climb rate: 6 mins 30 secs to 7620 m (25,000 ft.)

Combat radius: 600 km (370 mi.) on lo-lo-lo mission with cannon and two Maverick missiles

Service ceiling: 12,800 m (42,000 ft.)

Weights: empty equipped 3500 kg (7,700 lb.); maximum take-off 6300 kg (13,860 lb.)

Armament: one 30-mm cannon or two 12.7-mm (.50 cal.) machine-guns, plus up to 2250 kg (4,950 lb.) of assorted unguided and guided weapons

Dimensions:
span	10.60 m	(34 ft. 9 in.)
length	12.50 m	(41 ft.)
height	4.25 m	(13 ft. 11 in.)
wing area	20 m²	(215 sq. ft.)

E.25 MIRLO

Mirlo (Blackbird) XE.25-04 was the fourth C.101EB-01 prototype, flying in April 1978. In 1986, it was based at Torrejón with Grupo 54, a trials unit formally known as Escuadrón 406.

An internal windscreen is fitted between the two cockpits. In the event of a bird strike, the instructor in the rear seat is protected from debris and air blast and can maintain control of the aircraft.

Two of Garrett's TFE731 turbofans power the C.101 family. Spanish E.25s use the TFE731-2-2J variant rated at a modest 15.6 kN (3,500 lb. thrust). Export models optimised for ground attack operate at higher weights and have additional power (up to 19.13 kN/4343 lb. thrust in the C.101CC).

For ease of design and building, the C.101 is of modular construction, which also affords cost benefits. During design, ample internal space was left for electronic equipment to meet future needs.

Fuel tanks are situated behind the cockpit and in the wings. Total fuel tank capacity is 1259 litres, of which 1222 litres are usable.

Two Martin-Baker E10C ejection seats are fired by a single handle situated between the crewman's knees. The E10C is a 'zero-zero' seat, able to be used at up to 15,240 m (50,000 ft.) at 1110 km/h (688 m.p.h.). Staggered command ejection by the instructor is possible.

The C.101's nose landing gear retracts forward into the front portion of the nose. The rest of the nose carries radio and avionics equipment.

An equipment bay below the rear cockpit is employed for the storage of oxygen and some avionics. On armed aircraft, it may hold a cannon pack or electronic countermeasures (ECM) equipment.

Designed with help from Northrop in the US, the C.101's mainplane has 5° of dihedral and no de-icing provision. Export aircraft have three hardpoints per wing.

ACTION DATA

THRUST

In its improved C.101CC variant, the Aviojet's engines deliver a far better thrust figure than the original C.101EB training version. This makes the aircraft suitable for the attack role.

C.101CC AVIOJET	19.13 kN (4,300 lb. thrust)
S.211	11.12 kN (2,500 lb. thrust)
IA-63 PAMPA	15.57 kN (3,500 lb. thrust)

G LIMITS

Modular construction gives the Aviojet a surprisingly strong airframe, making it capable of higher-g manoeuvres than either the IA-63 or the S.211. Aerobatic ability is an important feature of any training jet. In the attack role, with a weapon load, g limits are considerably reduced to -1/+5.5 at maximum take-off weight.

S.211 -3/+6
IA-63 PAMPA -3/+6
C.101CC AVIOJET -3.9/+7.5

CLIMB RATE

The C.101's straight wing gives the aircraft a good climb rate, but limits its top speed. The Argentine FMA IA-63 also has straight wings, while the SIAI-Marchetti S.211 has swept wings.

S.211 1280 m/min (4,200 f.p.m.)
C.101CC 1494 m/min (4,900 f.p.m.)
IA-63 PAMPA 1560 m/min (5,120 f.p.m.)

CASA training aircraft

■ **1.131 JUNGMANN:** Among several German types for which production licences were obtained was the Bücker Jungmann trainer.

■ **1.133 JUNGMEISTER:** As well as 500 Bü 131s, CASA built about 50 Bü 133 single-seat trainers for the Spanish air force.

■ **C.212E1 AVIOCAR:** Known as the TE.12B in Spanish air force service, this variant of the Aviocar is employed as dual-control trainer.

■ **C.223 FLAMINGO:** Hispano (later part of CASA) built this version of the German SIAT (later MBB) light training aircraft from 1972.

CASA

C.212 AVIOCAR

● Twin turboprop ● STOL transport ● SAR, VIP and reconnaissance

As its name suggests, the Aviocar was designed with utility in mind. It turned out to be an extraordinarily useful aircraft, with big rear doors that provide unrestricted access to the square section fuselage. In addition to the original military transport and commercial passenger versions, later models have been adapted to fill a wide variety of roles. Well over 400 have been sold, and the aircraft was built by IPTN in Indonesia as well as in Spain.

▲ In its C.212-200 form the Aviocar is a far more capable aircraft than the original version. Maximum cargo load is increased from 2000 kg (4,400 lb.) to 2820 kg (6,200 lb.). Here a Jeep and crew enter via the rear door, ready for rapid offloading into combat.

CASA C.212 AVIOCAR

◀ **Saving lives**
The Spanish air force bought seven aircraft for the SAR role. Similar aircraft were purchased by Mexico, Sweden, Sudan and Venezuela. A search radar is mounted in the extended nose.

▼ **Fully loaded**
In an offensive role, the Aviocar may be armed with a range of weapons to suit a number of missions. Here the aircraft is shown with a Sea Skua anti-ship missile and Stingray light torpedo, in addition to gun and rocket pods.

▲ **Continued development**
The 300 series feature winglets and other changes. The US Air Force have used at least four on secret missions.

Far Eastern ▶ popularity
Malaysian Aviocars are built by Nurtanio. The Indonesian company builds the C.212 under license from CASA.

Worthy successor ▶
When the Spanish air force needed a replacement for its DC-3 and Ju 52/3m transports, CASA responded with the C.212. Its rugged construction and versatility have made it successful at home and on the export market.

FACTS AND FIGURES

➤ Reverse thrust was applied while the prototype was still airborne at the Paris airshow in 1971, damaging the wing.

➤ The C.212-100 could carry 16 troops with a flight crew of two.

➤ Of almost 450 in total, around 130 Aviocars have been built by Nurtanio.

➤ Top secret missions, possibly into Northern Iraq, have been flown by U.S. Air Force Aviocars.

➤ The Aviocar was built for operations from unprepared runways.

➤ To land from an altitude of 15 m (50 ft.) the Aviocar requires only a 462-m (1,500-ft.) run.

PROFILE

Multi-role STOL transport

There have been three basic production models of the Aviocar since the first Series 100 flew in 1971. The Series 200, flown in 1978, has more powerful engines and a higher gross weight, while the Series 300 added more payload as well as improving performance. There is also a version of the Series 300 with PT6 turboprop engines.

As a transport, the Series 300 can carry up to 26 passengers, 25 fully equipped troops or 24 paratroops plus an instructor/jumpmaster. Alternatively, it can be loaded with nearly three tons

of cargo, and the rear doors can be opened for low-level cargo dropping. Photographic versions have space for a darkroom as well as cameras.

Other missions for which the Aviocar has been adapted include anti-submarine warfare and maritime patrol. Operators as far afield as Sweden and Argentina have bought maritime models, which have a surveillance radar in the nose or a submarine detection radar under the fuselage. Weapons on these more aggressive variants include the Stingray torpedo, Sea Skua anti-ship

Above: The Chilean navy purchased C.212-100s. Variants of the 300 may also be in service.

missile and gun or rocket pods.

There have also been a handful equipped for electronic intelligence gathering and electronic countermeasures. These carry equipment for the interception and jamming of signals from hostile radars. One example was also used by the U.S. Army to test sensors for use in anti-drug operations.

Below: Swedish maritime patrol Aviocars are designated Tp 89 in service. Aircraft used for fisheries protection have side-looking radar and pollution detecting sensors.

C.212 Series 300

Type: utility transport

Powerplant: two 671-kW (900-hp.) Garrett TPE331-10-511C turboprops

Maximum speed: 370 km/h (229 m.p.h.)

Initial climb rate: 474 m/min (1,555 f.p.m.)

Range: 1433 km (890 mi.)

Service ceiling: 7925 m (26,000 ft.)

Maximum payload: 2820 kg (6,200 lb.)

Weights: empty 4280 kg (9,416 lb.); loaded 8000 kg (16,940 lb.)

Dimensions:
span	20.25 m	(66 ft. 5 in.)
length	16.15 m	(53 ft.)
height	6.30 m	(20 ft. 8 in.)
wing area	41 m²	(441 sq. ft.)

The high set tail has become a classic feature of transport aircraft design. It allows for easy and rapid loading of troops and their equipment.

C.212-200 AVIOCAR

This aircraft belongs to the Venezuelan navy and is configured for the maritime patrol role. SAR is a secondary role for these Aviocars.

Two Garrett TPE331 turboprops, producing 671 kW (900 hp.) each, drive four-blade propellers to give the Aviocar its exceptional range and STOL capabilities.

Attaching the wing at the fuselage shoulder allows the engines to be mounted away from any debris thrown from the airstrip. It also gives an unobstructed cabin.

In the patrol version, the AN/APS-128 search radar scans from this extended nose radome and is supplemented by a range of ordnance.

Vehicles are loaded using the built-in ramp. When retracted this forms the rear door of the aircraft, which may be opened inflight for dropping of paratroopers or supplies.

The fixed undercarriage is designed to withstand the rigors of continuous rough-field operations. Military transports frequently operate away from base.

In the maritime patrol and SAR variants the cabin contains special mission avionics and rescue equipment. In the transport role the C.212-200 carries up to 18 troops.

ACTION DATA

SPEED

The heavier but considerably more powerful Sherpa is closely matched with the Aviocar. The smaller, lighter and older Twin Otter lags farther behind the others in terms of speed, but it boasts a phenomenal STOL performance.

C.212-300 AVIOCAR	370 km/h (229 m.p.h.)
C-23B SHERPA	372 km/h (231 m.p.h.)
DHC-6 TWIN OTTER	350 km/h (217 m.p.h.)

PAYLOAD

Carrying a cargo 272 kg (600 lb.) greater than that of the C.212, the Sherpa appears to be the better aircraft. Its range, however, is less than the superb 1433-km (890-mi.) range of the Aviocar.

C.212-300 AVIOCAR	C-23B SHERPA	DHC-6 TWIN OTTER
2820 kg (6,200 lb.)	3221 kg (7,306 lb.)	1941 kg (4,270 lb.)

TAKE-OFF RUN

Although it is a smaller aircraft, the take-off performance of the DHC-6 is remarkable. Operating from damaged or unprepared airstrips, the C.212 has a huge advantage over the C-23B.

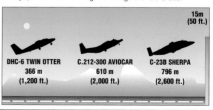

DHC-6 TWIN OTTER	C.212-300 AVIOCAR	C-23B SHERPA
366 m (1,200 ft.)	610 m (2,000 ft.)	796 m (2,600 ft.)

Military twin turboprop transports

■ **BAe JETSTREAM T.Mk 1:** Used by the RAF as a trainer, the Jetstream is capable of cruising at 454 km/h (281 m.p.h.).

■ **SHORTS SC-7 SKYVAN:** First flown in 1963, the Skyvan is a useful transport and patrol aircraft with impressive STOL performance.

■ **FAIRCHILD C-26:** Replacing Convair C-131s in the US Air National Guard, the C-26 features advanced avionics.

■ **ASTA (GAF) NOMAD:** Recent structural problems have caused the withdrawal of many Nomads from service.

CESSNA

T-37

● US Air Force primary trainer ● In service for over 40 years

▲ *Cessna*
stuck to conventional wisdom
by designing its T-37 trainer with side-by-side
seats. Like many air arms, the USAF is now turning
to a tandem arrangement for basic training.

N icknamed the 'Tweet' or 'Tweety Bird' after an appealing cartoon character, the Cessna T-37 has been the USAF's primary training aircraft since the mid-1950s. The visually pleasing design has not changed externally in 40 years, although the instruments and equipment beneath its skin have been constantly improved. Genuinely loved and admired, the T-37 will still be training most USAF pilots well into the 21st century.

PHOTO FILE

CESSNA **T-37**

▼ **First jet experience**
The T-37B is the first jet aircraft flown by most USAF pilots. Primary training takes between 80 and 85 hours of flight time, after which the student will graduate to advanced training on the T-38 Talon.

▲ **Mass production**
Around 1000 T-37s were built to meet the USAF's high demand for pilots during the 1950s and 1960s.

1980s upgrade ▶
Cancellation of the T-46A programme left the USAF without a successor to the T-37B and from 1989 it began to upgrade surviving Tweets for continued service. The T-37 began to be replaced by the T-6 Texan II from 2001.

▼ **Foreign 'Tweets'**
The T-37's excellent handling qualities make it the perfect mount for precision flying. T-37s are used by the Portuguese national aerobatic team.

▲ **Trainer with teeth**
Cessna developed an armed version of the T-37 for light attack as the A-37 Dragonfly. Sidewinder missiles were not part of the standard armament.

FACTS AND FIGURES

➤ Many student pilots briefly fly a propeller aircraft before advancing to primary training in the T-37.

➤ The USAF currently has about 550 T-37Bs in training squadrons.

➤ The prototype for the T-37 series made its first flight on 12 October 1954.

➤ Cessna began designing the T-37 as a private venture, aimed at introducing jet power to the primary training mission.

➤ In total, 1269 T-37s were manufactured for the US Air Force and for export.

➤ Cessna flew the first production T-37 on 27 September 1955.

PROFILE

Long-serving USAF trainer

Tens of thousands of USAF pilots have their first experience of jet flying in the T-37 'Tweet'. The T-37 was designed in 1952 to meet a USAF requirement for a jet-powered primary trainer and first flew on 12 October 1954. It was a very practical trainer design seating two side-by-side, with a low and wide-tracked undercarriage to ease landing and ground handling.

Cessna built 534 T-37As, and from 1959 switched production to the T-37B model with uprated J69 engines and improved navigation and communications

equipment. Provision was also made for wingtip fuel tanks. In all, 466 T-37Bs were built, including some for export, and all surviving A-models were brought up to T-37B standard.

The T-37C was the ultimate 'Tweet' and was never used by the USAF. Built solely for export, some 269 T-37Cs were sold to 10 foreign operators.

'Tweets' were to have been replaced during the mid-1980s by Fairchild T-46As but this new design was abandoned, and instead Sabreliner Corporation

Above: The Pakistan air force is one of the eight current operators of the T-37C. The others are Chile, Colombia, Greece, Jordan, Peru, Thailand and Turkey.

began supplying modification kits to the USAF which allowed T-37s to be rebuilt for extended service. The long-serving T-37 eventually began to be replaced by the Raytheon T-6A Texan II turboprop from 2001.

Below: Most USAF T-37s are based in Texas where flying conditions are ideal for much of the year.

T-37B

Type: two-seat primary trainer

Powerplant: two 4.56-kN (1,026-lb. thrust) Continental J69-T-25 turbojet engines

Maximum speed: 685 km/h (426 m.p.h.)

Cruising speed: 612 km/h (380 m.p.h.)

Initial climb rate: 1027 m/min (3,369 f.p.m.)

Range: 972 km (604 m.p.h.)

Weights: empty 1755 kg (3,869 lb.); maximum take-off 2933 kg (6,466 lb.)

Accommodation: instructor (right) and student (left) in side-by-side seating

Dimensions:
span	10.30 m	(33 ft. 10 in.)
length	8.92 m	(29 ft. 3 in.)
height	2.68 m	(8 ft. 10 in.)
wing area	17.09 m²	(184 sq. ft.)

T-37C

Turkey's air force, the Türk Hava Kuvvetleri (THK) received 20 ex-USAF T-37Bs and 50 new-build T-37Cs. Based at Cigli, they are operated by 122 Filo (squadron) of the Hâva Okullari Komutanligi (Air Training Command).

Turkish student pilots commence their primary flying training with 123 Filo at Gaziemir with a 10/15-hour course on propeller-driven Cessna T-41Ds and Beech T-34As. At Cigli, they complete a 90/100-hour basic training course on the T-37 before moving to the co-located 121 Filo for advanced training on Lockheed T-33 Shooting Stars and Northrop T-38 Talons.

The T-37's tailplane is set one-third of the way up the vertical fin to clear the efflux from the jet engines. As angle of attack increases, the tailplane remains in the relatively undisturbed airstream, thus preventing the aircraft from entering a deep stall.

T-37Cs have an armament training and light attack capability thanks to a single hardpoint under each wing. This can carry a multi-purpose pod containing a 12.7-mm (.50 cal.) machine-gun, two 70-mm folding-fin rockets and four 1.36-kg (3-lb.) practice bombs.

Four-digit codes on THK aircraft comprise the base identification number, followed by a three-number suffix which repeats the last three digits of the aircraft's serial.

Power is provided by two small J69 engines, which are licence-built versions of the French Turboméca Marboré used in the Fouga Magister. Buried in the wingroots and built by Continental, they deliver a total of over 9 kN (2025 lb.) thrust.

Wide track undercarriage makes the T-37 easy and stable to taxi. However, its relatively short stroke means that a tail bumper is necessary to protect the rear fuselage during take-off rotation and landing.

ACTION DATA

MAXIMUM SPEED

The single-engined Czech L-29, and the T-37B, have a comparable top speed, but both are out-paced by the French Magister. A higher top speed enables the French aircraft to transit to and from its training area more quickly, thus increasing training time.

T-37B	685 km/h (426 m.p.h.)
CM 170-1 MAGISTER	715 km/h (444 m.p.h.)
L-29 DELFIN 'MAYA'	679 km/h (422 m.p.h.)

CLIMB RATE

The twin-engined T-37B and Magister have a far superior climb rate to that of the L-29. The American trainer outclimbs the Magister on account of its more powerful engines which give a superior thrust-to-weight ratio.

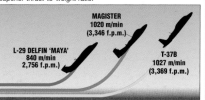

MAGISTER 1020 m/min (3,346 f.p.m.)

L-29 DELFIN 'MAYA' 840 m/min 2,756 f.p.m.

T-37B 1027 m/min (3,369 f.p.m.)

RANGE

With a standard fuel load, the T-37B can fly further or longer than either of its rivals. For a given flight condition, such as cruise, both twin-engined types can reduce their thrust settings to fly more economically than the single-engined L-29. Wingtip tanks were fitted to all three types to increase range.

T-37B 972 km (604 mi.)

CM 170-1 MAGISTER 925 km (575 mi.)

L-29 DELFIN 'MAYA' 640 km (398 mi.)

'Tweet' operators: American and export

USA: Since 1991 surviving USAF T-37Bs (which numbered 632 in 1989) have been cycled through an upgrade for continued service, until their eventual replacement in 2001.

CHILE: Chile received 22 ex-USAF T-37Bs and 12 T-37C trainers during the 1960s. Some 20-plus survivors serve with the training school 'Capitán Avalos' at Santiago-El Bosque air base.

PAKISTAN: Pakistan's air force received a total of 37 new-build T-37Cs and 28 ex-USAF T-37Bs. Two are used by instructors for the 'Sherdils' ('Lionhearts') aerobatic team.

CHENGDU

F-7

● Chinese-built MiG-21 derivative ● Updated variants ● Exports

Flown for the first time in January 1966, the Shenyang J-7 was a Chinese version of the Soviet MiG-21 'Fishbed'. By then Shenyang was working on the J-8, so development was transferred to Chengdu, where derivatives have been in production ever since. The J-7I, designated F-7B for export, was produced in small numbers before giving way to the J-7II, with an improved WP-7B engine. With Western avionics the J-7II became the F-7M Airguard. Development continues with the F-7MG, aimed at the export market.

▲ *Although essentially an updated MiG-21, the F-7M and F-7MG make use of Western avionics to enhance their capabilities. GEC-Marconi has been heavily involved.*

PHOTO FILE

CHENGDU F-7

▲ **Named for export**
Chengdu named the F-7M 'Airguard', with the Pakistani F-7P becoming 'Skybolt'. Neither name was adopted by other export customers.

▲ **Two-seat trainer**
In addition to the single-seat F-7, a two-seat version known as the JJ-7/FT-7 has been built. This FT-7P carries air-to-air missiles. It is primarily used as a trainer but can also adopt a secondary role as a fighter, if necessary.

◀ **Low-cost warplane**
Because of its simplicity and low unit cost, the F-7 has proved an ideal aircraft for small Third World air forces such as that of Sri Lanka.

▼ **In Chinese service**
The Air Force of the People's Liberation Army (AFPLA) continues to operate the J-7/JJ-7 in the fighter and training roles.

▲ **F-7MG at Air Show China '96**
Chengdu stated in 1996 that two of the updated F-7MGs had been built. Pakistan was expected to take delivery of the first service examples in 1997.

FACTS AND FIGURES

➤ Chengdu's all-weather J-7III, based on the MiG-21MF 'Fishbed-J', was built in limited numbers and not exported.

➤ The US-supported Super-7 project ended after 1989's Tiananmen Square massacre.

➤ Double-delta wings on the F-7MG offer an improved turn rate.

➤ The 'M' in F-7M signifies 'Marconi'; 'G' in F-7MG derives from the Chinese character 'Gai', meaning improved.

➤ Chengdu plans to install a new Western or Russian engine in the F-7MG in the future.

➤ Pakistan's first F-7Ps briefly had the name 'Skybolt' on their forward fuselages.

PROFILE

China's home-made 'Fishbeds'

Albania and Tanzania used the original J-7 as the F-7A, while F-7Bs were supplied to Egypt, Iraq and Sri Lanka. Bangladesh, Iran, Myanmar and Zimbabwe all received the F-7M Airguard, which is also used by the main export customer for the series, Pakistan. The F-7P variant was developed specifically to meet Pakistan's requirements.

Before the 1989 Tiananmen Square massacre in Beijing, Chengdu was collaborating with the American manufacturer Grumman on a Super-7 derivative for Pakistan. It was intended to use a US engine and carry the APG-66 radar used by the F-16, plus Sidewinder missiles. However, the US government suspended the collaboration.

Production of the two-seat JJ-7/FT-7 trainer variant is carried out at Guizhou. Another variant for the Chinese air force is the all-weather J-7III. Flown for the first time in April 1984, the III is powered by an up-rated 64.72-kN (14,650-lb.- thrust) Wopen WP-13 engine and also carries a new radar.

The latest version of the J-7 is the F-7MG which has a new wing, Western avionics and much improved weaponry.

Below: An updated version of the F-7 has been designated F-7MG in the Chinese inventory and features redesigned outer wings.

Above: The Bangladeshi air force's F-7s currently fly with two units, Nos. 5 and 35 Squadrons.

Known as the J-7 (for Jianjiji-7, or 'Fighter Aircraft Number Seven'), this development of the MiG-21 received the designation F-7 for export markets.

F-7M Airguard

Type: single-seat close support fighter

Powerplant: one 59.82-kN (13,460-lb.-thrust) Liyang Wopen WP-7B(BM) afterburning turbojet

Maximum speed: 2175 km/h (1,349 m.p.h.) above 12,500 m (41,000 ft.)

Endurance: 45 min on combat air patrol at 10,975 m (36,000 ft.) with three 500-litre (132-gal.) drop tanks

Initial climb rate: 10,800 m/min (35,425 f.p.m.)

Service ceiling: 18,200 m (60,000 ft.)

Weights: empty 5275 kg (11,605 lb.), normal take-off 7531 kg (16,570 lb.)

Armament: two NORINCO 30-mm cannon plus wing pylons for two PL-2, PL-5B, PL-7 or Magic air-to-air missiles, rocket pods or 500-kg (1,100-lb.) bombs on the inboard pylons

Dimensions:
span	7.15 m	(23 ft. 6 in.)
length	13.95 m	(45 ft. 9 in.)
height	4.10 m	(13 ft. 6 in.)
wing area	23 m²	(247 sq. ft.)

F-7P

An F-7P of the Pakistani air force, this machine was with No. 20 Squadron, based at Rafiqi, in 1991. It wears the air defence grey colour scheme with toned-down national markings.

Many export F-7s, including Pakistan's F-7Ps, have been fitted with Martin-Baker Mk 10 zero-zero ejection seats. Whereas early J-7I aircraft had single-piece canopies (as on the MiG-21F-13), later machines have more conventional two-piece units.

With a theoretical top speed of Mach 2.05 (with a full fuel load), the F-7P also has an excellent turn performance owing to its high power-to-weight ratio and low wing loading.

The engine air intake in the nose of the aircraft features a variable shockcone, as in the MiG-21. Computer-controlled, this is fully variable and houses a basic radar set. Western companies, including GEC-Marconi, supplied most of the avionics and other systems.

In Pakistani service, F-7P ordnance usually consists of a single centreline fuel tank and two AIM-9P Sidewinder or MATRA Magic air-to-air missiles. Four pylons are sometimes employed, and the aircraft has a limited air-to-ground capability.

Chengdu F-7Ps are powered by a single Wopen WP-7B afterburning turbojet producing 59.8 kN (13,460 lb. thrust). This engine is a copy of the Soviet Tumanskii R-11 found in early production MiG-21s.

COMBAT DATA

MAXIMUM SPEED

The Airguard and MiG-21bis 'Fishbed-L' share the same top speed as well as a common basic design. Northrop's F-5E Tiger II, though twin-engined, is designed for slightly slower speeds.

F-7M AIRGUARD	2175 km/h (1,349 m.p.h.)
MiG-21bis 'FISHBED-L'	2175 km/h (1,349 m.p.h.)
F-5E TIGER II	1700 km/h (1,054 m.p.h.)

THRUST

F-7s use an engine of earlier design than that of the MiG-21bis, producing less thrust. The F-5E's twin engines are comparatively small, producing just over two thirds the power.

F-7M AIRGUARD	59.82 kN (13,460 LB.)
MiG-21bis 'FISHBED-L'	69.65 kN (15,670 LB.)
F-5E TIGER II	44.40 kN (10,000 LB.)

INITIAL CLIMB RATE

In terms of its initial climb rate the MiG-21bis is the best performer of these types. Chengdu's F-7M has an inferior power-to-weight ratio and a climb rate little better than that of the F-5E.

F-7M AIRGUARD 10,800 m/min (35,425 f.p.m.)	MiG-21bis 'FISHBED-L' 13,800 m/min (45,265 f.p.m.)	F-5E TIGER II 10,455 m/min (34,300 f.p.m.)

China's modern jet fighters

■ **CHENGDU J-7 'FISHBED':** Early J-7s were broadly equivalent to the MiG-21F-13 and were built under licence from 1961.

■ **CHENGDU/GRUMMAN SUPER-7:** For sale to Pakistan, the cancelled Super-7 featured an American APG-66 radar and engine.

■ **SHENYANG J-8I 'FINBACK':** An all-weather version of the J-8 twin-engined fighter of 1968, the J-8I was produced from the mid-1980s.

■ **SHENYANG J-8IIM 'FINBACK':** After cancellation of the improved J-8II (with US radar), China used a Russian radar in the J-8IIM.

CNIAR/SOKO

IAR-93/J-22 ORAO

● Lightweight attack ● Conversion trainer ● Troubled development

▼ **Packing a punch**
With five weapons pylons and two twin-barrelled cannon, the Orao has impressive armament options.

▲ **Tandem trainer**
The 10 IAR-93A trainers featured an extended forward fuselage and sideways-opening canopies. However, they were found to be lacking in power and range.

▼ **Robust structure**
Designed from the outset to survive damage and for operating from rough airstrips, the Orao is a simple, but robust, design. It is fitted with a strong, twin-wheeled main undercarriage built by Messier-Hispano-Bugatti.

▼ **Cold War service**
Entering service in the early 1980s, the IAR-93 has survived the political upheavals in Romania.

Reconnaissance role ▶
Non-afterburning J-22 Orao 1s have been relegated to surveillance duties. This example, carrying a centreline camera pod, served with the Yugoslav air force and was based near Zagreb.

Designed jointly by Romania's CNIAR (now Avioane) and SOKO of Yugoslavia (now Bosnia), the twin-engined IAR-93/J-22 Orao has been built in single- and two-seat versions, both with and without afterburners. There were plans to upgrade the aircraft, but the two countries that collaborated to produce the IAR-93/J-22 Orao have undergone major upheavals in recent years, making these changes impossible.

▲ *Produced and designed equally by Romania and the former Yugoslavia, the IAR-93/Orao (Eagle) is a small, attractive twin-jet and is reminiscent of the larger SEPECAT Jaguar.*

FACTS AND FIGURES

➤ Romanian and Yugoslavian single-seat prototypes made simultaneous first flights on 31 October 1974.

➤ Early Orao 1s are now used for tactical reconnaissance and are designated IJ-22.

➤ The J-22 prototype is currently displayed in the museum at Belgrade airport.

➤ On 22 November 1984 a pre-production Orao became the first Yugoslav-built aircraft to exceed the speed of sound.

➤ Following the break-up of Yugoslavia, the Orao 2 is now operated by Serbia.

➤ Romania ordered 165 IAR-93Bs, including a number of two-seaters.

PROFILE

Lightweight strike-fighter collaboration

Single-seat prototypes of the IAR-93/Orao flew in October 1974, followed by two-seat prototypes in January 1977. The first production version was the IAR-93A/Orao 1, with non-afterburning engines, which was built in both single-seat tactical reconnaissance and two-seat operational trainer versions.

Afterburning engines were used for the Orao 2 and IAR-93B attack aircraft, first flown in 1983 and 1985, respectively. Most were single-seaters, but the Orao 2 was also built in a two-seat configuration.

A third version developed in Yugoslavia is the Orao 2D. This is a two-seat version of the Orao 2 and is used as a conversion trainer. The remaining two-seat Orao 1s were modified to the same standard, while the single-seaters were fitted with camera pods for reconnaissance.

The overthrow of the Communist government in Romania meant that plans to modernise the aircraft were left in limbo, and progress was halted in the former Yugoslavia when the SOKO factory at Mostar in Bosnia was demolished during fighting.

Oraos remain in service with the Serbian air force, and some were used operationally by the Serb forces in Bosnia before the imposition of the no-fly zone. The IAR-93B has remained in production after the revolution in Romania.

Above: Second-generation Orao 2s overcame the lack of power and range with afterburning engines and enlarged integral fuel tanks.

Below: This early IAR-93A, with four wing fences, wears the original Romanian air force insignia. This has since been replaced by a roundel.

IAR-93A

First flying in 1981, the IAR-93A was the first Romanian production version. CNIAR built 26 single-seat versions. They have been replaced in the attack role by the IAR-93B with afterburning engines.

J-22 Orao 2

Type: close-support and ground-attack aircraft

Powerplant: two 17.79 kN (4,000 lb.) Turbomecanica/ORAO-built Rolls-Royce Viper Mk 633-41 afterburning turbojets

Maximum speed: 1160 km/h (721 m.p.h.) at sea level

Climb rate: 4500 m/min (14,764 f.p.m.)

Range: 260–380 km (162–236 mi.) depending on load and mission profile

Service ceiling: 13,200 m (43,300 ft.)

Weights: empty 5700 kg (12,566 lb.); maximum take-off 11,200 kg (24,692 lb.)

Armament: two 23-mm cannon, plus up to 2800 kg (6,173 lb.) of bombs, rockets and air-to-surface missiles

Dimensions:
span	9.3 m (30 ft. 6 in.)
length	14.90 m (48 ft. 11 in.)
height	4.50 m (14 ft. 9 in.)
wing area	26 m² (312 sq. ft.)

Lacking a head-up display (HUD) and the latest avionics, the IAR-93A had fairly basic equipment. The updated Yugoslavian Orao 2 features a far more capable cockpit, with a Thomson-CSF HUD and other avionics from Honeywell and Collins. The pilot sits on a Martin-Baker Mk 10 ejection seat beneath a rearwards-opening canopy.

All operational versions of the J-22/IAR-93 have five weapons pylons: four on the wings and one beneath the fuselage. A wide variety of air-to-ground munitions can be carried, up to a total of 2800 kg (6,173 lb.). Orao 2s are capable of carrying the AGM-65 and AS-7 'Kerry' missiles.

The shoulder-mounted wing is of similar planform to that of the SEPECAT Jaguar. The early versions, such as this IAR-93A, did not have the leading-edge root extensions which gave later models better wing efficiency and manoeuvrability.

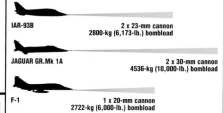

The strakes on the nose of the IAR-93A distinguish it from the prototypes and pre-production aircraft. The Orao 2 has a ranging radar in the dielectric nosecone.

A high degree of foreign-designed and imported equipment is used in the aircraft, including two Soviet GSh-23L twin-barrelled cannon in the forward fuselage.

All versions of the J-22 Orao and early versions of the IAR-93 have ventral fins. The IAR-93B is easily identifiable, however, as these fins were removed.

After problems and delays with the afterburning version of the Viper engine, the IAR-93A was fitted with two non-afterburning 17.79-kN (4,000 lb.) units. These engines did not provide the power to produce the desired performance.

SOKO-built aircraft

■ **G-4 SUPER GALEB:** This two-seat advanced trainer was designed to replace the G-2A Galeb and T-33 in this role.

■ **J-1 JASTREB:** Derived from the Galeb trainer, which saw service in the war in Bosnia, the Jastreb has been gradually replaced by the Orao.

■ **J-20 KRAGUJ:** Retired from Yugoslav service in 1990 after 20 years of operations, this close-support aircraft now serves with Slovenia.

■ **SA 342 PARTIZAN:** SOKO licence-built the Gazelle as the Partizan. It is used for liaison, anti-tank and anti-helicopter duties.

ACTION DATA

THRUST

Twin engines give greater chances of survival, especially after hits by ground-fire. As a consequence, all three of these aircraft feature twin afterburning engines. The lighter airframe of the IAR-93B requires less power than the F-1 to carry a similar load.

IAR-93B 44.48 kN (10,000 lb. thrust)

JAGUAR GR.Mk 1A 71.5 kN (16,080 lb. thrust)

F-1 64.98 kN (14,620 lb. thrust)

ARMAMENT

The IAR-93 can be loaded with a wide range of both Western and Eastern Bloc ordnance and can carry a reasonable load for a lightweight attack aircraft. The more powerful Jaguar can carry significantly more than the F-1 and the IAR-93B.

IAR-93B 2 x 23-mm cannon 2800-kg (6,173-lb.) bombload

JAGUAR GR.Mk 1A 2 x 30-mm cannon 4536-kg (10,000-lb.) bombload

F-1 1 x 20-mm cannon 2722-kg (6,000-lb.) bombload

COMBAT RADIUS

Although the IAR-93 resembles the Jaguar, it does not have the same capabilities. Both the F-1 and the IAR-93 are intended for operations close to the front line and possess poor range for modern combat aircraft.

IAR-93B 380 km (236 mi.)

JAGUAR GR.Mk 1A 852 km (529 mi.)

F-1 350 km (217 mi.)

DASSAULT

SUPER ETENDARD

● Carrier-based jet ● Anti-ship strike ● Maritime reconnaissance

Dassault's Super Etendard is a sleek, arrow-like aircraft which has achieved a superb military record with French and Argentine naval forces. The carrier-based Super Etendard can meet many challenges, including reconnaissance in its unarmed photo version. Most importantly, it can deliver the famous Exocet anti-ship missile with devastating results, using the aircraft's Thomson-CSF/EMD Agave multi-mode radar.

▲ Despite the age of the basic airframe design, the Super Etendard is a potent machine thanks to its avionics. It made history with the first ever air attack using a sea-skimming anti-ship missile.

DASSAULT SUPER ETENDARD

▼ **Etendard replacement**
The Aéronavale had proposed a navalised Jaguar for its strike squadrons, but this was cancelled and the Super Etendard entered production in the late 1970s.

▲ **Buddy refuel**
To extend its range, the Super Etendard can refuel from another aircraft fitted with a 'buddy' refuelling pack.

▲ **Nuclear missile**
For nuclear strikes, the Super Etendard is equipped with a single ASMP short-range nuclear stand-off missile. A fuel tank is carried on the port side to balance the weight.

▼ **Agave nose**
Distinguishing it from the previous Etendard IV, the Super Etendard has the Agave attack radar in its nose. This system detects maritime targets for the Exocet missile.

▲ **Argentina's revenge**
Exocet-armed Super Etendards sank the destroyer HMS Sheffield and the supply vessel Atlantic Conveyer in the Falklands war, despite being new in service.

FACTS AND FIGURES

➤ Reconnaissance versions can carry a Douglas 'buddy pack' and serve as air-refuelling tankers.

➤ Seventy-one Super Etendards were built for France and 14 for Argentina.

➤ More than 525,000 man-hours go into the production of a single Super Etendard.

➤ In the Falklands War, Argentine Super Etendards flew 580 sorties without a single aircraft being lost.

➤ The first flight of a Super Etendard prototype took place on 28 October 1974.

➤ The French navy first took delivery of the production aircraft on 28 June 1978.

PROFILE

Dassault's terror of the seas

From its first flight in 1974, the Super Etendard was an impressive machine for its small size. An updated version of the earlier Etendard IV, the Super Etendard featured a multi-mode attack radar, revised wing and more powerful Atar engine.

The Super Etendard served well with France, but this fine aircraft is mainly remembered as Argentina's cutting edge in the 1982 Falklands conflict. Best known was the sinking of the British destroyer HMS *Sheffield* by an Exocet, and the

subsequent sinking of the supply vessel *Atlantic Conveyor* which was carrying many helicopters for the land forces.

Iraq leased five Super Etendards with Exocets to attack Iranian oil tanker traffic in the Persian Gulf, causing havoc and marine insurance rates to skyrocket. French Super Etendards finally went to war in 1995, when one was hit by an SA-7 over Bosnia while flying a reconnaissance mission but managed to fly back home.

Uprated with a new avionics suite and the ability to use the

ASMP (Air-Sol Moyenne Portée) nuclear missile, the Super Etendard remain in service with France. In 1999 they began to be replaced as the first Rafale Ms entered service. The recently strengthened airframe could last until 2008.

Left: With new flaps and wing leading edge, the Super Etendard has the same performance as its predecessor, the Etendard IV, despite the extra weight.

Above: Aéronavale Super Etendards fly from the carriers Foch *and* Clemenceau.

Super Etendard

Type: single-seat carrier-based strike fighter

Powerplant: one 49.04-kN (11,000-lb.-thrust) SNECMA Atar 8K-50 turbojet

Maximum speed: 1380 km/h (856 m.p.h.) at high altitude

Combat radius: 850 km (527 mi.)

Service ceiling: 13,700 m (44,936 ft.)

Weights: empty 6500 kg (14,300 lb.); maximum take-off 12,000 kg (26,400 lb.)

Armament: underfuselage and underwing attachments for a variety of weapons, including AM39 Exocet or ASMP air-to-surface missiles, or AN52 tactical nuclear bombs; Sidewinder or MATRA Magic air-to-air missiles and rocket pods can also be carried

Dimensions:
span	9.60 m (31 ft.)
length	14.31 m (47 ft.)
height	3.86 m (13 ft.)
wing area	28.40 m² (306 sq. ft.)

SUPER ETENDARD

The 11 Flottille of the Aéronavale operates Super Etendards from the carriers *Clemenceau* and *Foch*, which carry 20 Super Etendards. Unit 11F is based at Landivisiau and the sister unit 17F at Hyères.

Another improvement to the Etendard is the Thomson-CSF head-up display (HUD) with TV or infra-red imaging. Threats received from the radar-warning receiver can be displayed on the HUD.

The Super Etendard wing uses blown flaps to allow take-offs from the short decks of the current French carriers.

The fuselage is of area-ruled design for supersonic flight.

Up to 3300 litres (500 gal.) of fuel are stored in the wing tanks. The four wing pylons can carry rocket pods, ECM pods or MATRA Magic missiles.

The cockpit has an improved HOTAS layout and VCN 65 electronic countermeasures display.

Aéronavale Etendards are now being updated with a new Anemone radar with ground mapping and search functions. The improved UAT 90 weapons computer is linked to the radar system.

One Exocet or ASMP missile can be carried with a fuel tank under the port wing, or an Exocet under each wing.

Power is provided by an ATAR turbojet, a slightly more powerful version of the original Etendard engine.

COMBAT DATA

MAXIMUM SPEED

Naval jet strike aircraft require range rather than speed. Designed to attack at sea level, high subsonic performance is more important than high speed at altitude.

SUPER ETENDARD	1380 km/h (856 m.p.h.)
A-4M	1038 km/h (644 m.p.h.)
A-7 CORSAIR	1123 km/h (696 m.p.h.)

ARMAMENT

The Super Etendard is a small aircraft, and carries a fairly light warload. For its size, the A-4M carries a hefty armament, although not usually a missile like the Exocet.

SUPER ETENDARD	2100 kg (4,620 lb.)
A-4M SKYHAWK	4153 kg (9,137 lb.)
A-7 CORSAIR	6804 kg (14,969 lb.)

COMBAT RADIUS

For such a small aircraft, the Super Etendard has impressive range, greater than the small A-4 and less than the larger A-7 with its efficient TF41 engine. Naval strike aircraft often have a short combat radius when flying at low level, which consumes more fuel than high-altitude flight.

A-4M SKYHAWK 547 km (339 mi.)

A-7 CORSAIR 1149 km (712 mi.)

SUPER ETENDARD 850 km (527 mi.)

Exocet attack

1 WEAPON LAUNCH: The ship's approximate position is confirmed by radar and passed to the missile's navigation computer.

2 SEA SKIMMER: Exocet has a radar altimeter which keeps the weapon at a set height, as little as 2 m (6 ft.). This height can be changed according to the target's height and the sea state.

3 RADAR LOCK: When only a few kilometres from the ship, Exocet's radar searches for the target, aiming for a point halfway along the hull.

4 DECOY: If a ship can launch chaff rockets in time, it can fool Exocet into aiming for the centre of the combined radar return from the ship and the chaff cloud.

DASSAULT-BREGUET
MIRAGE III/5/50

● 1960s design ● Fighter/attack/reconnaissance ● Upgrades

Between the late 1950s and 1992, Dassault and foreign licensees built more than 1,400 Mirage IIIs, 5s and 50s for 20 air forces. The same combination of performance, versatility and low cost that won the delta-winged fighter so many orders in the first place has encouraged several operators to embark on upgrade programmes. New avionics and weapons, plus airframe modifications, should keep them competitive well into the 21st century.

▲ *Although many larger operators have replaced their Mirage fleets, smaller users have seen a future in the type. Upgrading existing aircraft allows considerable cost savings.*

▼ Colombia's Mirages and Kfirs
As well as IAI Kfirs, Colombia operates Mirage 5COAs upgraded with IAI help. Canards and IFR probes are features.

▲ Chasing exports
Finishing this Mirage 50 demonstrator (a former Mirage IIIR) in desert camouflage made it clear that Dassault was seeking customers in the Middle East. However, the type has sold exclusively in South America.

▼ Venezuela
Dassault converted surviving Venezuelan Mirage IIIs and 5s to Mirage 50EV standard with Cyrano IV radar and Atar 09K-50 engines.

▲ Belgium's ill-fated Elkan Mirages
Mirage Safety Improvement Programme (MIRSIP) was the name given to an ambitious plan for the country's locally built Mirage 5s. Although post-Cold War defence cuts saw the type retired by Belgium, some Elkans were exported to Chile.

Brazil's F-103Es ▶
Mirage IIIEBRs flown by the Brazilian air force are known as F-103Es. The first were delivered in 1972. In 1989 work began on refitting these aircraft with canards and improved gun and missile armament.

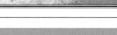

FACTS AND FIGURES

➤ Plans by Colombia to re-engine its Mirages with American J79 or F404 engines were cancelled on cost grounds.

➤ Dassault's Mirage prototype, a much smaller aircraft, flew in 1956.

➤ Mirage 5s were originally called 5Js; they were intended for Israel.

➤ With an eye to the upgrade market, Dassault built Mirage 50M, 3EX and 3NG prototypes to demonstrate new systems.

➤ The first Mirage 5 took to the air in May 1967; the Mirage 50 in April 1979.

➤ The Mirage 3NG offered fly-by-wire controls and Mirage 2000 systems, but did not sell.

PROFILE

Dassault's delta lives on

The Mirage IIIE, the main export model of the original series, remains in service with Argentina, Brazil, Pakistan and Switzerland. The latter two also fly the IIIR reconnaissance variant, along with France and South Africa. Abu Dhabi, Argentina, Chile, Colombia, Egypt, Gabon, Libya, Pakistan, Peru and Zaire still use the Mirage 5; Chile and Venezuela fly Mirage 50s.

More than half the air forces operating the various models have selected Dassault upgrades. New avionics options include head-up displays, inertial navigation systems, hands on throttle and stick (HOTAS) controls, and a multi-mode radar and/or laser rangefinder. Canard foreplanes improve take-off and manoeuvring performance.

Chile added new radars and air-to-air missiles to its Mirage 50s with the help of Israel Aircraft Industries to produce the Pantera, and bought 15 ex-Belgian Mirage 5s upgraded to Elkan standard.

IAI has helped Colombia and Argentina upgrade their Mirages, the Colombian aircraft having Kfir-style canards as well as improved avionics.

Below: Peru's Mirage 5Ps and 5P3s have been refurbished by Dassault with distinctive fixed in-flight-refuelling probes, Magic 2 air-to-air missiles and new avionics. The avonics include a new radar-warning receiver (RWR).

Above: Switzerland's Mirage IIISs are tasked with air defence. Survivors have been upgraded with canards, new avionics and other changes.

The Mirage family will survive for many years to come, thanks to upgrade packages that produce a modern warplane at a fraction of a new aircraft's price.

Mirage 50M

Type: single-seat interceptor/fighter-bomber

Powerplant: one 70.82-kN (15,930-lb.-thrust) SNECMA Atar 09K-50 afterburning turbojet

Maximum speed: 2338 km/h (1,450 m.p.h.) at 12,000 m (39,000 ft.)

Initial climb rate: 11,160 m/min (36,614 f.p.m.)

Combat radius: 1315 km (815 mi.) on a hi-hi-hi interception mission with two air-to-air missiles and three drop tanks

Service ceiling: 18,000 m (59,000 ft.)

Weights: empty equipped 7150 kg (15,730 lb.); maximum take-off 14,700 kg (32,340 lb.)

Armament: up to 4000 kg (8,800 lb.) of ordnance

Dimensions: span 8.22 m (26 ft. 11 in.)
length 15.56 m (51 ft. 1 in.)
height 4.50 m (14 ft. 9 in.)
wing area 35 m² (377 sq. ft.)

MIRAGE 50C

This aircraft was among the first Mirage 50s built, as part of an order for six 50s delivered to the Chilean air force in 1982 and 1983. All were operated by 4 Escuadron of Brigada Aérea 4 at Santiago.

Local technological expertise has been used in the Pantera, namely a Chilean-designed RWR (Caiquen III) and Eclipse chaff/flare dispensers, the former developed by ENAER (Empresa Nacional de Aeronáutica de Chile). A number of Mirage upgrade programmes have been undertaken locally to save money and take advantage of technology transfer.

Chile originally took delivery of eight ex-Armée de l'Air Mirage 5Fs, bought back by Dassault and rebuilt to 50FC standard. Six new-build Mirage 50Cs, with nose radar, followed, along with a pair of two-seat 50DCs, the latter with Atar 09C engines (as fitted to Mirage IIIs and 5s).

ENAER began a programme to upgrade the Chilean 50C fleet to Pantera (Panther) standard in the mid-1980s. With assistance from Israel Aircraft Industries (IAI), the airframe is being changed (including the addition of canard foreplanes) and new avionics are being fitted, resulting in effectively an Atar-engined Kfir. Funding problems have slowed the programme.

Canard foreplanes attached to the engine air intakes are a commonly specified addition to upgraded Mirage IIIs, 5s and 50s. On the Pantera, IAI-designed fixed canards are employed; they dramatically reduce take-off runs and improve manoeuvrability.

As built, Chile's Mirage 50s were believed to be equipped with Agave multi-mode radar. As part of the Pantera upgrade a 1-m (3-ft.) plug is inserted in the nose ahead of the cockpit to make room for avionics equipment, including a new Elbit EL/M-2001B radar.

Drop tanks of 600-litre (160-gal.) capacity are a common Mirage store. Rebuilt aircraft are often able to carry later, more capable variants of standard weapons systems, including air-to-air missiles. Agave radar-equipped machines can often carry Exocet anti-ship missiles.

Mirage 50s derive their designation from the SNECMA Atar 09K-50 engine fitted to what is otherwise a standard Mirage III/5 airframe. The afterburning 09K-50 was originally fitted to the Mirage F1 and offers more thrust.

COMBAT DATA

COMBAT RADIUS

Range has never been a strength of the Mirage family, though the 5 performs better in this respect than the Mikoyan-Gurevich MiG-27. SEPECAT's Jaguar has 50 per cent greater range.

MIRAGE 5	650 km (400 mi.)
MIG-27K 'FLOGGER-D'	540 km (335 mi.)
JAGUAR INTERNATIONAL	917 km (570 mi.)

Mirage IIIS rocket-assisted take-off

■ **FROM CONFINED SPACES:** Switzerland's air force faces unique challenges in its day-to-day operations in a small country that has limited areas of flat land on which to construct airfields. Its Mirages use thrust augmentation in order to take off from short runways.

■ **RATO BOTTLES:** Standard fit on Switzerland's Mirage IIIS/RS and BS are six rocket-assisted take-off (RATO) bottles under the wing centre-section. With the aircraft's engine producing maximum thrust, the bottles are lit and burn for a set duration.

■ **SPECTACULAR TAKE-OFF:** When used on a lightly loaded aircraft the result is spectacular. This aircraft is seen during an air show climbing almost vertically from the runway after a reduced take-off run with a minimal load.

DASSAULT

MIRAGE 2000

● Air superiority ● Low-level attack ● Agile dogfighter

I n 'clean' condition, whipping through the air without a clutter of weapons under its wings, the Dassault Mirage 2000 is one of the best-looking fighters ever built. This third-generation Mirage dates from 1978 and carries powerful radar, cannon, missiles and avionics. French pilots praise the delta-wing fighter mostly for its agility, claiming that an able pilot can fling the Mirage 2000 around as tightly as fighters like the F-16 or MiG-29.

▲ Although it is called a Mirage, the 2000 shares only a shape and a name with its older brothers. It is far more capable than any previous Dassault fighter, notably in terms of its weapons fit.

DASSAULT MIRAGE 2000

▼ Magic attack
For dogfighting, the Mirage 2000 is armed with the MATRA Magic infra-red missile, a short-range heat-seeker.

Strike role ▶
The Mirage 2000 can fire armour-piercing AS30L laser-guided missiles for pinpoint attacks on surface targets. AS30s were used with great success by the French air force during the Gulf War.

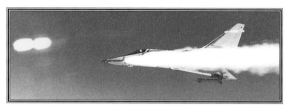

▲ Filling up
Without external tanks, the Mirage 2000 needs a fill-up from an aerial tanker to stay on combat air patrol for any length of time.

◀ Reliable turbojet
Power for the Mirage 2000 comes from a single SNECMA M53 turbojet. This relatively simple engine is reliable and performs well at most speeds.

Long-range missile ▶
The advanced MATRA Mica missile will give Mirage 2000s the ability to carry out medium- and long-range 'fire-and-forget' engagements against other aircraft.

FACTS AND FIGURES

➤ The RDF radar was test-flown in an old Mystère fighter-bomber, and the M53 engine in a Caravelle airliner testbed.

➤ The French fighter wing at Dijon began receiving its first aircraft in April 1983.

➤ The two-seat Mirage 2000B trainer made its maiden flight on 7 August 1983.

➤ India operates the Mirage 2000H fighter, armed with MATRA 530D missiles; it is known locally as the 'Thunderbolt'.

➤ Finland, Iraq, Jordan and Switzerland all considered buying the Mirage 2000.

➤ The Mirage 2000s serving with Abu Dhabi are fitted with Sidewinder missiles.

Dassault's deadliest fighter

The brilliant engineers at Avions Marcel Dassault began work on the Mirage 2000 in 1972. Three years later, France's Armée de l'Air sought a new fighter and backed development of this arrow-like craft.

Now standard equipment in the French fighter arm, the Mirage 2000 has a large wing with 'relaxed stability' and automatic flight control system, making this warplane extremely agile and giving better handling than traditional deltas. Lacking a

horizontal tail, the Mirage 2000 uses elevons at the trailing edge of its wing. The result is one of the world's most successful delta-winged fighters.

This is very much a pilot's aircraft – a 'Top Gun' in the world of modern dogfighting, especially when armed with the Magic 2 missile. The Mirage 2000 has become a popular export item, serving with Abu Dhabi, Egypt, France, Greece, India and Peru. Known for its air-to-air prowess, the Mirage 2000 also has considerable air-

The Mirage 2000 showed its mettle in the Gulf War, although it was never engaged in combat. It might have been exported more widely if it had not been so much more expensive than the F-16.

to-ground capability. A successful two-seat trainer variant has also been developed into France's Mirage 2000N nuclear strike aircraft.

Like earlier Mirages, the Mirage 2000 has large elevons for roll and pitch control. Carbon-fibre spoilers are mounted on the forward section of the wing. Trim change is made automatically by the flight-control computer.

The wing has a leading edge consisting of two large slats, which are deployed during high angle-of-attack manoeuvres.

061

Mirage 2000C

Type: single-seat fighter

Powerplant: one SNECMA M53-P2 turbofan rated at 64.33 kN (14,475 lb. thrust) dry and 95.12 kN (21,400 lb. thrust) with afterburning

Maximum speed: Mach 2.2 or 2338 km/h (1,453 m.p.h.) at 11,000 m (36,000 ft.)

Ferry range: 3335 km (2,072 mi.)

Service ceiling: 18,000 m (59,000 ft.)

Weights: empty 7500 kg (16,535 lb.); loaded 17,000 kg (37,479 lb.)

Armament: two DEFA 554 30-mm cannon with 125 rounds per gun; MATRA Magic 2 air-to-air missiles; up to 4500 kg (9,920 lb.) of bombs, rockets or ARMAT anti-radiation missiles

Dimensions:
- span 9.13 m (29 ft. 11 in.)
- length 14.36 m (47 ft. 1 in.)
- height 5.20 m (17 ft. 1 in.)
- wing area 41 m² (441 sq. ft.)

MIRAGE 2000P

The Peruvian air force was the third customer for the Mirage 2000, with 12 aircraft serving with Escuadron 412 at Base Aérea Meriano Melgar, La Joya. The unit operates in the ground-attack and air-defence roles.

The large avionics suite is carried in the fuselage spine. It includes a SAGEM ULIS 52 inertial navigation platform and the sophisticated CERVAL radar warning receiver.

The airframe is mostly of traditional alloys, but certain structural areas are made from titanium and steel, and extensive use is made of boron/epoxy and carbon-fibre panels.

The cockpit of the latest Mirage 2000 variants features four multi-function display screens, an advanced head-up display and a threat warning screen.

061

The radar is a Thomson-CSF RDM multi-mode set, with ground mapping, air-search and interception, maritime attack and terrain avoidance modes.

A fixed strake is fitted on the engine inlet fairing. This controls fuselage air vortices at high angles of attack.

A pair of DEFA 544 30-mm cannon, each with 125 rounds of ammunition, is housed in the wingroots. This gun can fire bursts at 1,800 rounds per minute for air-to-air engagements and at 1,100 rpm for air-to-ground firing.

COMBAT DATA

MAXIMUM SPEED

The Mirage 2000 is faster than its great rival, the F-16, since the American jet lacks the variable intakes which maximise supersonic performance. The MiG-29 is faster still, primarily thanks to the vastly greater power available from its twin engines.

MIRAGE 2000	2338 km/h (1,453 m.p.h.)
F-16 FIGHTING FALCON	2124 km/h (1,320 m.p.h.)
MiG-29 'FULCRUM'	2445 km/h (1,519 m.p.h.)

COMBAT RANGE

Modern fighter aircraft have considerably greater ranges than their immediate predecessors, and fighters like the Mirage 2000 can carry significant strike loads over great distances. However, the extended use of afterburning cuts their range considerably.

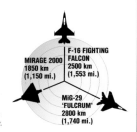

F-16 FIGHTING FALCON 2500 km (1,553 mi.)

MIRAGE 2000 1850 km (1,150 mi.)

MiG-29 'FULCRUM' 2800 km (1,740 mi.)

INITIAL CLIMB RATE

The Mirage is one of the fastest-climbing fighters in the world. It cannot match the MiG-29, again thanks to the immense power of the Russian fighter's twin jets. It can, however, climb faster than the American Fighting Falcon, although it cannot carry as heavy or as varied a weapons load.

MIRAGE 2000 17,000 m/min (55,774 f.p.m.)

MiG-29 'FULCRUM' 19,800 m/min (64,960 f.p.m.)

F-16 FIGHTING FALCON 15,250 m/min (50,033 f.p.m.)

Multi-mission Mirage

1 INTERCEPTOR: The Mirage 2000 was designed to defend France from air attack, and its first mission is to deter enemy bombers.

The Mirage has an exceptional climb rate, and can reach a height of 15,000 m (49,200 ft.) within four minutes of take-off. This means it should be able to intercept any bomber currently in service.

2 GROUND ATTACK: Modern fighters are extremely expensive, and are expected to be able to perform more than one task. The Mirage 2000 is a highly capable ground-attack aircraft, and has also been adapted to the nuclear strike role.

3 AIR SUPERIORITY: The Mirage's excellent radar and modern missiles mean that in well-trained hands it is a formidable and hard-hitting fighter.

The Mirage 2000 is highly manoeuvrable. French air force pilots claim that in a dogfight it is a match for any potential enemy, up to and including the superb MiG-29 'Fulcrum'.

DASSAULT-BREGUET

MIRAGE 4000

● Interceptor and attack prototype ● Mach 2 performance

Built as a private venture experimental prototype by Dassault-Breguet, the twin-engined Super Mirage 4000 drew on the experience gained in the development of the single-engined Mirage 2000 fighter. Capable of a speed exceeding Mach 2, it had the potential to be a worldbeater in its class. Budgetary cutbacks and the very high price tag of the new Mirage meant that it was not placed in production, despite its capability.

▲ *Powered by two SNECMA M.53 engines, as fitted to the smaller Mirage 2000, the 4000 prototype attained a speed of Mach 2.2 with ease on its sixth flight in April 1979.*

PHOTO FILE

DASSAULT-BREGUET MIRAGE 4000

▼ **Composite construction**
In order to save weight, extensive use was made of carbon fibre and boron composites in structures including the fin, rudder, elevons and foreplanes.

▲ **Mirage 2000 and 4000 prototypes**
The prototypes of the Mirage 2000 and 4000 flew within a year of each other, the former in March 1978.

▲ **Mock-up first**
Prior to assembly of the prototype, a full-scale mock-up was built. It was unveiled in December 1977.

▼ **Eight-tonne bombload**
The Mirage 4000 was able to carry over 8000 kg (17,600 lb.) of bombs, missiles and other equipment.

▲ **Delta wings**
The third-generation Mirages returned to the delta-wing design pioneered in the Mirage III/5 family of the 1960s.

FACTS AND FIGURES

➤ The Mirage 4000 design was heavily influenced by the cancelled Mirage F2 low-level attack aircraft.

➤ As many as 14 air-to-air missiles could be carried at once by the Mirage 4000.

➤ The prototype broke the speed of sound on its first flight, achieving Mach 1.2.

➤ Although a very capable aircraft, the 4000 offered little more than the smaller 2000, at considerably greater cost.

➤ Despite funding from Saudi Arabia, the type lost out to the F-15 and Tornado.

➤ Airbrakes are fitted above each wingroot leading edge.

PROFILE

Dassault's big delta prototype

Flying for the first time on 9 March 1979, the Mirage 4000 was a twin-engined interceptor and low-altitude attack prototype in the 20-tonne class. With a delta wing planform and canard foreplanes the Mirage 4000 employed fly-by-wire controls, but was a comparatively simple design with ease of maintenance on forward airfields in mind.

Its overall dimensions put it midway between the size of the F-14 Tomcat and the F/A-18 Hornet. The aircraft's twin engines provided a thrust-to-weight ratio greater than 1:1 in its original interceptor form.

The generous nose profile enabled the installation of a 80-cm (31-in.) radar dish which offered an effective range of 120 km (75 mi.).

Computer projection placed this apparently outstanding performance ahead of any other fighter in its class. Indeed, when the project was first announced in December 1975 the makers boldly assured potential export customers of the Mirage 4000's superiority over any similar aircraft in production or under development.

Although an operational version was envisaged, Dassault hoped to sell the type in export markets as well as to the Armée de l'Air as a replacement for the Mirage IV bomber, but orders did not materialise. What was destined to be the sole prototype has been used as a 'chase plane' during flight tests of the new Dassault Rafale advanced combat aircraft, the successor to the Mirage family.

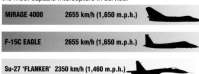

Above: At an early stage of development the Mirage 4000 was known as the Super Mirage Delta.

Above: The prototype featured desert camouflage while flying in the Middle East. Despite the success of earlier Mirages in that region, the price tag of the 4000 deterred buyers.

Mirage 4000

Type: single-seat multi-role combat aircraft

Powerplant: two 95.13-kN (21,400-lb. thrust) SNECMA M.53 afterburning turbofans

Maximum speed: 2655 km/h (1,650 m.p.h.)

Initial climb rate: 18,300 m/min (60,039 f.p.m.)

Combat radius: 1850 km (1,150 mi.)

Service ceiling: 20,000 m (65,600 ft.)

Weights: combat 16,100 kg (35,494 lb.)

Armament: over 8000 kg (17,630 lb.) of external stores including bombs, rockets, air-to-air and air-to-surface missiles and cluster munitions

Dimensions:
span 12.00 m (39 ft. 4 in.)
length 18.70 m (61 ft. 4 in.)
wing area 73 m² (786 sq. ft.)

MIRAGE 4000

The prototype Mirage 4000 took to the air for the first time in early 1979. Despite an aggressive sales campaign by the makers, the prototype remains the sole example.

The powerful 80-cm RDM multi-mode radar is the same as that fitted to the Mirage 2000C interceptor.

A two-seat version of the Mirage 4000 was under study by Dassault-Breguet, but was not built.

Dassault-Breguet hoped for sales of the 4000 in the Middle East. For sales tours in the region it therefore carried a 'desert' camouflage.

To provide extra fuel capacity, the tailfin of the 4000 contains a fuel tank; other tanks are found in the wings and fuselage. External tanks can also be carried.

The Mirage 4000's flight-control system has been used as a technology demonstrator for the Rafale combat aircraft.

Provision was made for two DEFA 30-mm cannon and up to 11 pylons for external stores, including weapons and fuel tanks.

MATRA Magic missiles were among the variety of air-to-air weapons which the 4000 could carry for self-defence.

Power was provided by two SNECMA M.53 turbofan engines, which gave the 4000 a thrust-to-weight ratio in the same class as that of the F-15 or Sukhoi Su-27.

The Dassault Mirage family

■ **MIRAGE III/5:** This Mach 2 delta-wing fighter and fighter-bomber provided the core of the French air forces in the 1960s and 1970s and won large foreign orders.

■ **MIRAGE IV:** This was a scaled-up, twin-engined bomber version of the Mirage delta, designed with a nuclear capability. The prototype first flew in 1959.

■ **MIRAGE F1:** The second-generation Mirage multi-role aircraft intended to replace the Mirage III and 5, the F1 discarded the delta wing for a more conventional layout.

■ **MIRAGE 2000:** Fly-by-wire controls solved the handling problems found in delta-winged aircraft. The prototype flew in 1978, and fighter, attack and reconnaissance versions followed.

COMBAT DATA

MAXIMUM SPEED

A top speed of over Mach 2 is a necessity for a modern, long-range, high-altitude interceptor designed to defeat waves of bombers or cruise missiles. The F-15 and Su-27 represent the most capable interceptors in service.

MIRAGE 4000	2655 km/h (1,650 m.p.h.)
F-15C EAGLE	2655 km/h (1,650 m.p.h.)
Su-27 'FLANKER'	2350 km/h (1,460 m.p.h.)

RANGE

The range of the Sukhoi Su-27 reflects the size and fuel-carrying capacity of an aircraft designed to defend the vast area of the Soviet Union. The first export customer for the Su-27, China, has similarly large areas to patrol. The F-15 and Mirage 4000 carry the same fuel load, with tanks, as an Su-27 carries internally.

F-15C EAGLE 1967 km (1,222 mi.)

MIRAGE 4000 3700 km (2,299 mi.)

Su-27 'FLANKER' 3000 km (1,864 mi.)

CLIMB RATE

Interceptors need to be able to climb quickly to the altitude of attacking aircraft. A power-to-weight ratio better than 1:1 allows excellent rates of climb. All three types have twin engines which give the aircraft exceptional power.

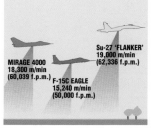

MIRAGE 4000 18,300 m/min (60,039 f.p.m.)

Su-27 'FLANKER' 19,000 m/min (62,336 f.p.m.)

F-15C EAGLE 15,240 m/min (50,000 f.p.m.)

DASSAULT

RAFALE

● Lightweight fighter ● Multi-role ● High-technology construction

▲ With pilots such as Guy
Mitaux-Maurouard at the controls, Rafale has
thrilled crowds at major air shows with its
exceptional agility. The first flight of the
technology demonstrator was in 1986.

Dassault's Rafale is a proud symbol of
France's independent spirit. Refusing
to rely upon other nations, the
French are staking their military readiness
on this superb machine, one of the best-
performing combat aircraft in the sky today.
Because nothing was spared in putting
21st-century technology into this futuristic
fighting jet, the Rafale can outclimb,
outmanoeuvre and outfight just about any
warplane now in service.

DASSAULT RAFALE

▲ Carrier fighter
France's navy was desperate to
replace its ageing F-8 Crusaders
with the Rafale M.

▲ 'Discreet' warplane
Air force operational
versions of the aircraft are
known as the Rafale D,
the 'D' standing for
'Discret'. This word is
meant to emphasise the
stealthiness of the
fighter.

▼ Engine testbed
The Rafale A testbed
aircraft at one point
featured two different
engines: a French-
built M88 in the left-
hand side of the
fuselage, and a US-
built F404 to the right.

▲ The Rafale family
The three operational
variants will be the two-
seat Rafale B (leading)
and single-seat Rafale C
(foreground) for the air
force, and the Rafale M
(background) for the
navy.

◀ Agility unlimited
Rafale's power and fly-by-wire
electronics make it
outstandingly agile, able to
defeat any current service
fighter in a low-speed dogfight.

FACTS AND FIGURES

➤ Composites and new materials make up
50 per cent of Rafale's weight.

➤ The twin-engine Rafale has 16 times as
much power as the Mistral, an early
French jet fighter.

➤ To decrease combat workload, most Air
Force Rafales will have a crew of two.

➤ Rafale was the result of France dropping
out of the European Fighter Aircraft
project in August 1985.

➤ The prototype Rafale A made 865 test
flights before being retired with honours.

➤ Naval Rafales will serve aboard the
nuclear carrier *Charles de Gaulle*.

Multi-mission workhorse

The Dassault Rafale is the air combatant of tomorrow, created by today's top scientists. Very soon, one- and two-seat Rafales will rise to take command of the sky, as France's navy and air force press these dart-shaped jets into action from carrier decks and airfields. Thanks to its advanced propulsion and flight controls, the Rafale can switch paths abruptly in mid-air. The pilot can steer in one direction and point his nose to shoot in another, making it look as if the

Rafale is flying sideways. Or it can snap into a 180° turn in less space than any other fighter. With this super agility, a Rafale pilot can rapidly get the aim on his opponent. The pilot's head need never leave his quarry as he manipulates his aircraft into firing position using his head-up display and voice-activated controls. Then he can launch several missiles or close in for the kill with his rapid-fire 30-mm cannon. The duel is likely to be over in seconds, with the Rafale the easy victor.

The French air force is getting a mix of one- and two-seat Rafales. The two-seaters will be used for both training and for difficult strike missions where the extra crew member is vital.

Fitted just forward by the main delta wing are the all-moving swept foreplanes. Constructed mainly of carbon-fibre, they give added manoeuvrability.

Rafale will be equipped with SPECTRA – Système pour la Protection Electronique Contra Tous les Rayonnements Adversés – a highly automated electronic protection system which includes radar warning and infra-red warning sensors, as well as radar jammers and chaff and flare dispensers.

RAFALE M

Designed to replace the ancient Vought F-8 Crusader aboard French carriers, the Rafale M will also be used as an anti-shipping strike and reconnaissance fighter, eventually also replacing the Super Etendard.

Rafale's futuristic cockpit will eventually be modified to allow the pilot to activate some controls by voice alone.

Rafale is powered by a pair of SNECMA M88-3 lightweight turbofans, each delivering around 86.99 kN (19, 570 lb.) of thrust with afterburning.

All Rafale variants will be equipped with an electronically-scanned multi-function radar with full air-to-air and air-to-ground capability.

The naval version of Rafale has a unique nose gear. Compressed before launch, it extends explosively, kicking the fighter's nose into the air as it leaves the deck.

In the air-to-air role, the Rafale can be armed with up to eight MATRA MICA advanced air-to-air missiles, or with six MICAs and two short-range Magic 2 dogfight missiles on wingtip launch rails.

Rafale D

Type: single-seat air combat fighter

Powerplant: two 86.99-kN (19,570-lb. thrust) SNECMA M88-3 turbofans with afterburning

Maximum speed: 2125 km/h (1,320 m.p.h.) at 11,000 m (36,000 ft.)

Combat radius: 1100 km (684 mi.) with typical weapons load; 1500 km (932 mi.) air-to-air

Service ceiling: 15,200 m (49,870 ft.)

Weights: empty about 9100 kg (20,060 lb.); maximum loaded 21,500 kg (47,399 lb.)

Armament: one 30-mm GIAT-built DEFA M791B cannon; up to 6000 kg (13,230 lb.) of air-to-air and air-to-ground ordnance

Dimensions: span 19.90 m (65 ft. 3 in.)
length 15.30 m (50 ft. 2 in.)
height 6.91 m (22 ft. 8 in.)
wing area 46 m² (495 sq. ft.)

COMBAT DATA

MAXIMUM SPEED
The current generation of fighters are not as fast as their immediate predecessors, but thanks to advances in engine efficiency they can maintain high speed for much longer periods, restricting the need for fuel-guzzling afterburners.

RAFALE 2125 km/h (1,320 m.p.h.)
EF 2000 2125 km/h (1,320 m.p.h.)
F-22 RAPTOR 2000 km/h (1,243 m.p.h.)

INTERCEPT RANGE
The Rafale and its contemporaries will be expected to fly many differing missions. In the intercept or long-range air-superiority role, they will be able to fly very long distances to reach their targets.

RAFALE 1500 km (932 mi.)
F-22 RAPTOR 2200 km (1367 mi.)
EF 2000 1100 km (684 mi.)

STEALTH
Stealth technology has revolutionised air warfare for those who can afford it, and all new fighters incorporate the expensive new features. Operational Rafales will be very stealthy, if not as elusive as the costly American F-22.

F-22 RAPTOR
RAFALE
EF 2000

Rafale M – jumping from the carrier

RUN-UP: With the nosewheel strut compressed to its minimum extent, the Rafale runs up its engines to full power and then is hurled down the deck by a powerful steam catapult.

SKI-JUMP: The carrier *Charles de Gaulle* will be equipped with a small ski-jump at the end of the catapult, which pushes the Rafale into the air. The ramp will retract to allow other types to be launched.

JUMP STRUT: As the aircraft hits the ramp, the compressed nose gear springs out to its maximum extent, literally jumping the fighter into the air at its most efficient low-speed angle of attack.

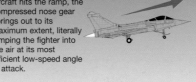

DASSAULT

ATLANTIQUE 2

● Maritime patrol ● Anti-submarine ● Shipping strike

Developed on a multinational basis for NATO, the Atlantic was created to shadow and, if necessary, attack the Soviet Union's imposing naval fleet. The Dassault Atlantic (Atlantique) has evolved into two generations of highly capable maritime patrol aircraft. Today's second-generation Atlantique 2 makes use of advanced technology to cope with undersea and surface warfare threats of many kinds, threats which persist even after the end of the Cold War.

▲ Always a force to be reckoned with at sea, the multinational Atlantique 2 has matured into a sophisticated sub-killer with a highly secret sideline in intelligence-gathering.

DASSAULT ATLANTIQUE 2

◄ 'Nouvelle Génération'
The latest version of this long-serving warplane is one of the world's most sophisticated maritime aircraft. Designed to hunt submarines, it can also carry a wide variety of high-performance anti-ship and anti-radar missiles.

European defender ▶
Designed originally by Breguet, the Atlantic was built by and is in service with four European nations. Only France operates the new Atlantique 2.

Heavy load ▶
This Aéronavale Atlantic displays the aircraft's capacious weapons bay which typically holds air-launched torpedoes and depth charges. The smaller doors aft of the bay are used to launch flares and sonobuoys.

▲ Computer cockpit
Every part of the Atlantique 2's avionics has been upgraded along with pilot-friendly screen displays replacing the plethora of dials and switches found on the original Atlantic.

◄ Flexibility
A typical mission load comprises torpedoes, air-to-surface missiles and more than 100 sonobuoys.

FACTS AND FIGURES

➤ The Breguet Br.1150, which became the Atlantic, entered service with the French and German navies in December 1965.

➤ Originally the ANG (Atlantic Nouvelle Génération), the Atlantique 2 entered service in 1989.

➤ French Navy Atlantique 2s will serve well into the 21st century.

➤ The Atlantique 2 can detect and attack ships or submarines with missiles, depth charges, bombs or torpedoes.

➤ The Atlantique 2 has a chin-mounted infra-red turret and revised wing and fin-tip antennas.

➤ Other proposed variants include the Atlantic 3 with upgraded engines.

NATO's multinational sub-hunter

The Dassault Atlantic was the result of thinking which dates back to the 1950s, when it was felt that long-range overwater patrol might best be carried out by a standard aircraft shared among the Western European Allies.

The Atlantic 1 first flew on 21 October 1961, and while it was not accepted by all Allied countries it became the backbone of maritime operations in France, Germany and Italy, and has also been adopted by Pakistan.

With its very thin wing and enormous fuselage, the Atlantic has the staying power for anti-submarine and other patrol missions of up to 18 hours. The pilots have great power and flexibility at their disposal, and crew members have ample space for work and occasional respite. The Atlantique 2, used only by France, has new avionics, sensors and equipment giving an old design 21st century capabilities.

One of the more important additions is the infra-red sensor

in a chin-mounted turret. Further changes are contemplated for Atlantic 3 and Europatrol versions, which may be built for service in the coming decades.

Above: The Atlantique Nouvelle Génération, or Atlantique 2, is identifiable by its chin turret and the antennas at the tip of the revised vertical tail.

Left: Although slower than its main contemporaries the Atlantique 2 combines impressive endurance with a modern and highly capable weapons lift.

Atlantique 2

Type: 12-seat long-range maritime patrol aircraft

Powerplant: two 4226-kW (5,670 hp.) thrust Rolls-Royce/ SNECMA Type 21 turboprops for take-off and emergency

Maximum speed: 648 km/h (402 m.p.h.)

Ferry range: 9000 km (5,580 mi.)

Service ceiling: 9150 m (30,000 ft.)

Weights: empty 25,700 kg (56,540 lb.); loaded 46,200 kg (101,640 lb.)

Armament: 2500 kg (5,500 lb.) of bombs, mines, depth charges or torpedoes internally and 3500 kg (7,700 lb.) externally; four AM39 Exocets may be carried on underwing pylons

Dimensions:
span	37.30 m	(122 ft. 4 in.)
length	33.63 m	(110 ft. 4 in.)
height	10.89 m	(35 ft. 9 in.)
wing area	120.34 m²	(1,295 sq. ft.)

ATLANTIQUE 2

Long after production of the original Atlantic had ceased, the French navy commissioned the improved Atlantique 2. It is similar in appearance to the original, but has improved sensors and avionics.

The small fin on the back of the Atlantique is a direction-finding aerial. On the original Atlantic, this stretched right back and blended into the tailfin.

The small radome at the tip of the Atlantique 2's tail houses an ECM antenna, designed to detect and identify enemy radar transmissions.

The Atlantique has a conventional flight deck with pilot, co-pilot and flight engineer. An observer can be carried in the glazed nose.

The tactical compartment in the fuselage houses the tactical co-ordinator, radio navigator, radar operator and two acoustic sensor operators.

Two visual observers can be carried in a rear compartment, looking through port and starboard bubble windows.

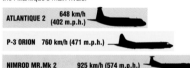

For anti-ship missions, the Atlantique is armed with up to four AM39 Exocet missiles.

The Atlantique can carry most NATO ASW weaponry internally. A typical load comprises eight air-launched torpedoes and four depth charges.

A smaller bay behind the main weapons bay houses sonobuoys and smoke markers. The Atlantique normally carries 100 buoys and 160 markers and flares.

The long tailboom houses a magnetic anomaly detector (MAD) sensor, which tracks down submarines by the effect they have on the local magnetic field.

COMBAT DATA

MAXIMUM SPEED

An anti-submarine mission might take place hundreds of miles out to sea, so the ability to transit fast and in comfort is essential. The Atlantique's two Rolls-Royce-designed turboprops are efficient, but cannot match the more powerful propulsion units of the Atlantique's main rivals.

ATLANTIQUE 2	648 km/h (402 m.p.h.)
P-3 ORION	760 km/h (471 m.p.h.)
NIMROD MR.Mk 2	925 km/h (574 m.p.h.)

FERRY RANGE

From the start the original Atlantic was designed with a very efficient wing for maximum economy when cruising over long distances. This gives the aircraft a very long range, enabling it to mount patrols up to two hours long at ranges of 3300 km from its base.

ATLANTIQUE 2	9000 km (5,580 mi.)
P-3 ORION	8900 km (5,520 mi.)
NIMROD MR.Mk 2	9250 km (5,735 mi.)

ENDURANCE

The key to successful anti-submarine warfare is endurance. Smaller than the Nimrod or the Orion, the Atlantique 2 uses less fuel. It can remain in the air for 18 hours, although crew fatigue usually limits mission length to between 10 and 12 hours.

ATLANTIQUE 2	**P-3 ORION**	**NIMROD MR.Mk 2**
18 hours	17 hours	15 hours

Submarine attack

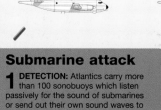

2 FIXING THE TARGET: Once a submarine has been detected, several more buoys are dropped. Triangulation of their signals pins down the exact position of the target.

3 ATTACK RUN: With the target position fixed, the Atlantic can attack. Weapon of choice will be a lightweight homing torpedo, but depth charges can also be used.

1 DETECTION: Atlantics carry more than 100 sonobuoys which listen passively for the sound of submarines or send out their own sound waves to locate the target by its echoes.

DASSAULT/DORNIER

ALPHAJET

● Advanced weapon trainer ● Light strike ● 'Hind' hunter

▲ The AlphaJet has been one of the most successful trainers, giving fierce competition to the BAe Hawk. Now in Luftwaffe service only in limited numbers, it is still an effective light strike aircraft.

The AlphaJet is an advanced trainer providing 'lead-in' instruction to pilots who will fly high-performance fighters. It is better known to the public for aerobatic displays with several nations, including single-ship performances in Belgium and formation exhibits by France's Patrouille de France. But the AlphaJet should not be dismissed as a 'feel good' aircraft: it is also a potent combat weapon.

DASSAULT/DORNIER ALPHAJET

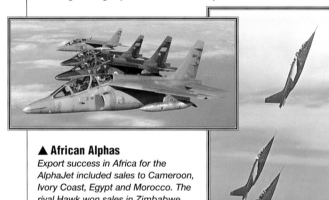

▲ **Patrouille de France**
The national aerobatic team of France flies the AlphaJet, which replaced the Fouga Magister as the team's aircraft. The crisp handling and high speed endear it to the pilots.

▲ **Tactical fighter**
French AlphaJets are advanced trainers, but armed with SNEB rockets and cluster bombs they have light-attack capability.

▲ **African Alphas**
Export success in Africa for the AlphaJet included sales to Cameroon, Ivory Coast, Egypt and Morocco. The rival Hawk won sales in Zimbabwe.

'**Hind' killer** ▶
The Luftwaffe used 175 AlphaJets in the light-attack role. Armed with a 27-mm Mauser cannon, they were seen as an answer to the threat from Soviet Mi-24 'Hind' helicopter gunships.

▲ **Twin-engine trainer** ▼
Over 500 AlphaJets have been sold. Part of the attraction of the AlphaJet over rival trainers is the safety of its twin-engine design.

FACTS AND FIGURES

➤ French AlphaJet trainers have rounded noses for good spin performance, while German attack craft have pointed noses.

➤ The first AlphaJet flew at Istres, France, on 26 October 1973.

➤ All but one of Belgium's 33 AlphaJets were assembled by SABCA at Gosselies.

➤ A German attack version with a supercritical wing flew for the first time on 15 November 1980.

➤ Egypt assembled 26 AlphaJet trainers at Helwan from September 1982 onwards.

➤ The first close support AlphaJet made its initial flight on 12 April 1978.

PROFILE

Strike trainer with the killer touch

A beautiful aircraft with both peaceful and warlike purposes, the Dassault/Dornier AlphaJet is the result of Franco-German efforts in the 1960s to develop an advanced jet trainer for the air forces of both countries.

The original purpose was sidetracked when Germany chose to continue training pilots in the US and decided to use the AlphaJet as a light-attack craft. Other nations, especially those with tight budgets in the military field, also sought the AlphaJet as a warplane or, in some instances, in both roles. Eleven countries now fly the aircraft. Several versions emerged from Dassault-Breguet and Dornier, including a pure trainer for French use, a close-support variant, the dual-role AlphaJet 2, and the proposed Lancier with advanced instruments.

Several nations emulate Qatar, which trains pilots in the AlphaJet but would form an attack unit, crewed by

Like the rival Hawk, the AlphaJet can be a dangerous threat when fully armed. It can even carry the potent AS.30 laser-guided air-to-ground missile.

instructors, in time of war. The versatility and performance of the AlphaJet has won it high praise from pilots and maintainers alike.

The rear seat is raised well above the front seat, giving the instructor an excellent view of the student's cockpit.

The proposed Lancier advanced trainer would have used twin multi-function cockpit displays, and advanced infra-red detection and radar systems.

Extra fuel can be carried in two 310- or 450-litre (82- or 120-gal.) underwing tanks.

AlphaJet E

Type: two-seat trainer and light-attack aircraft

Powerplant: two SNECMA/Turbomeca Larzac 04-C6 each rated at 13.24 kN (2,976 lb. thrust)

Maximum speed: 1000 km/h (621 m.p.h.) at 10,000 m (33,000 ft.)

Combat radius: 670 km (415 mi.)

Service ceiling: 14,630 m (48,000 ft.)

Weights: empty 3345 kg (7,359 lb.); loaded 8000 kg (17,600 lb.)

Armament: up to 2500 kg (5,500 lb.) of bombs, rockets or drop-tanks; one belly-mounted 27-mm Mauser MK 27 cannon pod (Germany); one 30-mm DEFA 553 cannon pod (France)

Dimensions:
span	9.11 m (30 ft.)
length	11.75 m (38 ft.)
height	4.19 m (14 ft.)
wing area	17.50 m² (188 sq. ft.)

ALPHAJET E

The Force Aerienne Belge uses AlphaJets in the advanced trainer role, serving with Nos 7, 9, 11 and 33 squadrons based at Brustem. No. 9 squadron is responsible for specialised instructor training.

German AlphaJets are fitted with American-made Stencel ejection seats, but French aircraft use Martin-Baker seats.

The wing has single-slotted Fowler flaps and outer-wing leading-edge extensions, allowing approach speeds of just 200 km/h (125 m.p.h.).

Despite wearing a tactical camouflage colour scheme, Belgian AlphaJets operate only as unarmed trainers.

Luftwaffe AlphaJets have advanced avionics, including a Lear-Siegler twin-gyro navigation system, Litton Doppler radar and a Kaiser head-up display.

The undercarriage is fitted with low-pressure tyres, allowing the AlphaJet to operate from rough 'tactical' sites near the front, just like its predecessor, the Fiat G91.

Many AlphaJets employ a podded DEFA 30-mm cannon with 150 rounds of ammunition for weapons training.

Although the AlphaJet has two engines, each has enough power to enable the aircraft to climb on one alone. This is a very useful asset in an aircraft flown at low level by junior pilots.

COMBAT DATA

MAXIMUM SPEED

Although a little slower than the lighter British Aerospace Hawk, the AlphaJet is capable of a useful turn of speed, its best performance being achieved at sea level. Both the AlphaJet and its great rival are swept-wing aircraft, and are faster than the straight-winged Italian Aermacchi M.B.339.

ALPHAJET E	1000 km/h (620 m.p.h.)
HAWK	1038 km/h (643 m.p.h.)
M.B.339C	900 km/h (558 m.p.h.)

CLIMB RATE

The AlphaJet's twin-jet power gives it a slight advantage over the single-engined Hawk, which is most clearly demonstrated in its improved climb performance. The M.B.339 has less available power than the other two jets, and cannot get aloft as quickly.

HAWK 2850 m/min 9,350 f.p.m.

ALPHAJET E 3660 m/min (12,005 f.p.m.)

M.B.339C 2225 m/min (7,300 f.p.m.)

COMBAT RADIUS

Trainers spend much of their time flying at low level, and on weapons training or light-attack flights will rarely climb very high. The AlphaJet has a reasonable strike radius, but the Hawk can carry a heavier load over greater distances and at faster speeds than either of the Franco/German and Italian jets.

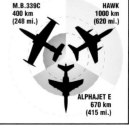

M.B.339C 400 km (248 mi.)

HAWK 1000 km (620 mi.)

ALPHAJET E 670 km (415 mi.)

Advanced flight and weapons trainers

■ **BRITISH AEROSPACE HAWK:** Britain's Hawk is slightly more capable than the AlphaJet, but both are among the best of their kind. The two jets have competed fiercely on the export market, where both have gained considerable sales success.

■ **NORTHROP T-38 TALON:** In service with the USAF, the T-38 was the first aircraft designed as a supersonic trainer. Exported to only two countries, the T-38 is expensive to operate but provides a unique training environment.

■ **AERMACCHI M.B.339:** Less complex and a little less capable than the AlphaJet, Italy's M.B.339 is cheaper than its advanced rivals, and has been sold to a number of countries. It was built in both basic and combat-capable versions.

EMBRAER

EMB-312 TUCANO

● Two-seat turboprop trainer ● Brazilian origin ● Fourteen operators

▲ One reason for the
Tucano's success is that its cockpit layout and
controls were designed from the outset to offer
'jet-like' training experience at speeds only
marginally slower than those of a jet.

Initially developed to meet a Brazilian air
force requirement and flown for the first
time in August 1980, the Tucano has
proved extremely successful. It sold well in its
original form, powered by a 559-kW (750-hp.)
PT6 engine, and has also been developed to
use much more powerful engines. It has
been built in two other countries. The latest
development is a single-seat light attack and
two-seat trainer version, again produced for
the Brazilian air force and known as the ALX.

EMBRAER EMB-312 TUCANO

▼ **Amazon warrior**
A one-tonne warload gives the
Tucano a useful weapons training
and secondary attack capability.

▲ **Prestigious British order**
The RAF operates extensively modified Tucanos
which are built under licence by Short.

▲ **British Tucanos**
Short-built Tucanos have considerably better
performance than their Brazilian counterparts.
They have been sold to Kenya and Kuwait.

▲ **South American exports**
The Tucano has been
especially successful in South
America. Among the operators
are Colombia and Paraguay.

Drug hunter ▶
Brazilian Tucanos are primarily
used as trainers, but some are
armed and used in the covert
fight against drug smuggling.

FACTS AND FIGURES

➤ Development of the Tucano began in
1978 in response to a Brazilian air force
requirement for a T-37 replacement.

➤ Brazil's Air Force Academy received its
first T-27 Tucano in September 1983.

➤ Egypt supplied 80 of its licence-built
Tucanos to Iraq.

➤ 'Escuadron de Fumaca', the Brazilian
national aerobatic team, replaced its
Harvards with the Tucano.

➤ Firm orders for 623 aircraft, excluding
demonstrators, have been received.

➤ The Super Tucano is 1.37 m (4 ft. 6 in.)
longer than the standard machine.

PROFILE

South American trainer design

As the Tucano entered Brazilian air force service during September 1983, EMBRAER was already receiving its first export order, from Egypt for 134 aircraft. Most were built in Egypt, and the majority were supplied to Iraq.

This was just the first of a flood of orders. Argentina, Colombia, Honduras, Paraguay, Peru and Venezuela all operate the type in South America and Iran in Asia. Many more machines were acquired by two European air forces, Britain and France, bringing the number of operators to more than a dozen.

The RAF bought 130 Tucano T.Mk 1s produced under licence by Short. These aircraft were strengthened and re-engined with an 820-kW (1,100-hp.) Garrett TPE331. Short also built armed versions for Kenya (T.Mk 51) and Kuwait (T.Mk 52). France bought 80 copies of the Brazilian Tucano fitted with a ventral airbrake, increased airframe life and French-manufactured avionics.

More recently, the Super Tucano, with a 1190-kW (1,595-hp.) PT6A-68 engine, was one of the unsuccessful finalists in the US competition to find a new trainer for the USAF and Navy. Using this new engine, the ALX light attack aircraft, with a head-up display, enhanced navigation systems and five hardpoints for weapons is being developed.

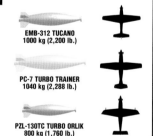

With its four wing hardpoints, the Tucano is able to carry a variety of weapons. Both single- and two-seat dedicated attack variants are planned, based on the uprated Super Tucano.

EMB-312 Tucano

Type: two-seat turboprop trainer

Powerplant: one 559-kW (750-hp.) Pratt & Whitney PT6A-25C turboprop

Maximum speed: 448 km/h (273 m.p.h.)

Endurance: 5 hours with internal fuel

Initial climb rate: 680 m/min (2,230 f.p.m.)

Range: 1844 km (1,143 mi.) with internal fuel

Service ceiling: 9145 m (30,000 ft.)

Weights: basic empty 1810 kg (3,982 lb.); normal take-off 2550 kg (5,610 lb.); maximum take-off 3175 kg (6,985 lb.)

Weapons load: 1000 kg (2,200 lb.) of light bombs, gun and rocket pods

Dimensions: wing span 11.14 m (36 ft. 6 in.)
length 9.86 m (32 ft. 4 in.)
height 3.40 m (43 ft. 6 in.)
wing area 19.40 m² (209 sq. ft.)

TUCANO T.MK 1

Two RAF Flying Training Schools (FTS) have been disbanded since the Tucano entered service. Only No. 1 FTS remains and ZF203 is currently on strength with the unit at Linton-on-Ouse, North Yorkshire.

A four-bladed Hartzell propeller drives the Tucano. It is fully feathering and offers reverse pitch to shorten the landing roll and for improved ground manoeuvrability.

A stronger canopy was required for RAF service to withstand birdstrikes when flown at low level. The two-piece Lucas canopy is able to withstand a 1-kg (2-lb.) strike at 444 km/h (275 m.p.h.).

The lightweight Martin-Baker 8LC Mk 1 ejection seats are suitable for ejection at zero altitude and speeds down to 130 km/h (80 m.p.h.). The seats may be fired through the canopy.

Dunlop produces the brakes, tyres and wheels of the Short aircraft. The nose undercarriage retracts backwards and the main units inwards.

Although it looks very similar to the EMB-312, the Short-built S312 has only 20 per cent commonality with the Brazilian aircraft. One significant recognition feature is the pair of large exhausts for the TPE331-12B engine.

A great deal of work was required to modify the cockpit to British standard. In its final form it is very similar to the RAF's Hawk advanced trainers.

Like the Brazilian aircraft, the T.Mk 1 is largely made of aluminium. The Short machine is strengthened to give an increased airframe life of 12,000 hours with increased manoeuvre loads. The wing leading edges are strengthened for improved birdstrike resistance.

COMBAT DATA

POWER

With its higher power the Turbo Orlik should be the more versatile aircraft, but engine problems have caused protracted development. The Tucano offers jet-like performance at a fraction of the cost of a jet-powered aircraft.

| EMB-312 TUCANO 559 kW (750 hp.) | PC-7 TURBO TRAINER 485 kW (650 hp.) | PZL-130TC TURBO ORLIK 798 kW (1,070 hp.) |

WEAPON LOAD

Many primary trainers have a secondary light attack role. Turboprop machines are especially useful for counter-insurgency and border patrol missions, where their ability to loiter for long periods and their relatively low noise level are an advantage.

EMB-312 TUCANO 1000 kg (2,200 lb.)

PC-7 TURBO TRAINER 1040 kg (2,288 lb.)

PZL-130TC TURBO ORLIK 800 kg (1,760 lb.)

CLIMB RATE

With its higher power output, the PZL-130TC offers the greatest climb performance. The Tucano and PC-7 are evenly matched and fierce competitors in the international trainer market. The RAF's uprated Tucano has an even better climb rate.

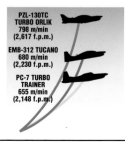

PZL-130TC TURBO ORLIK 798 m/min (2,617 f.p.m.)

EMB-312 TUCANO 680 m/min (2,230 f.p.m.)

PC-7 TURBO TRAINER 655 m/min (2,148 f.p.m.)

South American military trainers

 ■ **NEIVA T-25 UNIVERSAL:** After its first flight in 1966, the Brazilian air force ordered 150 T-25s to replace the North American Harvard.

 ■ **ENAER T-35 PILLÁN:** Piper developed the PA-28R-300 from the Saratoga as a primary trainer for licence production in Chile.

 ■ **ENAER T-35DT TURBO PILLAN:** This Allison turboprop-engined T-35, which first flew in 1986, has not found any customers.

 ■ **FAMA/FMA IA 63 PAMPA:** Now in service with the Argentine air force, the Pampa serves as a weapons trainer.

EUROFIGHTER

EF 2000

● Agile fighter ● Ground attacker ● Multinational

Embodying everything that aeronautical science has learned in the 20th century, the EF 2000 is destined to be the Top Gun of the 21st century. Developed by four nations, it will be one of the cornerstones of European air defence over the next 25 years. This is the fighter of tomorrow, bristling with the products of advanced science, relying on new technology for hi-tech victory in aerial combat.

▲ *Fast, agile and highly potent, the Eurofighter EF 2000 uses extremely advanced technology to provide Europe with one of the most flexible of the latest generation of superfighters.*

EUROFIGHTER **EF 2000**

▲ Euro-power
EFA's EJ200 engines are produced by a highly experienced consortium led by Rolls-Royce and MTU.

▼ Forward control
The rear-mounted delta wing and 'canard' foreplanes give the EFA incredible manoeuvrability at low and high speeds and altitudes.

▲ Europe's defender
Launched in a media spectacular, the EFA will provide the backbone of European air defence as well as deadly-accurate strike capability for the next 30 years.

▲ High-tech warrior
It doesn't look exotic, but the EFA incorporates the latest advances in airframe and engine design with new avionics, stealth and weapons technology.

◄ Multi-role, multinational fighter
Designed to meet exacting British, German, Italian and Spanish air force requirements, the EF 2000 will be a true multi-purpose fighter.

FACTS AND FIGURES

➤ The Eurofighter flies twice as fast as a 9-mm pistol bullet.

➤ Not only fast and high-flying, the futuristic EFA performs high-angle manoeuvres for victory in a close-up dogfight.

➤ Eurofighter simultaneously tracks a dozen targets, and engages six at once.

➤ Eurofighter design features were tested on British Aerospace's Experimental Aircraft Programme (EAP) demonstrator in the late 1980s.

➤ In common with most new-generation fighters, EF 2000 uses canards – small wings near the nose – to improve performance.

PROFILE

Defender of Europe's skies

Hard proof that Europe has a vision and that its nations can co-operate to produce the ultimate fighter for common defence, this purposeful, high-performance delta-winged jet offers significant advances in engines, radar, combat systems and weaponry. From nose to tail, the Eurofighter is one of the most advanced fighters in the skies today, equally at home as a highly agile interceptor and as a precision ground attacker.

It has not been easy for experts in Britain, Germany,

Italy and Spain to develop their new warplane. The original Eurofighter was even more capable than that now being built, but following considerable German opposition to the original price tag the consortium agreed to build a much less costly design now known as the EF 2000.

Even so, the EF 2000's advanced new radar, infra-red sensors and avionics mean that it is the best multi-role fighter flying today, which will form the backbone of Europe's fighter resources for many years.

The EAP trials confirmed that the canard layout and fly-by-wire controls would produce a superb fighter.

'Canard' foreplanes are primarily used to provide increased lift on take-off and at low speeds. This translates into greatly increased agility in dogfights.

Fuel-efficient EJ200 turbofan engines will allow the Eurofighter to cruise supersonically without the need for afterburning, greatly enhancing the fighter's range at high speed.

EF 2000's delta wing is very effective at high speeds and high altitudes, but slow-speed performance is equally good, thanks to computer-controlled fly-by-wire technology.

EF 2000

No single aircraft can perform every military role, but the EF 2000 will come closer than most. Agile, with good radar and a heavy weapons load, it will be called on to fight enemies both in the air and on the ground.

The advanced cockpit has been designed to reduce pilot workload. High-technology features include multi-function video displays, and some non-essential functions will be voice-activated.

The Eurofighter has no conventional tailplanes, climbing and diving being controlled by a combination of the aircraft's foreplanes and the control surfaces at the wing trailing edge.

ZH588

Eurofighter will enter service with the Marconi-developed ECR-90 radar. This will have lookup/lookdown air-to-air capability, and will be able to search for, track and engage multiple targets.

A passive infra-red search-and-track sensor mounted just to the left of the cockpit can detect and track multiple targets without any give-away radar signals.

Although weighing less than 10 tons, the EFA can carry more than six tons of weapons or fuel on nine hardpoints.

Eurofighter is designed to be armed with fire-and-forget active radar AMRAAM missiles and heat-seeking ASRAAM dogfight weapons, but will also be able to carry earlier-generation missiles such as the AIM-7 Sparrow and AIM-9 Sidewinder.

EF 2000

Type: high-performance jet fighter

Powerplant: two 60.02-kN (13,500-lb. thrust) Eurojet EJ200 engines, increased to 90.03 kN (20,257-lb. thrust) with afterburning

Maximum speed: Mach 2.0+, or 2125 km/h (1320 m.p.h.) at 6096 m (20,000 ft.)

Combat radius: up to 556 km (345 mi.) with full weapons load

Weights: empty 9750 kg (21,495 lb.); loaded 21,000 kg (46,297 lb.)

Armament: 6500 kg (14,330 lb.) of ordnance including up to eight missiles such as Sky Flash, ASRAAM, AMRAAM or Sidewinder, plus a 27-mm rapid-fire cannon

Dimensions:
span	10.50 m	(34 ft. 5 in.)
length	14.50 m	(47 ft. 7 in.)
height	4.00 m	(13 ft. 1 in.)
wing area	50 m²	(538 sq. ft.)

COMBAT DATA

MAXIMUM SPEED

The Eurofighter EF 2000 is one of the fastest of the latest generation of combat jets. However, although the phenomenally expensive American F-22 is slower, it can maintain supersonic speeds for longer periods.

EF 2000	Mach 2.0
JAS 39 GRIPEN	Mach 1.8
F-22 RAPIER	Mach 1.7

COMBAT RADIUS

EF 2000 is at a disadvantage in terms of combat radius. The single-engined Gripen is smaller and less fuel-hungry, and the F-22 is much larger and carries a bigger fuel load. But for most tactical purposes the EFA has enough range for its missions.

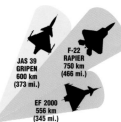

JAS 39 GRIPEN 600 km (373 mi.)

F-22 RAPIER 750 km (466 mi.)

EF 2000 556 km (345 mi.)

ARMAMENT

Most modern fighters carry a very large weapons load. Both the EF 2000 and the Gripen have been designed to be dual air-to-air and air-to-ground capable. The F-22 has the capability, but is more dedicated to the air-superiority role.

EF 2000 27-mm cannon 8–10 short- and medium-range AAM 6500 kg (14,330 lb.) of weapons and stores

JAS 39 GRIPEN 27-mm cannon 6-8 short- and medium-range AAM 6500 kg (14,330 lb.) of weapons and stores

F-22 RAPTOR 20-mm cannon AIM-120 AMRAAM and AIM-9 Sidewinders carried internally 10,000 kg (22,046 lb.) of air-to-surface weapons

Tomorrow's fighters today

■ SUKHOI Su-27 'FLANKER'
This is arguably the best fighter currently in service. The Eurofighter was designed to outperform advanced versions currently under development.

■ DASSAULT RAFALE
Developed after the French withdrew from the Eurofighter programme, the Rafale is a French national project. It is similar in design to the EFA, but is somewhat lighter.

■ SAAB JAS 39 GRIPEN
A product of Sweden's highly respected Saab concern, the Gripen is also a tail-less delta with canard foreplanes but is much smaller, and is powered by a single engine.

■ LOCKHEED F-22 RAPTOR
The F-22 incorporates a great deal of stealth technology, and is the most capable of the new batch of fighter designs. But that performance comes at phenomenal cost.

FAIRCHILD

A-10 THUNDERBOLT II

● CAS and anti-armour aircraft ● Gulf War veteran ● Forward air control

Built to attack the Warsaw Pact's main battle tanks, the Fairchild A-10 Thunderbolt II was named after a Fairchild Republic product from another era, the P-47 Thunderbolt of World War II. The twin-engined, single-seat A-10 'Warthog' showed its excellent air-to-ground capability in the unlikely setting of the Middle East during the first and second Gulf Wars, despite a proposed change of role for the A-10 in line with changes in USAF policy.

▲ *Plans for the withdrawal of the A-10 from the USAF inventory were well advanced by 1990, but events in the Persian Gulf meant that the retirement of the 'Warthog' was postponed.*

FAIRCHILD A-10 THUNDERBOLT II

◀ **Second prototype**
The two YA-10A prototypes flew for the first time in 1972. The second one is seen here carrying 'dumb' iron bombs. Service aircraft carry the Maverick air-to-surface missile as their primary anti-tank weapon.

▼ **Vulnerability issue**
Since the A-10's introduction debates have raged about the vulnerability of this relatively slow aircraft. As a result, the F-16 was chosen to replace it.

▲ **Camouflage**
Since the first Gulf War, all-over grey paintwork has replaced the grey/green scheme.

▲ **Avenger cannon**
The cannon is so powerful that it can be fired only in short bursts as it dramatically slows down the aircraft.

Countermeasures ▶
Even though it is relatively unsophisticated, the A-10 carries an electronic jamming pod.

FACTS AND FIGURES

➤ A-10s entered service in April 1976; 144 aircraft were committed to the Persian Gulf war zone in 1990/91.

➤ The first A-10 prototype made its initial flight on 10 May 1972.

➤ A-10s shot down two Iraqi helicopters during the first Gulf War.

➤ Although almost as large as the multi-crewed B-25 Mitchell bomber of World War II, the A-10 is flown by a single pilot.

➤ In 1994 plans to export 50 surplus A-10s to Turkey were cancelled.

➤ At its maximum rate of fire, a 30-round burst from the GAU-8 takes half a second.

PROFILE

Forward air control in the 'Warthog'

More than 100 A-10s were committed to the 1991 Gulf War and performed admirably in the air-to-ground and FAC roles.

The need for a close air support (CAS)/anti-armour aircraft was one of the lessons learned in the Vietnam conflict. The machine needed to be able to fly from rough forward airstrips, carry heavy weapon loads and withstand battle damage. Speed was not a major consideration.

Fairchild's A-10A was the design chosen to fill this 'A-X' requirement. A sturdy, somewhat heavy, single-seat attack aircraft, the A-10 was

said to be too slow; it flew at subsonic speeds in an era when fast anti-aircraft missiles were rapidly appearing on the scene.

Despite this, 713 A-10s were built, and the first entered service in 1976. Units in the continental US, Alaska, Europe and Korea were equipped with the type. However, the end of the Cold War meant that this specialist aircraft was no longer a vital requirement, and it was to be replaced by the Lockheed Martin F-16.

Surplus A-10s began to take over from the well-worn Rockwell OV-10 Broncos in the forward air control (FAC) role, with a number being redesignated OA-10A.

An AN/ALQ-184 electronic countermeasures (ECM) pod is a common fitting on both FAC OA-10s and tank-busting A-10s.

Split ailerons give the A-10 an exceptional rate of roll for the rapid low-level manoeuvres required for the anti-tank and FAC roles.

All A-10As have been redesignated OA-10A without undergoing any modifications, apart from changes to cockpit lighting to make them compatible with NVG equipment.

A-10A THUNDERBOLT II

The 706th Tactical Fighter Squadron, 926th Tactical Fighter Group, operated A-10As during Operation Desert Storm. After the Gulf War, the unit took on squadron/wing status and F-16C/Ds.

Survivability was one of the key considerations of the A-10's designers. The aircraft is able to fly on one engine or with one tailfin missing. The pilot sits in a titanium 'tub' as protection from ground fire.

Two General Electric TF34 turbofans power the A-10 and are high-mounted in pods to the rear of the aircraft to avoid debris when using rough airstrips. The nacelle design results in a low infra-red signature, which reduces vulnerability to heat-seeking missiles. This design also makes maintenance easier as access to the engine is less restricted than in other types.

In its original 'tank-busting' role the A-10's main weapon was the General Electric GAU-8/A Avenger 30-mm seven-barrelled Gatling-type cannon.

For the FAC role the OA-10 carries few weapons apart from two rocket pods for target marking and AIM-9 Sidewinder air-to-air missiles. The pilot is provided with NVG (night-vision goggles) for a night-time capability.

The main undercarriage retracts forwards into an underwing bay. In theory, once the aircraft's weapon load has been dropped, a safe wheels-up landing can be made with minimal wing damage.

This A-10 carries the 'NO' tailcode of the 926th Fighter Wing, based in New Orleans. In September 1996 it received A/OA-10As once again to take on the attack/FAC training role.

AGM-65 Maverick anti-tank strike

3 TERMINAL PHASE: As it approaches the target the Maverick glides in, using the image produced by its TV camera. The missile is able to follow slow-moving targets.

1 'POP-UP' APPROACH: When near the target, the pilot pops up from low altitude in his A-10 and acquires the target either visually or via the cockpit TV screen. The image on the screen is produced by the camera fitted in the missile's nose.

2 MAVERICK LAUNCH: During a shallow dive the pilot launches the Maverick, keeping the target in view to maximise the missile's speed and height.

ACTION DATA

WEAPON LOAD

The A-10A had an unmatched load-carrying ability in the CAS role, almost twice that of the Soviet's equivalent aircraft, the Sukhoi Su-25. The V/STOL Harrier is able to lift heavier loads with a short take-off than it can when taking off vertically.

7258 kg (15,950 lb.)	4400 kg (9,680 lb.)	4173 kg (9,180 lb.)
A-10A THUNDERBOLT II	Su-25K 'FROGFOOT-A'	HARRIER GR.Mk 7

MAXIMUM SPEED

The Thunderbolt II has been criticised throughout its operational career as being too slow and vulnerable for its CAS role. Both the 'Frogfoot' and Harrier are capable of speeds of around 1000 km/h (620 m.p.h.) at sea level without a load.

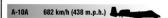

A-10A	682 km/h (438 m.p.h.)
Su-25K 'FROGFOOT-A'	975 km/h (604 m.p.h.)
HARRIER GR.Mk 7	1065 km/h (660 m.p.h.)

TAKE-OFF DISTANCE

The STOL ability of the Harrier gives it an unbeatably short take-off run, although this limits the aircraft's load-carrying ability. At maximum take-off weight both the A-10 and Su-25 require about 1200 metres of runway to get airborne.

HARRIER GR.Mk 7	Su-25K 'FROGFOOT-A'	A-10A THUNDERBOLT II
405 m (1,328 ft.)	1200 m (3,936 ft.)	1220 m (4,000 ft.)

FMA

IA-58 PUCÁRÁ

● Robust structure ● Counter-insurgency ● Hard-hitting turboprop

The FMA Pucará, built by Fabrica Militar de Aviones, is an ideal military aircraft for small countries. Argentina developed this twin-turboprop anticipating that an aircraft would be required to undertake anti-guerrilla and counter-insurgency (COIN) operations. Repeatedly upgraded and improved, the Pucará had limited success in the Falklands War. The COIN aircraft is better suited for counter-drug work in Colombia.

▲ Argentina's hard-hitting
Pucará is one of the best counter-insurgency planes ever built. It did not show its true potential in the Falklands War as many of the aircraft were destroyed on the ground.

FMA IA-58 PUCÁRÁ

▲ Silver Pucarás
These four Argentine Pucarás are wearing the original silver colour scheme. Subsequently most have been camouflaged.

▲ RAF evaluation
One of the Argentine Pucarás captured by British forces in the Falklands was flown and evaluated by test pilots at the UK test centre at Boscombe Down.

▲ COIN formation
This pair of IA-58As are armed with nose-mounted 20-mm Hispano DCA-804 cannon and pylon-mounted rockets and bombs.

▲ Arms assortment
In addition to the fixed cannon in the nose, the Pucará can carry up to 1620 kg (3,565 lb.) of mixed weapons and tanks on underfuselage and underwing racks.

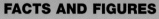

◀ Fast striker
With an unusual configuration that necessitates carrying stores externally, increasing drag, the Pucará still has a top speed of over 500 km/h (310 m.p.h.).

FACTS AND FIGURES

➤ The first aircraft, designed in 1966 and named the AX-2 Delfin, completed its maiden flight on 20 August 1969.

➤ The prototype was powered by two 674-kW Garrett TPE331-U-303 turboprops.

➤ The first production Pucará took to the air on 8 November 1974.

➤ Pucarás were ordered by eight countries but only Argentina, Colombia, Sri Lanka and Uruguay took delivery.

➤ In the Falklands a Pucará shot down a British Army Westland Scout helicopter.

➤ Most of the Pucarás in the Falklands were destroyed on the ground.

PROFILE

Close support in the Pucará

Named after the stone forts built by indigenous South American tribes, the Pucará is a manoeuvrable and rugged aircraft able to operate from small, rough airstrips – as short as 80 metres when boosted by JATO (Jet-Assisted Take-Off) bottles. With this ability to fight from primitive backwater bases, in the 1970s the Pucará proved that it would have been useful to US forces serving in Vietnam.

In fact, the Pucará dates back to the early 1960s and is a unique design. A tall, retractable tricycle undercarriage provides ample space for weapons and the generous propeller ground clearance needed for flights from unpaved ground. The two crewmembers are strapped into Martin-Baker Mk 6 ejection seats, with the rear-seat positioned 25 cm higher. In practice, many missions are flown by a single pilot. Without exception, pilots are pleased with the stability and responsiveness of the Pucará.

The IA-58 has been successful against lightly armed rebels in Argentina, but during the Falklands War nearly all of the aircraft flown to the islands were lost to sabotage, or were captured by the advancing British Army.

Above: The view from the cockpit is excellent, with the seats positioned in a staggered arrangement. Both crewmembers have a rearview mirror and unobstructed and almost undistorted vision.

Above: This Pucará, in landing configuration, shows its fully extended flaps and tall, stalky tricycle undercarriage. The legs are long to give good ground clearance on irregular surfaces.

IA-58A Pucará

Type: two-seat close air support and reconnaissance aircraft

Powerplant: two 729-kW (975-hp.) Turboméca Astazou XVIG turboprop engines

Maximum speed: approx. 500 km/h (310 m.p.h.) at sea level

Range: 1500 km (930 mi.)

Service ceiling: 10,000 m (33,000 ft.)

Weights: empty 4020 kg (8,800 lb.); maximum take-off 6800 kg (14,960 lb.)

Armament: two 20-mm Hispano cannon under the nose and four 7.62-mm (.30 cal.) Browning machine-guns abreast of the cockpit, plus up to 1620 kg (3,565 lb.) of external bombs or rockets

Dimensions:
span	14.50 m	(47 ft. 6 in.)
length	14.25 m	(46 ft. 9 in.)
height	5.36 m	(17 ft. 7 in.)
wing area	30.30 m²	(326 sq. ft.)

IA-58A PUCARÁ

Uruguay received six IA-58As prior to the Falklands War in 1982. They equipped the Grupo de Aviación 2 of Brigada Aérea II at Durazno.

The crew are protected by armoured plate glass in the canopy.

The moulded Plexiglas canopy covers both cockpits in a single unit that hinges upwards from the rear. Martin-Baker APO6A ejector seats, which can be used at zero speed and at zero height, are fitted.

The tall, all-metal T-tail has a fixed tailplane with manually driven control surfaces and electric trim tabs on the trailing edges.

Two 20-mm Hispano DCA-804 cannon are carried in the nose, each equipped with up to 270 rounds.

The French Ratier Forest three-blade propellers have fully feathering blades of solid forged duralumin.

Fuselage attachments can carry tandem pylons, and stores pylons are permanently attached under the wings at the junction between the rectangular centre section and the outer panels. These carry triplets of 110-kg (242-lb.) high-explosive bombs.

Most of the rear fuselage is empty apart from control rods leading to the tail surfaces, air bottles and radio/electronics racks. The centre section contains a large fuel tank and the machine-guns and cannon.

COMBAT DATA

MAXIMUM SPEED

Not surprisingly, the twin turbojet-powered Cessna A-37 Dragonfly is appreciably faster than the twin turboprop Pucará. The two turboprop aircraft can operate closer to the frontline due to their STOL performance.

IA-58A 500 km/h (310 m.p.h.)

A-37 DRAGONFLY 843 km/h (523 m.p.h.)

OV-10 452 km/h (280 m.p.h.)

ARMAMENT LOAD

Although the Dragonfly is only equipped with a single 7.62-mm Minigun it also has eight underwing hardpoints to carry a large weight of bombs and rockets. The Pucará and Bronco can only carry two-thirds of the A-37's munitions load in a combat situation.

IA-58A PUCARÁ 1620 kg (3,565 lb.)

A-37 DRAGONFLY 2268 kg (4,990 lb.)

OV-10 BRONCO 1633 kg (3,593 lb.)

COMBAT RADIUS

The Pucará's combat radius with a 1000-kg (2,200-lb.) warload flying at low level is 400 km (250 mi.), rising to 650 km (400 mi.) flying a hi-lo-hi profile. The A-37's radius with a similar warload is much less if flown at low level and 370 km (230 mi.) on a hi-lo-hi attack. With its lower overall performance, the OV-10 has a reasonable combat radius with a full weapons load.

A-37 DRAGONFLY 370 km (230 mi.)

AIA-58A PUCARÁ 400 km (250 mi.)

OV-10 BRONCO 367 km (228 mi.)

Falklands wipe-out

HELICOPTER DOWNED: In April 1982 the Argentine air force flew 25 Pucarás to newly captured Port Stanley and Goose Green. They found strong British resistance and the only success was the downing of a British army Scout helicopter.

BOMB TARGETS: As early as 1 May 1982 an Argentine Pucará about to take off was blasted by a cluster bomb released by a Sea Harrier. Worse was to come. On 15 May six aircraft were destroyed on Pebble Island by a raiding force of the SAS. Several more were shot down by infantry arms and missiles, and one by a Sea Harrier's guns. The remaining Pucarás were captured.

FOKKER

F50

● Transport duties ● Missile attack ● Intelligence gathering

F okker used its 50-seat twin-turboprop airliner as the basis for a range of military models. Using similar equipment to that carried by derivatives of its predecessor, the F27, they were designed to meet a wide variety of requirements, from transport and maritime patrol, to electronic surveillance and airborne early warning. However, targeting the aircraft at a very crowded market resulted in few production orders.

▲ Utilising
successful building techniques developed on the F27, the F50 incorporates all the latest advances in airframe technology, coupling this with a sophisticated radar system.

FOKKER F50

▼ Far East operations
Singapore operates four F50s, replacing Shorts Skyvans, in the transport role. Five Maritime Enforcer examples are to follow these aircraft into service to patrol coastal waters.

▲ More capability
Its lengthened fuselage is helping the F50 prove to be an even more capable aircraft than the F27 Fellowship that it is replacing.

Search radar ▶
A blister containing a 360-degree search radar is positioned on the underside of the fuselage. This allows the aircraft to locate ships at great distances in all weathers.

▲ Ship killer
The Enforcer Mk 2 has provision for four torpedoes or depth charges, along with Exocet, Harpoon, Sea Eagle or Sea Skua anti-ship missiles.

Airliner guise ▶
Resplendent in a high-visibility gloss white scheme, this F50 operates as a VIP transport for high-ranking officers in the Dutch air force.

FACTS AND FIGURES

➤ The Republic of China (Taiwan) air force was the first customer for the Fokker 50 transport aircraft in 1992.

➤ First flight of the Fokker 50 occurred on 28 December 1985.

➤ The aircraft is basically a lengthened, re-engined development of the F27.

➤ The aircraft was initially intended purely for the civil airline market, but has seen numerous military applications.

➤ A complete F-16 engine can be carried within the F50's fuselage.

➤ Fokker has developed an electronic reconnaissance version of the F50.

PROFILE

Airliner to ship-killer

Taiwan was the first nation to acquire the military Fokker 50, purchasing three examples for use as general transports. Singapore bought another four to replace its ageing Skyvans, but the more specialised variants of this former airliner have found few takers.

For naval operations, there was the unarmed Maritime Mk 2 for coastal surveillance, and the Maritime Enforcer Mk 2, which flew for the first time in 1992. Both these types carried a surface search radar but the Enforcer had

added provision for the carriage of external stores. The Republic of Singapore Air Force eventually bought five Enforcers.

These machines could be armed with a choice of American, Italian or British torpedoes, with depth bombs available as alternatives if customers wished. For operations against surface ships, the armament options included a pair of Exocet, Maverick, Harpoon, Sea Skua or Sea Eagle missiles. Other military variants of the Fokker 50 are the Black

Crow signals intelligence aircraft, the radar-carrying Sentinel for overland reconnaissance, the Troopship Mk 3 transport and an airborne early-warning aircraft dubbed 'Kingbird'. More successful was a transport version of the stretched Fokker 60. Used by the Dutch air force, it can carry up to 50 paratroops and can readily be converted for the medical evacuation role.

Left: Now wearing a more 'warlike' camouflage, this Dutch F50 operates on combat support missions. Later variants will have an improved ECM suite fitted to the wing tips.

Right: With the ability to fly long patrols over coastal waters and, if the need arises, to attack hostile shipping, the F50 may yet achieve substantial sales, as many nations need to upgrade their maritime fleets.

Maritime Enforcer Mk 2

Type: armed maritime patrol aircraft

Powerplant: two 1864-kW (2,500-hp.) Pratt & Whitney Canada PW 125B

Maximum speed: 480 km/h (298 m.p.h.); patrol speed 277 km/h (172 m.p.h.) at 610 m (2,000 ft.)

Combat radius: 2224 km (1,379 mi.)

Range: 6820 km (4,230 mi.)

Service ceiling: 7620 m (25,000 ft.)

Weights: empty 12,520 kg (29,300 lb.); maximum take-off 19,900 kg (47,400 lb.)

Armament: four Sting Ray torpedoes, depth bombs, two or four Harpoon anti-ship missiles

Dimensions:
span	29.00 m	(95 ft. 2 in.)
length	25.24 m	(82 ft. 9 in.)
height	8.31 m	(27 ft. 3 in.)
wing area	70 m²	(753 sq. ft.)

F50

Singapore was an early customer for the Fokker 50, receiving four transport examples in early 1994. These operate with No. 121 Sqn, replacing old Skyvans; an additional purchase of three aircraft seems likely.

An advanced cockpit is provided for the two pilots with multi-function displays and FLIR available for particular customers. Pilots have found the aircraft a delight to fly.

The F50 was equipped with improved engines to increase performance. This particular variant is fitted with two Pratt & Whitney turboprops which are linked to an advanced six-bladed composite propeller blade system, a combination that is proving very satisfactory.

Retained from the earlier F27 Friendship, the large fillet positioned ahead of the tail offers the F50 superb lateral stability, a quality of particular value during a search pattern.

The increased fuselage length allows the F50 to carry either more specialised avionics for maritime operations, or more cargo in its transport guise.

REPUBLIC OF SING

711

Maritime attack versions of the F50 are fitted with fuselage hardpoints that allow the aircraft to carry anti-ship missiles.

A large access door is retained from the airliner versions. This is positioned on the rear fuselage to facilitate the loading and unloading of cargo.

The tall tail of the F50 offers the aircraft excellent handling characteristics, particularly at low level during long patrol missions over the ocean.

COMBAT DATA

MAXIMUM RANGE

With the need to patrol for long distances over the oceans, range is of vital importance for maritime aircraft. Leader in this field is the Nimrod. The small size of the Enforcer means that only a relatively modest internal fuel load can be carried.

CP-140 AURORA 8339 km (5,170 mi.)

NIMROD MR.Mk 2 9266 km (5,745 mi.)

F50 MARITIME ENFORCER 6820 km (4,230 mi.)

MAXIMUM SPEED

With its four jet engines the Nimrod easily out-performs many other maritime patrol aircraft. Powered only by two turbo-props the Enforcer's speed is much less.

CP-140 AURORA	732 km/h (454 m.p.h.)
NIMROD MR.Mk 2	926 km/h (574 m.p.h.)
F50	480 km/h (298 m.p.h.)

WEAPON LOAD

Mines, depth charges and anti-ship missiles all need to be carried by maritime aircraft. For its size, the F50 Enforcer can carry a reasonable amount of ordnance, though it is a lot less capable in this respect than the CP-140.

CP-140 AURORA 9072 kg (8,778 lb.)

NIMROD MR.Mk 2 6124 kg (19,958 lb.)

F50 MARITIME ENFORCER 3990 kg (13,473 lb.)

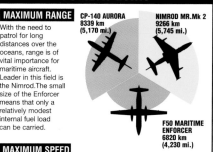

Patrolling the oceans on propellers

■ ATLANTIQUE 2: Continually upgraded, Dassault's Atlantique operates with many NATO forces and Pakistan.

■ EMB-111: Despite its small size, Embraer's maritime patrol aircraft is proving very successful in South America.

■ S-2 TRACKER: Now fitted with improved avionics, the Grumman Tracker continues to serve with smaller nations.

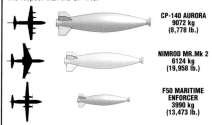

GENERAL DYNAMICS

F-111F

● Swing-wing strike fighter ● Gulf War precision laser-bomber

The F-111F was the ultimate combat variant of the amazing General Dynamics F-111. Known to its pilots as the 'Aardvark', the F-111 has a slender fuselage, side-by-side seating and 'swing' wings. In its day it was a revolutionary warplane of unrivalled all-weather striking power, and the modern F-111F, with a Pave Tack targeting device bulging in its belly, could hit targets with uncanny accuracy.

▲ *A Gulf War F-111 pilot checks the mighty TF30 turbofan. The F-111 was a superb performer in the Gulf, showing that after 20 years it remained almost unique in its long-range strike capability.*

GENERAL DYNAMICS F-111F

▼ **In-flight refuelling**
The F-111 was designed to strike deep into Russia from bases in England. Fuelling in flight extended its range still further.

▲ **Massive payload**
Few attack aircraft had as many armament options as the 'Aardvark'. Together with the F-15E, it was the only aircraft capable of delivering the GBU-28 'bunker buster' used to devastating effect in the Gulf War.

◀ **Precision strike**
Key to the F-111's performance is its ability to carry a heavy load of laser-guided bombs, which are able to strike to within centimetres of a designated target.

Desert strike ▲
Carrying a large load of 'iron bombs', an F-111F heads for a target somewhere in Iraq.

▼ **Capsule cockpit**
Instead of having ejection seats, the entire cockpit of the F-111 detaches as a parachute-retarded escape capsule.

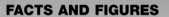

▲ **Take-off position**
The F-111's wings sweep forward for take-off and landing.

FACTS AND FIGURES

➤ The first F-111A made its maiden flight on 21 December 1964.

➤ The F-111 was originally called the TFX (Tactical Fighter Experimental).

➤ After a tragic start, F-111s returned to Vietnam in 1972 and flew 4030 successful sorties in five months.

➤ The F-111F, with more powerful engines, improved avionics and Pave Tack, served with the USAF until July 1996.

➤ One F-111F was lost during the air attack on Libya in April 1986.

➤ The 66 F-111Fs at Taif in Saudi Arabia flew 4000 sorties during the Gulf War.

PROFILE

'Aardvark' – the laser-bomber

The F-111 supersonic fighter-bomber was the world's first operational aircraft with a variable-sweep wing, and for two decades was the most advanced strike bomber. Introduced in 1968, it has flown in a number of versions, including the nuclear-armed FB-111A strategic bomber and the EF-111 electronic warfare aircraft.

The complex F-111 suffered a tortuous development process, culminating in the F-111F. Although the earlier F-111D had more advanced electronics, the 'F' model was much more reliable. Above all, it had more powerful and fuel-efficient engines than previous variants.

The F-111F has seen more action than other 'Aardvarks'. It performed well in a long-range counter-terrorist strike against Libya in 1986. During Operation Desert Storm the F-111F was a workhorse, accurately delivering more precision ordnance than

A typical mission load included a pair of 'Paveway' 1000-kg (2,200-lb.) laser-guided bombs, two AIM-9 'Sidewinder' missiles for self-defence, and the huge AVQ-26 Pave Tack laser-designation turret mounted under the fuselage.

any other warplane.

When they were retired in 1996 the F-111Fs were replaced by F-15E Eagles. The remaining airframes are in storage and could be returned to operational status in a time of crisis.

Paveway III bombs have an advanced proportional guidance system, and are distinguishable from earlier laser-guided weapons by their long fixed noses.

The wing is swept to the forward position of 16° for landing and back to 72.5° for high speed.

F-111F

Type: two-seat tactical strike fighter

Powerplant: two 111.65-kN (25,050-lb.-thrust) Pratt & Whitney TF30-P-100 afterburning turbofans

Maximum speed: Mach 1.2 or 1468 km/h (910 m.p.h.) at sea level; 2655 km/h (1,646 m.p.h.) clean at altitude

Radius of action: more than 2200 km (1,365 mi.)

Service ceiling: 18,300 m (60,000 ft.)

Weights: empty 21,500 kg (47,300 lb.); loaded 45,360 kg (99,792 lb.)

Armament: up to 14,228 kg (31,302 lb.) of ordnance, including bombs, missiles or gun pods. Normal tactical load of two or four precision-guided weapons plus AIM-9 Sidewinder missiles

Dimensions:
span	19.20 m (63 ft.)	
length	22.40 m (73 ft. 6 in.)	
height	5.21 m (17 ft.)	
wing area	48.77 m² (525 sq. ft.)	

The F-111F could carry up to 14228 kg of ordnance on its underwing and under-fuselage hardpoints, including air-to-air missiles and Vulcan cannon pods.

F-111F

The F-111Fs of the 48th Tactical Fighter Wing, based at RAF Lakenheath, were sent to the Taif airfield in Saudi Arabia during the 1991 Gulf War. They were arguably the most accurate and lethal bombers of the war.

The F-111 is one of the fastest aircraft in the world at low level. The main factor limiting an F-111 pilot who wishes to run his aircraft flat-out is that the canopy would melt due to air friction heating after 10 minutes.

The F-111 may have a fighter designation, but it was an out-and-out attack aircraft. Pilot visibility to the rear is poor, but thanks to the downward slope of the nose the forward visibility is excellent for a fast strike aircraft.

The complex system of moving wing glove and variable inlets are designed to cope with the conflicting requirements of Mach 2 flight and variable-geometry wings.

The F-111 has a fuel emergency jettison pipe between the afterburner nozzles. Dumping fuel with afterburner on results in a spectacular 'torch'.

The multimode APQ-144 attack radar and the APQ-146 terrain-following radar allows the aircraft to fly terrain-hugging attacks at low level day or night, whatever the weather.

The Pave Tack pod housed in the weapons bay has a stabilised turret containing an infra-red sensor and a laser designator. It enabled the F-111F to drop laser-guided munitions autonomously at night.

The GBU-24 is a BLU-109 907-kg (2,000-lb.) steel-jacketed penetration bomb fitted with a Paveway III laser-guidance kit.

The ALQ-131 jamming pod mounted on the rear fuselage gives the F-111F additional defence against hostile radar.

Chaff and flare dispensers are fitted on the underside of the tail. These were designed to decoy enemy radar-guided and heat-seeking missiles.

COMBAT DATA

SPEED AT LOW LEVEL

The F-111F had one of the longest operational service lives of any modern combat jet and was also one of the world's fastest jets, especially at low level. With its wings swept back it could penetrate the air more cleanly, suffering less turbulence than most of its rivals.

F-15E EAGLE
1400 km/h (1,678 m.p.h.)

F-111F
1468 km/h (910 m.p.h.)

Su-24 'FENCER'
1320 km/h (818 m.p.h.)

RANGE ON INTERNAL FUEL

The F-111F was designed at the height of the Cold War, and from the start was tasked with penetration missions. These involved flying very fast and very low through enemy air defences, striking at key command and communications targets deep inside enemy territory.

F-15E EAGLE 2500 km (995 mi.)

F-111F 4700 km (2,914 mi.)

Su-24 'FENCER' 2000 km (1,240 mi.)

WEAPONS LOAD

F-111F 14 228 kg

F-15E EAGLE 11 100 kg

Su-24 'FENCER' 8000 kg

The F-111F's internal bomb-bay was designed to carry two nuclear bombs or missiles. However, it usually housed a cannon pod or a Pave Tack guidance pod. But the bomb-bay was only part of the story. More than 14 tons of weaponry could be carried on six swivelling underwing pylons.

Pave Tack attack

DETECTION: An F-111F crew could detect their target visually via the infra-red sensor mounted in the Pave Tack turret under the fuselage. This allowed the attackers to acquire aiming points by day or by night at ranges of several kilometres.

WEAPONS RELEASE: The fire-control computer calculated the optimum point for dropping weapons. Releasing the bomb in a climb 'tossed' it further than would be possible in a level release or a diving attack.

ILLUMINATION: As the bomber turned away, the Pave Tack turret swivelled to keep the target in sight. Just before the weapon arrived, the F-111F illuminated the target with a laser beam onto which the bomb steered with deadly accuracy.

GRUMMAN/GENERAL DYNAMICS

EF-111A RAVEN

● Supersonic electronic warfare aircraft ● Converted F-111A

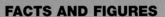

T he EF-111 Raven was until recently the USAF's 'secret weapon' – an electronic wizard that jams and confounds enemy radar and communications. Converted from the famous F-111A 'Aardvark' this big, variable-sweep veteran carried no weapons but relied on the magic of electrons to clear a path through enemy defences for other warplanes. The Raven saw action during the 1991 Gulf War.

▲ The Raven's role was 'non-lethal defence suppression', which involves jamming enemy radar defences, but the aircraft did not carry air-to-surface weapons to destroy them. That task is left to F-16Cs armed with AGM-88 HARM anti-radar missiles.

GRUMMAN/GENERAL DYNAMICS EF-111A RAVEN

◀ **Jammer's cockpit**
Dominating the control panel in front of the electronic warfare officer's right hand station is a large tactical situation display screen providing threat information.

Air-to-air refuelling ▶
As with the F-111 'tanking' was used to extend the already long range of the EF-111. Here a KC-10 is about to refuel a Raven.

◀ **Afterburners lit**
The immensely powerful TF30-powered F-111 was the ideal platform for a tactical jammer as it was able to keep up with F-111 strike aircraft on long-range missions such as those to Libya and Iraq.

▼ **Two-tone grey**
The Raven fleet was always painted in this two-tone grey colour scheme, the darker shade is on the upper surfaces of the aircraft. This makes it less conspicuous when viewed from above.

▲ **'Electric Fox' and 'Spark Vark'**
After the F-111 'Aardvark', the EF-111 was known as the 'Spark Vark'. The type was also called the 'Electric Fox' before 'Raven' was coined by the USAF.

FACTS AND FIGURES

➤ Skilful manoeuvring by an EF-111 pilot caused an Iraqi Mirage F.1 to crash into the ground early in the first Gulf War.

➤ The EF-111 has only one set of pilot's controls compared to the F-111's two.

➤ An EF-111 aerodynamic prototype flew in 1975 and the first full conversion in 1977.

➤ Though EF-111s used a similar ALQ-99 system to the four-seat EA-6B, greater automation allowed just one operator.

➤ The EA-6B differs from the Raven in being armed with anti-radar missiles.

➤ The last EF-111s were replaced with a version of the F-15E Strike Eagle.

PROFILE

Supersonic radar jammer

The 1973 Yom Kippur War demonstrated that tactical aircraft were extremely vulnerable to an enemy's large integrated air defence system of the type favoured by the Soviets and Warsaw Pact states. The USAF's Tactical Air Command (TAC) had invested little in electronic warfare and was about to retire its EB-66 stand-off jammers.

Grumman had experience with tactical radar jamming systems, having combined the ALQ-99 system with the A-6

Intruder attack aircraft to create the EA-6B Prowler carrier-based jammer.

TAC, however, needed a faster platform on which to mount this system so that it could keep up with its 'strike packages'. It therefore chose the long-range, Mach 2-capable General Dynamics F-111.

The EF-111 combined the proven airframe of a fast, sturdy, long-range strike aircraft with a 'package' of electronic equipment which would enable bombers to reach their targets.

By late-1985 Grumman had converted 42 redundant F-111As. Their first use 'in anger' came the following year, supporting the US raids on Libya. At the start of the first Gulf War, the Raven was one of the first aircraft to challenge Iraq's air defences.

The USAF's fleet of Ravens was retired in 1998, after a long-running deployment in the Southern no-fly zone over Iraq.

Above: EF-111A serial number 66-0041 was the second F-111A to be converted to Raven standard, but the first to have a full electronics suite installed.

Left: EF-111As drawn from units of the 66th Electronic Combat Wing from RAF Upper Heyford, Oxfordshire, and the 388th Tactical Fighter Wing from Mountain Home AFB, Idaho, performed a vital role in Operation Desert Storm, based at Incirlik, Turkey and Taif, Saudi Arabia, respectively.

EF-111A Raven

Type: two-seat supersonic electronic warfare aircraft

Powerplant: two 82.28-kN (18,460-lb.-thrust) Pratt & Whitney TF30-P-3 afterburning turbofan engines

Maximum speed: 2272 km/h (1,408 m.p.h.)

Combat radius: 1495 km (927 mi.)

Service ceiling: 13,715 m (45,000 ft.)

Weights: empty 25,072 kg (55,158 lb.); loaded 40,347 kg (88,763 lb.)

Armament: usually none, but able to carry two AIM-9 Sidewinder air-to-air missiles

Equipment: AN/ALQ-99E tactical jamming suite (TJS) consisting of a System Integrated Receiver (of hostile radar emissions) and jamming transmitters; self-defence avionics; mapping radar and terrain-following radar

Dimensions:
span (spread)	19.20 m	(63 ft.)
span (swept)	9.74 m	(32 ft.)
length	23.16 m	(70 ft.)
wing area	48.77 m²	(525 sq. ft.)

EF-111A RAVEN

This Raven belonged to the 430th Electronic Combat Squadron, 27th Fighter Wing, at Cannon Air Force Base, New Mexico. The last unit to fly the EF-111A operationally was the 429th Electronic Countermeasures Squadron.

The 168-kg (370-lb.) 'football' pod on the top of the fin holds 264 kg (580 lb.) of receiver antennas and related equipment, including an infra-red warning system.

The crew consists of a pilot and an electronic warfare officer, the latter in place of the weapons systems officer of the F-111.

The main jamming equipment is housed in the former weapons bay, the 10 transmitters filling a 4.9-m (16-ft.) long 'canoe' fairing. These cover seven frequency bands.

Up to four wing pylons can be fitted, two on each wing, for the carriage of such items as fuel tanks and datalink pods.

The only armament carried by the EF-111 is a pair of AIM-9 Sidewinders for self-defence. Its best means of defence, however, remains its sheer speed and acceleration.

The Raven retains both the F-111A's APQ-160 attack radar and APQ-110 terrain-following radar equipment.

The EF-111A uses the basic airframe of the F-111A, including the engines, two Pratt & Whitney TF30-P-3 turbofans.

The EF-111A's mission

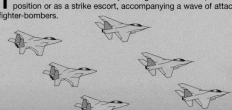

1 Ravens can undertake radar jamming from a distant (stand-off) position or as a strike escort, accompanying a wave of attacking fighter-bombers.

2 One or more EF-111s precedes the strike 'package', detecting hostile radar emissions and transmitting 'noise' so that the enemy is unable to detect the attackers.

3 Without the capacity to detect an attack, the enemy cannot direct anti-aircraft fire or fighters on to the strike force.

COMBAT DATA

MAXIMUM SPEED

Based on the Mach 2-capable F-111A strike aircraft, the Raven possessed a similarly impressive performance. The Su-24MP is also based on a supersonic attack aircraft.

EF-111A RAVEN	2216 km/h (1,408 m.p.h.)
EA-6B	982 km/h (609 m.p.h.)
Su-24MP	1435 km/h (890 m.p.h.)

DEFENSIVE ARMAMENT

While the EA-6B is capable of carrying up to four AGM-88 HARM anti-radar missiles, it is not equipped with defensive weaponry. The AIM-9 Sidewinder has a considerably better range than the R-60.

2 x AIM-9 Sidewinder missiles — EF-111A RAVEN

None — EA-6B PROWLER

2 x R-60 air-to-air missiles — Su-24MP 'FENCER-F'

RANGE

The F-111 family has an unrivalled range performance in the supersonic deep strike role. All three types may be refuelled in the air.

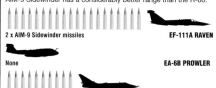

EF-111A RAVEN	2990 km (1,854 mi.)
EA-6B PROWLER	1769 km (1,096 mi.)
Su-24MP 'FENCER-F'	1300 km (806 mi.)

GRUMMAN

S-2E/F/G/UP TRACKER

● 1950s design ● US and foreign service ● Turbine conversions

T he first carrier-borne anti-submarine aircraft to combine the 'hunter' and 'killer' functions, detecting and tracking submarines and attacking them with bombs and depth charges, the S-2 Tracker entered US Navy service in 1954. The Tracker seemed an ideal counter to the Soviet Union's vast fleet of attack submarines threatening US warships. Many were exported and a few remain in service, some fitted with new engines and avionics.

▲ *While originally intended as a carrierborne aircraft, most S-2s that are still in service are land-based and equip the navies of smaller nations which require an affordable ASW platform.*

GRUMMAN S-2E/F/G/UP TRACKER

▼ **Folding wings**
Designed to operate aboard aircraft-carriers, the S-2 has folding wings to ease storage below deck. Until recently Canada operated its S-2s in this low-visibility dark grey colour scheme.

▲ **Prototype Turbo Tracker**
Built as an S2F-3S (S-2E after 1962) and retired by the US Navy years before its designation changed, this S-2T still carries US Navy markings. Taiwan's conversions were completed under a USN Foreign Military Sales contract.

▼ **Argentine S-2A**
Having retired its S-2As, Argentina is having its S-2Es refurbished by Israel Aircraft Industries.

▲ **Republic of China naval service**
Taiwan's original fleet of S-2Es and Fs has been retired or converted. This example has now received turbine engines.

◀ **Fire-bomber S-2F1T**
Marsh Aviation offers turboprop conversions for both civil fire-bomber and military aircraft.

FACTS AND FIGURES

➤ The first S2F Tracker completed its maiden flight from Long Island, New York, on 4 December 1952.

➤ Navy crews nicknamed the Tracker the 'Stoof' after its S2F designation.

➤ The first S-2G conversion was undertaken by Martin, the rest by the Navy using kits.

➤ In all, 1269 Trackers were built, including 100 under licence by de Havilland Aircraft of Canada.

➤ The S-2G variant was modified to carry Bullpup air-to-surface missiles.

➤ Marsh S-2 turboprop conversions employ a five-bladed propeller.

PROFILE

Breathing new life into the 'Stoof'

By the early 1960s, the S-2 had been in US Navy service for almost 10 years. In 1962 the new S-2E variant was introduced. This benefited from AQA-3 'Jezebel' passive long-range acoustic search equipment used in conjunction with a 'Julie' active acoustic echo-ranging by explosive charge device. The equipment was installed in the lengthened S-2D airframe, which offered more internal room than earlier versions.

The S-2F (an S-2B with 'Jezebel' and 'Julie' fitted) followed. In 1972, 50 S-3Es were converted to the more capable S-2G, an interim aircraft pending the introduction of the all-new Lockheed S-3 Viking. These were the last carrier-borne USN Trackers and made their final cruise in 1975.

The Tracker was eagerly snapped up by foreign navies, with surplus S-2Es and Gs going to Australia, Turkey and various Asian and South American nations. An affordable anti-submarine platform, the Tracker has become a candidate for major upgrades with new engines and avionics gear. Argentina, Brazil and Taiwan have taken delivery of rebuilt Turbo Trackers.

Above: Taiwan's Trackers carry one of two colour schemes, either grey or two-tone blue and dark grey. All were surplus ex-US Navy aircraft.

Right: Brazil continues to fly S-2Es and re-engined S-2Ts from its carrier Minas Gerais. Operated by the air force, they are designated P-16E and P-16T.

S-2T TURBO TRACKER

Taiwan ordered 32 S-2T conversions, the first two of which were carried out by Grumman and delivered in 1989. The remainder were tackled in Taiwan using kit sets of parts.

Tracker variants from the S-2D onwards had a lengthened forward fuselage with accommodation for two pilots and two radar operators. New navigation systems and radios are fitted as part of the S-2T conversion.

A key change made in the S-2T is the replacement of the original Wright R-1820 Cyclone 9 piston engines with 1227-kW (1,645-hp.) Garrett TPE331 turboprops, which produce about 10 per cent more power. Pratt & Whitney Canada PT6As have also been offered in other conversion packages.

The new engines and their Dowty advanced technology four-bladed propellers boost top speed to 500 km/h (310 m.p.h.) at 1525 m (5,000 ft.) and the payload by 500 kg (1,100 lb.). Cruising speed, field length, single-engined performance and time-between-overhauls are also improved.

As well as having new engines, the Tracker has improved avionics. These include the magnetic anomaly detector (MAD) and radar as well as the acoustic receivers and processors.

The later versions of the Tracker (from S-2D) had a longer wing span, enlarged tail surfaces and greater fuel capacity.

2143

S-2E Tracker

Type: carrier-borne anti-submarine warfare aircraft

Powerplant: two 1137-kW (1,525-hp.) Wright R-1820-82WA Cyclone radial piston engines.

Maximum speed: 426 km/h (264 m.p.h.) at sea level

Patrol speed: 241 km/h (149 m.p.h.) at 455 m (1,500 ft.)

Endurance: 9 hours with maximum fuel and 10 per cent reserves

Weights: empty 8505 kg (18,711 lb.); maximum take-off 13,222 kg (29,088 lb.)

Armament: one Mk 47 or Mk 101 nuclear depth charge or similar in weapons bay, 60 depth charges in fuselage, 32 sonobuoys in engine nacelles, plus a variety of bombs, rockets or torpedoes on six underwing hardpoints

Dimensions:
span	22.12 m	(72 ft. 7 in.)
length	13.26 m	(43 ft. 6 in.)
height	5.05 m	(16 ft. 7 in.)
wing area	46.08 m²	(496 sq. ft.)

ACTION DATA

PATROL SPEED

Contemporary carrier-borne ASW types include the Fairey Gannet and Breguet Alizé, only the latter of which remains in service along with a small numbers of Trackers. A great deal of ship-borne ASW work is now carried out by helicopters like the Sea King.

S-2E TRACKER	241 km/h (149 m.p.h.)
BR.1150 ALIZÉ	232 km/h (144 m.p.h.)
SEA KING Mk 42B	90 km/h (56 m.p.h.)

ENDURANCE

Larger fixed-wing aircraft have a considerably longer endurance than helicopters and operate at greater distances from the carrier or land base. The Alizé is smaller than the Tracker and thus carries less fuel, hence its shorter endurance.

S-2E TRACKER	BR.1150 ALIZÉ	SEA KING Mk 42B
9 hours	7 hours 35 min	3 hours

CLIMB RATE

A better climb rate than any fixed-wing aircraft is inherent in the design of a helicopter, due to its ability to rise vertically. The Tracker and Alizé have comparable climb rates, which are fairly typical for this type and size of aircraft.

S-2E TRACKER 425 m/min (1,400 f.p.m.)
BR.1150 ALIZÉ 420 m/min (1,380 f.p.m.)
SEA KING Mk 42B 661 m/min (2,170 f.p.m.)

Post-war US Navy ASW aircraft

■ **GRUMMAN AF GUARDIAN:** A replacement for the TBM Avenger, there were two versions of the AF, the radar-equipped AF-2W 'hunter' (below) and the weapon-carrying AF-2S 'killer'.

■ **GRUMMAN TBM-3E:** Famous during World War II as a torpedo-bomber, the TBM was used after the war by the US Navy as an anti-submarine aircraft equipped with radar.

■ **LOCKHEED S-3 VIKING:** The only carrier-borne type ever produced by Lockheed, the jet-powered Viking replaced the S-2 from 1974 and is still in service.

GRUMMAN

A-6 INTRUDER

● Classic naval aircraft ● Three decades of service ● Many upgrades

▲ A familiar sight on US carrier decks in both Navy and Marine Corps markings, the A-6 proved a highly capable aircraft in many combat actions.

On 28 February 1997 a ceremony was held at NAS (Naval Air Station) Whidbey Island to celebrate the retirement of the A-6 Intruder from the US Navy. The aircraft had provided more than three decades of service, most recently by A-6E variants equipped with advanced laser and infra-red (IR) targeting systems. In the course of its career the A-6 was involved in several combat actions and fought superbly during the first Gulf War.

GRUMMAN A-6 INTRUDER

▲ HARM compatibility
From 1990 the A-6E was given AGM-88 HARM (High-Speed Anti-Radiation Missile) capability.

◄ Into the storm
Wearing mission symbols and heavily armed, this A-6E prepares for launch on a Desert Storm raid.

▲ Intruder's last war
Both A-6E strike aircraft and KA-6D tankers were involved in the 1991 Gulf War.

▼ Tacit Rainbow
Designed to attack enemy radars, the AGM-136 Tacit Rainbow was tested on this A-6E.

▲ Protecting the Kurds
After the Gulf War Intruders were involved in Operation 'Provide Comfort' – the protection of Kurdish people returning to Northern Iraq.

FACTS AND FIGURES

➤ VA-75 squadron introduced the Intruder into service in 1963 and was the last unit to fly the type in 1997.

➤ Neither the advanced A-6F nor the cheaper A-6G entered production.

➤ F/A-18C/D Hornets currently undertake the missions once flown by Intruders.

➤ Several US Marine Corps A-6Es were passed to the Navy when the Marines retired their A-6s.

➤ The US Navy and Marines Corps intend to replace their A-6Es with F/A-18E/Fs.

➤ Some 240 A-6As became A-6Es; 12 were built per year between 1972 and 1977.

PROFILE

At the front line to the last

New avionics and radar were primary features of the A-6E Intruder when it first flew in 1970. In order to achieve rapid procurement of the new model within a limited budget, the US Navy began a programme of upgrading A-6As to the higher standard while new A-6Es were being built.

Further upgrades were added to the Intruder, including a navigation system that was used in the F-14A Tomcat. The most important modification, however,

was the addition of a Target Recognition Attack Multi-sensor (TRAM) turret beneath the nose. This contained laser, IR and video sensors, allowing accurate targeting and compatibility with smart, laser-guided munitions.

A programme to fit the A-6 fleet with new composite wings was started in 1988. In addition, the capability to fire stand-off missiles, including the AGM-84E SLAM, was added in the early 1990s, making the last of the Intruders highly capable attack platforms.

A removable air-to-air refuelling probe was normally mounted on the centreline, aft of the nose radome. Refuelling was possible from KA-6Ds and other hose-equipped tankers.

Short-sighted US Navy officials cancelled the formidable A-6F in favour of the A-12. This was later scrapped.

Early in the Intruder programme, it was realised that the rear fuselage-mounted airbrakes interfered with airflow around the tail. Hence split airbrakes were employed at each wingtip.

Intruders proved vulnerable to small-arms fire over Vietnam, a problem which was to surface again when the type was used at low level in the Gulf. The prominent exhausts could also attract heat-seeking surface-to-air missiles.

For stowage aboard the carrier, the Intruder's wings were folded hydraulically at a hinge line just outboard of the outer pylon.

A-6E Intruder

Type: all-weather shipborne attack aircraft

Powerplant: two 41.40-kN (9,040-lb.-thrust) Pratt & Whitney J52-P-8B turbojets

Maximum speed: 1037 km/h (643 m.p.h.) clean at sea level

Maximum climb rate: 2323 m/min (7,620 f.p.m.)

Range: 1627 km (1,008 mi.) with maximum military load; ferry range 5222 km (3,240 mi.)

Service ceiling: 12,925 m (42,400 ft.)

Weights: empty 12,132 kg (26,690 lb.); maximum for catapult launch 26,580 kg (58,478 lb.)

Armament: a maximum of 8165 kg (17,963 lb.) ordnance and external fuel

Dimensions:
span 16.15 m (53 ft.)
length 16.69 m (54 ft. 9 in.)
height 4.93 m (16 ft. 2 in.)
wing area 49.13 m² (529 sq. ft.)

A-6E INTRUDER

In service with VA-42 'Green Pawns', this A-6E wears the low-visibility camouflage which was common at the end of the type's career. VA-42 was the Atlantic Fleet Replenishment Squadron.

Both the pilot and navigator sat on Martin-Baker GRU-7 ejector seats. The bombardier/navigator was positioned to starboard, slightly below and behind the pilot, and was responsible for operating the attack systems.

FLIR and laser-designator systems were located in the TRAM turret, at the heart of the A-6E's attack avionics.

Shown here with a load of 18 Mk 82 227-kg (500-lb.) bombs, the A-6E was also able to carry stand-off weapons such as the AGM-84E SLAM.

Single-piece, all-moving tailplanes provided pitch control and all flying controls were hydraulically powered. The pipe beneath the rudder hinge line allowed fuel to be jettisoned from the fuselage tanks.

COMBAT DATA

THRUST

With its afterburning engines, the F/A-18C is a more powerful aircraft than the A-6E or A-7E which it has replaced. It has shorter range than the A-6E, however.

A-6E INTRUDER 82.80 kN (18,080 lb. thrust)

A-7E CORSAIR II 66.60 kN (14,982 lb. thrust)

F/A-18C HORNET 142.40 kN (32,034 lb. thrust)

BOMBLOAD

As a dedicated attack aircraft, the A-6E could carry a formidable bombload. The A-7E was the US Navy's second attack platform, but did not have the weapons-carrying ability of the A-6E.

A-6E INTRUDER 8165 kg

A-7E CORSAIR II 6804 kg

F/A-18C HORNET 7031 kg

INITIAL CLIMB RATE

Comparing aircraft in clean condition, the F/A-18C has by far the most impressive climb rate. When the F/A-18E/F is introduced, the Navy hopes to overcome the range deficiencies of the F/A-18C/D.

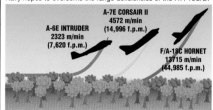

A-7E CORSAIR II 4572 m/min (14,996 f.p.m.)

A-6E INTRUDER 2323 m/min (7,620 f.p.m.)

F/A-18C HORNET 13715 m/min (44,985 f.p.m.)

TRAM attack

Gyro-stabilisation allows the TRAM turret to remain locked on to the target, even as the aircraft overflies it.

1 TARGETING INFORMATION: Using its Forward-Looking Infra-Red (FLIR) and laser-targeting systems, the A-6E is able to calculate precise targeting information for dumb or laser-guided munitions.

2 OVER THE TARGET: FLIR allows the A-6E to attack the hottest parts of a target; the engine room of a ship or a moving tank. The TRAM turret rotates to keep the target designated and in view of the IR system.

3 POST-STRIKE ASSESSMENT: After the attack the FLIR is able to look backwards from the turret. TV-like pictures are produced, which are viewed in the cockpit and recorded by an onboard video recorder for damage assessment.

GRUMMAN
EA-6B PROWLER

● Electronic warfare aircraft ● In combat from Vietnam to the Gulf

▲ *The jamming systems of the EA-6B are some of the most sophisticated in the world. A handful of these aircraft can 'black out' an area the size of France with their powerful electronic systems.*

Based on the Grumman A-6 Intruder, the EA-6B Prowler harnesses the electron to 'clean up' combat zones so that friendly warplanes can attack in safety. The Prowler takes a pilot and three operators into action with a powerhouse of 'black boxes', intent on jamming an enemy's radar. But it does more than jam; with its HARM missiles, the EA-6 is a fearsome radar-killer in its own right.

GRUMMAN EA-6B PROWLER

▼ **Electronic power**
The Prowler's systems are never turned on when it is on deck, as they emit enough energy to microwave anyone passing by.

▲ **ADVCAP Prowler**
In 1990 the advanced capability (ADVCAP) variant of the EA-6B was introduced. This is fitted with a global positioning kit for pinpoint navigation, and chaff, flare and self-protection jamming systems.

Folding wings ▶
With its wings folded up, the EA-6 has a narrow profile. Under the fixed wingroot is the massive TJS jamming pod, containing a high-powered noise generator and a tracking receiver. Operating power is generated by a wind turbine on the pod's nose.

▼ **Gulf strike mission**
Prowlers were vital components in the first Gulf war, protecting the massive Coalition air offensive which destroyed Saddam Hussein's air defences.

▲ **Catapult launch**
The EA-6B is a heavy machine, and a catapult launch is essential for it to reach flying speed. If for any reason the launch fails, the four-man crew will instantly eject as the aircraft clears the deck.

FACTS AND FIGURES

➤ The first EA-6 Prowler flew at Calverton, New York, on 25 May 1968.

➤ The Prowler has a black radiation warning symbol on its nose so that deck crews do not get 'fried' inadvertently.

➤ Home port for Navy EA-6Bs is Whidbey Island Naval Air Station, north of Seattle.

➤ The Prowler has been through five electronics upgrade programmes.

➤ When the EF-111 Raven fleet was retired in 1998, EA-6Bs were deployed in their place.

➤ The HARM missile used by some Prowlers has a launch weight of 361 kg (749 lb.).

Jamming with the fleet

Prowlers are in short supply and are sorely needed. Modern air power demands electronic warfare aircraft, and the US Navy developed the Grumman EA-6B to give its Carrier Air Wings a trump card in today's hi-tech warfare. The Prowler fought in Vietnam (1972), and in every action since – Grenada (1983), Libya (1986), both Gulf Wars, Bosnia (1995) and Afghanistan. The final Prowler was delivered

in 1991 and the final 'upgrade' programme curtailed two years later. The Prowler is 1.37 metres longer than the A-6 Intruder and substantially heavier. It sends out jamming transmissions from underwing pods, and analyses hostile signals received by equipment in a bulge on its tail.

Although well into middle age, the Prowler remains one of the best electronic warriors and saw service in Afghanistan

The Prowler is one of the most expensive aircraft in the US Navy inventory. The huge cost of the EA-6B is offset, however, by the lives and aircraft saved by the protection it can provide.

and the 2003 Gulf War. Prowlers replaced US Air Force EF-111 Ravens even though Prowlers are slower and lack the Raven's 'reach' to accompany strike aircraft on some missions.

The pilot sits in the front port cockpit, surrounded by three electronic countermeasures officers (ECMOs). ECMO one sits by his side and operates the navigation, radar and communications equipment, with ECMO two and three operating the tactical jamming suite.

ECMO two operates the ground-mapping Norden APS-130 radar system, a downgraded version of the A-6E's APQ-156 with attack functions deleted.

The large HARM missile has a passive seeker head and can be used in standby or pre-programmed modes.

The EA-6B has wingtip speed brakes, similar to those of the Sukhoi Su-25 'Frogfoot'.

The Prowler has wing spoilers for primary roll control, assisted by flaperons at low speeds. The large flaps are almost full-span, and the wing has upper-surface blowing to increase lift at low airspeeds.

EA-6B PROWLER

This EA-6B 'ICAP-II' Prowler flies with VMAQ-2, one of four US Marine Corps squadrons based at the Marine Corps Air Station, Cherry Point. The unit is fully carrier-capable and often deploys with the fleet.

The large pod on top of the tail fin houses the system integration receiver, which detects hostile radar emissions and sends them to a central computer for threat analysis.

163031

Cy

VMAQ-2 MARINES

17

Self-protection jamming to decoy enemy radar-guided missiles is provided by a deception jamming suite. The antenna for this is located next to the refuelling probe.

The ICAP-II improvement programme allows the pair of underwing TJS pods to jam in any one of seven frequency bands. They can also simultaneously interfere with more than one enemy radar, even when they are using widely different frequencies.

The Prowler can carry an internal fuel load of 6995 kg (15,390 lb.), with 4547 kg (10,000 lb.) in underwing tanks.

A large avionics pallet and fuel tanks occupy the fuselage area behind the engines. The J52 turbojet was also used in the McDonnell Douglas A-4 Skyhawk.

The aft-facing cylindrical pod on the fin is the ALQ-136 deception countermeasures system, known as the 'beercan' to crews.

EA-6B Prowler

Type: four-seat electronic warfare aircraft

Powerplant: two Pratt & Whitney 49.80-kN (9,300-lb.-thrust) J52-P-408 turbojets

Maximum speed: 1048 km/h (650 m.p.h.) in 'clean' condition at sea level

Range: 1770 km (1,097 mi.)

Service ceiling: 12,550 m (41,164 ft.)

Weights: empty 14,588 kg (32,028 lb.); loaded 24,703 kg (54,347 lb.)

Payload: four AGM-88A HARM (High-speed Anti-Radiation Missiles), AN/ALQ-99 emitter pods, or Aero 1-D 1136-litre (300-gal.) drop-tanks; some with AN/ALQ-149 jamming system

Dimensions:
span	16.15 m (53 ft.)
length	18.24 m (60 ft.)
height	4.95 m (16 ft.)
wing area	49.13 m² (529 sq. ft.)

COMBAT DATA

MAXIMUM SPEED

The Prowler was derived from a subsonic carrier bomber which was able to fly and fight in all weathers, by day or night. The EA-6 lacks the Mach 2 performance of the EF-111, but since its main function is to escort formations of heavily-laden strike aircraft at subsonic speeds this is no real handicap.

EA-6B PROWLER
1048 km/h (650 m.p.h.)

EF-111 RAVEN
2272 km/h (1,409 m.p.h.)

Yak-28 'BREWER-E'
1200 km/h (744 m.p.h.)

RANGE

The EA-6 has a shorter range than its land-based equivalents. Nevertheless, thanks to its ability to launch from a carrier anywhere on the world's oceans it can reach a much greater range of potential targets than aircraft like the EF-111, which can only operate from a few high-tech air bases.

EF-111 RAVEN
3000 km (1,860 mi.)

EA-6B PROWLER
1770 km (1,087 mi.)

Yak-28 'BREWER-E'
1900 km (1,078 mi.)

ELECTRONIC WARFARE CAPABILITY

The Prowler and the EF-111 have a similar electronics fit, but the 'Spark Vark' is a more recent adaptation, and greater computerisation means that one electronic warfare officer can do the job of three aboard the Prowler. Both are a great deal more sophisticated than the 'Brewer', which was operational with Soviet forces until the break-up of the USSR.

EF-111 RAVEN
EA-6B PROWLER
100% **90%**
40%
Yak-28 'BREWER-E'

Location of enemy radar transmitters

Prowlers will often operate in pairs, both to produce wider and more powerful jamming transmissions and, as depicted here, to locate and fix enemy radar sites.

LEAD PROWLER: ➤ One aircraft flies close enough to the enemy to persuade him to activate his radar. The 'senso' notes the exact bearing of the enemy transmitter.

◀ **TRAILING PROWLER:** Close enough to pick up the enemy radar, but far enough behind for any radar beams to be too weak to return an echo to the enemy, the second Prowler also notes the bearing of the radar site.

MISSION ACCOMPLISHED: Once the two Prowlers have noted the radar's bearing, they can turn away before coming within range of enemy missile defences.

LOCATION FIXED: A simple triangulation calculation exactly fixes the location of the enemy radar.

GRUMMAN

C-2A GREYHOUND

● COD aircraft ● Derived from the E-2 Hawkeye ● Twin turboprop

During the 1960s Grumman built the Greyhound for hauling supplies and people from land bases to the decks of the US Navy's aircraft-carriers. This is known in jargon as the COD (carrier on-board delivery) mission. The Greyhound draws its fundamental design features from the better-known Grumman E-2 Hawkeye airborne early-warning aircraft. It is a superb aircraft with a fine record of safety and performance.

▲ *The US Navy's C-2 Greyhound fleet was delivered in two batches, beginning in the mid-1960s and ending in the late 1980s. Most of the original batch have now been retired.*

PHOTO FILE

GRUMMAN C-2A GREYHOUND

▼ **Atlantic and Pacific C-2s**
Two transport units are equipped with C-2s and are based in the US. A detachment is also stationed in Japan. Training is carried out at NAS Norfolk, Virginia.

▲ **Carrier on-board delivery**
COD squadrons are attached to Hawkeye-equipped airborne early warning wings.

◄ **Folding wings for easy stowage**
The Greyhound has the same wing as the E-2 Hawkeye. Wing folding is a necessity for aircraft moving within the confines of a fleet carrier.

▼ **Mail call**
One of the Greyhound's most important deliveries, at least from the sailors' point of view, is the cargo of mail for crews.

▼ **Different cargoes**
As well as ferrying personnel, the C-2 delivers weapons for the carrier's combat aircraft. Among the weapons shown here are three AIM-54 Phoenix air-to-air missiles for an F-14 Tomcat.

FACTS AND FIGURES

➤ The Greyhound prototype completed its maiden flight on 18 November 1964.

➤ Fifty-eight Greyhounds were produced in two batches – between 1964 and 1968 and between 1985 and 1989.

➤ A proposal to re-open the Greyhound production line was rejected in 1991.

➤ Plans to replace the Greyhound with a version of the Lockheed S-3A Viking met with only limited success.

➤ The C-2A replaced the Grumman C-1A Trader, which was based on the S-2.

➤ Grumman considered a jet-powered version of the C-2 but it was never built.

PROFILE

Delivery van of the US Fleet

The Grumman C-2A Greyhound was developed in the early 1960s by mating a deeper, more capacious fuselage to the basic wings and tail of the E-2 Hawkeye. The result was a highly effective transport for the essential task of delivering supplies to aircraft-carriers at sea.

Although it is equipped with a tailhook and folding wings for carrier operations, the Greyhound is not intended to be stationed aboard a carrier. Instead, it is operated by a shore-based squadron placed in a strategic location to resupply ships at sea. The C-2A Greyhound is also successful in its secondary duty as a training aircraft, and has been used for training Hawkeye crews.

Before the cockpits of combat aircraft were opened up to women in 1993, the Greyhound was one of the very few carrier-capable aeroplanes to be flown by female pilots. Unlike the crews of fighters and bombers, these transport pilots fly a real-world mission every time they take off and land. Great care has to be taken when landing the Greyhound on an aircraft-carrier because its large wingspan leaves little room for manoeuvre on a crowded deck. But, for its size, the Greyhound is relatively easy to fly.

Above: Carrying the 'RG' tailcode of the since-disestablished VRC-50, this Greyhound was based at Cubi Point in the Philippines.

Below: This photograph of 162153, one of the batch built in the 1980s, shows the wing and tail design to good effect. These are shared by the E-2 Hawkeye.

C-2A Greyhound

Type: twin-engine carrier onboard delivery (COD) transport

Powerplant: two 3663-kW (4,900-hp.) Allison T56-A-425 turboprop engines

Maximum speed: 574 km/h (356 m.p.h.)

Range: 1930 km (1,792 mi.)

Service ceiling: 10,210 m (33,500 ft.)

Weights: empty 16,486 kg (36,269 lb.); maximum take-off 26,081 kg (57,378 lb.)

Accommodation: two pilots, up to 39 passengers or 20 stretchers plus four attendants or up to 6800 kg (14,960 lb.) of palletised cargo

Dimensions:
span	24.56 m	(80 ft. 6 in.)
length	17.32 m	(56 ft. 10 in.)
height	4.84 m	(15 ft. 10 in.)
wing area	65.03 m² (700 sq. ft.)	

C-2A GREYHOUND

Aircraft 155124 was one of the original batch of 19 Greyhounds delivered from the mid-1960s. 'JM' is the tailcode of Fleet Logistics Support Squadron 24 (VR-24), 'Lifting Eagles', based at Sigonella, Italy.

In all, including prototypes, 58 Greyhounds have been delivered to the US Navy. The 39 built in the 1980s differ from earlier C-2s in having uprated engines and an auxiliary power unit fitted.

The Greyhound's engines are the same 3663-kW (4,900-hp.) Allison T56-A-425 turbines as those fitted to the E-2C Hawkeye. This commonality between the two aircraft eases maintenance and reduces the need to carry different spare parts in the cramped confines of an aircraft-carrier.

Redesigned for the transport role, the Greyhound's fuselage is considerably larger than that of the Hawkeye. When configured for passengers, the Greyhound can carry up to 39 people. Twenty stretchers can also be installed.

The tail design is another feature shared with the E-2. Four fins are required to provide sufficient tail area, but must still fit within the cramped confines of the carrier hangar. All except the port inner fin have a rudder fitted.

Mission profiles for the Greyhound centre on its role for the delivery of high-priority cargo and passengers to and from carriers at sea. Its range of 1900 km (1,180 mi.) when fully loaded is far greater than that of land-based helicopters.

For the loading of bulky items like aircraft engines and weapons, the C-2 has a rear ramp. An arrester hook is fitted for carrier landings.

ACTION DATA

LOAD CAPACITY

The tilt-rotor Osprey, if funded, will greatly enhance the COD capabilities of the fleet. It has almost twice the capacity of the C-2. For land-based operations the C-2 has a maximum load of 6800 kg. The Viking, based on the S-3 ASW aircraft, has a limited capacity.

C-2A GREYHOUND	6800 kg (14,960 lb.)
V-22A OSPREY	9072 kg (19,958 lb.)
US-3A VIKING	2600 kg (5,720 lb.)

RANGE

When fully loaded and making a short take-off, the Osprey has an impressive range performance – an improvement on that of the C-2. The US-3A also has an excellent range.

C-2A GREYHOUND 1930 km (1,197 mi.)
US-3A VIKING 3700 km (2,294 mi.)
V-22A OSPREY 3336 km (2,068 mi.)

TAKE-OFF RUN

The Viking has the shorter take-off distance of the two fixed-wing aircraft. The Osprey tilt-rotor has a vertical take-off capability, but uses a short take-off run when carrying all but the smallest payloads.

C-2A GREYHOUND	932 m (3,057 ft.)
V-22A OSPREY	152 m (499 ft.)
US-3A VIKING	670 m (2,198 ft.)

Carrier on-board delivery aircraft

■ **GRUMMAN TBM-3R AVENGER:** As well as carrying personnel, COD Avengers delivered nuclear weapon components in times of crisis.

■ **GRUMMAN C-1 TRADER:** The Trader was a variant of the S-2 Tracker, which had its ASW equipment removed to make room for freight.

■ **GRUMMAN US-3A VIKING:** To supplement the C-2 fleet, a small number of anti-submarine S-3A Vikings have been converted for COD tasks.

■ **FAIREY GANNET COD.Mk 4:** In common with American COD designs, the British Gannet COD.Mk 4 was based on an existing design.

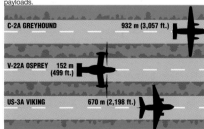

GRUMMAN

E-2 HAWKEYE

● Combat proven ● Airborne early warning ● Fighter controller

D esigned as a flying radar station, the Hawkeye is the US Navy's eye in the sky. Sometimes called 'the affordable AWACS' (Airborne Warning and Control System), it is just what the US Navy requires to guard its aircraft-carrier battle groups and to direct friendly warplanes when the action begins. This twin-engined aircraft, with its long, slender wing, huge tail, and saucer-shaped rotodome, is now a familiar sight in every US Navy carrier air wing.

▲ Throughout 22 years of service the E-2 Hawkeye has become an indispensable part of US naval operations. The latest E-2C Group II aircraft are far more capable and are likely to remain in use for some time.

PHOTO FILE

GRUMMAN E-2 HAWKEYE

▼ Fuel venting
An anonymous E-2, probably flying a research and development mission, dumps fuel from the rear-mounted fuel vent pipe.

▲ Rotodome
An E-2C from USS Constellation shows off its enormous radar rotodome.

Catapult launch ▶
The Hawkeye runs its engines up to full power before the steam catapult hurls it from the carrier deck at take-off speed.

▼ Feet-dry Hawkeye
All US Navy E-2s have a permanent shore base and most export customers fly their E-2s solely from airbases. This aircraft flies from NAS Norfolk, Virginia.

▲ Folded Hawkeye
With its wings folded the Hawkeye presents a more compact shape for stowage aboard the crowded decks of an aircraft-carrier.

FACTS AND FIGURES

➤ The Hawkeye was the last propeller-driven naval aircraft built by Grumman, the world's primary naval aircraft builder.

➤ In December 1971 Israel purchased four Hawkeyes equipped with APS-125 radar.

➤ Other users of the Hawkeye include Egypt, Japan, Singapore and Taiwan.

➤ The Hawkeye made its first flight from Grumman's Peconic River, Long Island, facility on 21 October 1960.

➤ The Hawkeye is now back in production, equipped with the AN/APS-145 radar.

➤ Hawkeyes are launched ahead of other carrier aircraft and are the last to return.

PROFILE

Eyes of the fleet

Nicknamed the 'Hummer' by its crews, the E-2 Hawkeye was designed to replace the earlier E-1B Tracer, the first radar plane in the fleet. The Hawkeye, with turboprop engines, a higher speed and a higher ceiling, was a great improvement over its predecessor. The Hawkeye introduced a General Electric APS-96 radar, the antenna of which revolves at six revolutions per minute inside the disc shaped radome. The first production Hawkeyes began

reaching squadron VAW-110 'Firebirds' based at North Island, California, in 1964. In Vietnam, the Hawkeye performed its primary mission of protecting aircraft-carriers with its radar 'eyes', but it also served as a flying headquarters for F-4 Phantom IIs and F-8 Crusaders on combat air patrols.
The Hawkeye's radar unit has

changed again, to APS-138, APS-139 and APS-145. The APS-145, now being retrofitted to aircraft in the fleet, offers better resistance to jamming. Although it is now getting old, the present E-2C Hawkeye is an up-to-date, state-of-the-art military fighting machine.

Japan received the first of its E-2s in 1982 and it is known as Daya (kite) in Japanese service. Several countries fly the E-2, including Egypt, Israel and Singapore.

Avionics systems create a vast amount of heat and must be kept cool to maintain their efficiency. A large dorsal radiator cools the fluid of the E-2's cooling system.

Remaining on station for four hours, 300 km (186 mi.) from the carrier and without inflight refuelling, the Hawkeye requires long endurance. This is achieved by its long, slender wings.

E-2C Hawkeye

Type: carrier-based airborne early warning aircraft

Powerplant: two 3661-kW (4,910-hp.) Allison T56-A425 turboprop engines

Maximum speed: 598 km/h (374 m.p.h.)

Endurance: 6 hours 6 min

Ferry range: 2583 km (1,602 mi.)

Service ceiling: 9390 m (30,000 ft.)

Weight: maximum take-off 23556 kg (51,900 lb.)

Accommodation: crew of five; fuel load of 5624 kg (12,399 lb.)

Dimensions:
span	24.56 m (80 ft. 7 in.)
length	17.54 m (57 ft. 7 in.)
height	5.58 m (18 ft. 3 in.)
wing area	65.03 m² (2,593 sq. ft.)

E-2C HAWKEYE

This aircraft belongs to VAW-126 'Seahawks', part of CVW-3, aboard the USS *John F. Kennedy*. The unit is home based at NAS Norfolk, Virginia, and proved invaluable during Operation Desert Storm.

A crew of five is normally carried, including pilot and co-pilot, a combat information centre officer, air control officer and radar operator.

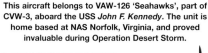

With a diameter of 7.32 m (24 ft.) the rotodome houses the AN/APS-139 radar and 'identification friend or foe' systems. It is lowered on jacks for parking on the carrier.

A four-fin tail arrangement was required to give the Hawkeye sufficient directional stability, but the tail had to be small enough to fit in a carrier's hangar.

Very strong undercarriage units are features of all ship-borne aircraft designed to be launched by steam catapult. This bar on the nosewheel leg connects with the catapult shuttle on the deck.

Although the original E-2C was powered by the 3661-kW (4,910-hp.) T56-A-425, the latest E-2C Group IIs are fitted with the even more powerful 3803-kW (5,096-hp.) T56-A-427.

US Navy E-2Cs have been slow to take on the low-visibility markings of the rest of the fleet, retaining colourful squadron markings and grey and white camouflage.

COMBAT DATA

SERVICE CEILING
The Hawkeye requires a good service ceiling because the higher the radar is, the further it can see. The E-2 is being fitted with the exceptional AN/APS-145 radar, giving it stunning performance.

E-2C HAWKEYE 9390 m (30,000 ft.)

P-3 AEW ORION 8625 m (28,297 ft.)

E-3C SENTRY 8840 m (29,003 ft.)

RADAR RANGE
Using the latest AN/APS-145 radar the P-3 AEW will be able to locate low-flying aircraft targets at very long range. In its E-3D and E-3F variants the Sentry is much more capable than the E-3C.

E-2C HAWKEYE 480 km (300 mi.)

P-3 AEW ORION 556 km (345 mi.)

E-3C SENTRY 470 km (291 mi.)

CREW
As it is a small aircraft the E-2C carries few crew. This means a necessary reliance on automation and a heavy workload for operators. In larger aircraft there are more crew to divide the work between.

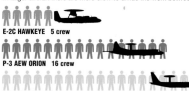

E-2C HAWKEYE 5 crew

P-3 AEW ORION 16 crew

E-3C SENTRY 20 crew

Controlling the air war

OVER THE HORIZON: Acting as an extension of the aircraft-carrier's own radar, the E-2C is able to monitor possible threats at greater distances.

AIRBORNE CONTROLLER: When the E-2 detects enemy aircraft or anti-ship missiles (ASMs) it alerts F-14 Tomcats, which are sent on barrier combat air patrol to intercept.

F-14

E-2

9150 m (30,000 ft.)

AIRCRAFT-CARRIER

Tu-22M

ASM

RANGE km	900	800	700	600	500	400	300	200	100
miles	500		400		300		200		100

GRUMMAN
F-14A TOMCAT

● Long-range fleet interceptor ● Recon platform ● Fighter bomber

▲ Tomcat aircrew are an elite
within an elite. The pilot and backseat Naval Flight
Officer act as a carefully co-ordinated team to wring the
best from the awesome combination of performance,
sophistication and firepower at their command.

With its high speed and ultra-long-range weapons, the Tomcat is the main defender of the US fleet and can operate hundreds of miles away from the carrier. Its AWG-9 radar can engage six targets at once and its Phoenix missiles can kill hostile bombers 150 km away before they can launch their attacks. The Tomcat is one of the world's true 'Top Guns'.

GRUMMAN F-14A TOMCAT

▲ **Fleet defender**
The main threat to US Navy carriers is posed by long-range bombers armed with sea-skimming missiles. Only the Tomcat can intercept the bombers before they get within lethal range.

▲ **Power to protect**
The F-14's high-thrust TF-30 turbofans and swing wing allow it to operate from short carrier decks. Take-offs are made using a powerful steam catapult.

▼ **Detecting the enemy**
As well as its own radar, the F-14 operates with an E-2 Hawkeye, a flying radar station with a huge rotating antenna above the fuselage.

Deadly performer ▶
The F-14 has Mach 2+ performance, a sparkling rate of climb and good manoeuvrability – all the hallmarks of a great fighter.

▲**Combat-proven**
The F-14 opened its score on 19 August 1981, when F-14 pilots Lt Larry Muszynski (above left) and Cdr Hank Kleeman of VF-41 'Black Aces' squadron destroyed a pair of marauding Libyan Sukhoi Su-22 'Fitters'. Two MiG-23s fell to F-14s in a similar incident during 1989.

FACTS AND FIGURES

➤ The Tomcat's AWG-9 radar can detect, track and engage targets at ranges of more than 150 km (93 mi.).

➤ One Tomcat can engage the same number of targets as three F/A-18 Hornets.

➤ The AIM-54C Phoenix is the world's longest-range air-to-air missile.

➤ The Tomcat's high magnification TV camera enables visual target identification at more than 50 km (30 mi.).

➤ Forming the outer edge of a battle group's defences, the Tomcat can engage enemy bombers and missiles more than 800 km (497 mi.) out from its home carrier.

PROFILE

Defender of the fleet

The Tomcat has been one of the great superfighters of the world since its first squadron took to the skies in 1972. It packs a massive punch, performs superbly and is the warplane of choice for many aspiring military pilots. Nothing is more calculated to worry an enemy than to know Tomcats are on his track.

And yet this tremendous fighting machine can operate from a 110-m (360-ft.) strip of aircraft carrier deck, in all weathers and around the clock.

Working with E-2C Hawkeye radar planes and using air-to-air refuelling, a squadron of Tomcats can sanitise the airspace 650 km (404 mi.) out from the Carrier Battle Group, allowing no hostile aircraft to threaten the warships below.

Even sea-skimming missiles can be killed by Tomcats using their Phoenix and AMRAAM missiles.

The fact is that Tomcats and their aircrews have to be good – they are protecting a 10-warship, $15-billion battle group manned by 10,000 sailors projecting as much firepower as the United Kingdom's entire armed forces.

The F-14's swing wings allow it to combine high-speed performance and supersonic manoeuvrability with docile low-speed handling.

F-14A Tomcat

Type: two-seat long-range shipboard fleet defence interceptor, tactical reconnaissance aircraft and fighter-bomber

Powerplant: two 92.97-kN (20,920-lb.-thrust) Pratt & Whitney TF-30 turbofans with afterburning

Maximum speed: 2485 km/h (1,544 m.p.h.)

Combat radius: 525 km (326 mi.) on internal fuel; 1210 km (752 mi.) with two 409-litre (90-gal.) tanks

Service ceiling: 15,515 m (50,900 ft.)

Weights: empty 18,191 kg (40,104 lb.); maximum take-off 32,098 kg (70,764 lb.)

Armament: one 20-mm Vulcan cannon, six AIM-54 Phoenix missiles or six AIM-7 Sparrow plus four AIM-9 Sidewinder missiles

Dimensions:
span	19.54 m (64 ft. 1 in.)	
	(11.65 m/38 ft. 3 in. swept)	
length	19.10 m (62 ft. 8 in.)	
height	4.88 m (16 ft.)	
wing area	52.49 m² (565 sq. ft.)	

This Tomcat is armed with two short-range Sidewinder missiles outboard with four longer-range Sparrows inboard.

F-14A TOMCAT

An F-14A Tomcat of VF-143, an Atlantic Fleet fighter squadron nicknamed the 'Pukin' Dogs'. This world famous unit fought in Korea, Vietnam and the Gulf War, and has flown the Tomcat for 20 years.

The Tomcat carries a crew of two – pilot up front and Naval Flight Officer behind, controlling the radar and weapons systems.

The key to the F-14's success lies in its powerful Hughes AN/AWG-9 radar, which can detect fighter-sized targets at very long range, and even allows the F-14 to shoot down cruise missiles.

The 150-km- (93-mi.-) ranged AIM-54 Phoenix missile steers itself towards the target using an onboard inertial navigation system, then homes in using its own onboard radar.

The Tomcat can extend its range or endurance by using inflight refuelling, or by carrying external fuel tanks.

The F-14's powerful TF-30 turbofans give the aircraft superb performance and economy, but have proved troublesome and unreliable.

Highly colourful squadron markings have given way to a subdued low-visibility grey camouflage on all US Navy aircraft.

REACH

The Tomcat's fuel capacity and highly efficient turbofan engines allow it to operate further out from the carrier than its F/A-18 Hornet counterpart. Once at its patrol station it can see further and reach further with its Phoenix, destroying enemy fighters before they can launch their own missiles against the fleet or the Tomcat itself.

The MiG-29 'Fulcrum' has about the same radar and missile range as the F/A-18, which is much less than that of the Tomcat.

F-14 Tomcat has long-range radar (290 km/180 mi.) and missiles (150 km/93 mi.).

MiG-29 'FULCRUM'

F/A-18 Hornet has relatively short-range radar (80 km/50 mi.) and missiles (45 km/28 mi.).

AIRCRAFT CARRIER

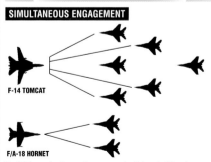

SIMULTANEOUS ENGAGEMENT

F-14 TOMCAT

F/A-18 HORNET

The F-14 can simultaneously engage up to six targets flying at different altitudes, airspeeds and in different directions. Because the Phoenix missile has its own radar it is independent after launch. The F/A-18 can fire only two Sparrows at a time against targets which are close together. Unlike the Phoenix, the Sparrow requires the Hornet to continue flying towards the enemy using its radar, making it vulnerable to a return missile shot.

Weenons of the Tomcat

AIM-9 SIDEWINDER: The highly agile Sidewinder is used against manoeuvring targets. It homes in on heat from the enemy's jetpipes. **Range 8 km (5 mi.).**

AIM-7 SPARROW: The Sparrow homes on radar energy reflected from the target, which must be illuminated by the F-14's radar for the whole of its flight. **Range 45 km (28 mi.).**

AIM-54 PHOENIX: Weighing in at almost 450 kg, costing $2m and with a range in excess of 150 km (93 mi.), the AIM-54 is the world's biggest, most costly and longest-ranged air-to-air missile. A Tomcat can launch six AIM-54s simultaneously against separate targets. The missile's onboard radar lets the F-14 turn away after launch. **Range 150 km (93 mi.).**

BOMBCAT: The Tomcat can carry a range of 'dumb' (unguided) bombs for use against ground targets. Tomcat squadrons began training in the bombing role in 1991.

HAWKER SIDDELEY

NIMROD R.MK 1

● RAF electronic intelligence aircraft ● Three examples in service

▲ *The Nimrod is a heavily modified version of the Comet airliner, and further modification to R.Mk 1P standard has only served to add to the number of protuberances and aerials on the basic airframe. However, they serve the serious task of collecting electronic signals from potentially hostile forces.*

Three specialised and highly classified conversions of the Nimrod maritime reconnaissance aircraft gather electronic intelligence (Elint) on hostile powers for the Royal Air Force. Packed with sophisticated sensors and designated Nimrod R.Mk 1, they entered service in May 1974 and fly with No. 51 Squadron. Although their operations are shrouded in secrecy, they were used during both the 1982 Falklands and 1991 Gulf conflicts.

HAWKER SIDDELEY NIMROD R.MK 1

Combat operations ▶
R.Mk 1P operations are highly secretive, but it is thought that they flew combat Elint-gathering missions from Chile during the 1982 Falklands War.

◀ 'New' Nimrod R.Mk 1P
Following the crash of one of its R.Mk 1Ps (XW666) in May 1995, the RAF received a 'new' Nimrod R.Mk 1 (XV249) in May 1997.

New base ▶
No. 51 Squadron's R.Mk 1Ps were at RAF Wyton for more than 20 years, but are now based at Waddington.

◀ Experienced crew
Packed with highly sophisticated sensors, the Nimrod R.Mk 1 is believed to fly regularly with more than 25 crew, many of whom are experienced sensor operators chosen for their discretion as well as their skill.

Elint and nav sensors ▶
The R.Mk 1P's sensors comprise a wide range of receivers to pick up signals. A comprehensive navigation suite was also fitted for extremely accurate flight around the borders of the former USSR.

FACTS AND FIGURES

➤ Originally, three R.Mk 1 aircraft were converted from Nimrod MR.Mk 1 airframes (XW664, XW665 and XW666).

➤ XW666 was lost in May 1995, after engine failure over the Moray Firth.

➤ All of XW666's sensitive equipment was recovered from the sea.

➤ A Battle Honour was awarded to No. 51 Squadron for its combat service during the Falklands conflict.

➤ Nimrod R.Mk 1Ps share their Waddington base with E-3D Sentry AEW.Mk 1s.

➤ An endurance of 19 hours is possible with one refuelling.

Highly secretive RAF 'ferret'

A version of the Nimrod maritime reconnaissance aircraft, the Nimrod R.Mk 1P is a specialised electronic intelligence-gathering aircraft. The type was developed in the early 1970s for use during the Cold War. Its role was to patrol just outside Warsaw Pact airspace in order to record the signals from ground and airborne radars and other emitters, as well as monitoring communications traffic. The R.Mk 1s carry more radio-frequency sensors than the maritime reconnaissance

Nimrods. They have multiple antennas on the fuselage and wing tanks, but do not have the tail-mounted magnetic anomaly detector (MAD). With the addition of refuelling probes for operations in the South Atlantic in 1982, they became designated R.Mk 1P, and there have been other modifications since.

Generally carrying a crew of 25 or more, the R.Mk 1Ps are believed to have operated from bases on the South American mainland during the Falklands War in 1982. They were also used operationally during the

Gulf War in 1991, when they were based at RAF Akrotiri in Cyprus. Since 1995 they have been based at RAF Waddington, alongside the RAF's force of E-3D Sentry airborne early warning aircraft.

Above: The main feature that distinguishes the Nimrod R.Mk 1P from its maritime counterpart is the lack of a MAD boom at the tail.

Above: Entering service in 1974 the RAF's R.Mk 1Ps were used extensively to probe Soviet defences during the Cold War. These missions remain shrouded in secrecy.

Nimrod R.Mk 1P

Type: electronic intelligence aircraft

Powerplant: four 54.00-kN (12,150-lb. thrust) Rolls-Royce RB168-20 Spey Mk 250 turbofans

Maximum speed: 926 km/h (575 m.p.h.)

Endurance: typically 12 hours; maximum 15 hours without refuelling and 19 hours with one in-flight refuelling

Ferry range: 5000 km (3,107 mi.)

Service ceiling: 12,800 m (42,000 ft.)

Weights: typical empty 39,010 kg (86,000 lb.); normal maximum take-off 80,514 kg (176,709 lb.)

Accommodation: 25 to 28 crew

Dimensions:
span	35.00 m	(114 ft. 10 in.)
length	36.60 m	(120 ft. 1 in.)
height	9.08 m	(29 ft. 9 in.)
wing area	197.04 m²	(2,121 sq. ft.)

NIMROD R.MK 1P

Three standard Nimrod MR aircraft were delivered to RAF Wyton in 1971 for fitting out with mission equipment. Flight trials took place during 1973 and the type entered operational service in May 1974.

During Cold War operations, Nimrod R.Mk 1s frequently operated in international airspace around the peripheries of the Soviet Union, making extremely accurate navigation essential. Accordingly, they received a Delco AN/ASN-119 Carousel Mk IVA inertial navigation system and an upgraded EKCO 290 weather radar.

The R.Mk 1P's fuselage is covered with various aerials and antennas which serve its sensors. The main receivers cover the widest possible range of frequencies, with DF (direction finding) and ranging, and are thus able to record and locate the source of hostile radar and radio emissions The aircraft almost certainly have a computerised 'threat library', allowing a detailed 'map' of potential enemy radar stations, fighter radars, navaids and air defence systems to be built up.

In addition to their mission and navigation equipment, the R.Mk 1Ps have also received Loral ARI.18240/1 wingtip pods containing ESM (electronic support measures) gear. Increased equipment internally has led to the deletion of several cabin windows, and in recent years the aircraft have started carrying BOZ chaff/flare dispensers.

All three Nimrod R.Mk 1s gained a refuelling probe for combat operations in the Falklands in 1982, thus adding a 'P' to their designation. Tanker support is invaluable for the R.Mk 1's long-endurance sorties.

Three R.Mk 1Ps were deployed to Cyprus for combat operations during Desert Storm in 1991. However, their role was fictitiously reported as 'radar and radio aid calibration'.

XW666

Nimrod variants

MR.Mk 1: The prototype Nimrod first flew in 1967 and was followed by 46 production MR.Mk 1s which entered RAF service in 1969. The type eventually equipped five squadrons.

MR.Mk 2: From 1975, the remaining 35 MR.Mk 1s were upgraded to MR.Mk 2 standard with improved mission equipment. The first example was redelivered to the RAF in 1979.

AEW.Mk 3: Developed during the 1980s to fulfil the airborne early warning role, the Nimrod AEW.Mk 3 was cancelled because of technical difficulties and spiralling costs.

NIMROD 2000: The Nimrod remains the RAF's standard maritime recce aircraft. Around 20 have recently been upgraded with new engines, mission equipment and armament.

COMBAT DATA

MAXIMUM SPEED

The Nimrod and RC-135 are much faster than the turboprop-powered 'Coot'. The Nimrod is marginally faster than the RC-135, and has a far better unrefuelled endurance, thanks to its more economical Spey turbofan engines. The R.Mk 1P can fly on just one engine to conserve fuel on long-endurance missions.

NIMROD R.Mk 1P	926 km/h (575 m.p.h.)
RC-135C STRATOTANKER	901 km/h (560 m.p.h.)
Il-20DSR 'COOT-A'	674 km/h (419 m.p.h.)

ILYUSHIN

IL-20/22 'COOT'

● Intelligence-gatherer ● Il-18 derivative ● Russia and Ukraine

F lown for the first time in July 1957 as a 75-passenger airliner, the Il-18 'Coot' entered service with Aeroflot in April 1959. Later versions used more powerful engines to carry more passengers and additional fuel; more than 700 were built. Most were used by Aeroflot, others being exported. Military derivatives include the Il-20 'Coot-A' and Il-22 'Coot-B', top secret variants used for intelligence-gathering and command post duties.

▲ As in the
West, the Soviet Union chose to modify an existing airframe for the Elint/reconnaissance role, choosing the reliable and sufficiently roomy Il-18 turboprop airliner.

ILYUSHIN IL-20/22 'COOT'

◀ Snooping flight
Elint and Sigint aircraft often shadow large 'enemy formations' of the type found during military exercises by Western forces.

▼ Airliner roots
Retention of its cabin windows betrays the origins of this Il-20 as an Il-18 airliner.

▼ Developed in the 1970s
First observed by the West in 1978, about 40 Il-20DSRs were converted. Other variants include the Il-22 'Coot-B' command post aircraft.

▼ Covert snapshot
Presumably at considerable risk to the photographer, this shot of an Il-20 was taken through an airfield's perimeter fence.

▲ Close up
Encounters between Western interceptors and 'snooping' Soviet intelligence aircraft have yielded close-up photographs like this one, useful to Western analysts.

FACTS AND FIGURES

➤ The Il-24N is an Il-20DSR derivative for fishery observation, retaining the SLAR but with Elint equipment deleted.

➤ About 20 Il-22s were operated by the CIS after the splitting-up of the USSR.

➤ One Il-22 'Coot-B' based in Belarus flies in Aeroflot colours.

➤ Il-22s are identified by a fin-top bullet fairing, a long container below the fuselage and numerous blade aerials.

➤ Il-20DSRs have a similar cruising speed to the Il-18M – around 625 km/h (388 m.p.h.).

➤ Il-20s are believed to have performed a secondary weather reconnaissance role.

PROFILE

Listening in on the West

Designated 'Coot-A' by NATO, the original Il-20 is an electronic intelligence (Elint) and reconnaissance version of the Il-18D. It carries a large fairing for a side-looking airborne radar (SLAR) under its fuselage, and pods for optical sensors are mounted on the forward fuselage sides. There are big blade antennas on top of the forward fuselage, and a series of three blister fairings on the fuselage underside, aft of the SLAR housing.

The aircraft are most often encountered by Western fighters 'scrambled' to intercept them on a 'snooping' flight, or while they are shadowing a large military exercise in order to glean information from intercepted communications.

The Il-22 'Coot-B' has a fin-tip pod plus many blade antennas above and below the fuselage. It is believed to be used as a communications relay aircraft and command post. Most 'Coots' are converted airliners, the Il-22s often being repainted in Aeroflot airline markings after

Below: Before the end of the Cold War, this was the closest that the West got to Il-20s and Il-22s – interception by an air defence fighter.

Above: This unknown variant of the Il-18 is equipped as a flying laboratory and features dielectric panniers and electro-optical sensors.

conversion. At least one has been seen since the end of the Cold War in Ukrainian air force colours. 'Coot-As' fly with Russia and the Ukraine.

Il-20DSR 'Coot-A'

Type: Elint/Sigint/reconnaissance platform

Powerplant: four 3169-kW (4,250-hp.) Ivchenko AI-20M turboprops

Accommodation: flight crew of 4 or 5, plus 20 mission specialists

Dimensions:
span 37.42 m (122 ft. 9 in.)
length 35.90 m (117 ft. 9 in.)
height 10.17 m (33 ft. 4 in.)
wing area 140 m² (1,507 sq. ft.)

Originally converted from Il-18s for the Soviet armed forces, since the end of the Cold War the Il-20 fleet has been divided between the Russian Federation and Ukraine. Each state is believed to operate at least five aircraft, including three used by Russian naval aviation.

Il-20DSR 'Coot-A'

About 40 Il-18s were converted in the 1970s to Il-20DSR electronic intelligence (Elint) and signals intelligence (Sigint) platforms for the Soviet forces.

Square-section pods approximately 4.4 m long are fitted to both fuselage sides. They have a small door near the forward end for a camera or other optical sensor.

A major feature of the Il-20DSR is the side-looking airborne radar (SLAR) fairing under the forward fuselage. It is approximately 10.25 m (33 ft. 8 in.) long and 1.15 m (3 ft. 9 in.) in diameter. In addition to this, most aircraft also carry 12 to 15 extra antennas, the functions of which are not entirely clear to Western observers.

Powerplants on the Il-20 are four standard Ivchenko AI-20Ms rated at 3169 kW (4,250-hp.), which drive AV-68I four-bladed reversible propellers. These engines, like similar Western designs, date from the 1950s.

Like civil Il-18Ds, the 'Coot-A' has a flight crew of four or five, including two pilots, a navigator, radio operator and flight engineer. A mission crew of about 20 is carried in the main cabin to operate the aircraft's systems.

To avoid drawing attention to their special mission, Elint aircraft tend to carry low-visibility colour schemes, for example all-over grey or an unpainted 'natural metal' finish.

Weather reconnaissance in the West

■ **BOEING WB-47E STRATOJET:** This conversion of the B-47E bomber was employed by the MATS Air Weather Service until 1969.

■ **BOEING WC-135B STRATOLIFTER:** This C-135B was one of 11 converted for weather reconnaissance by Hayes International.

■ **LOCKHEED HERCULES W.Mk 2:** A sole Hercules C.Mk 1 was converted to W.Mk 2 standard for RAF service.

■ **LOCKHEED WP-3D ORION:** The US Department of Commerce operates two Orions from Florida on 'hurricane hunting' duties.

ACTION DATA

CREW

Mission specialists operate the top secret sensors and signals processing equipment aboard these Elint aircraft, the exact numbers varying according to the precise nature of a given mission. The RAF's BAe Nimrod R.Mk 1s have a comparatively large crew, but the USAF's RC-135V 'Rivet Rider' has just 21 crew.

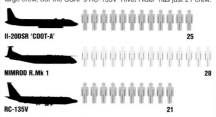

Il-20DSR 'COOT-A' — 25
NIMROD R.Mk 1 — 28
RC-135V — 21

ILYUSHIN
IL-38 'MAY'

● Sub hunter ● Maritime patroller ● Based on Il-18 airliner

Just as the American P-3 Orion was developed from the Lockheed Electra and the British Nimrod from the de Havilland Comet, the Soviet Il-38 was derived from the Il-18, an airliner and military transport that first flew in 1957. The 'May' has a longer fuselage and the wings are mounted farther forward. Stores bays are ahead of and behind the wing structure and there is a long magnetic anomaly detector (MAD) stinger extending from the tail.

▲ The 'May' is one of Russia's two main sub hunters and maritime patrollers. Around 50 are estimated to remain in service with the Russian navy, as well as in India and the Ukraine.

PHOTO FILE

ILYUSHIN IL-38 'MAY'

▼ Airliner roots
Like its Western counterparts, the Nimrod and Orion, the Il-38 is developed from an airliner, the 122-seat Il-18 "Coot."

▲ Deployment
'Mays' have been deployed under Soviet control all over the world, from the Baltic, to Yemen, Libya, Syria, northern Asia, Vietnam and Egypt.

▼ 'May' in the tropics
The only export customer has been the Indian navy. Entering service in 1977 with No. 315 Squadron was the first of five Il-38s. These are based at INS Hansa, at Dabolim. Interestingly, India also operates eight Tu-142 'Bear-Fs'.

▲ Shadowing the US fleet
An A-6 Intruder intercepts a snooping 'May'. One of the Il-38's missions is to keep a close watch on the activities of U.S. Navy carrier battle groups.

◄ Caught in the act
A Swedish interceptor snaps an Il-38 dropping a sonobouy. The 'May' carries two types of this acoustic sensor: passive and active. Ejected in a predetermined pattern, they are designed to pinpoint the location of hostile submarines.

FACTS AND FIGURES

➤ In order to adjust the center of gravity of the heavier Il-38 compared to its parent Il-18, the wings are set farther forwards.

➤ Yemen and the former USSR signed a treaty allowing 'Mays' to fly from Yemen.

➤ Four pressure refueling points serve the Il-38's 30,000-litre (7,926-gal.) fuel tanks.

➤ Shrouded in secrecy for some time was the conversion of 22 'Mays' to airborne command posts as the Il-20 'Coot-B'.

➤ The Il-20 'Coot-A' is an electronic intelligence rebuild of the Il-38.

➤ Eight engine-driven generators supply electrical power for the avionics.

PROFILE

Soviet eye above the seas

The bulk of the former Soviet Il-38s (about 59 aircraft in 1993) remain in service with the AV-MF, the air arm of the Russian navy. Lack of significant upgrades for the 'May' and continuing production of the Tu-142 seem to indicate that the latter is Russia's preferred maritime patrol and ASW aircraft.

As well as the tail-mounted MAD sensor, which detects the small variations in the earth's magnetic field caused by passing submarines, the 'May' carries a big 'Wet Eye' search radar under the forward fuselage. It can remain on patrol for up to 12 hours at a time, fly at speeds as low as 190 km/h (118 m.p.h.), and land in as little as 850 m (2,790 ft.) using reverse thrust from its propellers.

In addition to the two pilots and flight engineer on the flight deck, the aircraft carries a crew of nine systems operators in the main cabin. Their job is to monitor the displays showing targets detected by the radar and MAD sensors, and to track submarines using sonobuoys dispensed from the stores bays. Contacts may be destroyed using depth charges, torpedoes or missiles.

Only one export customer for the 'May' was found and a handful of Il-38s are operated by the Indian navy's No. 315 Squadron from its base at Dabolim. Before the Soviet Union disintegrated, 'Mays' were also deployed to bases in Yemen, Libya and Syria. And during the early 1970s, Soviet aircraft were flown in

Egyptian markings from bases located in Egypt.

Il-38 'May'

Type: medium-range anti-submarine and maritime patrol aircraft

Powerplant: four 3169-kW (4,250-hp.) ZMDB Progress AI-20M turboprops

Maximum speed: 722 km/h (448 m.p.h.) at 6400 m (21,000 ft.)

Take-off run: 1300 m (4,264 ft.)

Endurance: 12 hours

Weapons: Attack weapons and sonobuoys carried in two lower-fuselage bays.

Weight: 63,500 kg (140,000 lb.) max. take-off

Dimensions: span 37.42 m (122 ft. 9 in.)
length 39.60 m (131 ft.)
height 10.16 m (133 ft. 4 in.)
wing area 140 m² (1,506 sq. ft.)

Compared to its Western counterparts, the P-3 Orion, Atlantique and Nimrod, the Il-38 does not appear to have been upgraded with sophisticated sensors such as low-light level TV, FLIR or electronic surveillance measures equipment.

A massive radome dominates the Il-38's forward fuselage. It houses a search radar, NATO codename 'Wet Eye', which is used for detecting submarine periscopes and surface vessels.

Il-38 'May'

Former Soviet Il-38s are now flown by Russia's naval air arm (AV-MF). Only one export customer was found. India received five aircraft.

The Il-38 carries three flight crew. Separated from the flight deck by a pressure bulkhead is the main cabin, which houses the equipment and operating consoles for nine mission specialists.

In modifying the Il-18 airliner for the sub-hunting role, Ilyushin stretched the fuselage by about 12 feet. The weight of the special mission equipment so affected the aircraft's center of gravity, that the wings were moved forward to compensate.

Four powerful and efficient turboprops power the Il-38. Identical to those fitted on the Il-18D 'Coot' airliner, they give the 'May' a respectable top speed of 722 km/h (448 m.p.h.), and a patrol endurance of 12 hours.

'Mays' have only been seen in this overall gray camouflage scheme. Apart from national markings (the Soviet red star) and small identification numbers, the aircraft is entirely devoid of other markings.

The Il-38 has two weapons bays fore and aft of the wing spars. These can carry torpedoes, depth charges, mines and sonobuoys.

The Il-38's featureless fuselage contains few windows. Observation blisters allow the crew to photograph ships and intercepting aircraft.

The MAD (magnetic anomaly detector) projecting aft of the tail is used to give the general location of hostile submarines. The device picks up the disturbance in the Earth's magnetic field caused by a large metallic mass such as a submarine.

ACTION DATA

SPEED

Maritime patrol aircraft frequently have to reach a distant part of the ocean quickly, perhaps to check a contact or to assist in a rescue. The P-3C arrives first, but the Il-38 is not far behind.

Il-38 'MAY'	722 km/h (448 m.p.h.)
ATLANTIQUE 2	648 km/h (402 m.p.h.)
P-3C ORION	761 km/h (472 m.p.h.)

ENDURANCE

Patrol aircraft must spend a long time on station. The less fuel-efficient 'May' loses out to the other aircraft. The Orion achieves its endurance by shutting down two engines.

Il-38 "MAY" 12 hours / ATLANTIQUE 2 18 hours / P-3C ORION 17 1/2 hours

WEAPONS

Having found an enemy target, it must be destroyed with depth charges, torpedoes or missiles. The smaller load of the Il-38 relates to its lack of external weapons stowage.

Il-38 'MAY' 3000 kg (6,600 lb.) / ATLANTIQUE 2 6000 kg (13,200 lb.) / P-3C ORION 9072 kg (19,958 lb.)

From airliner to maritime patroller

■ **PILATUS BRITTEN-NORMAN MARITIME DEFENDER:** This version of the original Islander has proved popular with smaller air forces.

■ **BRITISH AEROSPACE NIMROD:** Developed from the world's first jet airliner, the superb Nimrod will serve for many years to come.

■ **LOCKHEED CP-140 AURORA:** Lockheed redesigned the Electra to build the Orion and Canada adopted its own CP-140 variant.

■ **AIRTECH (CASA/IPTN) CN-235 MPA:** In competition with the Maritime Defender, this more modern aircraft is becoming popular.

ILYUSHIN

IL-76 'CANDID'

● Tactical transport ● Strategic airlift ● Airborne command post

Capable of carrying a 40-tonne payload onto a battlefield airstrip, the massive Il-76 is one of the world's most impressive transports. Even larger than the Lockheed StarLifter, the Il-76 has short-field capability, long range and can carry huge loads. Despite being designed for the military transport role, the Il-76 has also been converted into an airborne command post and a water-bomber, and is also used by many civilian operators.

▲ Like most Soviet aircraft, the Il-76 is extremely rugged; in the words of an RAF C-130 pilot, 'the thing is built like a bridge'. It remains the principal equipment of the Russian military transport force.

ILYUSHIN IL-76 'CANDID'

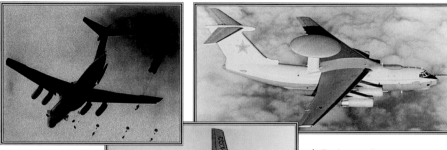

▲ **Para drop**
The Soviet army's paratroop force relies on the Il-76M to go to war. The aircraft can deploy 125 fully-equipped paratroops at a time. They exit the aircraft over the rear ramp to avoid the engine efflux.

▲ **Early warning**
The Il-76 carried out trials for the Soviet Il-78 'Midas' airborne early warning aircraft, which is comparable to the Boeing E-3.

◄ **Record breaker**
In 1975 an Il-76 flew a 60-ton payload for 2000 km (1,240 mi.) at 875 km/h (543 m.p.h.).

▼ **Aeroflot colours**
Despite its airline colour scheme, the Il-76 was mostly dedicated to military service; many Aeroflot aircraft flew to in Kabul in Afghanistan to offload Soviet garrison troops.

▲ **Ramp loading**
Unlike most of the An-12s it was designed to replace, the Il-76 has an integral rear door and ramp for fast loading.

FACTS AND FIGURES

➤ The Il-76 has been exported to Algeria, China, Cuba, Hungary, India, Iraq, Libya, North Korea and Syria.

➤ In Indian service the Il-76 is called 'Gajaraj' (cock elephant).

➤ The Il-76MDK allows trainee cosmonauts to experience weightless conditions.

➤ The 'Candid' can be converted into the Il-76DMP firefighter, carrying 42,000 litres (11,000 gal.) of water or retardant.

➤ The Il-76 transport can airdrop light tanks, pallets and amphibious vehicles.

➤ The new Il-76MF, carrying a 52,000-kg (114,000-lb.) payload, first flew on 1 August 1995.

Russia's military heavyweight lifter

Designed to replace the turboprop An-12, the Il-76 first flew in 1971 and entered service with a development squadron in 1974. Series production began in 1975 in Tashkent, and by 1993 more than 750 had been built, with production then continuing at the rate of one aircraft per week.

Immensely strong, the Il-76 has a titanium floor in the hold, a multi-wheel undercarriage, a wing fitted with various high-lift devices and four powerful Lotarev turbofans to allow short take-offs from rough airstrips. The 'TD' variant has uprated engines for 'hot-and-high' performance, and other Il-76s have been converted for airborne early warning and as command and control aircraft and tankers.

Military Il-76s differ from their civilian brothers by having a prominent rear gun turret with two 23-mm cannon, chaff and flare dispensers, and small fairings for electronic countermeasures gear. With the delays in the An-70 programme, the Il-76 remains a vital aircraft to the Russian tactical airlift force.

An adaptable aircraft, the Il-76 has also found use with Aeroflot as a freight transport and airliner. At least one, equipped with buffet kitchen, sleeping area and various cold-weather modifications is used in support of Russian Antarctic operations.

Il-76M 'Candid-B'

Type: medium military transport, command post, tanker (Il-78) and AEW aircraft (A-50)

Powerplant: four 117.68-kN (26,575-lb.-thrust) PNPP Soloviev D-30KP-1 turbofans

Maximum speed: 850 km/h (527 m.p.h.)

Maximum cruising speed: 800 km/h (496 m.p.h.) at 12,000 m (39,350 ft.)

Range: 5000 km (3,100 mi.) with maximum payload of 40,000 kg (105,600 lb.)

Service ceiling: 15,500 m (50,850 ft.)

Weights: max. take-off 190,000 kg (418,000 lb.)

Armament: optional two 23-mm GSh-23L twin-barrelled cannon in tail turret

Dimensions:
span 50.50 m (165 ft. 8 in.)
length 46.59 m (152 ft. 10 in.)
height 14 76 m (47 ft. 5 in.)
wing area 300 m² (3,228 sq. ft.)

The undercarriage doors close when the wheels are down to prevent the entry of mud, snow and ice. Braking is hydraulic and the tyre pressure can be altered from the cabin. Two packs of 96 50-mm flares can be carried on the landing gear fairings and a further two on each fuselage side.

Power is supplied by four reliable Lotarev turbofans, replaced on the stretched Il-76MF by Aviadvigatel PS-90ANs. The new MF's fuselage length is increased by 6.6 m (22 ft.).

The wing is high mounted and built in five pieces with a fail-safe, multi-spar construction.

IL-76TD 'CANDID'

The Russian air force operates around 300 Il-76 transports, plus an additional number of testbeds, labs, AEW aircraft, tankers, Il-76VPK naval command posts and various electronic aircraft.

The cockpit seats a crew of seven, including two freight handlers. The glazed nose houses a navigator for negotiating combat landings without the use of the chin radar. All systems are designed for all-weather, day or night operations.

The 'Candid' has a hold with reinforced titanium flooring and folding roller conveyors. In the roof are two travelling lifter cranes each with two hoists of 2500-kg (5,500-lb.) capacity. At the front of the hold are twin winches for loading cargo. The hold can accommodate up to three specially designed modules for medical evacuation, passenger transport, supply or maintenance.

The large fuselage hold is fully pressurised and accommodates 140 troops or 125 armed paratroops. Alternatively freight containers, cranes, trucks, APCs, artillery or light tanks can be carried.

CCCP-76482

ИЛ-76ТД

АЭРОФЛОТ

The tail ramp can be used as an additional hoist, with a 30,000-kg (66,000-lb.) capacity for loading heavier caterpillar-tracked vehicles.

The military-tasked Il-76 generally carries a tail turret containing two 23-mm twin-barrelled guns.

COMBAT DATA

MAXIMUM CRUISING SPEED
The C-141 is more streamlined and can cruise at a higher speed than the Il-76. The Polaris is based on the A310 airliner. All three would normally cruise at between 800 and 880 km/h (495 and 545 m.p.h.).

Il-76M 800 km/h (496 m.p.h.)
C-141B STARLIFTER 910 km/h (564 m.p.h.)
CC-150 POLARIS 850 km/h (527 m.p.h.)

PAYLOAD
The StarLifter and Il-76 are of similar design and perform similar tasks, both being able to carry around 40000 kg of cargo. The CC-150 cannot transport as much or such a range of freight.

Il-76M 'CANDID-B' 40,000 kg (88,000 lb.)
C-141B STARLIFTER 41,222 kg (90,688 lb.)
CC-150 POLARIS 33,780 kg (74,316 lb.)

RANGE WITH PAYLOAD
The Il-76 and StarLifter are used to transport troops and equipment on a global scale. They both regularly extend their range by the use of air-to-air refuelling to allow quick deployment.

Il-76M 'CANDID-B' 5000 km (3,100 mi.)
C-141B STARLIFTER 4725 km (2,930 mi.)
CC-150 POLARIS 6100 km (3,780 mi.)

Red star airlifters

ILYUSHIN Il-14 'CRATE': Now thoroughly obsolete, the Il-14 enjoyed great success as the standard Eastern Bloc military transport aircraft throughout the 1950s and 1960s.

ANTONOV An-26 'CURL': Derived from the An-24, the An-26 is a very successful transport aircraft which has found widespread use in both military and civilian markets.

ANTONOV An-72 'COALER': This turbofan-powered STOL transport was designed to replace the turboprop An-26. It can carry freight, troops or paratroops, with entrance via a rear ramp.

ILYUSHIN/BERIEV

IL-78 'MIDAS'/A-50 'MAINSTAY'

● Flying tanker ● Airborne command post ● Transport aircraft

As the effectiveness of Boeing's E-3 Sentry AWACS (Airborne Warning and Control System) aircraft became apparent, Soviet designers began working on an equivalent. The Ilyushin Il-76 'Candid' formed the basis of Beriev's A-50 response to the requirement, while Ilyushin itself had been working on a further modification of the Il-76, this time to tanker configuration. The definitive Il-78M emerged as a useful three-point in-flight refuelling tanker.

▲ With the ending of the Cold War, Russian crews unloading baggage from their Il-78 'Midas' aircraft at a British airfield have become a common sight.

ILYUSHIN IL-78/A-50

▼ **Early warning**
Beriev developed a specialised airborne early warning aircraft from the Ilyushin Il-76 transport aircraft.

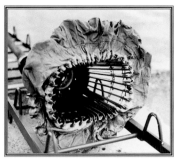

▲ **Fuelling the fighters**
In its tanker role the Il-78M can refuel three aircraft at the same time, using hose and drogue units like the one illustrated here.

◀ **On the approach**
The high-set tail and multi-wheeled undercarriage allow the 'Midas' to have a relatively short landing run. In this view the three refuelling points under the wings and rear fuselage are seen.

Watching and waiting ▶
Orbiting at high altitude, the A-50 'Mainstay' is charged with directing Su-27 'Flankers' and MiG-29 'Fulcrums' on intercept missions.

◀ **Funding problems**
Russian technology is now regarded as being the equal of its Western counterparts, but recent funding problems look set to hinder development of the A-50.

FACTS AND FIGURES

➤ The Il-78 'Midas' is a three-point tanker which carries the fuel internally on two pallet-mounted tanks.

➤ Ten mission operators are carried within the fuselage of the A-50 'Mainstay'.

➤ 'Midas' tankers were given a civilian airliner colour scheme.

➤ During the Gulf War 'Mainstays' operated over the Black Sea observing American air strikes flown from Turkey.

➤ The 'Mainstay' is said to be inferior to NATO's E-3 Sentry.

➤ China is seeking to purchase A-50s to support its 'Flanker' fleet.

PROFILE

The Soviets' all-seeing eye

During 1978, work began on a replacement for the primitive Tu-126 'Moss' AWACS platform in service with the Soviet forces. An all-new radar system, with its associated computer equipment and other sensors, was to be incorporated into the Il-76 airframe by Beriev.

Production of the A-50 'Mainstay' began in 1983 and, although there were a number of early problems, the aircraft has matured into an effective radar and command asset. It has demonstrated simultaneous operations with MiG-31 interceptors, Tu-22M bombers and submarines. A less capable aircraft, which retains the glazed nose of the Il-76, is known as the Be-976 and is used to support missile test programmes.

In an unrelated programme, Ilyushin converted an Il-76 to act as the prototype of the Il-78 'Midas' in-flight refuelling tanker. With some 28 tonnes (28 tons) of fuel in cylindrical tanks within the hold, the aircraft was initially equipped with a single hose drum unit (HDU) crudely attached to its rear fuselage. After 10 years of development 'Midas' finally entered service in 1987 and further modifications have seen the development of the much-improved Il-78M with two additional HDUs beneath the wings.

Below: Operational use of the A-50 has remained limited. Despite this Russia claims to have 12 examples flying.

Above: The 'Midas' is the principal Russian air-to-air refuelling platform. It uses a probe and drogue system like most European air arms.

A-50 'Mainstay'

Type: airborne early warning and control aircraft

Powerplant: four 117.68 kN (26,475-lb.-thrust) PNPP 'Aviadvigatel' (Soloviev) D-30KP turbofans

Maximum speed: 850 km/h (527 m.p.h.) at optimum altitude

Cruising speed: 800 km/h (496 m.p.h.)

Endurance: 4 hours

Radar detection range: 350–400 km (217–249 m.p.h.)

Operational ceiling: 10,000 m (32,000 ft.)

Accommodation: five flight crew; 10 mission specialists

Dimensions:
span	50.50 m	(165 ft. 8 in.)
length	46.59 m	(152 ft. 10 in.)
height	14.76 m	(48 ft. 5 in.)
wing area	300 m² (3,228 sq. ft.)	

A-50 'MAINSTAY'

Having observed America's success with the Boeing E-3 AWACS, the Russian air force requested an aircraft with similar capabilities. Despite its capabilities the A-50 faces budgetary restrictions.

Within the fuselage a single large screen is used for controlling fighters, smaller screens are used for monitoring the tactical situation on the ground.

Influenced by the design of America's E-3 Sentry, the 'Mainstay's' main radar is positioned in a rotodome mounted above the fuselage.

Crews used to operating in the Tu-126 'Moss' have found the conditions within the A-50 particularly unpleasant, because of the high noise levels.

Two A-50 'Mainstays' flew round-the-clock monitoring flights during the Gulf War from orbits high over the Black Sea. They observed combat strikes and US cruise missile launches.

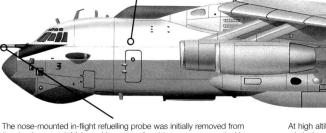

The nose-mounted in-flight refuelling probe was initially removed from the developmental 'Mainstay' because of problems encountered with the airflow across the aircraft during the fuel transfer phase.

At high altitude the stability of the A-50 was found to be relatively poor. Additional finlets were added to the lower fuselage above the undercarriage bays to alleviate the problem.

Deleted from both the AEW and tanker variants is the rear tail turret. On this particular variant the A-50 'Mainstay', the glazing is retained but additional avionics radomes are installed. This allows the aircraft to detect any rearward-approaching enemy aircraft. During flight operations this position is unmanned.

ACTION DATA

MAXIMUM TAKE OFF WEIGHT

The need to lift all the required radar equipment associated with airborne control requires the 'Mainstay' to have a large take-off weight. Offering an improvement over the Boeing Sentry, the 'Mainstay' is fitted with more bulky equipment.

A-50 MAINSTAY 190,000 kg (418,000 lb.)
E-3C SENTRY 147,420 kg (324,300 lb.)
E-4B 362,874 kg (798,320 lb.)

MAXIMUM SPEED

Weighed down as they are with heavy equipment, tairborne control aircraft can never reach high speeds. They normally orbit over friendly territory well protected by escort fighters, so their operational speeds are related to their radar capabilities.

A-50 MAINSTAY 850 km/h (527 m.p.h.)
E-3C SENTRY 853 km/h (530 m.p.h.)
E-4B 969 km/h (600 m.p.h.)

OPERATIONAL CEILING

Operating at high altitude allows the the aircraft to extend the range of their radar and contact friendly fighters for intercept duties at greater distances. One of the highest flying in its class, the 'Mainstay' operates at a much higher altitude than the Sentry but is unable to equal the E-4B.

A-50 MAINSTAY 10,000 m (30,000 ft.)
E-3C SENTRY 8840 m (29,000 ft.)
E-4B 13,715 m (45,000 ft.)

Controlling the skies

■ **E-3A AWACS:** Operated by the US Air Force and NATO, the AWACS is the West's primary airborne control aircraft.

■ **E-3F SENTRY:** The turbofan-powered E-3D and E-3F are the most capable European-owned AEW aircraft in service.

■ **Tu-126 'MOSS':** Derived from an airliner, the 'Moss' was the first Soviet aircraft to be fitted with a radar rotodome.

ISRAEL AIRCRAFT INDUSTRIES

KFIR

● Multi-role fighter ● 'Top Gun' aggressor ● Combat veteran

The Kfir (Lion Cub) has cemented a worldwide reputation for Israel Aircraft Industries, an aggressive and innovative builder of hi-tech warplanes in a very small country. The Kfir, based on France's remarkable Mirage III, appeared in the mid-1970s and became a key weapon in the Israeli arsenal, as well as a successful export product. Although originally designed as an interceptor, it has been developed into one of the world's finest strike aircraft. To fighter pilots the Kfir is fast, nimble and potent – enjoyable to fly, and proven in combat in the Lebanon.

▲ The Kfir is a generation ahead of early Mirage models. It has a more powerful engine and a much more modern cockpit, including advanced head-up and multi-mode displays.

IAI KFIR

▼ Strike jet
Although designed as a fighter, the Kfir is extremely versatile and has given Israel excellent service as a strike fighter-bomber.

▲ Marine aggressors
The Kfir was used in aggressor training by the US Navy and Marine Corps.

▼ Canard nose
The canard foreplanes are the most obvious difference between the Kfirs and the Mirage family, which are far less capable.

◀ On patrol
Armed with four missiles and two cannon, the Kfir is still a dangerous foe, despite the age of the Mirage airframe on which it was based.

▼ IAI factory
This is the Kfir-C2's assembly line in Israel. The success of the Kfir family has been a very valuable source of work for the company.

FACTS AND FIGURES

➤ Israel hastened development of the Kfir by testing the Technolog, a two-seat Mirage III with canards.

➤ The Kfir was not shown in public until Israel unveiled the aircraft in 1975.

➤ The US prevented Israel from exporting J79-powered Kfirs to Taiwan.

➤ Israel lent two squadrons of Kfirs to the US Navy and the US Marines, used for dissimilar air combat training.

➤ To avoid a US embargo, Israel developed a Kfir powered by an Atar engine.

➤ Israel successfully exported the Kfir to Ecuador and Colombia.

PROFILE

The Lion Cub from Israel

Israel operated the tailless, delta-winged Mirage III long before the revolutionary design of this French fighter was proved in combat. The Mirage was one of the great successes of the 1967 Six Day War, but when France embargoed a shipment of 50 aircraft, Israel became determined to offset its reliance on overseas suppliers.

This process began when agents of Mossad, the Israeli secret intelligence service, stole plans for the Mirage III, which were used to produce the Nesher, a pirated Israeli Mirage.

Then, in great secrecy, Israeli engineers worked on a programme called Black Curtain to adapt the Mirage III airframe to take a more powerful American-designed J79 engine. In 1975, this produced the Kfir. Although it originally resembled the Mirage 5, a version first seen in 1976 introduced small, swept-back foreplanes which improved handling, agility and low-speed performance.

From 1983 Israel began operating the Kfir-C7, which is an upgraded aircraft fitted with advanced radar and avionics

The Kfir was a potent addition to the Israeli air force, and performed well during the battles over Lebanon in 1982. Although used primarily in the ground attack role, it scored several kills against Syrian MiG-23s.

and a boosted engine. A highly capable interceptor, it is also as good a ground attack aircraft as can be found anywhere in the world.

Kfirs built after 1983 have an engine overspeed capability. This allows the J79 to give even more boost under combat conditions, although at the expense of engine life.

One of the many changes to the Mirage design was the pronounced 'dogtooth' in the wing leading edge.

Kfir-C7

Type: single-seat interceptor, fighter and fighter-bomber

Powerplant: one 79.63-kN (17,864-lb.-thrust) (83.36 kN/18,700-lb-thrust) with emergency boost afterburning General Electric J79-J1E turbojet

Maximum speed: Mach 2.3 or 2440 km/h (1,523 m.p.h.) above 11,000 m (36,000 ft.)

Combat radius: 880 km (546 mi.)

Service ceiling: 17,680 m (58,000 ft.) or 22,860 m (75,000 ft.) in a zoom climb

Weights: empty 7285 kg (16,027 lb.); maximum loaded 16,500 kg (36,300 lb.)

Armament: two 30-mm DEFA cannon with 280 rounds; up to 6085 kg (13,400 lb.) of bombs, rockets or missiles

Dimensions: span 8.22 m (27 ft.)
length 15.65 m (51 ft.)
height 4.55 m (15 ft.)
wing area 34.80 m² (374 sq. ft.)

KFIR-C2

Ecuador was one of two main export customers for the Kfir. The aircraft are primarily used as interceptors, and equip Escuadrón de Combate 2113, part of Grupo 211, based at Taura.

Small strakes are fitted to the nose just behind the radar. These generate vortices for increased control at high angles of attack.

Ecuador's aircraft are nominally Kfir-C2s, but have been upgraded with many of the advanced avionics systems of the Israeli Kfir-C7.

The intake design of the Kfir series was modified to cope with the greater mass flow of the J79 engine.

The Kfir can carry a huge variety of weapon stores, including Shafrir and Python dogfight missiles, Shrike anti-radar missiles, Maverick air-to-surface missiles, and various types of bombs.

The dorsal airscoop on the Kfir is necessary to provide cooling air for the J79 engine, which generates much more heat than the Atar engine powering the original Mirage.

The Kfir-C2 has a relatively simple ranging radar, as the aircraft is primarily a ground-attack type and only carries infra-red missiles.

The Kfir is powered by a single General Electric J79-J1E augmented turbojet, the most powerful variant of this American-designed engine.

COMBAT DATA

MAXIMUM SPEED

A combination of light weight, clean design and a powerful engine gives the Kfir a small edge in maximum speed over the lightweight MiG-21 and the far heavier F-4 Phantom.

KFIR-C7 — 2440 km/h (1,513 m.p.h.)
F-4 PHANTOM — 2390 km/h (1,482 m.p.h.)
MiG-21 'FISHBED' — 2230 km/h (1,383 m.p.h.)

CLIMB RATE

Although the Kfir is generally used as a ground attack aircraft, it is no mean performer as an interceptor. It cannot match the Phantom in a climb – even though the American jet is much heavier, the power of two J79s instead of one puts the F-4 in front – but the Kfir still climbs very fast, and it easily outpaces the older, lighter and less powerful MiG-21.

F-4 PHANTOM 18,700 m/min (61,336 f.p.m.)
KFIR-C7 14,000 m/min (45,920 f.p.m.)
MiG-21 'FISHBED' 7200 m/min (23,616 f.p.m.)

ARMAMENT

KFIR-C7 6085 kg (13,400 lb.)
F-4 PHANTOM 7260 kg (15,972 lb.)
MiG-21 'FISHBED' 2000 kg (4,400 lb.)

The large delta wing and powerful engine give the Kfir excellent striking power, allowing it to lift almost as much as the F-4 and far more than the much less versatile MiG-21 'Fishbed'.

History of a Lion Cub

■ MIRAGE ANCESTOR: The classic Dassault Mirage III was used to great effect as an air-superiority fighter by Israel during their amazing triumph in the Six Day War of 1967.

■ PIRATE COPY: Driven to desperate measures by an arms embargo, the Israelis built Mirage copies with stolen plans. Some were sold to Argentina and used in the Falklands.

■ AMERICAN POWER: Fitting a larger and more powerful American-designed General Electric J79 engine into a Mirage airframe, IAI produced the first Kfir in the early 1970s.

■ AERODYNAMIC REFINEMENT: The canard foreplanes are the most obvious feature of the Kfir-C2, designed to improve the delta-winged fighter's low-speed handling.

■ STATE OF THE ART: New radar, cockpit, avionics and a boosted engine have turned the Kfir-C7 into one of the most potent ground-attack fighters in service today.

KAWASAKI

C-1

● Twin-jet transport ● JASDF service ● Engine testbed

▲ *A competent,*
medium-ranged military transport,
the C-1 has served with the JASDF for 22 years.
No export customers were found and only
31 aircraft were built.

Designed in the late 1960s as a medium transport to replace the C-46 Commando in Japanese Air Self-Defence Force (JASDF) service, the C-1 has a typical military transport configuration. Kawasaki flew the first example in November 1970, and delivered 31 aircraft in October 1981. Proposed tanker, reconnaissance and other military variants were abandoned, but one C-1 has been used for research into blown flying surfaces for improved field performance.

PHOTO FILE

KAWASAKI C-1

▼ STOL testing
Four 47.07-kN (10,600-lb.-thrust) turbofans and a powerful flap blowing system allow a landing distance of only 853 m (2,800 ft.).

▲ Kawasaki camouflage
Deliveries of the C-1 were completed in 1981, and by 1982 all were camouflaged.

▲ Silver C-1
Sleekly-podded turbofans and large fairings over the flap hinges are characteristics of the C-1 design. All were originally natural metal.

▲ Rear ramp and clamshells
Kawasaki followed the accepted formula for tactical airlifter design, fitting the C-1 with a rear loading ramp and clamshell doors.

Two squadrons ▶
The stylised bird marking of the 402 Hikotai also appears on the unit's NAMC YS-11s. The C-130H is Japan's other principal airlifter.

FACTS AND FIGURES

➤ The C-1 needs only 439 m (1,440 ft.) to take off and only 853 m (2,800 ft.) to reach a height of 15 m (50 ft.).

➤ Nihon Aeroplane Manufacturing Company began designing the C-1 in 1966.

➤ Two prototypes completed C-1 test flying in March 1973.

➤ Five long-range versions were built with an additional 4732-litre (1,250-gal.) wing tank.

➤ Kawasaki was responsible for final assembly and testing of the C-1.

➤ One of the potential replacements for the C-1 is the C-17A Globemaster III.

PROFILE

Japanese STOL transport

With its high wing, fuselage-mounted undercarriage sponsons and hydraulically-actuated rear loading ramp, the C-1 Asuka resembles other tactical transport aircraft. Designed to provide maximum internal cargo space for troops, vehicles and freight, it is powered by turbofan engines but carries a smaller payload than the Lockheed C-130 Hercules or Transall C.160.

Construction of the C-1 was a collaborative effort involving the four major Japanese aircraft manufacturers, with Fuji, Mitsubishi and Nihon all contributing major sub-assemblies. The Asuka was used to equip two Japanese Air Self-Defence Force (JASDF) transport squadrons, the 402nd based at Iruma and the 403rd at Miho. One C-1, known as the EC-1, was modified as an electronic warfare training aircraft, with massive bulges and radomes to house the necessary sensors. Another was used as a testbed for the T-4 trainer's Ishikawajima-Harima F3 engine and the MITI/NAL FJR710 high-bypass turbofan.

Another modified C-1, the National Aerospace Laboratory Asuka, a quiet short take-off and landing (QSTOL) research aircraft, uses the FJR710/600S powerplant. Although the C-1 was designed to a JASDF specification, its limited payload has ultimately restricted its versatility in service and a replacement is being sought.

Above: For air-dropping freight or paratroops, the rear loading ramp and clamshell doors can be opened in flight. Typical loads include a 105-mm howitzer, three jeeps, a 2.54-tonne (2½-ton) lorry or two 0.76-tonne (¾-ton) trucks. Alternatively, three standard freight pallets may be accommodated.

Below: This take-off shot shows the C-1's extensive flaps and leading-edge slats to advantage.

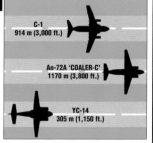

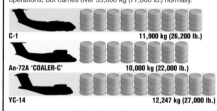

C-1

Type: tactical military transport aircraft

Powerplant: two 64.5-kN (14,500-lb.-thrust) Pratt & Whitney JT8D-M-9 turbofans

Maximum speed: 806 km/h (500 m.p.h.) at 7620 m (25,000 ft.)

Range: 1297 km (800 mi.) with 7900-kg (17,400-lb.) payload

Service ceiling: 11,580 m (38,000 ft.)

Weights: empty 24,300 kg (53,460 lb.); maximum take-off 45,000 kg (99,000 lb.)

Accommodation: five crew plus 60 fully-equipped troops, 45 paratroops, 36 stretchers with attendants or 11,900 kg (26,200 lb.) of cargo

Dimensions:
span 30.60 m (100 ft. 4 in.)
length 29.00 m (95 ft. 2 in.)
height 9.99 m (32 ft. 9 in.)
wing area 120.5 m² (1,297 sq. ft.)

EC-1

Extensively modified, this EC-1 is nominally used for electronic countermeasures (ECM) training with the 501st Hikotai. It is likely to have an additional electronic intelligence (Elint) role.

Large fairings festoon the EC-1, the most unusual being the giant radomes on the nose and beneath the tail. Kawasaki modified the 21st C-1 airframe to this standard, to meet a 1983 Defence Agency contract.

Setting the wings high up on the fuselage ensures that the wing carry-through structure does not affect cabin volume. The outer wings were built by Fuji, with Nihon producing the engine pods and control surfaces.

Although some American ECM and Elint avionics are employed by the EC-1, Elint equipment from Toshiba and the XJ/ALQ-5 ECM suite from Mitsubishi Electric are the heart of the onboard system.

Contrary to the solution adopted by Lockheed for the tail unit on its C-130, Kawasaki used a high-set horizontal surface on the C-1. This keeps the tailplane clear of the jet wash.

Using the upswept tail arrangement that has become characteristic of tactical transports, the C-1 offers easy loading. Three separate hydraulic units operate the aircraft's systems, one of which is dedicated solely to the rear ramp.

COMBAT DATA

PAYLOAD

While the C-1 can carry a greater payload than the An-72C, it does not have the capacity required by a primary airlift asset. The YC-14 can lift a maximum of 12,247 kg (27,000 lb.) for STOL operations, but carries over 35,000 kg (77,000 lb.) normally.

C-1 — 11,900 kg (26,200 lb.)
An-72A 'COALER-C' — 10,000 kg (22,000 lb.)
YC-14 — 12,247 kg (27,000 lb.)

TAKE-OFF RUN

With maximum payload the C-1 requires a respectable 914-metre run to clear a 15-metre obstacle. Antonov's An-72C needs a longer runway to attain a height of 10.7 metres, while Boeing's incredible YC-14 requires just 305 metres to become airborne.

C-1 914 m (3,000 ft.)
An-72A 'COALER-C' 1170 m (3,800 ft.)
YC-14 305 m (1,150 ft.)

MAXIMUM RANGE

Japan's C-1 has adequate range compared to other contemporary types. However, its range is sufficient for tactical in-theatre operations, and five examples of an extended-range version were built. Greater range would give the fleet added versatility.

C-1 3353 km (2,084 mi.)
YC-14 4828 km (3,000 mi.)
An-72A 'COALER-C' 2000 km (1,243 mi.)

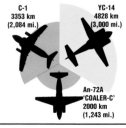

Electronic transports

BEECH RC-12 'GUARDRAIL': Several variants of the RC-12, most dedicated to communications intelligence, have been used by the US Army. The latest version is the RC-12P.

BOEING RC-135 'RIVET JOINT': Ordered as RC-135Bs, the 'Rivet Joint' strategic reconnaissance aircraft were delivered as RC-135Cs and updated to RC-135Vs.

LOCKHEED EC-130E 'RIVET RIDER': Highly modified EC-130Es are used as Airborne Battlefield Command and Control Centres and also flew broadcast duties during the Gulf War.

NAMC YS-11E: Three YS-11s were modified for electronic warfare training as YS-11Es. The aircraft shown has since been modified to YS-11EA standard for the Elint role.

KAWASAKI

T-4

● Modern jet trainer ● Indigenous design ● Highly versatile

Japan's T-4 was developed as a replacement for the Japanese Air Self-Defence Force's Lockheed T-33 and Fuji T-1 trainers. The new aircraft is sourced almost entirely from Japanese industry and offers excellent performance in the training role, as well as providing a useful liaison capability. Production deliveries began in September 1988 and since 1996 the T-4 has been the mount of the famous 'Blue Impulse' aerobatic team.

▲ Kawasaki's
T-4 is the standard medium jet trainer of the Japanese Air Self-Defence Force (JASDF) and looks likely to continue in service well into the 21st century.

PHOTO FILE

KAWASAKI T-4

▼ Joint-venture
The T-4 is a collaboration between Kawasaki, Mitsubishi and Fuji. Kawasaki is the lead contractor.

▲ Japanese exclusive
A T-4 prototype in flight. The type equips several JASDF units, though no export orders have so far been secured.

Aerobatic performer ▶
In addition to various training wings, the Japanese aerobatic team 'Blue Impulse' also flies the T-4, as seen here.

▼ First prototype
Identified by its red and white pitot head, the first prototype T-4 (66-5601) sits at rest. The first flight took place on 29 July 1985.

'Blue Impulse' ▶
The acclaimed aerobatic team has only recently re-equipped with the T-4 after operating the Mitsubishi T-2 for several years. Here one of its aircraft makes a low 'n' slow flypast with its gear lowered.

FACTS AND FIGURES

➤ Fuji builds the rear fuselage, supercritical-section wings and tail unit of the T-4.

➤ Some T-4s used by front-line squadrons are camouflaged.

➤ T-4s have replaced the T-33 in F-1, F-4 and F-15 units.

➤ Training T-4s are flown by 31 and 32 Flying Training Squadrons of the 1st Air Wing at Hamamatsu, Tokyo.

➤ Mitsubishi has responsibility for the centre fuselage and air intakes.

➤ Kawasaki has so far made no provision for the T-4 to be armed.

PROFILE

Indigenously designed trainer

Pilots from Japan might consider themselves proud to have been trained on a fully indigenous aircraft. On 4 September 1981, Kawasaki was chosen as prime contractor for the T-4. Although production aircraft are assembled by Kawasaki, the company shares manufacturing responsibility with Fuji and Mitsubishi.

Four XT-4 prototypes were funded, the first flying on 29 July 1985. Almost three years of testing followed, before the first production aircraft was delivered in 1988, and by 31 March 1996, 171 out of a total requirement for 200 aircraft had

been delivered. Similar in configuration to the Franco-German Alpha Jet, the T-4 offers greater versatility thanks to its in-built baggage compartment. This centre-fuselage hold allows the aircraft to fulfil its secondary liaison and high-speed, light transport duties. Many front-line JASDF squadrons have one or two T-4s on strength for use in this liaison role, or as 'hacks'.

Other missions within the capabilities of the T-4 include target-towing, electronic countermeasures (ECM) training and air sampling, with special equipment carried on three external pylons.

Despite its versatility and

Above: The T-4 features relatively large trailing edge flaps allowing a low approach and landing speed.

Above: Underwing hardpoints enable the T-4 to carry 450-kg (990-lb.) drop tanks. Additionally, a centre-line pylon permits the carriage of a target winch, ECM pod, or chaff flare dispenser.

excellent manoeuvrability, Kawasaki's T-4 has yet to find an export customer, but nevertheless is set to serve the JASDF for years to come.

Many modern jet trainers feature a relatively large vertical tail structure and the Kawasaki T-4 is no exception. The low-set tailplane (below the main wing) was designed to avoid adverse effects should the aircraft accidentally go into a spin.

T-4

Type: two-seat tandem intermediate jet trainer and liaison aircraft

Powerplant: two 16.28-kN (3,660-lb.-thrust) Ishikawajima-Harima turbofan engines

Maximum speed: 1038 km/h (644 m.p.h.) at sea level

Initial climb rate: 3048 m/min (10,000 f.p.m.)

Take-off run: 610 m (2,000 ft.)

Range: 1297 km (800 mi.) (on internal fuel)

Service ceiling: 15,420 m (50,600 ft.)

Weights: empty 3790 kg (8,338 lb.); maximum take-off 7500 kg (16,500 lb.)

Dimensions:
span	9.94 m	(32 ft. 7 in.)
length	13.00 m	(42 ft. 8 in.)
height	4.60 m	(15 ft. 1 in.)
wing area	21 m²	(226 sq. ft.)

T-4

This particular T-4, serial number 56-5601, was the first of four prototypes, originally designated XT-4 and is seen here wearing the markings of the Air Proving Wing.

The T-4 is jointly manufactured by three different companies, Fuji, Kawasaki and Mitsubishi. Kawasaki builds only the forward fuselage but is responsible for all flight testing.

Like many modern jet trainers, the T-4 features a raised, staggered cockpit offering excellent visibility for both pupil and instructor. The large canopy features a wraparound windscreen and separate main unit which hinges to starboard for entry/exit.

Conventional in design, the relatively high-set wing gives the T-4 excellent high-subsonic manoeuvrability and docile handling characteristics. Although it is not configured for combat, hardpoints under the wings permit the carriage of various external stores.

Japan's newest intermediate jet trainer was designed to withstand hard and heavy landings; consequently, the undercarriage is extremely strong and has anti-skid brakes, which are located on the main units.

Being of twin-engined configuration, the T-4 enjoys a distinct performance advantage over many other single-engined, contemporary jet trainers. Its two Ishikawajima-Harima turbofans put out a considerable amount (32.56 kN/7,320 lb. thrust) of thrust.

ACTION DATA

THRUST

In comparison with the Polish PZL I-22 and the older Dassault/Dornier Alpha Jet, the T-4 has more than adequate thrust and performance, thanks to its small but powerful locally designed and built F-3 IHI turbofans.

T-4 32.6 kN (7,320 lb. thrust)
ALPHA JET E 26.5 kN (5,960 lb. thrust)
I-22 IRYDA 21.6 kN (4,860 lb. thrust)

CLIMB RATE

Although powerful for its size, the T-4's overall performance is somewhat less than that of the Alpha Jet. All three types can out-perform several current front-line combat aircraft, however.

T-4 3048 m/min (10,000 f.p.m.)
ALPHA JET E 3660 m/min (12,000 f.p.m.)
I-22 IRYDA 1500 m/min (4,900 f.p.m.)

g LIMITS

Modern advanced trainers are capable of pulling higher-g manoeuvres than their predecessors without coming apart. This allows pilots to develop their skills and awareness before being assigned to front-line combat units.

T-4 +7.33/-3
ALPHA JET E +8/-4
I-22 IRYDA +12/-6

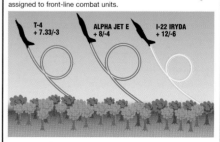

Asian jet trainer designs

■ **AIDC AT-3 TSU CHIANG:** The first military jet developed by Taiwan, the AT-3 performs both basic training and light attack roles.

■ **CNAMC/PAC K-8 KARAKORUM:** Jointly financed by China and Pakistan, the K-8 serves as a basic jet trainer with both air forces.

■ **FUJI T-1A/B:** This was Japan's first indigenous jet trainer, though it is now largely out of service, having been replaced by the T-4.

■ **MITSUBISHI T-2:** The T-2 serves as the JASDF's standard advanced trainer and shares many components with the F-1 fighter variant.

LOCKHEED
C-5 GALAXY

● Strategic transport ● Heavylift heavyweight

This monster aircraft, the world's biggest transport for two decades, hauled cargoes in American military actions from Vietnam onwards. Although not as large as the Antonov aircraft of today, the C-5 Galaxy has an unmatched service record for transporting the weaponry of war. To pilots, perched 10 m (30 ft.) off the ground before starting engines, the Galaxy is rated as the biggest and the best.

▲ Slowly disappearing into the opened 'mouth' of a C-5 Galaxy, a mothballed F-5 fighter demonstrates the huge Lockheed transport's unrivalled ability to handle large loads.

LOCKHEED C-5 GALAXY

▼ Global reach
Inflight refuelling means that the C-5 can deliver its outsize loads anywhere in the world.

▲ Rear loader
The C-5's tail is upswept, enabling a huge rear-loading door and ramp to be fitted.

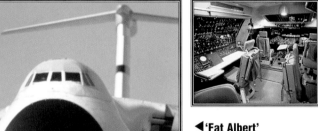

◀ Flight deck
The C-5 is flown by a pilot and co-pilot, with flight engineer and navigator facing outwards at the rear of the flight deck.

◀ 'Fat Albert'
Nicknamed with back-handed affection by its crews, the C-5 was for two decades the biggest and heaviest aircraft in the world.

◀ Easy to fly
The Galaxy's four-man flight crew sit high in the upper decking of the forward fuselage. In spite of its size, the C-5 is reasonably easy, if a little sluggish, to fly.

FACTS AND FIGURES

➤ The C-5 was chosen by the Air Force over transports proposed by Boeing and Douglas.

➤ Eighty-one C-5A transports were built in 1967-71; 50 similar C-5Bs were built when production resumed between 1984-89.

➤ Many C-5 loadmasters have logged 20,000 flight hours, more than most airline pilots.

➤ The crash of a C-5A at Ramstein, Germany, on 29 August 1990 was the only loss of a transport plane during the massive Desert Shield airlift preparing for the Gulf War.

➤ Lockheed claims that the C-5's four engines have the same power as 48 railroad locomotives.

PROFILE

Giant from Georgia

The revolutionary thing about the Lockheed C-5 Galaxy is its sheer size. Many big aircraft have won fleeting cameo roles in history's cast of aviation characters, but few of the real giants actually register a full working day, all day, every day, doing a real job in the real world. The C-5 combines greatness with unromantic achievement.

At over 300 tonnes, the C-5 was the biggest and heaviest aeroplane in its class when test pilots thundered aloft in the first example on 30 June 1968. Since then, even larger Antonov transports have appeared in the former Soviet Union, but for its first two decades of operation the Galaxy was without rival.

The C-5 can carry almost any item in the US military inventory, from Abrams main battle tanks to over 360 fully-equipped paratroops. It was the backbone of the 1991 Desert Shield airlift, the entire force of 85 Galaxies being used to carry 42 per cent of all air-delivered cargo – nearly a quarter of a million tonnes.

The C-5 was vital to the success of the Gulf War. Its record-breaking effort saw the Galaxy lifting a heavier tonnage in the first 21 days of Desert Shield than was carried in the entire Berlin airlift.

There are three inboard and three outboard sets of slotted flaps on the trailing edge of the wing, with slotted slats on the outboard leading edge.

The tip of the C-5's nose houses a Bendix APS-133 digital colour weather radar. The entire nose hinges upwards for access to the hold.

The T-tail is fitted with hydraulically-actuated four-section elevators and a twin-section rudder. There are no trim tabs; the whole of the horizontal tail can be adjusted.

The original C-5A had considerable problems with wing fatigue, which was corrected in the C-5B. In the 1980s the entire fleet was given new, stronger wings at a cost of more than one billion dollars.

The bullet fairing at the top of the huge T-tail houses an air data recorder as well as a flight data and crash recorder – the so-called 'Black Box'.

C-5B Galaxy

Type: heavy, long-range logistic freighter

Powerplant: four 191.24-kN (41,000-lb.-thrust) General Electric TF39-GE-1C turbofans

Maximum speed: 760 km/h (570 m.p.h.) at 10,000 m (32,800 ft.)

Range: 6033 km (3,700 mi.) with max. payload

Service ceiling: 10,900 m (34,000 ft.)

Weights: empty 170,000 kg (375,000 lb.); loaded 380,000 kg (838,000 lb.)

Payload: Up to 120,200 kg (264,440 lb.) in main freight compartment plus 73 passengers or fully-equipped combat troops

Dimensions:
span	67.88 m	(222 ft. 8 in.)
length	75.54 m	(247 ft. 10 in.)
height	19.85 m	(63 ft. 2 in.)
wing area	576 m²	(6,200 sq. ft.)

C-5B GALAXY

First built in the 1960s, the C-5 went back into production as the improved C-5B in the 1980s. There are more than 120 C-5s in service with the US Air Force, 50 of which are 'B' models.

Aircraft of the Galaxy's size became possible only with the development of large, powerful jet engines. The C-5 is powered by four General Electric TF39-GE-1C twin-shaft high bypass turbofans, each delivering 191.24 kN (41,000 lb. of thrust).

The main landing gear of the Galaxy consists of four bogies each with six wheels, two forwards and four aft.

The massive hold can accommodate a wide variety of outsize loads, from helicopters and tanks to trucks and cargo containers. It can also carry over 360 fully-equipped troops.

COMBAT DATA

RANGE

The arrival of the Galaxy in the late 1960s meant that for the first time the US military had the capacity to deliver outsize loads anywhere in the world at jet speeds. The Galaxy can fly intercontinental distances even when carrying a payload of 118 tonnes (118 tons); the huge Antonov An-124 is its only rival. The An-124, known as 'Condor' to NATO but called 'Ruslan' after a fairytale giant by its makers, can carry even heavier loads, but not over such great distances.

5200 km (3,200 mi.)	**6033 km (3,400 mi.)**	**4400 km (2,700 mi.)**
C-17 GLOBEMASTER III	C-5B GALAXY	An-124 RUSLAN

Heavylift specialist

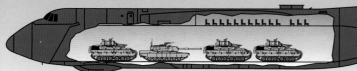

ARMOURED TRANSPORT: Hoisting just one 60-tonne M1 Abrams main battle tank would be beyond most other transport aircraft, but the C-5 can carry it with ease, along with its crew and mechanics, three 20-tonne M2 Bradley infantry fighting vehicles plus their crews and mechanics – all in airline comfort in the passenger compartment on the top deck.

HELICOPTER MOVER: Galaxies were vital during Operation Desert Shield, especially when they were used to fly Apache gunship helicopters out to Saudi Arabia. The AH-64s were packed two by two, six at a time, and three C-5 trips could move a whole battalion. Once in the Gulf, the helicopters were re-assembled and operational within 24 hours.

LOCKHEED

EC-130

● Electronic warfare Hercules variants ● Highly classified equipment

U nder the designation EC-130, the USAF operates four special mission variants of the ubiquitous Hercules transport. One is an airborne control centre, while the other three have a much more sensitive role: electronic warfare. Although routinely seen on the outside, the inside is a secret world. To gain access to the interior of the aircraft a top-secret codeword is required, as the task of the EC-130E and EC-130H is to listen to and disrupt enemy communications.

▲ The USAF operates an EC-130E version as an airborne battlefield command and control centre. Internal consoles can display digitised maps covering any area of the world.

PHOTO FILE

LOCKHEED EC-130

EC-130H Compass Call ▶
The EC-130H is used for communications intrusion and jamming duties. Previously operated from Sembach in Germany, the 10 operational aircraft are now based at Davis-Monthan in Arizona.

▲ Jamming equipment
An array of wire antennas is suspended on a gantry under the tail. Blisters on the rear fuselage contain two further antennas.

▲ EC-130(RR) Rivet Rider
Working in conjunction with the EC-130H is the EC-130(RR) Rivet Rider, which is also tasked with jamming enemy communications. It can tap into and rebroadcast radio and TV transmissions for propaganda and psychological warfare missions.

▲ Rivet Rider antennas
The Rivet Rider is easily identified by a single, large axehead antenna under each wing.

TACAMO – TAke Charge And Move Out ▶
A US Navy C-130Q relays communications to its ballistic nuclear missile submarines.

FACTS AND FIGURES

➤ EC-130 crew often exceed the USAF's recommended maximum of 155 days away from home each year.

➤ Incredibly, the original C-130 airframe made its first flight on 23 August 1954.

➤ US Navy EC-130Q aircraft were replaced in 1989 with the Boeing E-6 Mercury.

➤ Comfy Levi, Rivet Rider and ABCCC EC-130Es and EC-130Hs were operational during Operation Desert Storm.

➤ The US Coast Guard operates an EC-130E as an electronic calibration aircraft.

➤ A major role during the Cold War was eavesdropping in the Berlin Corridor.

PROFILE

USAF electronic warriors

The EC-130 may look like a transport aircraft but it is a saboteur with wings, using the marvel of electronics to break up an enemy's military radio and television broadcasting.

The USAF operates several intelligence-gathering versions of the Hercules transport under the designation EC-130E. A Hercules version, unofficially designated EC-130E and now retired, operated from Frankfurt and gathered signals, electronic and communications intelligence. Another EC-130E version, the ABCCC, is an airborne battlefield control aircraft.

There are two types of intelligence-gathering EC-130Es, both operated by the 193rd Special Operations Squadron,

based at Harrisburg in Philadelphia.

The EC-130E(CL) Comfy Levi undertakes Elint (electronic intelligence) and probably jamming missions under the codename 'Senior Scout'. Special mission equipment uses antennas that are fitted to removable undercarriage doors and fairings. Five of these aircraft carry sensor operators in the cargo hold, who use black boxes to intrude into an enemy's communications and extract information.

The most heavily-modified version, the EC-130E(RR) Rivet Rider, intrudes into enemy radio and television broadcasts and flies under the name 'Commando Solo'.

Above: The huge blade antenna on the fin leading edge and the Vietnam-style camouflage distinguishes early Rivet Riders. The latest upgraded version wears a smart two-tone grey scheme.

Above: For anti-drug trafficking duties, the US Coast Guard bought an early-warning EC-130V fitted with an APS-145 search radar. High costs, however, forced it out of service and the role was taken over by Customs Service P-3s. The EC-130 was reported to have gone to the USAF for an undisclosed 'black' programme.

EC-130H Hercules

Type: electronic warfare aircraft

Powerplant: four 3020-kW (4,050-hp.) Allison T56-A-15 turboprop engines

Maximum speed: 611 km/h (379 m.p.h.)

Range: 4100 km (2,540 mi.)

Service ceiling: 13,225 m (43,400 ft.)

Weights: empty 34,105 kg (75,031 lb.); maximum take-off 74,202 kg (163,244 lb.)

Accommodation: two pilots, navigator, electronic warfare officer, flight engineer, loadmaster and five electronic equipment operators

Dimensions: span 40.41 m (133 ft.)
length 29.79 m (98 ft.)
height 11.66 m (38 ft.)
wing area 162.11 m² (1,744 sq. ft.)

EC-130E(RR) HERCULES

All EC-130E(RR)s are operated by the 193rd Special Operations Squadron, Pennsylvania Air National Guard. They are based at Harrisburg International Airport.

EC-130Es are powered by four Allison T56-A-15 turboprops, as fitted to the standard C-130H transport variant.

The dark 'European One' colour scheme, as shown here, replaced the earlier Vietnam 'Southeast Asia' camouflage.

The Rivet Rider has recently been extensively upgraded. The latest model differs considerably from the one shown here. Current versions have worldwide colour television broadcast capabilities. Externally, these aircraft have four bullet fairings on the fin and two large pods under the outer wings.

The most prominent feature of the early Rivet Riders was the blade aerial ahead of the tailfin. This was believed to be related to TV broadcasting.

There are two retractable trailing antennas: a high-frequency one reeled horizontally behind the aircraft and a 304-metre AM-band antenna held in a near-vertical position by a weight.

An in-flight refuelling receptacle is fitted above the cockpit. Refuelling capability means that crew fatigue is the limiting factor during a mission.

The Rivet Rider's mission is to disrupt enemy communications. It can broadcast on any frequency, including AM/FM radio, black and white and now colour TV, as well as short-wave (HF) and other communication bands.

Underwing stores include long-range fuel tanks, as on standard Hercules, a pod containing a trailing aerial and an 'axe-head' antenna.

COMBAT DATA

MAXIMUM SPEED

All manner of different aircraft have been used as ELINT platforms. The Soviet An-12 is broadly similar to the C-130 in size and configuration, whereas the C-47 is a cheap and reliable alternative.

EC-130E HERCULES 612 km/h (379 m.p.h.)
An-12 'CUB-C' 777 km/h (482 m.p.h.)
C-47 346 km/h (215 m.p.h.)

RANGE

A useful feature of the Hercules is its range. Long range allows long-distance ELINT missions to be carried out or, alternatively, shorter range flights can be made with longer 'loiter' times in the air over the 'target'.

EC-130E HERCULES 7560 km (4,687 mi.)
An-12 'CUB-C' 5700 km (3,534 mi.)
C-47 2430 km (1,507 mi.)

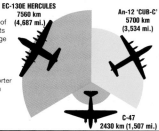

EC-130 Hercules missions

The C-130, with the minimum of modification to the basic airframe, has proved ideal for the various EC-130 roles.

1 COMMAND MODULE: The ABCCC is a regular Hercules transport fitted with a removable battle command module. This houses equipment for 16 mission specialists.

2 COMMUNICATIONS JAMMER: The EC-130E(RR) Rivet Rider is fitted with comprehensive jamming equipment in the tail, fuselage and wings to disrupt enemy communications.

3 RADAR CALIBRATION: Air traffic search and control radars need to be constantly checked. The US Coast Guard uses the Hercules to calibrate these.

LOCKHEED

C-141 STARLIFTER

● Strategic freighter ● Troop carrier ● Long-range heavy lifter

Lockheed's C-141 StarLifter is the heavy muscle of the American military air transport fleet. Although growing old and being replaced, slowly, by the McDonnell Douglas C-17 Globemaster III, the C-141 has logged millions of miles since entering service in the mid-1960s. As the principal long-range airlifter for US forces (helped by smaller numbers of the outsized C-5 Galaxy), the C-141 has carried equipment and freight to and from every crisis in recent history.

▲ The USAF's first purpose-built, long-range jet cargo and troop transport, the C-141 StarLifter was designed with its own ground-based handling system.

LOCKHEED C-141 STARLIFTER

▲ Short-field performance
A large wing area and full deflection, 60 per cent span Fowler-type flaps allows a fully laden C-141 to clear a 15-m (50-ft.) obstacle with a roll of just 1731 m (5,675 ft.). It also has a very impressive short landing run.

▲ Inflight refuelling
The C-141B introduced air-to-air refuelling to the StarLifter, increasing it to a potential global range. It has a prominent fairing on the top of the forward fuselage to receive the boom from the refueller.

▲ Clamshell doors
The C-141's large rear cargo doors allow vehicles and equipment to be loaded via a ramp that lowers to ground level.

▲ First paradrop jet
The first paradrop from a jet transport aircraft was made from a C-141 in August 1965. It made its first heavy cargo drops from the ramp later in the year.

◄ Long range
Cruising at 800 km/h (500 m.p.h.), a fully laden C-141 StarLifter can fly nearly 5000 km (3,100 mi.) on internal fuel, and much further with inflight refuelling.

FACTS AND FIGURES

➤ The StarLifter first flew on 17 December 1963, 60 years after the Wright Brothers.

➤ The first operational C-141A was delivered to Tinker AFB, Oklahoma, in October 1964.

➤ The C-141B has a 7.11-m (23-ft.) longer fuselage and inflight refuelling capability.

➤ The C-141B can carry 205 passengers or 168 fully-equipped paratroopers.

➤ In 1984, C-141Bs carried tents, water, blankets and 118,000 kg (259,000 lb.) of foodstuffs to famine victims in Sudan.

➤ The last of 270 rebuilt C-141Bs was delivered to Military Air Command in 1982.

PROFILE

The USAF's strategic lifter

Famous for finally bringing home the Prisoners of War from Vietnam in 1973 and for dramatic paratroop drops in Panama in 1989, the C-141's main task is far less glamorous but equally as important. For over 30 years the C-141 StarLifter has supplied US military and sometimes civilian installations around the world with vital supplies and reinforcements. In times of crisis the C-141 can, in partnership with the massive C-5, fully equip an entire army in a matter of days anywhere in the world.

StarLifters began hauling supplies to Vietnam in the 1960s. A decade later, Lockheed won an ambitious contract to 'stretch' the 263-plane C-141A fleet by 7.11 m (23 ft.) and to add an air refuelling receptacle. The lengthened StarLifter, known as the C-141B, flew for the first time on 24 March 1977 and was put into service soon after. The improvements have given the StarLifter global reach and made it a familiar sight almost everywhere. Except for a couple of test aircraft, all of today's StarLifters are lengthened C-141B variants.

Wearing the original Military Airlift Command colour scheme, this is the first C-141B StarLifter. The scheme was later changed to the drab green and grey 'lizard' European camouflage. They have now been repainted in overall medium-grey.

The StarLifter is powered by four Pratt & Whitney TF33-P-7 turbofan engines, each rated at 93.42 kN (20,950 lb. thrust), mounted in underwing pods and fitted with clamshell-door thrust reversers.

A conventional two-spar, box-beam, cantilever high-wing is mounted on top of the fuselage with 25° sweepback. It has Fowler-type trailing-edge flaps and hinged spoilers on the upper and lower wing surfaces.

An all-metal, variable-incidence tailplane is mounted at the top of the fin. Elevators are controlled by dual hydraulic units with manual reverse.

C-141B StarLifter

The StarLifter was the USAF's first pure-jet transport designed to meet a Specific Operational Requirement for a strategic transport.

The spacious cockpit accommodates a flight crew comprising two pilots, flight engineer and navigator. It contains modern instrumentation for all-weather operations around the world.

The raised area above the forward fuselage houses the inflight-refuelling receptacle, into which the tanker's boom is connected to pass fuel to the StarLifter.

Modification of the C-141A to the C-141B involved the insertion of newly-fabricated fuselage sections ahead of and behind the wing, resulting in a stretch of 7.11 m (23 ft.). This gave an increase in the volume of cargo that could be carried. The C-141B also had a new, more streamlined wingroot fairing and inflight-refuelling capability.

The stretched C-141B can house three extra pallets, although the weight capacity is no greater. Volumetric limitations of the C-141 have therefore been overcome.

The swept vertical fin and rudder has a prominent bullet fairing where it meets the horizontal tailplane. The rudder is hydraulically controlled by electric trim tabs.

The nosewheel retracts rearwards into the fuselage and is enclosed by two doors.

The four-wheel bogie main undercarriage units retract forwards into fairings on the sides of the lower fuselage. To assist with short-field landings the aircraft has hydraulic, multiple-disc, anti-skid brakes.

The large rear ramp doors can be opened fully in flight for aerial load dropping, while a built-in loading ramp can be extended and lowered for vehicle access when on the ground.

C-141B StarLifter

Type: strategic airlifter (troop/cargo transport)

Powerplant: four 93.42-kN (20,950-lb.-thrust) Pratt & Whitney TF33-P-7 turbofan engines

Maximum speed: 933 km/h (578 m.p.h.)

Maximum cruising speed: 911 km/h (565 m.p.h.)

Range: 4773 km (2,960 mi.) with max. payload

Service ceiling: 12,879 m (42,250 ft.)

Weights: empty weight (C-141A) 60,678 kg (133,491 lb.); (C-141B) 67,187 kg (147,811 lb.); maximum take-off 155,585 kg (342,287 lb.)

Accommodation: has carried every cargo from vehicles to a whale; normal payload is 32,135 kg (70,697 lb.); maximum payload 41,223 kg (90,690 lb.)

Dimensions:
span   48.74 m (159 ft. 10 in.)
length   51.29 m (168 ft. 3 in.)
height   12.15 m (39 ft. 10 in.)
wing area 299.90 m² (3,227 sq. ft.)

COMBAT DATA

PAYLOAD

The USAF had a small number of Boeing 707s adapted as C-135s for interim cargo transport before the C-141 came into service. With no ramp or rear loading doors, the volume of freight was limited. The Russian Il-76 has a similar weight-lifting capacity to the C-141, but its smaller fuselage limits the size and volume that can be accommodated.

C-141 STARLIFTER   41,000 kg (90,200 lb.)

C-135A   37,650 kg (82,830 lb.)

Il-76 'CANDID'   40,000 kg (88,000 lb.)

Lockheed's 'Star' lifter

BULK CARRIER: The C-141's hold is of almost constant cross-section along its entire length. This gives a usable cargo volume of 322.79 m³ in the C-141B, enabling it to transport up to four military vehicles.

CONVERTIBLE: An extensive array of internal equipment, including fold-away floor rollers, tie-down points and seat tracks, enables the passenger/cargo mix to be changed rapidly.

HEAVY LIFTER: In terms of tonne/miles per flying hour, one C-141 could equal four C-124 Globemasters. Just 18 StarLifters could have accomplished the same as 142 C-54 Skymasters in the Berlin Airlift of 1948/49.

FAST FREIGHTER: In Vietnam, under combat conditions, the C-141 could offload in 17 minutes using its special handling equipment. A full palletised load could be installed in only 30 minutes and flown to its destination in half the time of the C-124 it replaced.

LOCKHEED

S/ES-3 VIKING

● Twin-jet anti-submarine ● Elint version ● Gulf War veteran

A lthough it may not be as glamorous as the F-14 and F/A-18 'fast jets' which also serve aboard the United States' super-carriers, the S-3 Viking has, arguably, a more crucial role. One of the biggest enemies of a carrier battle group is the submarine. The Viking's task is to find these undersea machines and stop them in their tracks. For this role Lockheed packed sophisticated electronics and potent weapons into a surprisingly compact airframe.

▲ The S-3's main task is outer-zone anti-submarine warfare (ASW). Inner-zone ASW is tackled by carrier-borne helicopters, such as the SH-3 Sea King and SH-60 Seahawk.

LOCKHEED S/ES-3 VIKING

◄ **Improved Viking**
Most surviving S-3As were converted to S-3B standard in the late-1980s, with the addition of Harpoon anti-ship missiles and new avionics. Number 159742 was the first conversion.

▲ **Carrier-borne transport**
Six US-3A COD aircraft deliver vital replenishment supplies to the Pacific Fleet.

▼ **'Bombed-up' Viking**
Vikings were active in the Gulf War, undertaking bombing missions against land targets and small vessels in the Persian Gulf.

▲ **ES-3A eavesdropper**
Packed with extra sensors and a third systems operator, the ES-3A is an electronic intelligence (Elint) variant of the Viking. Sixteen conversions are deployed in pairs aboard US carriers.

'Stinger' deployed ►
With its boom extended, this Viking drops a torpedo. The weapons bay can hold up to 1814 kg (4,000 lb.) of ordnance, which, until recently, included nuclear depth charges.

FACTS AND FIGURES

➤ In partnership with Lockheed, Vought designed and built the wings, tail, landing gear and engine pods for the Viking.

➤ The US-3A COD transport aircraft have been stripped of their ASW gear.

➤ ES-3A Elint Vikings have replaced the last carrier-based EA-3B Skywarriors.

➤ Modified, so-called 'Brown Boy', Vikings were used to drop ground movement sensors in Bosnia.

➤ At one time the S-3A equipped 14 squadrons.

➤ In February 1974 the S-3 made its first carrier landing, on USS Forrestal.

PROFILE

US Fleet's Nordic sub-hunter

In 1964 the US Navy began its search for a replacement for the proven Grumman S-2 Tracker. Lockheed, a company with comparatively little experience in building carrier-borne aircraft, teamed with Vought to build the S-3 Viking.

After a January 1972 first flight, a further seven development airframes and

179 production aircraft were built. Operations began in 1974 and the last S-3As were delivered in 1978. A number have been modified for the carrier onboard delivery (COD) role as US-3As, and a dedicated in-flight refuelling version, the KS-3A, was trialled but did not go into production. There are also 16 ES-3A electronic intelligence variants operating in pairs from US Navy carriers.

The current ASW version is the S-3B, introduced in 1987. This aircraft features greatly improved avionics and a Harpoon air-to-surface missile capability.

This Viking is in its natural environment, in search of submarines. All S-3s are operated by the US Navy and represent the most capable carrier-borne anti-submarine force in the world.

S-3B VIKING

Air Antisubmarine Squadron 30 flew from the USS *Saratoga* during the Gulf War. Facing an enemy without submarines, VS-30 undertook bombing raids against Iraqi land targets.

Two General Electric TF34 turbofans provide the power for the S-3 family. Both main wings fold inwards and the vertical tail to the left on the Viking, to make it relatively compact and easy to manoeuvre on a crowded aircraft-carrier deck.

Two 1136-litre auxiliary fuel tanks are often carried to improve range. An in-flight refuelling probe is also fitted. In the 'buddy' refuelling role a D-704 'probe-and-drogue' refuelling pod is carried on the port wing pylon.

Vikings have a crew of four. Two pilots sit side-by-side and handle flight control and navigation. Behind them are the mission crew of Tactical Co-ordinator ('Tacco') and Sensor Operator ('Senso'). All sit in ejection seats.

The chief sensors aboard the S-3 include a large APS-137(V)1 search radar in the nose, for the detection of surface vessels and submarine periscopes, and a retractable forward-looking infra-red (FLIR) turret under the forward fuselage.

Apart from the FLIR turret and radar, the Viking's most important sensor is the magnetic anomaly detector (MAD) 'sting' deployed from the rear of the aircraft. This detects changes in the earth's magnetic field caused by a large metallic mass like a submarine.

The S-3B is virtually indistinguishable from the S-3A. However, the later version has a small chaff dispenser fitted to the rear fuselage.

As well as carrying 60 sonobuoys in the aft fuselage, the two internal weapons bays can hold bombs, torpedoes or depth charges. Harpoon missiles are carried on the wing pylons.

USS SARATOGA
NAVY
VS-30
VS 30 006
159390
700

S-3B Viking

Type: carrier-borne anti-submarine aircraft

Powerplant: two 41.2-kN (9,270-lb.-thrust) General Electric TF34-GE-2 turbofans

Maximum speed: 814 km/h (505 m.p.h.) at sea level

Ferry range: more than 5558 km (3,445 mi.)

Service ceiling: over 10,670 m (35,000 ft.)

Weights: empty 12,088 kg (26,594 lb.); maximum take-off 23,832 kg (52,430 lb.)

Armament: up to 3175 kg (6,985 lb.) of ordnance (up to 1814 kg/4,000 lb.) in internal weapons bays), including bombs, depth charges, torpedoes and AGM-84 Harpoon air-to-surface missiles

Dimensions: span 20.93 m (68 ft. 8 in.)
length 16.26 m (53 ft. 4 in.)
height 6.93 m (22 ft. 9 in.)
wing area 55.56 m² (554 sq. ft.)

COMBAT DATA

MAXIMUM SPEED

Powered by turbofan engines, the Viking has an impressive top speed compared to propeller-driven aircraft – almost twice that of the S-2E. When the Viking is loaded this speed is appreciably reduced, but it can still reach its given patrol area faster than other carrier-borne, fixed-wing ASW machines.

S-3B VIKING	814 km/h (505 m.p.h.)
S-2E TRACKER	426 km/h (264 m.p.h.)
Br.1150 ALIZÉ	323 km/h (200 m.p.h.)

ENDURANCE

The Viking has a shorter patrol endurance than the propeller-driven aircraft, but has the ability to be refuelled in the air, which greatly increases its flexibility. Vikings have a secondary in-flight refuelling role, for which they can be fitted with 'buddy' refuelling tanks. A tanker version of the Viking was also used until recently.

S-3B VIKING	**S-2E TRACKER**	**Br.1150 ALIZÉ**
7 hours 30 min	9 hours	7 hours 40 min

Multi-role Viking at work

ANTI-SUBMARINE WARFARE: ASW remains the S-3's most important task. The S-3B is found aboard all of the US Navy's super-carriers, providing protection from the ever-present underwater threat. During the Gulf conflict the S-3 displayed its versatility, and was deployed as a bomber.

IN-FLIGHT REFUELLING: Development of a specialised KS-3A tanker variant of the Viking was abandoned and ASW Vikings were modified to carry 'buddy' IFR equipment. The 'probe-and-drogue' gear is carried in a pod attached to the port underwing pylon.

CARRIER ONBOARD DELIVERY: A small number of S-3As were modified as COD aircraft to supplement the Pacific Fleet's C-2 Greyhounds. Avionics equipment was removed to make space for passengers and cargo.

ELECTRONIC INTELLIGENCE: Elint is the role assigned to the small ES-3A fleet. A large collection of new sensors (and their associated antennas) was installed in the aircraft modified and these are used in pairs from carriers.

133

LOCKHEED

F-117 NIGHTHAWK

● 'Stealth' fighter-bomber ● Fly-by-wire control ● Gulf War veteran

▲ Two weapons bays in the F-117 are equipped with a trapeze to carry bombs weighing up to 907 kg (2,000 lb.). The usual weapon for raids on Iraq was the laser-guided GBU-27. AGM-65 Maverick or AGM-88 HARM missiles can also be carried.

Developed in great secrecy, the F-117A Nighthawk quickly became one of the world's best known aircraft after its success in the first Gulf War. Making use of the stealth technology that renders the aircraft virtually invisible to radar, the USAF's F-117s attacked important targets in Iraq from the opening moments of Desert Storm. Not only did they reach Baghdad unseen, but they hit their assigned targets with pinpoint accuracy using laser bombs.

LOCKHEED F-117 NIGHTHAWK

▼ **Baghdad bombers**
Striking unexpectedly at night, F-117s flew missions against heavily defended positions in central Baghdad during both Gulf conflicts.

▲ **Under cover of darkness**
As during the first seven years of its existence, the F-117 flew almost exclusively at night to maintain the secrecy of its missions and capability.

▲ **Protective shelter**
This Nighthawk is seen inside its hardened shelter, in which the F-117s spent much of their daylight hours between night attack missions.

▲ **Rarely seen**
There was little evidence at their bases at home or overseas that the Nighthawks were operating, other than the standard joke signs.

First major deployment ▶
Apart from the invasion of Panama in 1989, the first Gulf War was the first major use of the F-117A. Nighthawks were assigned nearly one-third of the Baghdad targets during the first 24 hours.

FACTS AND FIGURES

➤ Laser-guided bombs used by the F-117 are specially modified with 'clipped' fins so that they will fit in the weapons bay.

➤ The most missions flown by an F-117 pilot during Desert Storm was 23.

➤ Successive missions were flown over different routes to confuse the Iraqis.

➤ Khamis Mushait airfield was at an altitude of 2073 metres, which affected take-off and necessitated in-flight refuelling.

➤ On rare occasions F-117 missions were supported by EF-111s and F-4Gs.

➤ The 1271 sorties undertaken totalled around 7000 flight hours.

Unseen bomber of Baghdad

High-tech 'stealth' capabilities allowed the F-117A to operate undetected at night in Iraqi airspace until it reached Baghdad. Transferred in great secrecy from its home base in Nevada to Khamis Mushait in the south of Saudi Arabia, the F-117A spearheaded the opening of the air war by coalition forces in January 1991. The dual infrared weapons delivery system and laser-guided bombs gave it the means to attack targets with the utmost precision. In addition to attacking important military areas in central Baghdad, the Nighthawks hit strategic targets such as communications facilities, bridges, airfields and command centres. In all, 1271 combat missions were flown by the F-117s, with each pilot averaging 21 sorties. Despite an estimated 3000 Iraqi anti-aircraft artillery (AAA) pieces and 60 surface-to-air missile (SAM) sites in the areas attacked, no F-117 was hit while dropping around 2000 laser-guided bombs (LGBs) onto targets deep inside Iraq. The normal flight-time for a Gulf War mission which included air-to-air refuelling was just over five hours.

In-flight refuelling played a vital part in most raids during the war, not least those flown by F-117s.

F-117A Nighthawk

Type: single-seat strike fighter

Powerplant: two 48.04-kN (10,800-lb. thrust) non-afterburning General Electric F404-GE F1D2 turbofans

Maximum speed: Mach 1 (estimated) or 1040 km/h (2,293 m.p.h.)

Combat radius: 1200 km (746 mi.) unrefuelled, with a 2250-kg (4,960-lb.) weapon load

Armament: up to 2268 kg (5,000 lb.) carried internally

Weights: empty 13,600 kg (29,983 lb.); maximum take-off 23,814 kg (52,500 lb.)

Dimensions:
span	13.2 m	(43 ft. 4 in.)
length	20.08 m	(65 ft. 11 in.)
height	3.78 m	(12 ft. 5 in.)
wing area	about 105.9 m²	(1,140 sq. ft.)

A receptacle incorporated in the spine running along the top of the Nighthawk's fuselage is used for in-flight refuelling, via the USAF's standard 'flying boom' system.

The F-117's wings are swept at 67°. This is again intended to reduce radar reflections as well as being for high-speed performance.

Tailfins are carefully positioned to keep radar reflections to a minimum and to help shield the engine exhausts from infra-red sensors of a pursuing fighter or missile.

The F-117 is manufactured from aluminium and composites with radar-absorbing material (RAM) sprayed onto the surface and key points, such as the joints between each facet of the fuselage and the wing leading edges.

F-117A NIGHTHAWK

The 37th Tactical Fighter Wing, based at Tonopah Air Force Base, Nevada, is the sole F-117A operator, and sent 44 aircraft to the Gulf.

The pyramid-shaped cockpit canopy restricts the area around the pilot's shoulders and head. The cockpit itself is a modern 'all-glass' environment dominated by large video displays.

All air data for the F-117's instruments are collected by four faceted plastic and metal sensor probes in the aircraft's nose.

Two imaging infra-red (IR) turrets (FLIR and DLIR) are recessed into the aircraft's nose. They are fully integrated with, and provide data for, the weapons release system.

Weapons are carried internally, to avoid the radar reflections associated with external stores. In the Gulf, F-117s were normally armed with 907-kg (2,000-lb.) laser-guided bombs.

The two General Electric turbofans are buried in the fuselage. The unique 'platypus' exhaust system mixes hot gasses with cold air, reducing the aircraft's infra-red signature.

The Nighthawk's sharply swept twin butterfly tailplanes act both as rudders and elevators. The 'ruddervators' work in opposition for yaw control and together for pitch control.

COMBAT DATA

MAXIMUM SPEED

Maximum speed and other performance parameters do not have the same relevance in an aircraft like the F-117. Its shape is optimised for stealth rather than speed.

F-117A	1040 km/h (646 m.p.h.)
F-15E EAGLE	2655 km/h (1,650 m.p.h.)
F-111F	2655 km/h (1,650 m.p.h.)

BOMBLOAD

The F-111F has been unequalled for its range and load-carrying capabilities for many years, and performed well in the Gulf. However, like other conventional aircraft, it was heavily reliant on its low-level speed and electronic countermeasures support.

F-117A NIGHTHAWK	2268-kg (5,000-lb.) bombload
F-15E EAGLE	11,113-kg (25,000-lb.) bombload
F-111F	14,228-kg (25,550-lb.) bombload

Black jets over Iraq

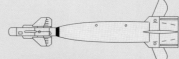

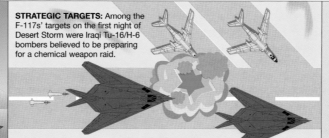

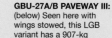

DESERT SHIELD: The Iraqi invasion of Kuwait and the decision by the coalition powers to come to Kuwait's aid gave the USAF its first opportunity to test the F-117 on a large scale.

TANKER SUPPORT: As the F-117s' Saudi base was situated at high altitude, the aircraft were required to take off with a reduced fuel load and 'top up' their tanks from a KC-135 once airborne.

STRATEGIC TARGETS: Among the F-117s' targets on the first night of Desert Storm were Iraqi Tu-16/H-6 bombers believed to be preparing for a chemical weapon raid.

GBU-27/B PAVEWAY III: (above) This laser-guided bomb, seen here with tail wings deployed, was one of the F-117s' primary offensive weapons. It has a standard 907-kg (2,000-lb.) Mk 84 general-purpose warhead.

GBU-27A/B PAVEWAY III: (below) Seen here with wings stowed, this LGB variant has a 907-kg BLU-109 'I-2000' penetrator warhead for use against hardened targets. The F-117's weapons bay is limited to two LGBs.

LOCKHEED

U-2R

● **High-altitude reconnaissance** ● **Earth resources survey**

Today's high-flying Lockheed U-2R is an improvement on the Cold War's most famous reconnaissance plane, updated with microchip technology. The U-2R is easy to spot with its huge, sailplane-like wing. Painted black and flown by a pilot in an astronaut-style pressure suit, this remarkable craft can loiter for hours higher than most planes can fly, gathering intelligence with its cameras and electronic sensors.

▲ *Clarence L. 'Kelly' Johnson was one of the best-known aircraft designers. He was responsible for the U-2 series, the F-104 Starfighter and the SR-71 'Blackbird'. Here he is seen in front of a NASA ER-2, a special version of the U-2R.*

PHOTO FILE

LOCKHEED **U-2R**

◀ **Dragon Lady**
The sinister black paint and elegant manoeuvres of the U-2 earned it this nickname. Its huge wings carry it to extreme altitude, from where its sensors can peer sideways many miles into denied territory. With radars, cameras or electronic receivers onboard, little escapes the watchful eye of the U-2R.

The first ▶ generation
Today's U-2R is based on the original U-2, which was developed by Lockheed's famous 'Skunk Works' under the direction of Clarence L. Johnson.

▶ **Delicate wings**
The wings are very fragile, and the pilot has to take great care not to overstress them.

▲ **Motor glider**
The U-2 has often been likened to a giant glider with a jet engine. Like gliders, the Dragon Lady is very efficient in the air, but is also very tricky to land. A second pilot drives behind the U-2 and gives a running commentary of the approach to aid the pilot.

◀ **Black paint**
The U-2 is coated with a special paint containing iron. This makes the aircraft difficult to see on radar.

FACTS AND FIGURES

➤ The original U-2 prototype, for the series that preceded today's U-2R, first flew on 4 August 1955.

➤ The prototype of the enlarged U-2R initially flew on 28 August 1967.

➤ A total of 49 U-2Rs and TR-1s were built in two batches.

➤ Lockheed's production line was reopened in November 1979 for the TR-1 (now also known as the U-2R).

➤ The U-2R and TR-1 employ ASARS-2 battlefield surveillance radar.

➤ Some U-2Rs have a satellite communication system.

PROFILE

Lockheed's black dragon

First introduced in the Vietnam era, the U-2R is similar to but bigger and more powerful than the U-2 in which Francis Gary Powers was shot down over Russia on 1 May 1960. A few identical aircraft used for battlefield surveillance in the 1980s were known by the designation TR-1.

The 'Dragon Lady', as this unique aircraft is sometimes called, is designed to monitor potential enemy forces or to police arms agreements. It carries photographic, radar and electronic sensors in a long, detachable nose cone, in the fuselage and in wingpods. The sensor fit is changed depending on the mission.

Although the basic design is nearly 50 years old, the U-2R still flies higher than all but a handful of aircraft. It is difficult to fly, with a cramped cockpit and challenging handling properties. It lands and takes off using an odd bicycle-style landing gear with outrigger wheels at the wingtips which detach and fall away after take-off. Recent missions have involved flights over Bosnia, which helped locate mass graves.

NASA uses two ER-2s, which are based on the U-2R airframe. They are employed for high-altitude research into the ozone layer and for monitoring the earth's crust.

U-2R

The U-2R's altitude performance and incredible endurance make it the perfect vehicle for maintaining a long watch on hostile territory. The small hand-built fleet is very important to the US Air Force, which has re-engined the aircraft. Radar reconnaissance and communications intelligence gathering are the U-2's main tasks, although the type still carries traditional cameras on some missions.

U-2R

Type: single-seat high-altitude reconnaissance aircraft

Powerplant: one 75.61-kN (16,950-lb.-thrust) Pratt & Whitney J75-P-13B turbojet engine

Maximum speed: Mach 0.8 or 960 km/h (595 m.p.h.) at sea level

Cruising speed: 692 km/h (429 m.p.h.) at 10,000 m (33,000 ft.)

Range: 10,060 km (6,237 mi.)

Service ceiling: 24,835 m (81,459 ft.)

Weights: empty 7031 kg (15,468 lb.); maximum take-off 18,733 kg (41,213 lb.)

Dimensions:
span	31.39 m (103 ft.)
length	19.13 m (63 ft.)
height	4.88 m (16 ft.)
wing area	92.9 m² (1,000 sq. ft.)

The U-2 has only a central mainwheel and a small tailwheel. When it lands, it topples over on to specially toughened wingtip skids. Groundcrew then come and fix the 'pogo' wheels back on to allow the aircraft to taxi.

For taxiing, the U-2 is fitted with outrigger wheels under each wing. On take-off these keep the wings level until the aircraft leaves the ground. These 'pogo' wheels then drop free.

The U-2R pilot has a mirror to look behind to see if the aircraft is leaving a contrail – a giveaway sign to those on the ground. If there is a trail, he can change speed or altitude to prevent it.

Power for the U-2R was provided by the Pratt & Whitney J75, but in the mid-1990s these were replaced by General Electric F101s, similar to the engine which powers the B-2 stealth bomber. The U-2R's designation changed to U-2S.

U-2Rs usually carry 'superpods' on each wing, used for the carriage of sensors. These are mainly electronic receivers for intercepting communications.

Immediately behind the cockpit is a large space known as the Q-bay. When the U-2R carries enormous downward-looking cameras, this is the only place big enough to fit them. The bottom door of the bay often has glass windows for the lenses.

The cockpit is fully pressurised, but if this failed at high altitude the pilot would die almost immediately without protection. For emergency situations, he wears a full pressure suit, very similar to that worn by astronauts flying the Space Shuttle.

The nose of the U-2R carries yet more sensors and is interchangeable. Two favourite noses are the ASARS-2 stand-off radar and the LOROP side-looking camera.

UPLINK: Some U-2s are fitted with the Senior Span pod on their backs. This digitally processes the intelligence gathered by the sensors, which can be relayed to a military communications satellite.

STAND-OFF: From high altitude the U-2's sensors can penetrate the target area without the need for the aircraft to enter hostile airspace.

COMBAT DATA

SERVICE CEILING

The U-2 is renowned for its altitude capability and is only bettered by the Lockheed SR-71. However, the U-2's main advantage is its ability to remain in the same area at this incredible altitude for hours at a time, whereas the SR-71 has been and gone in a matter of seconds. The Russian M-55 'Mystic' has some of the U-2's capabilities, but cannot achieve the operational altitude of the 'Dragon Lady'. It is slightly faster, but the U-2R has a much greater endurance and can carry a far heavier load of sensors.

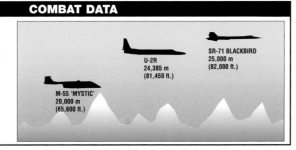

M-55 'MYSTIC'
20,000 m
(65,600 ft.)

U-2R
24,385 m
(81,459 ft.)

SR-71 BLACKBIRD
25,000 m
(82,000 ft.)

Stand-off reconnaissance

ASARS RADAR: Among the U-2R's sensors is the ASARS-2 radar, which peers sideways from the aircraft's nose.

RADAR PICTURES: The radar produces pictures of military and industrial installations deep within foreign territory. These are recorded digitally and can be datalinked to ground stations.

DOWNLINK: The images are relayed down from the satellite straight into a command post anywhere in the world. This allows battle staff to view the U-2's intelligence the moment it is gathered.

LOCKHEED
P-3 ORION

● Maritime patrol ● Anti-submarine warfare ● Electronic listener

Adapting airliner designs to the maritime reconnaissance role has long been an inexpensive solution adopted by nations requiring an airborne sea-search capability. The Lockheed Orion, based on the civil Electra, offered four-engined reliability and the necessary range and 'loiter' time for hours of patrol duty. Capable of considerable modification and updating, the Orion has served the US Navy and other air arms for nearly four decades.

▲ *The four-turboprop Lockheed Orion maritime patrol aircraft has remained virtually unchanged in appearance from the initial P-3 to the US Navy's latest P-3C Update IV.*

PHOTO FILE

LOCKHEED P-3 ORION

▲ Overseas equipment
P-3s have been supplied to 13 air arms around the world, including Australia, Canada, the Netherlands (P-3C-II above) and Spain, in addition to the US Navy.

▲ Anti-submarine
When a submarine or ship is identified on the surface, it is visually identified and photographed using the fixed KA-74 camera and hand-held equipment.

▲ Updates
Older P-3s are being updated to incorporate the latest equipment. Australian P-3s, for example, are having new data processors and weapons fitted.

▲ Attack
Various offensive weapons can be carried on underwing pylons, including mines, rocket projectiles or Harpoon medium-range anti-ship missiles. In addition, the P-3 can carry torpedoes, mines and depth bombs internally.

◀ Maritime patrol
The Lockheed P-3 Orion's primary task is to detect, identify and track submarines. For this role it is equipped with a variety of sensors, including a sting-tail mounted MAD and electronics equipment.

FACTS AND FIGURES

➤ The first flight of the P-3 derivative of the Lockheed Electra airliner took place on 19 August 1958.

➤ P-3Cs delivered to Norway and South Korea are named Update IIIs.

➤ Orions have been in production for nearly 40 years, the most recent going to Korea.

➤ To keep its crew alert on long missions, the P-3 has two rest bunks and a dinette to serve food around the clock.

➤ EP-3 is an electronic intelligence-gathering (ELINT) version of the P-3C.

➤ US Coast Guard Orions are used for anti-smuggling patrols.

PROFILE

Lockheed's sub-hunter

One of the most enduring maritime reconnaissance aircraft in service today, the Lockheed P-3 Orion is a powerful submarine hunter. Equipped with an array of advanced sonics equipment including DIFAR (Directional Acoustics-Frequency Analysis and Recording) sonobuoy processing gear and APS-115 search radar, the P-3 can find a periscope in a choppy sea or listen to the noise of a propeller in deep water. The first P-3 flew in the summer of 1962.

The upgraded P-3B with better engines but similar mission avionics flew in 1965. The P-3C which first flew in 1968, and remains in service today, has achieved great export success with countries as far apart as New Zealand and Norway.

To undertake its new military role, the P-3 inherited good shortfield performance and handling as well as ample fuselage space. A flight crew of four flies the Orion, while a team of six operates the sonics, electronic surveillance and radar equipment in the centre fuselage section. Update programmes have kept the P-3 abreast of advances in military technology, and a new version has been offered to the RAF to replace its current Nimrod patrol aircraft.

The US Navy received large numbers of all three main production models: the P-3A/B from 1961 and P-3C from 1968. The latter version remains in service to this day, also equipping the forces of Australia, Canada, Japan, Norway, the Netherlands and Pakistan.

P-3C Orion

Type: long-range anti-submarine patrol and early-warning aircraft

Powerplant: four 3661-kW (4,900-hp.) Allison T56-14 turboprop engines

Maximum speed: 761 km/h (472 m.p.h.)

Mission radius: 2494 km (1,546 mi.)

Service ceiling: 8625 m (28,290 ft.)

Weights: empty 27,890 kg (61,358 lb.); loaded 64,410 kg (141,702 lb.)

Armament: up to 9076 kg (19,967 lb.) of torpedoes, mines and depth charges internally, plus depth bombs, torpedoes, Harpoon anti-ship missiles on 10 pylons

Dimensions:
span	30.37 m (100 ft.)
length	35.61 m (117 ft.)
height	10.27 m (34 ft.)
wing area	120.77 m² (1,300 sq .ft.)

The tail unit is made from aluminium alloy. The tailplane has dihedral and there is a dorsal fin. The leading edges of the tailplane and fin have an electrical anti-icing system.

The pylons between the fuselage and inboard engines usually carry a Loral AN/ALQ-78A ESM pod.

Conventional aluminium-alloy construction fin and rudder are fitted, the latter being hydraulically-boosted.

The main cabin is the tactical centre and contains advanced electronic, magnetic and sonar detection systems. Computers and data processing equipment analyse inputs from the sensors.

The tailcone has been adapted to house electronic equipment, namely the AN/ASQ-81 magnetic anomaly detector (MAD) for detecting and tracking submerged submarines.

P-3C ORION

The land-based Lockheed P-3 Orion has been the premier maritime patrol and anti-submarine warfare aircraft with the US Navy and many other nations since its introduction in 1962.

The crew consists of 10 – four on the flight-deck, plus the tactical co-ordinator who has a team of five in the main cabin.

Four Allison T56A turboprops power the Orion, each driving four-bladed Hamilton Standard constant-speed propellers.

A tricycle-type undercarriage has hydraulically, forwards-retracting twin-, main- and nosewheels.

There are two weapons pylons permanently fitted outboard of the engines.

Launch tubes for sonobuoys and sound signals carried internally run along the rear, lower fuselage.

LE

161329

NAVY
VP-11

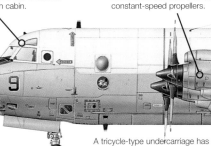

Ship attack

COMBINED OPERATIONS: The enemy warship is tracked by the Orion's search radar, infra-red detector and electronic support measures. In addition, a submarine uses its sonar devices to help the P-3C to fire its sea-skimming missile towards its target.

MISSILE: Fired from the P-3C, the subsonic, turbojet-powered Harpoon anti-ship missile uses a radar altimeter to remain just above the surface of the water.

ON TARGET: The missile's inertial guidance system is programmed to fly towards its target and an active radar controls its terminal guidance. The Harpoon then 'pops-up' before descending to impact the target with its warhead.

COMBAT DATA

ENDURANCE

The twin-engined Atlantic has a staggering 18 hours' endurance on its maximum fuel load, although this is at the expense of speed (315 km/h/195 m.p.h.). With a normal endurance of 13 hours at a patrol speed of 381 km/h (236 m.p.h.) the P-3C can increase this to over 17 hours by flying on two engines. The Russian Ilyushin Il-38 derivative of the Il-18 airliner has an endurance of 12 hours at a patrol speed of 400 km/h (248 m.p.h.).

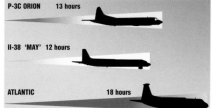

P-3C ORION	13 hours
Il-38 'MAY'	12 hours
ATLANTIC	18 hours

LOCKHEED

CP-140 AURORA

● Anti-submarine platform ● Canadian service ● Special duties

▲ *The first CP-140 Aurora was handed over to the CAF at Greenwood, Nova Scotia. Seventeen more machines followed until 1981, finally replacing the 20-year-old Bristol Britannia-derived Argus.*

A special version of the famous P-3 Orion anti-submarine warfare (ASW) aircraft, Lockheed's CP-140 Aurora is optimised for the maritime patrol requirement of the Canadian Armed Forces (CAF). The CP-140A Arcturus is based on the same airframe, but without submarine detection gear or weapons, and is used for crew training and environmental and fisheries work. These aircraft are a familiar sight around the coastline of Canada.

LOCKHEED CP-140 AURORA

▼ **Specialist weapons**
The Aurora is unique among Orion variants with its ability to carry eight Mk 44/46 torpedoes, one of a number of specific requests from the Canadian Armed Forces.

▲ **Anti-submarine sensors**
The Aurora is fitted with the US Navy S-3A Viking's APS-116 search radar, ASQ-501 MAD and AN/AYK-10 computer. A full crew consists of 11.

◄ **New missions**
Canada's CP-140 fleet has become increasingly involved in anti-drug smuggling operations.

▼ **Canadian colours**
Initially delivered in patriotic red and white colours, the fleet later reverted to an all-over grey.

◄ **CP-140 future upgrade**
Paramax Systems has submitted a bid for a C$750-million upgrade of the acoustic sensors, radar, ESM and communication/navigation systems.

FACTS AND FIGURES

➤ Canada's four Aurora and Arcturus squadrons are based at two locations, Greenwood and Comox.

➤ The first CP-140 completed its maiden flight on 22 March 1979.

➤ The last Canadian Aurora was delivered in July 1981.

➤ Lockheed built 18 CP-140 Aurora and three CP-140A Arcturus aircraft for Canada's armed forces.

➤ The CP-140 Aurora replaced the piston-engined Canadair CP-107 Argus.

➤ A No. 405 'Eagle' Squadron CP-140 won the Fincastle ASW competition in 1996.

Canada's coastal patroller

A machine of the Cold War and a reminder of the days when the Soviet Union had more than 450 nuclear submarines, the Lockheed CP-140 Aurora was Canada's answer to the undersea threat. Although the Cold War has ended, the submarine fleets belonging to Russia and other nations must still be watched closely. The four-engined, turboprop-powered Aurora allows Canadian combat crews to guard their nation and to secure the ocean approaches hundreds of miles from the shoreline.

The CP-140 Aurora uses the proven airframe of the famous Lockheed P-3 Orion – the world's most popular ASW aircraft – and is equipped with an avionics system based on that of the Lockheed S-3A Viking. This includes radar, magnetic anomaly detection (MAD) gear, and a basic computer. The CP-140 crew can detect a submarine from a considerable distance and attack with a variety of weapons.

The CP-140A Arcturus looks like the Aurora but it is not armed. The Arcturus has been used to train hundreds of ASW crews for the Canadian forces, and is also very successful for environmental and fisheries patrol duties.

A proposed upgrade of some of its systems will allow the fleet to continue operations to 2010 and beyond.

Above: The Aurora serves with the CAF in relatively large numbers. Eighteen are currently operational, in addition to three CP-140A environmental aircraft.

Below: Like the Orion, the Aurora's distinctive tail spikes contain a magnetic anomaly detector for the location of submerged enemy submarines.

CP-140 Aurora

Type: long-range maritime reconnaissance and anti-submarine patrol aircraft

Powerplant: four 3661-kW (4,910-hp.) Allison T56-A-14 turboprops

Maximum cruising speed: 732 km/h (454 m.p.h.) at optimum altitude

Maximum range: 8339 km (5,170 mi.)

Combat radius: 1853 km (1,150 mi.)

Service ceiling: 8610 m (28,250 ft.)

Weights: empty 27,892 kg (61,690 lb.); maximum take-off 64,411 kg (141,704 lb.)

Armament: 9071 kg (19,955 lb.) of stores

Dimensions:
span	30.37 m (99 ft. 8 in.)
length	35.61 m (116 ft. 10 in.)
height	10.29 m (33 ft. 9 in.)
wing area	120.77 m² (1,300 sq. ft.)

CP-140 AURORA

The CAF operates CP-140s from Greenwood, Nova Scotia (Nos 404, 405, 415 Squadrons), and Comox in British Colombia (Nos 407 and 409 Squadrons). No. 409 is the reserve squadron and No. 404 is also tasked with training.

On a typical patrol the CP-140 will carry a crew of 11 on an ASW mission of approximately 8 hours' endurance. Each of the Aurora's four Allison turboprops provides at least 3661 kW of power.

The Aurora can carry 2247 kg (4,945 lb.) of weapons in its forward fuselage stores bay alone, in addition to a wide array of wing-mounted weapons. Typically, depth charges, sea mines and torpedoes will be stowed internally, with anti-ship missiles and electronic equipment located on the twin wing hardpoints.

A secondary role for the CAF's Aurora fleet is search and rescue, for which the weapons bay can be quickly adapted to carry a special search-and-rescue package. In terms of anti-submarine capability, the Aurora is generally deemed to have a superior tactical compartment layout to that of the Orion.

The Aurora's mission profile has been widened to include the post-Cold War roles of pollution monitoring, resources surveying, ice reconnaissance and Arctic surveillance. The Aurora is destined to remain in service into the 21st century.

A battery of anti-submarine sonobouy launching tubes is carried in the lower fuselage behind the wing. In addition, powerful searchlights may be fitted underwing.

The primary conventional submarine detector aid is the tail-mounted MAD boom. This is used to locate submerged vessels, by detecting their magnetic presence in the water.

COMBAT DATA

WEAPONS LOAD

A maritime patrol aircraft has to have sufficient ordnance to deliver a decisive punch against a target at very long range. The CP-140 is well armed compared to the other aircraft.

CP-140 AURORA	9071 kg (19,955 lb.)
Il-38 'MAY'	6000 kg (13,200 lb.)
NIMROD MR.Mk 2	6124 kg (13,473 lb.)

MAXIMUM SPEED

High speed is a useful asset as it allows rapid transit to the combat zone or the scene of a rescue. The speed of the Nimrod enables it to search large areas relatively quickly. The CP-140 has a good top speed for a turboprop aircraft.

CP-140 AURORA	732 km/h (454 m.p.h.)
Il-38 'MAY'	722 km/h (448 m.p.h.)
NIMROD MR.Mk 2	926 km/h (574 m.p.h.)

MAXIMUM RANGE

The Nimrod is used for long over-water missions and therefore requires a good range. The CAF tends to use its aircraft for coastal duties, and therefore range is less important. Illyushin's Il-38 is much shorter ranged than either of its competitors and sees only limited use.

CP-140 AURORA 8339 km (5,170 mi.)

Il-38 'MAY' 7200 km (4,465 mi.)

NIMROD MR.Mk 2 9266 km (5,745 mi.)

Canada's post-war maritime aircraft

■ **LOCKHEED PV-1 VENTURA:** The PV-1 Ventura served the CAF from the mid-war period and continued post-war as a target-tug before it was retired.

■ **AVRO LANCASTER Mk 10MR:** The veteran Lancaster Mk 10MR, built by Victory Aircraft of Canada, was the CAF's standard patrol aircraft of the 1950s.

■ **LOCKHEED P-2 NEPTUNE:** The widely exported P-2 Neptune served as an interim aircraft until the Argus was available. This P-2 flew with No. 404 Squadron.

■ **CANADAIR CP-107 ARGUS:** The CP-107 Argus was a Canadian-built patrol version of the British Bristol Britannia airliner. It was finally retired in 1981 when the Aurora arrived.

LOCKHEED MARTIN

C-130H HERCULES

● Four-engine turboprop transport ● Used worldwide

▲ The 'Herc' was designed to meet a US Air Force requirement for a tactical transport able to use rough airstrips and carry 18 tonnes (24,950 lb.) of cargo, 92 ground troops or 64 paratroops.

There have been so many versions of the "Charlie One-Thirty" during its 40 years of service that it is hard to imagine it ever being grounded because of old age. Over the years it has undertaken dozens of useful tasks ranging from maritime patrol to secret agent support. Its main task, however, remains in the STOL transport role for which it was designed. The prototype first flew in August 1954, and the C-130H version was the biggest seller.

LOCKHEED MARTIN C-130H HERCULES

▼ **Desert airlift**
The Gulf War of 1990-91 brought together numerous C-130s from several nations as part of the Coalition force.

▲ **Providing relief**
Worldwide, the C-130's airlift tasks today often involve mercy flights and supply drops.

First exports ►
The first export customer was Australia, which received 12 C-130As in 1958 and later batches of both the E and H models.

▼ **Swedish 'Hercs' over Bosnia**
Due to the country's neutrality, few units of Sweden's air force deploy overseas. An exception has been its C-130 unit, F7, which deployed to the former Yugoslavia.

▲ **Stretched 'Dash-30s'**
Originally known as the C-130H(S), C-130H-30s have been delivered to several air forces including those of Algeria, France, Indonesia and Saudi Arabia.

FACTS AND FIGURES

➤ There is also a civilian version of the C-130, which is known as the L-100.

➤ US Air Force C-130s have seen combat in Vietnam, Grenada, Panama and the Persian Gulf.

➤ The US Navy tested a scale model of an amphibious version of the C-130.

➤ New Zealand's air force regularly uses its C-130Hs in Antarctica; the USAF also deploys ski-equipped 'Hs' to the Arctic.

➤ The first USAF C-130Hs were search-and-rescue HC-130Hs built in 1964.

➤ RAF Hercules are based on the C-130H with British radar and other equipment.

H-model Herky-bird

The C-130H was fitted with a redesigned and strengthened wing box, additional power (provided by uprated engines), and better brakes to distinguish it from the C-130E, the earlier main production variant of the Hercules. The first H model aircraft flew on November 19, 1964. Two years later, examples were delivered to the Royal New Zealand Air Force, the initial customer for the new model in Lockheed-Martin's already impressive catalog of aircraft.

The C-130H has since entered service with over 50 air forces around the world and although originally intended for export only, has also been ordered by the United States Air Force.

An important version of the C-130H was the Dash-30 which has a 4.57-m (15-ft.) fuselage extension to significantly increase payloads without any detrimental effect on performance. The first examples of this model were delivered to Indonesia in September 1980 and this stretched version has

since found wide appeal.

Built-in adaptability has also enabled a number of other major modifications to be made to the basic C-130H for a variety of extra roles.

Above: The basic soundness of the original 1950s design is reflected in the fact that the C-130H and earlier versions have been adapted for roles as diverse as gunships and mobile hospitals.

Above: Cameroon, another operator of the C-130H-30, has its aircraft painted in a sand camouflage scheme. These aircraft often carry civilians during the Haj pilgrimage season.

C-130H

Type: medium-range STOL transport

Powerplant: four 3362-kW (4,500-hp.) Allison T56-A-15 turboprop engines

Maximum speed: 618 km/h (383 m.p.h.)

Service ceiling: 10,058 m (33,000 ft.)

Range: 3791 km (2,350 mi.) with max payload

Maximum payload: 19,350 kg (42,570 lb.)

Weights: empty 34,357 kg (75,585 lb.); loaded 79,380 kg (174,636 lb.)

Dimensions:
span	40.41 m (132 ft. 6 in.)
length	29.70 m (97 ft. 9 in.)
height	11.66 m (34 ft. 3 in.)
wing area	162.12 m² (1,744 sq. ft.)

C-130H HERCULES

The Algerian air force operates 12 C-130Hs that were delivered between 1981 and 1990, replacing Antonov An-12s, on the understanding that the aircraft would not be used on operations against Polisario guerillas.

The bulbous 'Pinocchio' nose of the C-130H contains a navigational radar set.

C-130 Hercules in the transport role generally fly with a crew of five: aircraft commander, co-pilot, flight engineer, navigator and loadmaster.

The new Allison T56-A-15 engines introduced on the C-130H removed the need for rocket-assisted take-off equipment as fitted to some earlier models. Four-blade propellers are standard.

External fuel tanks, each holding 5150 litres (1,360 gal.), are fitted between the engines of each wing and are standard on all C-130Hs.

Algerian air force C-130s carry quasi-civilian registrations that are used when the aircraft fly overseas. The camouflage is a USAF-style, Vietnam-era scheme.

The rear loading ramp gives access to a hold capable of accommodating over 19 tons of cargo. A Low-Altitude Parachute Extraction System (LAPES) is used to make drops in combat zones.

ACTION DATA

SPEED

The jet-powered Kawasaki C-1 has a higher top speed than the An-12 and C-130, both of which are powered by turboprop engines. While the C-130 has a considerably lower top speed than the An-12, it has a better range, especially with a maximum fuel load on board.

C-130H	618 km/h (383 m.p.h.)
An-12	777 km/h (482 m.p.h.)
KAWASAKI C-1	806 km/h (500 m.p.h.)

PAYLOAD

The C-130 and C-1 have a rear loading ramp, while the An-12 has a pair of clamshell doors. The C-130 and C-1 are able to lower their ramps in flight so that troops and equipment can be deployed, usually with the aid of parachutes. The C-130 and An-12 are large enough to carry a medium-sized armored vehicle.

C-130H	An-12	KAWASAKI C-1
19,350 kg (42,570 lb.)	20,000 kg (44,000 lb.)	11,900 kg (26,180 lb.)

TAKE-OFF RUN

The engines on the jet-powered C-1 are positioned so that the exhaust is directed over the lower surface of the aircraft's flaps to provide more lift. Take-off distance is therefore shortened. Short take-off runs are particularly important for a tactical transport that needs to land in confined spaces near the battlefield.

KAWASAKI C-1	An-12	C-130H
640 m (2,100 ft.)	700 m (2,300 ft.)	1000 m (3,300 ft.)

The many labours of Hercules

■ **HERCULES W. MK 2 'SNOOPY':** Modified in 1973 from a standard Hercules C Mk.1, XV208 replaced a Vickers Varsity operated by the RAF Meteorological Flight for weather research.

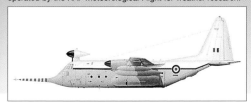

■ **EC-130E:** Codenamed 'Rivet Rider', four C-130Es were rebuilt by the USAF as airborne radio/television transmission stations to provide broadcasts in the event of a major disaster or emergency.

■ **MC-130E:** USAF MC-130s use the folding nose-mounted 'forks' of the Fulton recovery system to retrieve special operations personnel without having to land in hostile territory.

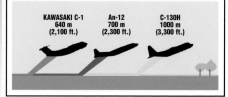

LOCKHEED MARTIN

F-16A FIGHTING FALCON

● Lightweight fighter ● Multi-mission capable ● 'The Electric Jet'

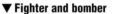

T he F-16 Fighting Falcon is 20 years old, but remains a star performer. A fast and potent dogfighter, it is equally at home destroying enemy tanks or positions at tree-top level. This relatively lightweight and inexpensive warplane introduced electronic flight controls and other hi-tech wizardry, and its radar, missiles and cannon make it a genuine 'Top Gun', respected by friend and foe alike.

▲ The F-16 pilot has at his command the West's premier light-fighter. The view from the cockpit is outstanding, thanks to the massive one-piece bubble canopy.

LOCKHEED MARTIN F-16A FIGHTING FALCON

◄ Head-up fighting
The F-16 pilot reclines at 30° and flies the fighter using a pressure-sensitive sidestick with his right hand.

▲ Flying the flag
Perhaps the best-known F-16s are those of the USAF's Thunderbirds team. The F-16 gives them excellent agility matched with noise and speed.

◄ Combat success
Israel has been using the Fighting Falcon since the early 1980s. The aircraft's combat debut came with the destruction of Iraq's Osirak nuclear facility in 1981, and over Lebanon in 1982 Israeli F-16s shot down 44 Syrian MiGs without loss.

▼ Fighter and bomber
Originally devised as a lightweight fighter, the F-16 emerged as a warplane capable of lifting just about every ground-attack store available.

▲ Air defender
Falcons can launch the latest AMRAAM air-to-air missile. Using this weapon, a USAF F-16 shot down a MiG-25 over Iraq.

FACTS AND FIGURES

➤ Lockheed acquired General Dynamics, who created the F-16, in March 1993.

➤ The company says it can build a new F-16 today for $20 million, less than half the price of an F-15E Strike Eagle.

➤ The F-16 ejection seat works safely at any speed and altitude.

➤ More than 4,000 F-16s serve in the US, NATO, Asia and Latin America.

➤ A delta-winged test version, the F-16XL, has wing area increased by 120 per cent.

➤ F-16 pilots flew 13,500 combat sorties in Operation Desert Storm, more than any other aircraft.

PROFILE

Lightweight superjet

The F-16 is proof that one aircraft can move back the boundaries of aviation. This marvellous warplane introduced lightweight computers, 'fly-by-wire' electronic controls and a breathtaking arsenal of hi-tech weaponry.

No longer new, the F-16 is a boon to those who fly it. Pilots say the F-16 is a super aircraft, without equal from the viewpoint of the airman at the controls.

Engineers saw the F-16 as a no-frills 'hot rod'. It gained weight with the addition of improved radar and weaponry, but is smaller and more nimble than many fighters. Used mainly to drop bombs, the Fighting Falcon can turn and fight with unbridled fury when provoked and was one of the first operational 'fly-by-wire' aircraft, its controls being electronically-operated and computer-controlled. The pilot sits in a seat which reclines at 30° to withstand high-g manoeuvres, allowing the gut-wrenching turns that give the F-16 an advantage over its rivals.

Halfway along its back the F-16 has a refuelling receptacle so that it can take on fuel in flight. This is now standard on most military fighting planes.

Despite its amazing agility, the F-16 is rock-steady when it needs to be – diving in to attack a target with gun or missiles. Here a two-seater lets fly with a Maverick missile, a favourite against tanks.

Nearly all F-16s are painted in shades of grey. This colour was found to be the most difficult to see across a wide range of different weather conditions.

F-16s are powered by a Pratt & Whitney F100 engine. It is extremely powerful, and very resistant to changes in airflow.

F-16A Fighting Falcon

Type: single-seat multi-role fighter

Powerplant: one 106.05-kN (23,800-lb. thrust) Pratt & Whitney F100-P-100 afterburning turbojet

Maximum speed: Mach 2.05 or 2173 km/h (1,350 m.p.h.) at 12,190 m (40,000 ft.)

Combat radius: 1300 km (808 mi.) with drop tanks

Service ceiling: 15,240 m (50,000 ft.)

Weights: empty 6607 kg (14,566 lb.); maximum take-off 14,968 kg (32,999 lb.)

Armament: one M61 Vulcan 20-mm cannon, up to 6900 kg (15,212 lb.) of air-to-air and air-to-ground weaponry

Dimensions:
span 9.45 m (31 ft.)
length 15.03 m (49 ft. 4 in.)
height 5.01 m (16 ft. 5 in.)
wing area 27.87 m² (300 sq. ft.)

F-16A FIGHTING FALCON

In service with many nations, the F-16 can rightly be regarded as the world's standard fighter. This example is one of Pakistan's aircraft, which have shot down several Russian types along the border with Afghanistan.

With its curved surfaces blending the fuselage and wing together, and its fly-by-wire electric flight control system, the F-16 ushered in a new era of fighter design. The radical shape had far better aerodynamics than earlier designs, making the F-16 more agile for dogfighting.

84717

The radar of the F-16 is as versatile as the aircraft. With a flick of a switch the pilot can change from air-to-air operation to air-to-ground. When dogfighting, the radar automatically follows the enemy and gives the pilot a steering cue on the large head-up display in front of him.

AIM-9 Sidewinders are the main air-to-air weapon of the F-16, seen here carried on the wingtips and on underwing pylons.

The AIM-9 is a heat-seeking missile, homing in on the heat of the enemy's exhaust. It is very difficult to counter and is far more manoeuvrable than an aircraft, so cannot be shaken off.

COMBAT DATA

AGILITY

The F-16 was a revelation when it first appeared, being the most agile fighter in the world. Both the Mirage 2000 and the MiG-29 were designed to try to match the smaller American jet's superb handling.

MIRAGE 2000
F-16A FIGHTING FALCON
MiG-29 'FULCRUM'

SPEED

Although capable of twice the speed of sound at altitude, it is the F-16's performance at lower level and its acceleration at lower speeds which make it such an outstanding fighter.

MIRAGE 2000 1100 km/h (684 m.p.h.)
F-16A FIGHTING FALCON 1450 km/h (901 m.p.h.)
MiG-29 'FULCRUM' 1300 km/h (808 m.p.h.)

Speeds at sea level

Multi-role fighter

POINT DEFENCE: In the interceptor role, the F-16 can launch in next to no time, scream upwards and shoot down incoming bombers before they can launch their weapons.

CLOSE SUPPORT: Over the battlefield the F-16 can use a variety of bombs and missiles against enemy tanks and positions.

AIR SUPERIORITY: The F-16 can be used to keep the battle zone clear of enemy fighters.

DEFENCE SUPPRESSION: In this role, the F-16 uses high-tech missiles to kill enemy radars. This allows other friendly aircraft to operate in safety.

PRECISION STRIKE: With laser-guided bombs, the F-16 can attack strategic targets such as nuclear installations and power stations.

LOCKHEED MARTIN (ROCKWELL)

AC-130U SPECTRE

● Airborne gunship ● Special Forces ● Improved model

After its successful combat debut in Vietnam, the AC-130 Spectre became the standard USAF night attack gunship. The early 'Herc' gunships were subsequently upgraded, up-gunned and, more recently, replaced by newer airframes. The ultimate model is the AC-130U, which carries fewer guns than its predecessor but, with its computer-controlled 105-mm (4.13-in.) howitzer, can bring down devastating firepower on the enemy.

▲ Ungainly in looks, the AC-130U is extremely simple in concept. The airborne gunship looks set to remain in the front line for the future, providing fire support for ground troops.

LOCKHEED MARTIN (ROCKWELL) AC-130U SPECTRE

◀ **State of the art**
The AC-130 was used to develop the gunship role in Vietnam. The AC-130U is equipped with the most advanced avionics available.

Old colours ▶
Early AC-130Us wore the old-style European One colour scheme. Later models wear an overall Gunship Gray camouflage.

◀ **Test flights**
Equipped with a nose-mounted probe, the prototype AC-130U undertook a long series of developmental flights. Crews found the aircraft was ideal for the role.

▼ **Special crews**
Because of the unique requirements of AC-130U operations, only the very best Hercules crews are selected to fly the specialised aircraft.

▲ **Broadside attack**
Retained on the latest Hercules gunship variant is the positioning of the cannon and guns along the port side of the fuselage. During combat missions the AC-130U maintains a circular orbit to maximise fire accuracy.

FACTS AND FIGURES

➤ Rockwell was awarded a $155 million contract to develop the new C-130 gunship for the USAF.

➤ The first AC-130U was rolled out on 20 December 1990.

➤ Flight trials were conducted at Edwards AFB during 1992–93.

➤ Thirteen aircraft were delivered to the 16th Special Operations Squadron at Hurlburt Field, Florida, in 1995.

➤ The radar of the AC-130U is derived from that of the F-15E Strike Eagle.

➤ The calibre of the guns aboard the aircraft ranges from 25 mm (1 in.) to 105 mm (4.13 in.).

PROFILE

Prowler of the battlefield

In the Vietnam air war, one of the more important developments was that of the aerial gunship. This involved heavily armed converted transport aircraft orbiting a point and delivering deadly firepower with great precision. From its origins in the crude 'Spooky' AC-47s left over from an earlier war, 'hosing' the target with multiple Miniguns, the gunship concept has developed into a highly sophisticated combination of sensors and weapons able to bring each round to the target. The AC-130A of the Vietnam era

had up to eight machine-guns. The AC-130U developed by Rockwell International has only three guns – one 25-mm (1-in.) multi-barrelled cannon, a 40-mm (1.57-in.) Bofors and a 105-mm (4.13-in.) howitzer. However, the guns can be brought to bear with greater precision – even engaging two targets at once – by the four mission computers and the extremely accurate GPS-based navigation system. For self-defence, the AC-130U is equipped with powerful jammers, together with a number of radar-warning antennas. On

the underside are three combined chaff/flare launchers. Although the AC-130U has yet to prove itself in combat, the other post-Vietnam version, the AC-130H, saw action in Grenada in 1983, Panama in 1989 and over Iraq during the Gulf War. It has gained a reputation as an efficient destroyer of enemy vehicles and troops.

Left: Retained on the new model is the 'Spectre' nose art. This dates back to the earliest days of gunship operations over Vietnam.

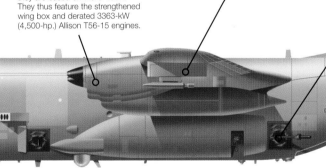

Above: The AC-130U can be distinguished from earlier models by the lack of the distinctive nose-mounted radome.

AC-130U Spectre

Type: aerial gunship

Powerplant: four 3363-kW (4,500-hp.) Allison T56-A-15 turboprops

Cruising speed: 602 km/h (373 m.p.h.)

Initial climb rate: 597 m/min (1,960 f.p.m.)

Range: 7876 km (4,883 mi.) with maximum fuel

Service ceiling: 10,060 m (33,000 ft.)

Weights: operating weight 34,356 kg (75,583 lb.); maximum take-off 79,380 kg (174,636 lb.)

Armament: GAU-12/U 25-mm (1-in.) cannon with 3000 rounds; 40-mm (1.57-in.) Bofors cannon; 105-mm (4.13-in) howitzer

Dimensions:
span	40.41 m (132 ft. 7 in.)
length	29.79 m (97 ft. 9 in.)
height	11.66 m (38 ft. 3 in.)
wing area	162.12 m² (1,744 sq. ft.)

AC-130U HERCULES

The gunship has proved itself in Vietnam and the Gulf War. The latest development of the Hercules gunship is the AC-130U, equipped with state-of-the-art avionics.

Dramatic improvements in the survivability for the crew have been made since the first AC-130A was developed. Crews are now surrounded by Spectra ceramic armour and the fuel is carried in explosion-suppressing fuel tanks.

AC-130Us are unique among the gunship Hercules variants in that they are based on the C-130H. They thus feature the strengthened wing box and derated 3363-kW (4,500-hp.) Allison T56-15 engines.

Required to operate over hostile territory, the AC-130U is equipped with an extensive array of electronic countermeasures equipment. This includes wing-mounted ALQ-172 jammers and less sophisticated chaff/flare dispensers.

The heavy punch of the AC-130U is provided by the 105-mm (4.13-in) howitzer and the 40-mm (1.57-in) Bofors cannon. They are positioned in the rear of the fuselage. Situated opposite these guns are racks for the vast amount of ammunition required.

The observer's station is on the rear loading ramp. This crewman is equipped with a small clear dome from which to observe firing by the aircraft. Firing corrections can then be reported to the pilot.

GUNSHIP HISTORY

'STINGER': Having developed the concept of airborne artillery with the AC-47, the USAF looked round for a more suitable aircraft to lift the necessary equipment into the air. The result was the conversion of the large twin-boom C-119 Flying Boxcar. Emerging as the AC-119K 'Stinger' (pictured below), the aircraft was soon pressed into combat against the North Vietnamese. The 'Stinger' was highly successful in this role, although limitations of the design soon became apparent. The aircraft was extremely vulnerable to ground fire, and soon operations switched to night-time to offer some degree of protection.

'SPECTRE': Already a well proven transport aircraft, the Lockheed C-130 was soon adapted to the gunship role. Known as the AC-130A 'Spectre' (below), the design was one of the most valued aircraft in Vietnam for supporting ground forces. Equipped with Miniguns, the 'Spectre' proved to be the ideal platform for 'truck-busting' along the network of trails that the North Vietnamese used for transporting troops and materials. The 'Spectre' took part in some of the final missions of the war, and after returning to the United States remained in front-line service with the USAF Special Operations Squadrons.

Legendary Lockheed C-130s

AUSTRALIA: Providing the heavy lift element of Australia's air force are C-130Hs, which continue in front-line service.

FRANCE: Operated alongside France's C.160 Transalls, the Hercules has been used on countless French combat operations in Africa.

NEW ZEALAND: The C-130H has been in production for over 30 years. The first C-130H built was sold to New Zealand in 1965.

SAUDI ARABIA: Resplendent in an overall desert camouflage, Saudi Arabian C-130s are often used as VIP transports.

147

McDonnell Douglas

A-4 Skyhawk II

● Light attack ● 1950s design ● Upgraded for the 21st century

Originally called the A4D, the Douglas A-4 Skyhawk was conceived in the 1950s to carry an atomic weapon on a one-way mission if a third world war was declared. In practice, the Skyhawk provided the US Navy and Marines with an impressive, conventional light-attack aircraft for the next 20 years. The improved A-4M Skyhawk II flew in 1970 and more recently several nations have updated their early-model A-4s with new engines, avionics and weapons.

▲ While no two-seat Skyhawk IIs were built, a number of early-model two-seaters have been included in the upgrade programmes carried out by the Malaysian and New Zealand air forces. The US Marine Corps also rebuilt a number of TA-4Fs to OA-4M standard for forward air control duties.

PHOTO FILE

McDonnell Douglas A-4 Skyhawk II

▼ **AGM-12 Bullpup**
The main air-to-surface missile carried by Skyhawks before recent upgrades was the Bullpup.

▲ **Singaporean two-seater**
The Royal Singaporean Air Force TA-4S is a rebuilt A-4B and is unique in having two cockpits each with a separate canopy.

▲ **Skyhawk II for the Marines**
Entering service in the mid-1970s, the A-4M operated until about 1994 mainly in the close air support role. This example is firing an unguided Zuni rocket during exercises.

▲ **From 'dumb bombs' to LGBs**
The refurbished A-4s are able to deliver laser-guided bombs and missiles and later versions of heat-seeking air-to-air missiles like the Sidewinder.

Combat in the Gulf ▶
Twenty Kuwaiti A-4KUs escaped to Bahrain during the 1991 Iraqi invasion and later flew daylight attack missions from Dhahran, Saudi Arabia. Kuwait also has one two-seat TA-4KU remaining in service.

FACTS AND FIGURES

➤ New Zealand's A-4Ks contain the APG-66 radar, as fitted to the F-16, in the nose to improve capability.

➤ Designed by Ed Heinemann, the A-4 has been nicknamed 'Heinemann's Hot Rod'.

➤ On their first Gulf War mission, Kuwaiti A-4s mistakenly bombed Saudi Arabia.

➤ F404 turbofans fitted to Singapore's A-4s are heavier than the J52 but are more fuel efficient and cheaper to maintain.

➤ Pave Penny laser designators, used on USAF A-10s, may be fitted to RSAF A-4s.

➤ American companies Lockheed and Grumman have updated foreign A-4s.

Bantam bomber reborn

The A-4 Skyhawk became a classic of US naval aviation, but it began as an extraordinary design. Douglas' famous designer Ed Heinemann created the Skyhawk at half of the specified weight. When the 'bantam bomber' was ordered in 1952 it was remarkably light,but nothing had been stripped from the design or omitted. The Skyhawk was easy to fly and an effective attack aircraft, and because of its small size it did not require folding wings for use aboard carriers.

In Vietnam, Skyhawks performed traditional bombing raids and 'Iron Hand' missions against North Vietnamese surface-to-air missile sites.

Intended for production from 1954 until 1957, the Skyhawk was produced for a further 26 years in many variants. Significant numbers were exported, some operating from land bases. More recently, retired ex-Navy aircraft have been refurbished and sold overseas. Malaysia and Singapore operate updated

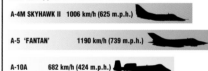

Above: Malaysia bought 88 ex-US Navy A-4s in 1979, but abandoned a major upgrade. Grumman refurbished 40 examples which now carry Maverick and Sidewinder missiles.

Below: With the GE F404 fitted to Singapore's A-4S aircraft, Skyhawks have used three types of engine, including the Wright J65 fitted in very early marks and the Pratt &Whitney J52 in versions after the A-4E.

former USN machines, while New Zealand's upgraded A-4s were delivered new in the 1970s.

A-4S-1 Super Skyhawk

Type: single-seat attack aircraft

Powerplant: one 48.04-kN (10,800-lb. thrust) General Electric F404-GE-100D non-afterburning turbofan

Maximum speed: 1128 km/h (701 m.p.h.) at sea level

Initial climb rate: 3326 m/min (10,912 f.p.m.)

Range: 1158 km (720 mi.) with max. ordnance

Service ceiling: 12,190 m (40,000 ft.)

Weights: empty 4649 kg (10,249 lb.); maximum take-off 10,206 kg (22,500 lb.)

Armament: two Mk 12 20-mm cannon, plus external ordnance

Dimensions:
span	8.38 m	(27 ft. 6 in.)
length	12.72 m	(14 ft. 9 in.)
height	4.57 m	(15 ft. 4 in.)
wing area	24.14 m²	(260 sq. ft.)

A-4M SKYHAWK II

US Marine Corps Attack Squadron 324 operated the first production A-4M Skyhawk IIs from 1971. By 1976 five USMC squadrons used the variant.

Skyhawk IIs introduced a more bulged cockpit canopy giving improved visibility.

Upgraded A-4s often carry an attack radar, equipment which was not fitted on the production line.

Intended to hold avionics, 'humps' were fitted to early versions of the Skyhawk, starting with the A-4F of 1966. Some upgraded A-4s have had these removed.

This A-4M carries the high-visibility markings common to US Navy and Marine aircraft in the 1970s. Today 'low-viz' colour schemes are more usual.

Skyhawk IIs have a later version of the Pratt & Whitney J52 turbojet engine. Singapore's 'Super Skyhawks' use a non-afterburning variant of the F-18's General Electric F404 turbofan.

Marine Corps aircraft generally carry a two-letter unit tailcode and the last four digits of the aircraft's 'BuNo', or serial number.

Two 20-mm Mk 12 cannon were fitted to the A-4M. Singaporean A-4S aircraft have been equipped with two 30-mm ADEN cannon, as carried by the SEPECAT Jaguar and the BAe Sea Harrier.

In its day the Skyhawk could carry a substantial weapons load. While this is modest by modern standards, upgraded A-4s can deliver much more up-to-date and effective weapons than before.

COMBAT DATA

MAXIMUM SPEED

The twin-engined A-5 is a relatively fast aircraft compared to the Skyhawk. The straight-winged A-10 was designed for low-speed close air support missions over a battlefield.

A-4M SKYHAWK II 1006 km/h (625 m.p.h.)

A-5 'FANTAN' 1190 km/h (739 m.p.h.)

A-10A 682 km/h (424 m.p.h.)

COMBAT RADIUS

The A-10's longer range is used to give it extended loiter time over a battlefield. The range of both the A-4 and A-10 can be extended by using air-to-air refuelling, unlike the A-5.

A-4M SKYHAWK II 547 km (340 mi.)

A-10A THUNDERBOLT II 1000 km (621 mi.)

A-5 'FANTAN' 600 km (373 mi.)

BOMBLOAD

The design of the A-5 was based on that of a lightweight fighter, and therefore could not carry as much ordnance as the A-4 and A-10 which were designed from the outset as attack aircraft.

A-4M SKYHAWK II 4153 kg (9,156 lb.)

A-5 'FANTAN' 2000 kg (4,409 lb.)

A-10A THUNDERBOLT II 7258 kg (16,000 lb.)

Fighter upgrade projects

F-5E TIGER IV: With the equipment installed in the Tiger IV, Northrop hopes to capture some of the market for updated F-5s.

MIRAGE 50CN PANTERA: Chile's Mirage 50Cs are being rebuilt with canards and new avionics with help from Israel Aircraft Industries.

F-4E KURNASS 2000: Originally intended to include new engines, this Israeli project is now restricted to an avionics and airframe upgrade.

MIG-21-2000: First flown in May 1995, the Israel Aircraft Industries MiG-21-2000 has a comprehensive Western avionics fit.

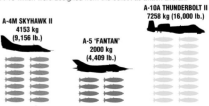

McDONNELL DOUGLAS

C-9 NIGHTINGALE

● VIP carrier ● Airborne ambulance ● Civilian design

After its successful introduction into the civil airline market during the mid-1960s, the McDonnell Douglas DC-9 was selected by the USAF in 1967 as its dedicated aeromedical evacuation aircraft. Experience in Vietnam showed just how vital such an aircraft was in modern war theatres. Ordering such an aircraft 'off-the-shelf' kept costs low, and the enduring nature of the type has ensured that it remains in service more than 30 years later.

▲ Essentially
based on the commercial DC-9 Series 30, the C-9A Nightingale has given sterling service to the USAF, yet it is often overshadowed by more glamorous aircraft.

▼ **Cargo carrier**
When operated by the US Navy, the type is known as the C-9B Skytrain II. For this role it is equipped with a large cargo door.

▲ **International rescue**
With a large Red Cross on its tail, a C-9 Nightingale lands at the scene of another disaster.

Naval reserve ▶
After a review of its transport assets, the US Navy turned over its fleet of Skytrain IIs to the naval reserve. In time of war, however, the aircraft would be deployed to front-line naval bases.

◀ **Angel in the air**
The US Navy has operated the C-9B Skytrain II since the early seventies. The aircraft required minor modifications for military service but retained the grace of its civilian counterparts.

Great white bird ▶
Throughout their entire service life the aircraft have retained a smart white and grey colour scheme. This has proved to be very appropriate for missions involving high-ranking personnel or government figures.

FACTS AND FIGURES

➤ C-9A Nightingales flew home the American hostages released from Iran in 1981.

➤ One C-9A Nightingale is configured as a VIP transport within Europe.

➤ Flight crew consists of two pilots with a crew chief or loadmaster.

➤ On aeromedical missions, the C-9A Nightingale can accommodate 40 stretcher patients or 40 seated patients.

➤ One C-9A was lost in a mishap at Scott Field on 16 September 1971.

➤ In March 1981 C-9Bs replaced the long-serving C-118B Liftmaster in the USN.

PROFILE

America's airborne saviour

From Vietnam to the Gulf War, the C-9A Nightingale has become indispensable in support of front-line US troops. Up to 40 stretcher cases or 40 walking wounded can be accommodated along with trained medical staff on these vital evacuation flights.

Based on the DC-9 Series 30, the Nightingale entered service in June 1968. Modifications to the standard airliner included a new access door with an in-built hydraulic ramp for the loading of stretchers, and a specialist medical care compartment.

The USAF also received three C-9C VIP transport versions.

The success of the DC-9 in military service was soon appreciated by the US Navy which ordered the C-9B Skytrain II in an effort to modernise its small but important logistics support service. First entering service in 1972, a dozen aircraft were acquired along with two for the US Marine Corps. Also based on the Series 30, the C-9B features additional fuel capacity for extended range and can operate in all-cargo, all-passenger or mixed configuration. The

aircraft were deployed to Saudi Arabia during the Gulf War.

Other military users include Kuwait and Italy which operate two examples on light transport and VIP duties.

Above: Operated on behalf of the special air missions airlift wing, this particular Nightingale is used as a personal VIP transport. The aircraft is especially configured for the role.

Above: Taxiing to the main runway, this C-9B Skytrain II operates with the US Navy on support duties. This example is capable of airlifting 107 naval personnel.

C-9A Nightingale

Type: transport/medical evacuation aircraft

Powerplant: two 64.5-kN (14,500-lb.-thrust) Pratt & Whitney JT8D-9 turbofan engines

Maximum cruising speed: 907 km/h (562 m.p.h.) at 7620 m (25,000 ft.)

Initial climb rate: 885 m/min (2,900 f.p.m.)

Range: ferry range 3327 km (2,060 mi.); range with full accommodation 2388 km (1,480 mi.)

Weights: empty 25,940 kg (57,068 lb.); maximum take-off 54,885 kg (120,747 lb.)

Accommodation: four crew; 30 to 40 stretcher patients with medical attendants

Dimensions:
span	28.47 m (93 ft. 5 in.)
length	36.37 m (119 ft. 3 in.)
height	8.38 m (27 ft. 6 in.)
wing area	92.97 m² (1,000 sq. ft.)

C-9B SKYTRAIN II

Though not as glamorous as the fighters operated by the US Navy, the C-9B Skytrain II has proved to be the ideal aircraft for transporting personnel and cargo to various naval bases throughout the world.

A flight deck crew of three is used for standard operations. Positioned on the port side of the nose is a set of hydraulically-operated self-contained airstairs. Often flown by reserve crews, who are full-time commercial airline pilots, the aircraft has proved itself to be a highly versatile transport asset for the USN.

Despite being in military service, the C-9B Skytrain II retains a smart civil-looking colour scheme. Although it rarely enters a combat zone, the aircraft is equipped with an infra-red jammer on the tail. This reduces the risk of attack by missiles.

To allow the C-9B to undertake cargo operations the aircraft is equipped with a large cargo door. This is hydraulically raised to ease loading and is operated from within the cockpit.

With room for 107 passengers, sufficient safety equipment is of vital importance. For ditching at sea, the aircraft is equipped with four 25-man life rafts located at various positions along the fuselage.

The fuselage area of the C-9B Skytrain II can contain up to eight standard military freight pallets when in all-cargo configuration. For these operations the aircraft is fitted with a specially adapted cargo roller floor to reduce the loading and unloading times.

Airliners in military service

■ BOEING E-4B: Adapted from the Boeing 747 Jumbo, the military E-4B is used as an Advanced Airborne Command Post. The aircraft is equipped with highly sophisticated communications equipment. Four aircraft are currently in service.

■ BOEING KC-135A: Operated both as an airborne tanker and transport aircraft, the KC-135 has served with the USAF since the 1960s. Current upgrades of the aircraft involve the adoption of more fuel-efficient engines.

■ DOUGLAS EC-24A: Serving with the US Navy as an Electronic Warfare Support aircraft, the EC-24A is used against naval vessels to assess their ability to defend themselves against attack during military exercises.

ACTION DATA

MAXIMUM SPEED

With the need to reach an emergency situation in the shortest period of time, the speed of the C-9A Nightingale is high compared to that of its contemporaries. Fastest of all the current military airliners is the CT-43A.

C-9A NIGHTINGALE	907 km/h (562 m.p.h.)
Tu-134 'CRUSTY'	900 km/h (558 m.p.h.)
CT-43A	927 km/h (575 m.p.h.)

RANGE

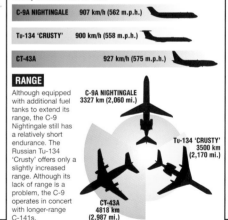

Although equipped with additional fuel tanks to extend its range, the C-9 Nightingale still has a relatively short endurance. The Russian Tu-134 'Crusty' offers only a slightly increased range. Although its lack of range is a problem, the C-9 operates in concert with longer-range C-141s.

C-9A NIGHTINGALE 3327 km (2,060 mi.)

Tu-134 'CRUSTY' 3500 km (2,170 mi.)

CT-43A 4818 km (2,987 mi.)

SERVICE CEILING

Designed originally for the civil airliner market, the C-9 Nightingale has retained its ability to operate at high altitudes. When operating with a full load of casualties its performance is significantly reduced, however. The highest performer is the Tu-134 'Crusty'.

C-9A NIGHTINGALE	Tu-134 'CRUSTY'	CT-43A
11,280 m (37,000 ft.)	11,900 m (39,000 ft.)	10,668 m (35,000 ft.)

McDONNELL DOUGLAS

C-17 GLOBEMASTER III

● Modern airlifter ● Next-generation technology ● Service proven

At first glance the C-17 could be mistaken as a run-of-the-mill transport, but those who have been inside the Globemaster III never forget it. This four-turbofan, hi-tech aircraft's interior is like a giant cavern. The C-17 can carry huge cargoes and can be 'turned around' quickly thanks to its 'roll-on, roll-off' capability. This is achieved by locating the ramp near ground level and using a palletised system with floor-mounted rollers for rapid loading.

▲ *Providing*
relief to crisis-hit regions and delivering military supplies around the world, the C-17 is said by pilots to handle more like a fighter than an airlifter in spite of its large size.

PHOTO FILE

McDONNELL DOUGLAS C-17 GLOBEMASTER III

◀ **Squadron service**
Lockheed C-141B Starlifters began to make way for the Globemaster III at Charleston AFB in June 1993. The 17th Airlift Squadron was the first unit to receive production aircraft.

▼ **Fighter or freighter?**
For the first time on a transport aircraft, the C-17 introduced twin, fighter-style, head-up display units for the two flight crew.

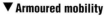

▲ **Always ready**
The C-17, carrying heavy and bulky loads, can be rapidly deployed to unprepared airstrips, by night and day, and in all weathers.

▼ **Armoured mobility**
One of the C-17's load requirements was the ability to accommodate large armoured vehicles, such as this 28,349-kg (62,368-lb.) payload of an M110A2 self-propelled Howitzer and support vehicles.

▲ **Global reach**
Air-to-air refuelling, which allows worldwide transport missions, is vital for any airlifter.

FACTS AND FIGURES

➤ In honour of the Douglas C-74 and C-124, the Globemaster III name was given to the C-17 in February 1993.

➤ The USAF is aiming for 140 C-17s, 70 of which have currently received funding.

➤ The C-17 is the world's third most expensive aircraft, after the B-2 and E-3.

➤ The C-17's fin contains a tunnel which enables a crewmember to climb up inside for stabiliser maintenance.

➤ In 1993 C-17s flew their first operational mission from the US to Kenya.

➤ The C-17 prototype completed its first flight on 15 September 1991.

PROFILE

Transport for the next century

Left: A parachute fixed to a freight pallet drags cargo from the C-17's cabin as the Low-Altitude Parachute Extraction System (LAPES) is used.

Combining long range, a capacity to carry heavy cargoes and the capability to land near the front line, the C-17 Globemaster III is the world's newest military transport. The high-wing aircraft is able to carry almost any cargo and it bears a slight resemblance to the airlifter it is replacing, the C-141 Starlifter. The C-17 boasts an ergonomic

flightdeck (that is, one optimised for pilot comfort) with digital displays. The C-17's two pilots sit side-by-side and the plane is flown with a control stick instead of the yoke which is traditionally used on transport aircraft. The wing is swept at 25° and has winglets for fuel

efficiency. The wing accounts for almost one-third of the aircraft's structural weight.

This fine aircraft is only just beginning to prove its global airlifting abilities. It is the hi-tech hauler of the future, and the USAF expects to establish a fleet of more than a hundred aircraft.

Above: All aircraft likely to be deployed anywhere in the world must be able to operate in extreme conditions. This C-17 is undergoing cold weather trials.

C-17A Globemaster III

Type: long-range transport

Powerplant: four 185.49-kN (41,730-lb.-thrust) Pratt & Whitney F117-PW-100 turbofan engines

Maximum cruising speed: 648 km/h (402 m.p.h.) at low altitude

Ferry range: 8710 km (5,400 mi.)

Service ceiling: 13,715 m (45,000 ft.)

Weights: empty 122,016 kg (268,435 lb.); maximum take-off 263,083 kg (578,783 lb.)

Accommodation: two pilots, one loadmaster and up to 102 troops/paratroops in stowable seats or 48 stretchers with attendants, or up to 76,658 kg (169,000 lb.) of cargo including an M1 Abrams main battle tank

Dimensions: span 50.29 m (164 ft. 11 in.)
length 53.04 m (174 ft.)
height 16.79 m (55 ft. 1 in.)
wing area 353.02 m² (3,798 sq. ft.)

C-17A Gʟᴏʙᴇᴍᴀꜱᴛᴇʀ III

This C-17A is the first production aircraft and was used for tests at Edwards AFB. It was successfully tested at 100 per cent loading before its first flight and was subsequently used for in-flight load tests.

The C-17 carries a large amount of internal fuel. Six wing tanks are positioned between the main spars and fill almost the entire wing span, giving a capacity of 102,614 litres (27,110 gal.).

A front view of the C-17A shows how close to the wing the engines are positioned. This is a result of the complex propulsive-lift technology used to give the aircraft its short take-off and landing (STOL) capability.

Four F117-PW-100 turbofan engines give outstanding fuel economy and a combined maximum thrust of 742 kN (1662,920 lb. thrust). The engine is based on the PW2040 turbofan, which powers many Boeing 757s and has already achieved in excess of six-million flying hours in regular service.

In common with many long-range airliners, the C-17A is fitted with winglets. These provide greater range and improved cruising characteristics.

A flight crew of two fly the C-17A. Two extra seats are provided at the rear of the flightdeck to accommodate a relief aircrew on long flights.

Only one loadmaster is required to supervise and handle the C-17A's large payload, using an internal cargo handling system to load up to 18 standard 463L cargo pallets.

Each main undercarriage unit has six wheels and, when retracted, is accommodated in a fairing against the lower fuselage.

USAF 80265

A quadruple-redundant fly-by-wire system operates the C-17A's 29 control surfaces. As well as the complex wing systems, these include the twin rudders, tailplanes and four elevators.

When retracted, the rear loading ramp is able to carry heavy cargo, including two 463L pallets for air-dropping.

ACTION DATA

MAXIMUM PAYLOAD

Compared to other similarly sized four-jet transports, and particularly the C-141B which the C-17A is partly replacing, the Globemaster III offers exceptional payload capabilities.

| C-17A GLOBEMASTER III 76,658 kg (169,000 lb.) | C-141B STARLIFTER 41,222 kg (90,688 lb.) | Il-76 'CANDID-B' 40,000 kg (88,000 lb.) |

RANGE

McDonnell Douglas' C-17A has only slightly better range than that of the Il-76M, but the American aircraft achieves this figure with almost twice the payload. Air-to-air refuelling is an important part of the C-17A capability and is also available to extend the range of the C-141B.

C-141B STARLIFTER 4725 km (2,930 mi.)

C-17A GLOBEMASTER III 5190 km (3,220 mi.)

Il-76M 'CANDID-B' 5000 km (3,100 mi.)

LANDING DISTANCE

Ilyushin used advanced systems to give the Il-76M excellent field performance, with a maximum payload only slightly below that of the C-141B. The C-17A is equally impressive, requiring twice the distance of the Il-76M for landing but with twice the payload.

C-17A GLOBEMASTER III ———— 914 m (3,000 ft.)
C-141B STARLIFTER ———— 1128 m (3,700 ft.)
Il-76M 'CANDID-B' 450 m (1,475 ft.)

USAF's Douglas airlifter dynasty

■ **C-54 SKYMASTER:** Douglas flew the first C-54 in 1942 and more than 1000 were delivered to the US Army Air Force and Navy.

■ **C-74 GLOBEMASTER I:** Having flown for the first time in September 1945, many C-74s were cancelled at the end of the war.

■ **C-124 GLOBEMASTER II:** The C-124 was produced by fitting the C-74 with 2610-kW (3,500-hp.) engines, a deeper fuselage and nose doors.

■ **C-133 CARGOMASTER:** Only 35 of these advanced turboprop transports were built. They were retired in 1971 after fatigue problems.

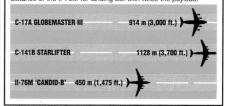

MCDONNELL DOUGLAS
F-15E EAGLE

● Two-seat fighter-bomber ● F-111 replacement ● Gulf War service

Strike Eagle – the McDonnell Douglas F-15E – is one of the fastest and deadliest warplanes. Developed from the F-15 air-superiority fighter, this 'smart' two-seat aircraft uses advanced radar and avionics to deliver a vast array of weapons at night and in all weathers to targets many kilometres away. One of the stars of the Gulf War, the F-15E has at the same time retained the single-seat Eagle's excellent air-to-air capability.

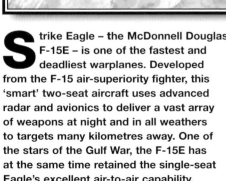

▲ Without doubt the most advanced tactical bomber in the West, the F-15E provides the USAF with a unique night/all-weather capability and replaces the capable but ageing F-111.

MCDONNELL DOUGLAS F-15E EAGLE

▲ 'Buckets of instant sunshine'
An early production 57th Fighter Wing 'Strike Eagle' carries two Dayglo-painted dummy B61 nuclear weapons. The B61 can be fitted with a warhead up to 25 times more powerful than the Hiroshima bomb.

▼ Range enhancement
F-15Es refuel from a KC-10A Extender. One criticism of the F-15E has been its lack of range compared to aircraft it has replaced, like the F-111F.

▲ LANTIRN pods
The AAQ-14 targeting pod is fixed to the right intake, with the AAQ-13 navigation pod on the left.

◀ Wing tanks
Up to three 2309-litre (580-gal.) drop-tanks are often carried on operations.

▲ Anti-radar missiles
This aircraft is armed with AGM-88 HARMs, one of a number of weapons options for the F-15E.

FACTS AND FIGURES

➤ Although the last of 209 'Strike Eagles' was delivered in 1994, the USAF has ordered further attrition replacements.

➤ The first production F-15E made its initial flight on 11 December 1986.

➤ F-15Es are known by the nicknames 'Beagle' (Bomber Eagle) and 'Mud Hen'.

➤ Fighter-bomber F-15s similar to the F-15E are currently being produced for Saudi Arabia (F-15S) and Israel (F-15I).

➤ Two F-15Es were lost in combat during Operation Desert Storm.

➤ USAF orders for the F-15E were cut to protect funding for the Lockheed F-22.

PROFILE

'Strike Eagle' tactical bomber

McDonnell Douglas' F-15E 'Strike Eagle' – the fast and far-reaching fighter-bomber version of the famous F-15 – has replaced Genral Dynamics' F-111 as the US Air Force's long-range tactical strike aircraft and equips eight squadrons.

The original plans for a ground-attack Eagle were abandoned in 1975 but revived in 1982 when trials began using a two-seat TF-15A. The first production aircraft flew in 1986 after competition from the F-16XL had been seen off.

Although government budget cuts reduced deliveries to just over 200, the F-15E performed with distinction in the 1991 Gulf War, attacking a variety of targets on missions that included hunting for 'Scud' missile sites during sorties lasting up to six hours.

The F-15E has acquired its bomb-carrying capacity without giving up any of its air-to-air ability. This is where it differs from the F-111, which used sheer speed to escape from hostile fighters. The 'Strike Eagle' can fight back and win.

The broad wing of the F-15E has a reputation for subjecting crews to a rougher ride in low-level, high-speed flight than the F-111.

Late-production F-15Es have two Pratt & Whitney F100-PW-229 Improved Performance Engine (IPE) afterburning turbojets giving Mach 2 capability.

As on fighter versions of the F-15, an M61 20-mm rotary cannon is mounted in the starboard wingroot.

For self-defence AIM-9 Sidewinder, AIM-7 Sparrow and/or AIM-120 AMRAAM air-to-air missiles may also be carried. This example carries two Sidewinders.

F-15E Eagle

Type: two-seat strike fighter-bomber

Powerplant: two 129.45-kN (29,000-lb.-thrust) Pratt & Whitney F100-P-229 afterburning turbofan engines

Maximum speed: 2655 km/h (1,646 m.p.h.)

Range: 4445 km (2,756 mi.)

Service ceiling: 18,290 m (60,000 ft.)

Weights: empty 14,379 kg (31,634 lb.); maximum take-off 36,741 kg (80,830 lb.)

Armament: one 20-mm M61 Vulcan rotary cannon and up to 11,000 kg (24,000 lb.) of weapons, including AIM-7, AIM-120 or AIM-9 air-to-air missiles, AGM-65 or AGM-88 HARM air-to-ground missiles, laser-guided or 'iron' bombs and cluster and nuclear munitions

Dimensions: span 13.05 m (43 ft.)
length 19.43 m (64 ft.)
height 5.63 m (18 ft.)
wing area 56.48 m² (608 sq. ft.)

F-15E EAGLE

Veterans of action against Libya and in the Gulf, USAFE's 48th Fighter Wing, based at RAF Lakenheath, traded its venerable F-111Fs for F-15Es in 1992. 90-0248 was their first example.

At the heart of the F-15E's capability is the APG-70 radar. As well as air-to-air modes it offers high-resolution ground mapping for accurate weapons aiming.

The cockpit is state-of-the-art. The pilot has a wide-angle head-up display (HUD) and three multi-function displays (MFDs). The Weapons Systems Officer (WSO) has four MFDs.

To improve range performance Conformal Fuel Tanks (CFTs) are fitted to either side of the fuselage. These each hold 2653 litres (700 gal.) of fuel and have pylons attached for the carriage of weapons.

Complementing the radar is the LANTIRN (Low-Altitude Navigation and Targeting Infra-Red for Night) system, consisting of two pods under the engine intakes; one with terrain-following radar and a forward-looking infra-red sensor, the other with FLIR and a laser designator.

This aircraft is loaded with 14 SUU-30H cluster bombs for a close air support/battlefield air interdiction mission. A vast array of 'smart' and unguided weapons can be carried.

COMBAT DATA

GBU-28
The GBU-28 is one of a family of 'laser-guided' bombs used in the Gulf. The seeker head and moving fins are fitted to a standard 'dumb' bomb and provide precision guidance.

CBU-87
For use against 'soft-skinned' targets the CBU-87 cluster bomb contains a variety of sub-munitions, including armour-piercing and anti-personnel devices.

AGM-88 HARM
HARM, or the High-speed Anti-Radiation Missile, is a specialised weapon for use against radar installations, especially those used to guide surface-to-air missiles, homing in on their radar emissions.

'Strike Eagles' strike Iraq

KEY WEAPON: The F-15E was one of the key aircraft of the Gulf conflict, able to make precision attacks in all weathers and at night.

STRATEGIC TARGETS: One mission of the F-15Es was to hit strategic targets, including bridges, using laser-guided bombs.

'SCUD' HUNTING: 'Scud'-busting missions were guided by AWACS aircraft and involved the use of cluster munitions against the launchers.

SAM THREAT: Heat-seeking surface-to-air missiles (SAMs) were a threat to F-15Es on daytime missions.

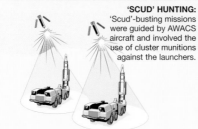

'TURN AND BURN': When chased by a SAM during a bombing run, a quick escape could be attempted by the pilot by jettisoning fuel tanks and firing 'chaff' and flares to confuse the missile.

McDonnell Douglas

F-4 Phantom II

● Air superiority ● Long-range strike ● Modernised classic

Although the last American Phantoms have been withdrawn from service, the amazing F-4 story continues all over the world. Several nations have decided that the best value for money in military aviation is to upgrade the mighty F-4 with new cockpits, avionics, engines and missiles, making the 40-year-old fighter as good as many new types.

▲ Like its classic adversary, the MiG-21, the F-4 is a highly versatile aircraft that sold in the thousands. An upgrade can cost as little as one-sixth of the cost of a new fighter, but can deliver performance that in many ways is as good as that of the latest tactical aircraft.

McDonnell Douglas F-4 Phantom II

◀ 'Wild Weasel'
The last Phantoms in US service were the F-4G 'Wild Weasel' defence suppression aircraft. Armed with HARM missiles, they flew with distinction in the Gulf.

◀ Turkish F-4s
An upgrade by Israel Aircraft Industries for Turkey includes a new radar from Elta and advanced multi-function displays.

▼ Kai upgrade for Japan
Japan's F-4EJ Phantoms were upgraded with a new AN/APQ-172 radar, new cockpit displays and avionics, but externally look almost unchanged.

'Kurnass' Phantoms ▶
Israel has upgraded its Phantoms, calling the new version 'Kurnass' (hammer). These have seen action over South Lebanon.

◀ Luftwaffe ICE
The upgrade for 110 of the Luftwaffe's F-4Fs included a ring laser-gyro, APG-65 radar, smokeless engines, radar-warning receiver and the ability to fire four AMRAAM missiles.

FACTS AND FIGURES

➤ The powerplant for the F-4F ICE consists of two German-assembled J79-MTU-17A turbojet engines.

➤ Israel's Kurnass Phantoms can launch the large Popeye stand-off weapon.

➤ The F-4G has been retired, but no fully satisfactory replacement yet exists.

➤ Israel's Super Phantom prototype was fitted with Pratt & Whitney PW1120 engines in trials.

➤ Forty Luftwaffe F-4Fs were upgraded to a lower standard than ICE/KWS.

➤ Upgraded Phantoms will remain in service until at least 2008.

PROFILE

New life for the great Phantom

Though the time-honoured Phantom is now a very old design, the F-4F ICE (Improved Combat Efficiency) upgrade will be flying with the Luftwaffe well into the 21st century, until the Eurofighter Typhoon enters full service. Improved radar, long-range AMRAAM missiles and advanced multi-function cockpit displays to ease the pilot's workload are all features of the upgraded aircraft. It also has a revised control stick for the pilot and improved avionics.

While Germany is the world leader in breathing new life into the Phantom, advanced versions of this super aircraft are being flown in Japan, Korea, Israel and Turkey. The Israeli Phantom 2000 incorporates strengthening and new avionics, while the proposed Super Phantom was equipped with a canard wing and new engines for greatly superior performance and economy.

The combination of modifications like new avionics and engines makes the F-4 feel like a new aircraft.

Japan's F-4EJ Kai aircraft also has improved weapons, radar and avionics, and has the ability to deliver the ASM-1 anti-ship missile.

Pilots say that new models like the F-4F ICE can take on any fighter in the world in a long-range air-to-air duel and come out victorious.

The addition of new armament to the F-4 is one of the most important parts of the upgrade programmes, enabling it to deliver precision-guided munitions like Popeye and Paveway.

Most upgraded F-4s have a new radar-warning receiver. The ICE has a Litton system with receiver aerials in the wingtips.

F-4F ICE Phantom

Type: two-seat fighter/fighter-bomber

Powerplant: two 79.63-kN (17,917-lb. thrust) GE J79-MTU-17A afterburning turbojets

Maximum speed: Mach 2.17 or 2304 km/h (1,432 m.p.h.) without weapons

Ferry range: 2593 km (1,611 m.p.h.)

Service ceiling: 18,975 m (62,250 ft.)

Weights: empty 14,556 kg (32,090 lb.); loaded 28,055 kg (61,850 lb.)

Armament: four AIM-120 AMRAAM or AIM-7 Sparrow medium-range radar-guided air-to-air missiles; AIM-9 Sidewinder heat-seeking missiles

Dimensions:
span	11.68 m	(38 ft. 4 in.)
length	18.96 m	(62 ft. 2 in.)
height	5.05 m	(16 ft. 5 in.)
wing area	49.24 m²	(530 sq. ft.)

F-4F ICE PHANTOM

The Luftwaffe's improved F-4F Phantoms are now entering service with JG 71 and JG 74. They are the only operational F-4s armed with AMRAAM missiles.

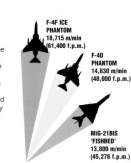

The dials and knobs of the old F-4E cockpit are being replaced by TV-type displays.

The pilot flies the new F-4 with a HOTAS (hands-on-throttle-and-stick) cockpit system. Elta of Israel is offering an advanced head-up display in its upgrades.

The aerodynamics of the F-4 are a generation behind today's fighters. Generally, it is only worth upgrading Phantoms with relatively low airframe hours; many F-4s are too old to be worth modifying.

Improved engines for the F-4 give little extra thrust, but offer much better fuel consumption and need far less maintenance.

The multi-mode APG-65 radar is also used in the F-18 Hornet. It can perform in ground-mapping, search-and-track and dogfight modes.

The new F-4Fs will have special Frazer-Nash ejector rails, allowing the carriage of the AMRAAM fire-and-forget missile.

Unlike the MiG-21, most Phantom upgrades have not included major changes of engine; the proposed PW1120 engine for the Israeli Super Phantom was not adopted.

COMBAT DATA

TURN RATE

Increased thrust and reduced weight give the newer F-4s a better instantaneous and sustained turn rate than older F-4s, especially those with unslatted wings. The upgraded MiG-21 with an RD-33 engine could probably still out-turn the F-4.

F-4D PHANTOM
F-4F ICE PHANTOM
MiG-21BIS 'FISHBED'

CLIMB RATE

Increased engine efficiency gives the new generation F-4s a superior climb rate to the older models. The F-4D had a slightly better rate than the standard MiG-21bis, thanks to its high thrust-to-weight ratio; the latest upgraded MiG-21s would probably have a better climb rate due to the power of the RD-33 engine. The F-4 ICE's climb rate would challenge many more modern fighters.

F-4F ICE PHANTOM 18,715 m/min (61,400 f.p.m.)
F-4D PHANTOM 14,630 m/min (48,000 f.p.m.)
MiG-21BIS 'FISHBED' 13,800 m/min (45,276 f.p.m.)

MISSILE RANGE

Like the MiG-21, the F-4 has been made vastly more capable with the addition of new fire-and-forget missiles, allowing the aircraft to turn away from its opponent as soon as it fires its weapons.

MiG-21BIS 'FISHBED' 50 km (31 mi.)
F-4D PHANTOM 45 km (28 mi.)
F-4F ICE PHANTOM 50+ km (31+ mi.)

The Phantom generation

■ **US NAVY F-4B:** The first major F-4 variant was the US Navy's F-4B, an interceptor with ground-attack capability that saw widespread service in Vietnam and inspired the USAF F-4C.

■ **EGYPTIAN F-4E:** Egypt received 35 ex-USAF F-4Es. This variant had a slatted wing to enhance manoeuvrability, and an internal cannon as a result of combat in Vietnam.

■ **JAPANESE F-4EJ:** The last Phantom built was one of 140 F-4EJs licence-produced by Mitsubishi, serving in the air-defence role. They were fitted with Japanese-built radar.

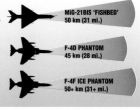

McDonnell Douglas

F/A-18 Hornet

● Carrier fighter ● Multi-role strike ● Anti-ship/radar bomber

McDonnell Douglas' F/A-18 can vault from a carrier deck, bomb a target, and stay to dogfight the enemy's top guns. The US Navy is delighted with this versatile warplane, its first jet intended for double duty against air and ground enemies. Marines and overseas operators also love the Hornet. The coming F/A-18E/F is a bigger, more robust version of this superb fighter for carrier squadrons in the 21st century.

▲ Being an F/A-18 Hornet pilot is perhaps the ultimate aviation job flying a single-seat high-performance jet from a carrier, tasked with both air-to-air combat and dropping bombs.

PHOTO FILE

McDonnell Douglas F/A-18 Hornet

▲ Angels of thunder
The US Navy's elite 'Blue Angels' formation team flies the Hornet. It offers outstanding agility while thrilling air show crowds with explosively noisy power displays.

▲ Export success
Nations which have chosen to operate the Hornet include Australia, Canada and Spain.

◄ Fighting office
The Hornet had the first truly modern cockpit aboard a carrier jet, designed around large TV-style screens and a head-up display.

▼ Marine mud-mover
The Marine Corps uses the two-seat F/A-18D Hornet on night attack missions, armed with laser bombs and other 'smart' weapons.

▲ Carrier-borne versatility
The Hornet is one of the world's most capable and versatile warplanes, and yet it still finds room to combine its talents with the demanding requirements of operating from the carrier deck.

◄ Killer on the prowl
Armed with Sparrow and Sidewinder missiles, and with an internal cannon, the F/A-18 can fight and win against the world's best air-to-air combatants.

FACTS AND FIGURES

➤ Land-based F/A-18 Hornets make up the front line of defence in Australia, Canada, Finland, Kuwait and Spain.

➤ About 65 crack pilots apply for three or four annual vacancies with the US Navy's Hornet-equipped 'Blue Angels'.

➤ An RF-18 Hornet photo ship was tested but not adopted.

➤ NASA uses a much modified F/A-18 to explore manoeuvring at extremely high angles of attack.

➤ The digital cockpit of the sophisticated Hornet has been described as a cross between 'Star Wars' and a video game.

➤ First flight of an F/A-18 Hornet took place on 18 November 1978.

PROFILE

Multi-mission master

This magnificent fighting jet from McDonnell Douglas has established a place as the backbone of US Navy and Marine aviation; sailors and marines wanted the F/A-18 Hornet so badly they relinquished other aircraft to get it. Their faith is justified: the F/A-18 performed superbly in raids on Libya and in Operation Desert Storm.

To keep the F/A-18 on top in the crucible of air combat, they

are improving the Hornet constantly. Better flight instruments and avionics have been added to new aircraft along with the capability to use far-reaching missiles. None of these changes detract from the manoeuvrability of the Hornet, an exceedingly agile adversary.

The future F/A-18E (single-seat) and F/A-18F (two-seat) will be 86 cm (2 ft. 10 in.) longer and carry 1360 kg (2,998 lb.) more fuel. Navy carrier air wings will

Defender of the frozen North – Canada has Hornets standing by to deter any attack across the vast areas that straddle the north of the country. The Hornet can react quickly to any intruder.

soon boast as many as four Hornet squadrons, giving a formidable stirke and fighter capability. With the F/A-18 on board the US Navy can project power globally knowing it has the best aircraft in the world.

The ends of the Hornet's wings fold up so that the aircraft does not take up much room in the confines of the aircraft-carrier deck or hangar.

Long strakes ahead of the wing give the Hornet pilot outstanding control of his aircraft when flying very slowly.

F/A-18C Hornet

Type: carrier-based naval strike fighter

Powerplant: two 71.2-kN (16,020-lb. thrust) afterburning General Electric F404-GE-400 turbofans

Maximum speed: Mach 1.8 or 1915 km/h (1,190 m.p.h.) at 12,190 m (40,000 ft.)

Combat radius: 1060 km (659 mi.)

Service ceiling: 15,240 m (50,000 ft.)

Weights: empty 10,455 kg (23,049 lb.); loaded 22,328 kg (49,225 lb.)

Armament: one Martin Marietta M61A1 Vulcan 20-mm cannon; two AIM-9L Sidewinder missiles; 7000 kg (15,432 lb.) of ordnance

Dimensions:
span	11.43 m	(37 ft. 6 in.)
length	17.07 m	(56 ft.)
height	4.66 m	(15 ft. 3 in.)
wing area	37.16 m²	(400 sq. ft.)

F/A-18C HORNET

Popularly called the 'Swing Fighter' because it can swing between air-to-air fighting and ground attack with great ease, the Hornet can perform a wide range of missions, including radar-killing and 'Fast FAC' – guiding other attack aircraft to their targets.

VFA-204

VFA-87

400

NAVY

164632

Above the radar is the trusty M61 20-mm Vulcan cannon which is used for close-range air-to-air combat. A drum containing 570 rounds of ammunition is mounted below the gun and aft of the radar.

Under the rear fuselage of the Hornet is an arrester hook for carrier landings. When lowered, this hook catches wires which are strung across the deck of the carrier.

The Hornet's undercarriage is immensely strong, since it has to withstand the repeated 'controlled crashes' of carrier landings.

This Hornet carries a mixed load of weapons – Sidewinders and Sparrows for enemy fighters, and Mk 82 bombs for ground targets.

In the nose of the Hornet is the APG-73 radar, which is at the heart of the aircraft's versatility. It can see and track other aircraft at great distances, while also mapping the ground to make precision bombing easy.

COMBAT DATA

SPEED

F/A-18C	1915 km/h (1,190 m.p.h.)	
MIRAGE 2000	2330 km/h (1,448 m.p.h.)	
TORNADO GR.Mk 1	2300 km/h1,429 m.p.h.)	

The Hornet is optimised for subsonic combat and weapons delivery, so while it is comfortably supersonic its simple intake design limits it to about 1.8 times the speed of sound.

LOW-LEVEL COMBAT RADIUS

Hornets have always had the reputation of being 'short-legged', even though they have longer range than the preceding F-4 Phantom. However, this is no real handicap in these days of aerial refuelling, and the F/A-18's superb fighting ability more than makes up for any minor defect, as shown in Operation Desert Storm.

TORNADO GR.Mk 1 1400 km (870 mi.)

MIRAGE 2000 750 km (466 mi.)

F/A-18C HORNET 600 km (373 mi.)

WEAPONS LOAD

Although the Hornet is one of the most manoeuvrable fighters in the world, it carries almost as large a weapons load as a specialised bomber like the Tornado. And with its sophisticated targeting and laser designation system it is one of the most accurate bombers currently in service.

TORNADO GR.Mk 1 9000 kg (19,842 lb.)

F/A-18C HORNET 7000 kg (15,432 lb.)

MIRAGE 2000 6300 kg (13,889 lb.)

Killing radars with the Hornet

PRE-EMPTIVE SHOT: As the main attack force approaches the target, an F/A-18 lobs a HARM anti-radar missile over the top of the attack force. If any enemy radars are up and running, they will be destroyed immediately before the attackers enter the lethal zone.

DETECTION ZONE

ATTACK FORCE

LETHAL ZONE

ANTI-RADAR ESCORT: After the pre-emptive HARM missile has been fired, other HARM-carrying Hornets lead the attack force into the lethal zone. Any enemy radars that attempt to turn on are fired at by these strike escort aircraft.

ENEMY MISSILES AND RADAR BATTERY

McDonnell Douglas

KC-10 Extender

● USAF tanker ● Strategic transport role ● Gulf War veteran

In a reversal of the Boeing KC-135 Stratotanker's production history, McDonnell Douglas built the KC-10A Extender tanker/transport after it had established the DC-10 airliner design. The aircraft has revolutionised USAF overseas deployments, with the ability not only to refuel formations of tactical jets, but also to carry their support equipment and personnel. The Extender is now a key element in USAF operations.

▲ *Supporting USAF aircraft deploying to bases all over the world, the Extender has become a symbol of US power projection. Forty-six KC-10As flew 25 per cent of the tanker missions over the Persian Gulf.*

PHOTO FILE

McDonnell Douglas KC-10 Extender

▼ **Gulf-bound Extender**
During Desert Storm, 46 of the USAF's 59 surviving KC-10As were used to support coalition air power. The KC-10A enabled the deployment of US-based fighters.

▲ **Refuelling options**
The principal Extender tool is the 'flying boom', but for refuelling US Navy and other NATO aircraft a hose drum unit is also carried.

◄ **KC-10A achievements**
In September 1982, seven KC-10As met 20 C-141Bs over Goose Bay, Labrador, delivering an incredible 29,484 kg (64,865 lb.) of fuel to each. The C-141Bs went on to drop troops over West Germany.

▼ **Premier tanker**
The Extender can transfer 90,720 kg (200,000 lb.) of fuel to one or more receivers.

▲ **Changing colours**
Originally operated in a blue and white colour scheme the KC-10 fleet has appeared in number of different colours including lizard green, dark grey and the current light grey scheme.

FACTS AND FIGURES

➤ During its initial operational assessment, the KC-10A supported eight A-7Ds on a deployment to the UK.

➤ McDonnell Douglas based its KC-10A on the DC-10-30CF airframe.

➤ Royal Netherlands Air Force KDC-10 tankers are conversions of DC-10s.

➤ A typical KC-10A mission might involve accompanying and refuelling eight fighters, while carrying 25 cargo pallets.

➤ A digital fly-by-wire control system is fitted to the air-refuelling boom.

➤ A six-month evaluation was carried out on the KC-10A before it entered service.

PROFILE

USAF's tactical Extender

Ordered off-the-shelf as a version of the DC-10 airliner to satisfy a USAF requirement for a dual-role Advanced Tanker/Cargo Aircraft, KC-10A deliveries began in 1981. Unlike the KC-135, the Extender has a permanent probe-and-drogue refuelling system in addition to its flying boom, allowing the support of USAF and USN aircraft on the same mission.

Officially credited with the best USAF aircraft safety record (only one aircraft has been lost, in a ground fire), the KC-10A was involved in the 1986 raids on Libya, operations in Panama in 1989, and in the Gulf War.

While the KC-135 force is mostly tasked with the support of strategic bombers, the KC-10A mission is almost wholly tactical. The KC-10A currently forms part of the USAF's primary tactical force, which is capable of rapid deployment to foreign airfields.

The Extender offers an unrivalled combination of capabilities. A full payload of 76,843 kg (169,055 lb.) can be carried over a 7033-km (4,360-mi.) range.

Just prior to Desert Storm, an experiment to fit additional, British-built hose refuelling pods beneath each wingtip was completed, providing a three-point refuelling capability.

This 2nd Wing KC-10A, seen on take-off from Barksdale AFB in Louisiana, has its crew provided by the Air National Guard.

KC-10A Extender

During the Libyan Crisis of 1986, Extenders were based at RAF Mildenhall, tasked with the support of the USAF strike force of F-111s.

Power for the Extender's long-range activities is provided by three General Electric turbofans, fitted with thrust reversers for shortening landing distances. For improving its own endurance, the KC-10A has a refuelling receptacle fitted.

The KC-10A fuselage can accommodate up to 25 freight pallets, or mixed loads. A typical mixed load might be 75 seated troops and 17 pallets.

The KC-10A has a 2.59-m (8-ft. 5-in.) by 3.56-m (11-ft. 8-in.) upward-hinged door in the fuselage side. Rollers and winches are fitted within the freight compartment.

No navigator is needed, thanks to the KC-10A's comprehensive navigation systems. On long-range missions, the flight deck accommodates a pilot, co-pilot and a flight engineer. The flight engineer has a secondary role as loadmaster when cargo is being carried.

The last KC-10A to be built carries a single Flight Refuelling Limited Mk 32B probe-and-drogue refuelling pod beneath each wing. The remainder of the fleet may be similarly equipped.

Additional or emergency power is provided by a Garrett TSCP-700-4 auxiliary power unit.

Manufactured by McDonnell Douglas, the Advanced Aerial Refuelling Boom (AARB) is located opposite an additional refuelling hose reel unit for probed aircraft.

Lacking the nuclear flash curtain and electro-magnetic pulse shielding of the KC-135, the KC-10A is unable to support strategic nuclear strikes.

For tanker missions, the lower fuselage carries fuel bladder cells, taking maximum usable capacity to a total of 206134 litres.

The KC-10A is favoured over the KC-135 by boom operators at least, for its comfortable aft-facing seating position in the rear fuselage.

KC-10A Extender

Type: in-flight-refuelling tanker/strategic airlifter

Powerplant: three 233.53-kN (52,535-lb.-thrust) General Electric CF6-50C2 turbofans

Maximum speed: 982 km/h (609 m.p.h.) at 7620 m (25,000 ft.)

Range: 18,507 km (11,475 mi.) in ferry configuration

Service ceiling: 10,180 m (33,400 ft.)

Weights: operating empty 108,891 kg (240,100 lb.)as a tanker; maximum take-off 267,620 kg (588,764 lb.)

Max payload: 76,843 kg (169,055 lb.) cargo, plus max. internal fuel 161,508 kg (355,310 lb.)

Dimensions:
span 47.34 m (155 ft. 3 in.)
length 55.35 m (181 ft. 7 in.)
height 17.70 m (58 ft.)
wing area 358.70 m² (3,860 sq. ft.)

Douglas airliners in military form

■ **DC-3:** From its world-beating DC-3, Douglas developed the C-47 Skytrain for military operations. A mainstay of the Allied transport fleet during World War II, the aircraft also served as a gunship in Vietnam. Several remain in service.

■ **DC-6:** While the USAF and US Navy both operated military versions of the DC-6, several other air forces flew DC-7 airliner conversions. A number of nations, mostly in South America, still had DC-7s on strength in the mid-1990s.

■ **DC-9:** McDonnell Douglas sold military variants of the DC-9 to the USAF as the C-9 Nightingale, primarily for use in the aeromedical evacuation role. The USN uses the C-9 Skytrain II on fleet logistic support duties.

COMBAT DATA

INTERNAL FUEL CAPACITY

A huge amount of internal fuel allows the KC-10A to refuel fighters several times on long missions, while retaining enough fuel for its own needs. The KC-135A does not fly such support-type missions, although the RAF's Tristar does.

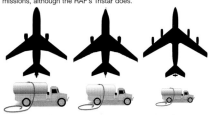

KC-10A EXTENDER	TRISTAR K.Mk 1	KC-135A STRATOTANKER
161,508 kg (353,310 lb.)	142,111 kg (312,644 lb.)	86,047 kg (189,303 lb.)

McDonnell Douglas

T-45 GOSHAWK

● US Navy trainer ● Navalized BAe Hawk ● Latest technology

When it wanted a new trainer, the Navy looked at several aircraft before deciding on Britain's well-established Hawk. Given the designation T-45 and named Goshawk, the aircraft is manufactured in the U.S. This well-known British jet is becoming the standard flying schoolhouse for all who earn the wings of gold worn by US Naval aviators. The T-45 replaces the Rockwell T-2 Buckeye and the Douglas TA-4J Skyhawk.

▲ Many modifications to the basic Hawk produced the T-45. The nose undercarriage unit is a completely new, stronger unit and features twin wheels and a catapult launch bar.

PHOTO FILE

McDonnell Douglas T-45 Goshawk

▼ **Carrier launch**
Steam rises from the catapult as a Goshawk crew prepare to leave the carrier. The T-45 launches at 224 km/h (139 m.p.h.).

▲ **Trainer supreme**
Sitting on a raised ejection seat, the instructor has an excellent view forward over the student's head. Carrier landings demand optimum visibility.

▲▼ **Flying 'dirty' and flying 'clean'**
The robust undercarriage, flaps, slats, airbrakes and arrestor hook are all deployed (above) in the landing configuration above while the aircraft is seen below in 'clean' cruising configuration.

▲ **Complex wing design**
Full-span hydraulically operated leading-edge slats were developed by McDonnell Douglas and are not found on the simpler wing of the BAe Hawk.

FACTS AND FIGURES

➤ Compared to previous U.S. Navy training, the cost saving T-45 system uses 42 per cent fewer aircraft.

➤ First squadron to with the T-45A is VT-21 Fighting Redhawks at Kingsville, Texas.

➤ French navy Rafale pilots will be trained in the US using the Goshawk.

➤ Compared with the British Hawk, the T-45 has an extra ventral fin and a tailfin heightened by about six inches.

➤ The T-45A will train about 600 new naval pilots each year.

➤ Each Navy T-45 is expected to make 16,000 carrier deck landings.

PROFILE

Navy trainer for the next century

Development of the T-45 Goshawk was criticized for taking a long time and costing plenty, but the result gives the U.S. Navy an advanced trainer second to none in the world. Looking very much like a fighter and performing in many ways like one, the T-45 Goshawk is an extensively altered version of the British Hawk, strengthened to permit operation on aircraft carriers.

The T-45 Goshawk is operated as a land-based trainer re-placing both the intermediate and advanced trainers of the past and it also operates from aircraft carriers as part of the student pilot program.

Since the Goshawk began carrier trials in 1991, the Navy has been generally pleased with its performance and has moved – too slowly, according to critics – to place the Goshawk in service with training squadrons.

Initially flying from Kingsville, Texas, and now operating at four locations, the

T-45 is be the first jet flown by Navy, Marine and Coast Guard aviators (after they fly the Beech T-34 Turbo Mentor) and student pilots fly it until they graduate with their wings.

SMURFS (Side-Mounted Unit horizontal Root tail Fins) help to limit aerodynamic interference between the deployed flaps and the tailplane.

A HUD in the front cockpit can show navigation, flight instrument and weapon aiming data. Two underwing pylons may carry practice bombs.

All Hawk variants are fitted with a gas turbine starter unit for starting the engines and onboard systems. The unit exhausts through this distinctive aperture on the spine.

T-45A GOSHAWK

This aircraft belongs to VT-21 Red Hawks, Training Wing Two and was based at NAS Kingsville, Texas, in 1995 in standard high-visibility markings.

All Goshawks will eventually be fitted with Cockpit 21. This development replaces the original instruments with two multi-function display screens in each cockpit.

Student and instructor each sit on a Martin-Baker Mk 14 NACES (Naval Aircraft Common Ejection-Seat). The seat allows safe escape at zero height and zero air-speed.

Power comes from a single F405-RR-401 engine. With this engine the T-45 burns 55 per cent less fuel than its T-2 Buckeye predecessor.

With a launch weight of 5787 kg (13,675 lb.), the T-45's catapult launch bar withstands huge stress. The catapult launches the aircraft at flying speed even with the brakes on.

In order to accommodate the new nose undercarriage unit, a deeper nose section was designed. The nosewheel doors close once the leg is locked down.

The strengthened rear fuselage has two side-mounted airbrakes and a modified F/A-18 arrestor hook, which is capable of holding the T-45 in the event of an accidental snagging of the arrestor cable while the aircraft is still airborne.

USS FORRESTAL
NAVY
TW-2
T-45A
163615
DANGER ARRESTING HOOK

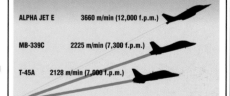

T-45A Goshawk

Type: two-seat intermediate and advanced flight trainer

Powerplant: one 26.00-kN (5,850-lb.-thrust) Rolls-Royce/Turboméca F405-RR-401 turbofans

Maximum speed: 997 km/h (618 m.p.h.)

Rate of climb: 2128 m/min (7,000 f.p.m.) at sea level

Ferry range: 1854 km (1,147 mi.)

Service ceiling: 12,875 m (42,240 ft.)

Weights: empty 4, 251 kg (9,374 lb.); maximum take-off (5,773 kg (12,731 lb.)

Dimensions:
span	9.39 m	(30 ft. 9 in.)
length	11.97 m	(39 ft. 3 in.)
height	4.24 m	(13 ft. 11 in.)
wing area	16.69 m²	(180 sq. ft.)

ACTION DATA

SPEED

High speed is important for a jet trainer, both to give the student pilot a taste of fast-jet speeds and to shorten any time spent flying between home base and the training area. In the case of the Goshawk, for example, this might allow extra carrier training.

T-45A GOSHAWK	997 km/h (618 m.p.h.)
ALPHA JET E	1000 km/h (620 m.p.h.)
MB-339C	902 km/h (559 m.p.h.)

CLIMB RATE

Rate of climb is important in a similar way to maximum speed. Much training takes place at high altitude in order to give the student room for mistakes. The T-45 loses out here due to the extra weight of its unique naval systems.

ALPHA JET E	3660 m/min (12,000 f.p.m.)
MB-339C	2225 m/min (7,300 f.p.m.)
T-45A	2128 m/min (7,000 f.p.m.)

THRUST

Although some critics have suggested that the Goshawk is underpowered, its upgraded F405-RR-401 engine provides adequate thrust for carrier operations and is extremely fuel efficient. The MB-339C is unusual amongst modern trainers in having a turbojet engine that is much less fuel efficient.

ALPHA JET E	26.48 kN (5,960 lb. thrust)
MB-339C	19.57 kN (4,400 lb. thrust)
T-45A GOSHAWK	26.00 kN (5,850 lb. thrust)

Carrier-capable trainers

■ **NORTH AMERICAN T-28B TROJAN:** From 1952 the T-28 was the US Navy's standard on-and-off-ship basic trainer.

■ **ROCKWELL T-2 BUCKEYE:** Entering service in 1959, the T-2 is now being replaced in service by the T-45A Goshawk.

■ **GRUMMAN TF-9J COUGAR:** Developed from the 1950s fighter, the trainer variant continued in service into the 1970s.

■ **McDONNELL DOUGLAS TA-4 SKYHAWK:** A two-seat version of the highly successful attack jet.

McDonnell Douglas/BAe

AV-8B Harrier II Plus

● Latest Harrier variant ● Air-to-air capability ● Export orders

I nternationally recognised as one of the most potent and versatile warplanes in service, the original second-generation Harrier II was penalised by its lack of radar. In the UK, British Aerospace (BAe) had produced the Sea Harrier by adding radar to the basic Harrier, a trend that has been repeated with the Harrier II Plus. With the APG-65 radar from the F/A-18A Hornet, the Harrier II Plus has gained a formidable beyond-visual-range (BVR) capability.

▲ Outwardly almost indistinguishable from the standard AV-8B, the Harrier II Plus embodies many improvements, including a new radar, new weapons and an upgraded engine.

PHOTO FILE

McDonnell Douglas/BAe AV-8B Harrier II Plus

▼ European operators
Italy and Spain have procured the latest AV-8B. Both countries employ the aircraft primarily in the air defence role.

▲ First rebuild
Unpainted and showing the various different structural materials, the first rebuilt Harrier II Plus performs a hover.

'Flying Tigers' ▶
The first unit of the US Marine Corps to receive the Harrier II Plus was VMA-542, which took delivery of its first example in 1993. One of its aircraft is seen here dropping Mk 82 Snakeye bombs during a training sortie.

◀ Variation in colours
Different paint schemes can be seen on the Harrier II Plus. Most sport two-tone Ghost Grey, though these two examples have much darker upper surfaces.

Reduction in orders ▶
Originally it was hoped that the entire USMC fleet would be upgraded to Harrier II Plus standard, but defence cutbacks during the 1990s have reduced the total to 99 aircraft.

FACTS AND FIGURES

➤ Since the first Harrier II Plus took to the air in 1992, engine failure has resulted in one of the prototypes crashing.

➤ A primary motivation for the programme was experience from the first Gulf War.

➤ All of the improved AV-8Bs were delivered by 2002.

➤ All the Harrier II Plus variants receive entirely new fuselages. This is cheaper than modifying the old ones.

➤ The introduction of the new aircraft has resulted in a true multi-role Harrier.

➤ Italy has been the first country to acquire trainers before single-seat variants.

PROFILE

Harrier II receives an update

Already a proven dogfighter with the short-range AIM-9 Sidewinder air-to-air missile (AAM), the Harrier II has now matured into an all-weather fighter, with the capability to engage BVR targets using AIM-7 Sparrow and AIM-120 AMRAAM radar-guided AAMs. The Harrier II Plus retains the close-support capability of its predecessor, but adds an important air defence role. In June 1987 McDonnell Douglas and BAe announced

their intention to develop a radar-equipped Harrier as a private venture. By late 1990, Italy, Spain and the US had signed a joint agreement for Harrier II Plus funding. The first prototype flew on 22 September 1992.

Since then, the USMC has received 27 new aircraft, andanother 72 were converted from AV-8Bs. Spain has received eight machines, and Italy has received 16, with options on a further eight.

Above: Another feature has been to increase the number of wing pylons from six to eight, in line with the RAF's aircraft. The new APG-65 radar and AIM-120 AMRAAM can be carried.

Left: Pilots have welcomed the introduction of the new aircraft and one, serving with VMA-542 'Flying Tigers', went so far as to describe it as a 'quantum leap for the Marines'.

AV-8B Harrier II Plus

Type: single-seat air-defence/close-support V/STOL aircraft

Powerplant: one 105.9-kN (23,825-lb.-thrust) Rolls-Royce Pegasus vectored-thrust turbofan

Maximum speed: 1065 km/h (660 m.p.h.)

Endurance: 3 hours

Combat radius: 1101 km (683 mi.)

Range: 3035 km (1,882 mi.)

Weights: empty 6336 kg (13,939 lb.); loaded 14,061 kg (20,552 lb.)

Armament: one 25 mm GAU-12/A cannon plus 11 hardpoints for various external stores

Dimensions:
span	9.25 m	(30 ft. 4 in.)
length	14.55 m	(47 ft. 9 in.)
height	3.55 m	(11 ft. 8 in.)
wing area	21.37 m²	(230 sq. ft.)

AV-8B Harrier II Plus

BuNo.164553 was one of the first Harrier II Plus variants to be delivered, being taken on charge by VMA-542 'Flying Tigers' at NAS Cherry Point in North Carolina, which has been a centre of US Marine Corps Harrier operations since the early 1970s.

Unlike early Harriers, the second-generation aircraft have retractable refuelling probes, which can be fitted to the port side of the fuselage above the intake. They are not always fitted, as is shown on this particular example.

Compared to the original Hawker design, the AV-8B series makes greater use of composite materials and graphite epoxy. The fuselage is somewhat longer and also stronger, with a much longer fatigue life than that of the early variants.

The lack of an adequate radar remained a handicap of the Harrier force for many years. Fitting the APG-65 into the AV-8B has resulted in a vastly superior machine, and has turned it into an effective sea defence fighter, offering better capability than the British Sea Harrier.

One improvement of the Harrier II Plus has been to increase the number of underwing hardpoints from six to eight. The latest AV-8B is also capable of carrying the AIM-120 AMRAAM (Advanced Medium-Range Air-to-Air Missile).

For self-defence, the latest AV-8B is fitted with a forward- and aft-looking RWR (radar warning receiver), a Goodyear AN/ALE-39 chaff dispenser and a Doppler MAW (missile approach warning) radar. This last item is fitted to the protruding tail boom unit.

COMBAT DATA

MAXIMUM SPEED

As the only truly effective V/STOL combat aircraft in service, the Harrier II has an impressive turn of speed. It is quicker than the Russian Sukhoi Su-25, which was also designed for battlefield support, but the Jaguar A is quicker still.

AV-8B	1065 km/h (660 m.p.h.)
Su-25K	950 km/h (589 m.p.h.)
JAGUAR A	1350 km/h (837 m.p.h.)

COMBAT RADIUS

Today's attack aircraft are designed to reach their targets at low level, in order to avoid tracking by enemy radar. Compared to the Jaguar and Su-25, the Harrier II Plus has a greater radius of action which is also a great improvement over the original Harrier.

Su-25K 'FROGFOOT-A' 495 km (307 mi.)

AV-8B HARRIER II PLUS 1101 km (683 mi.)

JAGUAR A 852 km (528 mi.)

CLIMB RATE

With its twin afterburning Adour turbofans, the SEPECAT Jaguar A (for Attack) has a phenomenal climb rate. The Su-25K 'Frogfoot' is not far behind, nor is the Harrier II, both of which can carry a greater amount of external stores.

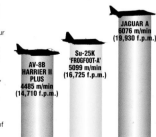

| AV-8B HARRIER II PLUS 4485 m/min (14,710 f.p.m.) | Su-25K 'FROGFOOT-A' 5099 m/min (16,725 f.p.m.) | JAGUAR A 6076 m/min (19,930 f.p.m.) |

Evolution of the Harrier

■ **HAWKER P.1127:** Forerunner of what became known as the Harrier, the P.1127 performed its first hover in October 1960.

■ **HAWKER KESTREL FGA.Mk 1:** With the success of the P.1127, nine development aircraft, known as Kestrels, were procured.

■ **HAWKER SIDDELEY AV-8A HARRIER:** First-generation Harriers were acquired by the USMC. They have been replaced by AV-8Bs.

■ **HAWKER SIDDELEY HARRIER GR.Mk 3:** Representing the pinnacle of early Harrier development, the GR.Mk 3 served until 1993.

MIKOYAN-GUREVICH

MiG-21BIS 'FISHBED'

● Interceptor ● Ground attack ● Most numerous fighter

Mikoyan-Gurevich's MiG-21bis 'Fishbed' is an advanced version of the fighter that has become one of the world's most successful. The MiG-21 was initially regarded as deficient in fuel capacity and lacking in adequate air-to-air radar, but improvements to the single-seat delta-winged fighter resulted in the MiG-21bis which was produced in huge numbers. Despite having a poor combat record, the MiG-21bis was being made as late as 1987.

▲ Like many
Soviet fighters, the MiG-21 was a simple design at first, but evolved steadily with better equipment to become a fine aircraft. It was far cheaper than its Western rivals.

▼ Dogfighter
MiGs have always enjoyed a reputation as good dogfighters, and the MiG-21bis was no exception. Its R-60 missiles and GSh-23 cannon were a great improvement on the MiG-21F.

▲ India's defenders
The MiG-21 remains the most numerous aircraft in the Indian air force, serving alongside other MiGs and SEPECAT Jaguars.

◄ Hungary squadron
Despite having retired two squadrons of MiG-21MFs, the Hungarian air force retains a squadron of MiG-21bis, which will probably be upgraded.

▼ Gone to the scrapyard
When Germany reunified, 'Fishbeds' from the DDR were retired to comply with the CFE treaty.

◄ Bigger engine
To increase power, the MiG designers replaced the earlier R-13 and R-11 engines with the R-25. This could be used at a special peak power rating for a limited time in combat.

FACTS AND FIGURES

➤ Production of all MiG-21 versions is at least 10,000, making it the world's most numerous jet fighter.

➤ India was granted the production rights to the MiG-21bis in 1974.

➤ Yugoslav MiG-21s were used during the nation's civil war in the early-1990s.

➤ MiG-21bis 'Fishbeds' still fly operationally with the air forces of over 40 nations from Afghanistan to Zimbabwe.

➤ Afghan Mujahideen shot down a large number of MiG-21s with Stinger missiles.

➤ Updated 'Fishbeds' may still be flying as late as 2015 with new engines and radar.

PROFILE

Making the old MiG better

MiG designers knew that their MiG-21 was a sound design but it suffered from a lack of fuel capacity and needed better equipment. The advanced MiG-21 appeared in the late Vietnam years. Although little different outwardly from earlier MiG-21s, the MiG-21bis introduced a large fairing atop the fuselage that raised its fuel capacity to 2900 litres contained in seven tanks.

The MiG-21bis also introduced the new R-25 engine, which had a much higher afterburner thrust

ratio than the R-13. It contained improved electronics such as the RP-22 Sapfir radar, RSBN short-range navigation system and a new instrument approach system. Armament was much improved as the result of the experience in Vietnam and the Middle East, with a GSh-23 revolver cannon and R-60M missiles that replaced the earlier R-13 'Atoll'.

The MiG-21bis was used in operations in Afghanistan, the Middle East and the former Yugoslavia, and often suffered heavy losses due to the poor

quality of pilot training. The aircraft is still widely used and will continue to give valuable service well into the next century.

Left: Take-off performance was drastically improved by the extra power of the R-25 engine. Two SPRD-99 solid rocket boosters could be fitted to assist take-off.

Right: Finland received its MiG-21bis aircraft in 1980, replacing its MiG-21Fs. The 'bis' was such a radical overhaul of the design that it almost received a new MiG Design Bureau number.

MiG-21bis 'Fishbed'

Type: single-seat fighter-bomber

Powerplant: one 73.55-kN (16,500-lb.-thrust) Tumanskii R-25 afterburning turbojet

Maximum speed: Mach 2.3 or 2230 km/h (1,383 m.p.h.) at high altitude

Initial climb rate: 17,680 m/min (57,900 f.p.m.)

Range: 1470 km (911 mi.)

Service ceiling: 16,100 m (52,800 ft.)

Weights: empty 5200 kg (11,440 lb.); normal take-off 7960 kg (17,513 lb.)

Armament: one twin-barrel 23-mm GSh-23 cannon with 200 rounds; four wing pylons for 'Atoll' missiles, bombs (two 500 kg/1,100 lb. and two 250 kg/550 lb.), rocket pods, or 490-litre (127-gal.) drop-tanks

Dimensions:
span	7.15 m (23 ft.)	
length	15.76 m (52 ft.)	
height	4.10 m (14 ft.)	
wing area	23 m² (247 sq. ft.)	

MiG-21BIS 'FISHBED'

The MiG-21bis was first accepted into VVS fighter regiments in 1972, and was mass produced in the Gorki factory. India was granted the production licence in 1974, and the type is still in service.

The first MiG-21s actually had better visibility than later versions with the high spine like the MiG-21R and MiG-21bis. New avionics for the 'bis' version included RSBN navigation equipment and an instrument approach system. The 'bis', and other MiG-21 models after the PFM variant, had a two-piece canopy hinging to starboard and a fixed windscreen.

The R-25 fuel system had to be modified to cope with the demands of the new engine. The R-25 offered superior performance at low level. The MiG-21R used the older R-11.

Like the MiG-21R, the 'bis' version had increased fuel capacity in the dorsal spine. This was something of a mixed blessing in some variants as it affected stability.

The MiG-21bis was fitted with an SPO-3 radar-warning receiver. The tailfin was topped by an aerial in a dielectric fairing. The fin chord was increased after the first MiG-21 versions to increase stability.

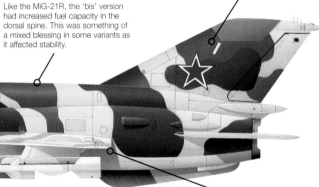

Some of the first MiG-21 variants were not fitted with a gun, but when it was realised how unreliable early missiles were, the gun was reinstated. India was one of the first customers to demand this.

The standard Soviet short-range air-to-air missile was the K-13 (NATO codename 'Atoll'). This MiG-21 carries the improved 'Advanced Atoll' in both infra-red and radar-homing versions.

For short take-offs from rough strips at high all-up weights, two solid rocket boosters could be fitted under the fuselage of the MiG-21bis. These produced 450,000 W of power for several seconds.

COMBAT DATA

SPEED (SEA LEVEL)

The R-25 engine delivered more thrust at low level than the older R-11 and R-13 fitted in earlier versions of the MiG-21. The Starfighter was even faster still.

MiG-21F 'FISHBED'	1150 km/h (713 m.p.h.)
MiG-21bis 'FISHBED'	1300 km/h (806 m.p.h.)
F-104G STARFIGHTER	1400 km/h (868 m.p.h.)

RANGE

With the additional fuel in its spine, the MiG-21bis had better range than the first-generation MiG-21s, and was even better than the short legged F-104G.

MiG-21F 'FISHBED' 1300 km (806 mi.)

F-104G STARFIGHTER 1200 km (744 mi.)

MiG-21bis 'FISHBED' 1470 km (911 mi.)

ARMAMENT

Performance was gained at the expense of weapon load, and so the MiG-21 and F-104 were designed to fire a pair of missiles and a few bursts from their cannon.

MiG-21F 'FISHBED'	1 x 23-mm cannon 2 x air-to-air missiles
MiG-21bis 'FISHBED'	1 x 30-mm cannon 4 x air-to-air missiles
F-104G STARFIGHTER	1 x 20-mm cannon 4 x air-to-air missiles

MiG-21 variants

■ **MiG-21F-13:** The first MiG-21 to carry air-to-air missiles, the 'F' was a very simple model, also built in China, Czechoslovakia and India. It was built between 1960 and 1965 in the USSR.

■ **MiG-21PF:** The MiG-21PF used the more powerful R-11F engine and the new 'Sapfir' radar. The 'PF' variant had the weakness (later corrected) of not having a cannon.

■ **MiG-21MF:** Demand for more power led to the MiG-21MF, which was an 'M' model fitted with the R-13-300 engine and a GSh-23 cannon. It was produced between 1970 and 1975.

■ **MiG-21bis:** The more powerful R-25 engine and improved radar and missiles made the MiG-21bis the best of the MiG-21 series. It could navigate accurately in any weather conditions.

MIKOYAN-GUREVICH
MiG-23 'FLOGGER'

● Swing-wing fighter ● High-performance interceptor

▲ Written off initially
as a 'poor man's Phantom', the MiG-23 is not easy to fly. But it has extremely good acceleration, high top speed and simple-to-use avionics, and is highly adaptable.

To most of the world, the word 'MiG' means 'Soviet fighter'. The MiG-23 'Flogger' is perhaps the least glamorous warplane bearing its famous name. Derided over the years as being ineffective, this tough and reliable swing-wing fighting jet has come in for a reappraisal. Available in interceptor and ground-attack versions, 'Floggers' have been built in large numbers and have seen action all over the world.

MIKOYAN-GUREVICH MiG-23 'FLOGGER'

▲ Polish air defender
Armed with a brace of R-60 missiles under the belly and wing-mounted R-23s, a Polish MiG-23 stands ready to scramble.

Mixed MiG formation ▶
A 'Flogger' flies with two 'Fulcrums', slower but more agile successors to the MiG-23.

▲ Dogfight story
Soviet MiG-23 pilots re-live a training fight. Not the most agile of fighters, in experienced hands the 'Flogger' could nevertheless give a good account of itself.

▼ Eastern favourite
The MiG-23MF was exported to Czechoslovakia, Germany, Hungary, Poland and Romania.

Bullet nose ▶
The sharp profile of the MiG-23 shows that it was meant to go very fast if need be. Later versions could even out-accelerate the Lockheed Martin F-16 Fighting Falcon.

▶ Mission ready ▲
A MiG-23 prepares for flight. Like most jets designed in the Soviet era, the MiG-23 can operate from semi-prepared strips, thanks to its swing wing and tough undercarriage.

FACTS AND FIGURES

➤ Development of the MiG-23, successor to the MiG-21, began in the early 1960s.

➤ The MiG-23 was first seen by the West at an air show near Moscow in June 1967.

➤ A typical MiG-23 carries 5380 litres (1,400 gal.) of internal fuel and up to 2370 litres (616 gal.) in external tanks.

➤ Its variable-geometry wing allows the MiG-23 to fly from short tactical runways.

➤ Two Libyan MiG-23s were shot down by US Navy F-14 Tomcats in 1989.

➤ Export MiG-23s have not done well in combat, due mainly to pilot inexperience and their downgraded avionics fit.

PROFILE

The variable-geometry 'Flogger'

More of a bully than a beauty, the MiG-23 'Flogger' is a contemporary of the West's F-4 Phantom. Both are powerful. Both are versatile. Both are rewarding aircraft from the pilot's point of view, and both succeed at their grim military business. Both make effective use of powerful engines, superb radar and muscular weapons-carrying capacity.

But while the Phantom is a two-seater with a fixed wing, most MiG-23s are single-seat aircraft with a variable-geometry wing which sweeps forward for good performance at low speeds and backward for high-speed flight.

The MiG-23 equipped nearly all allies of the former Soviet Union, and was still being refined and improved three decades after entering service. Its combat record was mixed. Arab forces lost large numbers of the aircraft to the Israelis, but this was more to do with disparity in training than any superiority of Western designs.

The MiG-23 may have been overshadowed by its successors, but the sheer numbers of this aircraft mean that it will remain an important combat type for many years to come.

No longer at the cutting edge of technology, the MiG-23 'Flogger' remains amenable to further development even as it gathers age, and it remains a hard-hitting weapon of war.

With its wing in the forward position, the MiG-23 can safely land slowly on rough surfaces. With the wing swung back, it can outrun almost anything in the skies.

MiG-23ML 'Flogger-G'

Type: single-seat strike fighter

Powerplant: one Soyuz (Tumanskii) R-35-300 turbojet rated at 127.5 kN (22,050-lb.-thrust) with afterburner

Maximum speed: 2500 km/h (1,550 m.p.h.) at 12,500 m (41,000 ft.)

Range: 2800 km (1,736 mi.)

Service ceiling: 18,000 m (59,000 ft.)

Weights: empty 8200 kg (18,040 lb.); loaded 17,800 kg (39,160 lb.)

Armament: one 23-mm GSh-23L twin-barrel cannon; 2000 kg (4,400 lb.) of ordnance

Dimensions: span 13.95 m (46 ft.)
length 16.70 m (53 ft.)
height 4.80 m (13 ft.)
wing area 37.35 m² (402 sq. ft.)

MiG-23MS 'Flogger-E'

Libya has received large numbers of the MiG-23MS, and has used them in action over Chad and Egypt. Two were shot down during a confrontation with US Navy F-14 Tomcats in January 1989.

The fact that the MiG-23 was not designed to dogfight can be seen in its cockpit. Rearward visibility is very poor, even with mirrors fitted on the canopy arch.

The MiG-23 gains its speed from its small frontal area, coupled with the huge power of the Tumanskii R-29 turbojet, which has a massive jetpipe.

The MiG-23 was always constrained by the performance of its radar, which lacked a true 'lookdown' capability until the final 'ML' variant was introduced.

The air intake of most MiG-23s had moveable 'splitter plates' to control airflow when flying at high speeds. The plates are fixed in the MiG-27 (the ground-attack variant of the MiG-23), which operates at lower speeds.

Export MiG-23s are often armed with the basic infra-red K-13 missile, known in the West as the AA-2 'Atoll'. This is a copy of a very early version of the American AIM-9 Sidewinder.

All Russian fighters have large mudguards to allow flight from rough airstrips in snowy weather.

COMBAT DATA

MAXIMUM SPEED

Even today, some three decades after its first flight in 1967, the MiG-23 remains one of the fastest fighters in the world. Its immensely powerful Tumanskii turbojet propels the fighter to Mach 2.5 with wings swept back at 72°. With wings at a minimum sweep of 16°, speed is limited to the subsonic regime, with a maximum of 940 km/h (580 m.p.h.).

F-4E PHANTOM
2390 km/h (1,482 m.p.h.)

MiG-23MLD
2500 km/h (1,550 m.p.h.)

MIRAGE F1C
2340 km/h (1,450 m.p.h.)

CLIMB RATE

Although powered by a potent engine, the MiG-23 cannot match the sheer brute twin-engined power of its great American rival. But the big and heavy Phantom cannot climb as high as the 'Flogger', nor can it accelerate as rapidly in level flight.

F-4E PHANTOM
18,000 m/min (59,040 f.p.m.)

MiG-23MLD
10,000 m/min (32,800 f.p.m.)

MIRAGE F1C
12,000 m/min (39,360 f.p.m.)

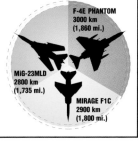

RANGE

No fast jet combat aircraft developed in the 1960s is notable for its range, although all have respectable ferry ranges. In combat, however, radius of action is dramatically reduced, and using the afterburner cuts endurance to a matter of minutes.

F-4E PHANTOM
3000 km (1,860 mi.)

MiG-23MLD
2800 km (1,735 mi.)

MIRAGE F1C
2900 km (1,800 mi.)

Swing-wing solutions

FULL WING SWING: The Panavia Tornado's wings swing from the wingroots, necessitating an extremely complex hinge construction built onto the fuselage. This allows all of the wing to be swept for high speeds and extended for low speeds, but presents a considerable engineering challenge and one that costs a great deal of time and money to perfect.

SWINGING FROM THE MIDDLE: The MiG-23 was one of the first operational variable-geometry aircraft. To simplify engineering problems, MiG's designers decided to move only those sections of the wing that were clear of the fuselage, leaving a small part fixed. That way, they could move the wing hinges away from the body of the plane, making for much less complex construction.

WINGTIP SWING: The huge Tupolev swing-wing bombers like the 'Backfire' and 'Blackjack' utilise the simplest swing wings, pivoting only the outer portions. While less efficient at low speeds than a fully moveable wing, they still significantly cut landing speeds. Fully swept, they are just as effective.

MIKOYAN-GUREVICH
MiG-25R 'FOXBAT'

● Soviet spy plane ● Exported ● Mach-3 flights

Expanding on knowledge gained in the design of the interceptor version of the 'Foxbat', the Soviets realised that the MiG-25 would make an ideal reconnaissance platform. Still often deployed along the Russian borders, the aircraft is tasked with looking deep into NATO countries to monitor military exercises and the like. Cameras were used at first; later versions employ a large side-looking airborne radar (SLAR).

▲ *Maintenance*
personnel lend scale to the huge size of the Foxbat. A development of the fighter version, the MiG-25R will serve in the Russian air force for the foreseeable future.

MIKOYAN-GUREVICH MiG-25R 'FOXBAT'

◀ **Border missions**
Taking-off from an airfield in East Germany, a MiG-25RBF displays the small dielectric panels on the nose. These aircraft were active along NATO's borders.

▼ **Stopping distance**
Because of the enormous size of the MiG-25, two large braking chutes are deployed to slow the aircraft.

▲ **Camera bay**
Lowered for servicing is one of the five cameras installed on the MiG-25 which allow high-altitude images to be taken.

▼ **Rare bird**
This complex camouflage scheme of green, brown and sand shades is seen on a few examples.

▼ **Indian operations**
A highly capable aircraft, reconnaissance versions of the 'Foxbat' have not been widely exported because of their advanced systems.

FACTS AND FIGURES

➤ The reconnaissance version of the Foxbat first flew on 6 March 1964, six months before the fighter variant.

➤ Five cameras are fitted in the nose of the aircraft in vertical and oblique positions.

➤ The MiG-25RB operates in a dual reconnaissance-bomber role.

➤ A detachment of four pre-production models was deployed to Egypt under the designation X-500.

➤ For training future reconnaissance pilots a dedicated two-seat trainer exists.

➤ Overseas operators of the aircraft have included Algeria, India, Libya and Syria.

PROFILE

Soviet high-speed snooper

Highly regarded as a Soviet Mach-3 fighter, the 'Foxbat' first flew in its reconnaissance variant six months before the interceptor. The most noticeable change was a longer, slimmer nose, the fighter's radome having been removed. Other modifications were shorter span wings and the addition of a constant leading-edge taper to improve handling.

Following a protracted development phase, two main variants were identified by the West. The 'Foxbat-B' version employed five oblique cameras and a small side-looking

airborne radar (SLAR), whilst the 'Foxbat-D' variant has no cameras fitted and relies on a much larger SLAR panel. Since the appearance of these aircraft, numerous upgrades of the type's reconnaissance systems have led to a host of sub-types becoming operational within the Soviet and Russian air forces. These have included reconnaissance/bomber versions. Requests for the aircraft from Soviet client states were initially turned down, but after a covert deployment to the Middle East during the 1970s the type became available for export. Algeria, India, Syria and Libya

are all believed to continue operating MiG-25R/RB ('Foxbat-B') aircraft, but with assistance from Russian advisors or even Russian pilots.

Above: The huge twin Tumanskii engines of the MiG-25 are powered up prior to propelling this reconnaissance aircraft on another intelligence-gathering mission.

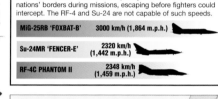

Above: India operates five MiG-25RBs, having lost one in an accident. They serve with No. 102 Squadron which also flies two MiG-25RUs, specialised training versions used to instruct future MiG-25RB pilots.

MiG-25RBF 'FOXBAT-B'

Developed from the interceptor variant, the MiG-25RBF is the latest of a number of reconnaissance versions, many of which have been brought up-to-date with the addition of more sophisticated equipment.

The twin tails allow the aircraft to be much more stable at high speeds, particularly during the photographic runs where the images obtained must be extremely clear.

Lacking the large distinguishing SLAR panels on the nose, the improved reconnaissance variants rely on dielectric panels symmetrically positioned around the nose of the aircraft to gather information.

The pilot is seated in a pressurised cockpit deep within the fuselage of the aircraft, restricting the field of view. Operating at high altitude with little risk of interception the pilot requires a minimum view of the outside world during a mission.

On early variants of the MiG-25R, wingtip mass-balances were fitted to improve the handling of the aircraft at high speed. Though standard, variants are often seen flying without them.

Reconnaissance variants of the Foxbat have a smoother nose profile than interceptor versions, this aerodynamic change allowing them to reach higher speeds.

The vertical camera window is retained on this version, although most of the intelligence collected is obtained by the small dielectric panels on the nose.

Two Tumanskii turbojets power the 'Foxbat', these being improved versions originally employed in the interceptor variants. The high speed achieved by these engines allowed the Foxbat to outrun Israeli F-4 Phantoms and Mirages.

COMBAT DATA

MAXIMUM SPEED

For sheer speed the MiG-25 has become a legend within aerospace circles. The reconnaissance versions are the fastest of the MiG-25 variants and have frequently been flown over various nations' borders during missions, escaping before fighters could intercept. The RF-4 and Su-24 are not capable of such speeds.

MiG-25RB 'FOXBAT-B'	3000 km/h (1,864 m.p.h.)
Su-24MR 'FENCER-E'	2320 km/h (1,442 m.p.h.)
RF-4C PHANTOM II	2348 km/h (1,459 m.p.h.)

Middle East missions

SPY FLIGHT: Arriving in total secrecy during March 1971, two MiG-25Rs were deployed to Cairo West air base in Egypt, and were code-named X-500s.

BEIRUT

Etam

Cairo West • CAIRO

Hatzerim
Ramon
Ovda

Etzion

IMMUNE TO INTERCEPTION: Despite repeated attempts by Israeli F-4 Phantoms and Mirages, the Foxbats were never attacked during their flights. Flown by Soviet pilots throughout the deployment, the aircraft were operated under strict control from Moscow.

'Foxbat' variants at home and abroad

■ MiG-25 'FOXBAT-A': Still in front-line service with the Russian air force, this example displays a typical mixed war load of heat-seeking and radar-guided missiles.

■ MiG-25P 'FOXBAT': An export fighter variant was supplied to a number of Soviet client states, including Syria, whose examples have seen considerable action in the Middle East.

■ MiG-25RU 'FOXBAT-C': India operates a number of examples of the MiG-25 reconnaissance variant. Two two-seat training examples are used to convert pilots on to the type.

MIKOYAN

MiG-27 'FLOGGER-D/J'

● Ground attack ● Close air support ● Anti-shipping strike

Based on the MiG-23BM, the MiG-27 is a dedicated ground-attack aircraft and is equipped with a six-barrelled 30-mm cannon for use against ground targets. The undercarriage is strengthened so that it can carry the additional weight of air-to-surface stores, including nuclear weapons, and the air intakes are simplified. It is fitted with a comprehensive array of antennas and sensors for targeting and self-protection.

▲ The MiG-27 was popular with the pilots who flew the aircraft in combat over Afghanistan, improving their operational techniques. Various modifications to the aircraft resulted from these operations.

MIKOYAN MiG-27 'FLOGGER-D/J'

◀ **The Indian Valiant**
India licence-builds the MiG-27M, and in Indian air force service it is known as the 'Bahadur' (Valiant).

▼ **Frontal aviation**
The MiG-27 has been an important asset to Russia's air armies since the mid-1970s.

▲ **Tactical deployment**
MiG-27s armed with tactical nuclear weapons were on strength at Soviet bases across East Germany until 1992.

▼ **Commonality**
The Soviet MiG-27 shared components with the MiG-23 but was dedicated to the ground-attack role.

▲ **Rough-field capability**
The rugged MiG-27 has been designed to operate from hastily prepared forward air bases with minimum ground support. Take-offs are kept as short as possible by using reheat.

FACTS AND FIGURES

➤ The Mikoyan MiG-27 was chiefly developed because of the Soviet's dissatisfaction with the MiG-23BN.

➤ For ground-strafing MiG-27s carry SPPU-22 gunpods with articulated barrels.

➤ To confuse enemy defences the MiG-27 has a powerful thermal jammer.

➤ The MiG-27 can be distinguished from the MiG-23BN by its fixed intakes and splitter plates 80 mm (3 in.) from the fuselage wall.

➤ Russian air force MiG-27s can carry the TN series of tactical nuclear weapons.

➤ The MiG-27K has an internal smoke emitter for laying battlefield screens.

PROFILE

'Ducknose', the strike fighter

Both the original MiG-27 and the MiG-27K were known in the West by the NATO designation 'Flogger-D'. However, the -27K had a new navigation and attack system, including a laser rangefinder in the nose, that made it capable of highly accurate blind bombing.

Further equipment improvements produced the MiG-27M, or 'Flogger-J'. This is equipped to launch missiles and precision-guided munitions. Later versions carried various additional systems, including forward-looking infra-red sensors and specialised navigation systems for the nuclear strike role.

Soviet forces used MiG-27s during the later stages of the war in Afghanistan in 1987–89. They were fitted with dispensers for chaff and flares to help protect them against surface-to-air missiles used by the Mujahideen guerillas.

The subsequent break-up of the Soviet Union left MiG-27s in the hands of several of the newly independent states, like the Ukraine. Other than these, however, the only MiG-27s to serve outside Russia are those operated by India, which actually built many of its own MiG-27Ms.

Above: The Russian air force is now beginning to phase out its older MiG-27s in favour of newer multi-role types. The aircraft remains a very important weapon for India, however.

Below: The original MiG-27K 'Flogger-D' has now been supplanted in the Russian air force by the improved MiG-27M 'Flogger-J' and '-J2', with provision to carry more precision-guided munitions.

MiG-27M 'Flogger-J'

Type: single-seat ground-attack and close air support aircraft

Powerplant: one 112.77-kN (25,370-lb.-thrust) MNPK Tumanskii R-29B-300 turbojet

Maximum speed: 1885 km/h (1,169 m.p.h.)

Initial climb rate: 12,000 m/min (39,360 f.p.m.)

Combat radius: 540 km (335 mi.) at low level

Service ceiling: 14,000 m (45,900 ft.)

Weights: maximum take-off 20,300 kg (44,660 lb.)

Armament: one GSh-6-30 six-barrel 30-mm gun, plus 5000 kg (11,000 lb.) of weapons on seven pylons

Dimensions:
span	13.97 m	(45 ft. 10 in.)
length	17.08 m	(56 ft.)
height	5.00 m	(16 ft. 5 in.)
wing area	37.35 m²	(402 sq. ft.)

MiG-27K 'FLOGGER-D'

In the 1980s the West's intelligence sources were confident that the MiG-27 had been widely exported to the Soviet's allies, including Syria (whose markings are shown below). However, India and the former Soviet republics are the only operators of the aircraft.

The MiG-27's broad, flat nose contains a small ranging radar and a laser rangefinder which are capable of locking on to laser energy from a marked target. The nose also holds air data probes and other antennas. The MiG-27 is known to the Russians as 'utkanos' (ducknose).

Large, heavy-duty armoured panels are scabbed onto the sides of the cockpit to protect the pilot from shrapnel and gunfire. The pilot's windscreen is also heavily armoured.

There are seven external stores pylons, including the centreline for carrying a 790-litre drop-tank. Other stores include: 23-mm gunpods; 20-, 130- or 240-mm rockets; 500-kg (1,100-lb.) bombs; bomblet dispensers; air-to-air and air-to-surface missiles including the Kh-29 and Kh-31.

The wing can be continuously swept or set to any of three pre-selected positions for different flight patterns. The hydraulically powered wings can be set to 16°, 45° or 72° sweep.

The tailcone contains a large brake chute normally deployed just prior to landing.

The sturdy forward undercarriage is designed for adverse terrain operations and features twin nosewheels, low-pressure tyres and mudguards.

A powerful GSh-6-30 Gatling gun, with six 30-mm barrels and provision for 260 rounds of ammunition, is housed in a bulge under the belly. The gun is especially useful for attacking ground targets and armoured vehicles.

A single Tumanskii turbojet with two-position afterburner provides up to 112.77 kN (25,370 lb.) thrust.

A stabilising ventral fin automatically folds up when the undercarriage is lowered.

Combat missions

AIRFIELD STRIKE: Armed with 500-kg (1,100-lb.) bombs and KMGU bomblet dispensers, the MiG-27 is suited to low-level attacks.

TANK BUSTING: The MiG-27 is a formidable anti-tank aircraft, using its 30-mm Gatling gun combined with Kh-29 precision-guided air-to-surface missiles. For self-protection it is equipped with chaff, smoke and flares.

ANTI-SHIPPING: Russian navy MiG-27Ms are equipped to carry the Kh-31 long-range ramjet-powered anti-ship missile. These aircraft are tasked with the protection of Russian shipping lanes and are based on the Kola Peninsula.

COMBAT DATA

TAKE-OFF DISTANCE

Ground-attack aircraft can extend their time over the target by using forward air strips, which are often very short pieces of disused road or damaged airfields. The figures given are for maximum weapon load, typical for a front-line mission.

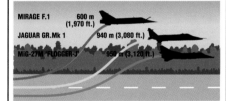

MIRAGE F.1	600 m (1,970 ft.)
JAGUAR GR.Mk 1	940 m (3,080 ft.)
MiG-27 'FLOGGER-J'	950 m (3,120 ft.)

INTERNAL GUNS

Unlike dedicated air-defence aircraft, which are equipped with less devastating but higher velocity cannon, the MiG-27 and its rivals in the ground-attack role use 30-mm (1.18-in) cannon. These rounds are far heavier than those used by the air-defence machines.

MiG-27M 'FLOGGER-J'	30-mm, 260 rounds
JAGUAR GR.Mk 1	30-mm, 300 rounds
MIRAGE F.1	30-mm, 250 rounds

COMBAT RADIUS

Equipped with two Kh-29 missiles and three 790-litre (210-gal.) drop-tanks, the MiG-27 has a useful range. With full weapon load, range is reduced to 225 km (140 mi.) with internal fuel only. The Jaguar has especially long range due to its efficient Adour engines.

MiG-27M 'FLOGGER-J'	540 m (335 mi.)
MIRAGE F.1	425 m (265 mi.)
JAGUAR GR.Mk 1	940 m (580 mi.)

MIKOYAN

MiG-29 'FULCRUM'

● Multi-role fighter ● Highly agile ● Advanced weapon systems

T he MiG-29 is a killer. This jet fighter from Russia is agile and potent, a challenge to America's best. Western fighters may be expensive limousines, but the 'Fulcrum', with its high manoeuvrability, resilient engines and excellent missiles, is like a hot racing car, not easy to fly but formidable in battle. And now the MiG-29K has been developed to fly from aircraft-carriers – even without the help of steam catapults!

▲ The advent of the MiG-29 in the 1980s gave the highly professional Russian fighter pilot a combat aircraft second to none.

MIKOYAN MiG-29 'FULCRUM'

▼ Afterburning power
A MiG-29 'Fulcrum' blasts into the sky, twin Klimov/Sarkisov RD-33 turbofans blazing. It can get airborne in less than 250 m (800 ft.).

Supremely agile ▲
Although some of its systems are old-fashioned, the MiG's advanced aerodynamics and great power give it unsurpassed manoeuvrability.

► Export success
'Fulcrums' are being operated by the air forces of nearly 30 nations, including Slovakia.

▲ Old enemies, new friends
For 10 years the MiG was a threat to Western air forces, but it is now more likely to be encountered as a friend.

◄ Rough-field performer
As with most Soviet-designed aircraft, the MiG-29 is designed to operate from rough fields. Braking parachutes are used to bring the 15-ton fighter to a halt.

FACTS AND FIGURES

➤ For a 'stealthy' intercept the MiG-29 can use an infra-red imaging device rather than its radar.

➤ The MiG-29 has an outstanding ejection seat, the Zvezda K-36, which works even at Mach 2.5.

➤ The MiG's AA-10 'Alamo' missile can destroy enemies 40 km (25 mi.) away.

➤ When the air forces of East and West Germany combined, the MiG-29 was the only Russian combat type good enough to be retained by the 'new' Luftwaffe.

➤ Unlike Western fighters, the 'Fulcrum' readily performs the tailslide, the aircraft falling backwards at the apex of a vertical climb.

PROFILE

Mikoyan's fantastic 'Fulcrum'

Russia's Mikoyan-Gurevich bureau came up with a real winner when the MiG-29 burst on the scene in 1977. Using advanced technology to make the 'Fulcrum' a real slugger in medium-range and close-quarter combat, engineers created a fighter which is one of the world's most manoeuvrable. In the right hands a MiG-29 can fight and win a close-in, gloves-off dogfight against any warplane in service today.

Seen by the West as a rival to the F-16, the MiG-29 offers far superior detection capabilities, and the AA-10 and AA-11 missiles it carries are much better

than their Western counterparts. However, it does not have much of an air-to-ground repertoire, although the second-generation MiG-29M can carry a wide array of precision weapons.

Though it offers super performance, the MiG-29 is practical, and less expensive than Western fighters. But the 'Fulcrum' never fails to command respect: in the heat of battle, it is always a lethal foe.

With the end of the Cold War, new customers are considering purchasing this superb fighter. The offer of a state-of-the-art machine at a bargain price is too good to refuse.

India is one of many countries to have bought the MiG-29. Its high performance and low cost has made it attractive to air forces worldwide.

The carrier version of the MiG-29 is thought to be based on the advanced 'Fulcrum-M', with more powerful engines, improved radar and avionics.

Before the fall of the Soviet Union the MiG-29 was flown by many of the elite Guards Aviation Regiments.

The MiG-29's wing and leading-edge extensions were designed at TsAGI, the Soviet equivalent of NASA. They are extremely efficient aerodynamically, and contribute to the 'Fulcrum's' superb performance.

MiG-29 'Fulcrum-A'

Type: single-seat multi-purpose fighter

Powerplant: two Klimov/Leningrad RD-33 afterburning bypass turbofan engines rated at 81.40-kN (11,100-lb.-thrust) static thrust

Max speed: Mach 2.2 or 2445 km/h (1,520 m.p.h.) at 10,000 m (32,800 ft.)

Range: 1200 km with an average weapons load

Service ceiling: 17,000 m (35,800 ft.)

Weights: empty 10,900 kg (24,000 lb.); maximum take-off 18,500 kg (40,800 lb.)

Armament: GSh-301 single-barrel lightweight 30-mm cannon, six to eight AA-8, AA-10 or AA-11 air-to-air missiles, or rocket pods and free-fall bombs for ground attack

Dimensions:
span	11.36 m	(37 ft. 4 in.)
length	17.32 m	(56 ft. 10 in.)
height	4.73 m	(15 ft. 7 in.)
wing area	38 m²	(410 sq. ft.)

MiG-29K 'Fulcrum'

The MiG-29K is a dedicated maritime aircraft, and underwent trails on the carrier *Kuznetsov* during 1992/1993.

The ball in front of the MiG-29's cockpit houses the laser and infra-red sensors of the infra-red search-and-track system.

Although the 'Fulcrum' has a much less obstructed view from the cockpit than previous Soviet designs, it does not match its Western rivals such as the F-15 and F-16 for pilot visibility.

The MiG-29's radar is a multi-mode lookup/lookdown system. It is extremely powerful, although data handling is a little less sophisticated than in the latest Western systems.

MiG-29s are fitted with shields for their air intakes which close when the aircraft is on the ground. This is designed to prevent debris entering the engines in rough-field operation.

Standard weapons on the MiG-29 include the AA-10 'Alamo' for beyond-visual-range engagements and the exceptionally agile heat-seeking AA-11 'Archer' for dogfights.

The carrier-capable MiG-29K is fitted with folding wings and an arrester hook.

Infra-red tracker

HEAT SOURCE: All powered machinery generates infra-red energy in the form of heat. Jet engines are particularly powerful heat generators.

DETECTABLE ENERGY: The heat generated by the engines and by air friction on the aircraft's skin is broadcast for miles around. This heat is detectable by another aircraft equipped with a heat sensor. The MiG-29 an aircraft-sized heat source at more than 80 km (50 mi.).

RANGE-FINDING: Once a target has been detected, the MiG-29 uses a laser beam to measure its distance and bearing. Weapons can then be locked on without the need for giveaway radar transmissions.

COMBAT DATA

MAXIMUM SPEED

The MiG-29 is one of the fastest fighters in the world, although supersonic flight cuts its range considerably.

MiG-29 'FULCRUM'	2445 km/h (1,520 m.p.h.)
F/A-18	1915 km/h (1,200 m.p.h.)
MIRAGE 2000	2340 km/h (1,450 m.p.h.)

COMBAT RANGE

Thanks to more efficient engines and greater fuel capacity, the MiG-29 has twice the range of earlier Soviet tactical jets such as the MiG-21 and MiG-23. Even so, the 'Fulcrum' has a relatively short range compared to its Western contemporaries.

F/A-18 HORNET 2000 km (1,240 mi.)

MiG-29 'FULCRUM' 1200 km (745 mi.)

MIRAGE 2000 1500 km (930 mi.)

SERVICE CEILING

The MiG is not really an interceptor, but its high speed and good ceiling mean that it can be pressed into service to catch high-flying bombers and reconnaissance aircraft.

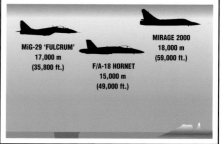

MiG-29 'FULCRUM' 17,000 m (35,800 ft.)

F/A-18 HORNET 15,000 m (49,000 ft.)

MIRAGE 2000 18,000 m (59,000 ft.)

MIKOYAN

MiG-31 'FOXHOUND'

● Long-range interceptor ● High-speed fighter ● Advanced radar

▲ *Without equal in the West, the MiG-31 is a unique aircraft, developed to meet the requirement of defending what was the world's largest nation with a relatively small number of interceptor units.*

MiG's 'Foxhound' is at the cutting edge of Russian air defence. The world's largest and most powerful fighter, the MiG-31 was designed to use the latest radar and missile technology to find and destroy bombers or cruise missiles threatening Russia. Able to control intercepts for other aircraft and engage targets from sea level to the edge of space, the 'Foxhound' is still being improved, and the more potent MiG-31M may yet enter service.

MIKOYAN MiG-31 'FOXHOUND'

Guess from the West ▶
This drawing was produced by intelligence officers in the United States, based on satellite pictures of MiG-31 prototypes and reports from defecting MiG-25 pilot Victor Belenko. Despite early assessments, the MiG-31 is far more than a 'super-Foxbat'.

▼ First appearance
'Foxhounds' began appearing over the Barents Sea in 1985. This example has the full armament fit of AA-9 'Amos' and AA-8 'Aphid' missiles.

▲ Stealthy search
Like the MiG-29 and Su-27, but not most Western types, the MiG-31 can detect aircraft passively with its retractable infra-red search-and-track sensor.

▼ Mother of all radars
The mighty 'Zaslon' radar's beam can even be swung to the side of the aircraft if required.

▲ Advanced Foxhound
The improved MiG-31M, easily recognisable by the four wing pylons for R-77 missiles and one-piece 'wrap-around' front canopy, is unlikely to be built in quantity.

FACTS AND FIGURES

➤ A fully loaded MiG-31 weighs as much as four unloaded MiG-29s, or two English Electric Canberra bombers.

➤ The MiG-31's GSh-23 cannon fires at a rate of 6000 rounds per minute.

➤ The SBI-16 (S-800) 'Zaslon' radar can engage several targets simultaneously.

➤ A MiG-31 prototype, the Ye-155, broke the payload-to-height record in 1977, climbing to 37,080 m (121,622 ft.) with 2000 kg (4,400 lb.).

➤ A MiG-31 shot down a low-level cruise missile from 20 km (12 mi.) away and 6 km (4 mi.) high.

PROFILE

Russia's fighting Foxhound

Developed as a specialised interceptor to defend Russia's extensive borders, the MiG-31 is arguably the most advanced air-defence aircraft ever built. Derived from the MiG-25 'Foxbat', the MiG-31 has the same blistering top speed as its ancestor, but also has a second crewmember who operates a massive phased-array 'Zaslon' radar (the first ever fitted to a fighter, and probably the most powerful). Also equipped with a search-and-track infra-red system, advanced datalink and the long-range AA-9 'Amos' missile, the 'Foxhound' can engage difficult targets (like cruise missiles) from almost surface level to maximum altitude, working in concert with other fighters and ground stations. Unlike the MiG-25, the MiG-31 has demonstrated impressive range, even allowing overflights of the North Pole.

The new MiG-31M has even more advanced defensive avionics, 'glass' cockpit displays, leading-edge root extensions and a new radar to allow it to fire active radar missiles. Despite its superb capabilities, the MiG-31M faces an uncertain future because of defence cuts.

Below: Despite being optimised for long-range engagements, the MiG-31 can take on short-range targets with missiles like the R-60 as well as with its 23-mm cannon.

Above: The MiG-31 can act as a fighter-control aircraft. Four aircraft in line formation can protect over 10,000 km² (3,680 sq, mi.) when used in this way.

One improvement in the MiG-31M is the addition of leading-edge root extensions, which improve the aircraft's high-alpha ability.

MiG-31 'Foxhound'

Type: twin-engine high-performance interceptor

Powerplant: two PNPP (Soloviev) D-30F6 turbofan engines each rated at 93.19 kN (20,904-lb.-thrust) or 152.06 kN (34,111-lb.-thrust) with afterburner

Maximum speed: 3000 km/h (1,860 m.p.h.) at 17,500 m (57,400 ft.)

Ferry range: 3300 km (2,046 mi.)

Service ceiling: 20,600 m (67,568 ft.)

Weights: empty 21,825 kg (48,115 lb.); normal take-off 41,000 kg (101,640 lb.); maximum take-off 46,200 kg (191,851 lb.)

Armament: one GSh-6-23 six-barrelled 23-mm Gatling-type cannon with 250 rounds; various air-to-air missiles

Dimensions:
span	13.46 m	(44 ft.)
length	22.68 m	(74 ft.)
height	6.20 m	(20 ft.)
wing area	61.60 m²	(663 sq. ft.)

MiG-31M 'FOXHOUND'

The seventh prototype MiG-31M, '057' may be the last of this unique aircraft to be built. The first fighter in the world equipped with a phased-array radar, the MiG-31 serves only with the Russian PVO air defence force.

A distinct clue as to the MiG-31's ancestry, the wing consists of a welded steel and titanium box containing a very large fuel tank. This acts as a heat sink because at maximum speed the MiG-31's skin can reach 300°C (572°F).

Some MiG-31Ms have this ECM pod on the wingtip, with radomes on each end and on the outer side.

Half of the airframe is constructed from advanced steel, with one-third duralumin and 16 per cent titanium.

Visibility is somewhat limited for the backseater, whose attention is focused on a very large radar scope and multifunction displays. He sits on the K-36 ejection seat.

Power is provided by a pair of D-30 turbofans derived from the engine in the Tu-134 airliner. These offer considerably better fuel consumption (and have longer life) than the MiG-25's R-15 turbojets.

Another unusual feature of the MiG-31 is the tandem mainwheel configuration of the undercarriage designed for operating in the snowy Russian climate.

By using electronic beam control the size of the aerial can be maximised, giving greater range than conventional radars. The 'Zaslon' radar can detect a fighter at over 200 km (125 mi.).

COMBAT DATA

MAXIMUM SPEED

The MiG-31 is not quite as fast as its predecessor, the MiG-25, but it can easily outrun any other fighter in service. In practice, few fighters ever reach such speeds for more than a few minutes, and only then without their full load of fuel and weapons.

TORNADO F.Mk 3	2340 km/h (1,451 m.p.h.)
F-14A TOMCAT	2480 km/h (1,537 m.p.h.)
MiG-31 'FOXHOUND'	3000 km/h (1,860 m.p.h.)

ARMAMENT

Missiles like the R-33 (AA-9 'Amos') give the MiG-31 the ability to destroy enemy aircraft up to 110 km (70 mi.) away. Although it can carry eight missiles, six is a more usual load, with just two R-60s.

MiG-31 'FOXHOUND'
1 x 23-mm cannon
4 x short-range R-60 AAMs
4 x long-range R-33 AAMs

TORNADO F.Mk 3
1 x 27-mm cannon
4 x short-range Sidewinder AAMs
4 x medium-range Skyflash AAMs

F-14A TOMCAT
1 x 20-mm cannon
2 x short-range Sidewinder AAMs
2 x medium-range Sparrow AAMs
2 x long-range Phoenix AAMs

RADAR RANGE

The powerful 'Zaslon' radar system has very long range, surpassing even the AWG-9 radar in the F-14. The Tomcat's radar can track more targets at the same time.

MiG-31 'FOXHOUND'	200 km (125 mi.)
F-14A TOMCAT	180 km (111 mi.)
TORNADO F.Mk 3	185 km/h (115 mi.)

The ultimate air-defence team

BOMBER THREAT: By the early 1980s, the threat varied from high-flying cruise missile-armed B-52s to low-level aircraft like the FB-111A and Rockwell B-1 and ground-launched cruise missiles.

TARGET DATA TRANSFER: The MiG-31's PD-518 datalink can transfer target information to other air-defence aircraft like the Su-27 or MiG-29. Four MiG-31s can sweep an area 900 km (560 mi.) wide.

MINI-AWACS: MiG-31s can act like a small AWACS craft, with the leader of a four-aircraft formation linked to a ground radar station and AEW aircraft.

MITSUBISHI

MU-2

● STOL design ● Built in Japan and USA ● Civil and military users

A fine light business transport, the Mitsubishi MU-2 has gained popularity in a wide range of civilian and military duties. Several versions of this twin-engined, high-wing aircraft are in operation, some with evocative names like Marquise and Solitaire. The MU-2 has a truly international flavour, with examples flying in at least 19 countries, and many of these Japanese aircraft were assembled at an American plant in Texas.

▲ *The design of the MU-2 began in Japan in the late 1950s, but the bulk of the production was carried out in Texas. The US represented the largest potential market for the aircraft.*

MITSUBISHI MU-2

▼ **Reconnaissance MU-2C**
Ordered by the Japanese Ground Self-Defence Force as the LR-1, this was an unpressurised version of the MU-2B and was fitted with cameras and radar.

▲ **High-speed MU-2M**
Publicity for the MU-2M emphasised its 590 km/h (367 m.p.h.) speed.

▼ **Astazou power**
The earliest MU-2As, which flew in 1963, were powered by Turboméca Astazou engines.

▲ **MU-2P becomes Solitaire**
The MU-2P was built in the US as the Solitaire and had more powerful engines. With a crew of two, the cabin can carry six or seven passengers.

Long-fuselage Marquise ▶
The MU-2N, with its lengthened fuselage and four-bladed propellers, was fitted with more powerful Garrett turboprops and named Marquise.

FACTS AND FIGURES

➤ Rhein Flugzeugbau obtained rights from Mitsubishi to assemble and maintain MU-2s in Germany.

➤ The prototype aircraft made its first flight on 24 September 1963.

➤ In all, 831 Mitsubishi MU-2s were built; only 57 were for users in Japan.

➤ The MU-2 was initially sold in the US by Mooney, until Mitsubishi established its own plant in Texas.

➤ Japan's Air and Ground Self-Defence Forces ordered 53 military examples.

➤ MU-2Cs and Ks operated by the JGSDF can carry two 12.7-mm (.50 cal.) machine-guns.

PROFILE

Japan's little turbine twin

The Mitsubishi MU-2 was a result of plans in 1959 for a STOL (short take-off and landing) utility transport. Mitsubishi developed a twin-engined, high-wing aircraft with wingtip tanks as standard.

The MU-2 immediately proved efficient and economical to civilian purchasers, who used it as an executive transport and feeder airliner. A few were adapted for military duties, including airfield radar calibration, target-towing and search and rescue.

The MU-2 has gained a reputation as a relatively fast aircraft, although not an easy one to fly; it can 'get away' from any pilot who forgets

that it is a high-performance machine.

Operators who want effective transport for key personnel praise the MU-2. The operating costs of this turboprop machine are 65 per cent of those of a jet aircraft with similar capacity. And with its short take-off run, the MU-2 can use smaller airfields that are not available to most jets.

Production ended in 1986 after 831 MU-2s in 15 different versions had been produced. Marquise and Solitaire production in the United States totalled 282.

Above: A stretched version, the MU-2G, was offered by Mitsubishi. The fuselage was lengthened by 1.88 m (6 ft. 2 in.) to increase seating.

Above: The majority of civil MU-2s were sold in the United States, although it had some sales success in Europe and Asia. This is a French-registered example.

MU-2C

Type: twin-engined STOL liaison aircraft

Powerplant: two 540-kW (725-hp.) Garrett TPE331-6-251M turboprops

Maximum cruising speed: 590 km/h (366 m.p.h.) at 4575 m (15,000 ft.)

Maximum rate of climb: 945 m/min (3,100 f.p.m.)

Maximum take-off distance: 520 m (1,706 ft.) to 15 m (50 ft.) altitude

Range: 2706 km (1,681 mi.)

Service ceiling: 10,110 m (33,170 ft.)

Weights: empty 2685 kg (5,919 lb.); maximum take-off 4500 kg (9,921 lb.)

Accommodation: two pilots and six or seven passengers

Dimensions:
span	11.94 m	(39 ft. 2 in.)
length	10.13 m	(33 ft. 3 in.)
height	3.94 m	(12 ft. 11 in.)
wing area	16.55 m²	(178 sq. ft.)

MU-2E

Derived from the MU-2K, the MU-2E serves with the Japanese Air Self-Defence Force under the designation MU-2S. Twenty-nine were built and are in use with the Air Rescue Wing at Iruma, with detachments elsewhere.

The Japanese Self-Defence Forces have been the only military operators of the MU-2, using the type in the SAR, training, reconnaissance, liaison, target-towing and radar calibration roles.

For its search-and-rescue role a Doppler search radar is fitted in the 'thimble' nose radome. The standard flight crew consists of one or two pilots. In this variant crew would also be carried as observers and to operate the radar.

Two 540-kW (725-hp.) Garrett TPE331-6-251M turboprops power the MU-2K and derivatives. Each drives a Hartzell fully-feathering, three-bladed, reversible-pitch, constant-speed propeller.

A sliding door is fitted to the MU-2E for air-dropping dinghies to the victims of maritime disasters, downed aircrew and the like. Although most MU-2 variants are pressurised, this version is not due to its role and the need to deploy dinghies.

The wingtip fuel tanks have a total capacity of 682 litres (150 gal.). Tanks in the wings hold 697 litres (153 gal.), giving a total fuel load of 1379 litres (303-gal.). The MU-2E utilised the original short fuselage of the original production versions of the MU-2.

The observation windows below each wing are bulged to improve the crew's view. The fuselage is painted in a high-visibility colour scheme to make the aircraft easier to see.

航空自衛隊 217 33-3217

ACTION DATA

MAXIMUM CRUISING SPEED

While some versions of the MU-2 were fast compared to their rivals, the MU-2N had a top speed closer to the 450 km/h average for turboprop twin-engined aircraft of the 1960s. All three aircraft have similar speed performances.

MU-2N	465 km/h (289 m.p.h.)
JETSTREAM SERIES 200	454 km/h (280 m.p.h.)
CONQUEST	426 km/h (265 m.p.h.)

RANGE

A range figure around 2300 km (1,430 mi.) was typical of the period. Range is an important consideration for buyers of executive aircraft which often fly long distances between cities.

MU-2N	2330 km (1,448 mi.)
JETSTREAM SERIES 200	2224 km (1,382 mi.)
CONQUEST	2995 km (1,861 mi.)

PASSENGER LOAD

Scottish Aviation's Jetstream (later built by British Aerospace) was able to carry a larger passenger load than both the MU-2N and the later Conquest. Limited size was a weakness of the MU-2 design.

MU-2N	11
JETSTREAM SERIES 200	16
CONQUEST	10

Other Mitsubishi aircraft

■ **F-4EJ PHANTOM II:** Mitsubishi licence-built 125 McDonnell Douglas F-4Es for the Japanese Air Self-Defence Force between 1971 and 1981.

■ **T-2:** Japan's first supersonic jet, the T-2 flew in July 1971. Used for the training role, the aircraft is powered by two Adour turbofans.

■ **F-1:** This fighter derivative of the T-2 flew in 1977. Its principal role is anti-shipping, for which it is equipped with missiles.

■ **MU-300/DIAMOND:** First flown as the MU-300 in 1978, the aircraft was marketed as the Diamond and later built in the US by Beech.

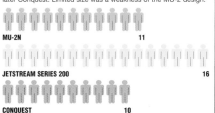

MITSUBISHI

T-2

● Advanced/combat trainer ● Supersonic ● Multi-role aircraft

 The T-2
trainer has proved a popular
and efficient aircraft in JASDF service, and
pilots benefit from its commonality with the
Mitsubishi F-1 fighter.

Japan's first indigenous supersonic jet, Mitsubishi's T-2 was designed to meet a Japanese Air Self-Defence Force (JASDF) requirement for an advanced training aircraft. Gaining inspiration from the SEPECAT Jaguar, a T-2A combat trainer variant, armed with a 20-mm cannon and hardpoints under the fuselage and wings, was also built. It provided a basis for subsequent development of the Mitsubishi F-1 close-support supersonic fighter.

MITSUBISHI T-2

Supersonic trainer ▶
Japanese officials were very impressed with the SEPECAT Jaguar, and when Mitsubishi designed the T-2 it incorporated many features which were similar to those of the European design.

◀ Training for combat
The T-2A combat trainer is fitted with a 20-mm M61 multi-barrel Vulcan cannon under the cockpit floor. It also has weapons stations on the centreline and under the wings, plus wingtip points for Sidewinder missiles.

Long service ▶
First flown as the XT-2 on 20 July 1971, the type has been in JASDF service since March 1975.

◀ Jaguar look-alike
Similarities with the Jaguar are evident in this view of a T-2 carrying four underwing rocket pods. The aircraft was also fitted with the Jaguar's engines.

F-86 replacement ▶
Entering service with the 4th Air Wing at Matsushima, the T-2 replaced the ageing, licence-built F-86 Sabre and T-33 in the advanced training role. Ninety-six T-2s were built, including two F-1 development aircraft.

FACTS AND FIGURES

➤ Mitsubishi was announced as the winner of the competition in September 1967, beating Fuji and Kawasaki.

➤ The T-2s of the 'Blue Impulse' aerobatic team have a secondary air defence role.

➤ AIM-9L Sidewinder AAMs can be carried on the T-2A's wingtips.

➤ One T-2 was extensively modified as the T-2CCV control-configured vehicle with test equipment in the rear cockpit.

➤ The T-2 can carry up to 2000 kg (4,400 lb.) of ordnance.

➤ The first prototype F-1 was a modified T-2A with a blanked-off rear cockpit.

PROFILE

High-performance Japanese trainer

As its first excursion into supersonic military aircraft design, Japan produced this two-seat combat trainer, which was intended to train pilots who would go on to fly the Lockheed F-104J Starfighter and the McDonnell Douglas F-4EJ Phantom. Mitsubishi's T-2, which became renowned as the mount of the 'Blue Impulse' aerobatic team, was also designed to give Japanese industry vital engineering experience that would eventually contribute to a home-built fighter – the F-1, which was based on the T-2. More recently, this engineering knowledge has been used to produce the F-2 strike fighter development of Lockheed's F-16.

When it first came on the scene in 1971, the T-2 astonished those who had not expected to see fighter-like features in a trainer. Using a Japanese-built version of the Rolls-Royce/Turboméca Adour turbofan engine and incorporating many hi-tech features both inside and out, the T-2 is equipped with licence-built American avionics. The successful Japanese trainer has also proved to be highly useful as a testbed for exploring fly-by-wire technology and other advanced systems.

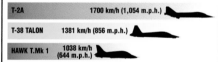

T-2/T-2A advanced and combat trainers are operated by the 4th Air Wing, based at Matsushima. Avionics systems include a J/AWG-11 nose-mounted search and ranging radar.

T-2A

Japan's national aerobatic team, 'Blue Impulse', has up to six T-2s allocated to it at any one time.

'Blue Impulse' T-2s are painted in this elaborate colour scheme and carry smoke-generating equipment. Based at Matsushima, the team is part of the 4th Kokudan (Air Wing) The T-2 was adopted by the aerobatic team, which previously flew licence-built F-86F Sabres, in 1982.

Instructor and pupil are accommodated in tandem under separate canopies in a pressurised and air-conditioned cockpit. The rear seat is elevated to give the instructor improved forward vision. Aerobatic displays are normally flown by a single pilot.

The T-2A has shoulder-mounted wings and fixed-geometry lateral air inlets for the pair of (licence-built) Rolls-Royce/Turboméca Adour afterburning turbofans.

The fuselage is of all-metal semi-monocoque construction, with titanium accounting for 10 per cent of the trainer's weight, mainly around the engine bays. Two airbrakes and a pair of ventral fins are located under the rear fuselage behind the wheel bays.

The T-2A's wings have electrically-actuated flaps and no conventional ailerons. Lateral control is maintained by hydraulically-actuated, slotted spoilers which move differentially and are located in front of the flaps.

Avionics systems include Mitsubishi Electric J/AWG-11 search and ranging radar, J/ARC-51 UHF radio, Nippon Electric J/ARN-53 TACAN and Tokyo Communication J/APX-101 SIF/IFF (Identification Friend or Foe).

29-5175

Armament comprises an M61 20-mm Vulcan cannon mounted on the left side of the fuselage under the cockpit. Early 'Blue Impulse' machines had the cannon port faired over.

All components of the tricycle landing gear retract into the fuselage, with the main units retracting forwards and the nosewheel rearwards.

A runway arrester hook is mounted beneath the rear fuselage and there is a brake parachute in the tailcone.

T-2A

Type: two-seat supersonic combat trainer

Powerplant: two Ishikawajima-Harima TF40-IHI-801A (Rolls-Royce/Turboméca Adour Mk 801A) turbofans, each rated at 22.75 kN (5,120-lb. thrust) dry and 32.49 kN (7,310-lb. thrust) with afterburning

Maximum speed: 1700 km/h (1,054 m.p.h.) at 10,975 m (36,000 ft.)

Service ceiling: 15,240 m (50,000 ft.)

Weights: empty 6307 kg (13,875 lb.); maximum take-off 12,800 kg (28,160 lb.)

Armament: one M61 20-mm Vulcan cannon, up to 2000 kg (4,400 lb.) of ordnance on one centreline and four underwing stations plus wingtip rails for AIM-9 Sidewinders

Dimensions:
span	7.88 m	(25 ft. 10 in.)
length	17.86 m	(58 ft. 7 in.)
height	4.39 m	(14 ft. 5 in.)
wing area	21.17 m²	(228 sq. ft.)

COMBAT DATA

MAXIMUM SPEED

Only two supersonic trainers have entered service in quantity, the T-2 and the Northrop T-38 Talon, of which the T-2 is by far the faster. Most air arms are not willing to pay the extra operating costs of a supersonic trainer and prefer high-performing subsonic types.

T-2A	1700 km/h (1,054 m.p.h.)
T-38 TALON	1381 km/h (856 m.p.h.)
HAWK T.Mk 1	1038 km/h (644 m.p.h.)

MAXIMUM CLIMB RATE

With its lower power, the Hawk has a slower rate of climb. It is, however, far more agile and its aerobatic capabilities more than compensate for its comparative lack of performance. The USAF is updating its T-38s to allow them to stay in service for several more years.

T-2A 10,670 m/min (35,000 f.p.m.)

T-38 TALON 10,241 m/min (33,600 f.p.m.)

HAWK T.Mk 1 2835 m/min (9,300 f.p.m.)

SERVICE CEILING

The Hawk and T-2 operate at similar altitudes, but the T-38 has a higher service ceiling. This has meant that it has been used for a number of special training and test roles, including training SR-71 and B-2 pilots.

T-2A 15,240 m (50,000 ft.)	**T-38 TALON** 16,335 m (53,600 ft.)	**HAWK T.Mk 1** 15,240 m (50,000 ft.)

Japanese trainers

■ **FUJI T-1:** This indigenous basic and intermediate trainer, based on the F-86, was the first post-war jet aircraft designed in Japan.

■ **FUJI T-3/BEECH T-34:** The T-3 (developed from the Beechcraft T-34) provides the initial 75 hours of primary pilot training in the JASDF.

■ **KAWASAKI T-4:** Built as a T-33 replacement, the T-4 is an intermediate jet trainer. The JASDF has a requirement for 200 aircraft.

■ **FUJI T-5:** This primary/basic aerobatic trainer and utility aircraft serves with the Japanese Maritime Self-Defence Force.

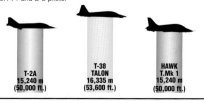

MITSUBISHI

F-1

● Single-seat close-support fighter ● Design based on T-2 trainer

M itsubishi's F-1 is a hard-hitting combat aircraft that draws its main features from the earlier T-2 supersonic trainer. The F-1 was developed for close air support and anti-ship operations, performing these tasks admirably in the robust Japan Air Self-Defence Force (JASDF). Seventy-seven F-1s were built, with the surviving aircraft equipping three squadrons.

▲ The F-1 was a straight development of the earlier T-2 trainer. In fact, their airframe dimensions are identical, with the rear cockpit canopy simply being faired over and extra avionics added.

MITSUBISHI F-1

▲ Brake parachute deployed
The fuselage tailcone at the base of the rudder contains a single 5.5-metre diameter ring-slot-type braking parachute. Anti-skid brakes and an airfield arrester hook are also fitted.

▲ Licence-built Adour turbofans
The IHI-built Adour turbofans fitted to the F-1 are comparable to those that equip the French versions of the Jaguar, which has a maximum take-off weight of some 2000 kg (4,400 lb.) more.

◀ T-2 heritage
It is very apparent that the single-seat F-1 was based on the two-seat T-2.

▼ F-1 number one
The first production F-1, 70-8201, left the Mitsubishi factory in June 1977.

▲ Three squadrons
The Japan Air Self-Defence Force's three F-1 units are based at Misawa in the north (two squadrons) and Tsuiki in the west (one squadron).

FACTS AND FIGURES

➤ The F-1 was belatedly given extra air-to-air capability with provision for up to four AIM-9 Sidewinder missiles.

➤ Two F-1 prototypes used British-built Adour engines.

➤ Up to three 821-litre (220-gal.) fuel tanks can be carried externally by the F-1.

➤ The first production Mitsubishi F-1 aircraft made its maiden flight on 16 June 1977.

➤ The last of 77 F-1s was delivered by Mitsubishi in March 1987.

➤ Japan's anti-military stance means that no F-1s have been exported.

PROFILE

From trainer to anti-ship striker

An island nation, Japan works hard to protect its shores. The Mitsubishi F-1 was created because of the threatening nature of Soviet naval activity around the Japanese home islands in the 1970s and 1980s.

Following the success of the T-2 twin-turbofan trainer, Mitsubishi went ahead with this close-support fighter version, intended primarily to fly from land bases on defence missions against enemy shipping.

The F-1 has a comprehensive avionics fit, its principal weapon being the Japanese-developed

Mitsubishi ASM-1 (Type 80) solid-propellant missile, which combines a similar range to that of the German Kormoran with a warhead comparable to the French Exocet. A secondary air-defence role is also fulfilled, and AIM-9 Sidewinders may be fitted for this purpose.

Very little is known of the F-1's overall performance, as limited information has been published in Japan and few foreign pilots have flown the aircraft. Published specifications suggest a fairly modest performance by modern standards, mainly due to its

Above: Most F-1s carry a three-tone camouflage, consisting of dark green, olive drab and light tan on the upper surfaces with a light grey underside.

relatively low-powered engines and small fuel capacity.

The F-1 remained in service until the end of the twentieth century, when it began to be replaced by the Mitsubishi F-2 – an adaptation of the F-16 Fighting Falcon.

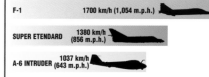

Above: Interviews with Japanese pilots suggest that the F-1's cockpit is 'optimised for the average Japanese physique' and has low stick forces and 'mild' control sensitivity.

F-1

Type: single-seat close-support fighter

Powerplant: two 32.49-kN (7,288-lb.-thrust) Ishikawajima-Harima TF40-IHI-801 (Rolls-Royce/ Turboméca Adour Mk 801A) afterburning turbofan engines

Maximum speed: 1700 km/h (1,054 m.p.h.) at 10,975 m (36,000 ft.)

Range: 2870 km (1,779 mi.)

Service ceiling: 15,240 m (50,000 ft.)

Weights: empty 6358 kg (13,988 lb.); maximum take-off 13,700 kg (30,140 lb.)

Armament: one JM61 Vulcan 20-mm rotary cannon and maximum of 2721 kg (6,000 lb.) of ordnance including four AIM-9L air-to-air missiles; two ASM-1 anti-ship missiles or combinations of other rockets and bombs

Dimensions: span   7.88 m (26 ft.)
length   17.86 m (59 ft.)
height   4.39 m (14 ft.)
wing area   21.17 m² (228 sq. ft.)

F-1

Aircraft 70-8203 carries the markings of 8 Hikotai (8th Squadron) of 3 Kokudan (3rd Air Wing) of the Northern Air Defence Command, based at Misawa Air Base on Honshu.

An American-designed zero-zero ejection seat is fitted to the F-1, which uses canopy penetrators to shatter the cockpit canopy when the seat is activated.

Dimensionally identical to the T-2, the F-1 uses the rear cockpit to house the fire-control system, bombing computer, inertial navigation and radar-warning system.

For self-defence the F-1 can carry two AIM-9L Sidewinder heat-seeking air-to-air missiles and has a Japanese-built M61 20-mm rotary cannon fitted in the forward fuselage.

When JASDF squadrons adopted individual markings in 1983, 8 Hikotai chose a black panther and the nickname 'The Panthers'.

F-1s use a J/AWG-12 dual-mode (air-to-air and air-to-ground) radar based on that fitted to Royal Air Force Phantom FGR.Mk 2s.

The principal weapon system for the F-1 is the Mitsubishi ASM-1 sea-skimming anti-ship missile, two of which may be carried. Each has a 150-kg (330-lb.) semi-armour-piercing warhead.

Two Rolls-Royce/Turboméca Adour afterburning turbofans, similar to those in early versions of the SEPECAT Jaguar, power the F-1.

COMBAT DATA

MAXIMUM SPEED

The F-1 was based on the Jaguar, which was designed to have a high penetration speed for ground attack. The A-6 and Super Etendard were both subsonic designs.

F-1	1700 km/h (1,054 m.p.h.)
SUPER ETENDARD	1380 km/h (856 m.p.h.)
A-6 INTRUDER	1037 km/h (643 m.p.h.)

COMBAT RADIUS

For the purpose of defending Japan, the F-1 did not need long range. The naval A-6 and Super Etendard both required much longer range to be effective rather than all-out speed.

F-1	555 km (344 mi.)
SUPER ETENDARD	850 km (527 mi.)
A-6 INTRUDER	1627 km (1,009 mi.)

WEAPON RANGE

Harpoon is one of the longest ranged naval missiles produced in the West, and is superior to the Exocet and ASM-1. The F-1's ASM-1 missile has enough range to avoid defensive naval missiles.

F-1	80 km (50 mi.) (ASM-1)
SUPER ETENDARD	60 km (37 mi.) (EXOCET)
A-6 INTRUDER	90 km (56 mi.) (AGM-84 HARPOON)

Fighters of the JASDF

■ **McDONNELL DOUGLAS F-4EJ PHANTOM II:** Japan continues to operate a number of Japanese-built F-4Es which are being upgraded. This is the RF-4EJ reconnaissance variant.

■ **McDONNELL DOUGLAS F-15J EAGLE:** Like the F-4EJ, most F-15Js were assembled in Japan by Mitsubishi. This is Japan's principal fighter aircraft.

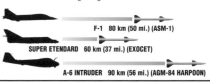

■ **MITSUBISHI/LOCKHEED F-2:** Originally known as the FS-X, this high-performance fighter is a local development of the Lockheed (General Dynamics) F-16C and will replace the F-1.

MYASISHCHEV

M-17/M-55 'MYSTIC'

● Balloon interception ● Reconnaissance ● Geophysical survey

I n 1982 Western intelligence reported the sighting of an unidentified Russian high-altitude reconnaissance aircraft. Satellite photographs of the Zhukhovskii flight test centre, known as Ramenskoye in the West, showed an aircraft with twin tail fins and long, unswept wings, suggesting that it was a Soviet counterpart of the American U-2. It was known as 'Ram-M', and several years passed before the mysterious aircraft was finally identified as the Myasishchev M-17.

▲ Russia's answer
to the U-2 has not achieved the
success or infamy of its American equivalent.
The M-17s and M-55s have performed useful
environmental research, however.

MYASISHCHEV M-17/M-55 'MYSTIC'

Record breaker ▶
During 1990 the single-engined M-17 Stratosphera
set a total of 25 speed/climb/height records.

▼ Environmental research
The M-55 Geofizika was developed to help to study
the problems of ozone depletion.

M-55 Geofizika ▶
The M-55 can carry equipment for Earth-resource missions,
agricultural surveying, ground mapping and ice reconnaissance.

▲ Air show star
Geofizika has appeared in
the West at the Paris and
Farnborough air shows.

Mystic power ▶
Two 88.30-kN (19,500-lb.-thrust)
Soloviev D-30-10V turbofans
power the M-55.

FACTS AND FIGURES

➤ Subject 34 was cancelled when the CIA stopped using high-altitude balloons as reconnaissance platforms.

➤ Eduard Chyeltsov flew the first M-17 Stratosphera on 26 May 1982.

➤ In 1992 an M-17 'Mystic-A' investigated the Antarctic ozone hole.

➤ Chyeltsov also flew the M-55 Geofizika on its maiden flight on 16 August 1988; at least three more have flown since.

➤ A projected M-55UTS trainer was to have a periscope to aid back-seat vision.

➤ The M-55 'Mystic-B' can climb to 21 km (13 mi.) in 35 minutes.

PROFILE

Master of the stratosphere

Originally planned in 1967 as an interceptor of high-altitude reconnaissance balloons under the designation Subject 34 and known as the Chaika (Gull), Myasishchev's new aircraft was first seen by NATO in the unarmed 'Mystic-A' form. Known as the Stratosphera in Russia, the M-17 retains some of its original mystery.

It resembles the U-2 in having a single engine with intakes on the sides of the forward fuselage, and was designed for a similar strategic reconnaissance role. But it has a greater wingspan and is

slightly longer overall, with a shorter, deeper fuselage and a long tailplane carried on twin fins.

It was intended to replace the Yak-25RD, but one of the two M-17s that were built is now housed in a museum. The second aircraft has been used to investigate the ozone layer and pollution in the upper regions of the atmosphere.

Since 1994 a twin-engined version, the M-55 Geofizika ('Mystic-B'), has appeared at Western air shows. Designed specifically for environmental and geophysical research, it can carry

Below: One of the two prototype M-17 Stratospheras (17103) survives in Aeroflot colours at the Monino aerospace museum near Moscow.

Above: According to Russian sources, development of the 'Mystic-B' as a strategic reconnaissance platform for military service is continuing.

a 1500-kg (3,300-lb.) payload and has an endurance of seven hours.

From its operational altitude of 21,500 m (70,500 ft.), the M-55 can photograph an area 120 km (75 mi.) wide, and can also glide for a distance of 200 km (125 mi.).

M-17 Stratosphera 'Mystic-A'

Type: single-seat high-altitude reconnaissance and research aircraft

Powerplant: one 68.65-kN (15,450-lb.-thrust) RKBM Rybinsk RD-36-51V turbojet

Maximum speed: 743 km/h (460 m.p.h.) at 20,000 m (65,600 ft.)

Endurance: 2 hours 25 min

Range: 1315 km (815 mi.)

Service ceiling: 21,550 m (70,700 ft.)

Weights: empty 11,900 kg (26,180 lb.); maximum take-off 19,950 kg (43,890 lb.)

Dimensions: span 40.32 m (132 ft. 3 in.)
length 22.27 m (73 ft. 1 in.)
height 5.25 m (17 ft. 3 in.)
wing area 137.70 m² (1,482 sq. ft.)

M-17 STRATOSPHERA 'MYSTIC-A'

Although it achieved a number of world records, the prospect of the M-17 becoming a Soviet counterpart of the U-2 faded. The aircraft moved on to investigation of the Antarctic ozone problem.

The M-17's single pilot is seated on a K-36L ejection seat, under an upward-hinging canopy. Carried just behind the pilot are two oxygen canisters.

Compared to the unusual inverted gull wing of the Subject 34 interceptor, the M-17's wing is much more conventional in layout. The engine is started by a turbo-starter and fed with fuel from five separate wing tanks, which hold a total of 10,000 litres (2,650 gal.).

The M-17s were built at Kumertau, Bashkiri, primarily from lightweight metals. The entire aircraft is comprehensively ice-protected for high-altitude operations. In normal conditions the reconnaissance-configured M-17 would have carried 1000 kg (2,200 lb.) of advanced cameras and sensors.

This M-17, serial CCCP-17401, was the aircraft used during trials and preparation work for the M-55. It flew missions to monitor Antarctica's atmosphere. A number of environmental slogans were subsequently added.

'Mystic-A' carries a PRNK-17 navigation system radio compass and an RSBN Kobalt radar. These were also used in the M-55 'Mystic-B'.

A novel feature of the M-17 'Mystic-A' is its retractable landing lights, stowed under the front of the tail booms.

Designed for high altitudes, the RD-36-51V is based on the engine core from which the MiG-31's powerplants were derived.

Both the M-17 Stratosphera 'Mystic-A' and M-55 Geofizika 'Mystic-B' feature an unusual twin-boom tail, with vertical surfaces bridged by a long horizontal stabiliser.

ACTION DATA

MAXIMUM TAKE-OFF WEIGHT

With its high maximum take-off weight, the M-17 is capable of lifting heavier loads to altitude than either of its most direct rivals. It does not have the hi-tech avionics of the U-2R, however.

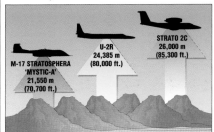

M-17 STRATOSPHERA 'MYSTIC-A' 19,950 kg (43,890 lb.)
U-2R 18,733 kg (41,213 lb.)
STRATO 2C 13,350 kg (29,370 lb.)

CEILING

Grob's all-composite Strato 2C uses specially tuned high-altitude piston engines to achieve its exceptional altitude capabilities. It is used solely as a research vehicle.

M-17 STRATOSPHERA 'MYSTIC-A' 21,550 m (70,700 ft.)
U-2R 24,385 m (80,000 ft.)
STRATO 2C 26,000 m (85,300 ft.)

ENDURANCE

With its two-seat cabin the Strato 2C is equipped for missions of long duration. Its engines are extremely fuel-efficient but do not deliver the climb and speed performance of the jet aircraft.

M-17 STRATOSPHERA 'MYSTIC-A' 2 hours 25 min
U-2R 12 hours
STRATO 2C 48 hours

Changing roles of the 'Mystic'

Since its conception in 1967, the 'Mystic' has seen its role change from balloon interceptor to research platform.

INTERCEPTOR: Armed with a turret-mounted GSh-23 cannon and two air-to-air missiles, the single-seat Subject 34 was intended to destroy spy balloons.

M-17 'MYSTIC-A': In its design role the M-17 would have flown high-altitude strategic reconnaissance missions over sensitive foreign installations.

M-55 'MYSTIC-B': An unusual role adopted by the M-55 is the conversion of hail into rain by the use of chemicals. Such weather alteration avoids excessive crop damage, helping the struggling Russian economy.

NANCHANG

A-5 'FANTAN'

● Ground attack ● Converted MiG ● Tactical fighter-bomber

▲ The A-5
might seem crude and old-fashioned, but price is important. The aircraft is an excellent low-cost 'bomb truck' in contrast to the Pakistan air force's high-tech F-16s.

Based loosely on the airframe of the Chinese-built MiG-19, the Nanchang A-5 'Fantan' (alias the Q-5) is a robust, capable warplane. The 'Fantan' airframe relies largely on technology of the 1950s, but incorporates more modern electronics, Sidewinder missiles and new ejection seats to ensure combat effectiveness. Although it is hardly at the cutting edge of fighter design, the A-5 has a very low price tag and suits the needs of Third World users.

NANCHANG A-5 'FANTAN'

▲ **Chinese weapon**
The 'Fantan' is offered on the export market with a range of Chinese weapons like this short-range PL-5.

▲ **Armed and dangerous**
Fitted with AIM-9P Sidewinders, Pakistan's A-5s are no easy target for a fighter. The original MiG-19 was known as a very dangerous dogfighter. There is also a nuclear-capable version of the Q-5 which can carry a 20-kT weapon.

▲ **Black Spiders**
Operating the A-5 from the large Pakistan air force base at Peshawar in North Pakistan, No. 26 squadron is known as the 'Black Spiders'. The PAF also operates the Shenyang F-6.

▲ **Home defence**
China is still the most numerous user, with hundreds of A-5s in service. China plans to introduce the F.10, derived from Israel's Lavi.

Flying to fight ▶
This A-5 is equipped with 57-mm rocket pods, MATRA Magic air-to-air missiles, 100-kg (220-lb.) iron bombs and a pair of 760-litre (200-gal.) drop-tanks.

FACTS AND FIGURES

➤ Over 1000 'Fantans' have been built, including 52 for Pakistan, 40 for North Korea and 20 for Bangladesh.

➤ China's 'Fantans' were used in the border conflict with Vietnam in 1979.

➤ Although design work began in 1960, the prototype A-5 first flew on 4 June 1965.

➤ An extended-range version carrying fuel in the bomb-bay has about a 35 per cent greater combat radius.

➤ The latest A-5 uses Italian-designed avionics and has additional pylons.

➤ The A5 carries 2827 kg (6,220 lb.) of fuel and up to 1178 kg (2,592 lb.) in drop-tanks.

PROFILE

Ground attack at low prices

The Nanchang A-5 'Fantan' gives China a low-cost, supersonic strike aircraft, demonstrating the country's ability to improve an existing military aircraft.

Although the A-5 is based on the proven MiG-19, Chinese designers created a new, stretched fuselage, an internal bomb-bay and a pointed nose. With work beginning in the early 1960s the 'Fantan' was designed, tested and produced without Soviet help and has evolved into a bomber that is

quite different from its Russian origins. The A-5 has less ability in a dogfight than its MiG cousin, but it carries more bombs, can fly further and is more accurate in its important duty of air-to-ground combat. The nuclear version of the 'Fantan' dropped a real atomic bomb during a test in 1970.

Export success has been considerable in the Third World due to the price tag. Pakistan's A-5s cost just $2.6 million each, about a quarter of the cost of a Jaguar or F-16A. Pakistan

upgraded its A-5s with better avionics and Sidewinder missiles, and China is now offering improved versions with laser rangefinder, head-up display, an IFF (Identification Friend or Foe) system and radar-warning receiver.

The cannon armament is carried in the wingroots. Unlike most modern ground-attack fighters, the A-5 uses 23-mm weapons with 100 rounds each.

The Pakistan air force A-5s have improved avionics and British Martin-Baker ejector seats.

A-5 'Fantan'

Type: single-seat ground-attack fighter

Powerplant: two Liming (previously Shenyang) Wopen-6A turbojet engines each rated at 29.42 kN (6,600-lb.-thrust) dry and 36.78 kN (8,250-lb.-thrust) with afterburning

Maximum speed: Mach 1.12 or 1190 km/h (738 m.p.h.) at 11,000 m (36,000 ft.)

Combat radius: 400 km (250 mi.) to 600 km (375 mi.)

Range: 2000 km (1,240 mi.)

Service ceiling: 15,850 m (52,000 ft.)

Weights: empty 6375 kg (14,025 lb.); maximum take-off 11,830 kg (26,026 lb.)

Armament: two 23-mm cannon each with 100 rounds, plus tandem pairs of pylons carrying up to 500 kg (1.100 lb.) of stores

Dimensions:
span	9.68 m (32 ft.)
length	15.65 m (51 ft.)
height	4.33 m (14 ft.)
wing area	27.95 m² (300 sq. ft.)

A-5 'FANTAN'

Still one of the most numerous aircraft in the People's Liberation Army Air Force, the Nanchang A-5 will probably be at least partially replaced by the F.10 fighter-bomber, derived from the IAI Lavi.

The A-5M is equipped with the avionics from the Italian AMX, including laser-rangefinder, Alenia head-up display and inertial navigation.

The A-5's original Chinese ejection seats are another feature which customers often replace, as they are not guaranteed below 270 m (900 ft.) or above 280 km/h (179 m.p.h.).

Almost all A-5 users have their aircraft painted in a three-colour stripe camouflage paint scheme.

Like the MiG-19, the A-5 has an all-moving slab tailplane.

The main clue to the A-5's MiG-19 ancestry is the swept tail.

The A-5 never received a radar, despite the removal of the original nose intake allowing for this. Future aircraft, if there are any, will use this space for avionics or a rangefinder.

The inboard wing pylons can carry 760-litre (200-gal.) fuel tanks and the outboard pylons 3,790-litre (1,000-gal.) tanks.

One of the most inhibiting features of the A-5 is the Wopen turbojet that powers the aircraft. This engine is an uneconomical design and requires a major overhaul every 100 hours.

COMBAT DATA

MAXIMUM SPEED

The 'Fantan' is limited by its old technology Wopen turbojets and the increased girth of the airframe compared to the original design. However, most ground-attack aircraft travel at around 800 km/h in combat, and theoretical maximum speeds are seldom reached.

A-5 'FANTAN'	1190 km/h (738 m.p.h.)
A-7D CORSAIR	1123 km/h (696 m.p.h.)
JAGUAR GR.Mk 1	1699 km/h (1,053 m.p.h.)

COMBAT RADIUS

Another victim of the poor engine technology is the A-5's range, which might have been improved with Western engines. Short range is generally a typical feature of second-generation MiGs, which had quite good performance.

A-7D CORSAIR 1149 km (712 mi.)

JAGUAR GR.Mk 1 852 km (528 mi.)

A-5 'FANTAN' 600 km (372 mi.)

BOMBLOAD

The 'Fantan' has quite a low bombload compared to the Jaguar and A-7, but the amount of weight carried per dollar cost of the airframe is about equal.

A-5 'FANTAN'	2000 kg (4,400 lb.)
A-7D CORSAIR	9072 kg (19,958 lb.)
JAGUAR GR.Mk 1	4536 kg (9,979 lb.)

Many faces of the MiG-19

■ **MiG-19PM:** This MiG-19 version introduced the K-5 missile system, guided by an Izumrud radar in the nose. It could carry rocket packs.

■ **SHENYANG J-6:** China built a straight copy of the MiG-19 fighter, which is also used by Pakistan and fought in the 1965 war.

■ **S-105:** This aircraft was a Czech-built MiG-19PM which was built by Aero Vodochody between 1958 and 1963.

■ **SM-12PMU:** An experimental version, the SM-12 used a mixed powerplant of turbojets and a rocket motor which could be re-lit.

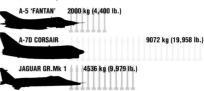

NORTHROP

F/RF-5E TIGER II/F-20 TIGERSHARK

● Upgraded 'Freedom Fighter' ● Lightweight, low cost ● Exports

▲ The F-5
family answered a request from
the US government for a relatively cheap fighter
for export to smaller nations under the Mutual
Assistance Plan (MAP).

As a result of the great success of Northrop's first F-5 – the 'Freedom Fighter' – the company won the contest to build its replacement as America's affordable, lightweight fighter for the world. The Tiger II, with more power and an emphasis on air-to-air capability, was a vast improvement over its predecessor. The Tiger II was a big seller, but the same could not be said of the Tigershark, which failed against F-16 opposition.

PHOTO FILE

NORTHROP F/RF-5E TIGER II/F-20 TIGERSHARK

▼ Ill-fated Tigershark
Three F-20s were built, and a fourth was started but never finished. Two were lost in fatal accidents due to pilot incapacity, and the third went to a museum.

▲ RF-5E Tigereye
Malaysia, Saudi Arabia and Singapore have taken delivery of this camera-equipped variant. Cameras are fitted in the nose, in place of the radar, and can include night-reconnaissance sensors.

▲ Taiwanese Tiger IIs
The Republic of China operates a sizeable fleet of locally-built F-5Es and Fs.

▲ Popular upgrades
Northrop Grumman is among several companies offering avionics upgrade packages for Tiger IIs.

◄ Increased capability
In addition to a top speed in excess of Mach 2, the F-20 had an avionics fit comparable to that of the F-16A and improved weapons capability.

FACTS AND FIGURES

➤ Total F-5 production, including 'Freedom Fighters', T-38 Talons and overseas production, totalled 3840.

➤ Overseas F-5E/F production has taken place in Korea, Switzerland and Taiwan.

➤ Israel's F-5 upgrade is known as Tiger III; Northrop Grumman's is the Tiger IV.

➤ The first F-5E flew on 11 August 1972, from Edwards Air Force Base, four months ahead of schedule.

➤ Taiwan is considering re-engined F-5Es with new radar and AIM-120 missiles.

➤ Only 12 RF-5Es were built; Singapore converted six F-5Es to RF-5E standard.

PROFILE

Feline son of the 'Freedom Fighter'

Skoshi Tiger was the name given to the evaluation of the F-5E's predecessor, the F-5A 'Freedom Fighter', in combat in Vietnam in 1965. The F-5A (and two-seat F-5B) were lightweight, low-cost fighters intended for export to 'approved countries'.

When, in 1970, the USAF asked for proposals for a new international fighter aircraft, Northrop successfully suggested an updated F-5, the F-5E, which was dubbed Tiger II to perpetuate the name

made famous in Vietnam.

Export sales have been numerous, with aircraft going to both existing F-5 customers and to new converts to this capable, yet affordable, tactical fighter. While the F-5A sold well to NATO countries, the Tiger II has been popular with Middle Eastern, Asian and South American states.

The re-engined F-20 (at first designated F-5G) flew in 1982, but failed to sell. F-5 production has ended, but upgrades will ensure long-term service.

The principal modification made to the F-5 design to produce the F-20 Tigershark, was replacing the two J85 turbojets with an F404 turbofan, as fitted to early F/A-18 Hornets.

Unlike earlier F-5s, the E model did not require wingtip fuel tanks but it did retain the rails for AIM-9 air-to-air missiles.

The F-5E was developed with emphasis on the air-to-air role, although ground-attack capability was not ignored. Indeed, the earliest customers, Iran and Saudi Arabia, both acquired the type for this role.

The standard radar of the F-5E was the Emerson Electric AN/APQ-159 search-and-track radar with a range of about 37 km (23 mi.).

Because the F-5E was designed as a counter to the Soviet MiG-21, it was also an ideal threat simulator for the USAF and US Navy Dissimilar Air Combat Training (DACT) schemes. The Navy continues to operate a small number of F-5Es in this role.

F-5E TIGER II

Once a renowned Hawker Hunter display team, Switzerland's Patrouille Suisse exchanged its elderly Hunters for Tiger IIs in 1994. J-3089 is one of the team's brightly-painted F-5Es based at Dubendorf Air Base.

The two-seat conversion trainer version of the F-5E was the F-5F, which has tandem cockpits in a 1.02-m (3-ft.) longer fuselage (from the USAF's T-38 Talon). It retains the combat capabilities of the E model, but is fitted with just one 20-mm nose cannon.

The available upgrades concentrate on improving the aircraft's avionics and weapons capability. The leading suppliers are Northrop Grumman and Israel Aircraft Industries (IAI).

Two Pontiac (Colt-Browning) M39A2 20-mm cannon are fitted in the nose of a standard F-5E. The RF-5E Tigereye and two-seat F-5F use just one, fitted on the left hand side.

Switzerland took delivery of 98 F-5Es and 12 two-seat F-5Fs, a number of which were assembled at FFA's Emmen factory. Originally tasked with air defence, some have been re-roled as ground-attack aircraft and replace Hunters.

The two 22.2-kN (5,000-lb.-thrust) General Electric J85 afterburning turbojets have separate, but cross-feedable, fuel supplies. The electrically-operated louvre doors supply additional air to the engines during take-off and in flight below speeds of Mach 0.4-0.35.

F-5E Tiger II

Type: light tactical fighter

Powerplant: two 22.2-kN (4,000-lb.-thrust) General Electric J85-GE-21B afterburning turbojets

Maximum speed: 1700 km/h (1,054 m.p.h.) at 10,975 m (36,000 ft.)

Service ceiling: 15,590 m (51,100 ft.)

Weights: empty 4349 kg (9,568 lb.); maximum take-off 11,187 kg (24,611 lb.)

Armament: two M39A2 20-mm cannon in the nose, two AIM-9 Sidewinder air-to-air missiles on wing-tip launchers plus up to 3175 kg (6,985 lb.) of ordnance on fuselage and wing pylons

Dimensions:
span	8.13 m	(26 ft. 8 in.)
length	14.45 m	(47 ft. 5 in.)
height	4.08 m	(60 ft. 9 in.)
wing area	17.28 m²	(186 sq. ft.)

COMBAT DATA

MAXIMUM SPEED

Among the world's most exported tactical fighters, the F-5E has an excellent speed performance which is only bettered by the MiG-21. Both the MiG and F-5E employ afterburning turbojet engines to achieve a high top speed. However, range tends to suffer as a result.

F-5E TIGER II	1700 km/h (1,054 m.p.h.)
MiG-21bis 'FISHBED'	2175 km/h (1,349 m.p.h.)
HAWK Mk 200	1065 km/h (660 m.p.h.)

ARMAMENT

The Tiger II represents a compromise between speed and range performance and lifting ability. Although limited to speeds of less than Mach 2 (unlike the MiG-21), the F-5 is able to lift more than 3 tons of ordnance. The smaller Hawk can also carry a good load.

F-5E TIGER II	2 x 20-mm cannon 3175 kg (6,985 lb.) of bombs
MiG-21bis 'FISHBED'	2000 kg (4,400 lb.) of bombs
HAWK Mk 200	2 x 25-mm cannon 3493 kg (7,685 lb.) of bombs

CLIMB RATE

The greater thrust of the MiG-21's powerful engine gives it the best climb rate. The Tiger II is not far behind, but the Hawk, powered by a non-afterburning engine, is significantly slower.

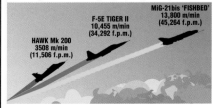

MiG-21bis 'FISHBED' 13,800 m/min (45,264 f.p.m.)
F-5E TIGER II 10,455 m/min (34,292 f.p.m.)
HAWK Mk 200 3508 m/min (11,506 f.p.m.)

Mutual Assistance Plan fighters

■ **REPUBLIC F-84F THUNDERSTREAK:** This French air force Thunderstreak was among a number of members of the F-84 family supplied, in particular, to NATO nations.

■ **NORTH AMERICAN F-100 SUPER SABRE:** Under the Mutual Assistance Plan, new-build F-100s were supplied by the USAF to Denmark, France and Taiwan.

■ **LOCKHEED F-104 STARFIGHTER:** The 'missile with a man in it' was built for the USAF under MAP contract in variants, like the F-104G, which did not actually serve with the USAF.

NORTHROP

B-2 SPIRIT

● Unique flying wing ● Advanced technology stealth bomber

▲ With its flowing, organic lines, the Northrop B-2 looks like no other aircraft in the world. But it offers power and combat capability unmatched by any other military aircraft.

The B-2 Spirit looks sinister because it has the dark mission of pressing into enemy territory in an atomic war. Northrop designed this charcoal-grey flying wing as the world's only stealth bomber, an invisible ghost to enemy radar operators. Long kept under a cloak of secrecy, the B-2 is out in the open today and is soon to be fully operational, with both nuclear and conventional bombing duties.

PHOTO FILE

NORTHROP B-2 SPIRIT

▲ **First flight**
Rolling out from the Northrop facility in Palmdale, the B-2 made its first flight, to Edwards Air Force Base, on 17 July 1989.

Stealth ▶ bomber revealed
When the B-2 was first rolled out, photos were taken only from certain angles to keep its stealth features as secret as possible.

▲ **Flying wing**
The B-2 has no conventional fuselage; its entire structure is contained within a smoothly-blended delta wing with 'W'-shaped trailing edges.

Compact ▶ power
By doing away with the fuselage, the B-2's designers have produced a very powerful and capable aircraft with enormous range and payload, in a surprisingly small package.

▲ **Long experience**
Northrop has amassed a great deal of experience with flying wings; its first full-sized bombers, such as this XB-35, flew in the 1940s.

FACTS AND FIGURES

➤ Two B-2s can complete a bombing raid which previously required 32 F-16s, 16 F-15s and 27 support aircraft.

➤ Before the B-2 ever flew, wind tunnel models were tested for 24,000 hours – a record.

➤ The radar-absorbing body of the B-2 contains 900 materials and a million parts.

➤ Almost invisible to radar, the B-2 was also made difficult to hear or see.

➤ The B-2 Spirit's engines are concealed deep within the structure to hide them from radar and heat-seeking sensors.

➤ The USAF's first B-2 was delivered exactly 90 years after the Wright brothers' first flight.

PROFILE

Northrop's amazing Flying Wing

The boomerang-like Northrop B-2 Spirit began as one of the best-kept secrets in history. Its sleek shape and special materials foil radar detection. The stealthy B-2 also flies very well with no fuselage or tail, using the flying-wing concept pioneered by earlier Northrop aircraft.

The B-2 is a triumph of technology in many ways, able to leap halfway around the globe on a strategic mission with just two pilots, located side-by-side in the crew compartment bulge. If the Cold War had continued, the B-2's stealth qualities, four powerful turbofan engines and lethal bombload would have made it the spearhead of nuclear forces. In today's changing world, the B-2 is flexible enough to fly long-distance to a crisis zone with highly accurate conventional bombs.

The B-2 is also the most expensive warplane ever built, with a price tag of $2 billion, so only 20 of these remarkable bombers will be produced.

Above: In common with most stealth aircraft, the B-2 carries minimal markings: a serial number on the fuselage and a low-visibility star-and-bar on the wing.

Below: Control of an aircraft without a vertical stabiliser is difficult, and led to the downfall of earlier flying-wing projects. The B-2 gets around the problem by using the kind of modern computer control that was unavailable to the pioneers of tail-less flight.

B-2A Spirit

Type: two-seat long-range strategic bomber

Powerplant: four 84.52-kN (19,017-lb. thrust) General Electric F118-GE-100 turbofan engines

Maximum speed: approx. 960 km/h (597 m.p.h.) above 12,200 m (40,000 ft.)

Range: 12,225 km (7,596 mi.)

Service ceiling: over 16,920 m (53,440 ft.)

Weights: empty 79,380 kg (175,995 lb.); loaded 181,437 kg (400,000 lb.)

Armament: eight B61 or B83 nuclear bombs or 16 stand-off nuclear missiles on rotary launcher in bomb-bay or 80 Mk 82 227-kg (500-lb.) bombs or up to 22,600 kg (50,000 lb.) of other weapons

Dimensions:
span	52.43 m (172 ft.)
length	21.03 m (69 ft.)
height	5.18 m (17 ft.)
wing area	196 m² (2,110 sq. ft.)

B-2A SPIRIT

Developed under great secrecy and at huge expense, the B-2 Spirit is the world's most advanced strategic bomber.

The B-2 has an advanced two-man cockpit with provision for a third crew member/observer. High technology has done away with the flight engineer and bombardier of earlier bombers.

The B-2 is powered by four General Electric F118 non-afterburning turbofans. They are buried deep within the aircraft, keeping the highly radar-reflective fan blades away from enemy radar transmissions.

The engines exhaust through 'V'-shaped outlets set back and above the trailing edges to hide these heat sources from the ground.

The 33° sweep of the leading edge and the 'W' configuration of the trailing edge are designed to trap and deflect radar energy away from a hostile transmitter.

The Hughes AN/APQ-181 attack radar has phased array transmitters buried in the fuselage, so there is no need for a dish aerial and its bulbous radome.

Extensive use is made of graphite/epoxy materials in the aircraft's structure. These are not good reflectors of radar energy, and contribute to the bomber's stealthiness.

The B-2's undercarriage has been adapted from a commercial design, used on the Boeing 757 and 767 airliners.

Vapour trails are the enemy of any aircraft claiming to be stealthy. Chloro-fluorosulphonic acid is injected into the exhaust gases of the B-2 to inhibit the formation of contrails at high altitude.

COMBAT DATA

RANGE

Thanks to its large fuel capacity and highly efficient turbofan engines, the Northrop B-2 has a truly global range. Others can fly as far, but not with such a heavy warload or such economy. Airborne refuelling allows the B-2 to strike anywhere in the world from its home base.

B-2A SPIRIT 12,225 km (7,596 mi.)

Tu-160 'BLACKJACK' 14,000 km (8,700 mi.)

B-1B LANCER 12,000 km (7,500 mi.)

Unrefuelled range

WEAPONS

Although it is much smaller than the massive 'Blackjack', the B-2 can carry a much heavier load. The B-1B can carry far more, but a heavy warload strictly limits the Lancer's range.

B-2A SPIRIT 22,600-kg (50,000-lb.) maximum weapons load

B-1B LANCER 60,000-kg (132,000-lb.) maximum weapons load

Tu-160 'BLACKJACK' estimated 16,500-kg (36,000-lb.) maximum weapons load

SPEED

Both the B-1B and the Tu-160 are designed to make the last portion of an attack at supersonic speeds, to give the maximum chance of survival. The B-2's stealthiness means that it does not need this highly expensive and fuel-hungry capability.

B-2A SPIRIT
Cruise: 750 km/h (466 m.p.h.)
Maximum: approx. 960 km/h (600 m.p.h.)

B-1B LANCER
Cruise: 960 km/h (600 m.p.h.)
Maximum: 1324 km/h (822 m.p.h.)

Tu-160 'BLACKJACK'
Cruise: 850 km/h (528 m.p.h.)
Maximum: 2000 km/h (1,240 m.p.h.)

Ancestry of the 'Flying Wing'

■ **PIONEERS OF WINGLESS FLIGHT:** Among the earliest pioneers were the German Horten brothers, whose radical Ho IX fighter evolved from pre-war gliders and which promised superb performance in 1945.

■ **SCALE MODELS:** American Jack Northrop had always been interested in flying wings, and his first designs for the US Air Force were scale designs exploring the potential of the configuration as a long-range bomber.

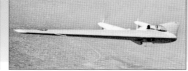

■ **AHEAD OF ITS TIME:** Northrop developed a full-size jet bomber to compete with the more conventional B-52, but control technology of the day meant that the resulting YB-49 of 1947 was not easy to handle in some conditions.

■ **LIFTING BODIES:** Between the demise of the XB-49 and the launch of the B-2, Northrop was involved in lifting bodies such as the X-24, shown here in 1969. These did away with wings, gaining lift from the shape of the fuselage.

PANAVIA

TORNADO GR.MK 1B/GR.MK 4

● Low-level bomber ● Stand-off missiles ● Ship-killer

▲ *In a world of increasing technology, the cover of night is the final sanctuary for attacking aircraft. In this environment Tornado pilots are suitably equipped with night-vision goggles (NVG).*

Although it is a well-proven strike aircraft, the Tornado's experiences in the first Gulf War highlighted its deficiencies. In a time of tightening defence budgets, a mid-life update was initiated for the Tornado to extend its service life. With an upgraded navigational suite and the ability to deliver stand-off weapons, the improved Tornados will remain the RAF's premier strike aircraft until the Typhoon is fully operational.

PHOTO FILE

PANAVIA TORNADO GR.MK 1B/GR.MK 4

◄ Pilot's delight
Improved versions of the Tornado have retained all the well-respected handling qualities pilots have come to expect from the aircraft.

Ship-killer supreme ▶
In its maritime role the GR.Mk 1B Tornado is able to deliver the Sea Eagle anti-ship missile, which has a range of over 92 km (50 mi.).

More power ▶
Despite the type's excellent low-level performance, an uprated turbofan engine was installed in the new models.

▼ Flight testing
In the hands of British test pilots, the Tornado GR.Mk 4 is proving to be an ideal interdiction aircraft. Overseas interest in the aircraft is increasing.

▲ Covert intruder
With an improved avionics suite linked to stand-off missiles, the Tornado is able to destroy enemy positions from afar.

FACTS AND FIGURES

➤ The first flight of the Tornado GR.Mk 4 prototype took place on 29 May 1993 from BAe's Warton Aerospace facility.

➤ On 14 July 1994 government approval was given to upgrade 142 examples.

➤ Tornado GR.Mk 4s entered RAF service in September 1998.

➤ Both cockpits are fully compatible with night-vision goggles, allowing missions to be flown in complete darkness.

➤ Principal characteristic of the GR.Mk 4 is an additional ventral under-nose fairing.

➤ Help for navigation is provided by a global positioning system.

PROFILE

Making the best even better

With the Warsaw Pact threat almost entirely removed, a radical review of the RAF's front-line capabilities took place in the early 1990s. In the absence of funding to develop a new strike aircraft, a series of modifications allowed the Tornado to replace the retiring Buccaneer in the maritime strike role. Equipped with Sea Eagle anti-ship missiles, the GR.Mk 1Bs operate with 12 and 617 Sqns from Lossiemouth in Scotland.

Externally the new aircraft is virtually indistinguishable from the GR.Mk 1. The GR.Mk 4's internal layout is where most changes have been made. A new wider head-up display allows the pilot to fly the aircraft while also receiving additional information from the forward-looking infra-red (FLIR) equipment. Below this is a head-down display for systems relating to the aircraft.

Both crew members can plot their position with the aid of a global positioning system and view the terrain below via a thermal imaging pod. The GR.Mk 4 enter service in 1998.

Above: A total of 142 Tornado GR.Mk 1/1As will be converted to GR.Mk 4s, taking the RAF's strike capability into the 21st century.

The improvements breathed new life into Strike Command's Tornado fleet, making the aircraft the equal of the latest Russian and American types. The Tornado will eventually be replaced by the Typhoon.

Above: Replacing the Buccaneer in maritime service, the Tornado is equipped with Sea Eagle anti-ship missiles.

Tornado GR.Mk 1B

Type: maritime strike aircraft

Powerplant: two 71.16-kN (16,008-lb.-thrust) Turbo-Union RB.199-34R afterburning turbofans

Maximum speed: 1482 km/h (919 m.p.h.) at sea level

Combat radius: 1335 km (828 mi.)

Service ceiling: 24,000 m (78,720 ft.)

Weights: empty 13,600 kg (29,920 lb.); maximum take-off 27,210 kg (59,862 lb.)

Armament: two 27-mm Mauser cannon, two fuselage-mounted Sea Eagle anti-ship missiles, plus AIM-9L Sidewinder AAMs or other stores

Dimensions:
span (swept)	8.60 m	(28 ft. 3 in.)
span (unswept)	13.90 m	(45 ft. 7 in.)
length	16.70 m	(54 ft. 9 in.)
height	5.79 m	(20 ft.)
wing area	30.00 m²	(323 sq. ft.)

GR.Mk 1B TORNADO

Operated by No. 12 Squadron, RAF, this GR.Mk 1B was one of 26 former Batch 3 Tornado GR.Mk 1s which were converted. The first flight of the GR.Mk 1B occurred on 18 September 1993.

Matched against the latest military aircraft, the cockpit of the Tornado was becoming dated, so a number of improvements were implemented. The cockpit is now fully NVG-compatible and incorporates new head-up and head-down displays.

Unique to British Tornados is the fuel tank in the fin of the aircraft, which means the Tornado can strike targets at great distances. Additional 2250-litre (594-gal.) fuel tanks can be carried under the wings.

A distinguishing feature of the GR.Mk 4 is an extra under-nose fairing housing a GEC TICM II forward-looking infra-red unit.

AIM-9L Sidewinder missiles can be carried on the inner wing pylons. Along with the two 27-mm cannon in the nose, this offers a limited self-defence capability

Dedicated Sea Eagle pylons are positioned on the underside of the fuselage. Control of the missiles is facilitated by an extra panel in the rear cockpit.

Plans have been outlined for at least some GR.Mk 1Bs to be modified to carry the Flight Refuelling Mk 20B HDU pods that were previously used by the Victor fleet. This would let Tornados operate in the buddy refuelling role, extending the strike range of the aircraft.

COMBAT DATA

PILOT'S OFFICE: The pilot's cockpit (pictured below) features a new, wide-angle holographic head-up display onto which both FLIR imagery and normal flight symbology can be displayed simultaneously. Positioned below this is a Smiths Industries head-down display (HDD), used for navigational purposes.

NAVIGATOR'S OFFICE: Despite undergoing only a modest upgrade, the navigator's rear cockpit (pictured below) is equipped with an advanced global positioning system. Maritime strike variants (GR.Mk 1Bs) are fitted with a Sea Eagle missile panel, which allows the navigator to operate and fire the weapon.

The next generation

■ **HARRIER GR.Mk 7:** Constant upgrades have now made the Harrier one of the most capable combat aircraft in the world. It can undertake attack missions at night.

■ **JAGUAR GR.Mk 1A:** Improvements to its navigational suite and attack avionics have kept the Jaguar in front-line service with the Royal Air Force into the 21st century.

■ **TORNADO F.Mk 3 ADV:** As a result of first Gulf War experience, improvements to the ADV fleet included the addition of radar-absorbent materials (RAM) along the leading edges.

PIAGGIO

P.180 AVANTI

● Radical design ● Composite construction ● High performance

F irst flown in September 1986, the Avanti was designed as a business aircraft. The distinctive airframe contains a host of innovative features which combine to provide the biggest possible cabin in an aircraft that also offers high speeds, long range and economy. Unfortunately, like the equally innovative Beech Starship, it has attracted few customers and the Italian air force has become its main operator.

▲ With its
distinctive looks and high speed the Avanti would make an ideal aircraft for the rapid transport of top-ranking military officers and VIPs.

PIAGGIO P.180 AVANTI

▲ Radical shape
From all angles the P.180 is a stunningly unusual aircraft. The propellers counter-rotate.

▼ Military colours
Italian air force machines are finished in overall white, with a smart blue cheat line.

▼ Avanti airborne
The P.180 is extremely graceful and very fast. National markings are restricted to small fuselage and underwing roundels.

▲ Low foreplanes
Fixed foreplanes are mounted low down on the nose. They combine with the tailplane to produce lift and allow a small main wing area.

◄ Assembly line
Carbon-fibre reinforced plastic is used for the high-stress parts of the airframe, while Kevlar and epoxy materials are employed elsewhere. The fuselage is stretch-formed in large sections, with the inner surfaces matching exactly.

◄ Super streamlining
Piaggio's attention to detail is evident in every feature of the Avanti. The powerful turboprops are carefully faired and blend into a large, pointed spinner.

FACTS AND FIGURES

➤ Gates Learjet was temporarily a partner in the P.180 project, joining in 1983 and leaving in 1986 for financial reasons.

➤ A standard P.180, complete with colour glass cockpit, costs $4.84 million.

➤ Composite airframe parts are built by Sikorsky and Edo.

➤ The P.180 design was initiated in 1979 and Piaggio announced its amazing new aircraft in 1983.

➤ Piaggio began assembly of the first Avanti at its Finale Ligne plant in 1986.

➤ Italy's air force also flies the Piaggio P.166 and PD-808 transport aircraft.

PROFILE

Piaggio's adventurous Avanti

There were sound reasons behind the apparently radical features of the Avanti. The designers' chief goal was to make the cabin interior as large as possible, giving passengers maximum headroom. The main wing was therefore placed at the rear of the fuselage rather than in a conventional location further forward, where the main spar would have occupied valuable cabin space.

Normally, this wing location would demand an impossibly large tailplane, but a small fixed wing on the nose provides additional lift and makes it possible to control the aircraft's pitch with elevators which are no bigger than normal. In addition, the fuselage is subtly shaped to reduce drag, while the 'delta fin' strakes under the tail help maintain controllability at high angles of attack. At the same time, the unusual configuration helps to keep the aircraft's weight low.

Despite the outstanding performance and advanced glass cockpit, buyers have proved difficult to find. The only substantial operator is the Italian air force, which ordered six for communications and general transport duties. These aircraft are attached to various operational units and the first was delivered on 14 May 1994.

Below: Large flaps are mounted on both outboard and inboard sections on the wing trailing edges. The flaps deploy along substantial tracks.

Above: Each main gear unit retracts rearwards into the lower fuselage. The nose unit retracts forwards and has twin wheels.

P.180 Avanti

Type: light transport

Powerplant: two 1107-kW (1,485-hp.) Pratt & Whitney Canada PT6A-66 turboprops

Maximum speed: 732 km/h (454 m.p.h.) at 8625 m (28,300 ft.)

Range: 3150 km (1,950 mi.) at 11,890 m (39,000 ft.)

Service ceiling: 12,500 m (41,000 ft.)

Weights: empty 3402 kg (7,484 lb.); maximum take-off 5239 kg (11,525 lb.)

Accommodation: one or two pilots, plus up to nine passengers

Dimensions:
span 14.03 m (46 ft.)
length 14.41 m (47 ft. 3 in.)
height 3.94 m (12 ft. 11 in.)
wing area 16 m² (172 sq. ft.)

P.180 AVANTI

Very few Avantis have been built and the type is represented here by the first prototype. A second aircraft joined I-PJAV in the air on 14 May 1987, and certification occurred in October 1990.

Two multi-function colour monitors display all the vital flight information. A colour display is also provided for the Collins WXR-480 weather radar.

A maximum load of nine passengers can enjoy the benefits of a galley, toilet and wardrobe. An alternative five-seat VIP interior is also available. Seats are of the armchair type, with multiple adjustments, and foldaway tables may be pulled out between them.

Each of the PT6A-66 turboprops drives a five-bladed Hartzell propeller. Some Italian air force machines have six-bladed propellers. The nacelles are constructed entirely from composites and represent the only break in the wing line.

Mounted high on the tail to clear the propeller wash, the sharply swept tailplane is electrically adjusted for trimming and also carries conventional elevators. The rudder is characterised by a very large trim tab.

I-PJAV

Fixed and carefully faired into the forward fuselage, the foreplane carries trailing-edge flaps. These are synchronised to operate with the wing flaps.

The wings are of high aspect ratio and of very limited area. This configuration minimises drag during high-speed flight. The main spar passes behind the passenger cabin.

Known as 'delta fins', the rear fuselage ventral strakes have no control surfaces but aid directional stability. The wings and tail section are manufactured by Piaggio in Genoa, while the forward fuselage is produced by Piaggio Aviation of Wichita.

ACTION DATA

MAXIMUM SPEED

Compared to other twin-turboprop light transports in military service, the Avanti has exceptional performance. It is capable of maximum and cruising speeds close to those of many jet transports and is also economical to operate.

P.180 AVANTI	732 km/h (454 m.p.h.)
SUPER KING AIR B200	545 km/h (338 m.p.h.)
TURBO CMDR 690	528 km/h (327 m.p.h.)

MAXIMUM PASSENGERS

As with their civilian counterparts, these aircraft rarely fly with a full passenger load. Five or six passengers would be typical and each therefore offers ample room. As a utility transport the P.180 is less useful, however, as it is a smaller aircraft.

P.180 AVANTI — 9 passengers

SUPER KING AIR B200 — 14 passengers

TURBO COMMANDER 690 — 11 passengers

RANGE

Beechcraft's Super King Air B200 offers impressive range and many serve with the US forces as the C-12. The P.180 Avanti cannot equal the B200 for range, but far exceeds the capabilities of the Rockwell Turbo Commander 690.

SUPER KING AIR B200 3656 km (2,267 mi.)

P.180 AVANTI 3150 km (1,950 mi.)

TURBO COMMANDER 690 2522 km (1,565 mi.)

Military light twin-turboprops

■ **BEECHCRAFT C-12:** A variety of missions are performed by C-12s in US service. All variants, apart from the C-12J, are based on the B200.

■ **BEECHCRAFT C-12J:** Based on the 1900C airliner, the C-12J flies operational support tasks for the US Air National Guard.

■ **EMBRAER EMB-121 XINGU:** Brazil and France both fly the Xingu. The French aircraft are used for training and fast communications.

■ **PIAGGIO P.166:** Developed from the earlier and much smaller P.136 amphibian, several P.166s remain in Italian air force service.

PILATUS
PC-7/PC-9

● Tandem two-seat trainers ● Turboprop power ● Swiss built

▲ The PC-9
introduced an 857-kW (1,150-hp.)
Pratt & Whitney Canada turboprop
compared to the earlier PC-7's 485-
kW (650-hp.) engine.

Using its 1950s designed P-3 piston-
engined trainer as a starting point,
Pilatus developed the PC-7 Turbo Trainer.
The aircraft became a best-seller around the
world and in 1984 it was joined in the air by the
new PC-9. Although it looked very similar to the
earlier machine, the PC-9 was in fact 90 per
cent new. A more powerful engine, stepped
cockpit and high performance make the PC-9
one of the world's most advanced and capable
turboprop trainers.

PILATUS **PC-7/PC-9**

▲ **Australian PC-9**
By far the largest operator to
date, the Royal Australian Air
Force operates 67 PC-9s, which
are designated PC-9As.

▲ **Civilian Pilatus in the US**
At least four high-performance PC-7 sports planes
are privately owned in the US. These two are
pictured at Wisconsin's Oshkosh Air Show in 1986.

▼ **PC-7 in Malaysia**
The Royal Malaysian Air Force is a major PC-7
operator, and the aircraft shown below are
members of its elite aerobatic team.

▲ **Joint Primary Aircraft Training System**
In co-operation with Raytheon Beech in the US,
Pilatus offered the PC-9 Mk II to fulfil the JPATS
requirement for the US Air Force and Navy. The
first orders were placed in late 1995. This
represents a major success for Pilatus since the US
is actively encouraging exports.

BAe demonstrator ▶
BAe, teamed with Pilatus,
offered the PC-9 to the RAF
in its bid to find a Jet Provost
replacement. The PC-9 lost
out to the Shorts Tucano,
possibly for political reasons.

FACTS AND FIGURES

➤ After BAe/Pilatus lost the RAF trainer
contract, BAe was instrumental in
winning a Saudi Arabian PC-9 order.

➤ In Germany, Holstenair operates a
target-towing PC-9 for the Luftwaffe.

➤ From 1985 Pilatus offered Martin-Baker
ejection seats as a retrofit for the PC-7.

➤ Swiss government regulations concerning
the export of arms caused Pilatus to lose a
Korean PC-9 order.

➤ Iran and Iraq used armed PC-7s against
each other during their long conflict.

➤ The PC-7 Mk II was developed for South
Africa and the aircraft were built by Atlas.

PROFILE

Pilatus' turboprop training twins

Installing a Pratt & Whitney Canada PT6A-20 turboprop in a Pilatus P-3 produced one of the world's earliest turboprop trainers. First flown in April 1966, the prototype suffered a landing accident, which caused the programme to be put on hold until 1973. A second P-3 was then modified and flew on 12 May 1975.

Incorporating a number of modifications to the basic P-3 airframe, the PC-7 Turbo Trainer was delivered to its launch customer, the Myanmar air force, in 1979. By early 1995 more than 440 aircraft had been delivered, the majority to military customers.

Comprehensively redesigned in the light of experience with the PC-7, the PC-9 was built from the outset with ejection seats allowing escape at sea level and speeds as low as 112 km/h (69 m.p.h.). The rear seat for the instructor was raised to give a good view over the student pilot's head.

A marketing agreement with

BAe has seen the PC-9 offered as the ideal lead-in trainer to the Hawk, with a number of countries, including Saudi Arabia, using the aircraft in this way.

Following the award of the JPATS (Joint Primary Aircraft Training System) contract to the PC-9, US Navy pilots will also be following the PC-9/Hawk path. Total JPATS procurement will be 711 aircraft over 20 years. With Pilatus and its US partner Raytheon Beech encouraged to seek export orders, the future of the PC-9 is assured.

Above: Since the prototype's first flight in 1984, the PC-9 has been ordered by nine countries.

Above: The French Patrouille Martini aerobatic team used the PC-7 for displays in the late 1980s.

PC-9

This PC-9 is in the colours of the Myanmar air force, one of the most recent customers for the high-performance trainer. This machine is unarmed, with the only armed aircraft in the series being South Africa's PC-7 Mk II Astra.

Instructor and pupil are seated on Martin-Baker adjustable ejection seats, with an integrated personal survival pack.

The structure of the PC-9 is all-metal with some composite materials used in the wings. A retractable 250-Watt taxiing light is stowed in each landing gear bay.

The 857-kW (1,150-hp.) Pratt & Whitney Canada PT6 turboprop drives an advanced Hartzell HC-D4N constant-speed fully-feathering propeller.

Both the PC-7 and PC-9 have retractable tricycle type landing gear with hydraulic disc brakes. The Australian version features low-pressure tyres for grass-field operation.

PC-9 design began in 1982, and its aerodynamic elements were tested on the similar PC-7. More than 200 military aircraft have been sold to Australia, Cyprus, Germany, Iraq, Myanmar, Saudi Arabia, Switzerland, and Thailand. In the future both the USAF and US Navy will fly the Beech/Pilatus PC-9 Mk II, powered by a 1274-kW (1,700-hp.) Pratt & Whitney Canada turboprop.

ACTION DATA

MAXIMUM SPEED

All three aircraft were designed to compete in the same marketplace and all are equally capable in terms of speed. Air forces demand jet-like speeds and handling at low cost.

PC-9	556 km/h (345 m.p.h.)
EMB-312H SUPER TUCANO	557 km/h (346 m.p.h.)
PZL-130 ORLIK	560 km/h (347 m.p.h.)

RATE OF CLIMB

EMBRAER's Super Tucano falls short on climb rate since it is a much heavier aircraft with similar power. The Orlik has suffered a protracted development period, although the introduction of US engine technology has produced a fine aircraft which should be capable of competing with the PC-9 on equal terms.

PC-9	EMB-312H SUPER TUCANO	PZL-130 ORLIK
1250 m/min (4,100 f.p.m.)	895 m/min (3,283 f.p.m.)	1236 m/min (4,054 f.p.m.)

RANGE

Poland's PZL-130 excels in this range comparison. The EMB-312H's range is much shorter, although the aircraft does offer the versatility of a range of missions outside the capabilities of its competitors. The Orlik is closely matched to the PC-9, but poses little threat since Pilatus is able to offer a complete training system.

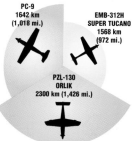

PC-9 1642 km (1,018 mi.)
EMB-312H SUPER TUCANO 1568 km (972 mi.)
PZL-130 ORLIK 2300 km (1,426 mi.)

Turboprop trainers

■ **SHORT TUCANO:** The RAF's licence-built version of EMBRAER's successful trainer, the Tucano T.Mk 1, has replaced the Jet Provost.

■ **DAEWOO KTX-1:** One hundred indigenous KTX-1 Yeo-Myoung (Dawn) trainers have been ordered by the Republic of Korea Air Force.

■ **BEECHCRAFT T-34C TURBINE MENTOR:** Redeveloped from an earlier piston-engined design, the T-34C serves with the US Navy.

■ **ENAER TURBO PILLAN:** Once known as the Aucan, this is the updated variant of the Chilean air force's original Pillan.

PILATUS/BRITTEN-NORMAN

DEFENDER

● Military Islander variant ● Piston and turbine versions

▲ Both large
air-to-air radar and smaller air-to-surface systems have been fitted to Defenders. These aircraft provide affordable coverage for smaller nations with limited budgets.

Civil operators of the Pilatus/Britten-Norman Islander are usually attracted by the aircraft's low cost, ease of maintenance and minimal support requirements. The same qualities are equally attractive to military operators, and the manufacturer has developed military variants to exploit the type's combination of long endurance and STOL ability. The military variants are known as Defenders and fill a wide variety of roles.

PILATUS/BRITTEN-NORMAN DEFENDER

▼ Rockets away!
Defenders have been widely exported, and have been optimised for the military role with four underwing hardpoints for various stores, including rockets.

▲ AEW Defender and MSSA
The AEW Defender testbed, G-TEMI, was later refitted with a Westinghouse APG-66SR radar, to become the Multi-Sensor Surveillance Aircraft.

▼ Maritime Defender
The Maritime Defender is an all-weather, day or night maritime coastal patrol aircraft and is available in piston or turbine form. A nose-mounted sector scan radar of the customer's choice is a standard fitting.

▲ Radar-equipped CASTOR
Corps Airborne Stand-Off Radar, or CASTOR, was a 1984 attempt to provide the British Army with a battlefield surveillance aircraft.

Popular with smaller nations ▶
The island state of Mauritania has an air force of just 12 aircraft, including six Defenders that can be fitted with rockets. The aircraft have a dual transport and counter-insurgency role.

FACTS AND FIGURES

➤ Originally a Britten-Norman design, the Islander/Defender family is now built by the Swiss company Pilatus/Britten-Norman.

➤ British Army Air Corps Turbine Defenders are designated Islander AL.Mk 1s.

➤ One RAF Islander CC.Mk 2A retains the ability to fire a torpedo.

➤ The BN-2T-4 Defender 4000 is a new version with a longer-span wing and a 100 per cent better payload capability.

➤ CASTOR Defenders were intended to operate with USAF E-8 J-STARS aircraft.

➤ Mexico's Presidential Flight is equipped with a Defender.

Low-budget muscle for small air forces

Like the Islander, the Defender is available in both BN-2 piston-engined and BN-2T turboprop versions. The aircraft can be fitted with equipment for electronic warfare, search and rescue, border surveillance and fisheries patrol. It can also be armed with machine-guns and rocket pods. In fact, the reduced size and weight of modern electronics mean that the Defender can be equipped with sensors that provide the surveillance capability of much bigger aircraft.

One variant is the Multi-Sensor Surveillance Aircraft (MSSA), which was developed together with Westinghouse in the United States. This combines

a Defender airframe with a version of the F-16 fighter's radar and an infra-red sensor.

The latest model is the BN-2T-4 Defender 4000, which has the enlarged wing of the Trislander, an increased fuel capacity and double the payload. In the BN-2T-4S version, the engines also drive 200-amp generators which provide electrical power for surveillance equipment.

Above: Botswana took delivery of both piston-engined and turbine-powered Defenders. This aircraft has four underwing hardpoints fitted.

Right: Seen here prior to delivery and still carrying their British delivery registrations, these Defenders were destined for Ghana's air force. Ghana also ordered Turbine Defenders.

BN-2T-4 Defender 4000

Type: twin-turbine multi-role transport

Powerplant: two 298-kW (400-hp.) Allison B250-17F turboprops flat rated at 238.5 kW (320 hp.)

Maximum speed: 326 km/h (202 m.p.h.) at sea level

Endurance: 8 hours

Service ceiling: 7620 m (25,000 ft.)

Weights: empty 2223 kg (4,890 lb.); maximum take-off 3856 kg (8,483 lb.)

Accommodation: up to 9 passengers plus pilot, or equivalent weight in mission equipment and associated crewmembers

Dimensions:
span	16.15 m (53 ft.)
length	12.37 m (40 ft. 7 in.)
height	4.18 m (13 ft. 8 in.)
wing area	31.31 m² (337 sq. ft.)

AEW DEFENDER

G-TEMI was the AEW (Airborne Early Warning) Defender demonstrator flown in the mid-1980s and later converted to MSSA standard as G-MSSA. An example of the latter has been sold to Turkey.

Marketed as an affordable airborne early warning (AEW) platform, the Defender featured a Thorn-EMI Skymaster radar in a large nose radome. In the 1990s a Westinghouse APG-66 radar was installed.

Turbine Islander/Defenders are powered by two 298-kW (400-hp.)Allison B250-17F turboprops, derivatives of the well-known 250-C turboshaft helicopter powerplant. They replace the Islander's Textron Lycoming O-540 or IO-540 flat-six piston engines.

The AEW version had one radar operator who was seated at a console in the aircraft's main cabin. An AEW/MR maritime version was equipped with a second console and operator to increase flexibility. Other systems available in the AEW Defender included electronic support measures and identification friend or foe.

To maintain directional stability with the bulbous radome fitted, the AEW Defender and MSSA aircraft had a fillet added forward of the tailfin. They also had the longer span wings which were introduced on the Defender 4000.

The Defender's STOL performance, inherited from the Islander, allowed it to be operated from forward, unprepared airstrips. Compared to many other AEW aircraft, the Defender had a smaller radar cross-section when airborne.

ACTION DATA

RANGE

In terms of its range capability, the Defender performs better than the Dornier Do 28D and DHC-6 Twin Otter. Defenders are able to carry extra fuel both internally and in external fuel tanks.

BN-2B DEFENDER	1965 km (1,218 mi.)
DHC-6 SERIES 300	1297 km (804 mi.)
Do 28D-1 SKYSERVANT	1810 km (1,122 mi.)

TAKE-OFF RUN

All three types are dedicated STOL designs and have good short-field performance. The Defender's take-off run at maximum weight is comparable to that of both the Twin Otter and the Do 28D Skyservant.

BN-2B DEFENDER	352 m (1,154 ft.)
DHC-6 SERIES 300 TWIN OTTER	366 m (1,200 ft.)
Do 28D-1 SKYSERVANT	347 m (1,138 ft.)

POWER

The piston-engined Defender has a modest power rating, which was addressed in the Turbine Defender. However, the Lycoming LTP-101 engine which was originally selected proved to be too powerful. The Do 28D is a piston-engined design and the DHC-6 is a turboprop.

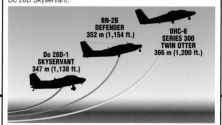

Do 28D-1 SKYSERVANT	BN-2B DEFENDER	DHC-6 SERIES 300 TWIN OTTER
566 kW (754 hp.)	448 kW (640 hp.)	924 kW (1,238 hp.)

Britten-Norman's STOL family

■ **BN-2/2A/2B ISLANDER:** Flown for the first time in 1965, the Islander nine-seater has been in production for 30 years in four countries.

■ **BN-2A Mk III TRISLANDER:** Introduced in 1970, this stretched, 18-seat, tri-motored BN-2 variant was built in limited numbers.

■ **BN-2T TURBINE ISLANDER:** To improve the Islander's performance, turboprop engines were fitted in 1980.

■ **BN-3 NYMPH:** This all-metal light aircraft flew in 1969, but failed to enter production before the Britten-Norman became bankrupt.

PZL

I-22/M-93 IRYDA

● Twin-engined jet trainer ● Polish design ● Export potential

While the Soviet's other Warsaw Pact allies adopted the Czech-built L-29 Delfin as their basic jet training aircraft, Poland chose to develop the indigenous TS-11 Iskra. When this first-generation local design needed replacing in the 1970s, Poland's highly developed PZL organisation came up with another new design, the Iskra-22, or I-22 Iryda. With the end of the Cold War, Poland has high export hopes for its new trainer.

▲ *Development of the I-22/M-93 series began in 1977. With the end of the Cold War, PZL now anticipates a worldwide market for the Iryda, but faces tough competition.*

PZL I-22/M-93 IRYDA

▼ **First production M-93K**
0204 was the first Iryda that was built to the initial Polish air force service standard and flew in July 1994. This aircraft entered service with the 58th Air School Regiment.

▲ **Numerous variants**
In addition to the M-93V, various other versions have been announced, including the M-93R two-seat reconnaissance aircraft and the M-93M maritime attack and reconnaissance platform.

Rolls-Royce power ▶
With airbrakes deployed, the fifth Iryda touches down. By this stage SP-PWE had been re-engined with Rolls-Royce Vipers for the export market. Designated M-93V, it flew in 1994.

◀ **Advanced trainer**
As the Iryda is expected to be used by the Polish air force for all aspects of pilot training, a weapon-carrying ability is an important feature.

Strength a strong point ▶
The I-22's name implies strength as Iryda (iridium) is a steel-grey metallic element with a very high melting point. The name Iryda is shared by a planned M-96 variant with improved aerodynamics.

FACTS AND FIGURES

➤ An ex-Vietnamese air force Northrop F-5 and Cessna A-37 were allegedly used in the development of the I-22.

➤ Including prototypes and 1996 orders, 25 Irydas had been built or ordered.

➤ The first I-22 deliveries were to the 58th Air School Regiment at Deblin-Irena.

➤ Proposed I-22/M-93 variants included two-seat reconnaissance and single-seat fighter/attack aircraft.

➤ At least two of the first 25 aircraft have been used as static test airframes.

➤ The PZL-Mielec factory was founded in 1938 and has built 15,000 aircraft.

PROFILE

Home-grown advanced jet trainer

Launched in 1977 as a replacement for the TS-11 and Lim-6 (MiG-17) tactical and advanced trainers, the I-22 was to be a combat-capable two-seater. Development has been prolonged, however, and the prototype did not fly until March 1985 and then crashed in 1987.

Four more aircraft flew between 1988 and 1991, the year in which the Polish air force announced its first order for nine aircraft. Five had been delivered by 1994, when it was decided to improve what was judged to be an underpowered

design by fitting new engines, ejection seats and avionics.

The Polish air force did consider buying ex-German Luftwaffe Alpha Jet trainers (to which the I-22 bears a strong resemblance), but this idea was abandoned. Instead, the I-22's 10.76-kN (2,420-lb.-thrust) PZL-5 engines were replaced by two new 14.71-kN (3,300-lb.-thrust) IL K-15 turbojets to produce the M-93K. A re-engined example flew in 1994 and this has become the main production variant. Twelve were ordered by the Polish air force and the

SP-PWC

Above: The third I-22 takes to the air with a load of assorted underwing stores. External loads are limited to 1100 kg (2,420 lb.).

surviving I-22s will be brought up to the new standard.

In an effort to secure foreign sales, the fifth I-22 has been fitted with two Rolls-Royce Vipers, as the M-93V. A number of other variants have also been discussed.

SP-PWB

Above: SP-PWB was the second I-22 prototype, and first flew in 1988. The crash of the first prototype and the political situation in Poland prolonged I-22/M-93 development.

M-93K Iryda

Type: two-seat basic and advanced trainer

Powerplant: two 14.71-kN (3,300-lb-thrust) Instytut Lotnictwa K-15 turbojets

Maximum speed: 950 km/h (589 m.p.h.) at 5000 m (18,000 ft.)

Maximum climb rate: 2520 m/min (8,265 f.p.m.) at sea level

Combat radius: 250 km (155 mi.) at 500 m (1,600 ft.) at maximum take-off weight

Service ceiling: 13,700 m (44,396 ft.)

Weights: empty equipped 4650 kg (10,230 lb.); maximum take-off 8700 kg (19,140 lb.)

Armament: one 23-mm twin-barrelled cannon in ventral pack, plus up to 1100 kg (2,420 lb.) of weapons on external pylons, including bombs, rockets, gun pods and air-to-air missiles

Dimensions:
span	9.60 m	(31 ft. 6 in.)
length	13.22 m	(43 ft. 4 in.)
height	4.30 m	(14 ft. 2 in.)
wing area	19.92 m²	(214 sq. ft.)

I-22 IRYDA

Aircraft '02' was the prototype of the I-22/M-93 series. After being lost in a crash on 31 January 1987, it was followed by four more airframes, the first of which flew in 1988.

The I-22's elevators and rudder are manually (rod) actuated. The flaps are hydraulic, although they can be pneumatically operated in emergencies. Hydraulic airbrakes are fitted in the upper fuselage.

Among the changes made to the I-22 to bring it up to M-93K standard were the installation of Western systems, including avionics, an inertial navigation system (INS) and Martin-Baker PL10LR zero/zero ejection seats.

PZL designed the Iryda to cover the full spectrum of pilot training, operating in all weathers from unprepared airstrips and carrying a variety of ordnance types. The airframe is able to withstand battle damage and is quick and inexpensive to repair.

The I-22 has an all-metal light alloy stressed skin structure and a two-spar wing with integral fuel tanks. The engine bays have titanium heatshields.

02

A twin-barrelled GSz-23L 23-mm cannon pack installed in a bay under the rear cockpit is standard on the M-93Ks. Up to 200 rounds of ammunition can be carried in the fuselage.

Two underwing pylons are fitted on either side of the aircraft. They may contain camera pods, fuel tanks or, for advanced training flights, an offensive load. In combat, air-to-air missiles can be carried for self-defence.

After initial flight trials of the I-22, powered by PZL-5s, showed the aircraft to be underpowered, two more powerful K-15 engines were substituted. For export, PZL has flown a Rolls-Royce Viper-powered variant.

ACTION DATA

MAXIMUM SPEED

The BAe Hawk has a marginal speed advantage over the Alpha Jet and a much higher top speed than the Iryda. New engines improved the Iryda's performance, especially its top speed.

I-22 IRYDA	840 km/h (520 m.p.h.)
HAWK T.Mk 1	1038 km/h (644 m.p.h.)
ALPHA JET E	916 km/h (568 m.p.h.)

CLIMB RATE

The twin-engined Alpha Jet E had a considerable power-to-weight advantage over the single-engined Hawk T.Mk 1. In its original form the under-powered I-22 showed an unimpressive performance, but this was rectified in later aircraft by fitting bigger engines.

ALPHA JET E 3660 m/min (12,000 f.p.m.)

HAWK T.Mk 1 2835 m/min (9,300 f.p.m.)

I-22 IRYDA 1500 m/min (4,920 f.p.m.)

Post-war PZL products

■ **M-15 BELPHEGOR:** Production of the jet-powered M-15 agricultural aircraft totalled 120. It ended in 1981, after the Belphegor proved to be uneconomical to operate.

■ **PZL-104 WILGA:** This radial-engined, light, general-purpose aircraft first flew in the early 1960s and remains in production. Roles include training and crop spraying.

■ **PZL-106 KRUK:** One of PZL's three dedicated crop-spraying/dusting designs, the piston-engined Kruk and turboprop Turbo-Kruk have secured export orders.

■ **PZL-230 SKORPION:** This turbofan-powered single-seat small agile battlefield attack (SABA) aircraft was proposed to the Polish air force in the 1990s, but did not proceed to prototype stage.

PZL

PZL-130 ORLIK

● Indigenous Polish trainer ● Jet-like performance

F lown for the first time in October 1984, the PZL-130 was conceived as part of a complete instruction system. As well as the aircraft itself, there was a simulator and an automatic inspection unit intended to diagnose faults with its systems or engine. The original aircraft was flown with two different piston engines, but after flight tests the Polish air force decided that it needed turboprop power. As a result, PZL has developed several versions of the PZL-130T.

▲ *Although it has suffered several setbacks and has taken a long time to develop, the indigenous Turbo Orlik basic turboprop trainer is now serving the Polish air force in large numbers.*

PZL PZL-130 ORLIK

▼ Pre-production
A small batch of pre-production Turbo Orliks was built in 1990–91. These all featured different powerplants in an attempt to determine the most suitable engine for air force use.

▲ Canadian force
A distinctive maple leaf on the tail identifies this aircraft as a pre-production example powered by a Pratt & Whitney Canada PT6A turboprop. This engine is used in the rival Swiss Pilatus PC-9 trainer.

Production differences ▶
In service, Orliks wear this attractive two-tone grey colour scheme. Differences from the prototype include a redesigned canopy.

◀ East meets West
When it was conceived during the Communism days in Eastern Europe, few would have envisaged that this aircraft would incorporate Western components.

Number three ▶
First flying in 1985 this aircraft was the third prototype of the original series and became the first turboprop conversion to take to the air, two years later.

FACTS AND FIGURES

➤ Two different engines are specified for the 130 Turbo Orlik, a Walter M601T or Pratt & Whitney Canada PT6A-62.

➤ An initial order for 12 aircraft was placed by the Deblin Training Academy.

➤ Development of the piston-engined variant was abandoned in 1990.

➤ A third pre-production Turbo Orlik flew in 1991, an incredible 10 years after design on the aircraft was first begun.

➤ Export orders have been sought but none has been achieved so far.

➤ The first turboprop conversion was destroyed in a crash in January 1987.

PROFILE

Poland's Spotted Eaglet

After flight tests of two pre-production Orliks (Spotted Eaglet), one powered by a 246-kW Vedeneyev M-14PM radial from the Soviet Union, and the other by one of PZL's own Kalisz K8-AAs, the piston-engined version was abandoned in 1990. This was partly because of the unreliable supply of the Russian engines but also through the advent of something better.

Using the existing airframe, PZL developed the Turbo Orlik. The first such machine was the third prototype piston Orlik fitted with a Pratt & Whitney Canada PT6A which flew for the first time in July 1986, but crashed the following January. A new airframe was fitted with a 560-kW (750-hp.) Motorlet M601E and flown in January 1989.

Subsequent prototypes included both PT6A and M601-powered versions, and in September 1991 PZL flew the first of 48 P-130TBs ordered by the Polish air force. The aircraft can be used for a wide range of training missions, and its six underwing hardpoints can carry a useful selection of armament.

After its long development, the P-130 finally entered service with the Polish air force in 1992. PZL has continued to develop the PT6A-powered versions, offering a range of models with engines varying in power from 410 kW (550 hp.) to 708 kW (950 hp.).

Left: All aircraft are delivered fully assembled from the PZL factory and are specifically made to order. Examples destined for overseas are certified by the Polish Ministry of Defence and Airworthiness.

Above: The most powerful Orlik is the PZL-130TC. Test pilots were reluctant to fly this machine after accidents in trials.

130 TB Turbo Orlik

Type: two-seat tandem basic trainer

Powerplant: one 560-kW (750-hp.) Motorlet M601E turboprop engine

Maximum speed: 501 km/h (310 m.p.h.)

Cruising speed: 454 km/h (281 m.p.h.)

Initial climb rate: 972 m/min (3,190 f.p.m.)

Range: 1905 km (1,180 mi.)

Service ceiling: 10,000 m (33,000 ft.)

Weights: empty 1450 kg (3,190 lb.); loaded 2700 kg (5,930 lb.)

External payload: 800 kg (1,760 lb.)

Load limits: + 6.5 g; -3 g

Dimensions:
span	9.00 m (29 ft. 6 in.)
length	9.00 m (29 ft. 6 in.)
height	3.53 m (11 ft. 7 in.)
wing area	13 m² (140 sq. ft.)

PZL-130 ORLIK

SP-PCA was the first Orlik to fly, taking to the air in October 1983. It was soon followed by a second, and later a third example, though by this time interest in the piston-engined version was waning.

With the original Vedeneyev M-14 radial, the PZL-130 featured a rather bulky front fuselage. Installing a turboprop not only improved performance, but also reduced drag, thanks to the slimmer cross-section of the new engine.

A tandem layout is incorporated, in common with many other modern basic trainers, with the rear seat set quite far back. The cockpit is well laid out and spacious. Full dual controls are featured and both crewmen sit on British Martin-Baker ejection seats which are fully automatic. A special command system enables the rear occupant to initiate the ejection sequence.

In line with many of its competitors, the aircraft is of all-metal, stressed-skin construction. The Orlik forms one element of the System 130 concept, the others being pilot simulator training and automatic diagnosis for ground crew. PZL designed the aircraft for ease of maintenance, to ensure maximum use of the fleet.

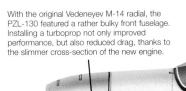

SP-PCA

002

Although the primary role of the aircraft is that of a trainer, a wide variety of external stores can be carried. In a war scenario, the Orlik would primarily be used for light-attack/close-support work.

All control surfaces are hydraulically powered and very light, giving the aircraft superb handling characteristics. PZL intended the Spotted Eaglet for both military and civilian operators and the aircraft is fully aerobatic.

Indigenous trainers from Poland

■ **PZL TS-8 BIES:** Roughly equivalent to the North American T-28, the Bies (fiend) entered service in 1958. It established several world records that remained unbeaten for 25 years.

■ **PZL TS-11 ISKRA:** Intended as a more advanced replacement for the TS-8, this aircraft represented a considerable coup for the Polish aviation industry, with some 500 built.

■ **P.Z.L IS-22 IRYDA:** Unlike other Eastern European countries which purchased the Aero L-39 Albatros, Poland chose to procure its own advanced trainer, resulting in the IS-22.

ACTION DATA

POWER
An interesting aspect of the Orlik is that its performance differs greatly depending on the engine fitted. The 130TM, with its M601 engine, is not as powerful as current Western types, though it can be specified with a much more potent Pratt & Whitney PT6A-25.

PZL-130TM 560 kw (750 hp.) **PC-9** 857 kW (1,150 hp.) **TUCANO T.Mk 1** 820 kW (1,100 hp.)

SERVICE CEILING
Despite having a less powerful engine, the Orlik has excellent performance and can reach an altitude of 10000 m with few problems. Its service ceiling is, surprisingly, greater than that of the much more powerful Shorts Tucano T.Mk 1.

PZL-130TM 10,000 m (33,000 ft.) **PC-9** 11,580 m (38,000 ft.) **TUCANO T.Mk 1** 9150 m (30,000 ft.)

CLIMB RATE
Not too long ago, a climb rate of 900 m/min was considered only attainable by jets. Improvements in technology and the advent of powerful turboprop engines have ensured that the latest generation of basic trainers can offer jet-like performance without the considerable cost.

PZL-130TM 972 m/min (3,180 f.p.m.) **PC-9** 1246 m/min (4,090 f.p.m.) **TUCANO T.Mk 1** 1070 m/min (3,510 f.p.m.)

ROCKWELL
B-1B LANCER

● Strategic nuclear bomber ● Supersonic swing wing ● Cruise carrier

▲ The B-1B combines stealth features with highly sophisticated defensive avionics. It has the ability to carry more bombs than the old B-52, and can fly low-level attack missions at high speed.

I t may lack the glamour of the stealthy B-2 flying wing or the reverence accorded to the 40-year-old B-52 Stratofortress, but the Rockwell B-1B Lancer is a highly advanced supersonic bomber. With its tremendous capacity to carry immense loads of nuclear and conventional weaponry, the Lancer has now become America's primary low-level, supersonic, nuclear strike asset.

PHOTO FILE

ROCKWELL B-1B LANCER

Fast dash ▶
With its wings swept, the Lancer can exceed Mach 1 at height, and gives a comfortable low-level ride at near-sonic speeds.

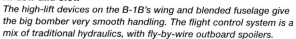

▲ Sleek and deadly
The long nose of the B-1B houses the Westinghouse AN/APQ-164 attack radar, derived from the F-16's APG-66. Most of the other electronic gear is classified.

▲ Low and slow
The high-lift devices on the B-1B's wing and blended fuselage give the big bomber very smooth handling. The flight control system is a mix of traditional hydraulics, with fly-by-wire outboard spoilers.

◀ High tail
Like the Russian Tu-160, the B-1B has a high-set tail to avoid the engine efflux. The bulge under the tail houses the defensive tail warning components of the AN/ALQ-161 system.

▼ Sweeping wings
Fuel is moved automatically to counter the large changes in trim as the wings change position. The variable geometry allows the B-1 to operate from relatively short runways.

▲ Loading the bomb
The main weapons for the B-1B are the SRAM nuclear missile and the B28, B61 and B83 free-fall nuclear bombs. Future weapons options include cruise missiles and advanced precision-guided conventional munitions.

FACTS AND FIGURES

➤ The all-white B-1A flew at Palmdale, California, on 23 December 1974.

➤ On 4 September 1984, the first B-1B was rolled out at Rockwell's Palmdale plant.

➤ The B-1B made its first flight on 18 October 1984, 15 years after design work began.

➤ One B-1B crashed in trials when the crew overrode the fuel transfer computer and unbalanced the aircraft.

➤ The first B-1Bs were assigned to the 96th Bomb Wing at Dyess AFB, Texas.

➤ The four crew sit in Weber-built ACES II (Advanced Concept Ejection Seats).

PROFILE

Low-level strategic striker

Making a low-level penetration of enemy territory, the B-1B crew flies 'zipped up', shielded from thermonuclear flash-blindness by blast curtains equipped with PLZT (polarised lead zirconium titanate).

The B-1B incorporates a number of stealth features, and has a radar cross-section one-fourth that of a B-52. This gives the Lancer an excellent chance of penetrating enemy defences and dropping its bombs without being detected.

Pilot and co-pilot sit side-by-side in a cockpit with both digital and analogue instruments. The B-1B is flown like a fighter, using a stick and rudder pedals.

Crew members 3 and 4, known as the OSO and DSO (offensive and defensive systems operators), sit side-by-side behind the pilots. They have small windows but cannot see a great deal outside the aircraft.

The B-1 entered service primarily as a carrier of free-fall nuclear bombs, with a maximum

load of 24 B61 devices. With minor modifications it can carry a heavy load of cruise missiles, and as the ageing B-52 fleet is retired the huge swing-wing bomber will probably become a cruise missile carrier.

Left: The evolution of the B-1B has not been easy. There have been many problems bringing into service such an advanced aircraft, especially involving the defensive ECM (electronic countermeasures) system and the engines.

Below: The B-1's origins date from the 1960s, when it was realised that Soviet air defences would imperil any high-flying aircraft, even the planned Mach 3-capable B-70 Valkyrie. But switching to low level presented designers with a whole new set of problems.

B-1B Lancer

Type: four-crew strategic bomber

Powerplant: four 133.57-kN (29,964-lb.-thrust) General Electric F101-GE-102 turbofans

Maximum operational speed: Mach 0.99 or 1207 km/h (748 m.p.h.), although the aircraft can reach Mach 1.2

Range: 11,675 km (7,239 mi.)

Service ceiling: more than 15,000 m (49,200 ft.)

Weights: empty 87,090 kg (191,598 lb.); loaded 216,368 kg (476,010 lb.)

Armament: eight cruise missiles or 12 B28 nuclear bombs, or 24 B61/B83 nuclear bombs; theoretical maximum conventional weapons load of 60,782 kg (133,720 lb.)

Dimensions:
span (unswept)	41.66 m	(137 ft.)
span (swept)	23.84 m	(78 ft.)
length	47.80 m	(157 ft.)
height	10.24 m	(34 ft.)
wing area	181.10 m²	(1,949 sq. ft.)

B-1B LANCER

The 95-strong B-1B force is operated by the US Air Force's Air Combat Command. This aircraft is assigned to the 28th Bomb Wing at Ellsworth AFB.

An advanced terrain-following radar system enables the huge bomber to make blind low-level attacks.

The wing has seven-segment leading-edge flaps and six-segment trailing-edge flaps. There are no ailerons, and roll control is effected by spoilers.

The engine intakes have been designed to shield the engine compressor fans from hostile radar beams. Since the compressor would otherwise give a strong radar return, this feature automatically reduces the bomber's signature.

All USAF strategic aircraft now carry low-visibility markings, with black lettering and reduced-size coloured unit emblems.

The original B-1A had an ejection capsule like the F-111, but the B-1B has separate crew compartments and individual ejection seats for the pilots and systems operators.

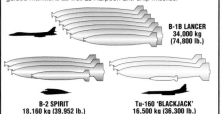

The B-1B has a pair of small composite vanes under the cockpit. These provide yaw and pitch damping, smoothing the ride at low level.

The fuselage structure is mainly aluminium and titanium alloy, with some composite glass fibre.

There are three internal weapon bays, two forward of the wing and one aft, covered by a large hydraulic-powered door. The bay can house the Common Strategic Rotary Launcher (CSRL) also used in the B-2 and B-52.

COMBAT DATA

CONVENTIONAL WEAPONS LOAD

Although the B-1B can carry up to 60 tonnes of conventional weaponry in its three bomb-bays and on 12 underwing weapons stations, operationally it will probably be limited to 85 Mk 82 227-kg general-purpose bombs or 20 AGM-86C conventionally-armed air-launched cruise missiles. As the B-52 force is retired, Lancers will acquire the ability to deliver a variety of precision-guided munitions as well as Harpoon anti-ship missiles.

B-1B LANCER
34,000 kg
(74,800 lb.)

B-2 SPIRIT
18,160 kg (39,952 lb.)

Tu-160 'BLACKJACK'
16,500 kg (36,300 lb.)

B-1 nuclear strike

STAND-OFF ATTACK: B-1s were designed to be armed with free-fall bombs, which could be 'tossed' several kilometres, or with SRAM nuclear missiles, with ranges of 50 km (30 mi.) at low level or more than 200 km (125 mi.) at altitude.

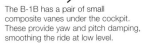

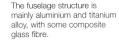

HIGH-LEVEL STRIKE: The original attack profile envisaged for the B-1A called for the aircraft to attack at high speed and from high level. But surface-to-air missiles would have made this suicidal long before the first metal was cut on the prototype.

LOW-LEVEL PENETRATION: The B-1's swing wings meant that it was a superb performer at low level, and it entered service as a low-level penetration bomber.

LAUNCH FROM SAFETY: The advent of the air-launched cruise missile meant that nuclear bombers could attack from ranges of 2000 km (1,240 mi) or more and still hit targets with pinpoint accuracy.

ROCKWELL

OV-10 BRONCO

● Forward air control ● Vietnam veteran ● Counter-insurgency

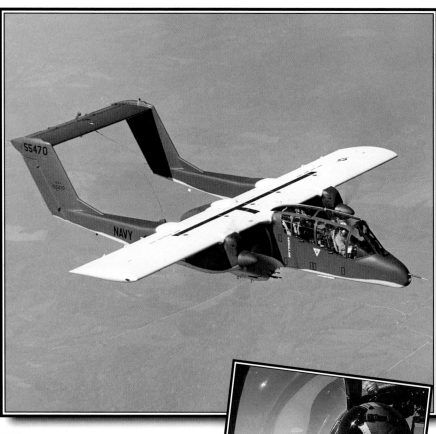

▲ Forward
air control is a demanding
mission, in which pilots must call in strikes while
they are exposed to gunfire. The excellent view
from the Bronco is appreciated by FAC officers.

Rockwell's OV-10 Bronco was a product from early lessons learned in the Vietnam War. Designed as a COIN (counter-insurgency) aircraft, it evolved into an armed, agile forward air control (FAC) machine directing fighter-bombers to their targets. The Bronco began as a US Air Force warplane, but performed its final service in the Persian Gulf War, where the US Marine Corps used it over the battlefield to great effect.

ROCKWELL OV-10 BRONCO

▲ Night striker
Marine Corps OV-10Ds have been updated for the night observation role. They are armed with the M197 20-mm cannon, which is aimed by an AAS-37 infra-red tracker and laser designator pod.

◄ Setting off
Despite its age, the Bronco was popular with crews, who enjoyed the excitement of low flying in a simple aircraft.

▲ USAF retirement
Repeatedly declared obsolete, the OV-10 was finally retired from the USAF's inventory. It has been replaced by the Fairchild OA-10.

Rocket launcher ▶
Standard armament for the FAC mission in Vietnam was the rocket pod, usually containing phosphorus markers.

▼ Strike pair
Armed with powerful fuel-air explosive bombs and machine-guns, the Bronco has a potent tactical strike capability.

▲ Marine favourite
The Bronco was favoured by the Marines, who see close support as a key mission. They also used the type for clandestine special forces insertions.

FACTS AND FIGURES

➤ Eleven companies participated in the early 1960s FAC aircraft competition.

➤ The Bronco prototype first flew on 16 July 1965 at Columbus, Ohio.

➤ The Marine Corps and USAF took delivery of their first Broncos on the same day, 23 February 1968.

➤ In Vietnam, the US Navy briefly operated a light-attack squadron, the 'Black Ponies', equipped with 18 armed Broncos.

➤ Two OV-10s were shot down during Operation Desert Storm.

➤ A Bronco was shot down in Venezuela in November 1992 during a coup attempt.

PROFILE

Tree-top flying on the front line

After almost two decades of soldiering, seeing combat from Vietnam to the Persian Gulf, the familiar, twin-boomed shape of the OV-10 Bronco is no longer seen in military colours – except, possibly, in Venezuela, where a few may still be in service. Nowadays, you can see Broncos in Montana working with the US Forest Service, or in Virginia flying law enforcement missions.

The OV-10 was ordered in 1964 and reached Vietnam in 1969. Bronco variants served in Germany (which used a turbojet-boosted model for target towing), Indonesia, Morocco and Venezuela. The most advanced version was the Marine Corps OV-10D-Plus, which incorporated night observation capability and forward-looking infra-red sensors and was employed on covert special forces insertion missions

as well as forward air control.

By the 1990s, many in the Corps were arguing that the OV-10 was too slow to survive in modern combat, when it might fall victim to shoulder-mounted heat-seeking missiles, but there was strong protest within Marine ranks when in 1993 the decision was made to retire the Bronco.

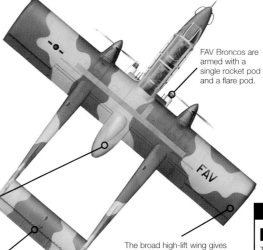

The OV-10 was the subject of much debate, and the future of forward air control missions by fixed-wing aircraft is still contested.

FAV Broncos are armed with a single rocket pod and a flare pod.

OV-10D Bronco

Type: two-seat forward air control aircraft

Powerplant: two Garrett 533-kW (715-hp.) T76-G-420/421 turboprops

Maximum speed: 452 km/h (280 m.p.h.)

Range: 2300 km (1,426 mi.)

Service ceiling: 7315 m (24,000 ft.)

Weights: empty 3161 kg (6,954 lb.); loaded 6552 kg (14,414 lb.)

Armament: one or two GPU-2/A lightweight gun pods containing an M197 Gatling gun coupled to a single-ended ammunition feed system with 300 rounds; high-explosive air-to-surface rocket pods

Dimensions:
span	12.67 m (40 ft.)
length	13.41 m (42 ft.)
height	4.62 m (15 ft.)
wing area	27.03 m² (291 sq. ft.)

Uprated engines with infra-red suppressing exhaust ducts were fitted to the OV-10D in an attempt to reduce vulnerability to shoulder-launched heat-seeking surface-to-air missiles.

The Bronco normally operates with a two-man crew, sitting in tandem.

The tailplane is a fixed-incidence unit with an inset elevator, providing excellent control at low speeds.

The broad high-lift wing gives the Bronco good low-speed handling and a short take-off capability. It can fly slowly enough to escort helicopters.

The long bulged canopy and short nose allows an excellent view of the target area. Both crew members have ejection seats.

Venezuelan Broncos are painted in a jungle colour scheme similar to US aircraft during the Vietnam War. The FAV operates in the surveillance role near the Colombian border.

The central fuselage pod can accommodate two stretchers and a medical attendant, or five paratroopers.

OV-10A BRONCO

The OV-10s of the Fuerza Aerea Venezuela (FAV) serve with two squadrons, the 'Geronimos' of 151 Escuadron and 'Zorros' of 152 Escuadron.

A 568-litre (150-gal.) drop-tank can be carried, in addition to the 976 litres (250 gal.) of internal fuel.

M60 machine-guns are mounted in pairs in each sponson.

The undercarriage is designed to permit operation from tactical airstrips just behind the front line.

COMBAT DATA

MAXIMUM SPEED

The Bronco and the US Army Mohawk were designed as military aircraft. Both served extensively in Vietnam, where they had a considerable performance advantage over the Cessna O-2, a twin-engined 'push-pull' light plane that was minimally adapted from the commercial Cessna Model 337 Skymaster.

OV-10D BRONCO 452 km/h (280 m.p.h.)

OV-1 MOHAWK 496 km/h (308 m.p.h.)

O-2 320 km/h (200 m.p.h.)

RANGE

All three of the observation aircraft were used to support US and South Vietnamese ground troops. They were deployed to American bases all over Southeast Asia, and the excellent range each displayed meant that they could provide overhead observation wherever US troops were in action.

O-2 1700 km (1,054 mi.)

OV-10D BRONCO 2300 km (1,426 mi.)

OV-1 MOHAWK 2000 km (1,240 mi.)

ENDURANCE

The ability to stay in the air for long periods is a definite asset in a forward air control machine. Directing support missions for units cut off on mountain tops or in isolated fire bases, or co-ordinating the rescue of pilots shot down in enemy territory could call for a FAC to stay in the air for several hours.

OV-10D BRONCO — 7 hours 40 minutes

OV-1 MOHAWK — 6 hours 30 minutes

O-2 — 6 hours

Forward observation in action

■ **UNDER FIRE:** Ground troops are advancing on a suspected enemy position when they come under artillery fire. Taking cover, they look for the enemy.

■ **CALLING FOR HELP:** The ground troops call the Forward Air Controller. The only information they can give is the general direction of fire. However, modern infantry are often equipped with locating radar, which tracks the shells in flight and makes a fairly accurate estimate of the position of the enemy battery.

■ **LOCATING THE ENEMY:** High above, an observer in an OV-10 follows the vector of the incoming shells, eventually spotting the enemy guns about 10 km away.

■ **GROUND ATTACK:** The observer calls in patrolling F/A-18 Hornets, which destroy the enemy artillery battery with a salvo of high-explosive air-to-ground rockets.

SAAB
105

- Saab private venture ● Trainer/ground attack ● Austrian air defence

▲ An entire family of highly successful light combat aircraft has evolved from the Saab private-venture trainer/business jet design.

Designed as a trainer and light attack aircraft for the Swedish air force, the Saab 105 has also been produced as an air defence fighter which is able to carry Sidewinder missiles. Other variants include a specialised reconnaissance aircraft and a four-seat liaison machine. After more than three decades of service, the Saab 105 is currently undergoing a major upgrade and the type looks set to serve well into the 21st century.

SAAB 105

Nose modifications ▶
In addition to its highly modified camera nose, the Sk 60C retains an attack capability.

◀ Initial variant
All 150 Sk 60As ordered by the Swedish air force had been delivered by 1968. These aircraft have formed the basis of all subsequent variants. In 1997 about 140 remained in service.

Dispersed attacker ▶
Sk 60Cs taxi at a dispersed airfield site in northern Sweden. The lead aircraft is armed with a dozen 135-mm rockets.

◀ Defending Austria
Saab 105OEs were Austria's sole air defence assets until delivery of Saab Drakens in 1987.

Offensive export ▶
Saab developed the 105XT as a more powerful attack variant for export. This aircraft is firing rockets.

FACTS AND FIGURES

- ➤ Saab designed the 105 as a replacement for the Vampire and the various piston-engined trainers of the Swedish air force.

- ➤ Karl-Erik Fernberg piloted the 105's first flight on 1 July 1963.

- ➤ By the summer of 1998 the 115th, and final, Sk 60 will have been re-engined.

- ➤ Most Sk 60 modifications have been carried out by the Swedish government's maintenance organisations.

- ➤ The first students began training on the Sk 60 on 17 July 1967.

- ➤ Sk 60B/C aircraft can carry 30-mm ADEN cannon pods.

PROFILE

Saab's most versatile product

Left: A huge Perspex canopy provides excellent visibility. Of value in the training role, this feature is also useful to the crew of the armed Sk 60C, seen here fitted with two ADEN gunpods.

F ive variants of the Saab 105 are in service with the Swedish air force. The Sk 60A was the original trainer, the Sk 60B added a ground attack capability and the Sk 60C is equipped with a nose-mounted reconnaissance camera and an infra-red search unit. A further trainer variant is the Sk 60D, with commercial avionics, which is used for the airline training of reserve officers. The ejection seats have been removed and two extra seats are installed in the rear cockpit. The Sk 60E also has four seats but is used as a liaison aircraft.

Forty of the 105XT model, with J85 turbojets, additional fuel capacity, strengthened wings and improved avionics, were built for Austria. Designated Saab 105OE in Austrian service, they can carry Sidewinder air-to-air missiles for air defence or camera pods for reconnaissance.

Most of the Swedish air force's remaining 105s are being modernised to extend their service lives to at least 2010.

In the late 1980s the SK 60s were fitted with new wings and ejection seats. Structural modifications also enabled them to carry out higher-g manoeuvres.

An upgrade programme started in 1995 to replace the original engines with 8.45-kN (1,900-lb.-thrust) Williams-Rolls FJ44 turbofans. The new powerplant will make the aircraft quieter and easier to maintain, as well as improving performance.

Left: This brightly coloured demonstrator shows off the 105's agility. Sweden's 'Team 60' aerobatic team use the Sk 60 as their display aircraft.

Sk 60B

Type: trainer and light attack aircraft

Powerplant: two 7.29-kN (1,640-lb.-thrust) Turboméca Aubisque turbofans

Maximum speed: 765 km/h (474 m.p.h.) at 6000 m (19,700 ft.)

Climb rate: 1050 m/min (3,445 f.p.m.)

Service range: 1400 km (868 mi.)

Service ceiling: 12,000 m (39,350 ft.)

Weights: empty 2510 kg (5,522 lb.); maximum take-off 4500 kg (9,900 lb.)

Armament: up to 700 kg (1,540 lb.) of bombs, rockets and air-to-air or air-to-ground missiles on six underwing hardpoints

Dimensions:
span	9.50 m (31 ft. 2 in.)
length	10.50 m (35 ft. 5 in.)
height	2.70 m (8 ft. 10 in.)
wing area	16.30 m² (175 sq. ft.)

Sk 60C

Combining the attack role of the Sk 60B with a useful tactical reconnaissance capability, the Sk 60C has an extended nose which houses a Fairchild KB-18 panoramic camera and its associated clear windows. The fairing beneath the nose houses an infra-red search unit.

Sk 60s serve with four squadrons of F5 and with 5 divisionen of F16 of the Swedish air force. All aircraft wear F5 unit identification, regardless of where they are based, since they are held in a central maintenance pool.

Saab designed the ejection seats of the 105. In four-seat configurations, these may be replaced by upholstered seats or more basic units, suitable for use with parachute and rescue packs.

Upwards- and downwards-hinging doors cover the engine compartment. With both sets of doors open, the majority of the engine's primary systems are revealed, allowing easy maintenance from ground level.

The large number on the tail identifies individual aircraft, while the nose number identifies the unit. Dayglo patches on the wing improve conspicuity.

Saab originally planned a four-seat business jet version of the 105. Although this never materialised, as a consequence the cockpit is very spacious.

Twin, hydraulically-actuated airbrakes are mounted behind the main landing gear doors. One is fitted on either side of the lower fuselage.

Early test flights showed that extensive redesign of the engine intakes and exhausts was necessary. To accommodate these major changes, the underside of the wingroot had to be altered. In addition, a great deal of work was necessary to rectify early engine reliability problems.

COMBAT DATA

THRUST

The Sk 60B appears to lack power when compared to the other two widely used light attack/trainer aircraft. The Saab machine's performance is, however, adequate and it offers the increased reliability and safety of twin-engined operations.

14.58 kN (3,280 lb. thrust) Sk 60B	15.17 kN (3,413 lb. thrust) STRIKEMASTER Mk 88	16.87 kN (3,795 lb. thrust) L-39 ALBATROSS

ORDNANCE

The Saab 105 is a very lightweight aircraft and is therefore restricted to a comparatively light weapon load. Saab has done its utmost to maximise the 105's potential in the attack role, however, by providing compatibility with a wide range of stores, including guided missiles.

Sk 60B 700 kg (1,540 lb.)

STRIKEMASTER Mk 88 1361 kg (2,994 lb.)

L-39 ALBATROSS 1000 kg (2,200 lb.)

CLIMB RATE

In a comparison of climb rates the Sk 60B cannot compete with the Strikemaster or Aero L-39. The ongoing Aubisque engine replacement programme will provide an improvement in performance, however, and neither of the other aircraft is as cost-effective as the Sk 60B.

STRIKEMASTER Mk 88 1600 m/min (5,248 f.p.m.)

L-39 ALBATROSS 1260 m/min (4,133 f.p.m.)

Sk 60B 1050 m/min (3,445 f.p.m.)

Side-by-side two-seat training jets

■ **CANADAIR CL-41 TUTOR:** Another private venture design which resulted in considerable sales, the Tutor was adopted by the Canadian forces and was also exported to Malaysia.

■ **CESSNA T-37:** Several hundred T-37s were delivered to the USAF from 1957. A number of aircraft were exported, including 34 to Chile.

■ **BAC (HUNTING) JET PROVOST:** Having adapted its piston-engined Provost design to turbojet power, Hunting was able to supply the RAF with its standard primary jet trainer.

SAAB

J 35J DRAKEN

● Upgraded version ● Highway fighter ● Double-delta

▲ Sweden's neutral situation has ensured that all its defence requirements are met without outside assistance. Here a pilot boards his aircraft on an air defence mission.

Delays to the original schedule for delivery of the Draken's replacement, the JAS 39 Gripen, led the Swedish air force to embark on an upgrade programme to keep two squadrons of J 35s operational until the Gripen was introduced. The aircraft selected were the best examples of the final air defence variant, the J 35F. With improved avionics and two additional wing pylons, the resulting J 35J served with the air force's 10 Wing alongside the Viggen.

SAAB J 35J DRAKEN

'Dragon trainer' ▶
A development of the J 35A was the Sk 35C pilot trainer; the instructor sits in the rear.

▼ **Landing roll-out**
Reduction of the landing run is accomplished with a drag 'chute and fuselage airbrakes.

◀ **Air-to-air armament**
The large wing area allows for a varied stores option, which could include Sweden's own AIM-9 Sidewinder derivative and, for longer range combat, the indigenous Rb 27 missile.

▼ **Draken overhaul**
As the Swedish aircraft were fitted with upgraded avionics an overall grey scheme was applied reflecting current camouflage trends.

▲ **Border patrol**
Austria received 24 aircraft during 1985. The war in former Yugoslavia ensured that they saw constant use patrolling Austria's border against any violations.

FACTS AND FIGURES

➤ Modifications to the J 35J consist of two additional pylons under the intake ducts as well as improved avionics.

➤ The undercarriage of the J 35J is narrow enough to operate from Swedish roads.

➤ The pilot of the Draken is seated in a reclined ejection seat as in the F-16.

➤ Despite a cramped cockpit with old technology the Draken was a much sought after posting within the air force.

➤ The Austrian Air Force is the only current operator of Drakens.

➤ A few early variants of the Draken still fly in Sweden for trials work.

PROFILE

The Nordic Dragon

Right: The Austrian air force chose the Draken instead of surplus Lightnings from the Saudi Arabian air force.

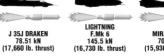

At least 64 J 35Fs were selected for the J 35J upgrade. This involved splitting the airframe in two. The front section was returned to Saab for modification while the rear part of the airframe was overhauled by FFV.

Externally, the most obvious difference is the extra missile pylon installed under each of the inboard wing sections. These can be used for short-range Sidewinder air-to-air missiles, allowing the original two wing and two fuselage pylons to be used for up to four fuel tanks, or a combination of fuel tanks and two Falcon air-to-air missiles.

Other important changes involved improvements to the aircraft's sensors and systems. New wiring was installed, the radar and infra-red tracker were modernised, and some additional cockpit instruments were also installed. New transponders and IFF systems were fitted. Originally given the designation J 35F-Ny (Ny from the Swedish for modified), the reworked aircraft were subsequently given the new 'J' suffix. They were returned to service over a 55-month period starting in March 1987. During subsequent major overhauls, they were painted in a new two-tone

grey colour scheme similar to that worn by many of the Swedish air force's Viggens.

The 'double-delta' design of the Draken wing allows good control at low speed. Lower speed improves the safety margin when landing at forward operational locations.

A single ADEN 30-mm cannon is positioned in the starboard wing root where it is easily accessible to ground crews. Gun gas is removed from the intakes by the natural airflow across the airframe.

Operating away from conventional airfields requires the Draken to have a small landing run. This is accomplished by the addition of a drag parachute at the base of the rudder and upper and lower fuselage-mounted airbrakes.

J 35J DRAKEN

This J 35J wears the colourful markings applied to the F10 display pilot's aircraft. The creature displayed on the wings represents a dragon. Flying with the last Draken unit the design has proved a huge success.

Despite the age of the Draken its cockpit was a sought-after position for Swedish fighter pilots, who were enthralled by the aircraft's performance, agility and high pilot workload. The bulged canopy gives adequate vision except to the rear.

The J 35J is fitted with a modified S71N Infra-Red Search and Track set under the nose. It has a range of about 16 miles under normal conditions which makes it a useful emission-free supplement to the radar.

The narrow tracked undercarriage is designed to allow easy operation from highway strips.

J 35J Draken

Type: single-seat interceptor

Powerplant: one 78.51-kN (17,660-lb.-thrust) Volvo Flygmotor RM6C afterburning turbojet

Maximum speed: over 2126 km/h (1,138 m.p.h.) at 10,975 m (36,000 ft.)

Initial climb rate: 10,500 m/min (34,500 f.p.m.)

Range: 720 km (446 mi.) combat radius with two drop tanks and two 454-kg (1.000-lb.) bombs

Service ceiling: 19,995 m (65,600 ft.)

Weights: empty 8250 kg (18,150 lb.), maximum take-off 15,000 kg (33,000 lb.)

Armament: one 30-mm cannon plus two Sidewinder and two Falcon air-to-air missiles

Dimensions:		
	span	9.40 m (30 ft. 9 in.)
	length	15.35 m (50 ft. 4 in.)
	height	3.89 m (12 ft. 9 in.)
	wing area	49.20 m² (529 sq. ft.)

COMBAT DATA

THRUST

The use of a licence-built Rolls-Royce engine fitted with a Swedish-designed afterburner allowed an exceptional thrust capability, although it didn't compare with the British twin-engined Lightning. Thrust is small compared with more modern designs.

J 35J DRAKEN 78.51 kN (17,660 lb. thrust)	LIGHTNING F.Mk 6 145.5 kN (16,730 lb. thrust)	MIRAGE 50M 70.82 kN (15,930 lb. thrust)

RANGE

The Flygvapen has always placed emphasis on the range of its combat aircraft, trusted with defending the skies against all intruders over inhospitable terrain. The J35s ferry range was excellent. When compared with France's Mirage or the Lightning, the J35 excelled.

J 35J DRAKEN 2890 km (1,796 mi.)
LIGHTNING F.Mk 6 1200 km (746 mi.)
MIRAGE 50M 1315 km (817 mi.)

CEILING

At high altitude the Draken was found to be a stable platform because of the 'cranked delta' wing design. Changes within the 'J' model brought a slight reduction in ceiling. Compared with contemporary aircraft the Draken design has proved extremely reliable.

J 35J DRAKEN 19,995 m (65,600 ft.)
LIGHTNING F.Mk 6 16,500 m (54,100 ft.)
MIRAGE 50M 18,000 m (59,000 ft.)

Draken developments

■ **J 35B DRAKEN:** To promote the Swedish military air service a formation team of four Drakens called the 'Acro Deltas' were fitted with smoke oil tanks and lines for formation aerobatics.

■ **J 35F DRAKEN:** Known as the F 35, the Draken's primary role in Danish service was ground attack. Some airframes were fitted with a camera nose for day photo-reconnaissance missions.

■ **J 35XS DRAKEN:** Finland modified its Drakens to allow installation of two cannon, and initial variants lacked the capability to carry the Falcon missile.

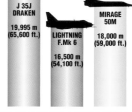

SAAB

TP 100 & 340 AEW&C

● Regional airliner ● Airborne early warning ● VIP transport

▲ Like its
NATO equivalents, Sweden's
AEW&C aircraft have armed guards placed
around the aircraft when making
public appearances.

With its strong stance of neutrality Sweden has found its airspace violated in the past by both NATO and Russian aircraft. Reluctant to purchase a foreign airborne early warning and control design, Saab undertook the conversion of a twin-turboprop regional airliner. The addition of numerous blisters and a roof-mounted fairing have seen the Saab 340 transformed into a highly capable aircraft for defending Sweden's airspace.

SAAB TP 100 & 340 AEW&C

◀ Eye on the future
Swedish defence officials had long been interested in providing their armed forces with a reliable command and control platform. The Saab 340 proved to be the ideal aircraft for the role.

◀ Advanced avionics
Using their Ericsson Erieye side-looking radar, operators can detect targets up to 300 km (200 mi.) away. The operators are also able to send information to orbiting friendly fighters on interception duty.

▼ Radar research
With its complete radar fit installed, the Saab 340 AEW&C entered operational service with Sweden's Flygvapen in early 1995.

Fabulous flight deck ▶
Developed from a regional transport airliner, the flight deck of the Saab 340 is equipped with multi-function displays and advanced flight controls for the pilots. This considerably reduces crew fatigue on long-standing patrols.

Executive model ▶
Designated the Tp 100, one example is operated from Stockholm-Tullinge as part of Sweden's Royal Flight. The aircraft wears a smart patriotic colour scheme and is suitably equipped internally. The aircraft is often used as a transport for government ministers attending meetings across Europe.

FACTS AND FIGURES

➤ The Saab 340 was originally developed in partnership with the American Fairchild aviation company.

➤ At present, Sweden is the only customer for the AEW&C variant.

➤ In November 1985 Fairchild dropped out of the development of the aircraft.

➤ The specialised radar-equipped Saab 340 is dubbed the 340 AEW&C, as it has a command and control role.

➤ Sweden first flew the AEW&C variant on 17 January 1994.

➤ Possible future customers for the radar variant include Australia.

PROFILE

Sweden's airborne watcher

Ever conscious of airborne trespass, Sweden regularly dispatched interceptors to shepherd away inquisitive intruders. Located within the heart of the Cold War arena, Swedish airspace was regularly violated by NATO and Warsaw Pact aircraft.

Responding to these never-ceasing intrusions, Sweden developed an air force that was equipped with fighters that could rise from a standard highway to intercept the high flying intruders 24 hours a day, 365 days a year. A key addition to their command

network was an airborne command and control aircraft as insurance for the future.

Initially working in partnership with Fairchild of America, Saab had already developed a highly capable turboprop airliner. After the withdrawal of American assistance, the aircraft was renamed the Saab 340. Quick to see the future potential in the design, the Flygvapen became the first military customer for the aircraft.

Equipped with an Ericsson Erieye side-looking airborne

radar (SLAR) in a canoe fairing above the fuselage, the Saab 340 AEW&C as it is now known, has become a valuable asset within Sweden's defence strategy.

The aircraft completed its flight testing phase in early 1995, amd five more examples were delivered to the Swedish air force.

Overseas interest in the 340 AEW&C has been shown from Australia although firm orders have yet to be received.

Left: Proving the concept of the sideways-looking airborne radar was the responsibility of Fairchild Merlin. The aircraft wore a complex splinter-camouflage during its testing phase.

Right: Sweden chose to use an Ericsson Erieye side-looking radar mounted in a canoe fairing above the aircraft. This allowed the maximum amount of coverage without being obstructed by the fuselage.

340B

Type: twin-engined VIP transport/airborne command and control aircraft

Powerplant: two 1394-kW (1,870-hp.) General Electric CT7-9B turboprops

Maximum cruising speed: 522 km/h (324 m.p.h.)

Initial climb rate: 610 m/min (2,000 f.p.m.)

Range: 1807 km (1,120 mi.)

Service ceiling: 7620 m (25,000 ft.)

Weights: operational empty 8036 kg (17,679 lb.); maximum take-off 13,063 kg (28,739 lb.)

Accommodation: two pilots and 35 systems operators

Dimensions:
span	21.44 m	(70 ft. 4 in.)
length	19.73 m	(64 ft. 9 in.)
height	6.87 m	(22 ft. 5 in.)
wing area	41.81 m²	(450 sq. ft.)

340 AEW&C

Equipped with a fuselage-mounted SLAR, the Saab 340 AEW&C is proving to be a highly capable command and control platform. At present the prototype remains on operational test duties.

The well equipped flight deck provides accommodation for two pilots and one observer. Positioned on the roof of the cockpit is an escape hatch.

By positioning the radar in a canoe fairing above the fuselage, unrestricted coverage can be achieved. During testing, the detection range of the Ericsson Erieye radar has been measured at over 300 km (200 mi.) against small airborne targets.

Since it has proved to be highly successful the Swedish air force has placed an order for five examples of the Saab 340 AEW&C. They will operate alongside Saab Viggens and Gripens.

005

A door positioned on the forward fuselage allows access to the flight deck. This is fitted with a small set of integral steps.

The additional weight of the radar equipment did not result in additional strengthening being required for the airframe of the Saab 340.

To compensate for the aerodynamic drag caused by the canoe fairing, additional finlets were installed at the rear of the fuselage to ease handling.

SWEDISH AIR FORCE

LOW-COST WATCHERS

UNITED STATES: The US Coast Guard operates a fleet of aircraft under the designation of HU-25 Guardians (pictured below). The aircraft, derived from the French Dassault Falcon 20, have been progressively upgraded to include an external SLAR mounted on the fuselage. Civilian roles for the Guardian are concerned with drug-interdiction and pollution monitoring.

BRAZIL: Unable to afford the expense of large, sophisticated, radar control aircraft, many countries have opted for a low-cost alternative. Initially marketed as a regional civil airliner the EMB-111 Bandeirante (below), now sports a large nose-mounted radar and under-wing hardpoints. With the addition of wingtip fuel tanks, mission endurance is increased to nine hours.

Sweden's airborne warriors

■ JAS 39 GRIPEN: Defending Sweden's neutrality, the Gripen represents the new cutting edge within the Flygvapen.

■ J 35 DRAKEN: First flying in 1955, the unique wing design of the Draken gave the aircraft an incredible performance.

■ SK 60: Used for both training and attack roles, the Saab 105, as it is more widely known, is also operated by Austria.

■ JA 37 VIGGEN: The backbone of Sweden's air defence system is the Viggen which has been produced in a host of variants.

SAAB

AJ/AJS 37 VIGGEN

● Double-delta canard wing ● Multi-role strike fighter

I t has been flying for nearly three decades, but the Saab 37 Viggen remains one of the most striking combat aircraft in the world. It is not just a fighter, it is a combat system built around one of the first of the modern 'canard', or tail-first, designs. As an interceptor, a ground attacker, a maritime striker, a reconnaissance platform or a trainer, the Viggen is an amazing warplane which upholds Sweden's tradition of independent, trailblazing aviation design.

▲ The first ground-attack Viggen unit converted to the type at Satenas in 1971. The fighter variant entered service at Norrköping in 1978, replacing the Draken.

PHOTO FILE

SAAB **AJ/AJS 37 VIGGEN**

▼ **Unique appearance**
The Viggen was the first modern fighter to be built with the now common 'canard' configuration, with control fins at the front of the airframe, pre-dating today's superfighters by two decades.

▲ **Low-level strike**
Armed for the low-level strike role, these AJ 37s are equipped with free-fall bombs, BOZ self-protection jamming pods and chaff and flare dispensers.

▲ **Chunky nose**
The classic profile of the Viggen gives an impression of strength and toughness. The cockpit area can withstand high-speed birdstrikes.

▲ **Ship killer**
The Rb 04 missile was once the main weapon of the AJS 37 for anti-ship attacks. It is now obsolete and has been replaced by the highly lethal Rb 15 missile.

Short take-off ▶
The Viggen has excellent short take-off capability, which makes the type ideal for operating from temporary bases on motorways.

▲ **Clean cockpit**
The AJ 37 cockpit is a very well-equipped design, with Doppler navigation, radar warning, ECM and head-up display systems.

FACTS AND FIGURES

➤ An uneventful flight test programme followed the Viggen's first flight on 8 February 1967.

➤ The Viggen carries about 600 kg of electronics gear in 50 'black boxes'.

➤ The Viggen fleet was grounded during 1981 due to an engine fatigue problem.

➤ The SF 37 single-seat reconnaissance version, a replacement for the Draken, first flew on 21 May 1973.

➤ The prototype Viggen two-seat trainer took to the sky on 2 July 1970.

➤ Australia, Austria, Britain, India and Norway all considered Viggen purchases.

PROFILE

The thunderbolt of Thor

Viggen is a thunderbolt in Nordic mythology, the hammer of the god Thor. Viggen the aircraft is, like Thor's hammer, a lethal weapon. Its primary purpose is to make an attack on Sweden so costly that any aggressor will bypass this customarily neutral nation.

The Viggen first appeared as the AJ 37 ground-attack aircraft in 1967. From the start its appearance was unusual, but the revolutionary wing form had a serious purpose. The

extra lift from the forward-mounted canard wings gives the Viggen fine short-field performance, allowing the powerful double delta to operate from unprepared surfaces, including roadways. This capability allows the Viggen force to be dispersed and hidden in time of war.

The Viggen incorporated many advanced features which have now become standard, including a head-up display and a navigation/attack computer for

accurate delivery of ordnance. One hundred and nine AJ 37s were built out of a total Viggen production run of 330. All remaining AJ 37s have been upgraded to AJS 37 standard, incorporating new avionics and weapons.

Saab knew that the Viggen had to be affordable, as effective as any potential opposition and built to cope with Swedish weather. It also needed to be simple to maintain, as all Flygvapen ground crew are conscripts.

AJ 37 Viggen

Type: single-seat all-weather attack aircraft

Powerplant: one 115.72-kN (25,960-lb.-thrust) Volvo Flygmotor RM8A turbojet

Maximum speed: Mach 2 or 2124 km/h (1,317 m.p.h.)

Combat radius: more than 1000 km (600 mi.)

Service ceiling: 18,300 m (60,000 ft.)

Weights: empty 11,800 kg (25,960 lb.); loaded 20,500 kg (45,100 lb.)

Armament: 6000 kg (13,200 lb.) of ordnance including bombs, air-to-surface or anti-ship missiles, air-to-air missiles, Bofors rocket pods or 30-mm ADEN gun pods

Dimensions:
span	10.60 m	(35 ft.)
length	16.30 m	(53 ft.)
height	5.80 m	(19 ft.)
wing area	46 m²	(495 sq. ft.)

AJ 37 VIGGEN

F7 wing, consisting of three Attackflygdivisions of AJ 37 Viggens, was the first to receive the type in 1972. The wing formerly included a JA 37 squadron.

The reconnaissance SF 37 has a special camera-equipped nose section.

The intakes are of the fixed type, as all-out speed is not so important in the ground-attack role.

The distinctive 'splinter' camouflage is applied to most Viggen variants, though the JA 37 fighters are now painted grey.

Unlike the fighter variant, the AJ 37 has no fixed gun. It can carry pod-mounted 30-mm ADEN cannon.

Ground-attack Viggens are easily identifiable since they lack the 'kinked' rudder fitted to the air-superiority fighter variant.

The Ericsson PS-37 radar is capable of ground mapping, air-to-ground ranging and ground proximity warning, and even has a limited air-to-air capability.

The canard foreplane is a fixed unit designed to generate lift, notably on take-off. It has its own moving trailing-edge flap.

The Viggen has a tandem mainwheel arrangement to allow operation from rough surfaces. This configuration gives good performance when taxiing in snow.

COMBAT DATA

MAXIMUM SPEED

The Viggen's clean airframe, powerful engine and efficient delta wings make it one of the fastest attack jets currently in service. It is considerably faster than near contemporaries like the Anglo-French Jaguar and the MiG-27, which were designed to perform the same strike role.

AJ 37 VIGGEN	2124 km/h (1,317 m.p.h.)
JAGUAR GR.Mk.1	1700 km/h (1,054 m.p.h.)
MiG-27 'FLOGGER-D'	1880 km/h (1,166 m.p.h.)

TAKE-OFF RUN

The virtue of the Viggen's large canard foreplanes and the extra lift they provide at low speeds is most aptly demonstrated by the Swedish jet's superb short-field performance. Its rivals can also take off in a short distance, but as soon as they carry any sort of warload they need a much longer runway.

AJ 37 VIGGEN 400 m (1,312 ft.)	JAGUAR GR.Mk 1 880 m (2,886 ft.)	MiG-27 'FLOGGER-D' 950 m (6,000 ft.)

Viggen anti-ship strike

TARGET DETECTION: The Viggen's PS-37 radar can detect surface targets from at least 50 km (30 mi.) – more than 100 km (60 mi.) at altitude. Target data is fed to the missile's guidance system before launch.

INERTIAL GUIDANCE: The Rb 04 missile and its successor, the Rb 15, drops to approximately 20 m (60 ft.) above the water and flies by inertial guidance to the general target location.

ACTIVE RADAR: As it approaches the target, the missile activates its onboard radar. Once it has locked on, it drops to sea-skimming level to ensure that it strikes the target's hull.

LAUNCH PHASE   **MID-COURSE PHASE**   **TERMINAL PHASE**

LOW-LEVEL COMBAT RADIUS

Fighting through the thick, resistant air at sea level forces a fighter's fuel consumption up dramatically. Although the Viggen has a ferry range in excess of 2500 km (1,550 mi.), on a strike mission flown entirely at low level its range is cut by at least 60 per cent. If part of the mission is flown at height, the aircraft's combat radius is extended to around 1000 km (600 mi.).

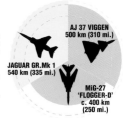

AJ 37 VIGGEN 500 km (310 mi.)

JAGUAR GR.Mk 1 540 km (335 mi.)

MiG-27 'FLOGGER-D' c. 400 km (250 mi.)

SAAB
JAS 39 GRIPEN

● High-tech multi-role lightweight ● Sweden's 21st-century defender

S aab's JAS 39 Gripen is a sensational fighter – one of the best in the world. With its canard layout and delta wing, hi-tech features and ability to operate from short airfields, Sweden's new warplane is also as fast and manoeuvrable as any plane in its class. First flown on 9 December 1988, the Gripen (Griffin) bears comparison with any of the latest generation of advanced fighters built for the 21st century, keeping Saab at the forefront of fighter design.

▲ Saab has long been in the forefront of aviation development, and the Gripen is equipped with the best of everything, including the latest Martin-Baker ejection seats, seen testing here.

PHOTO FILE

SAAB JAS 39 GRIPEN

▲ Reconnaissance
With a centreline camera pod, the Gripen will also carry out low-level reconnaissance missions.

Strike mission ▶
Armed with the Rb 75 and Rb 15 missiles and extra fuel tanks, the Gripen is perfectly equipped for a long-range anti-shipping mission.

▲ Single engine
Unlike most of its competitors in the super-fighter stakes, the Gripen is powered by a single engine. However, its small size and light weight mean that its performance does not suffer by comparison.

▼ Dogfighter
Armed with Sidewinder missiles and a powerful cannon, and not weighed down by underwing fuel tanks, the Gripen is a potent dogfighter.

▲ Pilot's-eye view
The Gripen has a very advanced cockpit, featuring a head-up display and three multi-function screens.

▲ Air defender
Gripens will be armed with four advanced medium-range missiles and two Sidewinders. Equipped with the powerful PS-05 radar they should be able to intercept any bomber currently in service.

FACTS AND FIGURES

➤ Rollout of the first Gripen, on 26 April 1987, marked Saab's 50th anniversary.

➤ Gripens have shown their ability to fly from airfields or roadways as short as 800 m (2,625 ft.) in length.

➤ Gripens will be produced at a rate of 20 to 30 per year until at least the year 2015.

➤ A milestone was reached on 21 April 1993 when Gripens logged their 1,000th test flight.

➤ Sweden has been producing its own fighters since World War II.

➤ The first Gripen prototype was lost in a landing accident on 2 February 1989.

PROFILE

Swedish superfighter for every mission

The sophistication of Sweden's aircraft industry is evident in this advanced, multi-role fighter, which promises as much as any warplane built in America, Europe or Russia. Thirty per cent smaller than an F-16, the Saab JAS 39 Gripen is a bantamweight – but in aerial combat it will be a superstar. The pilot has advanced avionics at his disposal and is pushed through the stratosphere by a Volvo-built version of the tried and tested General Electric F404 powerplant.

Even though the programme has been hampered by two spectacular aircraft losses – from which the same pilot twice

Blasting off from a runway, the Gripen sets off on patrol. Like previous Swedish jet fighters, the Gripen will often operate from remote semi-prepared strips.

ejected successfully – the two-seat JAS 39B will soon join the growing fleet of Gripens.

Gripens have already started augmenting highly capable Viggens in the Swedish air force. In the post-Cold War international climate, the government in Stockholm is hoping for export sales of this superbly performing and very promising lightweight fighter which is available years before the EF 2000 or F-22.

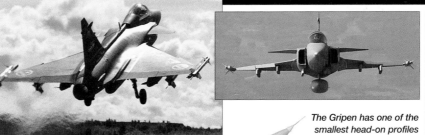

The Gripen has one of the smallest head-on profiles around. This is a useful combat asset, making the aircraft less easy to see or shoot down.

The Gripen has large canard foreplanes, which smooth the airflow over the wings and give enhanced low-speed manoeuvrability. They also act as airbrakes when landing.

The delta-canard configuration gives a good combination of high speed and load-carrying capability. The wing features leading-edge flaps, driven by the computerised flight control system.

JAS 39 Gripen

Type: single-seat high-performance fighter

Powerplant: one 54.0-kN (12,150-lb. thrust) Volvo Flygmotor RM12 turbofan (General Electric F404-GE-400); 80.49 kN (18,110-lb. thrust) with afterburning

Maximum speed: 2126 km/h (1,321 m.p.h.) at 11,000 m (36,000 ft.)

Service ceiling: over 14,000 m (46,000 ft.)

Weights: empty 6622 kg (14,600 lb.); loaded 8300 kg (18,298 lb.)

Armament: one 27-mm Mauser BK27 cannon; two wingtip Rb 74 (AIM-9L Sidewinder) or other air-to-air missiles; underwing air-to-ground or Saab Rb 15F anti-shipping missiles

Dimensions: span 8.00 m (26 ft. 3 in.)
length 14.10 m (46 ft. 3 in.)
height 4.70 m (15 ft. 5 in.)
wing area (est.) 80 m² (267 sq. ft.)

JAS 39A GRIPEN

Number '02' was the first production JAS 39 Gripen to be handed over to the Swedish air force in June 1993, when it flew to its new base at Satenas escorted by Saab Viggens.

The fuselage is approximately 30 per cent composite materials. The structure proved to be far stronger than designers had predicted when it was tested. The Gripen's airframe can withstand 9g manoeuvres.

The view from the Gripen cockpit is superb, and pilots will have a great all-round view in a dogfight.

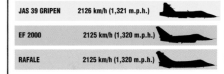

The Ericsson PS-05 is a lightweight multi-mode pulse-Doppler radar designed to perform air search and surface-attack functions.

The Gripen carries a 27-mm Mauser cannon under the port centre fuselage. This weapon is also used by the Tornado.

Power is provided by a single Volvo RM12 turbofan, which is a licence-built General Electric F404. This is the same engine that powers the McDonnell Douglas F/A-18 Hornet.

COMBAT DATA

MAXIMUM SPEED

All the current generation of fighters are supersonic with a similar 'clean' top speed, allowing them to make rapid intercepts of enemy aircraft as far away as possible from the area they are defending. But their speed is more than matched by their agility and handling, especially at subsonic speeds.

JAS 39 GRIPEN	2126 km/h (1,321 m.p.h.)
EF 2000	2125 km/h (1,320 m.p.h.)
RAFALE	2125 km/h (1,320 m.p.h.)

ENGINE POWER

The Gripen is unusual in being powered by a single engine. Both its European rivals are powered by two compact and advanced-design powerplants, delivering a great deal more thrust in total. But they are larger, heavier aircraft, and the Gripen's performance does not suffer by comparison.

JAS 39 GRIPEN	EF 2000	RAFALE
1 x Volvo turbofan delivering 80.49 kN (18,110 lb.) of thrust with afterburning	2 x Eurojet turbofans delivering 180.20 kN (40,545 lb.) of thrust with afterburning	2 x SNECMA turbofans delivering 174.07 kN (39,165 lb.) of thrust with afterburning

BOMBLOAD

The Gripen was designed from the outset as a multi-role aircraft and, although much less powerful than its rivals, it is capable of lifting just as great a warload. It has been cleared to carry anti-ship missiles, guided air-to-surface missiles, bombs, guided bombs, cluster bombs and unguided high-explosive air-to-surface rockets.

JAS 39 GRIPEN	EF 2000	RAFALE
6500 kg (14,330 lb.) of air-to-surface munitions	6500 kg (14,330 lb.) of air-to-surface munitions	6000 kg (13,228 lb.) of air-to-surface munitions

Sweden's tradition of aeronautical excellence

Saab 21R: Based on a wartime fighter with a pusher propeller, the 21R of 1947 was the first jet designed and built in Sweden.

Saab 29: Flown in September 1948, the Tunnan was the first swept-wing fighter to enter large-scale production in Europe.

Saab 32: The Lansen of 1952 was an elegant transonic design, contemporary with and comparable to the very capable Hawker Hunter.

Saab 35: The prototype of the 'double-delta' Draken flew in 1955. It was to become one of the world's first Mach 2-capable fighters.

Saab 37: The multi-role Viggen of 1967 anticipated by a quarter of a century the current trend for canard-winged combat jets.

SEPECAT

JAGUAR GR.MK 1/GR.MK 1B

● Anglo-French single-seat attack aircraft ● Gulf War veteran

One of the early successes of Anglo-French collaboration, the Jaguar fighter-bomber has been a mainstay of the RAF's first-line squadrons over the last three decades. With improved weaponry and avionics the Jaguar has developed into a useful tactical ground-attack and reconnaissance aircraft, despite a modest performance compared to some of its contemporaries.

▲ It was thought that the Jaguar was in the twilight of its career when both French and RAF aircraft were sent to the Gulf to participate in Operation Desert Storm. Since then a new RAF version, the GR.Mk 1B, has entered service equipped with the TIALD imaging and laser pod.

SEPECAT JAGUAR GR.MK 1/GR.MK 1B

B-24 bombload ▶
This GR.Mk 1 carries eight 454-kg (1,000-lb.) bombs, equivalent to the tonnage carried by a wartime B-24 Liberator bomber. A more normal load includes chaff and flare pods, fuel tanks and a pair of infra-red missiles.

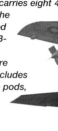

Multi-role aircraft ▶
When originally delivered to the RAF, Jaguars were tasked with nuclear strike, reconnaissance and conventional attack. Only the latter role is still performed.

◀ The 'front office'
This pilot's eye view of a single-seater's cockpit shows that it is fairly typical of a jet fighter-bomber of the 1970s.

▼ T.Mk 2 two-seater
The two-seat conversion trainer version of the GR.Mk 1 features a longer nose with the crew seated in tandem under separate canopies.

▲ Motorway take-off
Demonstrating its ability to operate from dispersed sites, this Jaguar lifts off from a stretch of motorway with a load of cluster bombs.

FACTS AND FIGURES

➤ During the Cold War there were up to five RAF 'Jag' squadrons in Germany, the theoretical 'front line' in a major conflict.

➤ A Jaguar was once accidentally shot down by an RAF Phantom in Germany.

➤ Jaguars in the Gulf were armed with iron bombs, cluster bombs and rockets.

➤ During Operation Desert Storm, 12 RAF Jaguars flew 618 war sorties during January and February 1991.

➤ The home base of the RAF's Jaguars is RAF Coltishall, home to three squadrons.

➤ An RAF Jaguar once survived a high-speed wire strike at an altitude of just 10 m (33 ft.).

The RAF's feline mud-mover

Throwing a fast fighter-bomber through mountains at night, without radar, alone and unaided by a navigator may seem a recipe for disaster, but this is what RAF Jaguar pilots do on a regular basis. They know that the Jaguar, with more than 25 years of service behind it, is a tried and tested weapon that will not let them down.

When it came to a real war situation in the Gulf in 1991, the Jaguar showed that it was able to fly missions as well as many aircraft that are considerably younger.

A Franco/British project, the result of collaboration between the British Aircraft Corporation (now British Aerospace) and Dassault-Breguet, the SEPECAT Jaguar was first flown on 8 September 1968 as a single-seat attack aircraft with limited all-weather capability. It was intended to serve both the Armée de l'Air and the RAF; the French Jaguar A entered service first, in May 1972.

The RAF took delivery of its first GR.Mk 1 in May 1973. A well-equipped tactical strike-fighter, its equipment included an inertial navigation system, a head-up display and laser rangefinder. From 1983 navigation upgrades resulted in the GR.Mk 1A. Some were able to perform a secondary reconnaissance role.

The GR.Mk 1B and two-seat T.Mk 2B were introduced in 1995, equipped with the TIALD (Thermal Imaging and Laser Designation) pod. This allows a Jaguar to deliver its own laser-guided weapons.

Jaguars are fitted with a retractable inflight-refuelling probe which greatly increases their range capability.

Jaguars were the first RAF attack aircraft sent to the Gulf after the Iraqi invasion of Kuwait.

RAF aircraft are equipped with 'zero-zero' ejection seats. These can be used at 'zero height' and 'zero forward speed'.

XZ364 is armed for a typical Gulf mission with four 454-kg (1,000-lb.) bombs, a jamming pod under the port wing, a chaff dispenser under the starboard and AIM-9 missiles for self-defence.

Jaguar GR.Mk 1A

Type: single-seat attack bomber

Powerplant: two 35.77-kN (8,048-lb. thrust) Rolls-Royce/ Turboméca Adour Mk 104 afterburning turbofans

Maximum speed: Mach 1.5 or 1690 km/h (1,050 m.p.h.) at altitude

Combat radius: 852 km (529 m.p.h.) on internal fuel

Service ceiling: 14,020 m (46,000 ft.)

Weights: empty 7000 kg (15,432 lb.); maximum take-off 15,442 kg (34,044 lb.)

Armament: two 30-mm ADEN cannon plus provision for two AIM-9L Sidewinder air-to-air missiles on overwing pylons, plus up to 4534 kg (9,996 lb.) of underwing stores on five pylons

Dimensions:
span	8.69 m (28 ft. 6 in.)
length	15.52 m (50 ft. 11 in.)
height	4.92 m (16 ft. 2 in.)
wing area	24.18 m² (260 sq. ft.)

JAGUAR GR.MK 1A

XZ364 'Sadman' was one of a detachment of Jaguars from the RAF Coltishall Jaguar Wing based at Muharraq, Bahrain, and one of two RAF 'Jags' that flew 47 missions each in the Gulf during 1991.

Nose art was a feature of RAF aircraft during the Gulf conflict. This one features a caricature of former Iraqi leader Saddam Hussein. The bomb symbols below the cockpit each represent missions flown.

Like the RAF Tornado bombers and Buccaneers in the Gulf, Jaguars were painted in a temporary 'desert pink' camouflage.

The Jaguar is unusual in being able to carry a pair of air-to-air missiles on overwing pylons. RAF Jaguars use AIM-9 Sidewinders.

The fin fairing contains a radar-warning receiver which warns the pilot when he is 'illuminated' by enemy radar.

RAF single-seat Jaguars are fitted with the 'chisel-nose' containing a Ferranti Laser Rangefinder and Marked Target Seeker (LRMTS).

Continuing the Rolls-Royce tradition of naming its engines after rivers, the Jaguar's Anglo-French Rolls-Royce/Turboméca Adour turbofans are named after a river in France.

COMBAT DATA

MAXIMUM SPEED

For ground-attack aircraft, speed at ground level is far more important than absolute maximum speed. All three aircraft have similar performance at lower levels.

JAGUAR GR.Mk 1A	1690 km/h (1050 m.p.h.)
MiG-27K 'FLOGGER-D'	1885 km/h (1,171 m.p.h.)
F-1	1700 km/h (1,056 m.p.h.)

ARMAMENT

The Jaguar is an excellent attack aircraft with the ability to carry a useful bombload, including laser-guided bombs, deep into enemy territory. The F-1 carries far less than the MiG-27 or the Jaguar.

JAGUAR GR.Mk 1A	MiG-27K 'FLOGGER-D'	F-1
2 x 30-mm cannon 4534 kg (10,000 lb.)	1 x 30-mm cannon 4000 kg (8,800 lb.)	1 x 20-mm cannon 2721 kg (6,000 lb.)

COMBAT RADIUS

With a typical bombload the Jaguar can strike deeper into enemy territory than the MiG-27 or the F-1. This capability was shown to good effect in the Gulf War when RAF and French Jaguars attacked targets deep inside Iraq.

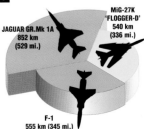

- MiG-27K 'FLOGGER-D' 540 km (336 mi.)
- JAGUAR GR.Mk 1A 852 km (529 mi.)
- F-1 555 km (345 mi.)

Jaguar ground attack

IN THE GULF AND BEYOND: Typical ordnance loads during the Gulf War included general-purpose iron bombs, cluster bombs and rocket pods. Since then the RAF has equipped a number of single- and two-seat Jaguars with the TIALD pod which was used briefly by Tornados during Operation Desert Storm. This allows Jaguars to deliver highly accurate laser-guided munitions autonomously as well as to 'illuminate' targets for other aircraft.

2 PRECISION GUIDANCE: The LGB homes in on the source of the reflected light for pinpoint accuracy.

TIALD ATTACK: The attacking Jaguar illuminates' the target with a laser beam, the reflected light forming a cone-shaped 'bucket' into which the laser-guided bomb (LGB) is dropped.

CRV-7 ROCKETS IN THE GULF: After it was decided that attacks would be made at medium rather than low level for safety, changes were made to the types of weapon used.

MACH 4 SPEED: The CRV-7 rocket, fired from a 240-kg (530-lb.) 19-tube pod, is accurate up to 6000 m (19,685 ft.).

SHENYANG
J-6 'FARMER'

● MiG-19 copy ● Built in huge numbers ● 40-year-old design

▲ *Although it appears to be little more than a copy of the Mikoyan-Gurevich MiG-19, the Shenyang J-6 has single-handedly helped to establish China as a major producer of military aircraft.*

Chinese production of the Soviet MiG-19 began at Shenyang and Nanchang in the late 1950s. The first aircraft actually to fly were assembled from Soviet parts. The first true Chinese-built J-6 followed in September 1959, with series production beginning soon after. The original J-6 was a copy of the MiG-19P all-weather fighter, but in 1961 production switched to the MiG-19S day-fighter variant. This variant has been widely exported.

SHENYANG J-6 'FARMER'

Sales success ▶
China saw the potential of the MiG-19 and was able to offer the aircraft at an unbelievably low price to other countries. Even more attractive is its simplicity and abundant spares situation.

◀ Longevity
Even today, large numbers of this 40-year-old design are in service.

▼ J-6 Xin
The word xin, meaning 'new', is applied to an upgraded variant with an air-intercept radar.

▼ Sub-continent Shenyangs
Pakistan was the first nation outside China to receive the F-6. Deliveries commenced shortly after the 1971 conflict with India.

Time warp ▶
Looking like a Frontal Aviation base in the 1950s, this scene actually dates from the 1980s. The Chinese pilots are even wearing leather helmets.

FACTS AND FIGURES

➤ All Pakistani air force F-6s have been retrofitted with British Martin-Baker ejection seats for better safety.

➤ The ground attack A-5 Fantan is based on a heavily modified F-6 airframe.

➤ Production of the J-6 was disrupted by the Cultural Revolution in the late 1960s.

➤ F-6s have been exported to Pakistan, Egypt, Vietnam, Bangladesh, Cuba, Tanzania and Somalia among others.

➤ In Chinese service the aircraft fulfils fighter, attack and reconnaissance roles.

➤ Nearly 5000 J-6s were produced, more than double the number of MiG-19s.

PROFILE

China's flying time capsule

During the 1960s, in addition to the J-6 fighter Shenyang produced a JJ-6 two-seat trainer and even a reconnaissance aircraft known as the J-Z6, based on the MiG-19R. The two-seater has been exported as the FT-6 to Bangladesh, North Korea, Vietnam and Zambia.

Although the J-6 became the standard fighter of the Chinese air force from 1962, the Cultural Revolution of the late 1960s badly hampered production. As a result, it was 1973 before

the first new model was delivered. Designated J-6III, it was a high-speed day fighter with cropped wings and more powerful engines.

The J-6C was an improved version of the basic J-6 and featured, among other things, a relocated brake parachute. China's Guizhou factory used this variant as the basis for the all-weather J-6A. It has a revised nose profile with a new radar and carries PL-2 missiles.

As F-6s, J-6s were exported to several countries, including

Above: Some ex-Pakistani F-6s were transferred to the Bangladesh Defence Force Air Wing. By 1994 only a handful were still flying.

Albania, Egypt, Iran, Iraq, Pakistan, Somalia, and Tanzania, as well as the four countries already listed as customers for the FT-6. Pakistan bought 120 F-6s and subsequently modified them with new avionics, Sidewinder missiles and a large fuel tank under the fuselage.

Above: Most 'Farmers' operated by the Pakistan air force wear this two-tone grey camouflage, though others sport an air-defence grey scheme or remain unpainted.

F-6 'Farmer C'

Type: single-seat fighter

Powerplant: two 31.88-KN (7,170-lb.-thrust) Limming (LM) Wopen-6 afterburning turbojets

Maximum speed: 1540 km/h (955 m.p.h.)

Initial climb rate: 9145 m/min (30,000 f.p.m.)

Combat radius: 685 km (425 mi.)

Range: 1390 km (862 mi.)

Service ceiling: 17,900 m (58,700 ft.)

Weights: empty 5760 kg (12,672 lb.); maximum take-off 10,000 kg (22,000 lb.) (est)

Armament: three 30-mm cannon

Dimensions:
span	9.20 m	(30 ft. 2 in.)
length	14.90 m	(48 ft. 10 in.)
height	3.88 m	(12 ft. 9 in.)
wing area	25 m²	(269 sq. ft.)

FT-6 'FARMER'

One of the many nations to purchase F-6s was Egypt. For conversion training on to single-seat F-6s, FT-6 trainers were also acquired. A small number of them were rumoured still to be active in the mid-1990s.

In common with early Mikoyan-Gurevich jet fighters, the F-6 features a large splitter plate at the mouth of the intake. This is contoured for more effective air flow to the twin turbojet engines.

A flat, almost razor-straight canopy profile identifies the two-seat 'Farmer'. The twin Shenyang ejection seats are woefully outclassed and are mounted high up, requiring tall pilots to wear old style leather flying helmets instead of modern 'bone domes'.

In comparison with the fighter variant, the two-seater is longer, with a fuselage plug of 84 cm (33 in.) forward of the wings. The rear cockpit is fitted in place of a fuel cell, and in an effort to restore fuel capacity the wing-root cannon were deleted and additional tanks substituted. Fit and finish are exceptional for an old design.

Large low-mounted stabilisers were fitted to the MiG-19 instead of the high-mounted units seen on its predecessors. The entire unit is able to move up and down. A small fairing at the base of the fin houses the relocated brake parachute.

Based on the airframe of the enhanced J-6C fighter variant, the trainer's improvements include nosewheel braking and tubeless tyres.

Conceived during the 1950s, the FT-6 suffers from the inadequate range that plagues all jets dating from this period. On most sorties drop tanks are fitted under the wings.

Twin Wopen WP-6 turbojets power the FT-6 variant. They are rated at 31.88 kN (7,170 lb. thrust) with afterburning and by modern standards are extremely crude and fuel thirsty.

COMBAT DATA

THRUST
Among the 1950s generation supersonic fighters still in service, the F-6 is not particularly powerful, especially considering that it is powered by two heavy turbojets. The slightly later MiG-21 had much greater performance despite having less thrust.

F-6 'FARMER'	63.76 kN (14,340 lb. thrust)
MIG-21 PFM 'FISHBED-F'	60.57 kN (13,625 lb. thrust)
F-104G STARFIGHTER	70.28 kN (15,810 lb. thrust)

MAXIMUM SPEED
Even today, these early supersonic fighters remain among the best-performing aircraft ever built, although the Starfighter was marred by poor handling. The F-6 retains the excellent performance of the MiG-19 but is a far more capable machine.

F-6 'FARMER'	1540 km/h (955 m.p.h.)
MIG-21 PFM 'FISHBED-F'	2125 km/h (1,318 m.p.h.)
F-104G STARFIGHTER	2338 km/h (1,450 m.p.h.)

RANGE
Drawbacks of the J/F-6 are numerous, especially range. The twin turbojets have horrendous fuel consumption and thus sorties are often very short, even with drop tanks fitted. Pakistani machines are sometimes fitted with an additional conformal tank under the fuselage in an effort to extend endurance.

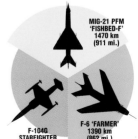

MIG-21 PFM 'FISHBED-F' 1470 km (911 mi.)

F-6 'FARMER' 1390 km (862 mi.)

F-104G STARFIGHTER 1200 km (744 mi.)

Indigenous combat jets of the People's Republic

■ **NANCHANG Q-5 'FANTAN':** Based on the airframe of the J-6, this dedicated ground attack aircraft features a redesigned nose housing an attack radar, and small fuselage air intakes.

■ **SHENYANG J-8II 'FINBACK-B':** Developed in conjunction with Grumman Aerospace, this promising aircraft was cancelled after the Tiananmen Square massacre of 1989.

■ **GUIZHOU JJ-7/FT-7:** Externally identical to Soviet-built MiG-21UMs, complete with bulged dorsal spine and broad fin, these aircraft serve as advanced trainers with the PLA AF.

SHENYANG

J-8 'FINBACK'

● Interceptor ● Ten-year test programme ● MiG-21 development

▲ China's self-imposed reliance on indigenous products has often led to problems in its aviation industry. The J-8 is no exception, and its development is in serious doubt.

First flown in June 1984, the F-8II was a development of the original Shenyang J-8, which had flown for the first time nearly 15 years earlier. Where the earlier aircraft had a configuration similar to that of the MiG-21, the F-8II has fuselage-side air intakes like those of the MiG-23 for its twin turbojets. It retains the J-8's combination of delta wings and sharply swept tailfin, but adds a folding fin below the tail.

PHOTO FILE

SHENYANG J-8 'FINBACK'

▼ **Missiles from abroad**
In 1987 Grumman received a contract to upgrade the avionics and missiles for the J-8. Political events prevented this contract from being completed, at great technological cost to China.

▲ **A big fighter**
Based loosely on the MiG-21 'Fishbed', the J-8 'Finback' is a considerably larger machine.

Familiar lines ▶
A wing plan similar to the MiG-21's is evident in this view of a J-8 'Finback' seen participating in a Chinese Armed Forces Air Display.

◀ **Future 'Finbacks'**
An improved version of the J-8 was developed as the J-8II 'Finback-B', incorporating upgraded avionics and more powerful engines.

Chinese counterfeit ▶
When viewing the aircraft, features of the MiG-21 and MiG-23 became apparent. They are the result of the inventive nature of the Chinese aviation industry, and the acquisition of different Soviet fighters from various sources.

FACTS AND FIGURES

➤ The J-8 originated from a 1964 PLA requirement for a fighter with superior performance to that of the MiG-21.

➤ In its configuration the J-8 'Finback' is described as a scaled-up MiG-21.

➤ Two prototypes were delivered, the first of which flew on 5 July 1969.

➤ Flight testing of the J-8 'Finback' lasted 10 years, because of various political interruptions to its development.

➤ An improved all-weather variant is equipped with an SR-4 radar.

➤ The improved 'Finback-B' first flew on 12 June 1984.

PROFILE

China on its own

Code-named 'Finback-B' by NATO and originally known as the J-8II, the F-8II does not seem to have entered Chinese air force service. As a result, the F that replaces J in the designation of export versions of fighters has become standard.

With side intakes instead of the nose intake of the J-8, the F-8II has room for a much more capable radar. Changes to export versions include the addition of a head-up display as part of a digital avionics suite.

A planned development using US avionics in a programme called Peace Pearl was halted after the 1989 Tiananmen Square massacre in Beijing. Under a contract awarded in 1987, Grumman had been working to integrate a version of the F-16's radar, along with other new systems. The aircraft would also have had a bubble canopy and an American ejection seat.

Even so, work on the fighter did not stop, and Shenyang went on to fly the first F-8IIM in March 1996. The flight came

only two years after drawings had been delivered, which constituted a record for the Chinese aircraft industry.

Recently, the future of the 'Finback-B' has been placed in further doubt by the purchase by the People's Republic of China of 24 Sukhoi Su-27 'Flankers'. The huge expense of these aircraft has restricted funding for the F-8II.

Left: No air force outside China operates the J-8. The recent purchase of Su-27 'Flankers' has placed the future of the fighter in serious doubt.

Above: When it was displayed at the 1989 Paris Air Salon, the J-8 'Finback' created much interest among Western observers, but no orders were received for the aircraft.

J-8 'Finback'

Type: single-seat interceptor

Powerplant: two 65.90-kN (14,825-lb.-thrust) Liyang (LMC) Wopen-13A II turbojets with afterburner

Maximum speed: 2338 km/h (1,450 m.p.h.)

Initial climb rate: 12,000 m/min (39,400 f.p.m.)

Range: 2200 km (1,365 mi.)

Service ceiling: 20,200 m (66,300 ft.)

Weights: empty 9820 kg (21,604 lb.); maximum take-off 17,800 kg (39,160 lb.)

Armament: one 23-mm ventral cannon with 200 rounds; plus various AAMs or 57-mm rockets

Dimensions:
span	9.34 m	(30 ft. 8 in.)
length	21.59 m	(70 ft. 10 in.)
height	5.41 m	(17 ft. 9 in.)
wing area	42.20 m²	(454 sq. ft.)

F-8II 'FINBACK-B'

The F-8II was developed from the earlier J-8 'Finback-A'. The aircraft's future is now in serious doubt after the withdrawal of American support and China's purchase of the Su-27 'Flanker'.

A bubble canopy was installed on later models at the request of pilots who found that vision to the rear of the aircraft was restricted. A modern ejection seat is fitted, as is a simple head-up-display.

The new side-mounted intakes of the 'Finback-B' give the aircraft greater airflow than the original nose intake, which fed a pair of the less powerful Wopen WP-7B turbojets. This design change was influenced by China's acquisition of several Egyptian MiG-23 'Floggers' during the late 1980s.

The 'Finback' is usually armed with a single 23-mm twin-barrelled cannon and a range of air-to-air missiles. Most Chinese copies of Russian weapons can be fitted. China also produces a missile that closely resembles the AIM-9L Sidewinder, plus a Sparrow copy. These, too, can be attached to the outer pylons.

An exact copy of the MiG-21 'Fishbed' fin is fitted to the F-8II. The wings follow a similar pattern but are increased in span and are equipped with extra hardpoints for missiles.

The large radome of the F-8II 'Finback-B' houses a modern fire control radar. Early models were built with a nose-mounted intake, leaving only a limited space.

Inspired by the Russian MiG-23/27 'Flogger', a folding fin is fitted on the lower fuselage to improve the directional stability of the aircraft.

Chinese copycats

XIAN F-7M AIRGUARD: Basically developed from the MiG-21, the F-7M was given an increased wingspan by Xian.

NANCHANG A-5M FANTAN: Exported to Pakistan, the A-5M 'Fantan' is used for ground attack duties using bombs and rockets.

SHENYANG J-6: After an agreement in 1958, China was allowed to produce a licensed copy of the MiG-19 'Farmer' for its air force.

SHENYANG J-8I: Known as the 'Flipper', this aircraft was the first indigenous fighter produced by China. It saw limited service.

COMBAT DATA

MAXIMUM SPEED

Using copied designs, China has often improved the capabilities of the Russian aircraft it has adopted. The gradual increase in speed of the various aircraft indicates that the manufacturers are constantly upgrading the types.

F-8II 'FINBACK-B'	2338 km/h (1,450 m.p.h.)
F-6 'FARMER'	1540 km/h (955 m.p.h.)
F-5 'FRESCO'	1145 km/h (710 m.p.h.)

COMBAT RADIUS

The size of the 'Finback' allows the aircraft to carry an exceptionally large fuel load, which can be improved even further by the addition of extra fuel tanks. The small dimensions of the F-5 'Fresco' restrict its fuel load, although additional tanks can be used, as on the 'Farmer'.

F-8II 'FINBACK-B' 800 km (500 mi.)
F-5 'FRESCO' 700 km (435 mi.)
F-6 'FARMER' 685 km (425 mi.)

CLIMB RATE

Equipped with two afterburning turbojets, the F-8's climb rate is exceptional compared to that of some previous Chinese fighters. This performance can be accomplished with a relatively large payload of weapons.

F-8II 'FINBACK-B' 12000 m/min (39,400 f.p.m.)
F-6 'FARMER' 9145 m/min (30,000 f.p.m.)
F-5 'FRESCO' 3900 m/min (12,800 f.p.m.)

223

SHINMAYWA

SS-2

● Long-range flying-boat ● Search and rescue ● Maritime patrol

▲ *Flying-boats are a dying breed, and it is a tribute to the SS-2 that it has been put back into production. The combination of large size, long endurance (thanks to its turboprops) and the ability to land on the sea are ideal for search-and-rescue missions.*

Introduced in 1967, the ShinMaywa SS-2 is one of the last great flying-boats. This aircraft served Japan's Maritime Self-Defence Force so well that in 1992 it was returned to production. Easily recognised with its watertight hull, high wing and T-tail, the ShinMaywa has been built in seaplane and amphibian versions and operates wherever water is found. This hard-working aircraft is successful and very popular with crews.

SHINMAYWA SS-2

◄ Water-bomber
Eight tonnes of water smothers the flames. The SS-2 shows much promise as a firefighting aircraft, with the ability to scoop up water from lakes or the sea to replenish its tanks.

▲ High wing
The high wing, designed to keep the propellers out of the sea, means that mechanics need platforms to carry out maintenance.

▼ Rescue colours
The later search-and-rescue mission SS-2 was painted with bright orange nose and tail. The old anti-submarine PS-1s were grey and white.

▲ Coastal patrol
The SS-2 spends its time on long, slow patrols around Japan's coastline, ready to mount rescues at a moment's notice.

Amphibian ▶
The later variants of the SS-2 had a wheeled undercarriage capable of landing on runways, unlike earlier models, which were pure flying-boats.

FACTS AND FIGURES

➤ The original SS-2 prototype went aloft for the first time on 5 October 1967.

➤ In its rescue configuration, the ShinMaywa can carry 20 seated survivors or 12 patients on stretchers.

➤ The amphibian SS-2A version was first flown on 16 October 1974.

➤ One SS-2 was converted for firefighting, using equipment from Comair in Canada.

➤ The US Navy retired the Martin P5M Marlin, its last flying-boat, two years before the first flight of the SS-2.

➤ ShinMaywa was formerly known as Kawanishi.

Japan's famous flying-boat

The ShinMaywa SS-2 flying-boat was ordered into production in 1966, and 23 aircraft were built for anti-submarine patrol duties using the military designation PS-1. During the Cold War, the threat from the Soviet Union's submarine force was viewed with alarm in Japan. These naval aircraft, from the same builder as the 'Emily' flying-boat of World War II, flew thousands of missions guarding against the threat until their retirement in 1989.

Because of its obvious utility to a nation of islands surrounded by ocean, the ShinMaywa

remains in service and re-entered production in the 1990s, now designated US-1. The seafaring capability of this aircraft makes it a 'guardian angel' to those in peril, and it is credited with several hundred rescues. Its comprehensive rescue equipment includes flares, float lights, droppable life raft containers, maritime markers and even a lifeboat with an outboard motor. The SS-2 with amphibious gear and more powerful engines is almost certainly the most hi-tech seaplane ever built, and will serve for many years.

It may look like an ungainly beast, but the SS-2 has advanced lift devices. Using upper surface blowing and slats, it can take off in only 80 metres and fly at very low speeds.

Like most maritime patrol aircraft, the SS-2 has a long, straight wing and four engines. The torpedo armament of the earlier versions was carried between the engines.

The SS-2 is almost unique in having a hidden fifth engine. The T-58, installed in the top of the fuselage, blows hot air through ducts to the wing and tail surfaces to help lift performance.

Most of the fuel capacity of the SS-2 is contained in large tanks between the wing spars.

SS-2

Japan remains the sole operator of the SS-2. This aircraft of the 75th Kokutai (squadron) entered service in 1976, and has saved many lives in rescues.

The fuselage carries all the essential rescue equipment along with the normal crew of nine.

For the rescue mission, the SS-2 can carry 12 stretchers or 20 seated survivors. The cabin can also store a rubber dinghy, which can be deployed through twin doors in the hull.

The nose houses a powerful search radar, although the sonar equipment fitted to the older anti-submarine aircraft has been deleted.

The hull of the SS-2 has a suppression system to deflect spray clear of the engines on take-off.

The boat-shaped hull of the SS-2 is an ingenious design, allowing very short take-offs despite its large size.

A rare feature of the SS-2 is its slatted tail. The 'T-tail' design helps keep this area clear of the sea.

SS-2

Type: anti-submarine aircraft (crew of 10); search-and-rescue aircraft (crew of nine)

Powerplant: four 2605-kW (2,850-hp.) Ishikawajima-built General Electric T64-IHI-10J turboprops; one 1014-kW (1,359-hp.) Ishikawajima-built General Electric T58-IHI-10J turboshaft

Maximum speed: 520 km/h (340 m.p.h.) at 3,040 m (10,000 ft.)

Range: 3800 km (2,360 mi.)

Service ceiling: 7195 m (29,500 ft.)

Weights: empty 25,500 kg (56,200 lb.); loaded 45,000 kg (100,000 lb.)

Dimensions:
span	33.15 m (107 ft. 3 in.)
length	33.46 m (109 ft. 11 in.)
height	9.95 m (31 ft. 10 in.)
wing area	135.82 m² (1,460 sq. ft.)

COMBAT DATA

RANGE

Designed for long-duration patrols, the big ShinMaywa boat has an extended range only bettered by the exceptional Russian Beriev Be-12. At normal cruise speeds the SS-1 and US-1 can stay aloft for at least nine hours at a time. Its turboprop engines give excellent fuel efficiency, increasing endurance.

Be-12 'MAIL' 5500 km (3,400 mi.)
ALBATROSS 2750 km (1,700 mi.)
SS-2 3800 km (2,360 mi.)

RESCUE CAPACITY

Flying-boats, with their high speed and long range, are particularly well-suited to mounting rescues far out into the ocean. Although their rescue capacity is no greater than that of the biggest of the current generation of helicopters, any fixed-wing aircraft is so much faster than a rotary-winged machine that it can make two or three trips in the time that a helicopter makes a single journey speeding recovery time. It is only the lack of hovering capability that stops the flying-boat from being the ideal rescue machine.

Be-12 'MAIL' 8 stretchers
ALBATROSS 10 stretchers
SS-2 12 stretchers

MAXIMUM SPEED

Turboprop power has revolutionised the performance of flying-boats. The Grumman Albatross is one of the best of the piston-engined boats, yet it would be left far in the ShinMaywa's wake.

SS-2	520 km/h (340 m.p.h.)
Be-12 'MAIL'	600 km/h (373 m.p.h.)
ALBATROSS	380 km/h (236 m.p.h.)

The Kawanishi connection

■ **KAWANISHI H6K 'MAVIS':** Built by one of Japan's oldest flying-boat makers, the Sikorsky-inspired 'Mavis' was the Imperial Navy's main patrol-boat in the first years of World War II.

■ **KAWANISHI H8K 'EMILY':** One of the biggest jumps in flying-boat technology ever devised, the 'Emily' was a heavily-armed boat which entered service as World War II started.

■ **SHINMAYWA:** The Kawanishi company was renamed Shin Meiwa (now ShinMaywa) in 1949. Their first post-war design was the piston-engined XS, which foreshadowed the PS-1.

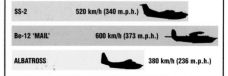

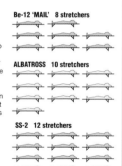

SIAI-MARCHETTI

SF.260

● Training and light attack aircraft ● 1960s design ● Turbine version

Designed by Stello Frati as a three-seat civilian aircraft for the Aviamilano company, the SF.260, as it became known, was put into production by SIAI-Marchetti. After disappointing sales in the civilian market, the aircraft's potential for training or light ground-attack duties was realised. Now in service with 19 air arms around the world, the SF.260 is ideal as a low-cost attack aircraft for less wealthy countries. It is currently available in turboprop form.

▲ Aviamilano flew the SF.260 as a two-seat type in 1964. Still in production (by SIAI-Marchetti, part of Agusta) more than 30 years later, the popular trainer has found numerous military buyers.

SIAI-MARCHETTI SF.260

◄ EFS contender
In the early 1990s, Agusta proposed the SF.260 in answer to the USAF's Enhanced Flight Screener (EFS) requirement for a replacement for the Cessna T-41A.

▼ Turbine-powered SF.260TP
Offering improved performance over its piston-engined counterpart, the Allison 250-powered SF.260TP has found six military customers.

▼ Pilot trainers
Belgium's 35 SF.260s are a mixture of military SF.260Ms and civil SF.260Ds.

▼ Somalian COIN
Until the mid-1990s, Somalia operated four SF.260Ws on counter-insurgency (COIN) duties.

◄ Aerobatic Belgian
In 1996, this colourful SF.260MB was a member of the 'Swallows', the Belgian national aerobatic team. ST-35 also carries the air force's 50th anniversary markings.

FACTS AND FIGURES

➤ By 1996, more than 900 SF.260s of all versions (including turboprops) had been ordered, most for military customers.

➤ In 1992, the first Turkish air force example built locally by TAI was delivered.

➤ The prototype SF.260M was first flown on 10 October 1970.

➤ Zimbabwe's SF.260TP turboprops were delivered as piston-engined, armed trainer SF.260WCs and converted locally.

➤ A search and surveillance SF.260SW Sea Warrior version with radar is available.

➤ In 1996, 20 countries continued to operate the SF.260 in various versions.

PROFILE

From sporty single to Warrior

With sleek lines and superb aerobatic qualities, the SF.260 recovered from a lack of interest in the civil market (as a result of its comparatively high cost) to become a great success in the military sector, with sales of more than 900. The first military version was the primary/basic training SF.260M which initially flew in October 1970. A strengthened airframe and more advanced equipment fit meant sales to five different air arms were forthcoming.

On the back of this success, SIAI-Marchetti developed the SF.260W Warrior. This aircraft retained the same training capability, but also featured two or four underwing hardpoints capable of carrying up to 300 kg (660 lb.) of ordnance. This versatility made the SF.260W ideal for a variety of roles such as air support, forward air control, armed reconnaissance and low-level strike. It achieved significant sales to a number of smaller air arms as a cost-effective multi-role aircraft.

Below: This pair of Sri Lankan SF.260TPs operate with No. 1 Flying Training Wing. Hardpoints allow carriage of light ordnance.

Above: Zambia has a small fleet of piston-engined SF.260MZs. The basic military SF.260 lacked the SF.260W's strengthened airframe.

The turboprop-powered SF.260TP is the latest military version. Among five customers are Ethiopia and Sri Lanka, who have used this version in the counter-insurgency role.

A cantilever, low-wing monoplane, the SF.260 has an all-metal stressed-skin structure. The original design introduced Frise-type ailerons and electrically-operated flaps. The aircraft's landing gear is also electrically retracted.

SF.260W Warrior

Type: single-engined light trainer and tactical support aircraft

Powerplant: one 194-kW (260-hp.) Avco Lycoming O-540-E4A5 piston engine

Maximum speed: 305 km/h (189 m.p.h.) at sea level

Range: 1104 km (684 mi.) with maximum internal fuel

Service ceiling: 4480 m (14,700 ft.)

Weights: empty 770 kg (1,694 lb.); maximum take-off 1300 kg (2,860 lb.)

Armament: two or four podded 7.62-mm (.30 cal.) machine-guns or up to 300 kg (660 lb.) of bombs or reconnaissance pods

Dimensions:
span	8.35 m	(27 ft. 5 in.)
length	7.10 m	(23 ft. 4 in.)
height	2.41 m	(7 ft. 11 in.)
wing area	10.10 m²	(109 sq. ft.)

SF.260WT WARRIOR

Tunisia operated a mixed fleet of SF.260CTs and WTs in the training and COIN roles in 1996. Aircraft 401 is one of the latter and carries the markings of the Tunisian air force.

Piston-engined SF.260s are powered by either a normally-aspirated Avco (now Textron) Lycoming O-540 air-cooled, flat-six, or a fuel-injected AEIO-540. Both variants are rated at 194 kW (260 hp.).

A distinctive feature of the SF.260 family is the wingtip fuel tanks, each able to hold 72 litres (20 gal.). Two or four underwing hardpoints on the SF.260W are able to carry up to 300 kg (660 lb.) of stores between them, including gun pods, bombs, camera pods and supply containers.

Originally designed as a two-seater, the SF.260 was soon available with a third seat, to the rear of the cockpit. While the SF.260M is essentially a training aircraft with improved cockpit instrumentation, the strengthened SF.260W Warrior adds other roles, including close support, forward air control (FAC), armed reconnaissance and liaison.

W41 401

Relatively high costs have resulted in only limited civilian SF.260 sales. In the US, the type was marketed as the Waco Meteor but, again, sales were disappointing and SIAI-Marchetti concentrated on developing military variants.

ACTION DATA

STORES LOAD

All three types are able to carry a variety of stores, including various types of ordnance and reconnaissance equipment. A load of 300 kg (660 lb.) is typical of these small aircraft, although the UTVA-75 is limited to just 200 kg (440 lb.).

SF.260W WARRIOR	RALLYE 235 GUERRIER	UTVA-75
300 kg (660 lb.)	300 kg (660 lb.)	200 kg (440 lb.)

MAXIMUM CRUISING SPEED

From the outset, the SF.260 was designed as a relatively fast sporting aircraft. This performance made the type attractive to military operators in a variety of roles, especially pilot training. Speed was also a useful attribute in the forward air control role.

SF.260W WARRIOR	281 km/h (189 m.p.h.)
RALLYE 235 GUERRIER	245 km/h (152 m.p.h.)
UTVA-75	185 km/h (115 m.p.h.)

TAKE-OFF DISTANCE TO 15-M HEIGHT

Compared to the SOCATA Rallye and UTVA-75, the SF.260 has a modest take-off distance performance of 825 m. The former designs are more useful aircraft when flown from confined airstrips.

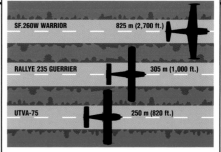

SF.260W WARRIOR	825 m (2,700 ft.)
RALLYE 235 GUERRIER	305 m (1,000 ft.)
UTVA-75	250 m (820 ft.)

Post-war armed piston-engined trainers

■ **NORTH AMERICAN T-6 TEXAN:** Famous as a wartime pilot trainer, the versatile Texan (Harvard in RAF and Commonwealth service) was often adapted as a weapons trainer.

■ **HUNTING PERCIVAL PROVOST:** As well as serving with the RAF, the Provost trainer of 1950 was sold in armed Mk 52 and Mk 53 versions to Rhodesia, Eire, Burma, Iraq and Sudan.

■ **SOCATA RALLYE 235G GUERRIER:** A military version of the 235E, the Guerrier had a strengthened airframe and underwing hardpoints. Only one example was completed.

■ **AEROSPATIALE TB 30B EPSILON:** Togo took delivery of an armed version of the French air force's two-seat basic trainer in 1986. Underwing pylons have a 300-kg (660-lb.) capacity.

SLINGSBY

T.67/T-3A FIREFLY

● Military trainer ● Aerobatic ● Glass-fibre construction

F ounded by Fred T. Slingsby in the 1930s, the Slingsby company became famous for producing highly respected gliders and sailplanes. By the 1980s the company's interests had diversified into other fields, and it was its experience in glass-fibre technology which lead to its success with the T.67 aerobatic trainer. Originally popular in the civil market, the aircraft has also achieved significant military sales in the more powerful T.67M form.

▲ Low operating
costs and impressive performance have led to significant orders from both civil and military customers. Glass-fibre construction also reduces maintenance costs.

PHOTO FILE

SLINGSBY T.67/T-3A FIREFLY

◀ Clear canopy
The single-piece canopy fitted to the T.67 gives the pilot excellent visibility, which is useful for aerobatics.

▼ Large span
A long wingspan plus large ailerons give the T.67 superb stability and control, particularly during aerobatics.

Island trainers ▶
Four T.67M-200s were acquired by the Royal Hong Kong Auxiliary Air Force as trainers.

▲ High visibility
The Joint Elementary Flying Training School (JEFTS) T.67s are colourfully painted to be easily visible.

◀ Training school
Based at RAF Barkston Heath, the JEFTS operates 18 T.67Ms under a civilian contract, currently held by Hunting, for the RAF, Royal Navy and Army Air Corps.

FACTS AND FIGURES

➤ Developed from the Fournier RF-6B, the T.67B gained British CAA certification on 18 September 1984.

➤ Slingsby also designs and manufactures hovercraft in composite materials.

➤ Dutch airline KLM operates nine T.67s for training future aircrew.

➤ Initial production cost for the USAF's 113 T-3A Fireflys was US$54.8 million, plus options for air conditioning and radios.

➤ Northrop Grumman is the sub-contractor for final T-3A assembly at Hondo, Texas.

➤ The T.67M Firefly, G-BKAM, first flew on 5 December 1982.

PROFILE

Elementary trainer for the 21st century

In 1979 the newly reformed French Fournier company granted a licence to Slingsby for the manufacture of the RF-6B wooden trainer/tourer. Named T.67A, an initial series of 10 was built before Slingsby decided its experience in glass-fibre design could be integrated into the aircraft, producing a new and superior product.

Having re-engineered the RF-6B in glass-reinforced plastic (GRP), the T.67M (indicating its 'military' role) first flew from the company's Kirkbymoorside factory in 1982. Civil versions,

named T.67B/C, achieved steady sales but it was the military interest which persuaded the company that the type had greater potential in this field.

Launched at the end of 1982, the T.67M Mk II Firefly was a dedicated military trainer with a new rear-hinged cockpit canopy, available with either 119-kW (160-hp.) or 149-kW (200-hp.) engines. Customers for this version to date have included the RAF and Royal Navy, and Norway's Flying Academy. A number of airlines in the UK and Japan also use the type for

Above: Seen prior to its entry into USAF service, this T-3A displays the 'RA' tailcode of Randolph AFB, Texas.

training. However, the type's greatest success has come in winning the USAF's Enhanced Flight Screener competition to replace the ageing T-41. Fitted with a 194-kW (260-hp.) engine and designated T-3A, 113 examples have been delivered, securing a healthy future for the company.

Below: Seen in the colours of Hunting Aircraft Ltd, this T.67M Firefly 2 deploys full landing flap for a short-field landing at its Topcliffe base.

Royal Hong Kong Auxiliary Air Force T.67s were painted in a high-visibility white-and-orange paint scheme. Two of these aircraft have since been sold to Hunting in the UK for training duties with the JEFTS.

T-3A Firefly

Type: two-seat military basic trainer

Powerplant: one 194-kW (260-hp.) Textron Lycoming AEIO-540-D4A5 flat-six piston engine

Maximum speed: 281 km/h (174 m.p.h.)

Maximum cruising speed: 259 km/h (161 m.p.h.)

Endurance: 5 hr 20 min (with 20 min reserve)

Initial climb rate: 480 m/min (1,575 f.p.m.)

Range: 755 km (470 mi.) (with 30 min reserve)

Weights: empty 807 kg (1,775 lb.); maximum take-off 1145 kg (2,520 lb.)

Accommodation: two seats side by side

Dimensions:
span	10.59 m	(34 ft. 9 in.)
length	7.57 m	(24 ft. 10 in.)
height	2.36 m	(7 ft. 9 in.)
wing area	12.63 m²	(136 sq. ft.)

T.67M-200 FIREFLY

Four T.67s were acquired by Hong Kong as training aircraft. Registered HKG-10 to -13, they have now been sold because of the handover of the colony to China.

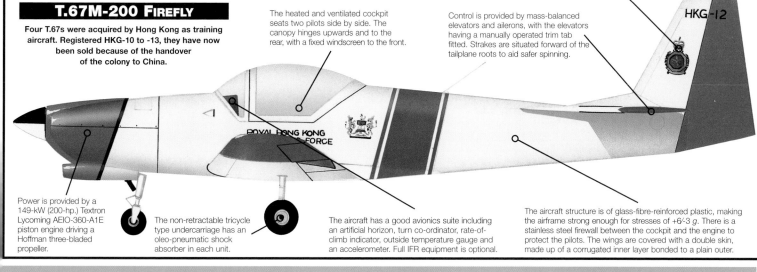

The heated and ventilated cockpit seats two pilots side by side. The canopy hinges upwards and to the rear, with a fixed windscreen to the front.

Control is provided by mass-balanced elevators and ailerons, with the elevators having a manually operated trim tab fitted. Strakes are situated forward of the tailplane roots to aid safer spinning.

Power is provided by a 149-kW (200-hp.) Textron Lycoming AEIO-360-A1E piston engine driving a Hoffman three-bladed propeller.

The non-retractable tricycle type undercarriage has an oleo-pneumatic shock absorber in each unit.

The aircraft has a good avionics suite including an artificial horizon, turn co-ordinator, rate-of-climb indicator, outside temperature gauge and an accelerometer. Full IFR equipment is optional.

The aircraft structure is of glass-fibre-reinforced plastic, making the airframe strong enough for stresses of +6/-3 g. There is a stainless steel firewall between the cockpit and the engine to protect the pilots. The wings are covered with a double skin, made up of a corrugated inner layer bonded to a plain outer.

Slingsby post-war designs

■ SLINGSBY KIRBY CADET: Designed to an Air Ministry specification for a two-seat glider, the Kirby Cadet first flew in 1946.

■ MOTOR TUTOR: Devised by fitting a Tutor glider airframe with an undercarriage and an Aeronca engine, only three examples were built.

■ T.61 FALKE: This side-by-side two-seat trainer was based on the Scheibe SF-24A. Licence-production began in 1970.

■ T.59 KESTREL: Based on the German Glasflügel Kestrel, 109 T-59s were produced by Slingsby between 1971 and 1974.

ACTION DATA

POWER

The Bulldog is the most powerful of these three training types, giving it better aerobatic and acceleration characteristics. More powerful versions of the Firefly can compete with the Bulldog on equal terms.

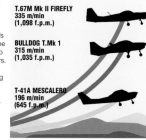

T.67M Mk II FIREFLY 119 kW (160 hp.)

T-41A MESCALERO 108 kW (145 hp.)

BULLDOG T.Mk 1 149 kW (200 hp.)

MAXIMUM SPEED

Despite having a less powerful engine, the Firefly has a better turn of speed than the Bulldog thanks to its more aerodynamic shape and lighter weight. The larger T-41 is a 1950s design and is slower.

T.67M Mk II FIREFLY 252 km/h (156 m.p.h.)

T-41A MESCALERO 224 km/h (139 m.p.h.)

BULLDOG T.Mk 1 241 km/h (149 m.p.h.)

CLIMB RATE

The use of lightweight glass-fibre-reinforced plastic in the T.67's structure allows the aircraft to outclimb its two competitors. It also has a long wing span creating greater lift and aiding climb rate. The T-41 is a four-seat design, and this extra weight hinders climb performance.

T.67M Mk II FIREFLY 335 m/min (1,098 f.p.m.)

BULLDOG T.Mk 1 315 m/min (1,035 f.p.m.)

T-41A MESCALERO 196 m/min (645 f.p.m.)

SUKHOI

SU-17 'FITTER'

● Strike fighter ● Swing wing ● Afghan war veteran

Although overshadowed by Russia's better-known MiGs, the Sukhoi family of ground-attack aircraft have proved capable, sturdy and reliable in service, and have seen extensive combat with many countries around the world. The Su-17 'Fitter-C' and Su-22 'Fitter-K' combine modern, variable-sweep wings with the rugged features of earlier Sukhoi warplanes in a package liked by the pilots who fly it.

▲ The Su-17 has evolved from a simple tactical fighter with limitations into a very capable strike machine. The latest versions can carry sophisticated precision-guided bombs and missiles.

SUKHOI SU-17 'FITTER'

▲ **Nose cone**
The shock cone in the nose is fixed, unlike the one in the earlier Su-7. It houses a laser rangefinder which may also be a marked target seeker.

▲ **Libyan 'Fitter'**
The Su-22s exported to Libya are armed with the K-13 'Atoll' infra-red missile, equivalent to early-model Sidewinders. The Su-22 lacks the modern avionics and weaponry of Russia's newer Su-17M-4.

▼ **Low pass**
An Su-17 pilot enjoys a high-speed pass over his home airfield at Templin.

▲ **Redundant**
The retirement of the Luftwaffe's Su-22s was resented by their pilots, who thought the aircraft was as good as the Tornado.

▲ **Well equipped**
This 'Fitter' is equipped with flare dispensers above the wingroots, a UV-32 rocket pod, an infra-red R-60 dogfight missile and the SPPU-22 wing cannon pod.

◄ **Rocket blast**
The Su-17's usual armament is the powerful UV-32 rocket pod, often used in Afghanistan for attacking rebel positions in caves.

FACTS AND FIGURES

➤ The prototype swing-wing Su-17 made its first flight on 2 August 1966.

➤ In a 1981 air-to-air engagement, a pair of Libyan Su-22s proved no match for US Navy F-14 Tomcats and were shot down.

➤ In the late 1980s Pakistan air force F-16s had tangles with intruding Afghan Su-22s.

➤ With wings swept forward, an Su-17 or Su-22 has a 100 km/h (62 m.p.h.) slower landing speed than earlier Sukhoi jets.

➤ An Afghan air force Su-22 pilot defected to Pakistan with his aircraft.

➤ All the Su-22s inherited by the Luftwaffe from East Germany have been retired.

PROFILE

Sukhoi's strike master

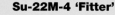

The original Sukhoi Su-7 'Fitter' was a swept-wing contemporary of the MiG-21. While Sukhoi jets were highly prized for their handling, their robust and rugged airframe and outright performance, they lacked the range to carry a heavy bombload over a long distance. The solution: variable-geometry wings, which can remain in the swept-forward position for low-speed performance when landing and taking off but can be swept back (as much as 62°) for high speed in combat.

Entering service with Frontal Aviation in the late 1960s, swing-wing 'Fitters' were upgraded several times to carry more fuel, weapons and better avionics. The aircraft was exported, as the Su-22, to Warsaw Pact air forces and to more than a dozen countries, from Afghanistan through Peru to the Yemen.

'Fitters' carried out thousands of attack missions in Afghanistan, flying precision strikes against the Mujahideen. More recently, they were in action in Peru in a

Dismissed by many as a revamped Su-7, the Su-17 is a capable aircraft with good performance at low level. The 'Fitter' is popular with its pilots and is nicknamed 'Swallow' by Russian crew.

border war with Ecuador, and in the Russian campaign in Chechnya. With the two-seat 'Fitter-E' and 'Fitter-G' providing excellent training, the Su-17 family will be around for many years to come.

The twin NR-30 30-mm cannon are mounted in the wingroots, with 80 rounds per gun.

Sukhoi swing wings have a large fixed wing glove, with a pivoting outboard section. A large hardpoint and the undercarriage are fitted on the fixed section.

Like all the Sukhois of the 1950s and 1960s, the Su-17 has large wing fences.

Su-22M-4 'Fitter'

Type: single-seat attack fighter

Powerplant: one Tumanskii R-29B augmented turbofan, rated at 122.34 kN (5,659 lb. thrust) with full afterburner

Maximum speed: 2335 km/h (1,448 m.p.h.) or Mach 2,20 at high altitude; 1400 km/h (868 m.p.h.) at sea level

Service ceiling: 15,200 m (49,869 ft.)

Weights: empty 11,000 kg (24,251 lb.); loaded 19,000 kg (41,887 lb.)

Armament: two 30-mm NR-30 or related cannon plus about 5000 kg (11,023 lb.) of weapons on two tandem pairs of pylons under the fuselage or under the wing

Dimensions:
span	14.00 m (46 ft.)
length	18.90 m (61 ft.)
height	5.18 m (17 ft.)
wing area	40.10 m² (431 sq. ft.)

SU-17 'FITTER-H'

Frontal Aviation of the Soviet air force was the largest user of the Su-17. This late model 'Fitter-H' version, with a pronounced dorsal spine, was based at Bagram in Afghanistan during the 1980s Soviet occupation.

A special TV-style display is installed in some Su-17s for the use of TV-guided weapons.

The Lyul'ka turbojet is cooled through a number of vents and intakes, including a large vent at the base of the fin.

The pilot aims his weapons using a head-up display and ASP-17BC gunsight.

The Su-17M-4 introduced further avionics updates including a mission computer and a navigation system that comprised Doppler, radio compass, inertial navigation system and improved IFF equipment.

Flare pods can be fitted to the fuselage to decoy infra-red missiles.

Underwing armament can also include TV-guided and laser-guided bombs, and the AS-11 'Kilter' anti-radar missile.

Although the Su-17 had better range/payload than the Su-7 series, external fuel tanks are commonly fitted for all but short-range missions.

The rearward-facing 'bullet' fairing covers an aerial for the 'Sirena' radar warning receiver.

COMBAT DATA

SEA-LEVEL SPEED

The 'Fitter' was designed as a Mach 2-capable fighter, and although current versions no longer carry any of the aerodynamic refinements necessary for such speeds they are still very fast at low level. However, achieving high speed requires plenty of afterburner, which uses fuel at such a rate that it cuts endurance to a matter of minutes.

JAGUAR GR.Mk 1	1350 km/h (837 m.p.h.)
Su-17 'FITTER'	1400 km/h (868 m.p.h.)
A-7 CORSAIR	1100 km/h (682 m.p.h.)

BOMBLOAD

The theoretical maximum bombload is almost never carried. Although a fighter like the Su-17 can lift over four tons of bombs, a normal combat load might consist of 1000 kg (454 lb.) of bombs, air-to-surface rockets, podded or unpodded rockets, ranging in calibre from 57 mm to 300 mm.

Su-17 'FITTER' 4250 kg (9,370 lb.)

JAGUAR GR.Mk 1 4500 kg (9,923 lb.)

A-7 CORSAIR 6800 kg (14,994 lb.)

COMBAT RADIUS

Flying through the dense air at sea level requires a great deal of power, and although a jet might be capable of flying thousands of kilometres at economical speeds, on a lo-lo-lo mission it is much more limited. The 'Fitter' has always been somewhat 'short-legged', but it still has a useful tactical range.

Su-17 'FITTER' 700 km (434 mi.)

JAGUAR GR.Mk 1 920 km (570 mi.)

A-7 CORSAIR 800 km (496 mi.)

Sukhoi's dynasty of fighters

■ **Su-7 'FITTER':** First seen in 1956, it was the standard Soviet fighter bomber in the 1960s and was the foundation of a line of combat aircraft.

■ **Su-9/11 'FISHPOT':** This had a small delta wing and radar in the intake cone. It equipped 25 per cent of the Soviet air defence force in the 1970s.

■ **Su-15 'FLAGON':** Supplementing the 'Fishpot', the very fast 'Flagon' was of similar configuration but had two engines and a large nose radar.

■ **Su-17 'FITTER':** Originally known as the Su-7IG, the swing-wing adaptation of the 'Fitter' first entered service in the early 1970s.

■ **Su-27 'FLANKER':** In the 1980s Sukhoi stepped away from previous designs and introduced the 'Flanker', arguably the world's best fighter.

SUKHOI

SU-24 'FENCER'

● Low-level strike ● Electronic warfare ● Nuclear bomber

Fast, long-ranged and deadly accurate, the Su-24 'Fencer' was the first Soviet warplane with an avionics system which integrated navigation, bombsight and weapons control via a central computer. An advanced swing-wing bomber, the Su-24 could mount high-speed nuclear strikes deep into NATO territory from far behind the Iron Curtain. The Su-24 also proved its high-level bombing capability during operations over Afghanistan.

▲ From bases in Poland or East Germany, the Su-24 could have hit air bases in eastern Britain. The huge increase in capability introduced by this aircraft caused NATO planners considerable headaches.

SUKHOI SU-24 'FENCER'

◀ **Reconnaissance bird**
The Su-24MR is equipped with advanced cameras and infra-red systems for the reconnaissance role. Electronic sensors can also be carried in pods.

▼ **Wings forward**
With its broad wings forward, the Su-24 can land at a sedate 230 km/h (143 m.p.h.). Full-span flaps and a slotted leading edge allow low-speed flight.

▼ **Afghan bomber**
The 'Fencer' first saw action in Afghanistan, flying long-range strikes in the Panjshir Valley from bases in the USSR.

▲ **Anti-ship missile**
Long-range naval strikes were another Su-24 speciality. This aircraft is armed with the lethal AS-11 'Kilter' missile, which has a 150-kg (330-lb.) warhead.

'Fencer-E' ▶
The reconnaissance 'Fencer-E' has dielectric panels on the nose sides. These cover the Shtik side-looking radar system, which has a moving target indicator and can be used to produce maps.

FACTS AND FIGURES

➤ The 'Fencer' was derived from a prototype that first flew in June 1967.

➤ The Su-24 entered squadron service in 1974 and appeared outside the USSR in 1979.

➤ The Su-24 was the first aircraft with the superb Severin K-36D ejection seat.

➤ About 700 'Fencers' of all versions have been manufactured.

➤ The reconnaissance 'Fencer-E' can use its cameras from altitudes of 150–2000 m (500–6,500 ft.).

➤ The Su-24 used laser-guided bombs to destroy bridges in Chechnya.

PROFILE

Sukhoi's long-armed striker

With side-by-side seating for its two-man crew and variable-geometry wings which can be swept back for high-speed flight, the powerful Su-24 has often been compared with the larger General Dynamics F-111. Like the American jet, the 'Fencer' is a long-range strike aircraft, but it also exists in reconnaissance and electronic warfare versions.

Improved Su-24s now in service make extensive use of smart weapons technology, including laser and TV designator/tracker systems. Like the F-111 and the smaller Tornado, the 'Fencer' can fly virtually all of a typical combat mission at treetop altitude, evading enemy radar and air defences and attacking with remarkable accuracy. Some versions of the 'Fencer' add in-flight refuelling capability, giving them strategic range.

Ironically, while the US Air Force is retiring the F-111 for economy reasons, the Sukhoi Su-24 is employed more widely than ever, as the forces of the former USSR are struggling to fund a replacement. This will probably be Sukhoi's Su-27IB strike fighter.

Seen here over the Baltic from a Swedish fighter, the 'Fencer' is a formidable machine. The loss of most Su-24s to other republics is keenly felt by the Russian forces.

'Fencer' has a twin nosewheel to allow operation from short unpaved runways at high all-up weights. A large mudguard is fitted behind the wheels to prevent the engines from ingesting snow.

The first 'Fencers' had a 30-mm cannon in the lower starboard fuselage, but this is replaced by cameras in the 'Fencer-E'.

Su-24 'Fencer-C'

Powerplant: two NPO Saturn (Lyul'ka) AL-21F-3A turbojets each rated at 76.49 kN (17,160 lb. thrust) dry and 110.33 kN (24,750 lb. thrust) with afterburning

Maximum speed: 2320 km/h (1,438 m.p.h.) at 11,000 m (33,600 ft.)

Service ceiling: 17,500 m (57,400 ft.)

Weights: empty 19,000 kg (41,800 lb.); loaded 36,000 kg (79,200 lb.)

Armament: one GSH-6-23m 23-mm cannon; provision for TN-1000 and TN-1200 nuclear bombs or for up to 8800 kg (19,360 lb.) of conventional bombs and missiles

Dimensions:
span (spread)	17.63 m	(34 ft.)
span (swept)	10.36 m	(21 ft.)
length	24.53 m	(80 ft.)
height	6.19 m	(20 ft.)
wing area	42 m²	(452 sq. ft.)

Su-24 'Fencer-C'

The 'Fencer-C' differed from the earlier 'Fencer-B' in having radar warning receiver fairings just above the intake doors. This version serves with Russia and Kazakhstan, and the later 'Fencer-D' with the Ukraine.

The crew sit side-by-side on K-36 ejector seats, which can be command-fired by either crew member. The canopy is a two-piece upward-hinging unit.

Outboard pylons can swivel to keep the wing stores facing into the airstream during wing sweep. An air-to-air missile, usually an R-60, can be carried under the outboard pylon.

The all-moving tail is responsible for roll control as the aircraft has no ailerons. The cylindrical fairing on the rear of the tail houses the large brakechute.

The pilot looks through a PPV head-up display, supplied with data from the PNS-24M navigation system. This allows him to aim weapons accurately, aided by the Kaira laser and TV sighting system.

The 'Fencer' has a forward-looking attack radar and a downward-facing terrain-following radar.

Almost any Russian air-to-surface weapon can be carried.

Power is provided by a pair of afterburning AL-21F turbojets.

Su-24 WEAPONS

AA-8 (R-60) MISSILE

The R-60 missile is a short-range infra-red homing weapon. The Su-24 usually carries at least one of these under the wing for self-defence against enemy fighters.

FAB-500 BOMB

The FAB-500 is the standard general-purpose Russian free-fall bomb. It is filled with 214 kg (471 lb.) of Torpex high-explosive, detonated by various types of fuses.

S-24 ROCKET

Designed to destroy large fixed installations such as aircraft shelters and missile launchers, the S-24 is unusual in that it relies only on fins for guidance. The weapon has a very powerful warhead. It is also carried by MiG-29 and Su-30 fighter-bombers.

Killing radar sites with 'Kegler'

4 RADAR DESTROYED: 'Kegler' flies down the radar beam, using inertial navigation until it acquires the signal. Travelling at Mach 4, the radar operator has very little time to turn off his equipment before the missile hits.

3 POP-UP AND DIVE: The missile can either be launched from high level for more range, or can pop-up from low-level and search.

2 MISSILE AWAY: When the systems operator acquires the radar signal on his ESM system, he fires the AS-12 'Kegler' anti-radar missile, at up to 70 km (40 mi.) from the transmitter.

1 TARGET ACQUIRED: The crew will have a general location of the target, and may get an exact fix from a 'Fencer-F' or other aircraft.

SUKHOI
SU-27 'FLANKER'

- Soviet superfighter ● Long-range interceptor ● Superb dogfighter

The Sukhoi Su-27 'Flanker' was the greatest success in the last days of the Soviet aviation industry. Holder of 27 absolute records, it is one of the great jet fighters. The Su-27 is not as heavy as it looks: it is exceptionally manoeuvrable and one of the most agile aircraft in the world. Small wonder, then, that the Su-27 performs with pride for international audiences with the 'Russian Knights' aerobatic team.

▲ Members of the 'Russian Knights' aviation display team pose with General Antoshkin, commander of the Moscow Military District, in front of one of their Su-27s. The 'Flanker' is one of the most powerful fighters ever used to perform team aerobatics.

SUKHOI SU-27 'FLANKER'

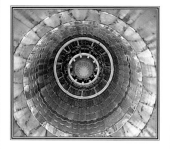

Old-style cockpit ▶
First generation 'Flankers' use old-style instruments. However, the display from the powerful lookdown/ shootdown radar (top right) makes the big Russian fighter a deadly opponent in air combat.

▲ **Superpower superfighter**
The Su-27's two Lyul'ka AL-31F turbofans are about the same size and diameter as the F100 jets used in the American F-15. But at nearly 13 tons of thrust the Russian engines are more powerful, yet consume less fuel.

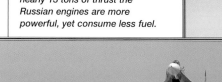

▲ **Long-range warrior**
For Soviet Frontal Aviation, as for its post-Soviet successors, the Su-27 was the long-range counterpart to the MiG-29. It specialises in long-range intercepts, escorting strike aircraft and counter-air missions against enemy air forces.

▲ **Quick reaction**
Immensely powerful and with sophisticated aerodynamics, the Su-27 can get aloft after a take-off run of only 500 m (1,640 ft.). Once in the air it climbs faster than any other fighter in the world, being rivalled only by the McDonnell Douglas F-15 Eagle.

◀ **Naval 'Flanker'**
The heavily-armed Su-27K is a navalised variant of the standard Su-27, and was designed to operate from the carrier Admiral Kuznetsov.

FACTS AND FIGURES

➤ The 'Flanker' prototype, known as the T-10, made its first flight on 20 May 1977.

➤ The Su-27 uses what Sukhoi calls an 'integrated airframe', with wing and fuselage blended to form a single 'lifting body'.

➤ The two-seat Su-27KU began as a demonstrator for carrier operations.

➤ The side-by-side two-seater is viewed as a possible replacement for the Su-24 'Fencer' as a long-range strike aircraft.

➤ Su-27s are operated by former Soviet states, but China is the only export user.

➤ A new-technology version, the Su-35, is being promoted for possible foreign sales.

PROFILE

The best fighter in the world

Looks are misleading. The Su-27 looks like a bigger MiG-29. But the 'Flanker' is not just the big brother of the 'Fulcrum'; it is an advanced design which demonstrates that the Sukhoi design bureau is neck-and-neck in the race for excellence with the better-known MiG organisation.

Chosen as the principal fighter of Soviet air forces, the 'Flanker' is beyond question an aerodynamic miracle. It was first seen in the West as a blurred image on grainy film, but the veil of secrecy has now lifted. In visits to air shows abroad the Sukhoi's incredible agility, including its tail-sitting 'Cobra' manoeuvre, has never been matched by any other performer. This is a pilot's aircraft: the man in the cockpit can fling this ship all over the sky.

Some experts say that the radar and missiles are not as advanced as the basic design of the aircraft, but Russian technology has improved greatly over the last decade and it would be a mistake to underestimate the Su-27.

The 'Flanker' is one of the fastest and most agile fighters in the world. It is the standard by which modern combat jets are judged.

In these post-Soviet days the Su-27s used by the 'Russian Knights' are colourfully painted in the markings of the old Imperial Russian Air Force.

SU-27UB 'FLANKER-C'

This 'Flanker-C' of the 234th 'Proskurovskii' Guards Fighter Regiment wears the colours of the 'Russian Knights'. Based at Kubinka, the team has demonstrated its extraordinary aircraft worldwide.

The Su-27UB's tailfins are taller than those on other 'Flankers', with an extra section added at the base.

Although primarily designed as a two-seat trainer, with a stepped cockpit giving both the trainee and instructor good forward visibility, the Su-27UB has full combat capability.

The 'Flanker' bears a marked resemblance to the smaller MiG-29 because both aircraft use an advanced wing designed at TsAGI, the Central Aerodynamics Institute, which is the Russian equivalent of NASA.

The sharply-swept wing leading-edge extensions provide extra lift at high angles of attack, and contribute to the Su-27's extraordinary agility.

On combat 'Flankers', the long fuselage protrusion houses an aft-looking radar.

The ventral fins fitted to all 'Flankers' greatly improve spin recovery.

The air intakes are fitted with a mesh debris screen which remains closed until the nosewheel has lifted off the ground.

A glazed ball mounted in front of the windscreen houses a laser rangefinder and an infra-red search and track system, which can detect enemy aircraft at up to 70 km (43 mi.).

Su-27 'Flanker-B'

Type: high-performance interceptor and fighter

Powerplant: two NPO Saturn (Lyul'ka) AL-31F turbofans each rated at 79.43 kN (17,872-lb. thrust), increasing to 122.58 kN (27,581-lb. thrust) with afterburning

Maximum speed: Mach 2.35 or 2350 km/h (1,460 m.p.h.)

Service ceiling: 18,000 m (59,000 ft.)

Weights: empty 17,700 kg (39,022 lb.); loaded 33,000 kg (72,753 lb.)

Armament: one GSh-30-1 30-mm cannon with 149 rounds; six AA-10 'Alamo' medium-range and four AA-11 'Archer' short-range missiles

Dimensions:
span	14.70 m	(48 ft. 3 in.)
length	21.90 m	(71 ft. 10 in.)
height	5.93 m	(19 ft. 5 in.)
wing area	46.50 m²	(501 sq. ft.)

COMBAT DATA

MAXIMUM SPEED

The 'Flanker' is one of the fastest jets around, if not quite as speedy as the American F-15 Eagle. At lower speeds, however, the Russian jet's powerful engines and advanced aerodynamics give it a slight handling advantage. The smaller F/A-18, as it is purely an interceptor, is not quite as fast.

Su-27 'FLANKER-B'	2350 km/h (1,460 m.p.h.)
F-15 EAGLE	2500 km/h (1,553 m.p.h.)
F/A-18	1900 km/h (1,181 m.p.h.)

SERVICE CEILING

Once again, the 'Flanker' and the Eagle are closely matched. The Su-27 was one of the first Soviet jets to be equipped with an effective lookdown/ shootdown radar, and operating at such heights means that it can protect an immense amount of air space. Both aircraft can zoom climb to intercept high-flying reconnaissance aircraft.

Su-27 'FLANKER-B' 18,000 m (59,000 ft.)
F-15 EAGLE 18,300 m (60,000 ft.)
F/A-18 HORNET 15,500 m (50,850 ft.)

COMBAT RADIUS

The 'Flanker' has a slightly smaller range than the F-15. However, the Russian jet achieves its long range on internal fuel alone; the American fighter needs auxiliary drop-tanks or conformal tanks to reach its intercept limits. All three types are able to be air-to-air refuelled to increase their range.

Su-27 'FLANKER-B'	F-15 EAGLE	F/A-18 HORNET
1500 km (932 mi.)	2000 km (1,243 mi.)	1000 km (621 mi.)

The Pugachev 'Cobra'

AEROBATIC PASS: First revealed at the Paris Air Show by Sukhoi's great test pilot Viktor Pugachev, the 'Cobra' is an astonishing manoeuvre no Western fighter can match.

NOSE HARD BACK: As the 'Flanker' makes a low-level pass, the pilot pulls the nose back sharply while the fighter carries on forwards.

STRIKING SNAKE: From the vertical or even beyond, the fighter's nose snaps back and then forwards like a striking snake. Loss of height in the manoeuvre is minimal.

COMBAT USE: The Cobra is more than an air show trick; it enables the 'Flanker' pilot to take a snap missile shot at an aircraft directly above or even behind his fighter.

SUKHOI

SU-27K/SU-33 'FLANKER'

● Ship-based interceptor ● Heavy missile load ● In service

Having previously operated only helicopters and the vertical take-off Yak-38 'Forger', the Soviet navy had an urgent requirement for a carrier-capable aircraft to equip its planned force of four new aircraft-carriers. Sukhoi responded with the powerful Su-27K 'Flanker-D' (sometimes known as the Su-33), an adaptation of the standard Su-27 'Flanker-B'. The aircraft has entered service, although only one carrier has been completed.

▲ By considerably modifying the land-based 'Flanker-B', Sukhoi produced a highly effective carrier-based interceptor which entered service on the Admiral Kuznetsov.

PHOTO FILE

SUKHOI SU-27K/SU-33 'FLANKER'

◄ Sukhois on deck
Visible behind this Su-27K is an Su-25, several of which have been modified for carrier training.

▼ Folding 'Flanker'
Folding wings and tailplanes allow the large Su-27K to be stored on the carrier deck.

▼ No 'cat' carrier
After deciding that a steam catapult could not be developed within the required timescale, the Soviet navy opted for a combination of a ski-ramp and deck restraints, which hold the aircraft against retractable thrust deflectors while it runs up to full power.

▼ 'Blue 109'
This aircraft was the last of the Su-27K prototypes, which were known as T10Ks. It was the closest prototype to production form and was deployed on the Kuznetsov's first cruise.

◄ Extra missiles
Two additional underwing hardpoints allow the carriage of two extra missiles. This gives the Su-27K a formidable eight-shot BVR capability when armed with the R-27 missile.

FACTS AND FIGURES

➤ Victor Pugachev, flying an Su-27K, performed the first Soviet landing on a conventional carrier in November 1989.

➤ Several Su-27s were used to test features of the new Su-27K.

➤ Production 'Flanker-Ds' are known as Su-33s by Sukhoi.

➤ In spite of Sukhoi's use of the Su-33 designation, the Su-27K is not a development of the advanced Su-35.

➤ The Su-27K is unable to operate at full weight from a carrier deck.

➤ Early take-off tests were performed on a land-based ski-ramp.

PROFILE

'Flanker' joins the navy

A fleet of four carriers was to be built for the Soviet navy, the first of which, the *Tbilisi*, was launched on 5 December 1985. Each carrier was to be equipped with an Airborne Early Warning and Control System (AWACS) platform, as well as a dedicated air defence aircraft derived from the Su-27 'Flanker-B' and a multi-role strike version of the MiG-29 known as the MiG-29K.

Budgetary problems after the break-up of the Soviet Union led to the completion of only one carrier, the *Tbilisi*, which entered service as the *Admiral Kuznetsov*. Consequently, production of the Su-27K was reduced from a potential 72

to a maximum of just 20.

In addition, the Su-27K found itself in competition with the MiG-29K, since only one aircraft type was to be ordered for the sole carrier. With its strong political position, Sukhoi was able to secure orders for its air-combat dedicated Su-27K, even though the multi-role MiG might have been the better choice for a single-type air wing.

Nevertheless, the 'Flanker-D' represents a highly capable aircraft, with powerful radar, a heavy air-to-air missile load and excellent range. Its lack of strike capability is being addressed in service and the aircraft seems likely to have gained a podded reconnaissance system.

This unusual angle shows the muzzle of the 30-mm cannon in the starboard leading-edge root extension (LERX) and the Su-27K's retractable refuelling probe to port below the cockpit.

SU-27K 'FLANKER-D'

Only one squadron flies the production Su-27K, the 1st Squadron of the Severomorsk Regiment of the AV-MF (Russian Naval Aviation). This aircraft was present during the type's first operational tour.

In order to fit the retractable in-flight refuelling probe, Sukhoi had to move the Infra-Red Search and Tracking (IRST) sensor slightly to starboard from its usual centreline position. The sensor allows the passive acquisition and tracking of targets by their heat signature.

Cockpit modifications were kept to a minimum in the Su-27K. The only additional equipment was that relating to a more precise landing approach system, plus tail hook and wing fold controls.

A typical load for the Su-27K is represented here. The AA-10 'Alamo' missiles provide a beyond-visual-range (BVR) kill capability and the smaller AA-11 'Archer' are used for close-in dogfighting.

Analogue fly-by-wire (FBW) controls are retained by the Su-27K. The canard-equipped Su-35 has a digital FBW system and is therefore a more capable aircraft.

In order to prevent tail scraping on take-off, the tailcone of the Su-27K was considerably shortened. This also allows slower landing speeds and a shorter landing run, but requires forward repositioning of the chaff and flare dispensers, which were also reduced in number.

'Slot Back' radar is common to both the Su-27 and MiG-29. The unit has excellent range performance and power, but scanning capacity is poor, with multiple targets causing problems. The Su-27K relies on AWACS or Ground Controlled Intercept (GCI) support.

A substantial square-section arrester hook was introduced on the first Su-27K prototype. The undercarriage is also modified to withstand carrier landings and twin nosewheels are fitted.

Su-27 'Flanker-D'

Type: carrier-based interceptor and air defence fighter

Powerplant: two 122.59-kN (28,170-lb.-thrust) Saturn Lyul'ka AL-31F afterburning turbofans

Maximum speed: 2300 km/h (1,426 m.p.h.)

Range: 3000 km (1,805 mi.) clean

Service ceiling: 17,000 m (55,800 ft.)

Weights: maximum carrier launch weight 29,940 kg (65,868 lb.)

Armament: one 30-mm cannon, plus up to eight R-27 (AA-10 'Alamo') air-to-air missiles, or a combination of R-27s and R-73 (AA-11 'Archer') air-to-air missiles

Dimensions:

span	14.70 m	(48 ft. 3 in.)
length	21.19 m	(69 ft. 6 in.)
height	5.85 m	(19 ft. 3 in.)
wing area	46.50 m²	(500 sq. ft.)

COMBAT DATA

THRUST

Powerful engines are vital for the heavy 'Flanker-D' to operate from carriers without catapults. The lighter MiG-29K was less powerful but offered comparable performance.

Su-27K 'FLANKER-D'	245.18 kN (56,380 lb. thrust)
F-14D TOMCAT	206 kN (46,342 lb. thrust)
MiG-29K 'FULCRUM'	173 kN (38,918 lb. thrust)

SERVICE CEILING

Reports suggest that the Su-27K has a slightly lower service ceiling than the Su-27 'Flanker-B'. It has a greater ceiling than its nearest Western counterpart, the F-14D, however, and is about 20 km/h (12 m.p.h.) faster than the standard 'Flanker-B'.

Su-27K 'FLANKER-D' 17,000 m (55,800 ft.)	F-14D TOMCAT 16,150 m (52,970 ft.)	MiG-29K 'FULCRUM' 17,000 m (55,800 ft.)

RANGE

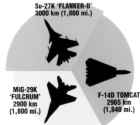

Long range is essential for the fleet defence role, in which missiles and aircraft must be intercepted long before they reach the naval battle group. Only the Su-27K is able to achieve a 3000-km (1,860-mi.) range without external fuel tanks taking up valuable pylons.

Su-27K 'FLANKER-D' 3000 km (1,860 mi.)

MiG-29K 'FULCRUM' 2900 km (1,800 mi.)

F-14D TOMCAT 2965 km (1,840 mi.)

'Flanker-D' at sea

DECK MANOEUVRES: Wing and tailplane folding is necessary to make the large Su-27K easier to handle on deck. To avoid collisions, flying surfaces are kept folded as long as possible.

FULL THRUST FOR TAKE-OFF: With the deck restraints engaged, the aircraft's AL-31F turbofans are wound up to full afterburning thrust. Retractable deflector plates move up behind the 'Flanker-D' to prevent damage from jet thrust.

SKI-RAMP: A conventional take-off by the 'Flanker-D' would be impossible if the *Admiral Kuznetsov* was not equipped with a ski-ramp. The aircraft leaves the ramp at a speed of about 148 km/h (92 m.p.h.) and at an angle of attack of 14°. The take-off run is a mere 100 m (300 ft.) when lightly loaded, or 180 m (600 ft.) at maximum launch weight. The aircraft launch is at full power.

SUKHOI

SU-34 'FLANKER'

● Advanced strike aircraft ● Long-range ● Side-by-side seating

▲ *The number of different variants that have already been derived from the original Su-27 interceptor is a credit to the versatility of this exceptional Russian design.*

Possibly one of the world's most admired and distinctive warplanes, the Su-27IB/Su-32FN/Su-34 is a formidable maritime strike aircraft. While some confusion exists, even among Sukhoi officials, as to the aircraft's true designation, there is no doubt about its incredible capabilities. Although a chronic shortage of funding continues to dog the programme, it seems likely that the Su-32FN will eventually enter service.

SUKHOI SU-34 'FLANKER'

▼ **Long range**
The Su-34 has a completely redesigned forward fuselage with side-by-side seating and full dual controls. It also has twin nose wheels and a longer wheelbase.

▲ **Uncertain future**
Despite funding problems, the Su-34 entered operational service in the mid-1990s.

▲ **Flying 'Platypus'**
The characteristic flattened nose profile has led to the universal nickname of 'Platypus'.

▲ **Big brute**
A pre-production Su-27IB inside the hangar at Kubinka dwarfs the MiG-29 'Fulcrum' in the background.

◄ **Carrier trainer?**
Taken by TASS, this photo apparently shows the Su-27IB poised for touchdown on the carrier Kuznetsov. Note the lack of an arrester hook, however.

FACTS AND FIGURES

➤ Sukhoi confirmed the Su-27IB designation after it was revealed accidentally by TASS photographers.

➤ Buddy refuelling is likely to be an important part of Su-27IB operations.

➤ A food heater and toilet are fitted in the cockpit of the Su-27IB.

➤ For its ASW role, the Su-32FN carries a magnetic anomaly detector and a pod containing up to 72 sonobuoys.

➤ By 1997 an order for 12 Su-32FNs had been placed by an unnamed country.

➤ Unit price of the Su-32FN in 1997 was quoted at roughly US $36 million.

Fearsome 'Flanker'

The heavier weight of the Su-32FN/Su-34 has resulted in a redesign of the undercarriage. This has given the aircraft a distinctive tail-up attitude on the ground, in contrast to fighter variants which are known as 'Cranes' because of their drooping noses.

A considerable redesign of the basic Su-27 'Flanker' produced the T10V-1 prototype in the early 1990s. Referred to originally as the Su-27KU, the aircraft appeared to be a carrier trainer, but when the true designation of Su-27IB became known, it was clear that the machine was destined for the strike role.

Features of the new machine included a side-by-side two-seat cockpit, situated in a completely new nose section. The entire undercarriage was strengthened and the machine optimised for low-level attack/maritime strike in all weathers.

When the Su-27IB was revised for production, twin-wheel main undercarriage bogies were introduced, along with a 'glass cockpit' and compatibility with a wide range of weapons. Intended primarily as a replacement for the Su-24 'Fencer', the Su-27IB is known to the Sukhoi design bureau as the Su-34.

An attack 'Flanker' appeared for the first time in the West at the 1995 Paris Air Salon. The aircraft was described as a maritime attack variant of the Su-27IB, designated Su-32FN. The programme was halted in 1997 because of a lack of

resources at Sukhoi, by which time the machine was described as an export version of the Su-27IB. By June 1997, however, the Su-32FN was back in action at the Paris Air Salon.

In addition to air-to-surface weapons, the Su-34 can also carry two AA-11 'Archer' air-to-air missiles on the wingtips.

Canard foreplanes have been seen on several late 'Flanker' variants and are a feature of the Su-34. They provide improved take-off performance and lift.

The Su-34 can carry a wide variety of external stores, virtually the entire inventory of Russian air-to-surface weapons. They include 100-kg (220-lb.) and 250-kg (550-lb.) bombs, SL25 laser-guided rockets, CBUs and, it is rumoured, long-range stand-off missiles.

Although the rear fuselage is similar to that of the tandem-seat Su-27, the tailcone has been completely recontoured and is presumed to house a rearward-facing radar related to the N012 fitted to the Su-27M, along with twin braking chutes.

SU-34 'FLANKER'

This particular aircraft, originally referred to as the Su-27KU, or carrier trainer, was later designated Su-27IB, signifying a strike role. It was first seen at the 1992 Moscow Aeroshow.

Strike variants of the 'Flanker' have a completely redesigned forward fuselage, an all-glass cockpit with side-by-side seating and full dual flight controls.

Unlike the single-seat and tandem-seat versions, the Su-34 features a new-profile, flat nose with a dielectric tip for the new attack radar.

Second generation 'Flankers' like the Su-34 boast a retractable in-flight refuelling probe, to extend their already formidable combat radius further.

Production Su-34s feature a redesigned nose gear along with tandem main gears, which help distinguish them from earlier 'Flanker' variants.

Despite the new forward fuselage, the rest of the airframe remains essentially unaltered from the original Su-27 Interceptor, including the twin tails, unlike the Su-27UB and Su-35 variants which have new fins.

Modern maritime strike aircraft

■ **BAe SEA HARRIER FA.Mk 2:** The new generation Sea Harrier provides the Royal Navy with an effective maritime strike force.

■ **McD D F/A-18 HORNET:** The Hornet continues to be one of the most capable and versatile aircraft in front-line service.

■ **PANAVIA TORNADO IDS:** For anti-ship work, the principal users of the Tornado are the RAF and the German Marineflieger.

■ **SEPECAT JAGUAR:** India is among several Jaguar users. In addition to ground attack, its aircraft also perform maritime strike duties.

TRANSALL
C.160

● Franco-German tactical transport ● Sigint and civil variants

TRANSALL C.160

▲ **Paradropping**
The main door on the right-hand side
of the aircraft, behind the main wing,
is used by paratroopers.

▲ **Fire-bomber role**
This Luftwaffe C.160 demonstrates a
secondary fire-fighting capability, with tanks
fitted in the cargo bay. The rear loading
ramp must be lowered for this role.

▲ **French relief flights**
This Armée de l'Air C.160F, in a
white colour scheme, has seen
service in a humanitarian role.

▲ **Turkish Transall**
Turkey's C.160s operate
alongside a smaller number
of C-130 Hercules and ageing
C-47 transports.

Updated C.160D ▶
The threat presented by
heat-seeking missiles was
addressed in the C.160 fleet
by fitting missile defence
systems, such as flares.

One of Europe's earliest multinational aircraft programmes was started in 1959 as a collaboration between France and Germany to develop a new military transport. Nord-Aviation, HFB and VFW formed Transport Allianz, or Transall. The resulting aircraft, designed to replace the Nord Noratlas, carries a payload of 16,000 kg (35,200 lb.). The prototype flew in February 1963, and deliveries to the French and German air forces began in 1967.

▲ *Built to replace the Nord
Noratlas, Transalls have, until recently,
single-handedly filled the tactical
transport requirement for the German and
French air forces.*

FACTS AND FIGURES

➤ Of the C.160NGs built for the French, 10 are fitted with a hose-drum unit in the port undercarriage sponson for the IFR role.

➤ The four French C.160H ASTARTE aircraft are fitted with IFR probes.

➤ The C.160SE electronic surveillance version was proposed but never built.

➤ Two C.160G GABRIEL electronic intelligence (Elint) aircraft replaced similarly equipped Noratlases.

➤ Some French Transalls are based overseas in Senegal and New Caledonia.

➤ The Transall programme is now controlled by Aérospatiale and DASA.

Transport Allianz collaboration

Initial production of the C.160 included 110 for Germany and 50 for France. All were completed by 1972, but France later bought another 29 new-generation C.160NGs with additional fuel tanks, in-flight refuelling (IFR) probes and new avionics. Ten are fitted with hoses allowing them to refuel tactical aircraft. An upgrade programme was started in the early 1990s to modernise the earlier aircraft and add defences against missiles.

Two of the newer aircraft were completed as C.160G GABRIEL signals intelligence

variants. They have a number of additional antennas to pick up emissions from radar and other systems. A further four, designated C.160H ASTARTES, were equipped to communicate with ballistic missile submarines. They use long trailing antennas to transmit very low frequency (VLF) radio signals which carry coded messages that can be received underwater. All six of these special mission versions have refuelling probes and hoses.

Germany sold 20 of its C.160s to Turkey, and the remainder operate as the Luftwaffe's main transport aircraft, equipping

three wings. South Africa bought nine C.160Zs as part of the original production batch, but these were retired in the early 1990s.

Among the projected versions that did not enter production was the C.160AAA (avion d'alerte avancée). This would have filled an airborne early warning role, with large radomes fitted in the nose and tail, in a similar fashion to the ill-fated British Aerospace Nimrod AEW.Mk 3.

Below: This Swiss-registered C.160 was used by the Red Cross. Other civil examples included four postal aircraft in Air France colours.

Above: The C.160NG (nouvelle génération) is distinguished by its in-flight refuelling probe above the cockpit.

C.160F

Type: military transport

Powerplant: two 4548-kW (6,100-hp.) Rolls-Royce Tyne RTy.20 Mk 22 turboprops

Maximum speed: 536 km/h (332 m.p.h.) at 4500 m (14,760 ft.)

Range: 4500 km (2,790 mi.) with 8000-kg (17,600-lb.) payload or 1182 km (733 mi.) with 16,000 kg (35,200 lb.)

Weights: empty 28,758 kg (63,268 lb.); maximum take-off 49,100 kg (108,020 lb.)

Payload: 93 troops, 88 paratroops or up to 16,000 kg (35,200 lb.) of cargo

Dimensions: span 40.00 m (131 ft. 3 in.)
length 32.40 m (106 ft. 3 in.)
height 11.65 m (38 ft. 3 in.)
wing area 160.10 m² (1,723 sq. ft.)

C.160D

This is one of 110 C.160s delivered to the German air force. More than 200 C.160s were built, initially for Germany and France, but new aircraft were also delivered to South Africa.

The flightdeck crew of the C.160 consists of a pilot, co-pilot and flight engineer. The aircraft is fully pressurised and air-conditioned in flight and on the ground.

Two Rolls-Royce Tyne turboprops power all Transall C.160s. This powerplant has also been used in the Atlantic maritime patrol aircraft. Two four-bladed British Aerospace Dynamics propellers are fitted.

The main cabin of the Transall will hold up to 93 troops, 61 to 88 fully equipped paratroops or 62 stretchers and four attendants. Other typical loads include armoured vehicles up to 16,000 kg (35.200 lb.) in weight.

The French air force's C.160H variant is used to communicate with missile-armed nuclear submarines in a similar role to the US Navy's E-6 Mercury. The cargo hold carries VLF communications equipment and associated crew.

In common with most tactical transport types, the C.160 has a rear loading ramp. This forms the underside of the upswept rear fuselage.

ACTION DATA

LOAD CAPACITY

Despite being only a twin-engined aircraft, the C.160 has a creditable load-carrying capacity. However, its performance with a full load aboard would not be as impressive.

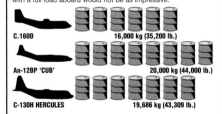

C.160D — 16,000 kg (35,200 lb.)
An-12BP 'CUB' — 20,000 kg (44,000 lb.)
C-130H HERCULES — 19,686 kg (43,309 lb.)

LANDING RUN

Being a smaller aircraft, the Transall has a shorter landing run than the larger types. Short take-off and landing runs are important for tactical transport aircraft which are required to use hastily prepared landing strips constructed in confined areas, possibly under enemy fire.

C.160D — 640 m (2,100 ft.)
An-12BP 'CUB' — 804 m (2,635 ft.)
C-130H HERCULES — 838 m (2,750 ft.)

RANGE

A negative factor of the Transall's small size is its correspondingly short range, approximately a third of that of the C-130 and An-12. This shortcoming was addressed in the C.160NG, which introduced in-flight refuelling. While later versions of the C-130 have also been equipped with IFR, An-12s have never been fitted with this feature.

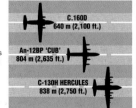

C.160D 1182 km (733 mi.)
An-12BP 'CUB' 3600 km (2,232 mi.)
C-130H HERCULES 3539 km (2,194 mi.)

C.160s in military and civil service

■ **C.160D:** The Luftwaffe has been the largest operator of the Transall. It is its principal transport machine and still equips three wings. Search and rescue is a secondary role for these aircraft.

■ **C.160P:** Air France operated four C.160Ps converted from French air force C.160Fs in 1970. Flown under contract to the French post office, they transported mail.

■ **C.160T:** In the early 1970s Turkey took delivery of 20 ex-German air force C.160Ds. These were redesignated C.160Ts and had a modified camouflage scheme applied.

TUPOLEV

TU-16 'BADGER'

● Tanker ● Anti-ship missile launcher ● Reconnaissance role

▲ The Tu-16 has proved capable of adapting to many roles. With the shortage of cash to fund a replacement in Russia, it will remain an important aircraft for many years to come.

Still in service after more than 50 years, the Tu-16 'Badger' remains a vital part of Russia's Long Range Aviation, serving as a tanker, electronic jammer and reconnaissance aircraft. The 'Badger' was also sold overseas, and remains in service in China, Ukraine and the Middle East. Despite its age, the 'Badger' is still a very useful aircraft and will almost certainly be flying somewhere in the world for many years.

TUPOLEV **TU-16 'BADGER'**

▼ Desert launch
Egypt still operates a handful of 'Badgers' based at Cairo West air base. They are equipped with the ageing 'Kelt' missile.

▲ Ocean snooper
This 'Badger-F' was spotted near a NATO surface fleet during an exercise. A small number of these dedicated reconnaissance aircraft serve with Russian naval aviation.

Chinese 'Badger' ▶
Probably one of the B-6 export aircraft subsequently delivered to Iraq, this aircraft was equipped to deliver the C-601 'Silkworm' missile. This system is large and slow, and a lot less dangerous than the Mach 3-capable AS-6 'Kingfish' missile normally used by the aircraft in Russian service.

▲ On patrol
This 'Badger-G' is one of the earlier model 'Gs' with missile-carrying ability but no ventral radar fairing.

Missile launcher ▶
A 'Badger-G Mod' carries an AS-6 missile. It has a range of 300 km (185 mi.) and can carry a nuclear warhead.

FACTS AND FIGURES

➤ 'Badgers' are believed to be in service in Belarus, China, Egypt, Iraq, Russia (naval aviation and air force) and the Ukraine.

➤ A small number of Tu-16PP 'Badger-Js' remain in service in the jamming role.

➤ 'Badgers' originally employed a wingtip-to-wingtip refuelling technique.

➤ About 20 Tu-16N tankers serve with the Russian air force (VVS) and six with the naval air force (AV-MF).

➤ Ukraine's Tu-16s serve with 251 HBAP at Belaya Tserkov and 260 HBAP at Stryy.

➤ F-117 bombers attacked three Iraqi 'Badgers' on the ground in the first Gulf War.

PROFILE

Half a century of 'Badger' power

Despite being obsolete in its original role of nuclear free-fall bombing, the Tu-16 'Badger' is still doing sterling work in the hands of a small number of pilots, most notably in Russia and China. The Tu-16 airframe was highly adaptable, and was soon pressed into service in the first Soviet air-to-air refuelling squadrons, a role in which the aircraft remains to this day, designated Tu-16N. Another role that the Tu-16 retained was as an airborne missile launcher, at first carrying the KS-1 'Komet' missile and then the faster KS-15. Chinese-built 'Badgers', known as Xian H-6s, carry the

C-601 anti-ship cruise missile, and also carry out test and development work. Other roles for the Badger are in electronic warfare, using chaff launchers and various active jammers (Tu-16PP 'Badger-J') and in long-range reconnaissance (Tu-16P 'Badger-F').

About 100 'Badgers' are still flying in China, with about the same number flying in Russia, and around 50 in the Ukraine. Quite how long the 'Badger' will remain in service is hard to determine, but the absence of any obvious replacement suggests that the aircraft could well survive to celebrate its fiftieth birthday.

Left: 'Badgers' used to be a common sight flying near every NATO exercise, but fuel availability constraints mean that the aircraft now rarely fly even at home.

The radar system in the nose is believed to be the system known to NATO as 'Short Horn'.

The few remaining Tu-16 tankers have replaced the old wingtip fuelling system with a probe-and-drogue system located in the capacious bomb bay.

The fin-tip has a dielectric antenna, probably used to relay high-frequency radio communications to surface vessels.

Above: Some 'Badger' variants retain a manned tail gun turret and are among the last aircraft to do so.

Tu-16 'BADGER-L'

The Tu-16PM is a dedicated electronic intelligence gatherer, with special electronic aids replacing the rear gun turret. The nose has a small thimble radome, and the aircraft retains its dorsal and ventral turrets.

A useful defensive armament is retained in the form of two NR-23 cannon in the dorsal and ventral turrets. The fit of this 'Badger' variant varies widely, but most have a camera window in the port forward fuselage.

Earlier Tu-16s were powered by the Mikulin AM-3 turbojet, but most current versions use the Tumanskii RD-3M engine rated at 93 kN thrust.

The nose of this Tu-16 has the pentagonal excellence award painted under the cockpit.

The underwing pods house electronic information-gathering equipment, and are also fitted to the earlier 'Badger-F'.

Like most Soviet designs from the 1950s, the Tu-16 has large overwing fences to reduce spanwise airflow and induced drag.

The extended tailcone is believed to house electronic counter-measures gear or very low frequency radio equipment for communications with submarines.

'Badger' missions

JAMMING: The 'Badger-J' has an on-board chaff-cutting system and active jammers, so that it can saturate a radar with false signals at exactly the right wavelength.

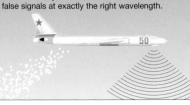

TANKER: The Soviet forces eventually settled on a probe-and-drogue technique similar to that used by most Western air forces and the US Navy. The thirsty MiG-31 interceptor needs frequent top-ups to remain on-station.

MISSILE ATTACK: A Chinese H-6 launches a C-601 cruise missile. This weapon is a relatively slow and high flying system, and is less of a threat than the new C-801. However, it has a very heavy payload and is still a potent weapon.

Tu-16 'Badger-G'

Type: twin-engined long-range anti-ship missile carrier

Powerplant: two 93-kN (20,920-lb.-thrust) Mikulin AM-3M turbojet engines

Maximum speed: 1050 km/h (651 m.p.h.) at 6000 m (19,700 ft.)

Endurance: 5 hours with maximum load

Range: 7200 km (3,675 mi.)

Service ceiling: 15,000 m (49,200 ft.)

Weights: empty 37,200 kg (81,840 lb.); maximum take-off 75,800 kg (166,760 lb.)

Armament: two K-26 missiles plus six 23-mm cannon in tail, dorsal and ventral turrets

Dimensions: span 32.99 m (108 ft. 3 in.)
length 36.80 m (120 ft. 8 in.)
height 10.36 m (34 ft.)

COMBAT DATA

MAXIMUM SPEED

Jet engines gave the 'Badger' higher speed than the bombers it replaced. The Tu-22, a smaller design with bigger engines, was faster still, but short ranged. The remarkable Tu-95/142 'Bear' was almost as fast by virtue of its swept wing and enormous propellers.

Tu-16 'BADGER-G' 1050 km/h (651 m.p.h.)

Tu-142M 'BEAR-F' 925 km/h (574 m.p.h.)

Tu-22 'BLINDER-A' 1480 km/h (918 m.p.h.)

COMBAT RADIUS

Range was an important feature of the early jet bombers, and the Tu-16 was one of many Soviet designs from the 1950s to suffer from the lack of efficient engines. For this reason, Tupolev designed the Tu-95 with the massive NK-12 turboprop engine.

Tu-16 'BADGER-G' 7200 km (3,675 mi.)

Tu-142M 'BEAR-F' 6200 km (3,970 mi.)

Tu-22 'BLINDER-A' 3100 km (1,920 mi.)

SERVICE CEILING

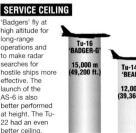

'Badgers' fly at high altitude for long-range operations and to make radar searches for hostile ships more effective. The launch of the AS-6 is also better performed at height. The Tu-22 had an even better ceiling.

Tu-16 'BADGER-G' 15,000 m (49,200 ft.)

Tu-142M 'BEAR-F' 12,000 m (39,360 ft.)

Tu-22 'BLINDER-A' 18,300 m (59,040 ft.)

TUPOLEV

Tu-22M 'BACKFIRE'

● Strategic bomber ● Missile carrier ● Reconnaissance

F ast, long-ranged and hard hitting, the Tu-22M remains one of the most capable bombers in the world. This large swing-wing bomber is tasked primarily with long-range missile strikes against shipping, serving with units of Russian naval aviation (AVMF). Equipped with powerful sensors and large supersonic missiles, the Tu-22M is even more important now that Russia has very few of its Tu-160s still in service.

▲ Together with the Tu-160 'Blackjack', the 'Backfire' makes up Russia's modern long-range bombing fleet. As a replacement for the Tu-22 'Blinder', the 'Backfire' serves in large numbers – 250 in total, with around 150 employed by the naval air arm. It may well drop decoy drones to confuse enemy air defences.

TUPOLEV Tu-22M 'BACKFIRE'

▲ Ultimate bomber
The Tu-22M-3 is the most advanced and formidable 'Backfire' development, with new radar, engines, intakes and more advanced electronic countermeasures systems.

▲ Anti-shipping strike
This Tu-22M is armed with the AS-4 'Kitchen' anti-ship missile. The 11-m (36-ft.) missile has a range of over 400 km (250 mi.) and can be nuclear armed.

▲ Maritime patrol and reconnaissance
The Tu-22M-3 'Backfire-C' is employed by the Russian navy for long-range destruction of enemy naval fleets. The M-3 can also carry six AS-16 'Kickback' attack missiles internally, plus four more externally. Defence is provided by a 23-mm tail gun.

▲ Interception
This Tu-22M-2 'Backfire-B' was intercepted over the Baltic by a Swedish Saab Draken fighter.

High-speed attack ▶
The Tu-22M-3 sweeps back its long wings for a rapid bomb run over the enemy fleet's shipping.

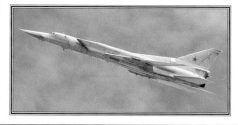

FACTS AND FIGURES

➤ For short landings the Tu-22M can deploy a large brake parachute, stored in the rear fuselage.

➤ The Tu-22M can carry external rocket packs to decrease take-off distance.

➤ The 'Backfire' can lift a maximum of 69 FAB-250 conventional bombs.

➤ Tu-22M-3s were first used operationally on bombing missions in the Soviet war in Afghanistan in October 1988.

➤ Video cameras are used on the Tu-22M for bomb aiming from high altitude.

➤ An inflatable LAS-5M dinghy is carried behind the cabin for emergencies.

PROFILE

Soviet swing-wing striker

First known in the West as the Tu-26, the Tu-22M 'Backfire' was developed at the same time as the Su-7IG variable-geometry prototype, and may have benefited from the same research by Soviet aerodynamicists. It is possible that early prototypes (Tu-22M-1) were in fact radically modified Tu-22 'Blinder' airframes, hence the Tu-22M designation. Alternatively, the name may have been adopted simply to confuse Western analysts.

Development began around 1965, and the production Tu-22M-2 'Backfire-B' first flew

in 1975. This machine featured a four-man crew, revised undercarriage and two GSh-23 twin-barrel 23-mm cannon in the tail. Typically this aircraft would be armed with up to three Kh-22 (AS-4 'Kitchen') missiles. After arms limitation treaties the bombers' refuelling probes were removed to reduce their strategic capability.

The later Tu-22M-3 'Backfire-C' introduced a recontoured nose, Kh-15 (AS-16 'Kickback') short-range attack missiles, single GSh-23 cannon, improved wedge intakes and two new NK-25 turbofans. The M-3 first entered

service with the Black Sea fleet in 1985, replacing the M-2 in production. A dedicated electronic warfare version, the Tu-22M-4, is also rumoured to exist.

For years the Tu-22M was a subject of debate. NATO argued with the Warsaw Pact about its role, and even its real name.

Tu-22M-3 'BACKFIRE-C'

This Tupolev Tu-22M-3 'Backfire-C' is a Russian navy aircraft configured for a long-range anti-shipping mission. The Russian navy has large numbers of 'Backfires', and as newer types begin to enter service with the other air forces, more will be transferred to the AVMF squadrons.

The Tu-22M-3 introduces not only more powerful turbofans, but reconfigured high-performance ramp-type intakes similar in shape to those on the Russian MiG-25 'Foxbat'.

Although no flight refuelling probe is normally carried, one can be bolted on quickly if required for a long-range mission.

Large variable-geometry wings are swept forward for cruise and swept back for a high-speed dash over the target.

The aircraft shown here carries only one of a possible three Kh-22 anti-ship missiles. Alternatively, up to 10 Kh-15s could be carried, or a combination of both weapons.

Two Kuznetsov KKBM NK-25 afterburning turbofans propel the Tu-22M-3 to 2125 km/h (1,317 m.p.h.) at an altitude of 11,000 m (33,000 ft.). Fuel reserves provide a 12000-km (7,440-mi.) ferry range and a 4000-km (2,480-mi.) combat radius.

For defence, a single GSh-23 twin-barrel 23-mm cannon and associated guidance radar are mounted in the tail.

The large missile targeting and navigation radar in the nose is codenamed 'Down Beat' and is coupled with very advanced electronic systems.

The 'Backfire-C' carries a crew of four, comprising a pilot and co-pilot side-by-side in front and two further crewmembers behind. All four have ejection seats under gull-wing doors.

For conventional missions 12,000 kg (26,400 lb.) of bombs can be carried in the weapons bay and another 12,000 kg (26,400 lb.) on underwing racks. The heaviest weapon is the FAB-3000 3000-kg (6,600-lb.) bomb.

The main undercarriage consists of two heavy-duty six-wheeled units, retracting neatly into the lower fuselage for storage.

Tu-22M-3 'Backfire'

Type: long-range medium bomber and maritime strike/reconnaissance aircraft

Powerplant: two 245.18-kN (55,000-lb.-thrust) Kuznetsov KKBM NK-25 turbofans with afterburning

Maximum speed: (clean and level) 2125 km/h (1,317 m.p.h.)

Service ceiling: 18,000 m (59,000 ft.)

Weights: maximum take-off 130,000 kg (286,000 lb.)

Armament: 12,000 kg (26,400 lb.) in weapons bay; 12,000 kg (26,400 lb.) on external pylons; three Kh-22 missiles or 10 Kh-15 missiles or bombs, plus one GSh-23 twin barrel 23-mm cannon in tail

Dimensions:
span	34.30 m (112 ft. 6 in.)
length	39.60 m (129 ft. 10 in.)
height	10.80 m (35 ft. 5 in.)
wing area	170 m² (1,829 sq. ft.)

'Backfire' over Afghanistan

STRIKE THE PANSHJIR: 'Backfire' squadrons based in the USSR could easily reach distant Afghanistan. They often headed for the Panshjir valley, north-east of Kabul. The Tu-22Ms were tasked with the destruction of towns, villages and the concealed guerrilla bases of Afghan rebels.

ROUTE IN: The 'Backfires' crossed into Afghanistan over high mountain ranges, often using them to help mask their presence.

SAFE FROM ATTACK: Flying high and fitted with decoy flares and chaff launchers, the Tu-22M was safe from the Afghans' Stinger missile system.

NO WARNING: Bombing from high altitude, the Tu-22M attacks were silent until the bombs were dropped. The 'Backfires' released conventional 'iron' bombs weighing 1500 kg (3,300 lb.), 500 kg (1,100 lb.) and 250 kg (550 lb.). From October 1988 the improved M-3 model joined the earlier M-2 over Afghanistan.

COMBAT DATA

MAXIMUM SPEED

Optimised for long-distance missions, the Tu-22M compensates for its slow speed with a very long range and heavy weapons load. The Mirage and FB-111 were designed for shorter missions.

Tu-22M-3 'BACKFIRE-C'	2125 km/h (1,317 m.p.h.)
FB-111A	2334 km/h (1,447 m.p.h.)
MIRAGE IVP	2338 km/h (1,450 m.p.h.)

AS-4 'KITCHEN'

Known in the West as the AS-4 'Kitchen', the Kh-22 anti-shipping missile has a range of over 400 km and can carry either a 350-kiloton nuclear warhead or a 1000-kg (2,200-lb.) high-explosive warhead. It makes very steep attacks at extremely high speed.

TUPOLEV

TU-95 'BEAR-D/E'

● Powerful strategic bomber ● Ultra-long-range maritime patrol

One of the most majestic sights in aviation is the Russian 'Bear' bomber, cruising at high altitude with bare metal surfaces gleaming in the sun and vapour streaming back from its huge engines. This incredible giant has served Russia valiantly for more than 40 years. Now almost all 'Bears' except the newest versions are close to retirement, and the big Tupolev bomber is becoming an increasingly rare sight.

▲ The 'Bear-D' was usually not far from any NATO exercise, and frequently flew down the North Sea coast of Britain testing the reaction times of the RAF's Lightning and Phantom interceptors.

TUPOLEV TU-95 'BEAR-D/E'

▼ A classic bomber
'Bear' sums up the Tu-95's power and strength superbly well: never was a NATO reporting name more aptly chosen.

▲ Pre-jumbo giant
The 'Bear' was used as the basis for the amazing Tupolev Tu-114, the largest and longest-ranged airliner before the Boeing 747. It could carry more than 200 passengers.

◄ Maritime scout
The 'Bear-D' was the most frequently encountered variant, growling over the world's oceans to gather maritime intelligence for the Soviet navy.

▼ East-West relations
Getting in close to a 'Bear' gave NATO pilots and Tupolev crews a chance for some good-natured rivalry – never forgetting that in war the rivalry would have been deadly.

▲ Eye in the sky
NATO navies could expect to pick up a shadowing 'Bear' almost anywhere in the world. In war, the bomber's task would have been to guide Soviet missiles onto US carriers. Other 'Bears' carried nuclear-tipped weaponry such as AS-3 missiles.

FACTS AND FIGURES

➤ Bombers are designated Tu-95; maritime reconnaissance and anti-submarine warfare variants are designated Tu-142.

➤ The 'Bear' prototype flew on 12 November 1952.

➤ The Indian navy operates a small number of naval 'Bears', known as Tu-142Ms.

➤ The 'Bear'-based Tu-114 airliner was the biggest aircraft in the world when it flew on commercial routes in the early 1960s.

➤ 'Bears' covered the world from bases in Cuba, Somalia, Angola and Vietnam.

➤ Over 400 'Bears' have been built in the type's four-decade production run.

PROFILE

In the shadow of the 'Bear'

Now in its fifth decade, the Tupolev Tu-95 'Bear' is one of the most visually stunning aircraft ever built. It is unique in having swept wings and turboprop engines, which use jet power to drive enormous contra-rotating propellers. Tupolev decided this was the only practical way to achieve long range and high-altitude flight for bombing and intelligence-gathering duties, given the limitations of early Soviet jet engines. The huge turboprops made the 'Bear' almost as fast as many jet bombers. The pilots in the big

maritime patroller's flight deck are at the controls of one of the biggest and heaviest military planes in history. A dozen versions of the 'Bear' were built, the 'Bear-D' acting first as a missile-guidance platform and then as a photo-reconnaissance machine when missiles no longer needed target updating. In the reconnaissance role, the 'Bear' could even communicate with Soviet satellites. The rarer Tu-95MR 'Bear-E' was a similar update of 'Bear-As', incorporating electronic intelligence-gathering equipment.

The 'Bear' was a truly international performer. The combination of its vast range and the Soviet Union's many bases in client states meant that there was almost no part of the world's oceans that could not be photographed, or attacked.

For decades, 'Bears' flew along the fringes of the West, shadowing NATO's fleets and prying out the secrets and testing the reaction times of opposing air defence systems. As long as they were in the danger zone they were invariably intercepted and escorted by Allied fighters.

The 'Bear-D' remains in limited service with about 15 examples on strength. The sight of a 'Bear', once a common occurrence, is now rare indeed.

NATO fighter pilots have had a lot of practice intercepting 'Bears', and most Western knowledge of the type has come from such regular encounters.

Tu-95RT 'Bear-D'

Type: long-range maritime reconnaissance/missile guidance aircraft

Powerplant: four 11,186-kW (15,000-hp.) Kuznetsov NK-12MV turboprops

Maximum speed: 925 km/h (573 m.p.h.) at 9000 m (29,500 ft.); cruising speed 710 km/h (440 m.p.h.)

Range: 13,500 km (8,730 mi.)

Service ceiling: 12,500 m (41,000 ft.)

Weights: empty 80,000 kg (176,000 lb.); loaded 188,000 kg (413,600 lb.)

Armament: two 23-mm cannon in manned tail turret (other 'Bears' had up to six cannon and a wide variety of bombs, cruise missiles, torpedoes and depth charges)

Dimensions:
span	51.10 m (167 ft. 7 in.)
length	49.50 m (162 ft. 4 in.)
height	12.12 m (39 ft. 8 in.)
wing area	297 m² (3,196 sq. ft.)

Tu-95RT 'Bear-D'

The mighty Tupolev 'Bear' was designed as a conventional bomber. Very early in its career, however, it was given a new role as a long-range target acquisition and maritime reconnaissance aircraft, finding targets for missile guidance.

The fuselage of the Tu-95 contains a unique aircrew escape system, in which a conveyer-belt style floor section carries the pilots to safety through an escape hatch. The tail gunner has a floor hatch.

The 'Bear' is powered by four massive Kuznetsov NK-12M turboprops, the most powerful engines of their type ever built. They drive massive contra-rotating propellers.

Huge engine power and a graceful swept wing push the 'Bear' faster than any other propeller-driven aircraft, achieving jet-like speeds in excess of 900 km/h (560 m.p.h.). Jet power was considered for the 'Bear' but never adopted.

The defensive armament of the 'Bear-C' included retractable dorsal and ventral turrets and a manned tail turret, each with two 23-mm cannon. The 'Bear-D' retained only the rear gun turret.

The 'Bear' has a gracefully swept vertical tailfin, which houses numerous electronic antennas.

The addition of a refuelling probe meant that the 'Bear's' already massive range could be extended indefinitely.

The blister under the nose housed a missile-guidance radar associated with the AS-3 Kangaroo cruise missile. The radar was kept in the RT version but bomb and missile capability was deleted.

Big Bulge is a very powerful radar, able to detect a large ship at over 250-km (155-mi.) range.

The blisters on the rear fuselage of the 'Bear' house electronic intelligence-gathering sensors. A reconnaissance camera port is also visible under the rear of the Elint blister.

Long eyes of the Soviet fleet

THE RED FLEET: Soviet naval doctrine called for the elimination of American carrier battle groups. As a result, Red Fleet warships were very heavily armed with large, long-range missiles with heavy conventional or nuclear warheads.

MID-COURSE GUIDANCE: The largest of the Soviet anti-ship missiles had very long ranges, far beyond any possibility of guidance from their launch platforms. For maximum accuracy they relied on mid-course targeting updates from the 'Bear'.

TARGET LOCATION: In its Cold War maritime role, the 'Bear' was tasked with locating American carrier battle groups either visually or by radar, and transmitting that location to the Soviet fleet.

COMBAT DATA

RANGE

B-52 STRATOFORTRESS 16,000 km (9,900 mi.)

Tu-95 'BEAR-D' 13,500 km (8,400 mi.)

P-3 ORION 7600 km (4,700 mi.)

The key to effective maritime reconnaissance and strike capability is long range and endurance. The Boeing B-52 is the 'Bear's' only rival in this regard, especially when carrying a heavy weapons load. More conventional maritime patrollers such as the Lockheed P-3 Orion are not in the same league.

VOUGHT

A-7 CORSAIR II

● Maritime strike ● Ground attack ● Two-seat trainer

O riginally designed in the early 1960s as a light attack aircraft for the US Navy, the Corsair was also developed as a land-based tactical fighter for the USAF. Various improved versions were projected for the export market but, until recently, only two other countries had bought the type. One was Greece, which acquired 60 A-7H and five TA-7H models, and the other was Portugal, whose A-7Ps and TA-7Ps are refurbished early-model Corsairs.

▲ Surprisingly,
the A-7 Corsair II has not found many export customers. It is a rugged, powerful attack aircraft which has good range and is able to carry a heavy weapons load.

VOUGHT A-7 CORSAIR II

◄ **Hellenic Corsair II**
Greek Corsair IIs were based on the US Navy's A-7E standard and designated A-7H. They were received in a camouflage scheme similar to that of early USAF A-7Ds. Of the 60 delivered, about 50 are still in service and operate in a similar anti-shipping role to Portuguese Corsair IIs.

◄ **Wishful thinking**
Although this aircraft is marked in Pakistani national markings, the country never received the A-7. A Canadian air force bid to obtain the Corsair II early in the programme also failed.

Two-seat TA-7H ▶
A two-seat trainer variant of the A-7E was produced for Greek air force conversion training. The Greek A-7 fleet has been strengthened by the addition of 36 A-7Es and a few TA-7Cs.

◄ **Portugal's A-7P**
A number of ex-US Navy A-7A and B airframes were rebuilt as A-7Ps with 59.6-kN (13,400-lb.-thrust) TF30-P-408 turbofans. About 30 A-7Ps remain in service, giving Portugal a potent attack capability.

Portuguese conversion ▶
Ex-US Navy TA-7Cs were supplied to the Portuguese air force as TA-7Ps, some wearing standard US Navy colours. All TA-7Cs were produced by converting A-7B or C airframes.

FACTS AND FIGURES

➤ The first flight of the Corsair II was on 27 September 1967; early A-7s flew from carriers during the Vietnam War.

➤ Greek TA-7Hs are fully combat-capable even though they are used for training.

➤ Some 80 per cent of the TA-7H's parts are common with those of the A-7H.

➤ Portuguese Corsair IIs are compatible with the ALQ-131 electronic countermeasures pod.

➤ Portugal received 50 aircraft, which were delivered in two batches from 1981.

➤ About 35 aircraft in Portuguese service remain airworthy.

PROFILE

Corsairs in foreign service

Greece was the first overseas customer for the Corsair. Its A-7H, a land-based version of the US Navy's A-7E, flew for the first time in May 1975. It was bought primarily for anti-ship missions and has no provision for in-flight refuelling. The TA-7H is a two-seat trainer. Portugal's Corsairs were originally A-7Bs. Fitted with avionics from the A-7E and USAF A-7D variants, the A-7P first flew in October 1984. It can carry Maverick missiles for use against ships.

Greece's original A-7 fleet has been strengthened by the transfer of a further batch of ex-US Navy Corsairs. The additional aircraft are mainly A-7Es plus a a small number of TA-7C trainers.

International Corsair II and III variants were studied in the mid-1980s, but nothing came of either project. Canada, Pakistan and Switzerland were also interested in acquiring Corsair IIs but no orders were ever placed. Interestingly, in 1994 the US Navy agreed to transfer 18 A-7Es to the Thai navy, opening a new chapter in the Corsair II's career.

Above: Portugal now operates its TA-7P and A-7P Corsair IIs in a wrap-around tactical camouflage scheme. All aircraft display their original US Navy serial numbers.

Above: Having been designed for operation from the US Navy's crowded carrier decks, the A-7 was produced with folding wings. This feature has been retained in all subsequent variants.

A-7H Corsair II

Type: light attack aircraft

Powerplant: one 66.6-kN (15,000-lb.-thrust) Allison TF41-A-2 turbofan

Maximum speed: 1123 km/h (696 m.p.h.) in clean configuration at sea level

Initial climb rate: 4572 m/min (15,000 f.p.m.)

Combat radius: 1151 km (715 mi.) on a hi-lo-hi mission profile

Weights: empty 8988 kg (19,774 lb.); maximum take-off 19,050 kg (41,910 lb.)

Armament: one 20-mm cannon and more than 6804 kg (15,000 lb.) of bombs and missiles, including AGM-65 Maverick air-to-surface missiles

Dimensions: span 11.81 m (38 ft. 9 in.)
length 14.06 m (46 ft. 2 in.)
height 4.88 m (16 ft.)
wing area 34.83 m² (391 sq. ft.)

A-7H CORSAIR II

Greek air force personnel know the A-7H as 'Koursaro' and operate the aircraft in the long-range strike and anti-surface vessel roles. The aircraft fly in USAF-style camouflage with three squadrons.

A pylon is mounted in this position on both sides of the fuselage. It is used exclusively for the carriage of AIM-9 Sidewinder missiles for self-defence. Principal among the offensive weapons in the Greek A-7 inventory is the AGM-65 Maverick, a weapon that is so accurate that the Israelis have found it to be effective against vehicles even without a warhead.

A high-set wing was chosen for the Corsair II so that adequate space was available beneath the wing to hang large and bulky stores, while maintaining deck clearance.

159662

For many years the standard US aircraft gun has been the M61A-1 Vulcan cannon. This powerful, reliable weapon has six rotating barrels and fires through this port on the lower fuselage.

Six pylons, three under each wing, inboard of the fold line give the A-7 the capability of carrying a heavy load of diverse weaponry. Each of the inboard pylons can carry a 1134-kg (2,500-lb.) load, while the outer two on each side can carry 1587 kg (3,500 lb.).

Another reminder of the A-7's naval origins is the underfuselage arrester hook. Although only the US Navy has operated A-7s from carriers, the hook is useful for emergency airfield landings.

A-7Hs were built with the TF41 engine, as introduced on the USAF's A-7D and later on the A-7E. This fuel-efficient powerplant was a variant of the Rolls-Royce Spey, licence-built by Allison.

COMBAT DATA

MAXIMUM SPEED

The Corsair II does not represent the sleekest of aircraft and this, combined with its non-afterburning engine, prevents it from keeping pace with these rival designs. The TF41 engine, however, makes the aircraft very fuel efficient.

A-7H CORSAIR II	1123 km/h (696 m.p.h.)
JAGUAR INTERNATIONAL	1352 km/h (838 m.p.h.)
MiG-27 'FLOGGER-D'	1352 km/h (838 m.p.h.)

COMBAT RADIUS

While the Jaguar International possesses a greater combat radius than the A-7H, it accomplishes this with a much lighter warload. Both aircraft have good range for tactical designs, however, especially when compared to the Russian MiG-27 'Flogger-D' which is barely capable of a tactical range mission.

A-7H CORSAIR II 1151 km (715 mi.)
JAGUAR INTERNATIONAL 3524 km (2190 mi.)
MiG-27 'FLOGGER-D' 950 km (590 mi.)

ARMAMENT

All of these aircraft feature powerful in-built cannon, but the A-7H carries by far the largest warload. Both the Jaguar International and the A-7H carry two air-to-air missiles for self-defence as standard equipment.

A-7H CORSAIR II 1 x 20-mm cannon 6804-kg (15,000-lb.) bombload
JAGUAR INTERNATIONAL 2 x 30-mm cannon 4763-kg (10,500-lb.) bombload
MiG-27 'FLOGGER-D' 1 x 30-mm machine-gun 3000-kg (6,600-lb.) bombload

US Naval aircraft abroad

■ **GRUMMAN F-14 TOMCAT:** Reports vary concerning the airworthiness of Iran's 79 F-14s. At least one was lost to an Iraqi Mirage F1.

■ **VOUGHT F-8 CRUSADER:** France's Aéronavale retired its F-8s in 1999, due to their replacement by the Rafale M.

■ **McDONNELL DOUGLAS A-4 SKYHAWK:** Skyhawks have been widely exported, with customers including Malaysia and New Zealand.

■ **McDONNELL DOUGLAS F/A-18 HORNET:** Another great export success, the numerous operators of the F/A-18 include Spain.

VOUGHT

F-8E(FN) CRUSADER

● Carrier fighter ● Variable-incidence wing ● Superb dogfighter

O ne of the most spectacular fighters ever, the Vought F-8 Crusader was chosen by the French Aéronavale in the early 1960s. At that time, the Crusader had already chalked up a superb record with the American Fleet and was soon to wage a near-perfect campaign against North Vietnamese MiGs. Entering French service in 1967, the Crusader became the backbone of France's naval air power aboard the aircraft-carriers *Clemenceau* and *Foch*.

▲ For all its success, the Crusader attracted few export orders and is now a very rare aircraft. The Aéronavale retired its ageing fighters in 1999, replacing them with Rafale Ms.

VOUGHT F-8E(FN) CRUSADER

◀ **Quad launcher**
One of the weaknesses of many fighters in the early 1960s was their lack of weapon load, with only two missiles carried. The F-8E solved the problem by having a new twin missile rail on each side of the fuselage and four cannon.

▼ **Turning tight**
The F-8E has excellent manoeuvrability, and pilots can out-turn many more modern fighters.

▲ **Navy blue**
In the early years the F-8E was painted light-grey, but the aircraft now wear this all-over blue paint scheme to blend in with the sea.

▼ **Sidewinder aboard**
Unusually for a French aircraft, this F-8E of 14F carries an American-made Sidewinder missile in place of the usual MATRA weapons.

▼ **Raised wing**
The flash of red paint above the fuselage shows the variable-incidence wing in the raised position.

FACTS AND FIGURES

➤ France acquired 42 single-seat Crusaders, but it cancelled plans for six two-seat variants.

➤ A Crusader can fly at about twice the speed of a bullet fired from a pistol.

➤ The test prototype for the French navy made its first flight in February 1964.

➤ The F-8E(FN) lands 50 km/h (30 m.p.h.) slower than American Crusaders, to permit duty on smaller French aircraft-carriers.

➤ The first production F-8E(FN) made its initial flight in June 1964.

➤ Pilots considered the Crusader difficult to fly, but a real pleasure when mastered.

Gunfighter of the Aéronavale

French officers made a dramatic choice when they turned to America for the F-8E(FN) Crusader in 1964; a quantum leap forward when chosen to replace the propeller-driven F4U-5N Corsair and jet Aquilon (developed Sea Venom). With minor changes to the wing and boundary layer systems fitted to the Crusaders in American service, the F-8E(FN) became a stunning performer in French hands. Even today, with the new-

generation Rafale having entered service as a repacement, many regard the Crusader as one of the finest fighters they ever flew.

Although the Crusader can drop bombs and attack ground targets, the Aéronavale chose to use the F-8E(FN) strictly as an air-to-air fighter. These Crusaders supported Allied operations in the Persian Gulf in 1987, although they were never employed in combat. Once a world-class air warrior,

the F-8E(FN), which lacks a multi-mode radar and long-range missiles, is now outclassed, and has been replaced in service by the naval Rafale M.

Left: The F-8E could carry the MATRA R.530 radar-guided missile. In firing trials this weapon had a poor record.

Right: The Aéronavale conducted acceptance trials of the F-8E onboard the American carrier USS Shangri La.

F-8E(FN) Crusader

Type: single-seat carrier-based fighter

Powerplant: one 47.60-kN (10,700-lb.-thrust) Pratt & Whitney J57-P-20A turbojet engine

Maximum speed: 1827 km/h (1,133 m.p.h.) at 10,975 m (36,000 ft.)

Cruising speed: 901 km/h (559 m.p.h.)

Range: 2253 km (1,397 mi.)

Service ceiling: 17,680 m (58,000 ft.)

Weights: empty 9038 kg (19,884 lb.); maximum take-off 15,420 kg (33,924 lb.)

Armament: four Colt-Browning Mk 12 20-mm cannon, plus two to four MATRA R.530 or 550 air-to-air missiles or two to four AIM-9 Sidewinder air-to-air missiles

Dimensions:
span	10.87 m	(35 ft. 8 in.)
length	16.61 m	(54 ft. 6 in.)
height	4.80 m	(15 ft. 9 in.)
wing area	32.51 m²	(350 sq. ft.)

F-8E(FN) CRUSADER

Now operated only by 12F at Landivisiau, the F-8E is one of very few American types used by the French forces since 1960. The Aéronavale was the last operator of the F-8E, which has also been retired by the US Navy and the Philippines.

The F-8E had a short-range radar for ranging use only. It could not detect aircraft at long range over water or search for targets at low altitude.

For escape from the aircraft, the F-8E was fitted with a Martin-Baker ejection seat. The Crusader had a comfortable cockpit for its era but rearward visibility was quite poor.

The F-8E was the only jet fighter ever with a variable-incidence wing. The wing used boundary layer control for extra lift during take-off and landing. Bullpup or Zuni rockets could be carried for ground attack, but the Aéronavale did not equip their aircraft with them.

Power was provided by a single J57 engine, as used in the B-52, U-2, B-57 and KC-135. The fixed intake limited the aircraft's speed to less than Mach 2. The F-8 has an all-moving tailplane.

Armament consisted of four Colt 20-mm cannon, with two MATRA 550 Magic infra-red homing missiles. In the 1960s Sidewinder and R.530 were carried.

The F-8E, like the RF-8A, had ventral fins fitted.

COMBAT DATA

MAXIMUM SPEED
The Crusader was a relatively small fighter with only a single engine, and was not as fast as the Phantom or MiG-21. However, in a subsonic dogfight, it was just as fast as any other fighter, and its legendary agility gave it the edge over many MiG-21s.

PHANTOM FG.Mk 1	2548 km/h (1,580 m.p.h.)
F-8E(FN)	1827 km/h (1,133 m.p.h.)
MIRAGE IIIC	2230 km/h (1,383 m.p.h.)

CEILING
On the power of one J57, the F-8E could climb to a very respectable altitude. The Phantom had twice the power and was one of the finest interceptors of its day. However, fuel and weapon load often meant a much lower ceiling was attained in flight.

PHANTOM FG.Mk 1 18,900 m (62,000 ft.) — MIRAGE IIIC 16,500 m (54,100 ft.) — F-8E(FN) CRUSADER 17,680 m (58,000 ft.)

RANGE
Naval fighters require range, and the F-8E had a good performance. Range is highly dependant on the use of afterburner, which gives a huge increase in thrust but uses fuel up at a massive rate. The Phantom consumed fuel quickly as it had twin engines.

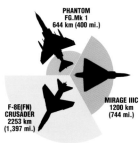

PHANTOM FG.Mk 1 644 km (400 mi.) — F-8E(FN) CRUSADER 2253 km (1,397 mi.) — MIRAGE IIIC 1200 km (744 mi.)

Variable incidence in action

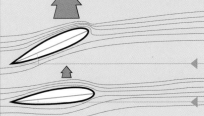

ANGLE OF ATTACK: Wings generate lift according to the angle of attack – the angle at which the wing meets the oncoming airflow. The lift generated increases with the angle of attack up to about 20° when the wing stalls.

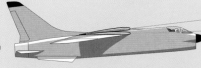

MOVING WING: The Crusader pilot can increase the incidence of the wing (the angle at which it is mounted on the airframe). This is carried out by a large hydraulic jack in the fuselage. For a given incidence the aircraft's attitude can be lowered, providing better cockpit visibility without losing lift.

LOWER NOSE: The Crusader has more lift for a given airspeed, and the pilot can fly with a lower nose attitude. This gives him a better view of the deck on approach.

YAKOVLEV

YAK-38 'FORGER'

● Vertical take-off ● Fleet air defence ● Maritime strike

Since 1976, the Yak-38 'Forger' has been Moscow's equivalent of the famous Harrier, but uses three powerplants instead of the Harrier's one for vectored-thrust performance. The vertical take-off jet was designed to spring from the decks of 'Kiev'-class carriers to defend the Russian fleet from Western patrol aircraft and saw service on Russia's last 'Kiev' carrier, *Gorshkov*.

▲ The Yak-38 gave the Soviet navy experience with high-performance jets at sea, and was a useful stepping stone towards the fixed-wing naval fighters now coming into service with the Russian navy.

YAKOVLEV YAK-38 'FORGER'

◀ **Conversion trainer**
The 'Forger-B' is the two-seat trainer variant of the Yak-38. This was a much-needed aircraft as the standard Yak-38 was always a very tricky aircraft to learn to fly. The trainer aircraft lacks underwing pylons, radar or infra-red systems, and is therefore not combat-capable.

◀ **'Freestyle'**
The Yak-141 'Freestyle' is the follow-on to the Yak-38, with advanced avionics and increased speed and range. It has not been produced in quantity, and needs a foreign buyer.

▲ **On deck**
The 'Forger' was not an impressive aircraft by itself, but the overall 'Kiev'-class package was capable and a real threat.

▲ **Hover practice**
This Yak-38 is hovering, with the lift-engine intake doors opened just behind the cockpit, and jet blast churning the sea.

Pacific fleet ▶
The Yak-38 could be seen all over the world as Soviet sea power expanded. The carrier Novorossiysk, based in Vladivostok, flew its 'Forgers' all over the Pacific.

FACTS AND FIGURES

➤ The Yak-36 'Freehand' of 1967 was the test ship for the better-looking 'Forger'.

➤ The Yak-38 first carried out sea trials on board the *Kiev* in the Black Sea.

➤ About 90 'Forgers' were built, but at least 37 have been lost in accidents (with 32 pilots ejecting safely).

➤ Each aircraft carrier had 12 single-seaters and a pair of two-seat trainers.

➤ Of four 'Kiev'-class carriers, only one remains in service with Yak-38s.

➤ The advanced Yakovlev Yak-141 'Freestyle', a supersonic replacement for the 'Forger', has not entered service.

PROFILE

Soviet naval 'jump-jet' fighter

The Yak-38 'Forger' stirred excitement in the West when first seen aboard the *Kiev* in the Mediterranean. Using a main turbojet with twin rotating nozzles plus tandem lift jets behind its cockpit, the 'Forger' performed well in its specialised domain as a V/STOL (Vertical/Short Take-off and Landing) naval fighter.

The Yak-38 was never designed to be in the class of conventional naval fighters; it was aimed at warding off NATO maritime patrol and strike aircraft such as the P-3 Orion and BAe Nimrod. Its radar has only a very limited range, and it carried only the short-range infra-red 'Atoll' missile and cannon. It had limited strike capability, with armament including the unguided UV-32 rocket pod and the short-range AS-7 'Kerry' tactical missile. Neither was suited to attacking a well-defended warship.

The 'Forger' was tested, not very successfully, in Afghanistan. Its main value to the Soviet navy was to give experience in operating jets at sea.

YAK-38 'FORGER-A'

The Yak-38 served aboard the 'Kiev'-class aircraft carriers *Kiev*, *Minsk*, *Novorossisyk* and *Baku* (now renamed *Admiral Gorshkov*). This Yak-38 carries the badge of the Red Banner Northern Fleet.

The Yak-36 could not carry a major warload and was no match for land-based fighters, but it was more than capable of destroying enemy bombers and anti-submarine aircraft.

The cockpit has a head-up display, but is otherwise very simple and quite cluttered compared to modern fighter aircraft.

Four pylons under the fixed portions of the wings can carry up to 2000 kg (4,400 lb.) of stores, including bombs, missiles and cannon pods.

Fences were later fitted to the upper fuselage above the intakes to improve the airflow.

The short-span wing folds for shipboard stowage, with a hinge between the flap and ailerons. A 600-litre (160-gal.) fuel tank can be fitted under each wing.

The traditional Yak-38 paint scheme was a naval blue, but this has been changed to a sea grey on the 'Forgers' remaining in service.

The air intake at the base of the fin directs cooling air into the aircraft's rear electronics bay.

The Yak-38 is unique in having an automatic ejection system, which is used in the dangerous transition phase when taking off or landing.

Twin Koliesov RD-36 lift engines are mounted behind the cockpit. They are not used during wingborne flight.

The Yak-38 radar is a simple model, with a surface search mode and capable of giving range data for infra-red missiles.

Auxiliary blow-in doors were added to the intake walls, to improve engine air flow while in the hover.

The Yak-38 uses a Harrier-like system of autostabilisers with reaction control jets in the wingtips, nose and tail.

The main Soyuz R-27 thrust engine exhausts through twin vectoring nozzles under the tail.

Yak-38 'Forger-A'

Type: single-seat VTOL fighter

Powerplant: one 66.68-kN (15,000-lb.-thrust) MNPK 'Soyuz' (Tumanskii) R-27V-300 turbojet; two 31.87-kN RKBM (Koliesov) RD-36-35FVR lift jets

Maximum speed: 1009 km/h (625 m.p.h.) in 'clean' condition at 11,000 m (36,000 ft.)

Service ceiling: 12,000 m (39,000 ft.)

Weights: empty 7485 kg (16,467 lb.); loaded 13,000 kg (28,600 lb.)

Armament: up to 2000 kg (4,400 lb.) of underwing stores or four AA-8 'Aphid' air-to-air missiles

Dimensions:
span	7.32 m (24 ft.)
length	15.50 m (51 ft.)
height	4.37 m (14 ft.)
wing area	18.50 m² (199 sq. ft.)

COMBAT DATA

MAXIMUM SPEED

When it first appeared, Western experts assumed that the Yak-38 was capable of travelling faster than sound, but it has since been discovered that the Russian jet is subsonic, and somewhat slower than Britain's Sea Harrier.

Yak-38 'FORGER'	1009 km/h (625 m.p.h.)
SUPER ETENDARD	1380 km/h (856 m.p.h.)
SEA HARRIER FRS.Mk 1	1185 km/h (738 m.p.h.)

COMBAT RADIUS

The penalty for carrying extra weight in the shape of lift engines, which also take up valuable space in the fuselage, is a noticeable deficiency in range. The 'Forger' could not match earlier versions of the Harrier, and while the British jet's capability has been greatly enhanced the Yak's range has remained limited.

SUPER ETENDARD 850 km (527 mi.)

SEA HARRIER FRS.Mk 1 970 km (600 mi.)

Yak-38 'FORGER' 370 km (230 mi.)

WEAPONS LOAD

The primary task of the 'Forger' was to destroy Western maritime and anti-submarine warfare aircraft, and although it has been given some air-to-surface capability it cannot strike as hard as land-based fighters. But, although limited, the Yak can match the French Etendard, although it is much less capable than the latest Sea Harrier.

Yak-38 'FORGER' 2000 kg (4,400 lb.) or 2 x AS-7 missiles

SUPER ETENDARD 2100 kg (4,620 lb.) or 1 Exocet missile

SEA HARRIER FRS.Mk 1 3600 kg (7,920 lb.) or 2 x Sea Eagle missiles

Soviet carrier evolution

■ **HELICOPTER CARRIER:** The 'Moskva' class appeared in the early 1960s. It was a cross between a carrier and a cruiser, and could only operate helicopters.

■ **'FORGER' CARRIER:** Carriers of the 40,000-ton 'Kiev' class had a through-deck, which enabled them to operate with a dozen Yak-38s as well as anti-submarine helicopters.

■ **SUPERCARRIER:** The last gasp of Soviet naval expansion was the supercarrier *Kuznetsov*, which was designed to operate with advanced fighters like the Su-33 'Flanker'. It has proved to be far too expensive, however, for financially challenged Russia to contemplate putting into service.

INDEX